JERUSALEM
in the Time of Jesus

JOACHIM JEREMIAS

JERUSALEM
in the Time of Jesus

An Investigation into Economic and
Social Conditions during the
New Testament Period

FORTRESS PRESS

PHILADELPHIA

This book is a translation by F. H. and C. H. Cave
(based on an earlier draft of a translation by M. E. Dahl)
of the third edition of
Jerusalem zur Zeit Jesu, copyright © 1962 by Vandenhoeck & Ruprecht
in Göttingen, Germany,
as amended by the author's own revisions up to 1967.

Library of Congress Catalog Card Number 77-81530
ISBN 0-8006-1136-5

First American Edition 1969 by Fortress Press
First Paperback Edition 1975

Printed in the United States of America   1-1136

00   99   98   97   96   10   11   12   13   14   15   16   17   18   19

CONTENTS

TRANSLATORS' NOTE

This is a translation based on the third German edition of 1962. The first part has been extensively revised to 1967 by Professor Jeremias, and the whole has been compared with the French edition, *Jérusalem au temps de Jésus*, Paris 1967.

The translators wish to thank Lady Bruce Lockhart for her skill and care in typing a much corrected manuscript.

EDITIONS USED

Mishnah, Stettin 1865. In doubtful cases, after the *ed. princ.* of the Jerusalem Talmud, Venice 1523. Cf. ET by H. Danby, Oxford 1933.

Tosephta, Pasewalk 1880 (reprinted Jerusalem 1963). In doubtful cases, MS Erfurt, now in Berlin, Staatsbibl. MS or. 2° 1220.

Mekilta Ex., Venice 1545 (cited by biblical chapter and verse, folio and column a–d); cf. ET by J. Z. Lauterbach, 3 vols., Philadelphia 1933–5 (reprinted 1949) (cited as L).

Siphra Lev., *ed. princ.*, Venice 1545 (cited in the same way as Mek. Ex.).

Siphre Num. and Deut., *ed. princ.*, Venice 1545 (cited in the same way as Mek. Ex.).

Jerusalem Talmud, *ed. princ.*, Venice 1523. Cf. French trans. by M. Schwab, 11 vols., Paris 1878–90, reprinted in 6 vols., Paris 1960. (Cited by chapter and section, followed by page, column and line of Schwab.)

Babylonian Talmud, Lemberg (Lvov), 1861. Cf. ET, ed. I. Epstein, 34 vols., London 1935–52.

Midrash Rabbah on the Pentateuch, Stettin 1864. Cf. ET, ed. H. Freedman and M. Simon, 10 vols. (published by the Soncino Press and referred to as Son.), London 1939. (Cited by Parasha, biblical chapter and verse, Soncino paragraph where this differs from the Stettin ed., and Soncino page.)

Midrash on the five Megilloth, *ed. princ.*, Pesaro 1519. Cited from Stettin ed. and Soncino ed. in the same as Midrash Rabbah.

Tanḥuma, Stettin 1864.

Pirqe de Rabbi Eliezer, Warsaw 1878.

Aboth de Rabbi Nathan (ARN), ed. S. Schechter, Vienna 1887. Cf. ET by J. Goldin, *The Fathers according to Rabbi Nathan*, New Haven 1955.

Pesiqta rabbati, ed. M. Friedmann, Vienna 1880.

Damascus Document, ed. L. Rost, Berlin 1933. (Cited as CD.).

Flavius Josephus, ed. B. Niese, Berlin 1885–94 (reprinted Berlin 1955). Cf. ET by H. St J. Thackeray and others, 9 vols. (Loeb Classical Library), London 1926–66.

Philo of Alexandria, ed. L. Cohn and P. Wendland, Berlin 1896–1926 (reprinted Berlin 1962–3). Cf. ET by F. H. Colson and G. H. Whitaker, 9 vols. (Loeb Classical Library), London 1929–41.

ABBREVIATIONS

Ant.	Josephus, *Antiquitates* (see p. xii)
ARN	*Aboth de Rabbi Nathan* (see p. xii)
Beginnings	See under Foakes-Jackson, p. xiv
Bill.	(H. L. Strack and) P. Billerbeck, *Kommentar zum Neuen Testament aus Talmud und Midrasch*, 6 vols., Munich 1923–61
BJ	Josephus, *Bellum Judaicum* (see p. xii)
BZAW	Beihefte zur *Zeitschrift für die alttestamentliche Wissenschaft*, Giessen, then Berlin, 1896ff.
CA	Josephus, *Contra Apionem* (see p. xii)
CCSL	Corpus Christianorum. Series Latina, Turnhout, 1959ff.
CIJ	*Corpus Inscriptionum Judaicarum* I–II (Sussidi allo studio delle antichità cristiane 1 and 3), ed. J.-B. Frey, Rome, 1936 and 1952
CSEL	Corpus Scriptorum Ecclesiasticorum Latinorum, Vienna, Prague and Leipzig, 1866ff.
ET	English translation
GCS	Die Griechischen Christlichen Schriftsteller der ersten Jahrhunderte, Leipzig and Berlin, 1897ff.
HTR	*Harvard Theological Review*, Cambridge, Mass., 1908ff.
HUCA	*Hebrew Union College Annual*, Cincinnati, 1924ff.
JE	*The Jewish Encyclopaedia*, 12 vols., New York 1901–6
JQR	*Jewish Quarterly Review*, London 1889ff.
LXX	The Septuagint
MGWJ	*Monatsschrift für Geschichte und Wissenschaft des Judent(h)ums*, Dresden, Leipzig and elsewhere, 1851ff.
MT	Masoretic text
MW	L. Mitteis and U. Wilcken, *Grundzüge und Chrestomathie der Papyruskunde* I.1, Leipzig 1912
NS	New series
NTS	*New Testament Studies*, Cambridge 1954ff.
PJB	*Palästinajahrbuch*, Berlin 1905ff.
PL	Patrologiae cursus completus accurante J.-P. Migne, Series Latina, Paris 1844ff.

PRE	*Realencyklopädie für protestantische Theologie und Kirche*, 3rd ed., Leipzig 1896–1913
RB	*Revue biblique*, Paris 1892ff.
REJ	*Revue des études juives*, Paris 1880ff.
RGG	*Die Religion in Geschichte und Gegenwart*, 3rd ed., Tübingen 1957ff.
Son.	See Midrash Rabbah, p. xii
SW	See under Dalman, below
TA	See under Krauss, p. xv
TWNT	*Theologisches Wörterbuch zum Neuen Testament*, ed. G. Kittel and G. Friedrich, Stuttgart 1932ff.
Vita	Josephus, *Vita* (see p. xii)
WB	See under Dalman, below
WJ	See under Dalman, below
ZAW	*Zeitschrift für die alttestamentliche Wissenschaft*, Giessen, then Berlin, 1881ff.
ZDPV	*Zeitschrift des Deutschen Palästina-Vereins*, Leipzig, then Wiesbaden, 1878ff.
ZNW	*Zeitschrift für die neutestamentliche Wissenschaft*, Giessen, then Berlin, 1900ff.

The following Works are cited by Short Title, as indicated by **Bold** type

W. Bacher, *Die Agada der Tannaiten* I, 2nd ed., Strasbourg 1903; II, Strasbourg 1890 (cited as **Ag. Tann.**)

A. Büchler, *Die **Priester** und der Cultus im letzten Jahrzehnt des jerusalemischen Tempels*, Vienna 1895

G. Dalman, *Sacred Sites and Ways: Studies in the Topography of the Gospels*, London 1935 (cited as **SW**; ET by P. P. Levertoff of *Orte und Wege Jesu*, 3rd ed., Gütersloh, 1924)
Aramäisch-neuhebräisches Handwörterbuch zu Targum, Talmud und Midrash, 3rd ed., Göttingen 1938 (cited as **WB**)
Die Worte Jesu I, 2nd ed., Leipzig 1930 (reprinted Darmstadt 1965); ET of 1st ed., *The Words of Jesus*, Edinburgh 1902 (cited as **WJ**)

F. Delitzsch, *Jewish **Artisan Life** in the Time of Jesus*, New York 1883, ET of *Jüdisches Handwerkerleben zur Zeit Jesu*, 2nd ed., Erlangen 1875

J. Derenbourg, ***Essai** sur l'histoire et la géographie de la Palestine d'après les Thalmuds et les autres sources rabbiniques*, Paris 1867

Festschrift A. Schwarz *zum siebzigsten Geburtstag*, ed. S. Krauss, Berlin and Vienna 1917

F. J. Foakes-Jackson and K. Lake, *The **Beginnings** of Christianity*, 5 vols., London 1920–33

M. Gottheil, 'Jerusalem', **JE VII**, 1904

H. Guthe, 'Jerusalem', **PRE VIII**, 1900, 666–93

H. Guthe, **Die griechisch-römischen Städte** *des Ostjordanlandes*, Leipzig 1918

J. C. **Hirschensohn**, *Sepher šebhaᵉ ḥokmoth*, Lemberg 1883

J. Jeremias, '**Sabbathjahr** und neutestamentliche Chronologie', *ZNW* 27, 1928, 98–103, reprinted in *Abba. Studien zur neutestamentlichen Theologie und Zeitgeschichte*, Göttingen 1966, 233–8

S. Krauss, *Talmudische Archäologie*, 3 vols., Leipzig 1910–12 (reprinted Hildesheim 1966), cited as **TA**

J. **Levy**, *Neuhebräisches und chaldäisches Wörterbuch über die Talmudim und Midraschim*, 4 vols., Leipzig 1889 (reprinted Darmstadt 1963)

E. Meyer, **Ursprung** *und Anfänge des Christentums* **II**, Stuttgart 1921 (reprinted Darmstadt 1962)

A. Neubauer, *La* **géographie** *du Talmud*, Paris 1868

W. Otto, **Herodes**. *Beiträge zur Geschichte des letzten jüdischen Königshauses*, Stuttgart 1913 (a reprint with the same column numeration of the article 'Herodes' in Pauly-Wissowa, *Real-Encyclopädie der classischen Altertumswissenschaft*, Supplement, vol. II, Stuttgart 1913, cols. 1–100)

A. Schlatter, **Geschichte Israels** *von Alexander dem Grossen bis Hadrian*, 3rd ed., Stuttgart 1925

Jochanan ben Zakkai, *der Zeitgenosse der Apostel*, Gütersloh 1899 (reprinted in A. Schlatter, *Synagoge und Kirche bis zum Bar-Kochba-Aufstand*, Stuttgart 1966, 175–237)

Die **Tage** *Trajans und Hadrians*, Gütersloh 1897 (reprinted in *Synagoge . . .*, 9–97)

Die **Theologie** *des Judentums nach dem Bericht des Josefus*, Gütersloh 1932

E. **Schürer**, *Geschichte des jüdischen Volkes im Zeitalter Jesu Christi*, 4th ed., I–III, Leipzig 1901–9 (reprinted Hildesheim 1964); ET by Sophia Taylor and P. Christie, *A History of the Jewish People in the Time of Jesus Christ* I.1–2, II.1–3, Edinburgh 1885–90

G. A. Smith, **Jerusalem**. *The Topography, Economics and History from the Earliest Times to AD 70*, 2 vols., London 1908

H. L. Strack, **Einleitung** *in Talmud und Midrasch*, 5th ed., Munich 1921 (reprinted 1961)

M. Weber, *Gesammelte Aufsätze zur* **Religionssoziologie III**, Tübingen 1921

J. Wellhausen, *Die* **Pharisäer** *und die Sadducäer. Eine Untersuchung zur inneren jüdischen Geschichte*, Greifswald 1874 (reprinted Hanover 1924, Göttingen 1967)

TRACTATES OF THE MISHNAH

Ab.	Aboth	M. Kat.	Moed Katan
A. Zar.	Abodah Zarah	M. Sh.	Maaser Sheni
Arak.	Arakhin	Naz.	Nazir
B.B.	Baba Bathra	Neg.	Negaim
Bekh.	Bekhoroth	Ned.	Nedarim
Ber.	Berakhoth	Nidd.	Niddah
Betz.	Betzah (or Yom Tob)	Ohol.	Oholoth
Bikk.	Bikkurim	Orl.	Orlah
B.K.	Baba Kamma	Par.	Parah
B.M.	Baba Metzia	Peah	Peah
Dem.	Demai	Pes.	Pesahim
Eduy.	Eduyoth	R. Sh.	Rosh ha-Shanah
Erub.	Erubin	Sanh.	Sanhedrin
Gitt.	Gittin	Shab.	Shabbath
Hag.	Hagigah	Shebi.	Shebiith
Hall.	Hallah	Shebu.	Shebuoth
Hor.	Horayoth	Shek.	Shekalim
Hull.	Hullin	Sot.	Sotah
Kel.	Kelim	Sukk.	Sukkah
Ker.	Kerithoth	Taan.	Taanith
Ket.	Ketuboth	Teb. Y.	Tebul Yom
Kidd.	Kiddushin	Tam.	Tamid
Kil.	Kilaim	Tem.	Temurah
Kinn.	Kinnim	Ter.	Terumoth
Maas.	Maaseroth	Toh.	Tohoroth
Makk.	Makkoth	Uktz.	Uktzin
Maksh.	Makshirin	Yad.	Yadaim
Meg.	Megillah	Yeb.	Yebamoth
Meil.	Meilah	Yom.	Yoma
Men.	Menahoth	Zab.	Zabim
Midd.	Middoth	Zeb.	Zebahim
Mikw.	Mikwaoth		

T. signifies Tosephta
b. signifies the Babylonian Talmud
j. signifies the Jerusalem Talmud

Bar. = Baraita (an ancient tradition not inserted in the Mishnah)
b. = ben
R. = Rabbi

PART ONE

ECONOMIC CONDITIONS IN THE CITY OF JERUSALEM

under Roman rule to the time of its destruction by Titus (AD 6–70)

In order to obtain a complete picture of the economic life of an ancient oriental city we must enquire into the nature of its industries, its commerce, and its traffic. Further, if the character of the city is to emerge from this enquiry, when we have established the existing conditions, we must then examine the causes which have brought them about.

I

INDUSTRIES

THE TYPICAL FORM of industry of the period was the crafts-man's shop; i.e. the producer owned the means of production, put them to use and sold his products directly to the consumer without intermediary.

The crafts were held in high esteem in Judaism at the time: 'He who does not teach his son a craft teaches him brigandage' (b. Kidd. 29a). We have special evidence in the case of Jerusalem: 'R. Johanan said three things in the name of the men of Jerusalem . . . treat your Sabbath like a week day rather than be dependent upon your fellow men' (b. Pes. 113a and parr.). Theory and practice went to-gether. When M. Bikk. iii.3 describes the entry of the first-fruits into Jerusalem, where the procession was met by the leading priests and Temple officials, special mention is made of the fact that even the craftsmen stood up and greeted the procession as it passed. This was an unusual sign of reverence, for whereas everyone else had to greet scholars by rising to their feet, craftsmen were exempt while engaged in their occupation (b. Kidd. 33a). The high value attributed to craftsmen and their work is above all attested by the fact that most of the scribes of the time plied a trade. Paul, who studied in Jerusalem (Acts 22.3), was a σκηνοποιός (Acts 18.3), a tent-maker (Knopf), or a carpet weaver (Achelis), or a weaver of tent curtains (Leipoldt). A list of the earliest scribes mentioned in the Talmud shows the following professions among others: nail maker, flax trader, baker, miller of pearl barley, currier, scrivener, sandal maker, master builder, asphalt merchant, tailor (Bill. II, 745f.).

This does not mean that there were no despised trades. Weaving, for instance, belonged to that category (p. 5). We have several lists of trades which, for various reasons, were despised. Some were dirty, some notorious for leading to fraud, others had to do with women. These are discussed on pp. 303–12.

After this survey of the status of craftsmen in Judaism at that time, we turn to the city of Jerusalem.

A. THE INDUSTRIES OF JERUSALEM AND THEIR ORGANIZATION

First of all we must try and establish the facts. Which industries do we find in Jerusalem, and how were they organized? Here the sources make it clear that the Temple, both by its rebuilding (pp. 21f.) and by the daily cult, provided a focal point for various industries. Therefore we must consider it separately from those industries which served the needs of the whole community.

1. *Industries which served the general public*

Geographically, culturally and politically the province of Judaea belonged to the province of Syria, but it is difficult to determine the relationship between the two Roman governors, though there is no doubt that the governor of the former was subordinate to that of the latter. The chief industrial products of the interior of Syria at that time were woollen goods, such as carpets, blankets, and woven stuffs; then came perfumed ointments and resins.[1] There is evidence that these commodities were also produced in Jerusalem.

Let us consider first those industries which produced commodities for domestic use, then the catering trades, the production of luxury goods, and finally the building trade.

(a) *Goods for domestic use*

M.B.K. x.9 reads, 'From women can be bought garments of wool in Judaea, and garments of linen in Galilee.' According to this, *woollen manufacture* was a speciality of Judaea. M. Ket. v.5 mentions work in wool as a task which married women should carry out. In Jerusalem wool was sold in one of the markets of the city. M. Erub. x.9 (cf. b. Erub. 101a) tells us, 'R. Jose said, It happened in the wool carders' market.' Levy (IV, 200a) translates the word ṣammārīm equally correctly as 'wool merchants' market', since the word used for wool dressers and for dealers in the finished goods is the same. *BJ* 5.331 tells us that the wool market at Jerusalem was to be found in the suburb known as the New City.

The dressed wool had to be spun into thread, and was then ready

[1] Guthe, *Die griechisch-römischen Städte*, 40.

for *weaving*, which was also carried on in Jerusalem. In the Syriac Apocalypse of Baruch, written soon after AD 70, the virgins of Jerusalem were addressed thus: 'And you, O virgins, who spin fine linen and silk with gold of Ophir' (10.19). From this statement, and from the fact that eighty-two virgins were known as skilled weavers of the Temple (p. 25), and finally, from a remark in Josephus, we may conclude that weaving was a task for women only. Indeed, Josephus speaks of two Babylonian Jews who learned the art of weaving, 'for it is not there (in Mesopotamia) considered unbecoming for men too to be weavers of cloth' (*Ant.* 18.314). It is true to say that weaving, when undertaken by men, was a despised trade in Palestine. Weavers were disqualified from the high priesthood. Their quarter in Jerusalem was the despised neighbourhood of the Dung Gate (M. Eduy, i.3). It is an example of great magnanimity, and was reported as such (M. Eduy. i.3), that Hillel and Shammai were prepared in a dispute to accept the witness of two respectable weavers of Jerusalem. It is not impossible that we have further evidence of weavers in Jerusalem in the form of the word *ṭarsiyîm*.[2]

Along with the craft of the weaver went that of the *fuller*, who had to render the cloth from the looms watertight by teasing together the fibres. The north-east corner of the northernmost wall formed the so-called 'fuller's tomb' (*BJ* 5.147). It was a fuller with his mallet who gave the death-blow to James the Just, brother of Jesus, when in AD 62 he was thrown by the Jews from the pinnacle of the Temple.[3]

From the fuller the material passed on to the *tailor*. According to *BJ* 5.331 there was a clothing market in the New City. In the Midrash Rabbah on Lamentations there is mention of the tailors of Jerusalem (Lam. R. 1.1, Son. 69).

Provision of clothing also occupied the *leather industry*. We do not know whether there were tanneries in Jerusalem. According to M.B.B. ii.9, tanneries had to be at least fifty cubits distance from a, or

---

[2] b.Meg. 26a refers to a synagogue of the *ṭarsiyîm* in Jerusalem. The word denotes either a gathering of people of Tarsus or a trade. If it is not translated 'synagogue of the people from Tarsus', which we hold to be right (p. 66), then it must mean people who are coppersmiths (Delitzsch, *Artisan Life*, 41; Schürer II, 524 n. 77, cf. II, 87 n. 247 [ET omits]), weavers or miners (Levy, II, 193b), skilled weavers or metal workers (Dalman, *WB*, 177a), or, better still, manufacturers of Tarsian garments (Krauss, *TA* II, 625 n. 67), for such is probably the meaning of ταρσικάριος in several papyri, as C. Wessely has shown (*Studien zu Palaeographie und Papyruskunde*, Leipzig 1901). He refers to the *edictum de pretiis* of Diocletian, 26–28, which deals with Tarsian and Alexandrian linen goods.

[3] Eusebius, *HE* II, 23.18; cf. *Ant.* 20.200.

the, city, and must be placed only to the east. Since Jerusalem is 'the city',[4] it is probable that this rule was originally intended for Jerusalem. At any rate, the associated ruling (M.B.B. ii.9) concerning graves was evidently carried out in Jerusalem. If the ruling was intended originally for Jerusalem, there must have been tanneries there, but they had to lie outside the walls. They had plenty of material, for R. Ḥananiah (some MSS read Hanina), the chief of the priests, reports (M. Eduy. ii.2) that the priests kept the hide of every animal they sacrificed, even if it was subsequently found unclean. We hear that the innkeepers of Jerusalem (b. Yom. 12a) used to take by force from the festal pilgrims the skins of the holy sacrifices, meaning principally the Passover sacrifices which were slaughtered by the owners, the hides of which did not belong to the priests. Sandal merchants are also mentioned in Jerusalem (Lam. R. 1.1, Son. 79).

We have evidence of certain other trades which served chiefly domestic needs. *BJ* 5.331 makes mention of the *smith*'s bazaar. This trade had its place in the New City. We are told that the high priest Joḥanan (John Hyrcanus, 134–104 BC) forbade 'workers in bronze and iron' to exercise their profession in Jerusalem on the lesser 'middle days' of the feasts (on which work involving noise was forbidden (T. Sot. xiii.10; 320)): these workers, mentioned in M.M. Sh. v.15 and M. Sot. ix.10, are the smiths. This industry seems to have converted itself into a war industry during the Roman-Jewish war of AD 66–70 in a very short time: 'In Jerusalem they busied themselves . . . with the preparation of engines of war, and in all the city missiles and suits of armour were being forged' (*BJ* 2.648f.; cf. 6.327).

According to b.B.K. 82b and b. Zeb. 96a *potteries* were not allowed in Jerusalem because of the smoke, but there is some doubt on the trustworthiness of this collection of laws of cleanliness concerning Jerusalem (see pp. 42ff., on gardens, and p. 47 on poultry). The fact that Jer. 18.2f. speaks of a house of a potter in Jerusalem, and Matt. 27.7 of a potter's field, weighs more heavily than the rabbinic tradition, although only the first passage is incontestable, since Matt. 27.7 may well be influenced by Jer. 18.2f. (p. 140).

(b) Food trades

The article to be mentioned here in the first place is *oil*. Eupolemos and Pseudo-Aristeas 112 say that olive trees took pride of place

[4] Cf. M. Sanh. i.5: 'They must add nothing to the city and to the courts of the Temple.'

among the crops in the neighbourhood of Jerusalem. As a matter of fact, the soil around Jerusalem is well suited to the cultivation of olives. Certainly there must have been much larger olive groves in the time of Christ than today, for as a result of bad economy under Turkish rule the planting of trees in the whole of Palestine became very restricted in comparison with earlier times. Place names near Jerusalem which contain the word 'oil' demonstrate this. To the east we find the name 'Mount of Olive Trees' (Mark 11.1), or 'Olive Grove' (Luke 19.29; 21.37; Acts 1.12; *Ant.* 7.202). The Talmud calls it *ṭūr zētā*, 'Mount of Oil' (cf. Targum; j. Taan. iv.8, 69a). This hill would scarcely have been so called if its groves had not been outstandingly luxuriant in comparison with the surrounding land, and the olives not of economic importance for the city. The Talmud actually attests that it was cultivated: according to b. Pes. 14a the Mount of Olives was ploughed at the time of the second Temple. For the south of Jerusalem, Jerome bears witness that there were olive trees in the valley of Hinnom (*Comm. on Jer.* II, 45 on 7.30).[5]

The olives were processed in and around Jerusalem. According to M. Men. viii.3, some of the oil that was needed for the Temple was brought from Peraea. The question of the purity of the oil being defiled by its journey through heathen territory was answered in j. Hag. iii.4,79c.3, namely that the whole olives should be obtained (from Peraea), and should then be pressed in Jerusalem. Several presses have indeed been found in the northern part of the city. Again, we read in the New Testament, 'And they came to a place named Gethsemane' (Mark 14.32; Matt. 26.36; cf. Luke 22.39). John 18.1 says of the place 'where there was a garden'. Gethsemane means an oil or perfume press.[6] The Mishnah has regulations regarding oil presses 'whose entrance lay within [the city] and their enclosed space outside' (M.M. Sh. iii.7). Since oil presses could hardly have been built in the actual wall of the city, we must assume that the area of Greater Jerusalem is meant rather than the actual city, or that the oil presses here serve merely as a casuistical illustration. The fact remains that oil presses in Jerusalem are taken for granted. Finally, it should be noted that oil was probably the only export of Jerusalem.[7]

Jer. 37.21 presumes the existence of a bazaar of *bakers* from ancient

[5] For a collection of place names comprising the word 'oil' in a wider area around the city, see Smith, *Jerusalem* II, 300 n. 3.

[6] Cf. G. Dalman, *Grammatik des jüdisch-palästinischen Aramäisch*, 2nd ed., Leipzig 1905 (reprinted Darmstadt 1960), 191.

[7] Smith, *Jerusalem* I, 15, 299f.

times, and Josephus (*Ant.* 15.309) mentions the bakers of Jerusalem in connection with a famine. The last passage makes it clear that this trade did not exist as a matter of course, since domestic baking was common.

The *butchers* were organized as elsewhere in guilds in the 'Butchers' Street' (T. Nidd. vi.17, 648; b. Nidd. 57b). The sellers of fattened cattle also had a bazaar in Jerusalem (Erub. x.9). An Athenian is said to have had cheese and eggs brought from a Jerusalem market (Lam. R. 1.10 on 1.1, Son. 1.9, 77).

There was also the occupation of *water seller*, an oddity to us. Josephus is witness to the fact that in years when rain was scanty, water was bought and sold: 'You know that before his [Titus'] arrival, the pool of Siloam and all other wells in front of the city dried up, so that water had to be sold in pitchers' (*BJ* 5.410). The water carrier in Mark 14.13 ('there shall meet you a man carrying a pitcher of water') belongs here, unless he was a domestic servant.

(c) *Luxury goods*

There is evidence for the manufacture of ointments and resins in Jerusalem. j. Yom. iv.5, 41d.37, says: 'The spice makers[8] of Jerusalem said: "If they had put a little honey into the incense the strong odour of it would be unbearable to the world." '[9] In this connection we should recall the legend in b. Shab. 63a: 'The woods of Jerusalem consisted of cinnamon trees; when men used these for fuel, a pleasant odour was diffused.' From this it would seem that cinnamon trees were cultivated in Jerusalem, which is out of the question. All we can be sure of is that cinnamon was used for incense in the Temple (*BJ* 6.390).

Mark 16.1 (cf. Luke 23.56f.) gives proof of the sale of ointments in Jerusalem when it speaks of the Galilean women who stood by the cross of Jesus, 'They bought spices (mixed with ointment), that they might go and anoint him'. John 19.39 mentions Nicodemus coming to the sepulchre of Jesus 'with a mixture of myrrh and aloes, about one hundred [Roman] pounds weight'. We may presume also that oil of roses was made in Jerusalem at the time, for while ornamental gardens were forbidden, according to b.B.K. 82b,[10] a rose garden is

---

[8] So Dalman, *WB*, 317b. Levy IV, 27a, says 'chemists'.

[9] It is also possible that in j. Sot. viii. 3, 22c.16, par. j. Shek. vi.1, 49c.47; M. Erub. x.9, spice-makers are meant where the word *paṭṭāmīm* is used. Usually the other translation of the word, 'a seller of fat cattle', is preferred.

[10] For a criticism of this see pp. 42ff.

expressly excepted (cf. T. Neg. vi.2, 625; M. Maas. ii.5). Dealers in ointments are repeatedly mentioned in rabbinic literature.[11] The court of Herod the Great, with its magnificent luxury and many women, contributed to the prosperity of this industry in Jerusalem.

The luxury trade in general increased greatly because of the Herodian court. This is specially true of *arts and crafts* whose centre was in the Upper City.[12] As early as the time of Pompey we hear of a unique masterpiece in gold that came from Judaea (meaning no doubt Jerusalem). 'Whether it was a grape vine or a garden, τερπωλή (delight) is what they call this work of art', says Strabo of Cappadocia (*Ant.* 14.35).

Frequent mention is made of a piece of jewellery called *'ir šel zāhāb*, 'the golden city' (M. Kel. ix.8; M. Shab. vi.1; b. Sot. 49b; j. Sot. ix.16, 24c.6). This ornament is also called 'golden Jerusalem', *yerūšalāyim dedahebā* (b. Shab. 59a; b. Ned. 50a). The question was discussed whether or not women should wear jewellery on the Sabbath, and the text reckons the 'golden Jerusalem' as a head ornament (T. Shab. iv.6, 115). In the *Aboth de Rabbi Nathan* 6a (Goldin 42) and elsewhere, it is said that only ladies of high rank wore this jewel. So the 'golden Jerusalem' was a costly head ornament for women. It may be imagined as a kind of *corona muralis*, and the name 'golden Jerusalem' suggests that the ornament was originally made in Jerusalem. Today, the manufacture of souvenirs forms a particularly flourishing branch of arts and crafts in Jerusalem. In Ephesus there is evidence of a similar industry in the time of Paul. Acts 19.23ff. gives an account of a riot among the makers of souvenirs there.[13] Bearing in mind the great significance of the annual pilgrim feasts for the Holy City, we may well conclude that such items of jewellery were widely bought as souvenirs there. Indirect evidence of the manufacture of signet rings with figured engraving is provided by R. Eleazar b. Zadoq (*c.* AD 100) when he says, 'All manner of seals were to be found in Jerusalem, with the exception of human faces.'[14]

Finally the profession of *scrivener* was included among the arts and crafts, and b. B.B. 14a describes the method the Jerusalem scriveners used to roll up a book.

On arts and crafts connected with building, see below pp. 15f.

[11] Krauss, *TA* I, 242.
[12] Delitzsch, *Artisan Life*, 61.
[13] Acts 19.24: 'a maker of silver shrines of Artemis'.
[14] *parsūpōt*, Gk. πρόσωπα. T.A. Zar. v.2, 468.15. The parallel in j. A. Zar. iii.1, 42c.58, names R. Eleazar b. Simon (*c.* AD 180) as the author.

(d) The building trade

(i) **Building activity**

The princes of the Herodian royal line were enthusiastic builders, and their example challenged imitation. As a result the building trade held an important position in Jerusalem under their rule and for some time afterwards. The most important building operations are the following:

(a) Under Herod the Great 37 BC–4 BC

1. The rebuilding of the Temple (20/19 BC–AD 62/64).[15]

2. The rebuilding of Herod's palace in the Upper City near the 'western gate which leads towards Lydda' (Lam. R. 1.32 on 1.5, Son. 1.31, 104), today the Jaffa Gate (*BJ* 5.176–83).

3. The building of three towers, Hippicus, Phasael and Mariamne, in the same area (*BJ* 5.161–76).

4. Dominating the Temple, in the north-west corner of the Temple area, at the supposed place of the former Temple fortress Bira or Baris (Neh. 2.8; 7.21), arose the huge fortress of Antonia (*BJ* 5.238–47).

5. The splendid tomb of Herod, which he had erected during his lifetime.[16] It remained unused, as he was buried in the Herodium.[17]

6. The theatre built by Herod in Jerusalem (*Ant.* 15.268).

7. The Jerusalem Hippodrome (*Ant.* 17.255; *BJ* 2.44), which may be attributed to Herod.[18]

8. A water-channel (see below p. 14).

9. The memorial over the entrance to David's tomb (*Ant.* 16.182; cf. 7.392ff.).

10. The five magnificent porticoes, about 27 feet high, around and

[15] See p. 21.

[16] *BJ* 5.108 etc.: 'up to the tomb of Herod'.

[17] Jebel el Fureidis, nine miles south of Jerusalem.

[18] Unless the 'place of exercise and training' (I Macc. 1.14; II Macc. 4.9, 12, 14) is to be considered as a stadium and identified with the Hippodrome (Dalman, *SW*, 278). That would place its erection between 174 and 171 B.C. But since II Macc. 4.14 speaks of a *palaestra*, it appears to have been a wrestling school. This 'place of exercise' is most probably identical with the Xystus, a covered colonnade, formerly a gymnasium (Guthe, *PRE* VIII, 684), which fits the topographical indications. The Xystus lies on the western hill of Jerusalem, in the north-east corner of the Upper City, opposite the western wall of the Temple area, whereas the modern street name Ḥaret el-Maidan ('street of the race-course') suggests that the Hippodrome was somewhat south-west of the Xystus; such names quite often reflect reliable tradition. Thus it is very likely to have been built by Herod. 'The very large amphitheatre in the plain' (*Ant.* 15.268) should be distinguished from the Hippodrome; it was probably located in the plain of Jericho (cf. *Ant.* 17.194; *BJ* 1.666).

across the twin pools of Bethesda (John 5.2) were probably erected in Herod's time.[19]

(β) Under Agrippa I AD 41–44

According to *BJ* 2.218; *Ant.* 19.326f.; *BJ* 5.149–55, Agrippa I built the northernmost wall of the city, which enclosed a very considerable area. Josephus says that it was almost exactly two miles long. (Three miles and three-quarters = 33 stades, the total circumference of the city according to *BJ* 5.159, minus about a mile and a half, the total of the pre-Agrippan west, south and east sides.) Josephus cannot praise the strength of this wall too highly. He says it was 10 cubits thick and built of blocks of stone 20 cubits long and 10 cubits wide, i.e. the blocks measured 10.5 by 5.25 metres (34 ft. 6 ins. by 17 ft. 3 ins.), and the wall was 5.25 metres thick.[20]

---

[19] Cf. J. Jeremias, *The Rediscovery of Bethesda* (New Testament Archaeology Series 1), Louisville, Ky., 1966.

[20] A word must be said here about the size of the cubit in Palestine of those days, since it will be used in our calculations. There is no agreement about its size. To begin with, different sizes of cubit were used within Jerusalem itself. M. Kel. xvii.9 says, 'There were two kinds of cubit [in one room of the Temple] . . ., one in the north-east corner and one in the south-east. The first was longer by half a finger-breadth than the Mosaic cubit, and the second half a finger-breadth longer still [i.e. a whole finger-breadth longer than the Mosaic cubit]. And why was there ordained a larger cubit and a smaller cubit? So that craftsmen might undertake their work to the measure of the smaller cubit, and fulfil it according to the measure of the larger.' In fact, work in gold and silver used the half finger-breadth longer. and other work the whole finger-breadth longer. The Rabbis go even further, and distinguish between no fewer than six kinds of cubit: the building cubit, the tool cubit, the land cubit, the circular cubit, the Mosaic cubit, the royal cubit. The Temple was built according to building cubits (F. Hultsch, *Griechische und römische Metrologie*, 2nd ed. rev., 1882, 441). Now it is remarkable that the measurements given by Josephus for the Temple are repeatedly in agreement with those of the Mishnah Tractate Middoth, e.g. as to the width and the height of the forefront of the Temple building. As far as Josephus is concerned, two measurements are in question: (*a*) The Roman cubit (*cubitus*) of six-hand-breadths of 74 mm., i.e. nearly 3 inches, each=444 mm., i.e. nearly 18 inches. (So Krauss, *TA* II, 388ff., following Lübker, *Reallexikon des klassischen Altertums*, 7th ed., Leipzig, 1891.) The likelihood that Josephus, although possessing estates in Judaea (*Vita* 422), lived and wrote in Rome (cf. e.g. his connection with the Roman emperors, *Vita* 422ff., Schürer I, 76, ET I.1, 80) would explain his use of the Roman cubit. (*b*) The cubit of the Phileterian system of measurement, called after the surname of the kings of Pergamum, which was standard in the eastern empire from the establishment of the province of Asia (133 BC). It measured 525 mm., i.e. almost 21 inches (Hultsch, *op. cit.*, I, 597ff.; O. Holtzmann, *Neutestamentliche Zeitgeschichte*, Freiburg 1895, 118; O. Holtzmann, *Middot* [coll. *Die Mischna*], Giessen 1913, 12–15). This measurement was in fact customary in Palestine and Egypt, as we know from Julian of Ascalon (a Byzantine writer; see *Metrologicorum scriptorum reliquiae* [coll. Teubner], ed. F. Hultsch, I, Leipzig 1864, 54f., 200f.), and was not displaced

Ninety massively built towers defended the wall (*BJ* 5.158); the strongest was the octagonal Psephinus tower situated to the north-west, which is said to have been seventy cubits (about 120 feet) high (*BJ* 5.159f.). The ban put on the building of the wall by the Emperor Claudius, as a result of a denunciation by the Syrian governor Vivius Marcus, interrupted the work (*Ant.* 19.326f.), and not until the beginning of the rebellion in AD 66 was it finished (*BJ* 6.323; 2.563; 5.152).

(γ) Under Agrippa II King of Chalcis AD 50–53; King of Batanea, Trachonitis, Gaulanitis, Abila and an area of the Lebanon known as the Eparchy of Varus, AD 53–100[21]

1. He enlarged the Hasmonean (Maccabean) palace. This lay at the north-eastern end of the hill on which stood the Upper City, west of the Temple, and above the Xystus (*Ant.* 14.5ff.; *BJ* 1.120f.; *Ant.* 14.58–63; *BJ* 1.142ff.; cf. Luke 23.6ff.). Probably this did not involve a new building, but only an extension of the old palace: 'He built a mighty building on to the royal citadel in Jerusalem, near the Xystus; the royal citadel itself had been erected earlier by the Hasmoneans' (*Ant.* 20.189f.). The result of the enlargement was that the king had a view from the palace of the whole Temple court, which had not been the case hitherto; the priests, therefore, had a wall built to block the view; the resultant quarrel was even brought before Nero (*ibid.* 194f.). In this palace there was perhaps an audience window (*BJ* 2.344), like the 'window of appearance' attested for Egypt by pictures and assumed for the palace of Ahab and Jezebel (II Kings 9.30–33) by H. Gressmann.[22] This building was set on fire by the insurgents at the beginning of the rebellion (*BJ* 2.426).

2. A further undertaking of Agrippa II was occasioned by the completion of the Temple between AD 62 and 64, an event which left

---

by the Roman cubit. Didymus (end of first century AD) provides evidence for Egypt, that this statement also applies to a time before Julian of Ascalon. He calculates the Egyptian cubit of Roman times as 1½ Ptolemaic feet (525 mm. or 21 inches), the same length that was in use as early as the third century BC in Egypt (Holtzmann, *Middot* 13). We are justified then in assuming that the Philetarian cubit was already standard for Palestine during the first century of the Christian era. Thus the cubit of rabbinic literature may be taken as 525 mm.=21 inches. We have already seen that Josephus has the same standard as the Mishnah for measuring the cubit, i.e. the Philetarian cubit of 525 mm.

[21] *BJ* 2.247; *Ant.* 20.138; Schürer I, 587, ET I.2, 193.
[22] *Der Messias*, 2nd ed., Göttingen 1929, 45f.

more than 18,000 workers unemployed. To provide work for these people was an act of social concern which the king, who had control of the Temple treasury, was urged to do by the whole population of Jerusalem. In order to relieve unemployment he had the city of Jerusalem paved with white stone, probably limestone, at the expense of the Temple treasury (*Ant.* 20.222).

Now a paved street has been found in Jerusalem which has been identified as being near the west wall and part of the south wall of the Temple court. The position of this pavement, which lies about 40 feet below the present surface, and supports the vaulted stones which bear 'Robinson's Arch' (so called after E. Robinson who discovered the remains of the arch which once joined the Temple court and the Upper City), indicates a date before AD 70.[23]

Another broader paved street, in places about 25 feet wide, probably a continuation of the first, was discovered by J. C. Bliss north of the pool of Siloam. It shows signs of heavy wear by pedestrians. As this lies in the southern part of the city, which after the time of the Emperor Hadrian no longer lay inside the city walls, the paving of this street also should be dated before the destruction of Jerusalem in AD 70. So it is possible that we have in these two places remains of the paving laid down by Agrippa II.

3. However, this employment was short-lived; so it is likely that it was to meet a new threat of unemployment among the Temple workers that Agrippa II, in co-operation with the high priests and the people, began new building works in the Temple before AD 66 (p. 22).

(δ) The Royal Family of Adiabene

This family, whose kingdom lay on the boundaries of the Roman and the Parthian states, erected other large buildings (*BJ* 2.250; 6.355; M. Naz. iii.6; j. Sukk. i.1, 51d. 22, 25; j. Naz. iii.6, 52d.38). We read in *BJ* 5.252 of a palace of King Monobazus, which according to the context, lay on the southern part of the eastern hill. Further, *BJ* 6.355 speaks of the palace of Queen Helena of Adiabene. This palace lay in the middle of the Acra, and so also on the eastern hill (*BJ* 5.138). The exact location of the palace of Princess Grapte of Adiabene is doubtful. According to the context it lay not far from the Temple; we should, perhaps, look for it also on the eastern hill (*BJ* 4.567). Finally, Queen Helena erected a tomb for herself three

---

[23] P. Thomsen, *Denkmäler Palästinas aus der Zeit Jesu*, Leipzig 1916, 29f.

stades north from Jerusalem, in the form of three pyramids. Eusebius mentions the pillars of the monument,[24] and Pausanias[25] compares its splendour with that of the tomb of Mausolus in Halicarnassus. It was, therefore, an unusually imposing building for the period.

(ε) *Pontius Pilate*

Next, as a building in the grand manner, the aqueduct built by Pontius Pilate deserves mention (*BJ* 2.175; *Ant.* 18.60). Because he financed the project from the Temple treasury, his action provoked a public uproar, and the furious crowd had to be quietened by soldiers with cudgels. The conduit was doubtless like that described by Pseudo-Aristeas 90, lined with lead and lime mortar.

The remains of two conduits which brought water to Jerusalem from the south have been discovered.[26] The 'higher' is Roman (the inscription indicates AD 165), the 'lower' is older, and in its construction shows a similar technique to the aqueduct laid out by Herod at the Wadi Artas (near Bethlehem) which once supplied the Herodium, the fortress built by Herod (*Ant.* 15.323ff.). This lower conduit is, without doubt, that built by Pilate.

Besides all this, we have reports of other building work; for example the construction and rebuilding of a synagogue, with an inn for strangers and with baths, on Ophel.[27]

(ii) The building workers

(a) *Ordinary building*

Stone was the most important building material. As the first step for rebuilding the Temple, Herod prepared a thousand wagons for transporting the necessary stone (*Ant.* 15.390). *BJ* 7.26–31 describes the flight of Simon, one of the leaders of the Jewish insurgents. He tried to escape with his companions by way of an underground passage, along with '*stonecutters*, bringing the tools necessary for their craft'. The 'Royal Caverns' mentioned in *BJ* 5.147 beside which, according to Josephus, the third northern wall later passed, must for a long time have served as a quarry. There still exists an enormous cave, the so-called Cotton Cave, which runs underneath part of the northern city, and extends from the present wall for about 200 yards under the city to the south. Its entrance is under the present north

[24] Eusebius, *HE* II, 12.3.
[25] *Descr. Graeciae* VIII, 16.
[26] Guthe, *PRE* VIII, 682, 686.
[27] According to the inscription found by R. Weill, *CIJ* II, 1404.

wall. The Talmud (b. Erub. 61b) speaks of a cave of Zedekiah at Jerusalem which was extraordinarily large and uninhabited; according to the Midrash Tanḥuma (*Bemidbar* 9, 485, 7; Bill. II, 592f.) it was said to extend for 12 miles (probably Egyptian miles, about 40 yards shorter than English ones). It is possible that this cave is identical with one of the two already mentioned. If the course of the northernmost wall (see p. 11) was the same as that of the present north wall, then there is some possibility of identifying all the three caves. According to M. Par. iii.2, 2, there were 'caves under the whole Temple hill and under the forecourts'. Underground passages in the city were very important during the capture of Jerusalem, and people hid there for some time afterwards.

There is evidence that a certain Simeon, from the village of Siknim, a '*digger of wells, mines and caverns*', lived in Jerusalem at the time before the destruction (Eccles. R. 4.18 on 4.17, Son. 125).

(β) Skilled craftsmanship in building

Most of the buildings mentioned on pp. 10ff. were very ornate, and provided plenty of scope for the *skilled craftsman*. Especially was the palace of Herod, according to Josephus (*BJ* 5.176), rich in unique works of art. Both in exterior decoration and interior appointment, in the selection of materials as in their treatment, in wealth of variety as in costly detail, the various crafts competed: the sculptor, the tapestry maker, the planner of fountains and ornamental gardens, the goldsmith and the silversmith, were all engaged in the work (*BJ* 5.178ff.).

Stone-masons had an important place among the craftsmen of Jerusalem. This is confirmed by what little remains of the architecture of the period, which comprises the so-called 'Royal Tombs' and three monuments in the Kidron Valley, now called 'Absalom's Tomb', 'St James' Cave' and 'the Tomb of Zechariah'.

The 'Royal Tombs' are identical with the tomb of Helena (pp. 13f. *BJ* 5.147: 'opposite the tomb of Helena'; *Ant.* 20.95: 'in the three pyramids that his mother had had erected at a distance of three stades from Jerusalem' (cf. *BJ* 5.55, 199). A moulded cornice has partly survived here, with fluted spirals decorated with fruit and foliage. Before the entrance to the grave lie the remains of columns, among them Corinthian capitals.

At 'Absalom's Tomb' Ionic and Doric capitals, once supported by half-columns and corner pilasters, are preserved. Immediately above the capitals is an ornamental frieze; the architrave is Doric.

Ionic capitals are to be found on the pyramid of the 'Tomb of Zechariah', and at 'St James Cave' pillars with Doric capitals and above them a Doric frieze with triglyphs.[28]

Most probably Jesus had in mind the 'Tomb of Absalom' and the pyramid of Zechariah when he uttered his woe against those who 'build the tombs of the prophets and adorn the monuments of the righteous' (Matt. 23.29f. par. Luke 11.47).[29]

These monuments are the only significant evidence we have for the contribution of Jerusalem to the sphere of architectural sculpture, from the time before its destruction by Rome.

We should conclude this survey of skilled craftsmen employed in building with a reference to the *mosaic makers*. In various parts of Jerusalem, e.g. south-east of the Cenaculum, mosaic floors have been found which must belong partly to the period before AD 70.

(γ) Building maintenance

In addition to labourers and skilled craftsmen, *maintenance workers* were necessary for buildings. Maintenance of 'the water-channel, of walls, towers and everything else needed by the city', was paid for from the Temple treasury (M. Shek. 4.2).[30] This included the maintenance of wells and cisterns, and the cleaning and supervision of streets. This agrees with the statement in b. Betz. 29a Bar. (cf. b.B.K. 94b) according to which misappropriated property, the ownership of which could not be decided, was used by the Temple treasurers for public works such as ditches, cisterns and caves, i.e. for the maintenance of the water supply of Jerusalem.

Road sweepers may be referred to in b.B.M. 26a (cf. b. Pes. 7a): 'According to R. Shemaiah b. Zeira the streets of Jerusalem were

---

[28] To determine the age of these monuments is a matter for the history of architecture. Absalom's tomb and the pyramid of Zechariah are first described by the Pilgrim of Bordeaux in AD 333 (P. Geyer, *Itinera Hierosolymitana saeculi IIII–VIII*, CSEL 39, 1898, 23, lines 10–13), but the origin of these four monuments is undoubtedly to be placed in the time before the destruction of Jerusalem in AD 70.

[29] J. Jeremias, *Heiligengräber in Jesu Umwelt*, Göttingen 1958, 68, 114.

[30] According to J. J. Rabe, *Mischnah* II, Onolzbach 1761, 147, on M. Shek. iv.2, the water-channel was that flowing from the Temple forecourt down into the Kedron Valley (p. 44). But the passage can also refer to the aqueduct mentioned above, p. 14. If this is true, Pilate, when drawing upon the Temple treasury to finance the project, did no more than punish a neglect on the part of Jerusalem's municipality, the Sanhedrin, by assuming, however illegitimately, the latter's duty. His action would have meant that the Temple money was spent for the purpose for which it was intended.

swept every day', evidently to secure the levitical purity of the city. The fact that the Valley of Hinnom was a dump for filth and rubbish agrees with this statement. The upper end of the valley, between the tower of Hippicus and the Gate of the Essenes in the south, was called βηθσώ or βησοῦ (*BJ* 5.145); according to A. Neubauer's etymological explanation, this means 'place of filth'.[31] The gate called the Dung Gate M. Eduy, i.3 (cf. p. 5), the quarter of the despised weavers, gave immediately on to the Valley of Hinnom at its debouchment into the Kidron Valley. This accords with the fact that the Valley of Hinnom was a place of abomination from ancient times, since it was connected with the worship of Moloch (II Kings 23.10; Jer. 2.23 and elsewhere), and was supposed to be the same as Gehenna (Hell), which took its name from it. It was still in modern times the place for rubbish, carrion and all kinds of refuse.

It should also be mentioned that Jerusalem had drainage canals which were constructed with an almost modern care and precision. Bliss has traced their course in several places. Inside, they were from 1.78 to 2.36 m. (5 ft. 10 ins. to 7 ft. 9 ins.) high and from 0.76 to 0.91 m. (28 to 36 inches) broad. There appear to have been sluice holes to take the water from the streets, and even manholes for cleaning.[32]

There may even have been *tomb guardians*, according to Krauss,[33] who refers to habitable rooms in the mausoleum (M. Erub. 5.1; b. Erub. 51a; T. Erub. vi.5, 144), and points to the 'Tomb of Absalom' in the Kidron valley as an example.

(e) Other trades

We should never dream nowadays of placing a *doctor* in the category of manual workers, but there is evidence that they were considered as such during that period. The word for manual work is *'ummānūt*, which can mean manual work, a profession, or a skill. An *'ummān* (*'ummānā*) indicates a labourer, an artist, a leech, a surgeon, a bath attendant, a circumciser. Consequently, we must deal with the medical profession along with trades.[34] According to the Talmud there were doctors in every city and in every large place. M.B.K. viii.1 decrees that, in cases of injury or wounding, the person responsible must pay the doctor's fee. We have rabbinic evidence for doctors in the first century AD at Pegae (T. Yeb. vi.7, 248) and at Lydda

---

[31] *Géographie*, 139.
[32] Thomsen, *op. cit.* 25.
[33] Krauss, *TA* II, 80f.
[34] See also p. 26 (Temple doctor).

(T. Ohol. iv.2, 600). Josephus (*Vita* 403f.) received medical care after a fall from his horse at Capernaum.[35] At one place on the Sea of Galilee, probably also Capernaum, a woman came to Jesus 'who had suffered many things from many doctors' (Mark 5.26; cf. Luke 8.43). A doctor called Tobias is mentioned by name at Jerusalem (M.R. Sh. i.7; b. R. Sh. 22a), and Herod had his own private physicians (*BJ* 1.657). An interesting point is that the Mishnah tells how the Jerusalem doctors had their way of treating the sick during a festival without incurring levitical uncleanness: 'For thus they used to do in Jerusalem, that were afflicted with boils: On the eve of Passover a man would go to the physician, and he would cut [the boil] and leave but a hair's breadth; he [the sick person] then stuck it on a thorn and drew himself [suddenly] away from it. Thus the man was able to bring his Passover offering, and the physician was able to bring his Passover offering' (M. Ker. iii.8).

Ezek. 5.1. suggests that there were *barbers* in Jerusalem (p. 26); *BJ* 1.547 and *Ant.* 16.387 speak of a court barber called Trypho.

Washing was usually done by the housewives, but there were also professional launderers (T. Mikw. iv.10, 656.36).

Finally, *money changers* are explicitly mentioned in connection with the Temple.[36] They must also have played a part in secular money transactions, as is suggested by what will be said on the different currencies, on pp. 32f.

To sum up: those industries which played the greatest part in Jerusalem were the arts and crafts, crafts connected with the building industry, building itself, weaving and the manufacture of oil.

We have now presented a general view of the industries in Jerusalem (with the exception of those employed in the Temple) for the time up to AD 70. However, this picture is not complete. In the Near East even today, industries and their organization stand in very close interdependence, and they did so 1900 years ago. Therefore, to complete the picture we must deal with the following topics.

2. Guilds within the individual industries

(a) The layout of the city

The city was divided into two parts by the Tyropoeon valley, the Upper City in the west (*šūq hāʿelyōn*), and the Lower City in the

---

[35] Kepharnokos=Kepharnomos=Kepharnaum, *BJ* 3.519.
[36] Bill. I, 761ff.

east (*šūq hattaḥtōn*) on the Acra (*BJ* 5.136ff.; T. Hull. iii.23, 505; T. Sanh. xiv.14, 437; Lam. R. 1.49 on 1.16, Son. 1.46, 128, *et passim*). The Greek equivalents 'Upper and Lower Acra' (*BJ* 5.137) are as characteristic as the local names. *Sûq* still means 'bazaar' in modern Arabic. The Upper and Lower Cities thus contained the two principal market streets. This is confirmed by the so-called Madaba map, found in the Greek church of Madaba, and dating from the middle of the sixth century AD. Because the east is conservative in matters of town planning, it is certain that at least the general scheme remained the same between AD 70 and the sixth century. According to this map, two parallel arcades ran through the city from north to south, the Great and Small market streets. The first of these, whose course corresponded to the modern Suq Bab el-'Amud (Bazaar of the Damascus Gate) and its southern prolongation, the Ḥaret en-Nebi Daud, ran through the suburbs and the Upper City. The second arcade corresponds to the modern El Wad street, and followed approximately the course of the Tyropoeon valley. Josephus (*BJ* 5.146) describes the second northern wall as running round the northern district of the Lower City called the Acra (*BJ* 5.137), and so attests the extension of the Lower City from the south-eastern hill (Ophel) towards the north (*BJ* 5.146). This extension leaves only the Tyropoeon valley as the link between the southern and northern parts of the Acra. This shows that the Tyropoeon valley and the small arcade formed part of the Lower City.

These two main commercial streets were linked by numerous side streets running from east to west, which led into the Tyropoeon valley (*BJ* 5.138ff.). The most important of these was the street which led from Herod's palace to the Temple, reaching it at the Xystus bridge. The present day Tariq Bab es-Silsele, one of the principal bazaars, corresponds to this street.

The suburb was located to the north of the Upper City and west of the Temple area, and still further north (in Jesus' days outside the city wall) was the New City called Bezata.

(b) *The distribution of industries in the city*

The craftsmen's shops, *ḥanūyōt*, were along these streets. The festal procession with the sheaf of the first-fruits probably passed along the small arcade, that is, the bazaar of the Lower City, and by the Xystus bridge to the Temple. Thus it was in the lower market that the craftsmen sat at work in their shops open to the street (M. Bikk.

iii.3; b. Kidd. 33a) when the procession passed (p. 3). It is likely
that there were shops even in the Temple court (b. R. Sh. 31a; b.
Shab. 15a; b. Sanh. 41a; b. A. Zar. 8b; Lam. R. 4.7 on 4.4, [other-
wise in Son. 220]; pp. 48f). Close by were the shops on the Mount of
Olives (Lam. R. 2.4 on 2.2, Son. 162), the shops of Beth Hino (b.
B.M. 88a; b. Hull. 53a) and those of the sons of Hanun or Hanan
(j. Peah i.6, 16c; Siphre Deut. 14.22, 105): these last two may be
identical. As mentioned above (p. 3), in these shops both the manufacture and the sale of goods took place.

Now we have already seen (pp. 4ff.) that each craft had its shops
in its own quarter, and in fact it is likely that each had its own bazaar
(*šūq*).

In Old Testament times, heathen tradespeople were situated in the
northern part of the city. Zeph. 1.10f. proclaims woes to the Fish Gate, the
Second Quarter, the hills and the Maktesh,[37] all situated in the north, thus
indicating that the enemy was coming from that direction. Verse 11 reads,
'Wail, O inhabitants of Maktesh, for the whole nation of Canaan is no
more.' The 'nation of Canaan' probably means Phoenician traders such as
are referred to in Jerusalem in Neh. 13.16. The Fish Gate, lying at the
point of intersection of the second north wall and the Tyropoeon valley
(Neh. 3.3; 12.39; Zeph. 1.10; II Chron. 33.14), took its name from Tyrian
fish merchants (Neh. 13.16). This, too, attests heathen traders in the north
of the city. The Jewish goldsmiths and perfumers mentioned in Neh. 3.8
presumably had their bazaar in the northern suburb west of the Temple.

In New Testament times the tailors evidently positioned themselves
near the gates. This is taken for granted for Jerusalem and Tyre in
Lam. R. 1.2 on 1.1. (Son. 69), and fits in with the fact that there was a
Clothes Market (*BJ* 5.331) in the northern suburb or New City.
Also in the New City were the bazaars of the wool carders or merchants (*šūq šel ṣammārim*; *BJ* 5.331; M. Erub. x.9; b. Erub. 101a) and
of the smiths (*BJ* 5.331).

Heathen fullers have been supposed to live in the Upper City, but
wrongly. There was a rule that spittle was regarded as clean in the whole
town except that found in the Upper City (M. Shek. viii.1); the Palestinian Talmud says that this was 'because a *qṣrn* of Gentiles was there'
(j. Shek. viii.1, 51a.20). The word, *qṣrn*, left untranslated, could mean
'fullers' (*qaṣṣārin*), but most probably it is to be derived from *qaṣrā*, 'citadel'.

[37] Literally 'the Mortar'; the meaning here is doubtful.

This makes excellent sense: it was the presence of the Roman garrison in Herod's palace which induced the rabbis to declare unclean the spittle found in the Upper City.

In the southern part of the Lower City, near the Dung Gate, the despised trade of weaving was quartered (p. 5).

(c) The organization of the trades

Here we have very little to go on. However, the very fact that the various industries were grouped together implies some sort of organization. Craftsmen of the same trade would settle down in the same part of the city, not only according to custom, but no doubt there was some pressure to do so.

From the fact that b. Sukk. 28a and b.B.B. 134a mention 'fullers' and fox fables', Delitzsch[38] concludes that the guilds 'formed a circle among themselves, and expressed themselves after a peculiar fashion, understood only by the initiated'; this last idea is suggested by the context.

We saw earlier (p. 18) that the Jerusalem doctors had their own ways of medical treatment. Tradition has it that the bakers of shewbread and the manufacturers of incense for the Temple had their own jealously guarded trade secrets (M. Yom. iii.11).

If the *tarsiyim* mentioned above (p. 5) were weavers or coppersmiths or makers of Tarsian garments in Jerusalem, we should have proof of the existence of a synagogue of whatever trade these people represented; but in my opinion the word means just 'Tarsians', though there is no doubt that it can mean all these trades.

The organization of the trades manifested itself in the first instance by localization, but there is some evidence that there was also some organization in the way of guilds.

3. Industries connected with the building of the Temple and its ceremonial

(a) The buildings

'Forty and six years was this Temple in building, and wilt thou raise it up in three days?' (John 2.20) said the Jews to Jesus about AD 27, and even then the building was not complete. Herod had begun it in 20/19 BC.[39]

---

[38] Delitzsch, *Artisan Life*, 40.
[39] 'In the eighteenth year of his reign' (*Ant.* 15.380) or 'in the fifteenth' (*BJ*

Only in AD 62–64, under the governor Albinus (*Ant.* 20.219), was the rebuilding of the Temple finally completed. Innovations were: the reconstruction of the Temple house, increasing its height from sixty to a hundred cubits; renovation of the holy Inner Court; the building of the large gate between the Court of Women and the Court of Israel; enlargement of the outer Court to the north and south by means of strong sub-structures; and adornment with colonnades which encircled the whole of the Temple area.[40] Shortly after the completion of the rebuilding, but before the outbreak of rebellion in AD 66, more building activity was projected, possibly as a means of social relief for the unemployed Temple workers (p. 13). This project included new foundations and a heightening of the Temple house by about twenty cubits. The timber had already been obtained from Lebanon by the time that the war against Rome broke out in AD 66 (*BJ* 5.36).

Upwards of 18,000 workmen are said to have been thrown out of work by the completion of the renovation of the Temple in AD 62–64. When the work began, 10,000 lay workers and 1,000 priests trained for the purpose are said to have been engaged. Even if we make allowance for Josephus' normal tendency to oriental exaggeration, it is clear that a whole army of labourers must have been involved.

Stone-cutters, carpenters, and craftsmen in gold, silver and bronze took a principal part in the work. For the construction of the consecrated area to which laymen had no access, priests had to be specially trained (*Ant.* 15.390). Some were taught masonry and some carpentry.

The stone-cutters had first to quarry their material. The largest possible blocks were of greatest value, but we need not take too seriously Josephus' statement (*BJ* 5.224) that these were blocks measuring 45 cubits by 5 by 6 (about 77 ft. 6 ins. by 8 ft. 8 ins. by 10 ft. 2 ins.). Some of the material was of great value. According to b. Sukk. 51b, the Temple was built of alabaster, stibium and marble. The courts were paved with different kinds of stone (*BJ* 5.192). Sculptors were also employed and, for example, in

---

1.401). Both statements point to the same year 20/19 BC, for Herod the Great was appointed King of Judaea in 40 BC but only succeeded in gaining possession of his kingdom in 37 BC with the conquest of Jerusalem. There were therefore two methods of reckoning the chronology of Herod's reign (*BJ* 1.665; *Ant.* 17.191) which differed by three years.

[40] Schlatter, *Geschichte Israels*, 240.

the 'royal' hall to the south, they had to make capitals for the 162 columns (*Ant.* 15.414). Furthermore, they had to carve the stone lattices three cubits high separating the Inner Court from the outer Courts of the Gentiles, and another, one cubit high, to separate the innermost Court of the Priests from the Court of Israel. They had also to carve stone tablets to be set up at regular intervals along the outer lattice, with Greek and Latin inscriptions warning Gentiles not to go beyond the lattice on pain of death. One of these stone tablets was found in 1871,[41] and another in 1936.[42]

The carpenters' task was to fix the beams, which were partly made of cedar wood (M. Midd. iii.5ff.; iv.5); the timber for these was brought from Lebanon. The colonnades which encircled the Temple court was roofed with cedar panelling, and cedar from Lebanon was also used for the sub-structure of the sanctuary.

Josephus in his account has depicted the Temple as gleaming all over with gold, even excelling the Mishnah account. The Talmud, on the other hand, warns us against taking these accounts too seriously: 'Moreover he (Herod) intended to overlay it (the Temple) with gold, but the wise men said to him, "Leave it alone, for it is more beautiful as it is, having the appearance of waves of the sea"' (b. Sukk. 51b). Still, Josephus, describing a view of the Temple building, says positively that its appearance was dazzling even where there was no gold (*BJ* 5.223); but even though we must take the statements of Josephus with critical caution, we cannot doubt that the Temple was built with the greatest possible splendour and provided great opportunities for craftsmanship in gold, silver and bronze. Indeed, on entering the Temple, no matter from what direction a man came, he would have to pass through double gates covered with gold and silver, with but one exception, as the Mishnah (M. Midd. ii.3) in agreement with Josephus (*BJ* 5.201) remarks: 'every gate there was gilded, except the Nicanor gates, for with them a miracle has happened; and others say, because their bronze shone like gold' (M. Midd. ii.3).[43]

[41] Ch. Clermont-Ganneau, 'Une stèle du Temple de Jerusalem', *Revue Archaéologique* NS 23, 1872, 214–34, 290–6.

[42] *CIJ* II, 1400.

[43] This Nicanor Gate, between the Court of Women and the Court of Israel, was made of Corinthian bronze (b. Yom. 38a; T. Yom. ii.4, 183), and the title 'the Gate Beautiful' given to it in Acts 3.2 confirms that it was out of the ordinary. This agrees with the tradition in Josephus (*BJ* 5.210ff.) that nine of the gates, together with their thresholds and lintels, were overlaid with gold and silver, but that one was made of Corinthian bronze and far exceeded the others in value (*BJ* 5.201).

Going further in, we should see in the Court of Women golden lamps, with four golden bowls hanging over them (M. Sukk. v.2). In a room of the treasury (Mark 12.41; Luke 21.1) we should see the sacred gold and silver bowls and vessels (M. Yom. iv.4, etc.). Some of these had no bases (*b^{e}siqin*, M. Pes. v.5; b. Pes. 64a), a sign that old tradition was kept up, but those used on the Day of Atonement had golden stems, which King Monobazus of Adiabene had had mounted (M. Yom. 3.10).

We find the greatest splendour on the Temple house itself, and in its interior. According to Josephus, not only was the whole façade, 100 cubits (150 feet) square, covered with gold plates, but also the wall and entrance between the porch and the sanctuary (*BJ* 5.207ff.). This was no exaggeration, as we see in T. Men. xiii.19, 533, which says that the whole porch was covered with gold plates '100 cubits in size in the thickness of a gold dinar'. On the roof were sharp spikes of gold to keep off the birds, as a scarecrow (M. Midd. iv.6; *BJ* 5.224). From the beams of the porch hung gold chains (M. Midd. iii.8). In the porch itself stood a marble and a golden table (M. Men. xi.7), the latter according to Josephus (*BJ* 6.388) of solid gold. Above the entrance, between the porch and the Holy Place extended a golden vine (*BJ* 5.210), and to this were brought gifts of golden tendrils which the priests added to the vine (M. Midd. iii.8), so that it was always getting larger. Above the entrance hung a concave mirror of gold which reflected the rays of the rising sun through the doorless main entrance of the porch (b. Yom. 37b). It was a gift of Queen Helena of Adiabene (M. Yom. iii.10). Doubtless other votive offerings stood in the porch, for Caesar Augustus and his consort had once given bronze wine-vessels (*BJ* 5.562) and other offerings,[44] and his son-in-law Marcus Agrippa had also dedicated gifts.[45]

In the Holy Place, lying beyond the porch, were unique masterpieces which later were to be the climax of Titus' triumphal procession (*BJ* 7.148f.), and were then exhibited in a temple at Rome among the most famous wonders of the world: the solid seven-branched candlestick of allegedly two talents' weight, and the equally solid and even heavier shewbread table.[46]

When the gates were burned during the destruction of the Temple, the metal coverings melted and allowed the flames to reach the wooden frames (*BJ* 6.233).

[44] Philo, *Leg. ad Cai.* 156, 312ff.

[45] *Ibid.* 296.

[46] *CA* 1.198; *BJ* 6.388; 7.148; b. Men. 98b, and compare the triumphal Arch of Titus in the *Via Sacra* in Rome.

We come at last to the empty Holy of Holies, whose walls were overlaid with gold (M. Midd. vi.1; T. Shek. iii.6, 178; cf. M. Shek. iv.4).

So great is the abundance of gold in Jerusalem, and especially in the Temple, said to have been, that after the sack of the city, the market in gold for the whole province of Syria was completely glutted, with the result, Josephus says, that 'the standard of gold was depreciated to half its former value' (*BJ* 6.317).

A skilled workman, who invented a machine for the water tanks in the Temple area, is mentioned by name in b. Tam. 28b and b. Zeb. 28b.

(b) The cultus

During the eighty-two to eighty-four years that the Temple was being built (pp. 21f.), the ceremonial was not interrupted for even an hour.

Its requirements were served by the bakers of shewbread and the makers of incense. The baking of shewbread was entrusted to the family of Garmo (M. Yom. iii.11; M. Shek. v.1; M. Tam. iii.8). In addition they had to supply the baked pieces of the daily meal-offering (Lev. 6.21) for the high priest (M. Men. xi.3; M. Tam. i.3; cf. T. Yom. ii.5, 183; T. Men. ix.2, 525; b. Zeb. 96a; M. Midd. i.6). The manufacture of incense was the hereditary right of the family of Euthinos (M. Shek. v.1; M. Yom. i.5; iii.11; M. Shek. iv.5). We are told—in a fragment only, b. Yom. 38a—that these two families once went on strike. When they returned to work they were given double wages, so we may conclude that it was a strike for higher pay.

Care of the Temple curtains was a constant occupation, as M. Shek. v.1 reveals in a list of the superior Temple officials: 'Eleazar was appointed to have new curtains made when necessary.' Skilled weavers and knitters had to produce annually two of the Temple curtains, twenty cubits wide and forty cubits long, which had to be hung in no less than thirteen places in the Temple (b. Yom. 54a; b. Ket. 106a). Each curtain had to be woven in six colours, on seventy-two strands, each with twenty-four threads (M. Shek. viii.5; b. Yom. 71b; T. Shek. iii.13, 178).[47] According to M. Shek. viii.5 (the variant readings differ: cf. b. Ket. 106a; j. Shek. viii.4, 51b.13) eighty-two maidens had to produce two curtains each year.[48]

[47] *BJ* 5.212 specifies four colours.
[48] See further, p. 36 n. 18.

Besides the goldsmiths employed in the construction, others had to be on hand for current work. According to M. Shek. iv.4, the surplus from the Temple tax of a didrachma which was levied on every Jew in the world, [49] was spent to supply the gold plating used to cover the Holy of Holies. According to T. Shek. i.8, 174, this was done with the surcharge that was added to the Temple tax if it was not paid in the prescribed Tyrian currency (M. Shek. i.6f.).

A master of trench digging (M. Shek. v.1) was responsible for the Temple water supply.

Mention should also be made of the Temple doctor (M. Shek. v.1; j. Shek. v.2, 48d.26). He was called upon, not only when the priests hurt themselves in the course of their duties (M. Erub. x.13f.), but beyond that had an extensive practice since the priests had to go around barefoot on the flagstones of the Temple floor even in winter time, and so easily fell ill. Even more injurious to their health was their diet, which had a high meat content with only water to drink, as wine was forbidden them (M. Shek. v.1; j. Shek. v.2, 48d.26).

Finally, there must have been barbers in the Temple. These would be necessary for the Nazirite vows, for initiation of Levites, and purification of those healed of leprosy.

(c) Organization of the Temple workers

The Temple had thus become a centre for crafts and industries because of its regular worship, but especially during the decades of its restoration. As time went on various customs became firmly established. The principle of piece work was established, and as a means of precaution against attempts to defraud the sanctuary, different measurements were employed for distribution and delivery of work (M. Kel. xvii.9; p. 11). On the other hand wages were generous[50] and were paid on the spot, even when a man had done only one hour's work (Ant. 20.220). The Temple treasury was also responsible for giving assistance to unemployed workers. The paving of the streets of Jerusalem, put in hand after the completion of the Temple, and possibly also the additional work that was undertaken at the Temple a little later, helped to do this (pp. 12f.). Favourable wage agreements made the Temple workers the most fortunately placed craftsmen in the city.

[49] Ex. 30.13; Matt. 17.24–27; Ant. 3.194; 18.313; BJ 5.187; 7.218; M. Shek.; T. Shek.; Philo, De spec. leg. I, 77f. et passim.

[50] Fantastic rates are mentioned in connection with the strike referred to on p. 25, above.

Certain crafts at the Temple, for example the preparation of shew-bread and of incense, were the prerogative of certain families, and became hereditary (p. 25).

B. THE INDIVIDUALITY OF JERUSALEM AND ITS INFLUENCE UPON TRADE

1. *The position of the city*

Jerusalem may be regarded as part of the province of Syria (p. 4) inasmuch as the most important industries of that province were also characteristic of Jerusalem.

Jerusalem, however, differed from the other large cities of that province in one important respect, that it lay in a part of the country quite extraordinarily unfavourable for trade. The only raw material that the area yielded in large quantities was stone. Otherwise, mountainous Judaea provided only the products and by-products of cattle and sheep rearing—wool and hides, and those of the olive trees—wood and olives. Most other raw materials were lacking, metals and rich ore were entirely absent, and the clay which the neighbourhood produces is of inferior quality. Most serious of all, water was lacking. Jerusalem possesses only one spring of any importance, that of Siloah in the south. Water had to be bought by the measure in times of drought (p. 8), and even in normal times it had to be used carefully from the cisterns or had to be brought from a distance by means of aqueducts. A proof of how unsuitably placed Jerusalem was for trade is the fact that in the entire course of her history, we find no single trade whose product had ever made her name famous.

2. *The political and religious significance of the city*

In spite of these disadvantages of position, Pseudo-Aristeas describes the city as 'rich in trade' (114), and with good reason. Precisely because of its unfavourable position, Jerusalem, a city of some 25,000 inhabitants in Jesus' time, had to resort to trade, for raw materials had to be imported. She depended less on trade with distant lands than on trade with her neighbours.

What revenues did the city have to promote such trade? We shall try and set out the most important factors:

(i) In the first place there are the enormous revenues of the Temple, made up of bequests coming in from all over the world, the world-wide levy of a fixed tax, that of the didrachma (p. 26), the sacrifices, the redemption of vows, the wood offerings, etc., as well as the produce of the land owned by the Temple. Against this, of course, we must set the vast expenses, notably of the rebuilding of the Temple.

(ii) Further revenue flowed into the city from foreign traffic, especially at the great pilgrim feasts, when it increased enormously. Every good Jew was committed to spending a tenth of the produce of his land in Jerusalem, the so-called 'second tithe' (M.M. Sh.; pp. 47 n.52, 57).

(iii) At least during those times when independent rulers resided in Jerusalem (Herod 37 BC–4 BC; Archelaus 4 BC–AD 6; Agrippa I AD 41–44) we must include the general taxes. Josephus writes that Archelaus collected six million drachmas a year from Idumaea, Judaea and Samaria (*Ant.* 17.320), and Agrippa I, from a considerably larger area, twelve million (*Ant.* 18.352). An important amount of these sums must have been spent in Jerusalem for the needs of the court and for buildings.[51]

(iv) Finally it should be remembered that owners of capital had always been attracted to Jerusalem; wholesalers, tax collectors, Jews of the Diaspora grown rich; quite a few people would also settle here from religious motives.

This enormous revenue paid for all the imports. At the same time, the city itself manufactured, in addition to articles for daily use, luxury products such as ointments. The 'alabaster jar of ointment of pure nard, very costly' (Mark 14.3) no doubt contained ointment made in Jerusalem.

This survey has already shown that it was the political and, above all, the religious significance of the Holy City which made its trades flourish.

From ancient times (cf. the record of Solomon in the Old Testament) enthusiasm for building and a taste for splendour had encouraged the building trade and its attendant crafts in the Holy City. In New Testament times Jerusalem was a royal city for only a short time, AD 41–44, under Agrippa I. Nevertheless, the members of the Herodian royal family (e.g. Herod Antipas, Luke 23.6ff., and Agrippa II) came to Jerusalem for the feasts, if indeed they did not

---

[51] On the purchasing power of such amounts, see below on wages, p. 111, and food prices, pp. 122f.

live there permanently. 'The first [to be arrested by the Zealots] was Antipas, one of the royal family, who had carried such weight in the city that he had been entrusted with charge of the public treasury. Him they arrested and imprisoned, and after him Levias, one of the nobles, and Syphas son of Aregetes, both also of royal blood' (*BJ* 4.140f.).[52] The rebuilding of the Hasmonaean palace by Agrippa II shows clearly that the royal family regarded themselves as belonging to Jerusalem.

The court and the rich people resident in Jerusalem led a life that generated a variety of needs; for instance, this favoured the growth of the luxury trade.

More than the political significance, the religious significance of Jerusalem was of decisive importance; it was the city of the Temple. Indeed, the very fact that a man lived in the Holy City imposed upon him certain commitments. Here the strict rules of the sabbath were rigorously observed, forbidding any kind of work (M. Shab.). Here too the rules of ritual purity, which involved numerous inconveniences in everyday life, played an entirely different role from what they would in a town with a substantial Gentile minority.[53] But the chances offered to craftsmen by the Temple far outweighed the disadvantages. From the Temple resources municipal building was kept up (p. 16), streets paved (pp. 12f.) and kept clean (pp. 16f.), and possibly an aqueduct maintained (p. 16 n. 30).

The importance of the Temple extended far beyond the boundaries of the city. Since the reforms of Josiah (621 BC), with the centralization of the cultus in Jerusalem on the Deuteronomic pattern, the city was the one holy place for Jews. The temple of Onias at Leontopolis in Egypt (*c.* 170 BC–AD 73) was totally unimportant; the Temple of Jerusalem in fact remained the single holy place in the world for Jews. Three times a year pilgrims journeyed there from all over the world. Among these pilgrims were certain wealthy people like the members of the royal house of Adiabene, whose noble building works (pp. 13f.) greatly helped the building trade, and the minister of finance of the queen of Abyssinia (Acts 8.27). The pilgrims provided the sanctuary with pious offerings which gave work to the Temple craftsmen (p. 24), and it was they also who made possible the souvenir industry (p. 9).

Finally, the Temple was the centre of a trading colony. An army

[52] Cf. Philo, *Leg. ad Cai.* 278.
[53] Cf. the sixth division of the Mishnah, called Tohoroth, i.e. Cleanliness.

of craftsmen was engaged in the building of it, and a permanent staff of workmen was employed for the cultus.

So we have a strange picture: although the position of the city was entirely unfavourable for the development of trade, nevertheless, because of its cultural importance, it evolved a flourishing commercial life in its midst.

II

COMMERCE

A. EVIDENCE OF COMMERCE IN JERUSALEM

1. *In general*

TRADE IN JERUSALEM before AD 70 had reached a stage of development corresponding to town economy, whether defined with Bücher[1] as a period when goods pass directly from producer to consumer, or with Schmoller[2] as a period in which the town supports the economic organization.

The profession of a merchant was held in great respect. Even priests engaged in commerce. T. Ter. x.9, 43 and j. Peah i.6, 16c.53 mention a priest's shop. T. Betz. iii.8, 205 tells of two scholars, Eleazar b. Zadoq, and Abba Saul b. Batnith who were merchants in Jerusalem 'all their life'.[3] The high-priestly family too carried on a flourishing trade (p. 49).

We must attempt first of all to trace the course of commercial traffic to Jerusalem, and inside it.

Camel caravans, often of impressive length, brought goods from a distance to Jerusalem; Lam. R. 1.2 on 1.1 (Son. 69) tells us of one such caravan, composed of 200 beasts, passing Tyre on the way to Jerusalem. For local transport the ass, too, was used (M. Dem. iv.7). Owing to the generally poor condition of the roads, wagons will have been used only for short journeys, such as the one which Herod's 1,000 wagons made to bring stone for building the Temple (*Ant.*

---

[1] C. Bücher, *Die Entstehung der Volkswirtschaft*, 8th ed., Tübingen 1911.

[2] G. Schmoller, *Grundriss der allgemeinen Volkswirtschaftlehre* II, Leipzig 1904.

[3] R. Eleazar b. Zadoq the Elder must have been born soon after AD 25, because he was still a boy at the time of Agrippa I (AD 41–44), and studied during the time of the famine in the second half of the forties (see p. 143). Proof that Abba Saul b. Batnith too lived in Jerusalem before the destruction of the Temple is given in the record of his over-conscientiousness in delivering to the Temple treasurer even the scum of the wine (b. Betz. 29a Bar.).

15.390). The produce of the neighbouring countryside was brought to the city by the peasants themselves.

The safety of the roads was of vital concern to trade. Herod took vigorous measures against the prevailing brigandage. He established peace in the interior, and pushed the roving Bedouin tribes back to their own territory. The Roman rule of the following decades was equally concerned to protect commerce. They reconstructed under Trajan a fortified frontier (*limes*) against the desert,[4] following the older line of fortifications which, according to Karge,[5] was already there from early times. However, the many references to robbers in Talmudic literature (M. Ber. i.3; M. Shab. ii.5; M.B.K. vi.1, etc.)[6] give the impression that bandit raids were by no means rare. We are often told of raids which were feared, or actually took place, particularly in the neighbourhood of Jerusalem, and of the necessity of controlling this outlawry.

Anyone who succeeded in reaching the market in Jerusalem had to pay duty to the tax-collector to whom the market of Jerusalem had been farmed out.[7] No doubt most of the tax-farmers were Jews, as the Gospels show. Payment was ruthlessly exacted; however, there was some relief from AD 37 when the governor Vitellius remitted the market duty on crops (*Ant.* 18.90).

After the duty had been paid, the seller would go next to the bazaar in which the particular article was sold. There were markets for corn, fruit and vegetables, livestock and wood, a market for fat cattle, and even a special stone on which slaves were put up for auction and sold. Buyers would be tempted by encouraging shouts extolling the goods; b. Pes. 116a makes it clear that Jerusalem was no exception to this rule. When a sale was negotiated, great care had to be taken over the weight, for Jerusalem had its own system. Weights were reckoned according to the *qab* and not, as elsewhere, by 'tenths of an *ēphāh*' (M. Men. vii.1, 2; T. Men. viii.16, 524); but even this *qab*-measure was distinctive, for b. Yom. 44b mentions a 'Jerusalem *qab*'. The larger measure of capacity, the *se'āh*, was about one-fifth larger in Jerusalem than in the 'wilderness', while at the same time one-sixth smaller than the *se'āh*-measure of Sepphoris (M. Men. vii.1; b. Erub. 83a, b; T. Eduy. i.2, 454). As to payment, merchants and pil-

[4] Guthe, *Die griechisch-römischen Städte*, 33ff.

[5] P. Karge, *Rephaim* (Collectanea Hierosolymitana 1), Paderborn 1917.

[6] Levy II, 503f. Krauss, *TA* II, 315f.

[7] *Ant.* 17.205: 'the taxes that had been levied upon public purchases and sales and ruthlessly exacted'.

grims would go to the money changers to exchange their foreign currency (M. Eduy. i.9f.; M. Shek. i.3). It is at first sight surprising to read that Jerusalem had its own coinage too. T.M. Sh. ii.4, 88 mentions *māʿot* of Jerusalem; j. Ket. i.2, 25b, a *silʿā*' of Jerusalem; M. Ber. viii.7 and T. Ket. xiii.3, 275, compare a Jerusalem silver coin with a Tyrian. The riddle of these coins is solved by a Tannaitic statement: 'What is a coin of Jerusalem? (one that shows) David and Shelomo (Solomon) on one side, Jerusalem on the other' (b.B.K. 97b). This refers to silver coins struck in Jerusalem in the fourth year of the first Jewish revolt. They bear the legend 'Shekel of Israel *Š D*', and on the reverse 'Jerusalem the Holy (City)'.[8] *Š D*, meaning *šenat 'arbaʿ* 'fourth year', was read as Sh(elomo) and D(avid).[9]

When it came to concluding a bargain, certain special rules had to be respected in Jerusalem, over and above the universal regulations regarding the keeping of the Sabbath and those concerning trade with Gentiles; b.B.K. 82b mentions one of these rules regarding the sale of houses. Above all, imports of unclean beasts, flesh or animal hides were strictly controlled. There is an edict on this matter, by the Seleucid king Antiochus III, the Great, for the time immediately after 198 BC (*Ant.* 12.146; see pp. 46f.). Provided that there were no obstacles of a cultic nature, the price could be fixed. Prices in Jerusalem were high, it being a large city. M. Maas. ii.5 gives an interesting example of this: In Jerusalem one *'isār* would buy only three or four figs, in the country the same money would buy ten or even twenty figs from the tree (M. Maas. ii.6). Prices for land around Jerusalem were particularly high.[10]

Police supervised trade. The Talmud has market inspectors (j. B.B. v.11, 15a.63; T. Kel. B.K. vi.19, 576; j. Dem. ii.1, 22c.21 (6, 9), assessors (b. A. Zar. 58a; b.B.K.98a), and overseers (b.B.B. 89a). There is a record of a decision given by one of the three 'criminal judges' on a point of commercial law, whether or not the sale of an ass included its harness (M.B.B. v.2). Again, we have evidence of an indirect attempt at maximum price fixing by Simeon, son of Gamaliel I (Paul's teacher, Acts 22.3), whom we meet as an influential member of the Sanhedrin at the time of the Jewish War.[11] 'Once a pair of doves (sold for an offering, cf. e.g. Luke 2.24, Jesus'

---

[8] A. Reifenberg, *Ancient Jewish Coins*, 2nd ed., Jerusalem 1947, 58 and pl. x, 143.
[9] L. Goldschmidt, *Der babylonische Talmud neu übertragen* VII, Berlin 1933, 337 n. 103.
[10] j. Yom. iv.1, 41b; cf. Levy II, 369b under *keseph*.
[11] He is asked to influence the authorities: *Vita* 189ff.

presentation in the Temple) was sold for two gold dinars. Then said Rabbi Simeon, son of Gamaliel, "By this dwelling (meaning the Temple)! I will not rest this night until I have made it so that they can be bought for one (silver) dinar." So he went into the court and taught thus: In certain cases only one offering need be brought instead of the five strictly necessary. (He was afraid that the high prices would prevent poor people from bringing any offering.) The same day the price of a pair of doves stood at half a silver dinar' (M. Ker. i.7). Since a gold dinar is worth twenty-five silver dinars, this decree of the Sanhedrin had, according to the Mishnah, caused a reduction of 99 per cent, to 1 per cent of the original price.

Now let us look at the merchant himself. The produce of the surrounding villages passed directly from producer to consumer. In Palestine at that time barter was still a common custom: Krauss, *TA* II, 351, gives instances. Lam. R. 2.20 on 2.12 (cf. Son. 2.16, 179) gives an example of this in Jerusalem: 'A woman said to her husband: "Take a necklace or a nose-ring and go to the market and buy there with it something for us to eat."' We should not infer too much from this reference, however, as it refers to special circumstances during the siege by the Romans in AD 70.

We are still dealing with small-scale trade where we meet with a single intermediary between producer and consumer, as were the shopkeepers of Jerusalem (T. Betz. iii.8, 205) or the hawkers. It may also have happened that private individuals engaged in trade, so that a tailor of Jerusalem might buy a large consignment of pepper from a caravan for resale to a colleague in the trade, who circulated it among the people (Lam. R. 1.2, Son. 69). We read in j. Pes. x.3, 37d.9 of street traders in Jerusalem who dealt in spices; the parallel in b. Pes. 116a calls them *tagg^erē ḥarāk*—'dealers in parched corn' (see p. 102 n.7).[12]

There were also merchants whom we might call wholesalers, who had employees working for them and who undertook journeys. It was they above all who used the counting house at Jerusalem (Pesiqta rabbati 41, 173a.7), where evidently there were considerable money transactions; it was said that some of the settlements could work out at such a figure that one could lose a fortune (Ex. R. 54.4 on 39.32,

---

[12] A variant reads: *tagg^erē ha-dāk*=dealers in crushed (corn). A conjecture reported by Krauss (II, 688 n. 314) suggests *tagg^erē ḥārān*='merchants from Haran'. This refers to merchants then in Jerusalem, from Haran in Mesopotamia (called Carrhae by the Romans); the most likely product to have been imported from Mesopotamia was spices (see p. 37).

Son. 52.5, 580).[13] Tradesmen in Jerusalem were cautious over settling up a business deal, and they would sign nothing unless they knew who were their co-signatories (Lam. R. 4.4 on 4.2, Son. 218).

2. *Foreign trade*

After this general survey we turn to the particular articles of trade. First we shall deal with foreign trade, beginning with Greece. The extraordinarily powerful influence of *Greece*, and of Hellenistic culture in general, on Palestinian trade is shown by the very large number of loan-words in all sections of everyday life, and especially of trade, which we find already in the Mishnah. Latin loan-words are also extant, but less frequently.[14] Bearing in mind that Jerusalem was of predominant importance in Judaea, we shall understand that the powerful influence of Hellenistic culture, as far as the period up to AD 70 is concerned, was concentrated mainly in Jerusalem; it had been introduced there chiefly through the court of Herod the Great.

We can quote specific examples of trade with Greece. At the time of Hyrcanus II (76–67 and 63–40 BC) there were Greek merchants from Athens in Jerusalem: this is doubtless the meaning of the statement that Athenians were in Jerusalem on private business as well as official. There must have been constant connections and considerable traffic between the two places, otherwise the Athenians would not have honoured Hyrcanus II with the Golden Crown of Athens as a sign of gratitude, nor set up a bronze statue of him in Athens (*Ant.* 14.153). The most valuable of the Temple gates was made of Corinthian bronze, according to both Josephus and the Talmud (p. 23 n. 43).

When Agrippa II, with the consent of the people and the chief priests, had decided shortly before AD 66 to provide the Temple building with new substructures and to raise it twenty cubits, he had timber imported from the *Lebanon* at enormous expense, nothing but long, straight beams (*BJ* 5.36). From the Lebanon also came the cedar wood to roof the arcades (*BJ* 5.190) and the slaughterhouse (M. Midd. iii.5).[15]

---

[13] According to this passage the counting house was outside Jerusalem, so that anyone who had incurred a heavy loss would not be melancholy in Jerusalem, for in that city one must always be joyful. The same idea is expressed in Lam. R. 2.24 on 2.15 (Son. 2.19, 182) with reference to Ps. 48.3, 'a joy of the whole earth!' This speculation has no historical value.

[14] Schürer II, 71ff., ET II.1, 37ff.

[15] For cedar wood used in building the Temple see also M. Midd. iii.8; iv.5.

The chief industry of *Sidon* was glassmaking.[16] M. Kel. iv.3 mentions bowls or dishes from Sidon. Jose b. Johanan of Jerusalem proclaimed, with Jose b. Joezer of Zerada, that glass vessels could become levitically unclean (b. Shab. 14b; j. Shab. i.7, 3d.37; cf. j. Ket. viii.11, 32c.4). These men, among the earliest scribes mentioned in the Talmud, flourished about 150 BC, so the import of glass to Jerusalem began at an early date.

We have already come across fish merchants and other traders from *Tyre*, who displayed their goods for sale in the northern part of the city (p. 20; Neh. 13.16). Tyre, like Sidon, was noted for its precious glassware, and also for the costly purple dye. There is also evidence of commerce with Tyre in the frequent equivalents drawn between the Jerusalem money and the Tyrian (p. 33). According to T. Ket. xiii.3, and elsewhere, the Jerusalem standard of currency was the same as the Tyrian. The prevalence of the Tyrian standard is explained not only by the brisk trade which went on, but also because in the Temple only Tyrian currency was allowed.

Tyre was a centre for the slave trade, and most of the heathen slaves of both sexes from Syria, and often even further away, came to Jerusalem through this slave market. The import of slaves was important; in Jerusalem there was a stone on which the slaves were displayed for auction.[17] There are frequent references in Josephus to male and female slaves, particularly in connection with the court of Herod the Great. Rabbinic literature, too, often mentions them, as for instance in the case of an Athenian who bought a male slave in Jerusalem (Lam. R. 1.13 on 1.1, Son. 1.12, 78).

It was from *Cyprus* that Queen Helena of Adiabene arranged for shiploads of dried figs to be brought to Palestine, during a famine there (*Ant.* 20.51).

Babylonia exported costly materials, woven from blue, scarlet and purple stuffs, and byssus (fine white linen). These materials were used for example, for the curtain in front of the Holy Place (*BJ* 5. 212f.),[18] and for the high priest's mitre (*BJ* 5.235); the priest on duty was clothed in byssus, and it was also used in the ceremonies of the Day of Atonement, when a sheet of it was held out between the high priest and the people (M. Yom. iii.4). In addition, large stocks of purple

---

[16] Schürer II, 81 n. 229, ET II.1, 45 n. 196.

[17] Siphra Lev. 25.42; Siphre Deut. 26 on 3.23; Krauss, *TA* II, 362.

[18] This passage is more credible than the Talmud accounts of the making of these curtains by eighty-two maidens in Jerusalem, p. 25; but it seems likely that repairs etc. were done on the spot.

and scarlet stuffs were kept for curtains in the Temple (*BJ* 6.390). Luke 16.19 implies that richer people were 'clothed in purple and fine linen'. The tyrant Simon wore a purple cloak when he attempted to escape in Jerusalem (p. 14) in order to alarm the Roman soldiers (*BJ* 7.29). The robe put on Jesus when he was mocked by the Roman soldiers (Matt. 27.28, the 'scarlet robe') was not of course of this purple material, but a soldier's cloak of a scarlet colour.

If the conjecture on b. Pes. 116a, reported by Krauss, is right, spices were brought from Mesopotamia (p. 34 n. 12). This seems to be borne out by a statement in Lam. R. 1.2 on 1.1 (Son. 69), that a caravan of two hundred camels carrying pepper travelled to Jersualem by way of Tyre.

On the east gate (the Shushan gate) of the Temple was a relief carving of, strangely enough, the city of Susa (M. Kel. xvii.9), which points to a connection with *Persia*. It may well have been a votive offering.

Fabrics for the Temple came even from *India*. 'In the afternoon (of the Day of Atonement, the high priest was clothed) in Indian linen' (M. Yom. iii.7).

Trade with the East, and particularly with *Arabia*, had always been very brisk. 'A great quantity of spices (probably the raw materials for the spice trade in Jerusalem, see p. 8), precious stones and gold is brought into the country by the Arabs' (Pseudo-Aristeas 114). The Old Testament already speaks of frankincense from Arabia (Isa. 60.6; Jer. 6.20). The incense used in the Temple came chiefly from the desert (*BJ* 5.218); again, cinnamon and cassia (*BJ* 6.390) are mentioned as spices for the Temple, and both grow in tropical or sub-tropical climates. Pseudo-Aristeas 119 suggests that copper and iron were imported from Arabia.

The lions and other wild animals needed by Herod for his sports in Jerusalem (*Ant.* 15.273) were also obtained from the Arabian desert. Eupolemus, in the second century BC, speaks of a supply of fat stock from Arabia;[19] but in this connection we should note what is said on p. 58 n. 21 below about the extension of the Nabatean state in the time of Eupolemus.

From *Egypt* Herod the Great imported grain during a famine (*Ant.* 15.307), and so did Helena of Adiabene when there was famine in her time (*Ant.* 20.51). T. Maksh. iii.4, 675 records the import of corn from Egypt into Jerusalem.

[19] See p. 28 and n. 20.

From the east of the Nile delta came the Pelusian fine linen which the high priest wore on the morning of the Day of Atonement (M. Yom. iii.7). In the gruesome family history of the Herods poison played a large part, and *BJ* 1.592 mentions poison which Antipater, son of Herod the Great, introduced from Egypt. According to j. Sot. i.6, 17a.19, the wife suspected of adultery was bound with Egyptian cord in the Temple court.

Although we depend entirely on chance information, the conclusion is reached that foreign trade had considerable importance for the Holy City. The Temple drew the largest share. For the rest, foreign trade consisted of food supplies, precious metals, luxury goods and clothing materials.

3. *Local trade*

In earlier times, as today, the main concern of local trade was to supply the large city with food. What were the chief provisions imported? We have two comprehensive accounts:

(1) Soon after 150 BC Eupolemus wrote his work *Concerning the Prophecy of Elijah* and in this is an imaginary letter from King Solomon to the King of Tyre, about food supplies for the workmen sent to Judaea by the latter: 'I have instructed Galilee and Samaria, Moab and Ammon and Gilead that they supply what is necessary for them from each country: each month, 10,000 *kōr* of wheat . . .; oil and other things will be supplied by Judaea, but fatstock by Arabia'.[20] According to this, the chief food supplies imported by Jerusalem were *wheat*, *oil* and *livestock*. Judaea supplied the oil, or olives; wheat came from the rest of Palestine and livestock from Transjordan.[21] There is no doubt that Eupolemus reproduces the conditions of his time;[22] nevertheless, the facts are also valid for the next two centuries after him.

(2) Rabbinic literature provides a further piece of evidence on the chief requirements of foodstuffs in Jerusalem. According to b. Gitt.

[20] Excerpt from Eupolemus in Alexander Polyhistor (*c.* 40 BC), *On the Jews*, preserved in Eusebius, *Praep. evang.* IX, 33.1 (GCS 43.1=Eus. VIII.1, 540f.).

[21] As regards the import of livestock from Arabia, it must be noted that Eupolemus wrote at a time when the Nabatean tribes were no longer restricted to the area round Petra, but had already extended their influence over part of Transjordan. Soon Egypt and Syria trembled before their attacks (I Macc. 5.25; 9.35; Justin, *Histor. Philippic.* XXXIX, 5.5f.). Thus the fatstock which came from Arabia would mostly be cattle from these areas east of the Jordan which, in the time we are dealing with, had been colonized by Jews though they were under Arab rule.

[22] Smith, *Jerusalem* I, 315.

56a there were three[23] councillors (probably members of the Sanhedrin)[24] who, at the time of the outbreak of rebellion against Rome, declared that they would supply the city with food for twenty-one years. The first intended to furnish wheat and barley, the second wine, salt and oil, the third wood. The only omission here is cattle.

(a) Grain

The two statements are right in putting grain in the first place. The existence of the citizens was directly dependent on the import of grain. In times of famine it was grain which failed first, and we must suppose that grain formed the greater part of food imports. Where did it come from?

Grain was grown in the neighbourhood of Jerusalem. Pseudo-Aristeas 112 says that the neighbourhood of Jerusalem was thickly planted with olive trees and crops of corn and pulse. Simon of Cyrene, who came to the city from the north or west, came 'from the country' (i.e. 'fields') when he was taken and forced to carry the cross of Jesus (Mark 15.21; Luke 23.26). The primitive Church in Jerusalem included landowners (Acts 4.34, 37; 5.1ff.). Josephus mentions the fields which he owned 'in Jerusalem' (*Vita* 422). M. Men. x.2 lays down that the wave-sheaf, made up of corn, must be taken from the neighbourhood of Jerusalem, and M. Bikk. ii.2 enlarges upon the subject of the first-fruits of grain, in cases where after being mixed with ordinary grain, they were used as seed in Jerusalem (here, too, this must mean the district around Jerusalem as in the passage on p. 7). M. Dem. vi.4 finds occasion for discussing the case of a countryman who has leased a field belonging to a citizen of Jerusalem. b. B.M. 90a mentions threshing within Bethphage.

The question, however, is whether these 'fields' or 'landed property' did not also include orchards. Pseudo-Aristeas says, in connection with the passage quoted above (112), that agricultural products came mostly from Samaria and the 'coastal plains . . . which adjoin the land of the Idumaeans' (107). It must also be remembered that the rocky limestone of the Judaean hill country is not entirely suitable for grain. M. Arak. iii.2 describes the soil of Jerusalem as

---

[23] So also Gen. R. 42.1 on 14.1 (Son. 340); Lam. R. 1.32 on 1.5 (Son. 1.31, 101) on the contrary says four, evidently as the result of a misunderstanding.

[24] Cf. Gen. R. 42 on 14.1 (Son. 340): 'chiefs of the city'; Eccles. R. 7.18 on 7.12, (Son. 193); Lam. R. 1.32 on 1.5 (Son. 1.31, 101): *bulewtes*=βουλευτής.

being of notoriously poor quality. Village names indicating the agricultural products of the place are frequent, but at the present day within a radius of eleven miles around Jerusalem, there is only one name made up of the word 'wheat'.[25] If we add all this to the statement of Eupolemus on the import of grain into Jerusalem (p. 38), we reach the conclusion that the country around Jerusalem, and Judaea, could have supplied only a small fraction of the necessary grain.

The flour for the Temple, which had to be of specially fine quality, was brought from Michmash and Zanoah, or failing that, from Ephraim 'in the plain' (M. Men. viii.1).[26] Michmash lay to the north-east, Zanoah to the south-west of Jerusalem; both were in Judaea. The third place, if identified as Ephraim,[27] lay about five miles east of Bethel (cf. John 11.54; b. Men. 85a). If this is correct, it would not be situated, as Neubauer[28] says in Samaria, which would be highly unlikely as a source of supply for Temple meal, but in Jewish territory (so also I Macc. 11.34; Ant. 13.127). However, as this third place is 'in the plain' we ought to read Hapharaiim (see n. 26), and to look for this in the western part of the fruitful plain of Jezreel. Thus it follows that meal for the Temple was brought mainly from *Judaea*. However, this does not permit any conclusions as to the importance of Judaea as a source of grain for the city, since we are concerned with grain for the Temple, and this could not have come from Samaria and Perea (p. 17).

Most of the grain was received from *Transjordan* (cf. Eupolemus above, p. 38). The Hauran was the granary not only for Palestine but also for Syria. Herod had enforced public security east of Jordan. He had achieved his purpose not so much by the settlement of three thousand Idumeans in Trachonitis as by settling, in the district of Batanea (west of Trachonitis), the fierce Babylonian Jew Zamaris and his dependants (*Ant*. 17.23–31). This measure was taken in the last years before our era, and it marked the beginning of the rapid rise of Transjordan.

Besides Transjordan Eupolemus lists *Samaria* and *Galilee* as grain-supplying areas. It was from the city of Samaria that Herod ordered

[25] Smith, *Jerusalem* I, 298.
[26] Hapharaiim? According to Prof. I. Kahan a place near Sepphoris (Josh. 19.19); and so read many MSS; cf. R. N. Rabbinowicz, *Sepher diqduqe sopherim* XV. Munich 1886, on M. Men. viii.1.
[27] Eusebius, *Onomast*. 223 (GCS 11.1=Eus. III.1, 28).
[28] Neubauer, *Géographie*, 155.

grain, wine, oil and livestock, when the Roman troops which had been sent to help him as he besieged Jerusalem complained of a shortage of food (*BJ* 1.297ff.). In connection with the wave-sheaf and the two Temple loaves, b. Men. 85a reads: 'They would also have brought the wheat from Karzaiim[29] and Kefar Akim, if these had been nearer Jerusalem.' These two places named here are doubtless the towns of Chorazin (Matt. 11.21; Luke 10.13) near Capernaum, and Capernaum itself.[30] This would suggest that Galilean grain was regarded in Jerusalem as being of the highest quality, fit for Temple use. However, because of its transport through heathen territory, it could not so be used, but only by the people in the city.

As for *trade in grain in Jerusalem*, we know that there was a grain market with a considerable turnover (Lam. R. 1.2 on 1.1, Son. 70) and that the sale of flour began immediately after the offering of the wave-sheaf on 16 Nisan (M. Men. x.5; b. Gitt. 56a).

It is remarkable how little information we have about the traffic in grain to Jerusalem. This is probably due to the fact that it had to be carried over considerable distances, and whereas with the produce of the immediate neighbourhood the retailer himself took his goods to the market, transport from greater distances meant caravans. This traffic—and this is as true today as it was in ancient times, as the topical allusions of the Old Testament prophets prove—provided a golden opportunity for the often unprincipled wholesaler (p. 34). So it comes about that the grain trade in the Jerusalem market was given less publicity than might be expected from its importance, but that most of this business was carried on behind the scenes.

(b) *Fruit and vegetables*

Eupolemus and b. Gitt. 56a (pp. 38f.) put in second place the import of fruit and its products. Our first question is: What do we know about the cultivation of fruit and vegetables around Jerusalem at that time?

The limestone soil around Jerusalem is suitable mainly for olive trees, and to a lesser degree for corn-growing and vineyards. Pseudo-Aristeas 112 keeps to this order exactly in his description of the neighbourhood: The land is 'thickly planted with olive trees, with crops of corn and pulse, rich moreover in vines and much honey, and

---

[29] Other versions: Barziim, Karwis; and in T. Men. ix.2, 525, Barhaiim; cf. R. N. Rabbinowicz, *op. cit.*

[30] Cf. E. Cashdan on b. Men. 85a in *The Babylonian Talmud* (Soncino ed.).

other fruits and dates beyond reckoning'. Josephus and the pseudepi-graphic Book of Enoch have similar statements. The Ethiopian Enoch (composed probably after the Parthian invasion of 40–38 BC) says of the area around Jerusalem, contrasting it with the Valley of Hinnom, 'To what purpose is this blessed land, which is full of trees, and to what purpose this accursed valley between?' (27.1; cf. 26.1).[31] Josephus tells us that when Herod laid siege to the city in 37 BC, he deforested the immediate neighbourhood of the city, probably only to the north (*BJ* 1.344). Yet the trees must have grown again, or else the deforestation was not complete, for when the Romans laid siege in AD 70 they deforested first the immediate neighbourhood of the city (*BJ* 5.264), then the land within a radius of 90 stades (10¼ miles; *BJ* 5.523; 6.5), and finally to the radius of 100 stades (11½ miles; *BJ* 6.151), thus turning to wilderness a district once adorned with trees and ornamental gardens (*BJ* 6.6). These included vineyards, as is shown by M. Taan. iv.8, in which R. Simeon b. Gamaliel describes the great national festival on 15 Ab, when the young maidens of Jerusalem danced before the young men in the vineyards.

We saw above (pp. 39f.) that the report of Pseudo-Aristeas about the amount of growing crops may have been exaggerated. We should therefore treat with caution the rest of his statements about the fruits in the area around Jerusalem. However, if we give due consideration to the damage wrought by Turkish mismanagement in the matter of tree-preservation, we can assume that in earlier times the country was much more thickly wooded than at present. Actually, there is evidence for this as much for Transjordan as for western Palestine. Though during the great sieges the neighbourhood of the city was deforested (by Pompey, 63 BC; by Herod, 37 BC, though probably only partly), the trees usually grew again very quickly and there were no sieges between 37 BC and AD 66. When we consider the suitability of the soil for olive trees and to a lesser extent for vines (p. 41) we may take it that the area was much more thickly wooded than it is now.

This conclusion can be checked by means of detailed evidence. According to b.B.K. 82b, gardens might not be laid out in Jerusalem itself. The Talmud (b.B.K. 82b; M. Maas. ii.5; T. Neg. vi.2, 625) quotes as the sole exception a rose garden dating from the times of the prophets (pp. 8f.). M.M. Sh. iii.7 discusses the case of a tree which stands inside the walls of Jerusalem with its fruit hanging outside or

[31] On the Valley of Hinnom see p. 17.

vice versa. According to John 12.13, people took branches of palm trees in Jerusalem. According to the parallel passage in the Synoptic Gospels, however, it was not the crowd going out from Jerusalem to meet Jesus which paid homage, but the festal pilgrims in whose train he approached the city, and it was not palm branches plucked in Jerusalem with which they decked his way, but bunches of leaves from the trees between Bethany or Bethphage and Jerusalem (Mark 11.1, 8; Matt. 21.1, 8). Yet if we recall that there are a few palm trees in Jerusalem even today and that Pseudo-Aristeas 112 enumerates dates among the products of Jerusalem (pp. 41f.), John's account appears to be within the bounds of possibility. As on p. 6 and p. 47, we shall have to reckon with the possibility that the prohibitions which b.B.K. 82b says were in force in Jerusalem are pure theory. In any case, there was in Jerusalem a rose garden in which incidentally also fig trees grew (M. Maas. ii.5), and other gardens (p. 47 n. 44). Now let us make a tour of the city. Let us remember first of all that we have already met olive trees east and south of the city (pp. 16f.). It was near the north-west tower of the northernmost wall, the Psephinus Tower, that Titus got into difficulties when on patrol, because of the innumerable walls and hedges of the cultivated land (*BJ* 5.57). The whole of the *northern part* had been cultivated as gardens (i.e. orchards) for a long time. Even before the erection of the third northern wall, built under Agrippa I (AD 41–44), there were gardens in the area which was then enclosed by this wall. This is indicated by the name of the gate which formed the starting point of the second wall: *Genath*, Garden Gate (*BJ* 5.146). On its exact position, we can be sure only that it was in the first north wall. For the rest, its position is disputed and constitutes a focus of topographical interest to Christian students of ancient Jerusalem; for on the position of this Garden Gate (i.e. the beginning of the second northern wall) partly depends the positioning of the hill Golgotha, and so the genuineness of the present-day site of the Church of the Holy Sepulchre. Near Golgotha, lying outside the second north wall and enclosed by the third since its erection in AD 41–44, lay the garden of Joseph of Arimathea, a member of the Sanhedrin (John 20.15; 19.41), a garden which was tended by a gardener (John 20.15). Even after these gardens, which had once lain outside the second northern wall, had been integrated into the city, other gardens remained outside further north. So in his advance upon Jerusalem from Mount Scopus in the north, Titus and his army came across gardens, woodlands and groves of cultivated trees (*BJ* 5.107).

We come next to the area *east* of the city. According to John 18.1 there was a garden in the upper Kidron Valley near an oil-press, which suggests it was a grove of olive trees. Trees stood along the road between Jerusalem and Bethany to the east (Matt. 21.8; Mark 11.8). No doubt the fig tree said in the Gospels to have been cursed (Mark 11. 13f.; Matt. 21.18–22) was an isolated example standing among other kinds of tree along this very way. On this road from Jerusalem to Bethany lay Bethphage, which should almost certainly be translated 'House of unripe figs'.[32]

If we turn next to the *south-east*, we reach the lower course of Kidron, whose valley was eminently suitable for planting gardens. Admittedly the Kidron valley is a *wadi*, with water flowing only in winter (*Ant.* 8.17; John 18.1), but an artificial supply which made the valley so extraordinarily fruitful was the blood of Temple sacrifices. The Temple floor was paved and sloped in particular directions, so that the blood from sacrifices could easily be rinsed away (Pseudo-Aristeas 88, 90). The channel which drained it away began by the altar (M. Midd. iii.2) and the blood of blemished offerings was thrown straight into it (M. Zeb. viii.7). This drainage channel led underground into the Kidron valley (M. Tam. iv.1; M. Midd. iii.2; M. Yom. v.6; M. Pes. v.8; M. Meil. iii.3, etc.). The gardeners bought the blood from the temple-treasurers for use as fertilizer, and to use it without paying for it was to incur sacrilege (M. Yom. v.6).[33]

On the western slopes of the Kidron valley, south of the Temple area, no doubt vines had been planted. G. Dalman has shown the likelihood of this, on the basis of excavations undertaken by R. Weill between 5 November 1913 and 8 March 1914 on the eastern slope of Ophel.[34] Weill found three terraced ledges on this slope with short pieces of wall, a crossing wall a little over 40 yards long and a round tower, which according to Dalman, belonged to a vineyard (cf. Zech. 14.10, see below).

Further south, below the pool of Siloam, the gardens of the Kidron valley were irrigated by the 'Well' of Siloam (actually the spring rises further north, at Gihon) (*BJ* 5.410). Near the confluence of the

---

[32] For alternative derivations see Dalman, *SW* 253 n. 4.

[33] A considerable quantity of blood must have been involved, especially at the festivals, as we see from b. Pes. 65b, according to which 'it was a boast of the sons of Aaron to wade up to their ankles in (sacrificial) blood'. This reference is to blood not in the channel but in the Court of the Priests.

[34] Cf. *ZDPV* 45, 1922, 27.

Kidron and Hinnom valleys grew from very early times the royal gardens in which a spring rose (*Ant.* 7.347) called, according to tradition, *En Rogel* (I Kings 1.9). In these gardens were the royal wine-presses (Zech. 14.10).[35]

In the *south-west* of the city the name of a village mentioned in *BJ* 5.507, 'Ερεβίνθων οἶκος 'house of chick-peas', suggests the cultivation of this vegetable.

The detailed evidence confirms the general assertion that there was considerable cultivation of fruit and vegetables in the immediate neighbourhood of Jerusalem. Crops included vegetables, olives, grapes, figs and chick-peas.

Besides fruit from the immediate neighbourhood, olives (oil) and grapes (wine) were imported, mostly from Judaea. Wine for the Temple, which was used for libations, was brought preferably from Qeruhim or Qeruthim (which probably lay in the Wadi Far'a north of Jericho) and from Hattulim (north of Gilgal). Less renowned were the vintages from Beth Rimmah and Beth Laban, both lying in the hill-country, and from Kephar Segana in the plain (M. Men. viii.6).[36] The context states that the remaining parts of Palestine were also qualified to supply the Temple with wine; this suggests that all five of these places were in Judaea, as is commonly accepted. If we consider the many Judaean place names which indicate vineyards, together with the numerous remains of wine-presses, and finally the fact that both the Old Testament[37] and the Talmud[38] describe Judaea as pre-eminently a vine-growing province, we may be certain that Judaea provided grapes and wine for Jerusalem.

The most important fruit, however, produced in Judaea was the olive. Eupolemus (p. 38) and Pseudo-Aristeas (112, see p. 41 '. . . thickly planted with multitudes of olive trees') entirely agree with this. Numerous Judaean place names,[39] as well as a glance at the quality of the soil (p. 7), confirm it. The oil needed for the Temple was brought from Tekoa in Judaea and from Regab in Perea (*Ant.* 13.398).[40] We read in j. Hag. iii.4, 79c.3 that Perea provided

[35] They are named as an indication of the city boundary in the south.

[36] On their positions see Neubauer, *Géographie*, 82ff.; S. Klein, 'Weinstock, Feigenbaum und Sykomore in Palästina', *Festschrift Schwarz*, 391.

[37] Smith, *Jerusalem* I, 303 and n. 2.

[38] S. Klein, *art. cit.*, 389–92.

[39] Smith, *Jerusalem* I, 300 n. 3.

[40] Today Rägib, probably to be identified with Erga, 15 miles west of Gerasa, mentioned by Eusebius (*Onomast.* 216, GCS 11.1 = Eus. III.1, 16).

olives but not oil (p. 7). T. Men. ix.5, 526 names Gesh Halab (called Giskala by Josephus) as the third source of supply, but this seems to be based less upon historical evidence, than upon the desire to name each of the three Jewish districts of Palestine.

An isolated passage (M. Maas. ii.3) mentions the transport of fruit from Galilee for sale in Jerusalem.

When we enter the fruit and vegetable market in Jerusalem we find figs, which could also be bought in the rose garden (M. Maas. ii.5), and sycamore fruit, one of which was all the nourishment taken by the devout Zadok, although he gave a hundred discourses a day (Lam. R. 1.32 on 1.5, Son. 1.31, 104). Certain vegetables and spices needed for the correct keeping of the Passover had to be brought to the market in great quantities, considering the large number of pilgrims. Lettuce was prescribed (M. Pes. x.3), but also allowed were chicory, pepperwort, snakeroot and dandelion (M. Pes. ii.6). Besides these, the market at Jerusalem at Passover time had to supply spices, wine and wine vinegar, which mixed with crushed fruits made up the prescribed fruit puree (harōset) (M. Pes. x.3). Wine had to be drunk as part of the rite, and even the poorest had to drink at least four cups (M. Pes. x.1). This, or perhaps a cultic purpose, seems to explain the import of three hundred barrels of wine from the Mount of Simeon.[41]

To summarize what we are told of the cultivation around the city and of the imports of grain, fruit and vegetables: grain was brought mainly from the non-Judaic parts of Palestine, especially Transjordan, and next from Galilee and Samaria. The city's requirements of fruit and vegetables were supplied mainly with olives, wine, figs and vegetables from the immediate neighbourhood, and with olives and grapes from Judaea.

(c) Livestock

Eupolemus says that, besides corn and fruit, livestock was imported (p. 38). Josephus tells us that Antiochus the Great (at times during 219–217 BC, and from 198 BC fully, ruler of Palestine), issued a decree for his whole kingdom concerning the import of livestock into Jerusalem: 'Nor let any flesh of mules or of horses or of asses, be brought into the city, whether they be wild or tame; nor that of

---

[41] Lam. R. 2.5 on 2.2. (Son. 2.4, 162), cf. j. Taan. iv. 8, 69a. According to the context, this export of wine was counted as credit to the Mount of Simeon. The parallel of the Mount of Olives (ibid.), on which were shops for sacrificial animals, points to the sale of wine for ceremonial purposes.

leopards or foxes, or hares, and in general, that of any animal which is forbidden for the Jews to eat: Nor let their skins be brought into it; nor let any such animal be bred up in the city. Let them only be permitted to use the sacrifices derived from their forefathers, with which they have been obliged to make acceptable atonements to God' (*Ant.* 12.146). This ordinance limited the import of livestock to beasts necessary for cultic purposes, and proves that livestock was imported in great quantity at the beginning of the second century BC.

We must first enquire where the livestock came from.

'There are cattle of all kinds in great quantities and rich pasturage for them,' says Pseudo-Aristeas 112. In fact, the grasslands in the hill-country of Judaea provide good pasture, but only for sheep and goats. This agrees exactly with the list in b. Men. 87a, which begins with the Tannaitic opening phrase 'Our Rabbis have taught', indicating that the passage to follow is earlier than AD 200. The list is concerned with the requirements of the Temple: 'Rams are brought from Moab, lambs from Hebron, calves from Sharon, doves from the Royal Mountain.' 'Sharon' means the coastal plain between Jaffa and Lydda (cf. Acts 9.35), an area ideally suited to cattle-breeding, the 'Royal Mountain' is the hill-country of Judaea.

If we now consider Eupolemus' statement (p. 38) that beasts for slaughter came from Arabia, or Transjordan, we have the following picture: Transjordan produced beasts for slaughter, especially rams, the coastal plain produced calves, the Judaean hill-country produced sheep, goats and doves.

Jerusalem had several cattle-markets for both secular and sacrificial purposes.

First, there was a market for trade in livestock (M. Shek. vii.2).[42]

Second, there was a market for fat-cattle, no doubt a meat-market.[43] Chickens were sold here.[44]

[42] This passage assumes that most of the livestock for sale here would be bought with 'second tithe' money. Every pious Israelite was obliged to spend one-tenth of the profits from his land, or perhaps even from his stock, in Jerusalem (the so-called 'second tithe'). This money was spent mainly on peace-offerings and thank-offerings, i.e. offerings which could be eaten after the priests had taken their share. The passage also seems to assume that this 'second tithe' money was spent in Jerusalem the whole year round, and therefore that people who lived in the country left such money behind with their friends in Jerusalem. This is of importance to the social situation in the city (cf. M.M. Sh.; and p. 29).

[43] On the ambiguity of the word *paṭṭāmîm* see p. 8n. 29; Levy IV, 27b.

[44] According to M.B.K. vii.7; T.B.K. viii.10, 361; b.B.K. 82b, it was forbidden to keep chickens in Jerusalem, because it was feared that their scratching would bring to light unclean things. Against this we have the record of the cock crowing at

Thirdly, after the secular cattle-markets we come to the markets for sacrificial animals.

On the Mount of Olives were two cedars, under one of which were 'four shops belonging to sellers of things necessary for sacrifices of purification', which suggests especially doves, lambs, sheep, oil and meal. 'From the other came forty *s^e'āh* of young doves every month for sacrifice' (Lam. R. 2.5 on 2.2, Son. 2.4, 162, cf. j. Taan, iv.8, 69a.36).[45] The position of *Migdal Sebo'ayya* (var. reading *Migdal Sabba'ayya*), which means Tower of the Dyers, is uncertain. Here were allegedly three hundred shops for the sale of clean animals for sacrifice (Lam. R. 2.5, Son. 2.4, 163), and eighty for fine woollen fabrics (j. Taan. iv.8, 69a.42). Neubauer's theory[46] that this place was near Tiberias has against it the fact that it would have meant the transport of sacrificial animals through heathen territory. It is more likely that there was a place of this name near Jerusalem. The story of a synagogue sexton who prepared the lamps for the Sabbath, went to Jerusalem to pray in the Temple and returned in time to light them, suggests a position very near the city (Lam. R. 3.9 on 3.9, Son. 3.3, 192). However, the whole statement must be treated with caution, since the context tells a similar story relating to the women of Lydda.

In the Temple area at Jerusalem there is clear evidence of trade in sacrificial animals. Jesus came into the temple court and over-turned the 'tables of the money-changers' (Mark 11.15; Matt. 21.12; cf. also John 2.14), and the 'seats of those who sold doves' (Mark and

---

Peter's denial (Mark 14.72; Matt. 26.74; Luke 22.60; John 18.27). According to the Mishnah, the crowing of a cock was a time-signal for the sanctuary: 'At cock-crow they blew . . . a blast' (M. Sukk. v.4; cf. M. Tam. i.2; M. Yom. i.8). A Jeru-salem cock is mentioned in the Mishnah, admittedly in a legendary context: R. Judah b. Baba testified (M. Eduy. vi.1) 'that a cock was stoned in Jerusalem be-cause it had killed a man' (it was said to have pecked a child's brains out). On the whole we can take it that the alleged prohibition against keeping chickens is no more credible than the others related in b.B.K. 82b (pp. 6; 42). This conclusion is all the more probable as T.B.K. viii.10, 361, says that chicken keeping was per-mitted in Jerusalem as long as there was a garden or dung-heap for the hens to scratch. This implies the existence of gardens in Jerusalem (pp. 42f.), and so con-firms the objections against b.B.K. 82b and parallels.

[45] A passage from Josephus may be relevant here: *BJ* 5.505, which, dealing with the wall built by Titus during the siege, says that it led to the Mount of Olives 'round the mountain up to the rock called the Dovecote'. This rock possibly had holes to serve as dovecotes, which gave it its name.

[46] Neubauer, *Géographie*, 217f.: cf. F. Buhl, *Geographie des alten Palästinas*, Freiburg-Leipzig 1896, 226.

Matt.). According to John this meant those 'who sold oxen, sheep and doves' (2.14).

The authenticity of this evidence has been questioned, but with no good reason. Zech. 14.21 (i.e. Deutero-Zechariah, fourth to third century BC) already speaks of traders in the sanctuary. M. Shek. i.3 and T. Shek. i.6, 174, give evidence of money-changers in the Temple court. The shops on the aqueduct (Lam. R. 4.7 on 4.4, Son. 220, cf. p. 14) were probably in the Temple court. These, then, would be the same shops in which the Sanhedrin was said to be housed for forty years before the destruction of Jerusalem; this reference is evidently an illustration of the withdrawal of the right of capital punishment (b. R. Sh. 31a; b. Sanh. 41a; b. Shab. 15a; b. A. Zar. 8b). Identification of these shops with those mentioned in Lam. R. 4.7 on 4.4 (Son. 220) is therefore inevitable, since it is stated positively that the Sanhedrin was only later driven 'into the city'. It is here therefore that we must look for the traders in doves for sacrifice, already discussed on pp. 33f. Now Mark (11.15) and Matthew (21.12) mention only traders in doves, but both of them previously speak of 'those who bought and those who sold', which may well have meant cattle dealers (John 2.14). Actually, there is a rabbinic tradition which indicates the sale of cattle in the Temple area. According to j. Betz. ii.4, 61c.13, R. Baba b. Buta (a contemporary of Herod the Great) had three thousand head of small livestock brought to the Temple hill to be sold for whole burnt-offerings and peace-offerings (cf. T. Hag. ii.11, 23b; Bill. I, 851f.). We also saw above (p. 20) that there were shops belonging to the sons of Ḥanun or Ḥanan, which possibly may have been the same as those at Beth Hino, and maybe those mentioned on p. 48. These shops apparently belonged to the high-priestly family.[47] We may add here that the high priest Ananias (in office AD 47 to about 55) was called the 'great procurer of money' by Josephus (*Ant.* 20.205), and that the Temple was said to be going to rack and ruin because of avarice and mutual hatred (T. Men. xiii.22, 534). So we are forced to conclude that in the Court of the Gentiles, in spite of the sanctity of the Temple area, there could have been a flourishing trade in animals for sacrifice, perhaps supported by the powerful high-priestly family of Annas.

(d) Raw materials and merchandise

(i) The main material for house-building was *stone* which could be

---

[47] So Derenbourg, *Essai*, 459.

procured from the land surrounding the city (pp. 14f.). The stone for the altar and the ramp was brought from Beth-Kerem (M. Midd. iii.4).[48]

(ii) *Wood* was also used, especially for beams to construct roofs (M. Ohol. xii.5f.; T. Ohol. v.5, 602). T. Eduy. iii.3, 459, and b. Zeb. 113a, expressly mention a woodshed in which human bones were found. If there were, in fact, three-storied houses which Lam. R. 1.2 on 1.1. (Son. 69) suggests was usual in the city, the demand for timber must have been quite considerable. We have seen (pp. 41–45) that the surrounding country was much more thickly wooded than now, and therefore most of the timber may have been obtained from the neighbourhood. Wood for fuel at any rate was found just in front of the city, as the report on the activities of the brigand leader Simon shows (*BJ* 4.541). The bundle of willow-twigs used for the Feast of Tabernacles was gathered from Mosah, (Arab Qaloniyeh), west of Jerusalem, on the road to Jaffa. If, as R. Jose the Galilean demanded, the Passover offering was roasted on a spit of pomegranate wood (M. Pes. vii.1), there must have been an enormous amount of this wood brought into Jerusalem at Passover time, in view of the thousands of animals sacrificed.

Wood was needed for the Temple, as well as for secular purposes. The wood mainly used for building in the Temple was cedar wood from the Lebanon (p. 35). The Ark of the Covenant was said to be made from acacia wood which Jacob had brought with him from *Migdal Sebo'ayya* or *Sabba'ayya* (Cant. R. 1.55 on 1.12, Son. 79; Gen. R. 94.4 on 46.1, Son. 871). For the daily burnt-offering wood from the fig, nut and pine trees was used (M. Tam. ii.3); wood from olive trees and vines was not allowed. The special pyre for burning the 'Red Heifer' on the Mount of Olives was built of cedar, laurel and cypress wood, as well as from fig trees (M. Par. iii.8, 10).

Since the Temple was built with the greatest possible splendour and had developed an ancient, firmly rooted tradition of ceremonial, cedar wood was preferred although it had to be transported from far away, whereas the wood at hand from the numerous olive trees could not be used.

The timber market mentioned by Josephus (*BJ* 2.530) as lying in the northern part of the city served secular needs.

---

[48] The place lay in Judaea, Jer. 6.1 and Neh. 3.14; according to Jerome, *In Hieremiam* II, 8, on Jer. 6.1 (CCSL 74. 63), it was on a hill between Jerusalem and Tekoa.

(iii) Country folk came to Jerusalem to sell *wool*, some of them from far away, since we hear in this connection that sellers stayed overnight in the city (Lam. R. 2.24 on 2.15, Son. 2.19, 182). Purple wool was used at the burning of the Red Heifer (M. Par. iii.10).

(iv) *Pottery* which came from a distance as far as Modiith (seventeen miles away) for sale in Jerusalem, was regarded as clean. Any pottery imported from further away was regarded as unclean (M. Hag. iii.5).

(v) *Slaves* of both sexes were regarded as merchandise in those days, and we have already noted that there was a stone in Jerusalem where they were put up for auction (p. 36). It has been wrongly said that Jewish slaves were not sold in Palestine.[49]

To summarize: by far the most important business of local trade was to supply Jerusalem with foodstuffs, and after that to provide raw materials for the trades of the city.

B. THE INFLUENCE OF JERUSALEM ON COMMERCE

1. The city's geographical position

As a result of both the extension of military security and the policy of colonization of the Roman government, the cultural sphere of Syria stretched further east than it does today. A flourishing culture was spreading beyond the Jordan. In fact the province of Syria, to which the province of Judaea really belonged (p. 4), 'was the equal of Egypt, as far as commerce and industry was concerned, among the provinces of the Roman Empire'.[50] So cultural conditions were favourable for commerce in Jerusalem.

Let us take a look at Jerusalem itself. The central position of the city is the first thing to strike us, a fact which contemporary writers strongly emphasized. Jerusalem lies in the middle of Judaea (Pseudo-Aristeas 83; BJ 3.52). Siloam, a synonym on the principle of *pars pro toto* for Jerusalem, is the centre of all Israel (j. Hag. i.1, 76a). Furthermore, Jerusalem was the centre of the inhabited world (Ezek. 5.5),[51] the mid-point of the whole earth (Ethiop. Enoch 26.1). For this reason it was called the 'navel of the earth' (Ezek. 38.12; BJ 3.52), to which

[49] Krauss, TA II, 83.
[50] Guthe, Die griechisch-römischen Städte, 40f.
[51] Cf. Gottheil, JE VII, 129.

the Gentiles and Satan must come up (Rev. 20.9); and Jubilees 8.19 even calls Mount Zion the 'centre of the navel of the earth'.

This central position was combined with favourable sea communications through the harbours of Ascalon, Jaffa, Gaza and Ptolemais. One point is of particular importance: Jerusalem was more or less equidistant from all of them, and therefore lay in a central position for all, as Pseudo-Aristeas 115 points out.

However, we should be mistaken if we assume too readily that the commercial connections were favourable. Of what use was the central position of Jerusalem in a province with considerable commerce and favourable sea communications, if it remained a remote upland city? For that, in fact, is what Jerusalem was.

In the past, and even up to modern times, the hill-country of Judaea with its countless caverns and hiding places provided excellent opportunities for brigandage even under a vigilant administration. Only last century whole villages were known to be nests of thieves (Abu Rosh, between Jaffa and Jerusalem; Abu Dis to the south-east of the city). We hear of raids by brigands either feared or actually happening along the roads leading to Jerusalem during the period before AD 70. M. Shek. ii.1 discusses the case of men bringing their Temple dues being attacked on the way to Jerusalem, and M.R. Sh. i.9 says the same about those 'bearing witness about the new moon'. In Luke 10.30–37, Jesus tells the story, albeit in a parable, of the traveller going from Jerusalem to Jericho who fell among thieves, and was robbed and half killed (nevertheless the parable assumes that three other travellers went that way unaccompanied). Again we must remember that Josephus reports the attacking and robbing of an imperial servant on his way to Jerusalem through the pass of Beth Horon: Rome took harsh reprisals and sacked the neighbouring villages. Jesus' exclamation to the Temple guard come to arrest him: 'Have you come out as against a robber with swords and clubs?' (Mark 14.48) assumes that the Temple guard was obliged to intervene against robbers; two robbers were crucified with Jesus (Mark 15.27). According to John 18.40 Barabbas had been condemned to death as a robber, but the synoptic description of him as a revolutionary and murderer suggests that he belonged rather to the anti-Roman party of the Sicarii.

As soon as the hands of the authorities in Jerusalem were tied because of the revolt in the city, brigandage became rampant throughout the land (*BJ* 4.406ff.). Possibly there was a special court in Jerusalem empowered to try cases of robbery (M. Ket. xiii.1),[52] and to take police measures against brigands.

An even greater drawback, however, than attacks by robbers was the inadequate system of roads leading to Jerusalem. As the map shows, the city is completely ringed round with high hills and lies on a south-south-eastern spur of the watershed, so that it is enclosed on the east, south and west by deep ravines. We must admit that this highland city, perched on this spur, is designed by nature not for a centre of commerce but a fortress.

Not one single pass cuts through the watershed near Jerusalem in an east-west direction; the nearest lies further to the north. Communications to Jerusalem are artificial and difficult in the west, and even more so in the east. All this kept Jerusalem from being a thoroughfare for the rich products of Transjordan which were increasingly plentiful at this time, or from becoming a commercial centre for nomadic tribes. This is why the ford over the Jordan near Jericho was quite unimportant for commerce, as also was the near-by one at the outlet of the Jabbok which provided a link with Samaria (Sebaste) by way of the Wadi Far'a. The main traffic from Transjordan to the sea would cross the Jordan immediately south of the Sea of Gennesaret by the Gadara-Tiberias road, or some twelve miles south of this on the Gadara-Scythopolis road, unless it preferred the ford eight miles north of the Sea of Gennesaret, by the bridge called Jisr-Benat Yakub, to follow the *Via Maris*, the ancient caravan route from Damascus to the Plain of Jezreel. This evidence is all the more conclusive since much of the merchandise, especially from Arabia coming by way of Bostra and Gadara, had to make a wide detour to use the two first-mentioned crossings.

Only one natural route passes near Jerusalem: that is the north-south road following the line of the watershed from Nablus (Sichem, Neapolis) to Hebron. This route, however, is one of the least significant in Palestine for commerce, and is of use only for inland trade. Any foreign trade would need to make for the sea, and this north-south road only became of value at points where it crossed an east-west route—but it is precisely that which nature has denied to Jerusalem. Consequently the main value of this route was that it linked Jerusalem with southern Palestine. Jerusalem therefore played a greater part for the semi-desert of southern Palestine than for Samaria in the north; Samaria moreover was at that time more

[52] If we adopt the reading *g^ezēlōt*, as does b. Ket. 105a.

civilized and more thickly populated than southern Palestine. In consequence, the link *via* the watershed made Jerusalem the natural trade centre only for southern Palestine.

Naturally, links from Jerusalem to east and west came into being, and achieved prominence because of the importance of Jerusalem and the extent of her requirements; but she still remained important simply for inland trade. Only for southern Palestine was Jerusalem the accepted centre of commerce.

Josephus puts this very clearly (*CA* 1.60): 'Ours is not a maritime country; neither commerce nor the intercourse which it promotes . . . has any attraction for us . . . and we devote ourselves to the cultivation of the productive country with which we are blessed.' Judaea played no part in world trade.

Yet, despite the geographical disadvantages, Jerusalem had a considerable commerce. How did this happen?

2. *Political and religious importance of the city*

Since parts of the land 'in so-called Samaria and bordering the land of the Idumaeans are level, but the rest is mountainous (especially that in the middle)', agriculture had to be 'extensively carried on, for so these people too (who lived in the mountains) had rich rewards' (Pseudo-Aristeas 107; cf. 108–12). We may smile at this reasoning by an obviously Jewish writer—that the plain-dwellers must toil, from the theoretical motive of encouraging the others to work—but he has grasped the state of affairs very well; he is indicating that the city is dependent on imports. To what extent this is true is proved by the food-shortage suffered by Antiochus in Jerusalem during the Maccabean war (*BJ* 1.46), by the famine there during the siege of 37 BC (*BJ* 1.347; *Ant.* 14.471), and by the conditions during the famines, under Herod and Claudius. The city had not only to maintain its own people but also, three times a year, teeming multitudes of pilgrims. Against that sort of demand, the first-fruits did not do much to feed the city. Several references in rabbinic literature cast doubts on how much these actually produced, and in any case they were perquisites of the priests (M. Bikk. ii.1); as for the other dues in kind, these could be delivered to the local priest of one's own region.

A further difficulty was the notorious unsuitability of the soil for grain (pp. 39f.) and the lack of cattle-breeding (pp. 46f.). Usually the city's demands could be met from the produce of Palestine: only in times of famine or after a war had it to fall back on foreign trade.

Besides essential food supplies, the position of the city caused another shortage, of raw materials, and especially metals, in consequence, the city had to import these also, partly from Palestine (pp. 49ff.), partly from foreign lands (pp. 35ff.).

What export would serve for foreign trade? 'Considering how thickly populated Syria is, it is likely that from its natural products of grain, oil, and wine, only wine was exported in quantity.'[53] Grain of course was out of the question for exporting, nor do we have evidence of a single outstanding industrial product which can be described as characteristic of Jerusalem (p. 27). On the other hand Eupolemus (p. 38) and Pseudo-Aristeas (pp. 41f.) both put oil as the main product of Judaea, or the district around Jerusalem (cf. p. 7: olives were processed in the area round Jerusalem). In addition, the demand for oil in Northern Syria was very heavy at times (*BJ* 2.591; *Vita* 74f.), so heavy that whereas in Gischala in North Galilee eighty sextares of oil cost no more than four drachmas, the price at Caesarea Philippi, about twenty miles away at the foot of Hermon, was one drachma for two sextares, which means that it was ten times as dear (*Vita* 75; *BJ* 2.592, says eight times). From this it seems possible that oil was exported from Jerusalem, as has been supposed;[54] but there is no conclusive proof. The only mention I know of exports from Jerusalem is to be found in Lam. R. 1.13 on 1.1, Son. 1.12, 79, which tells of a camel on the road from Jerusalem carrying two skins, one full of wine and the other of vinegar. The passage being an anecdote, we had better not draw from it conclusions on exportation from Jerusalem.

The political importance of the city had both a direct and indirect effect on trade. The direct effect was produced by the kings, and the demands stimulated by their sumptuous manner of life. When Herod built his palace, he had the most costly materials brought from all over the world (*BJ* 5.178), and in Josephus' opinion the palace exceeded even the Temple in magnificence. With the materials for this splendid architecture, brought by foreign trade, came the products of alien cultures. Herod prided himself on being 'more a Greek than a Jew' (*Ant.* 19.329), and this was displayed particularly in the way he kept court.

The indirect effect was due to the fact that from ancient times the

53 Guthe, *Die griechisch-romischen Städte* 40.
54 Smith, *Jerusalem* I, 15 and 335.

political centre had also been the centre of attraction for the national wealth. In Jerusalem sat the customs officials, not only those in charge of the market dues of the city (p. 32), but also those in control of much greater levies. An example of this is the tax-collector Joseph, in the second century BC (*Ant.* 12.160ff.). This man came from the village of Phicola, established himself in Jerusalem, and from there directed the collection of taxes from Syria, Phoenicia, Judaea and Samaria (*Ant.* 12.175ff.). He held this position for twenty-two years. He had an office in Alexandria from which his steward, acting on the instructions of the moment, made payments into the royal treasury. Such people as this often established themselves as bankers in the capital, and they must have been those who from ancient times (Isa. 5.8; Micah 2.1–5) mortgaged the land and crops of the needy peasants (p. 41). The money was deposited in the Temple, where according to IV Macc. 4.3, myriads of private fortunes were kept (cf. *BJ* 6.282). We come across the people as wholesale traders (p. 34). Some of them retired from business to Jerusalem, partly in order to spend their capital there, and partly to die in the Holy City.

The national capital influenced commerce in two ways. It drew trade towards Jerusalem by promoting business transactions, and it provided a ready market for trade because of the heavy demand for luxury in clothing, jewellery, etc., a demand met primarily by foreign trade.

What a huge volume of material had been consumed by the Temple in the eighty-two years or so of its construction! The status of the holy house demanded the greatest magnificence (one has only to think of the amount of gold used) and the highest quality of all materials. Stibium, alabaster and marble (b. Sukk. 51b) must be mentioned, as well as cedar wood: so it is understandable that the Temple is the most important item in any description of foreign trade (p. 38).

The *Temple ceremonial* required also the finest quality in wood, wine, oil, grain and incense. From as far as India came the material for the high priest's vestment for the Day of Atonement; and the twelve precious stones on his ephod (*BJ* 5.234) were chosen from the most valuable jewels in the whole world. But above all, what quantities of sacrificial animals, bulls, calves, sheep, goats and doves, were required there! Specifically defined offerings were brought daily as public sacrifices (*Ant.* 3.237); during the Passover feast the daily offering was two bulls, one ram and seven lambs for burnt-offering, and one kid as sin-offering (*Ant.* 3.249). Private daily offerings too were known to have been made, since sacrifices had to be offered to expiate numerous precisely defined transgressions which led to uncleanness, for the restoration of ritual purity. Hecatombs were offered on special occasions as when Herod offered three hundred oxen on the completion of the Temple buildings (*Ant.* 15.422); and when Marcus Agrippa, son-in-law of Augustus, visited Jerusalem, 'he offered a hecatomb' (*Ant.* 16.14). Especially at festivals did the number of sacrifices go up: 'Many sacrifices were necessarily brought every day, and particularly at general assemblies and feasts, on behalf of both individuals and all in common' (Philo, *De vita Mosis* II, 159). Pseudo-Aristeas 89 mentions the many thousands of sacrificial animals brought in on feast days. So great was the import of animals for sacrifice that all cattle found in the vicinity of Jerusalem, within a radius of the distance of Migdal-Eder, were without exception regarded as destined for sacrifice (M. Shek. vii.4).[55]

The most important factor, however, had not yet been mentioned: the tri-annual invasion of the city by multitudes of pilgrims, particularly at the Passover, when Jews came from all over the world. This host had to be fed. True, they catered for themselves in part, from the fruits of the Second Tithe (pp. 134ff.), i.e. the tenth part of all agricultural produce and perhaps also of cattle, which had to be consumed in Jerusalem; but transport of these goods themselves was possible only for the immediate neighbourhood. Those who lived at a distance were forced to convert their Second Tithe into money and spend it in the city, in conformity with regulations.

As well as food, at Passover there was a great demand for beasts for sacrifice. Since the reform of Josiah, 621 BC, it had been lawful to slay the passover lamb in Jerusalem only. Josephus (*BJ* 6.424) exaggerates grossly when he speaks of 255,600 (variant reading 256, 500) Passover victims, but certainly the figure ran into many thousands.

The Temple was the most important factor in the commerce of Jerusalem. By means of the Temple treasury, to which every Jew had to pay his annual dues, the whole of world-wide Jewry contributed to the commerce of Jerusalem.

[55] Migdal-Eder, cf. Gen. 35.21, was near Bethlehem.

IIII

FOREIGN VISITORS

A. EVIDENCE FOR FOREIGN VISITORS IN THE CITY[1]

1. *In general*

(a) *The Journey to Jerusalem*

IF WE HAD A WAY of drawing a statistical graph of the number of visitors to Jerusalem from abroad, it would show well-defined curves which remained fairly constant each year. We would record against February and March that 'the tourist season' began. This depended on the climate, for these months see the end of the rainy season, and people could begin to think about travelling. Before this the roads would be too deep in mud (M. Taan. i.3; cf. Matt. 24.20; 'Pray that your flight be not in the winter'). In consequence, Jerusalem saw most foreigners in the dry months, approximately March to September. On three occasions during these months the number of visitors increased by leaps and bounds to a prodigious height, at the three great festivals when pilgrims came from all over the world: Passover, Pentecost and Tabernacles (Deut. 16.1–16). The annual peak was reached at Passover.

Let us follow a traveller on his way to Jerusalem. When the rainy season ended, he made his preparations: if he were a merchant, he would prepare his merchandise. If he were going up for some religious purpose, perhaps a festival, he would take the opportunity of bringing his 'dues' to the Holy City, and these, according to custom at that time, included the 'second tithe', which though used privately and not 'given' had to be spent in Jerusalem. The tax of the didrachma, the *bikkūrīm* (first-fruits, which were of course generally sent to Jerusalem all together by each of the twenty-four courses, M. Bikk. iii.2ff.),

---

[1] To give a complete picture, we mention here all non-Jerusalemites, including for instance foreign troops.

and this 'second tithe': these were the 'dues' which had been brought to Jerusalem. In *Ant.* 18.313 we are told that the money dues were escorted from Nearda and Nisibis in Mesopotamia by 'many tens of thousands', making it clear that the festival caravans were used, at least in distant lands to bring the Temple dues to Jerusalem. M. Hall. iv.10f., dealing with instances of the delivery of first-fruits, obviously shows that individual offerings were also brought privately. Dough-offerings were also brought to Jerusalem (M. Hall. iv.10), although that was not required, as they could be given to the local priests. At any rate, however, each Israelite brought his 'second tithe' (p. 57), in money or in kind, with him to Jerusalem.

The traveller's preparations further included finding company for the journey, since the prevalent brigandage (pp. 52f.) made it hazardous for anyone to travel alone for any great distance. At festival times great caravans were formed. The 'many thousands' who assembled in Babylonia, referred to in *Ant.* 18.313, were no doubt some of these festival caravans. Luke 2.44 refers to the caravan from Nazareth in which were the parents of Jesus with their relatives and friends. It was a festival caravan coming through Jericho which Jesus joined the last time he came up to Jerusalem (Mark 10.46).

The journey was usually made on foot. Hillel the Elder is said to have made his pilgrimage from Babylon to Jerusalem on foot.[2] Of course, travel by donkey was quicker, as we see in the same reference, when a man riding an ass jeered at the pedestrian Hillel; and Jesus rode into Jerusalem on an ass (Mark 11.1ff.). Only occasionally was a chariot used for the journey to and from Jerusalem, as in the case of the treasurer of the Ethiopian Candace (Acts 8.27ff.). That the usual way was on foot appears from M. Hag. i.1; it was considered a very meritorious way.

On the whole the roads were bad (p. 58). As far as the Sanhedrin, as principal local authority, was concerned, very little was done about this, as perhaps the negligence over the Jerusalem aqueduct shows (p. 16 n. 30). Matters improved where the Romans had responsibility for the roads. The pilgrim road to Babylonia (linking north and south, p. 53) appears to have had more care devoted to it all along,[3] for Herod had been concerned for its safety. The Babylonian Jew Zamaris, whom he settled in the district of Batanea, protected the Babylonian festival caravans from marauding brigands from Trachonitis (*Ant.* 17.26ff.).

M. Taan. i.3 gives us information on the time such a journey would take, particularly when made in a large festival caravan with all its interruptions and delays. Here R. Gamaliel decrees that prayers for rain should first begin on 7 Marḥeshvan. He gives as a reason that this is the fifteenth day after the Feast (of Tabernacles, celebrated in the month Tishri), and so the festival pilgrims might reach the Euphrates dryshod. As this was a distance of over 375 miles, it implies that Gamaliel was reckoning more than 25 miles each day, which is too much for a caravan.

(b) Accommodation in Jerusalem

Having safely arrived in Jerusalem, our traveller's next concern was lodgings. Generally it was not difficult to find accommodation in one of the inns in Jerusalem (Lam. R. 1.2 on 1.1, Son. 70) such as all larger places had (Luke 2.7: Bethlehem). Fellow members of religious communities such as Essenes, Pharisees, Christians, were lodged by their friends. Those who lived in Cyrene, Alexandria and the provinces of Cilicia and Asia found shelter in the hospice connected with their synagogue on Ophel (see p. 66). An inscription found there by R. Weill says clearly that 'the rooms and cisterns at the Inn' have been set aside for 'the use of visitors'.[4] However, it was difficult to find shelter on feast days, for only a few foreigners owned their own houses in Jerusalem. The foreign princes of the Herodian royal house coming to Jerusalem on feast days (Herod Antipas, Tetrarch of Galilee and Perea, Luke 23.7; and Agrippa II), had a permanent lodging ready, the Maccabean Palace immediately above the Xystus, and the princes and princesses of Adiabene had their palaces on the eastern hill (pp. 11–14).

Where did the mass of the pilgrims stay? It is one of the ten wonders of God in the Holy Place, that all found shelter and none said to another: 'The crowd is too great, I cannot find shelter in Jerusalem' (M. Ab. v.5). Some of the pilgrims could live in the city itself, excluding the Temple area. There could be no question of its being used for shelter, if only because the prohibition in M. Ber. ix.5 (b. Yeb. 6b): 'No man may enter the Temple area with a staff, or sandals, or a wallet, or with dust on his feet.' It would be conceivable, however, that pilgrims might ask for shelter in some of the buildings

[4] *CIJ* II, 1404, lines 6–8.

belonging to the Temple, which had acquired vast properties by endowments; but even taking this into account, it is highly improbable that the huge crowds drawn into Jerusalem by the feasts could all find rooms inside the city walls. Some might stay in near-by places like Bethphage or Bethany, where Jesus found shelter during his last stay in Jerusalem (Mark 11.11f.; Matt. 21.17). The majority of pilgrims, however, had to have tents in the immediate neighbourhood of the city, since at Passover time it was still very cold at night and there could be no question of sleeping out in the open. Actually we have evidence of Festival pilgrims camping out at night: In *Ant.* 17.217 we hear of Passover pilgrims striking camp; and according to the parallel passage in *BJ* 2.12 this was apparently 'in the plain', which probably means the area opposite the present Damascus gate.

However, the participants in the Passover feast were obliged to spend the Passover night (14–15 Nisan) in Jerusalem. The city itself could not take the crowd of pilgrims, and so that they could fulfil the law the boundaries of Jerusalem were extended to take in even Bethphage (M. Men. xi.2).[5]

According to Mark 11.11f. and Matt. 21.17 Bethany was the place where Jesus and his disciples passed the nights just before his death. Luke 21.37 says instead: 'And every night he went out, and lodged in the mount that is called the Mount of Olives.' This can be interpreted as Bethany since it lies in the region of the Mount of Olives; but that does not make sense within the context of Luke's Gospel, since Luke 22.39 uses the same phrase ('He came out and went . . . unto the Mount of Olives') to describe Gethsemane. Now Luke 21.37 is obviously just an editorial summary of the Marcan tradition (Mark 11.11, 17, 19) written by Luke himself. Thus we are forced to conclude that Luke was ignorant of the local geography, and has mistaken the place where Jesus was arrested, i.e. Gethsemane, for the usual nightly lodging place. On the other hand the statement in Luke 22.39 comes from Luke's special source, as the phrase 'as his custom was' shows.[6] It is absolutely correct; for this phrase 'as his custom was' refers, as John 18.2 confirms, not to the nightly lodging but to the meeting of Jesus and his disciples at some definite place on the Mount of Olives. This place is undoubtedly identical with the Garden of Gethsemane (Mark 14.26, 32; Matt. 26.30, 36), which lay on the western slope of the Mount of Olives,

---

[5] Cf. Neubauer, *Géographie*, 147ff.; Dalman, *SW*, 251–4; above p. 7.

[6] In my opinion, the Lucan passion narrative, from 22.14 onwards, is based not on Mark, but on another tradition, cf. J. Jeremias, 'Perikopen-Umstellungen bei Lukas?', *NTS* 4, 1957–8, 115–19, reprinted in *Abba*, Göttingen 1966, 93–97.

that is, unlike Bethany, still within the boundaries of greater Jerusalem which must not be left during the passover night.

Each group of festival pilgrims had its fixed quarters for the feast, in conformity with the distribution of different sections of the population in different quarters of the town (see the inscription quoted on pp. 60 and 66). From the fact that Jesus used to spend his nights at Bethany, we may presume that the quarters for Galilean pilgrims were to the east of the city.

2. *Visitors from a distance*

Having imagined the journey of a traveller to the Holy City and his lodging there, let us survey visitors to the city with regard to their country of origin. As before, we shall deal first with those from a distance, then with those who lived relatively near by.

We find in Acts 2.9–11, included in the account of the miracle of Pentecost in the year of Jesus' death, a list of Jews from every nation, dwelling in Jerusalem. This refers to Jews and proselytes temporarily resident in Jerusalem as pilgrims. In this list we find representatives from all countries of the then known world, 'Parthians, Medes, Elamites, dwellers in Mesopotamia, Judaea, Cappadocia, Pontus, Asia, Phrygia, Pamphylia, Egypt, parts of Libya belonging to Cyrene, and visitors from Rome, both Jews and proselytes, Cretans and Arabians'.

This evidence will be verified later when we examine relationships between Jerusalem and foreigners from different countries. The list in Acts 2.9–11 is undoubtedly stylized, and we can only accept it in so far as its contents are verified by further witness. By way of comparison, however, we can cite two other lists:

(i) In Acts 6.9, within a context obviously not stylized (6.1ff.), is a reasonable and remarkably well informed statement. With reference to Jerusalem it says, 'Certain of them were of the synagogue called The Synagogue of the Libertines, and of the Cyrenians, and of the Alexandrians, and of them of Cilicia and Asia, disputing with Stephen.' This verse refers to Jews living permanently in Jerusalem. As Hellenists, they must have lived together in their own quarter of the city, as they had a common synagogue and guesthouse (p. 66), just as at the turn of our century the different Jewish groups lived in their own quarters of Jerusalem.

(ii) A passage from Philo (*Leg. ad Cai.* 281f.) quotes a letter from

Agrippa I to Caligula. In this he says that Jerusalem is the Mother City not only for the Jews of Judaea but also those of Egypt, Phoenicia, Syria, Coele-Syria, Pamphylia, Cilicia, Asia, Bithynia, Pontus, Europe, Thessaly, Boeotia, Macedonia, Aeolia, Attica, Argos, Corinth, the Peloponnese, the isles of Euboea, Cyprus, Crete, the lands beyond the Euphrates, Babylonia and its neighbouring satrapies. Although this list makes no specific mention of journeys to Jerusalem, the idea is implicit, since it was obligatory for all adult Jews to make the pilgrimage there.

Next we shall deal with those who came from each individual country.

(a) Gaul and Germany

Gauls and Germans were lodged within the walls of old Jerusalem. Caesar Augustus (29 BC–AD 14) had sent Herod the Great the personal bodyguard of Cleopatra, the last Egyptian queen, who committed suicide in 30 BC, and this consisted of 400 Gauls (*BJ* 1.397).[7] It was Gallic mercenaries whom Herod the Great employed to drown his brother-in-law Jonathan (only called so here, elsewhere always Aristobulos) in a bath at Jericho (*BJ* 1.437). In the description of Herod's funeral procession Germans are mentioned as forming part of the guard together with Thracians and Gauls (*Ant.* 17.198; *BJ* 1.672). After Herod's death these troops will have been taken over by his son Archelaus the Ethnarch (4 BC–AD 6) and, after his deposition (AD 6), by the Romans. However, they could scarcely have been left in Palestine after AD 6.

(b) Rome

After AD 6 Judaea was a Roman province with a Roman governor, Roman troops and Roman officials. Jerusalem had a Roman garrison, namely a *cohors miliaria equitata* under a tribune, which would ensure frequent contact with Rome. Before this we hear of journeys made to Rome by Herod and his son and later the two Agrippas, of embassies to Rome (*Ant.* 20.193ff.; *Vita* 13ff. *et passim*) and of Romans coming to Jerusalem, mostly in an official capacity. On the other hand, in the garrison at Jerusalem, as was proper for a procuratorial province, even the officers were not Roman (Acts 22.28); but in

---

[7] They could have been Gauls or Galatians, but the occurrence of the term Γαλάται in *BJ* 2.364, 371, and 7.76, cf. *CA* 1.67, indicates that only the first meaning is possible.

Caesarea, the procurator's residence, was the so-called 'Italian Cohort' (Acts 10.1), and these troops no doubt were part of the procurator's escort on his customary appearance in Jerusalem at Passover time. From Rome, too, returned most of the 'freedmen', who had been taken prisoner in Pompey's wars and then given their freedom (Philo, *Leg. ad Cai.* 155). They appear as attached to the synagogue mentioned in Acts 6.9 (the so-called 'synagogue of the Libertines', see p. 66), in which with its attendant guest house the Jewish pilgrims from Rome no doubt found shelter (Acts 2.10). Acts 28.21 assumes that there was regular correspondence and personal contact between the Jews in Rome and the Jewish supreme authority in Jerusalem, the Sanhedrin.

(c) Greece

The Hellenistic influence, which shows itself among other things in the profusion of Greek loan-words to be found in Rabbinic literature, depended not on politics but on culture. For this very reason therefore it had a stronger impact than the Roman influence.

As early as the time of Hyrcanus II (76–67 and 63–40 BC) we find Athenians in Jerusalem, the coming and going between the two cities being occasioned as much by official as by private affairs (*Ant.* 14.149ff., see p. 35). Herod had Thracian mercenaries in his bodyguard (*Ant.* 17.198; *BJ* 1.672), and Eurycles, a Lacedemonian, played a conspicuous role at Herod's court (*BJ* 1.513–31). The so-called second and third missionary journeys of Paul are proof of the relations between Jerusalem and Greece; and on his return from the third journey we find him on the way to Jerusalem accompanied by a delegate from the church in Berea and two from that in Thessalonica (Acts 20.4). Relations with Athens also loom large in the stories in Lam. R. 1.1 (Son. 74, 76f.), which mention people from Jerusalem journeying to Athens, and Athenians staying in Jerusalem.

(d) Cyprus

In Acts 11.20 we hear of men from Cyprus in Jerusalem. They were Jewish Christians, who because of anti-Christian persecution were obliged to leave the city and go to Antioch. There they preached the gospel to Greeks, that is to non-Jews, a very important development. Barnabas, who was a Levite from Cyprus, owned a field near Jerusalem (Acts 4.36f.; Gal. 2.1, etc.). We must also reckon Mnason of Cyprus, 'an early disciple' (Acts 21.16), among the first members of the early Christian community in Jerusalem.

(e) Asia Minor

Asia Minor had a considerable Jewish diaspora, and in Jerusalem we come across representatives of almost every part of it. We find inhabitants of:—

(i) The province of Asia

Jews from the province of Asia joined with other Hellenists in one synagogue (Acts 6.9). Among the delegates bringing the taxes who accompanied Paul were two from Asia. The Jews of Asia, in Jerusalem for the feast of Pentecost, who recognized Paul in the Temple and tried to lynch him (Acts 21.27) were probably from Ephesus, for they recognized Trophimus of Ephesus who was with Paul. Temple tax was brought to Jerusalem from the province of Asia, for Cicero (*Pro Flacco* 28) tells us that Flaccus, proconsul of Asia in 62/1 BC, had Temple tax confiscated in Apamea, Laodicea, Adramyttium and Pergamum.

(ii) The island of Cos

A man from Cos, named Evaratus, was in Jerusalem in the train of the Herodian princes. Money was also brought from the island to the Temple at Jerusalem, and Mithridates had Temple money confiscated there (*Ant.* 14.112).

(iii) The province of Galatia

Gaius of Derbe and Timothy of Lystra journeyed to Jerusalem with Paul (Acts 20.4; cf. 16.1–8). It is highly probable that the Judaizing missionaries attacked in the Epistle to the Galatians came from Jerusalem.

(iv) Pisidia

In *BJ* 1.88, we find Pisidians in Jerusalem in Alexander Jannaeus' army of mercenaries.

(v) Cilicia

Cilicians also served in Alexander Jannaeus' army (*BJ* 1.88). Paul, who was born at Tarsus, studied in Jerusalem (Acts 22.3). Cilicians settled in Jerusalem had joined with other Hellenists in one community with a common synagogue (Acts 6.9: 'them that were of the synagogue called the Synagogue of the Libertines . . . and of them of Cilicia and Asia'). We come across this synagogue also in Talmudic literature where it is sometimes called the synagogue of the Alexandrians (T. Meg. iii.6, 224; j. Meg. iii.1, 73d.35), sometimes of the Tarsians, i.e. Cilicians (b. Meg. 26a).[8] It was probably this synagogue which R. Weill discovered on Ophel. During his excavations in 1913–14 he found, among some remains of masonry, an inscription (see above p. 60 and n. 4), which said among other things that the synagogue had been built by Theodotus, son of Vettenos, priest and ruler of the synagogue; a guest house and baths were attached. The father's name, Vettenos, and the reference to the attached guest house led L. H. Vincent [9] followed by R. Weill and G. Dalman, to surmise that this was the Synagogue of the Libertines (Acts 6.9; see p. 62); according to our argument this synagogue is the synagogue of the Alexandrians or Tarsians.

(vi) Cappadocia

Archelaus, king of Cappadocia, visited Jerusalem (*BJ* 1.499ff.; cf. 1.456, 530, 538).

(f) Mesopotamia

There was a strong Jewish community in Mesopotamia from the time of the deportation of the Jews by Assyria (722 BC) and Babylonia (597 and 587 BC). We know this from direct evidence and also from the close intellectual ties between Palestine and Babylonia.

Accordingly traffic moved vigorously between Jerusalem and the Land of the Two Rivers. Josephus (*Ant.* 15.22, 39, 56) speaks of a Babylonian Jew, Ananel, who was High Priest from 37–36 BC, and again from 34 BC. M. Par. iii.5 speaks of Ḥanamel, a high priest under whom a 'Red Heifer' was burnt, as 'the Egyptian'. If, as is likely, this is the same man, we prefer Josephus' evidence (see p. 69f.).

---

[8] It has been disputed whether 'Tarsians' (*ṭarsiyyīm*) here means the inhabitants of Tarsus. Some hold that they are artisans (Schürer II, 87 n. 247; 524 n. 77 etc.; see pp. 5 and 21; for the geographical meaning see Derenbourg, *Essai*, 263; Neubauer, *Géographie*, 293 n. 5, 315; Gottheil, 'Jerusalem', *JE* VII, 129). However, against this interpretation we must record: (a) b. Meg. 7a uses the same word, obviously meaning people from Tarsus, since it says that they conversed in their mother-tongue. (b) We have no other proof of synagogues in Jerusalem belonging to a guild. (c) In b. Meg. 26a 'Tarsians' is a variant for the word 'Alexandrians' which appears in T. Meg. iii.6, 224, and j. Meg. iii.1, 73d.32; this would explain the variations in the name of the synagogue, and also the longish enumeration in Acts 6.9.

[9] 'Découverte de la "Synagogue des Affranchis" à Jérusalem', *RB* 30, 1921, 247–277.

M. Men. xi.7 reports that Temple priests of Babylonian descent in Jerusalem ate the flesh of the additional offering raw, on the Day of Atonement, since they were not squeamish. The noted scribe Hillel, who taught approximately at the beginning of our era, was called 'the Babylonian' and was said to travel from Babylonia to Jerusalem on foot.

Besides priests and scribes, we find other Babylonians in Jerusalem. *Vita* 47 speaks of 'some Babylonians . . . who were in Jerusalem'. The Babylonian Silas is a prominent leader in the revolt against Rome (*BJ* 2.520; 3.11, 19). A woman from Carchemish lived in Jerusalem (M. Eduy. v.6); the 'wise men from the East' are said to have enquired in Jerusalem for the king of the world (Matt 2.1–12), just as in AD 66 a Parthian delegation went to Nero to render him divine honours. It was Babylonians, too, who used to mock the scape-goat on the Day of Atonement and pull its hair, while it was on the way to the desert (M. Yom. vi.4). After the fall of Jerusalem (AD 70) Babylonians came to the Holy City to fulfil the Nazirite vow (M. Naz. v.5).

We hear of pilgrims from Mesopotamia meeting in their thousands in Nearda and Nisibis, bringing with them the Temple dues from the Mesopotamian community of Jews, to travel together to Jerusalem (*Ant.* 18.310ff., see p. 59; cf. M. Taan. i.3, see p. 60; M. Ned. v.4–5). On their journey they were protected in the region of Batanea by the Babylonian Jew Zamaris who was settled there (*Ant.* 17.26). These Jews delivered as tax the offering of the didrachma (M. Shek. iii.4; *Ant.* 18.312f.). On the other hand, gifts of first-fruits and first-born animals from Babylon were not accepted because of ceremonial purity (M. Hall. iv.11).

(g) Parthian territory east of Mesopotamia

At that time only an insignificant part of Mesopotamia, in the north-east, belonged to the Roman Empire. The rest of Mesopotamia and the land adjoining it in the east belonged to the Parthian empire.

The king of *Adiabene* was a vassal of the Parthian king. The ruling family of this land was favourably disposed towards Judaism and entered into close relations with Jerusalem. King Monobazus had a palace in Jerusalem (*BJ* 5.252f.), as had his mother Queen Helena (*BJ* 6.355).[10] The Mishnah says that Queen Helena came to Jeru-

---

[10] On their benefactions to the Temple see p. 24, and on the social conscience displayed by Helena during the famine in Jerusalem see pp. 36f.

salem after fulfilling her seven-year Nazirite vow (M. Naz. iii.6).
Other representatives of the royal house of Adiabene whom we meet in
Jerusalem are Grapte, who had a palace there, other relations of
King Monobazus (*BJ* 2.520), and sons and brothers of King Izates
(*BJ* 6.356). These princes fought on the side of the Jews against the
Romans (AD 66 and 70). The conflicts against Cestius Gallus (AD 66),
in which the princes of Adiabene mentioned in *BJ* 2.520 took part,
broke out at Passover time; this suggests that they were in Jerusalem
on a pilgrimage. A man of Adiabene called Chagiras also fought in
AD 70 on the side of the Jews (*BJ* 5.474).

From *Media* came the scribe Nahum the Mede (M. Shab. ii.1;
M. Naz. v.4; M.B.B. v.2; b. A. Zar. 7b), who according to b. Ket.
105a was a member of a Jerusalem court.

(h) *Syria*

Of all the lands outside Palestine Syria had the highest percentage
of Jews (*BJ* 7.43) and in fact there were many contacts between Syria
and Jerusalem. In contrast to Babylonia (see p. 67), first-fruits were
accepted from Syria (M. Hall. iv.11). To Syria were sent messengers
from Jerusalem to announce the appearance of the New Moon which
fixed the time of the feast (M.R. Sh. i.4). At the time of the conversion
of Paul the Sanhedrin kept up relations with the synagogues of
Damascus (Acts 9.2). Again the Christian community in Jerusalem
kept up specially lively intercourse with the capital city of Syria,
Antioch (cf. Acts 11.27; Gal. 1.19–21; Acts 15, especially vv. 2, 4, 30;
Gal. 2.11–12; also the collection at Antioch for Jerusalem: 11.29f.;
12.25). A proselyte from Antioch was a member of the primitive
church at Jerusalem (Acts 6.5). M. Naz. vi.11 mentions Miriam, a
Jewess from Palmyra (one of the cities of Syria recognized as auto-
nomous by the Romans), in connection with the sacrifice she presented
as a Nazirite.

(i) *Arabia (Nabatean Empire)*

During the first century BC there were political links between the
Jewish kings and Arabia. The Nabatean kings sent troops more than
once to help them, and supported them in other ways (*BJ* 1.124ff.,
187). At Herod's court we find an Arabian bodyguard, who was
arrested with two other Arabs on suspicion of trying to assassinate
Herod; one of the other two was a friend of Syllaeus, the steward of
the Nabatean King Aretas IV; the other was sheikh of an Arabian

tribe (*BJ* 1.577). The city of Damascus was evidently under the control of an ethnarch[11] of this same Aretas IV, when Paul had to flee from Damascus to Jerusalem (Acts 9.26; Gal. 1.18). Shortly after the conversion of Paul, Damascus seems to have passed from Roman rule, under which it was part of Syria, to Arabian.

(j) Egypt

Egypt, with its strong Jewish elements, contributed substantially to Jerusalem's foreign population. Egyptians living in Jerusalem joined with other Hellenists in one synagogue (Acts 6.9), and so this synagogue was sometimes called after them 'synagogue of the Alexandrians' (T. Meg. iii.6, 224; j. Meg. iii.1, 73d.32).

Herod made Simon, the son of an Egyptian Jew Boethus of Alexandria, high priest so that he could marry his daughter Mariamne. Subsequently five other men from this family became high priest. M. Par. iii.5 claims that the high priest Ananel (*Ant.* 15.22; M. Par. iii.5: Hanamel), who came from Babylon, was an Egyptian.[12]

One Jerusalem scribe, Hanan b. Abishalom, who was a member of a court of civil law in Jerusalem (M. Ket. xiii.1–9; b. Ket. 105a; p. 52f.) had the nickname 'the Egyptian'.

Philo, like many Egyptian Jews, made the pilgrimage to Jerusalem.[13] Priests living in Egypt (*CA* 1.30ff.) who wished to marry had the genealogy of their future wife checked according to requirements. All these details, as well as the fact that dough-offerings were brought to

---

[11] 'Ethnarch' can mean ambassador as well as governor, but this man apparently had military power in his hands: II Cor. 11.32; Acts 9.24f.

[12] It is strikingly apparent, though the reason for it is not clear, that people thought little of the Baylonian Jew in Palestine, and were much more kindly disposed toward the Egyptian Jew. At all events, where there was anything good to be reported about a Babylonian Jew, such as the fact that he had been high priest, he was said to have been an Egyptian (M. Par. iii.5). The statements about Babylonians do not redound to their credit: Babylonian priests eat raw flesh, which was an abomination to Jews; Babylonians mock the scape-goat (p. 67). Now the Babylonian Talmud asserts that these last two incidents referred to Alexandrians. In the exposition of the mocking of the scape-goat (M. Yom. vi,4: cf. b. Yom. 66b) it says: 'Rabba b. Bar-Hana says: These were not Babylonians, but Alexandrians; but because the Palestinians hated the Babylonians they called them (the Alexandrians whom the Babylonian Talmud says reviled the scape-goat) by their name (the innocent Babylonians).' Similarly on M. Men. xi.7 (see p. 67). However, the Babylonian Talmud is obviously trying to vindicate the Babylonians. The only true fact emerging from these Talmudic passages seems to be that the Babylonians were not in fact well thought of in Palestine.

[13] *Frag. de providentia*, preserved in Eusebius, *Praep. ev.* VIII, 14.64 (GCS 43.1 = Eus. VIII.1, 477).

Jerusalem from Alexandria (M. Hall. iv.10), though admittedly these were refused on ground of levitical purity, show us that the worship of all the Egyptian Jews was by no means fully concentrated on the temple of Onias (see p. 29). The same picture emerges from other references to this temple. Josephus (*Ant.* 12.388; 13.62ff., 285; 20.236f.; *BJ* 1.33; 7.421ff.) observes that structurally it was small and mean compared with the one at Jerusalem. M. Men. xiii.10 records the regulations made by the scholars at Jerusalem concerning the offerings and the priests of the temple at Leontopolis. According to these, for example, the priests who had ministered there were not allowed to officiate in the Temple of Jerusalem.

Evidence that Jerusalem was the religious centre for Egyptian Jewry too is the fact that the instigator of one of the numerous messianic movements centred on Jerusalem was an Egyptian. This man gathered around him a large following, according to Acts 21.38, four thousand Zealots (members of the fanatical revolutionary party), according to *BJ* 2.261, thirty thousand followers. He hoped to show his followers, from the Mount of Olives, the collapse of the walls of Jerusalem (*Ant.* 20.169f.), and to make himself lord of the city after this messianic marvel (*BJ* 2.262).

Finally we have Talmudic evidence for traffic between Egypt and Jerusalem. During the strike of those who supplied incense and baked shewbread for the Temple, men from these industries were brought in as substitutes from Egypt; but the experiment miscarried because these people were so inefficient (b. Yom. 38a, b). There was a similar failure with Alexandrian workmen brought in to repair the copper cymbal of the Temple, and others who had to mend cracks in the copper mortar used for pounding the spices for incense, and in both cases the operations had to be broken off (b. Arak. 10b Bar.; cf. Bill. III, 450). Finally, we have further proof of traffic with Egypt: R. Joshua b. Peraḥia fled with a disciple named Jesus, under Alexander Jannaeus (103–76 BC), from Jerusalem to Alexandria.[14] A letter from Jerusalem is said to have recalled him.

---

[14] b. Sanh. 107b, b. Sot. 47a. Bill. I, 85, sees here a confusion with the incident in *Ant.* 14.175, when Herod put to death the whole Sanhedrin except Shemaiah in 37 BC. However, we do not have to accept his hypothesis, since the Talmud repeatedly recounts how the scholar Simeon b. Shetaḥ was persecuted by Alexander Jannaeus, and we know from Josephus about the very long, bloody struggle between Alexander and the people influenced by the Pharisees. The fact that the parallel in j. Hag. ii.2, 77d, substitutes Judah b. Tabai (*c.* 90 BC) for Joshua also confirms the Talmudic chronology.

(k) *Cyrene*

The burial place of a Jewish family from Cyrene, or more precisely from Cyrenaica in Libya with Cyrene as capital city, was found in the Kidron Valley.[15] From Cyrene came that Simon who was compelled by the Roman soldiers to carry Jesus' cross to Golgotha (Mark 15.21; Matt. 27.32; Luke 23.26). The Jewish Cyrenians living in Jerusalem belonged to the synagogue mentioned in Acts 6.9. Some of the festival pilgrims from Cyrene would no doubt have stayed in the guest house attached to this synagogue. A section of this group was converted to Christianity; these Christian Cyrenians ventured into Antioch, with the Christian Cypriots, to preach the gospel to Gentiles there (Acts 11.20).

A high priest called Ishmael was beheaded in Cyrene (*BJ* 6.114), but for what reason we do not know.

(l) *Ethiopia*

Strangers came to Jerusalem even from Ethiopia. In Acts 8.27–39 we meet the treasurer of the Ethiopian Candace on his way back from a journey he had made to Jerusalem for some religious purpose.

To sum up: Travel from abroad to Jerusalem took place from the whole of the then known world. It was actuated mainly by religious motives, to a lesser extent by political and economic ones. The main participators were Syria, Babylonia, Egypt and Asia Minor.

3. *Visitors from within Palestine*

The greatest number of visitors to Jerusalem have always come from within Palestine. As we have seen, the commerce of the city attracted first and foremost those who lived in the immediate neighbourhood, and nature itself, as a glance at the road system shows (pp. 53f.), had likewise linked the inhabitants of southern Palestine commercially with the city. Judaea especially was more closely linked with Jerusalem than the rest of Palestine. The eleven toparchies into which Judaea was divided by the Romans (*BJ* 3.54), probably taking up the division of Palestine into twenty-four priestly districts (p. 199), surrounded Jerusalem. The police supervision of Judaea was partly the responsibility of the Jerusalem authorities and the Temple guard which was put at their disposal. The courts of justice of the Judaean

---

[15] N. Avigad, 'A Depository of Inscribed Ossuaries in the Kidron Valley', *Israel Exploration Journal* 12, 1962, 1–12.

province turned to Jerusalem for decisions in certain cases, and particularly difficult cases were referred to the Jerusalem Sanhedrin as
the highest court in the land. In cases of doubt the scribes came to
Jerusalem from the country, e.g. from Mizpah (M. Peah ii.6) to
obtain information.

In the Jerusalem cultus, too, the province of Judaea was more
closely involved than the rest of Palestine. Only a man living near the
city could come to worship at the Holy Place on the Sabbath, and the
witnesses who certified the arrival of the New Moon to the supreme
authority could only in the nature of things come from the city, or at
least from its immediate surroundings (M.R. Sh. i.7). Most of the
priests lived in Judaea. M. Ned. ii.4 says 'the Galileans know naught of
things devoted to (the use of) the priests' (since few priests lived there).
Within Judaea, however, priests did not by any means all live in
Jerusalem as did the high priests, the priest Zadok (Lam. R. 1.16,
Son. 127f., where he was called kōḥēn gādōl, i.e. a chief priest), and the
priest Josephus (*Vita* 7). We hear rather that the priest Zacharias
lived in the hill-country of Judah (Luke 1.39), according to tradition
in Ain Karim, west of Jerusalem. The priest Mattathias, ancestor of
the Maccabees, lived in Modin (I Macc. 2.1), and in Luke 10.31 we
find a priest, in the parable of the Good Samaritan, on the road from
Jerusalem to Jericho. According to Origen,[16] Bethphage was a village
of priests, and M. Ter. ii.4 gives the ruling that in any place where a
priest lived, the heave-offering must be given to him.

Thus we may take it that the references are likely to be true,
that the whole of Palestine was divided into twenty-four districts,
corresponding to the courses of priests, and that each district in turn
sent to the Temple its priests, Levites and some representatives of the
people (M. Taan. iv.2; M. Bikk. iii.2; M. Par. iii.11). But the province of Judaea, because of its proximity to Jerusalem, had most chance
of having a larger number of representatives in the pilgrimages. We
hear that in AD 66 a whole city of the size and importance of Lydda,
the capital of a toparchy (*BJ* 3.55), took part in the Feast of Tabernacles, so that only fifty persons were left in the whole place (*BJ*
2.515). This was possible only in Judaea.

Because of greater distances (p. 41) trade in the rest of Palestine
was dependent more on caravans and wholesale merchants, so for the
most part its travel from home was less for commercial reasons than
religious ones, with the exception of the Samaritans whose cultus

[16] *Comm. on Matt.* XVI,17, on Matt. 21.1 (GCS 40.2=Origen X.2, 531f.).

centred on Mount Gerizim (John. 4.20f.). We find the carpenter Joseph from Nazareth in Jerusalem with Mary and Jesus for a feast (Luke 2.41ff.); and also Queen Berenice, daughter of King Agrippa I and sister of Agrippa II, came probably from Caesarea Philippi[17] to 'discharge a vow to God' (*BJ* 2.313). Rich and poor alike came to the Holy City as a religious duty.

In times of national agitation the number of pilgrims rose enormously. Large assemblies of pilgrims in Jerusalem seem to have had a political significance, as diverse evidence shows. Thus it was a political reason which in AD 6 brought together in Jerusalem countless multitudes of armed Jews from Galilee, Idumea, Jericho, Perea and especially Judaea (*BJ* 2.43). The other factor which from time to time increased the size of caravans from other parts of Palestine to an exceptional degree, was the fact that Jerusalem was bound to be the objective of every messianic movement. Galilee was the main seat of anti-Roman feeling and messianic ideas, and Pilate's measures in the Holy Place against the Galilean Passover pilgrims (Luke 13.1) were scarcely taken without good reason. Most of Jesus' followers were in Galilee, but, most important of all, Galilee gave birth to the Zealot party who in time took into their hands the destiny of the whole nation. Judas, whose rebellion (AD 6–7) against the Romans gave the decisive impetus to the spread of the Zealot movement, came from Galilee, and his father Hezekiah was already leader of a partisan group who fought in Galilee against Herod. Judas' son Menahem was one of the chief leaders in the rebellion against Rome in AD 66 (*BJ* 2.433ff.). For these movements the journeys to Jerusalem at feast times were the accepted means of contact with the Holy City.

B. THE UNIQUE CHARACTER OF JERUSALEM AS AN ATTRACTION TO TRAVELLERS FROM ABROAD

1. *The city's geographical position*

The same applies here as in the case of the effect of its position on commerce (pp. 51ff).

2. *Political and religious importance of the city*

The economic circumstances of the city attracted visitors from

[17] AD 66: her marriage with Polemon of Cilicia must have been dissolved by then.

elsewhere in so far as they brought to Jerusalem merchants from all over the world, especially from Judaea and the rest of Palestine.

As a further stimulant there was the political importance of the Holy City. Jerusalem was the hub of Jewish politics. The city attracted visitors as much because of its status as the ancient capital city as because it was the seat of the highest authority and the objective of all festal pilgrimages.

Jerusalem was the *old capital city*. The court of Herod, which was entirely dominated by the spirit of Hellenism and game-hunting, gymnastics, musical performances, dramatic spectacles, chariot races, which Herod arranged in the hippodrome and theatre of Jerusalem (*Ant.* 15.268ff.), all constituted a powerful centre of attraction for strangers. Foreigners who took an active or a passive part in the contests, writers and other educated Greeks, were guests at the Herodian court. To these were added the many official connections which Herod maintained, as did Agrippa I; these brought ambassadors, messengers and foreign bodyguards. We have already seen (pp. 55f.) how the court formed a magnet of great attraction in the country, especially for the representatives of the national wealth.

Jerusalem further was the seat of the *highest authority*. In Jerusalem sat the Sanhedrin, which was in origin and effect the first authority in the land, and so its competence extended throughout world Jewry. At least it was so ideally; and although the enforcement of its decisions outside Judaea was difficult, its reputation as the highest authority guaranteed it the ear of world-wide Jewry. Acts 9.2 tells of Paul's letters for the synagogue at Damascus, which contained orders to seize Christians there and deliver them to the Sanhedrin. Acts 28.21 says that the Jews of Rome had received no written instructions concerning Paul from Judaea. The Sanhedrin's greatest influence was in Judaea, for after Judaea became a Roman province in AD 6, the Sanhedrin was its chief political agency. A committee of the Sanhedrin was in charge of finance in the eleven Jewish toparchies (*BJ* 3.54ff.) into which the Romans had divided the land. Furthermore, the Sanhedrin was at that time the first communal court of justice in the province, and finally it was the highest Jewish court of law in all Judaea.

In consequence of its importance, the Sanhedrin had links with the entire world of Jewry, and joined every little village in Judaea administratively with Jerusalem.

The three main festivals were celebrated at the Temple; and as we have seen (p. 73), in troubled years the political importance of these assemblies caused a tremendous increase in the size of caravans.

The fact that Jerusalem after AD 6 was a Roman provincial city with a garrison made very little difference to travel. At the Feast of the Passover the Roman Procurator came, doubtless as a matter of course, to Jerusalem from Caesarea with a strong military escort, and held assizes there.

Jerusalem, therefore, attracted an enormous influx of visitors, both official and private, because of its importance as the political centre of Jewry.

The religious importance of the city was absolutely decisive in attracting this influx.

In the first place, Jerusalem was one of the most important places for *Jewish religious education*. It attracted scholars from Babylonia and Egypt, and the world-wide reputation of its scholars attracted students.

Jerusalem had significance, too, for the most varied *religious movements*. Here was the focal point of Christianity (cf. Gal. 2.1–10), and here we find the Essenes. For Christianity the holy places must have been a permanent centre of attraction, and were no doubt revered from the very beginning. The earliest witnesses of the Gospel were there, too. It is clear from Gal. 2.10; I Cor. 16.1–4; II Cor. 8–9 (cf. Acts 20.4) that world Christendom sent its gifts to its Mother Church in Jerusalem.

Religious expectation looked to Jerusalem. Thus all the many messianic movements of the time aspired towards Jerusalem. Many people settled in Jerusalem, so that they might die in the Holy Place and be buried in the place of the Resurrection and the Last Judgement.

Most important of all, in Jerusalem was the Temple, the *home of the Jewish cultus*, the place of the presence of God on earth. Here men came to pray, because here their prayers went directly to the ear of God; here the Nazirite on completion of his vows and the Gentile wishing to become a proselyte offered their sacrifices (M. Ker. ii.1; b. Ker. 81a); here they brought the *sōtāh*, the wife suspected of adultery, to judgement. To the Temple people brought the first-fruits, and here the mother brought the customary offerings for purification after the birth of each child. To the Temple Jews from all over the world sent the Temple tax. To the Temple came each course of priests, Levites and Israelites in turn. To the Temple, three times a year, the whole of world Jewry streamed.

It is difficult to get a clear picture of the volume of the crowds at the three festivals, especially at Passover time. We can attempt it by studying the regulations governing participation and how they were carried out in practice, and then try to arrive at some conclusion as to the numbers of participants.

On the three major feasts 'all are subject to the command to appear (before the Lord) except a deaf-mute, an imbecile, a child, one of doubtful sex, one of double sex, women, slaves that have not been freed, a man that is lame or blind or sick or aged and one that cannot go up (to Jerusalem) on his feet' (M. Hag. i.i). The word for 'a child' is defined by the school of Shammai as, 'One who is not able to go up to the Temple hill riding on his father's shoulders' and by the school of Hillel, 'one who is not able to go up holding his father's hand' (ibid.). Correspondingly the term 'Israelites' may be paraphrased as 'those who go to Jerusalem'.

Did theory and practice agree? In Luke 2.41 we read that Jesus' parents 'went every year to Jerusalem at the feast of the Passover'. From this we may conclude, first, that the poorer people,[18] and those living at a greater distance, could afford the journey only at Passover time; secondly, that women took part in these journeys, though they were not obliged to (M. Hag. i.i); and, thirdly, we read in Luke 2.42 that 'when he was twelve years old' Jesus was brought by his parents on a journey at festival time; so we may conclude that it was the custom among people from a distance to bring their children when they reached twelve years of age. The priest Joseph even brought his children, not yet of age, and his household to the second Passover, that is to the Passover held a month later (M. Pes. ix) for those hindered from coming to the main one. However, he was turned back, so as not to set a precedent for the ceremony of the second Passover. This fact alone shows that Joseph was a man of excessive zeal (M. Hall. iv.ii). Incidentally the Talmud speaks of thirteen years as the border-line for the fulfilment of the law. Luke 2.42 is not in contradiction with this rule; the twelve-year-olds were brought on the pilgrimage in order to get them used to the event which would become a duty next year.

The fact that pilgrim caravans also came to the festivals from the Diaspora is borne out by the evidence compiled on pp. 62ff., by Josephus and also by Philo: 'Countless multitudes from countless

---

[18] In Luke 2.24 Jesus' parents take advantage of the concession that poor people need offer only two doves.

cities come, some over land, others over sea, from east and west and north and south, at every feast' (Philo, *De spec. leg.* I, 69). These pilgrims of the Diaspora certainly had at least the concession of a single journey each year (Luke 2.41), if not the full mitigation as known for instance in Islam, which says that under difficult circumstances it is enough to make the journey once in a lifetime.

Among the proselytes, the full proselyte was bound to make the pilgrimage (cf. Gal. 5.3, where Paul cites the Jewish regulations). But more than once we also come across so-called 'God-fearers' at the festivals in Jerusalem: 'Now there were certain Greeks among those who went up to worship at the feast' (John 12.20): these were the uncircumcised heathen 'God-fearers', as was the treasurer of the Ethiopian Candace (Acts 8.28ff.). Josephus in *BJ* 6.427, mentions 'any foreigners present for worship'. In such cases the people were no doubt taking part of their own free will.

This is what emerges from the regulations and the specific information: every male Israelite and full proselyte who could make the journey, was obliged to do so for the three main feasts; but certain concessions had grown up for those living at a distance. Josephus (*Vita* 354) provides numerical evidence for this conclusion; his statement is all the more credible since he was here in controversy with Justus of Tiberias, and so obviously took great care to be accurate. He was dealing with Tiberias, which had become the capital of Galilee under Herod Antipas and had a council of six hundred members (*BJ* 2.641) indicating a considerable population. Nevertheless, according to *Vita* 354, there were only two thousand men from Tiberias among those besieged in Jerusalem, that is, among the celebrants at the Passover of AD 70 (*BJ* 6.421).

EXCURSUS

The number of pilgrims at the Passover

Definite figures have been recorded for the numbers taking part in the Passover Feast, that is, of pilgrims as well as residents in Jerusalem, in four places. Apparently attempts have been made to calculate the number of pilgrims from the number of Passover victims.

1. According to b. Pes. 64b; Lam. R. 1.2 on 1.1 (Son. 70f.), Agrippa[19] ordered that a kidney be taken from each victim. The resulting number of

[19] Probably Agrippa II, see next paragraph.

victims was 'twice as many as those people who departed from Egypt (600,000 according to Ex. 12.37), excluding those who were unclean and those on a distant journey; and there was not a single Paschal lamb for which more than ten persons had registered' (b. Pes. 64b). According to Lam. R. the number of participants in each victim varied between 10 and 100, so this would amount to at least 600,000 × 2 × 10, or twelve million pilgrims.

2. According to Josephus (*BJ* 6.422ff.), between AD 63 and 66 a count of the victims showed 255,600 (variant 256,500) animals and 2,700,000 participants. The figure of three million which Josephus gives in *BJ* 2.280 is probably a round figure.

3. Josephus gives the following figures for those trapped in Jerusalem during the siege, which began suddenly during the Passover of AD 70:

Killed	1,100,000 (*BJ* 6.420)
Taken prisoner	97,000 (*BJ* 6.420)
Fled to the wooded ravine of Jardes	3,000 (*BJ* 7.210ff.)
Total	1,200,000 participants

4. We are indebted to Tacitus (*Hist.* V. 13) for a fourth piece of evidence, that a total of 600,000 people must have been trapped in Jerusalem in AD 70; but this must be treated cautiously, since Tacitus has probably made use of Josephus. In *BJ* 5.569 we are told that deserters reported that the number of corpses of poor people thrown out through the gates amounted to 600,000 and it was impossible to determine the number of the rest. It is likely that Tacitus has mistakenly reckoned this as the total of those besieged in the city.

These four sources give, without exception, such fantastic figures that we cannot regard them as historically accurate.

If we attempt to calculate the exact number of pilgrims, help may be found in M. Pes. v.5. Here we read that on 14 Nisan the Paschal lambs were slaughtered in three groups: 'When the first group entered in and the Temple court was filled, the gates of the Temple court were closed; (on the *šôpār*) a sustained, a quavering, and again a sustained blast were blown'; and v.7; 'When the first group went out the second group came in and when the second group went out the third group came in', which however was not as numerous as the first two.

It is a fact that in Jesus' time the Passover victims were always slain in the Temple and not in private houses. This was because the Passover lamb was a sacrifice and its blood had to be used ceremonially.[20] The Passover victim is expressly described as a sacrifice in Ex. 12.27; 34.25; Num. 9.7 and 13; *Ant.* 2.312f.; 3.248; *BJ* 6.423 (θυσία); Philo, *De vita Mosis* II, 224 (θύειν). In the NT, Mark 14.12; Luke 22.7; I Cor. 5.7 (θύειν, θύεσθαι).

[20] See II Chron. 35.11 on the sprinkling of the Altar, and cf. H. L. Strack, *Pesahim* (Schriften des Intsitutum Judaicum in Berlin 40), Leipzig 1911, 76*.

The prescriptions in Deut. 16.2, 6, the precept in II Chron. 35.5f. (cf. Jub. 49.19f.), and the rabbinic regulations concerning the 'lesser Holy Things' in M. Zeb. v.8 insist that the immolation take place in the Temple. This is indicated too by the fact that the bones or the kidneys of the Passover lambs were counted, a thing which would be possible only if all the slaughtering took place in the Temple. Finally, all those passages which show that the slaughtering could be done by laymen, say that it was done in the Temple: Philo (*De vita Mosis* II, 224; *De decalogo*, 159; *De spec. leg.* II, 145). This agrees with M. Pes. v.6 which says, 'An Israelite slaughtered his (own) offering and the priest caught the blood.' In the OT the regulation in Lev. 1.5 deals with laymen slaughtering the sacrifice. It follows therefore that this ceremonial act took place in the Temple.

Since we know the dimensions of the Temple from M. Middoth and from Josephus, we can calculate the approximate measurements of the space available for the three groups, and from that make a deduction of the numbers of pilgrims at the feast.

How much space did a group occupy when slaughtering the sacrifice?

By 'forecourt', into which one group was admitted we have to understand the area west of the Nicanor Gate, the 'inner court', in which were the place of slaughter and the Altar of Burnt Offering. Let us get a clear picture of the layout of the Temple area. M. Kel. i.6–9 describes the ten degrees of holiness which surround the Holy of Holies in concentric circles:

1. The land of Israel.
2. The City of Jerusalem.
3. The Temple Mount.
4. The *ḥēl*, a terrace with lattice work beyond which no Gentile could pass.
5. The Court of Women.
6. The Court of the Israelites.
7. The Court of the Priests.
8. The area between the Porch and the Altar.
9. The Sanctuary.
10. The Holy of Holies.

Using this layout as a frame of reference we see that the inner forecourt with which we are concerned comprises the sixth and seventh circles of holiness, i.e. the Court of the Israelites and the Court of the Priests. The eighth, ninth and tenth circles also belong to the inner forecourt, but laypeople were not in any circumstances admitted there. On the other hand, the space at the sides and back of the Temple building was not part of the area absolutely forbidden to lay people (*BJ* 5.226).

From the Mishnah we learn that the area of Circle 6, Court of the Israelites, 'a' in the plan, was $135 \times 11 = 1,485$ sq. cubits. The area of

INNER COURT OF TEMPLE

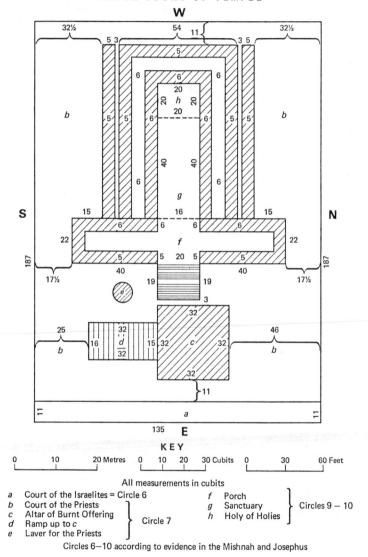

KEY

All measurements in cubits

a   Court of the Israelites = Circle 6
b   Court of the Priests
c   Altar of Burnt Offering   } Circle 7
d   Ramp up to c
e   Laver for the Priests

f   Porch
g   Sanctuary   } Circles 9 — 10
h   Holy of Holies

Circles 6–10 according to evidence in the Mishnah and Josephus

Circle 7 (Court of the Priests, 'b' in the plan) must be calculated by subtraction. Circles 7 and 8 (area between the Porch and the Altar, 'c') and 9/10 (Porch, Sanctuary and Holy of Holies, 'f', 'g', 'h') added up to a total of $135 \times 176 = 23,760$ sq. cubits. The area of 8 was $32 \times (19 + 3) = 704$ sq. cubits; the area of 9/10 is found by adding 'f', $100 \times 22 = 2,200$ sq. cubits, and 'g + h', $80 \times 70 = 5,600$ sq. cubits. If we subtract $8 + 9/10 = 8,504$ sq. cubits from the total of $7 + 8 + 9/10 = 23,760$ sq. cubits, we arrive at the area of $7 = 15,256$ sq. cubits. Of this area, the Altar ('c' in the plan) $32 \times 32 = 1,024$ sq. cubits, and its Ramp ('d') $32 \times 16 = 512$ sq. cubits, were forbidden to laymen. They must therefore be subtracted, leaving an available space of $13,720$ sq. cubits in 7. Adding to this the area of 6, $1,485$ sq. cubits, we arrive at a total of $15,205$ sq. cubits, or (1 sq. cubit equalling 3 sq. feet) of about $5,068$ sq. yards. From this we must again subtract the space occupied by the Laver ('e'), the pillars, etc., which cannot be calculated exactly. So we can reckon that about $5,000$ sq. yards were filled by each group while making the sacrifice.

We are in a position to check this figure. M. Pes. v.10, which discusses the case of 14 Nisan falling on a Sabbath, reports that the second group waited for nightfall on the *ḥēl*, the terrace enclosing the inner forecourt (as shown on the plan), the Court of Women and the buildings on the north, east and south sides (Circle 4).[21] So there was room for one group in 4. How big was 4?

[21] It is clear from Josephus and M. Midd. that the inner forecourt did not give straight on to the terrace, but that there were side buildings in between: M. Midd. i.1 speaks of the gates (i.5) leading from the *ḥēl* to the inner court as if they were buildings; this is confirmed by a closer description of the gate-buildings, especially the one described as a 'Chamber of the Hearth' in M. Midd. i.6–9 and which may be identified with one of the gates mentioned in ii.7. These gate-houses had an *exedra*, a hall provided with seats, and above this an upper room (M. Midd. i.5; *BJ* 5.203). This *exedra* was thirty cubits wide (*BJ* 5.203). But there were not only gate-houses between the *ḥēl* and the inner court, for connecting buildings linked the gate-houses. The connecting buildings to the north and south of the inner court housed the treasure chambers, according to *BJ* 5.200; while M. Midd. v. 3–4 tells of six rooms which were used for ceremonial and similar purposes. Between the Court of Women and the *ḥēl*, too, there were gate-houses and other buildings. Here we are told of four rooms four cubits square in the four corners (M. Midd. ii.5); these rooms, however, could not have been inside the Court of Women itself, since the Nicanor Gate, the fifteen semi-circular steps up to it, and the rooms mentioned in M. Midd. ii.7 as beneath the Court of Israel, would take up the whole 135 cubits of the west side of the Court of Women.

We cannot doubt, from this evidence, that there were side buildings which joined up to the gate-houses and enclosed the sacred area to the north, east and south. They were probably forty cubits wide, corresponding to the rooms at the Court of Women.

Between the Court of Women and the Court of the Israelites there seem to have been no buildings; this is suggested by the information in M. Midd. ii.7 concerning rooms under the Court of the Israelites, which were open towards the Court of Women.

Its inner circumference is equivalent to the circumference of the area enclosed, which was 187 (length of inner forecourt) + 135 (length of Court of Women) + 40 (side buildings to the east) = 362 cubits long; and 135 (breadth of the courts) + 40 + 40 (side buildings to north and south) = 215 cubits wide. Thus the inner circumference of the ḥēl was 1,154 cubits. Now the ḥēl was 10 cubits wide (M. Midd. ii.3; BJ 5.197). Its outer circumference is therefore 1,154 + (8 × 10) = 1,234 cubits. Accordingly, the area of the ḥēl measured $\frac{1,154 + 1,234}{2} \times 10 = 11,940$ sq. cubits, or 3,980 sq. yards.[22]

Since the actual slaughtering was in the place of slaughter, and the priests who stood in lines naturally claimed some of the space in the inner court, we should deduct approximately one-fifth of the available space for this, and the result is the same as our calculations. One group took up about 3,900 sq. yards when they were *not* slaughtering.

How many men would this space hold? The people were closely packed. It is the eighth of the ten wonders of the Holy Place that there was enough room for them all (M. Ab. v.5). However, things did not always go as well as that: in b. Pes. 64b we read that, 'The Rabbis taught:[23] No man was ever crushed in the Temple court except on one Passover in the days of Hillel, when an old man was crushed, and they called it "The Passover of the Crushed".' Josephus also knows about such crowded conditions. At one Passover between AD 48 and 52 on the fourth day, not on the Day itself, there was a panic in the Temple area and 30,000 people were crushed to death according to BJ 2.227. In such a restricted space we must reckon two men to a sq. m., each with one, or very occasionally with two (M. Pes. viii.2), animals for sacrifice; that is, about 6,400 men, which means about 6,400 animals for each group. This agrees with Josephus' account of the Passover of 4 BC, according to which the troops of Archelaus killed 3,000 people while they were sacrificing (BJ 2.12f.; Ant. 17.218), while the rest escaped.

There were three groups, of which the last was not as large as the other two, since everyone naturally tried to get in the earlier groups.

In this way we arrive at a figure of 18,000 Passover victims. How many

[22] It is possible that, besides the terrace, the second group could use the steps leading up to it. According to Josephus (BJ 5.195 and 198) there were fourteen steps between the Court of the Gentiles (the stone railing) and the terrace, and five steps between the terrace and the sacred enclosure. M. Midd. ii.3 mentions only twelve steps of a half-cubit in height and breadth, without more precise details. Taking these steps into account, then according to Josephus the area of 4 was about 7,900 square yards, and according to M. Midd. about 6,400 square yards. These higher figures too confirm our conclusion on p.81; we must then assume that people were not so closely packed in the ḥēl as in the inner forecourt.

[23] The Tannaitic introductory formula which is evidence of a date before AD 200.

pilgrims were there altogether? One victim was chosen for each table fellowship (φρατρία, ḥabūrāh, M. Pes. vii.3). How large were these groups? It was disputed whether one individual could slay a victim for himself (M. Pes. viii.7; according to *BJ* 6.423 it was forbidden). The upper limit is given in M. Pes. viii.7: 'They may not slaughter it even for a company of a hundred if they are not able to eat an olive's bulk', or in other words, this number was too big. M. Pes. ix.10f. mentions five, ten or twelve persons as typical table fellowships. If the Last Supper was a Passover meal, Jesus and his twelve disciples made up a complement of thirteen. Josephus (*BJ* 6.423), the Talmud (b. Pes. 64b) and the Midrash (Lam. R. 1.2 on 1.1, Son. 71) agree on ten as the average number of participants, and we must agree with this.

Thus we can take the number of participants in the whole feast as 18,000 × 10 = 180,000. If we subtract from that the approximately 55,000 inhabitants of Jerusalem,[24] this gives us a total of about 125,000 pilgrims. We shall probably not have to increase or decrease that number by more than half (see below p. 84).

So great was the number of pilgrims and other visitors to Jerusalem that at feast times it was far in excess of the normal population. In the economic life of the city, it was this sector which primarily gave Jerusalem its economic importance.

To recapitulate: Our enquiry shows us a highland city with a poor water supply, in a district poor in raw materials for industry, whose situation was highly unsuitable for trade and commerce. Despite this, within its walls this city contained flourishing industries, and main-

[24] Ancient figures for the inhabitants of Jerusalem are unreliable. (Pseudo-Hecateus, as quoted in *CA* 1.197, gives 120,000 for the period before 100 BC; Lam. R. 1.2 on 1.1, Son. 70f., gives figures amounting to 9½ billion.) Consequently we must try to calculate the number of inhabitants from the area of Jerusalem. Pseudo-Hecateus shows that the west, south and east sides together measured 2,575 metres (a little over 1½ miles) before the time of Agrippa I. To this must be added the third north wall begun by him. If we identify it with the present north wall, it was about 2,025 metres (about 1¼ miles) long; but if we accept Josephus' statements, p. 11, it was about 3,500 metres (nearly 2¼ miles). The perimeter of the city was therefore either about 4,600 metres (nearly 3 miles) or about 6,105 metres (about 3¾ miles). These figures give an area of either $(4,600 \div 4)^2 = 1,322,000$ square metres (about 330 acres, or just over half a square mile) or $(6,105 \div 4)^2 = 2,329,000$ square metres (about 625 acres, or approaching a square mile). Now the density of the population in Jerusalem, including the suburbs, fifty years ago was about one person to every thirty square metres (about 135 persons per acre), but since the ancient city consisted only of the area inside the walls, we may guess at a somewhat greater density, about one person to twenty-five square metres (about 160 per acre). So we have a figure for the population of ancient Jerusalem of about 55,000 to 95,000. The smaller figure is the more probable, and even that may still be too high.

tained a widespread trade. Above all it received a regular influx of people which linked it with all parts of the known world and at times completely outnumbered the inhabitants of the city. The reason for this is that the city contained the central shrine of world Jewry.

ADDITIONAL NOTE (1966) ON CALCULATING THE NUMBER OF FESTIVAL PILGRIMS (pp. 77ff.)

The ancient writers, with their exaggerations, are no help in finding a basis for calculating the number of pilgrims, and so the only way open to us is to calculate from the amount of space available for the slaughtering of the Passover lambs. I therefore still maintain (1966) that the method I followed in 1923 is correct. As for the result, I can still admit it; it was fortunate that I was careful enough to add that the number (125,000 pilgrims) I had arrived at could be halved (p. 83).

This now means that today I should set the figure somewhat lower. As regards the inhabitants of Jerusalem (see p. 83 n. 24), I may refer to my article on this subject,[25] in which (as above n. 24) I based my calculations on the size of the city, but arrived at a smaller figure because: (*a*) I subtracted, from the available space within the walls of Jerusalem of Jesus' time, the uninhabited Temple area, state buildings, etc. (*b*) I assumed, on the basis of archeological evidence, a more limited settlement in the area outside the city walls which Agrippa I (AD 41–44) enclosed with his north wall, and (*c*) I took into account an assessment of population density in Jerusalem made in 1881, which suggests a density inside the city in Jesus' time of one person for every thirty-five, not twenty-five sq. m. (about 116 persons per acre).

This results in a population of about 20,000 inside the city walls at the time of Jesus, and 5,000 to 10,000 outside. This figure, of from 25–30,000, must be the upper limit.

As regards the number of festival pilgrims, the calculations described on pp. 79–83, based on the space available for worshippers at the Passover, are probably quite right, but I now ask myself whether it should be assumed that the entire inner forecourt, including the space at the sides and back of the Temple building, was thickly packed with worshippers (though we cannot imagine the throng of men with their sacrificial animals on their shoulders, described on p. 82). As a consequence, is the figure of 6,400 for each of the three groups, and therefore the total of 180,000 participants including the population of Jerusalem, fixed a little too high? However, there can be no doubt that the influx of pilgrims at Passover time from all over the world was immense, and amounted to several times the population of Jerusalem.

[25] 'Die Einwohnerzahl Jerusalems zur Zeit Jesu', *ZDPV* 66, 1943, 24–31, reprinted in *Abba*, Göttingen 1966, 335–341.

PART TWO

ECONOMIC STATUS

IV

THE RICH

UNDER THE HERODIAN dynasty Jerusalem, as the capital city, was an example of royal splendour. Magnificent buildings arose (pp. 10ff.), splendid games were organized by Herod every four years (*Ant.* 15.268), and the cultus in the newly built Temple exhibited a magnificence scarcely known before.

The wealth of the rulers was displayed most conspicuously to the populace of Jerusalem in the glitter of the court. The court dominated public life; even under the foreign rule of Rome (AD 6–41, 44–66) the princely court was in evidence, though only a shadow of its former self. The following description is based mainly on conditions in the court of Herod the Great, about which we have most information.

If anyone wished to present himself at court he would have to pass the military bodyguard stationed at the gateway. Herod, who inevitably lived in constant fear of his own subjects, had every reason to maintain a strong bodyguard (δορυφόροι; σωματοφύλακες. These last should be distinguished from the chamberlains, who are given the same title). Herod once sent five hundred men from his own personal troops to help Caesar Augustus (*Ant.* 15.317). A further indication of the strength of this force is the report that besides the personal bodyguard (*Ant.* 16.182; 17.187) it included 'Thracian, German and Gallic troops' (*Ant.* 17.198; *BJ* 1.672). The Gallic section alone, which formed the bodyguard of Cleopatra of Egypt before entering Herod's service, numbered four hundred men (*BJ* 1.397).

Next, the doorkeepers would enquire the visitor's business (*Ant.* 17.90). These men belonged to the staff of servants, five hundred strong (*Ant.* 17.199; *BJ* 1.673), most of whom were slaves, though some were freedmen (*BJ* 1.673), and some eunuchs. Those given by Herod to the Cappadocian king Archelaus were slaves (*BJ* 1.511, cf. *Ant.* 17.44), while the chamberlains mentioned below may well have been freedmen. The household included the royal huntsmen under the chief huntsman (*Ant.* 16.316), and probably also the court barbers (*BJ* 1.547ff., cf. *Ant.* 16.387ff.), and the king's personal physicians (*Ant.* 15.246; 17.172; *BJ* 1.657). We have evidence from the Talmud (b.B.B. 133b) of someone responsible for plaiting the royal garlands during the reign of Alexander Jannaeus (103–76 BC).[1] The household also included torturers, who had such a grim role to play in Herod's last years (*BJ* 1.592, 635 etc.).

In the palace itself the visitor would find the court officials. Here is the king's secretary, through whose hands all his correspondence passes (*Ant.* 16.319; *BJ* 1.529). Commercial transactions, as for example, the purchase of a valuable pearl for the royal treasury (b. B.B. 133b), are handled by the chief treasurer Joseph (*Ant.* 15.185). Those two men deep in conversation are Andromachus and Gemellos, the tutors and travelling companions of the royal princes (*Ant.* 16. 242–5). Their sons are the σύντροφοι of the princes Alexander and Aristobulus, for we find at the Herodian court the same system as in Hellenistic royal houses, where the sons of leading families were educated with the princes. In Acts 13.1 we find Manaen, a σύντροφος of Herod Antipas, brought up with him in the court of Jerusalem.

Corinthus, called a σωματοφύλαξ, conducts the visitor to the royal apartments. The very fact that he was one of the most trusted of Herod's court officials (*Ant.* 17.55f.), even more that he was a σύντροφος of Herod (*BJ* 1.576: like Herod's mother Cypros he was of Arabian descent), rules out the possibility that he was a member of the body-guard, despite the title σωματοφύλαξ. This title should rather be taken to mean some high rank such as chamberlain, as it does in other Hellenistic courts.[2] In this connection, Otto[3] was the first to draw attention to this by pointing out that two other 'bodyguards' mentioned in *Ant.* 16.314, Jucundus and Tyrannus, are described as cavalry officers in the parallel passage in *BJ* 1.527. Three other of Herod's chamberlains, his cupbearer, steward and gentleman of the bedchamber, were eunuchs (*Ant.* 16.230; *BJ* 1.488; cf. *Ant.* 15.226). Josephus reports that these chamberlains were personages of great

---

[1] The Roman emperors appear on coins wearing garlands. The 'kingly crown', made of thistles or thorns, was placed in mockery upon the head of Jesus by the Roman soldiers (Mark 15.17; Matt. 27.29; John 19.2, 5).

[2] Otto, *Herodes*, col. 87 n. 1.

[3] *Ibid.*, cols. 86f. and n. 1.

influence; the third, he says, had access to the royal bedchamber, and was entrusted with government business of the greatest importance (*Ant.* 16.230). Blastus, who held a similar office at the court of Agrippa I in Jerusalem, negotiated the peace settlement between his master and the towns of Tyre and Sidon, probably in AD 44 (Acts 12.20).

In the royal apartments, among the king's associates are to be found his intimate friends, the 'cousins and friends', and 'cousins' does not necessarily mean relations. These 'cousins and friends' constitute the highest rank which we meet at all Hellenistic courts.[4] In addition to the cousins, nephews, brothers-in-law and other relatives of the ruler, a number of distinguished men, Greeks especially, belong to Herod's court (*Ant.* 17.219; *BJ* 2.14). Thus when the people demanded the removal of Greeks after his death, this was not directed against visitors, but against members of his retinue.[5] The best known of Herod's intimates is the cultured scholar, court philosopher and historian, Nicholas of Damascus, and next to him his brother Ptolemy (*Ant.* 17.225; *BJ* 2.21). Another Ptolemy is the royal minister of finance and privy seal (*Ant.* 16.191; 17.195; *BJ* 1.667), and there is also the Greek orator Irenaeus (*Ant.* 17.226; *BJ* 2.21), and a whole array of other 'friends' of Herod known to us only by name. At court too there will probably be the military commander-in-chief under Herod (*Ant.* 17.156; *BJ* 1.652), Archelaus (*BJ* 2.8)[6] and Agrippa I (*Ant.* 19.317, 353). At all events there is a camp commander Volumnius at court whom Otto, because of his name, has convincingly pictured as a Roman military instructor.[7] He was sent as ambassador to Caesar (*Ant.* 16.332, 354; *BJ* 1.535) with another 'friend' of Herod, called Olympus, and a retinue (*Ant.* 16.354). Finally, we repeatedly meet guests of Herod, Marcus Agrippa (*Ant.* 16.13f.; *Leg. ad Cai.* 294) the son-in-law of Caesar Augustus; the Cappadocian king Archelaus (*Ant.* 16.261; *BJ* 1.511); the Spartan Eurycles (*Ant.* 16.301; *BJ* 1.513ff.); Euarestus from Cos (*Ant.* 16.312; *BJ* 1.532); and Melas the ambassador of the king of

[4] Otto, *op. cit.*, col. 86.

[5] Nicholas of Damascus, Frag. 136.8, ed. F. Jacoby, *Die Fragmente der griechischen Historiker*, vol. 2A, Berlin 1926 (reprinted Leiden 1957), 424; cf. *Ant.* 17.207; *BJ* 2.7.

[6] *Ant.* 17.294 and *BJ* 2.74 name an officer, Joseph, cousin of Archelaus and nephew of Herod, who is probably commander-in-chief.

[7] Otto, *op. cit.*, col. 60. He was perhaps the commanding officer of the barracks adjoining and belonging to the palace, *BJ* 2.329, 440.

Cappadocia (*Ant.* 16.325–8). Most of these left the court considerably enriched by gifts from their host.

Although the court must have been, to outward appearances, Hellenistic, it was nevertheless basically oriental; as we shall see from this next paragraph on the harem. Polygamy was permitted to the king by law (Deut. 17.17, cf. *Ant.* 4.224). The Mishnah sets the limit at eighteen wives (M. Sanh. ii.4), and the Talmud gives twenty-four and forty-eight, both figures representing Tannaitic and so ancient teaching (b. Sanh. 21a Bar.). It is consequently no surprise to hear of the concubines of Alexander Jannaeus, 103–76 BC (*Ant.* 13.380; *BJ* 1.97). When Antigonus, the last Hasmonean king, wished to seize the Jewish throne in 40 BC with the help of the Parthians, he promised them among other things five hundred Jewish women (*Ant.* 14.331, 343, 365; *BJ* 1.248, 257, 273): he had in mind the entire female side of the royal court, that is of the ruling ethnarch of the Jews Hyrcanus, as well as of the two tetrarchs of Judaea, Herod (later king) and his brother Phasaelus, then resident in Jerusalem.[8]

Herod the Great (37–4 BC) had ten wives (*Ant.* 17.19f.; *BJ* 1.562, cf. *Ant.* 15.319; 17.14; *BJ* 1.477), and at least nine of these were still living at the same time about 7 or 6 BC (*BJ* 1.562); but the Hasmonean Mariamne alone seems to have borne the title of queen (*BJ* 1.485). The gift of a concubine to King Archelaus of Cappadocia shows that Herod's harem was even more extensive (*BJ* 1.511). It should also be remembered that Herod's mother, and at times his sister Salome,[9] and Alexandra the mother of Queen Mariamne (*Ant.* 15.183ff.), lived in the palace, and that the children's upbringing in their earliest years was in the hands of the mother, and consequently in the harem (cf. Prov. 31.1). There was also a large number of servants who belonged to this part of the court. We hear of a eunuch belonging to Queen Mariamne (*Ant.* 15.226), and of slaves belonging to Herod's consort Doris (*Ant.* 17.93).

Besides the royal household of the monarch, there were lesser households, perhaps living in the palace too: from 12 BC at least, those belonging to the royal princes Alexander, Aristobulus, Antipater

[8] According to *BJ* 1.257 this was the promise of 'most of the women belonging to them' (i.e. Hyrcanus and Phasaelus). According to *Ant.* 14.365 it meant the women who fled with Herod when he saved the entire court (*Ant.* 14.352ff.).

[9] After her first husband had been put to death (35 or 34 BC) until her marriage to her second after 30 BC (in that year she was still at court at Jerusalem, *Ant.* 15.184), and also after her second husband was put to death in 25 BC.

and Pheroras, Herod's brother.[10] Each had his own retinue of 'friends' and household of servants.[11]

As for the rulers' revenues, which allowed their vast expenditure, Josephus provides several details. He calculates the revenues of Herod's successors, among whom his kingdom was divided (*Ant.* 17.319; *BJ* 2.96). He says that Herod Antipas received 200 talents in revenue, Philip 100 talents, Archelaus 400 (*BJ*) or 600 (*Ant.*), and Salome 60. This would mean a revenue from the whole kingdom of 760 or 960 talents. According to the information we have about Agrippa I's revenue the higher is preferable. However the cities of Gaza, Gadara and Hippos also belonged to Herod's kingdom, though they reverted to the Roman province of Syria after his death; furthermore, at that time the district of Samaria had 25 per cent of its taxes remitted (*Ant.* 17.319; *BJ* 2.96). According to all this Herod's revenues from taxes amounted to over 1,000 talents.

Agrippa I's revenues came to twelve million drachmas (*Ant.* 19.352), and it is with silver Attic drachmas that Josephus usually calculates. Since Agrippa's realm was bigger than Herod's because of the possessions of Claudius in the Lebanon and the Kingdom of Lysanias (i.e. the area in the Lebanon around Abila, *Ant.* 19.275; *BJ* 2.215), it is quite reasonable to suppose that his revenue from taxes was much greater than Herod's.[12]

However, even with 1,000 talents Herod could not possibly meet all his commitments, nor could Agrippa I with 1,200 talents.[13] Herod had in addition considerable private possessions, as appears among other things from the terms of his will. The Jews' complaint brought against Herod in Rome in 4 BC rings true: it was that he derived great wealth by confiscating the goods of the leading men of his realm whom he had convicted (*Ant.* 17.307). A further source of wealth

[10] Otto, *Herodes*, cols. 87f.; cf. *BJ* 1.557ff.

[11] Alexander's and Aristobulus', *Ant.* 16.97; a freedman of Antipater, *Ant.* 17.79; Pheroras' freedmen, *Ant.* 17.61; and his female slaves, 16.194; cf. 17.61ff.; *BJ* 1.584.

[12] The standard of value of the talent on which this is based is that of the Hebrew talent of 10,000 Attic silver drachmas. This is shown, first, from a comparison of *Ant.* 17.146, 321f. with 17.190, where a legacy of 1,500 talents in Herod's will is expressed as fifteen million drachmas, and, secondly, from a comparison of Herod's revenues with those of Agrippa I. To appreciate the amount of these it may be recalled that Herod gave his daughter a dowry of 300 talents (*BJ* 1.483); that his brother Pheroras drew 100 talents a year from his possessions, in addition to the revenues from his tetrarchy of Peraea (*ibid.*); and that Zenodorus sold the Auranitis to the Arabs for 50 talents (*Ant.* 15.352).

[13] Otto, *op. cit.*, cols. 91f.

was the copper mine in Cyprus ceded to him in 12 BC by Caesar Augustus;[14] and, finally, regular gifts, or rather bribes, may be taken to have added considerably to the prince's income (cf. *Ant.* 17.308).

B. THE WEALTHY CLASS

1. *Extravagance*

The various extravagances of the rich in Jerusalem in their houses, their clothing, their servants, as well as their rich offerings and bequests to the Temple and their monuments has already been dealt with in the first part of this book. Occasionally the sources give indications of this luxury: two men wagered 400 *zūzīm* (denarii) on being able to provoke Hillel to wrath (b. Shab. 30b–31a Bar.). R. Meir records that the people of Jerusalem tied up their bundle of branches at Tabernacles with gold thread (M. Sukk. iii.8). The rich of Jerusalem had property in the country, and evidently among these was Ptolemy, Herod's chancellor, who owned the whole village of Arus (*Ant.* 17.289; *BJ* 2.69). Another indication is the statement that Queen Helena of Adiabene, whose visit to Jerusalem is recorded by Josephus (*Ant.* 20.49f.), is said to have had in Lydda a ritually approved tent for the Feast of Tabernacles (j. Sukk. i.1, 51d.22)[15]

The banquets given by wealthy people were an important part of life, and frequent references to customs peculiar to Jerusalem suggest that the city set the tone of contemporary etiquette throughout the land. We hear that the host weighed most carefully the social advantages of inviting a large number of guests against providing good entertainment (Lam. R. 4.2 on 4.2, cf. Son. 216). It was the custom to engage a cook for a handsome fee, and if his cooking was at fault he would have to compensate the master of the house for his shame, and pay a penalty in proportion to the importance of the host and guests (*ibid.*).[16] Undiluted wine was drunk from crystal drinking-glasses at table (Lam. R. 4.5 on 4.2; Son. 4.4, 219), and when spirits were high people might well start handclapping to accompany the dancing, as did for example the 'great men' of Jerusalem at the circumcision of Elisha b. Abuya whose father belonged to the aristocracy (j. Hag. ii.1, 77b.33; Bill. I, 682; Eccles. R. 7.18 on 7.8, Son.

---

[14] *Ant.* 16.128. It is not clear whether Herod got the whole mine at half the rent or half the mine rent free.

[15] Cf. Neubauer, *Géographie*, 77.

[16] Hirschensohn, 133; b.B.B. 93b.

184). The dance would be a men's round-dance, for which there is evidence at religious celebrations. Rigid etiquette controlled the procedure for invitations. The guest expected to be informed of the names of other guests (Lam. R. 4.4 on 4.2, Son. 218), and quite irrespective of an earlier invitation, to be summoned by a messenger on the actual day (ibid., 4.2 on 4.2, Son. 216). This seems to have been the usual custom in Palestine[17] and in Egypt (MW I, i.419). The fact that the written invitations found in Egyptian papyri had generally been sent only one day before the feast, or even on the day itself, can be explained only by assuming that they are repetitions of an earlier invitation. Furthermore, the guest took care to roll up the wide sleeves of his robe (Lam. R. 4.4. on 4.2 [cf. Son. 218]; cf. j. Dem. iv.6, 24a.53) perhaps so that he could reach out with ease during the meal. The length of time during which invited guests were welcomed was indicated by a cloth hung from the house, and this was removed only after the three introductory courses had been served.[18] There is reliable evidence[19] that at Passover time in Jerusalem poor people were invited in from the street. On certain political occasions there was a feast given for 'the whole populace' of Jerusalem, such as Marcus Agrippa gave on his visit there (Ant. 16. 14, 55), and Archelaus on the death of his father Herod (Ant. 17.200; BJ 2.1).

Wives formed a second important item of expenditure. Polygamy was allowed among Jews at the time.[20] However, the maintenance of a household with several women involved such heavy financial burdens that in general we find polygamy only among the rich. So b. Yeb. 15b attests levirate marriage among the wealthy classes in Jerusalem. A controversy arose over the well-known question of a brother marrying a widow of his brother who had died childless. What happens in the case of a dead man who leaves several wives, among them his niece? The brother naturally cannot marry his own

---

[17] Matt. 22.3 and especially Luke 14.16f., where the wording, taken with Matt. 22.11f. and the various rabbinic analogies, e.g. b. Shab. 153a, cf. Eccles. R. 9.6 on 9.8 (Son. 235f.) makes it clear that the reference is to a repeated invitation.

[18] T. Ber. iv.10, 10; Lam. R. 4.4 on 4.2 (Son. 219); b.B.B. 93b. This report goes back to R. Simeon b. Gamaliel II.

[19] M. Pes. ix.11, confirmed by the Passover Haggadah, Hā lahmā. The statement about the hospitality of the Jerusalem councillor, ben Kalba Shabua, who is said to have fed every hungry person, is merely a pun on his name, b. Gitt. 56a.

[20] Leipoldt, Jesus und die Frauen, Leipzig 1921, 44–49, gives many examples in the notes.

daughter, but what about the other wives? The school of Shammai permitted such levirate marriage, that of Hillel did not. In this connection R. Joshua b. Ḥananiah, a Levite, reports that two leading Jerusalem families, members of which officiated as high priests, were descended from such levirate marriages.[21] We thus hear of two cases of polygamy in Jerusalem,[22] at least for the first marriages of the wives. If we suppose that their second marriages were levirate marriages (as allowed by the school of Shammai),[23] then we would know more about the families from the fact that descendants of the two women were High Priests. Their second husbands being the brothers of the first, both would belong to high priestly families. In that case we should have evidence of polygamy in four high priestly families in Jerusalem.

Further examples of polygamy among the aristocracy of Jerusalem are found in Josephus. He says that the Tobiad Joseph had two wives (*Ant.* 12.186ff.), and Alexander Jannaeus several others besides his chief wife (*BJ* 1.97; *Ant.* 13.380). We also read of an administrative official of King Agrippa having two wives, one living in Tiberias and one in Sepphoris (b. Sukk. 27a).[24] There is therefore evidence of polygamy among the aristocracy of Jerusalem, but it was by no means the rule.

The aristocracy gave large sums for their daughters' dowries. An example of this was the marriage settlement of Miriam, daughter of Nicodemus (Naqdimon b. Gorion), which was said to have been a

---

[21] One such family was the 'house of Quphae', which Professor Kahan links with the NT high priest Joseph, called Qaiaphas (Caiaphas). The high priest of the house of Quphae can otherwise only be Elionaius (*c.* AD 44), who, according to Josephus, was the son of Kantheras (*Ant.* 19.342), called in M. Par. iii.5 'ben ha-Qayyaph'; or the high priest Joseph Qabi (up to AD 62), according to Josephus the son of the high priest Simon (*Ant.* 20.196). [For the sake of clarity Qaiaphas is written with a Q, since it is based on post-biblical Hebrew *qayyaph*; similarly, Qabi is written with a Q.]

[22] It is improbable that the two women, in their first marriages, were wives of the same husband; obviously it is rather a question of two analogous cases.

[23] Cf. the cases quoted by R. Tarphon and R. Gamaliel in b. Yeb. 15b–16a, and the wording of the description of the controversy at the time of R. Dosa b. Arkinus (16a), where the brothers who were allowed to marry the additional wives are expressly mentioned. Büchler explains the passage thus in 'Familienreinheit und Familienmakel in Jerusalem vor dem Jahre 70', in *Festschrift Schwarz*, 136, ET, 'Family Purity and Family impurity in Jerusalem before the Year 70 C.E.', *Studies in Jewish History: the Adolf Büchler Memorial Volume*, London 1956, 37f.

[24] This must refer to Agrippa I, since there is no evidence that Sepphoris belonged to the realm of Agrippa II. Tiberias was given to him by Nero (*Ant.* 20.159; *BJ* 2.252).

million gold denarii, to which was added a sum from her father-in-law (b. Ket. 66b). The demands of these ladies were correspondingly high, and in Jerusalem ten per cent of the dowry went to them by right (*ibid.*; b. Yom. 39b) to pay for luxuries alone—perfumes and ornaments (*ibid.*), jewellery (pp. 8f.; M. Kel. xii.7), false teeth fastened with gold and silver wire (M. Shab. vi.5), etc. There is disagreement as to whether this ten per cent was an annual payment or applied only to the first year.

The aristocratic ladies of Jerusalem had a reputation for being very pampered. Martha (p. 156), the widow of the high priest R. Joshua, is said to have been assured by the scribes of a daily allowance of two measures of wine, while the daughter-in-law of Naqdimon b. Gorion was given two *se'āh*, or more than twenty-six litres, of wine per week (Lam. R. 1.50 on 1.16, Son. 1.47, 128; b. Ket. 65a). The daughter of Naqdimon is reported to have cursed the scribes because under the agreement for her widow's maintenance they allowed her only 400 gold denarii a day for luxuries (b. Ket. 66b; Lam. R. 1.51 on 1.16, Son. 1.48, 129, says 500 denarii). No wonder that the same Martha could not withstand the misery of the siege of Jerusalem in AD 70, and when at her last hour she threw all her gold and silver in the street, she learnt too late the worthlessness of money (b. Gitt. 56a). It is interesting to note the growth of certain customs among the leading women of Jerusalem; e.g. they provided a narcotic wine mixed with myrrh to those led out to be executed.[25] According to Abba Saul they also undertook the maintenance of those women who brought up their children for the ceremonies of the Red Heifer (b. Ket. 106a).

2. *Representatives of the wealthy class*

From time immemorial Jerusalem had attracted the wealth of the nation—merchants, landowners, tax-farmers, bankers and men of private means.[26] Several members of the Sanhedrin came from these circles. The councillor Nicodemus (John 7.50; 3.1; cf. 12.42) was wealthy. It is said that he brought a hundred Roman pounds' worth of ointments and spices for Jesus' burial (John 19.39). Jerusalem merchants dealing in grain, wine and oil, and wood, who belonged to

[25] b. Sanh. 43a Bar., cf. the 'daughters of Jerusalem' who accompanied Jesus to his crucifixion (Luke 23.27ff.). It may have been these women who provided the wine mingled with myrrh offered to Jesus before his crucifixion (Mark 15.23; Matt. 27.34).
[26] See p. 56; also Smith, *Jerusalem* I, 367.

the Council between AD 66–70, are mentioned in rabbinic literature (pp. 38f.). There is a great deal of tradition about one of them, the corn merchant Nicodemus (Naqdimon b. Gorion).[27] We are told about the luxury that was prevalent in his household, and of the generous benefactions, not always free from ambition, and of the destruction of his wealth during the chaos which preceded the destruction of Jerusalem, when the mob fired his granaries full of wheat and barley[28] in the winter of AD 69–70, according to Josephus. When Joseph of Arimathea, another member of the Sanhedrin, is described as εὐσχήμων (Mark 15.43), the papyri make it clear that this means a wealthy landowner.[29] He was a rich man (Matt. 27.57) and owned a garden to the north of the city with a family grave hewn from the rock (John 19.41; cf. 20.15). The main part of his property would probably be in his native city, since the Jerusalem site had evidently not been long in the possession of his family, for the grave was newly hewn.

The priestly aristocracy belonged to the wealthy class. In the upper part of the city lived the high priest Ananias (*BJ* 2.426), Zadok the chief priest (Lam. R. 1.49 on 1.16, Son. 1.46, 128), and according to tradition Annas and Caiaphas. The house where lived the ex-high priest Annas, father-in-law of the officiating high priest, to whom John says Jesus was first taken after his arrest (John 18.13), had a spacious court (John 18.15). A woman doorkeeper (John 18.16) and other servants belonged to the household (John 18.18, where the group who took Jesus prisoner is no doubt included). Annas' grave, in the south-east of the city, must have been a large construction dominating the district (*BJ* 5.506). The officiating high priest Caiaphas, to whom Jesus was taken next, lived in a house large enough to accommodate an emergency session of the Sanhedrin (Matt. 26.57; Mark 14.53; Luke 22.66), and it apparently possessed

---

[27] Is he the same Nicodemus we meet in John's Gospel? Josephus mentions a distinguished and highly respected man of Jerusalem called Gorion (*BJ* 4.159), or Gurion (4.358). However the Gorion who was still playing a part in public life in AD 70 can scarcely have been born before the turn of the century, in which case his son Nicodemus cannot have been a grown man and a member of the Sanhedrin by the time of Jesus.

[28] b. Gitt. 56a. The burning of the grain stores by the Zealots during the Jewish War is well attested in *BJ* 5.24; Tacitus, *Hist.* V, 12; Lam. R. 1.5 (Son. 101); Eccles. R. 7.12 (Son. 193): Schlatter, *Jochanan ben Zakkai*, 62.

[29] Cf. Leipoldt's review in *Theol. Literaturblatt* 39, 1918, cols. 180f., of the papyri of Basle published by E. Rabel in *Abhandlungen der königlichen Gesellschaft der Wissenschaften zu Göttingen*, Phil.-hist. Klasse, 16.3, Berlin 1917.

a gate-house (Matt. 26.71; Mark 14.68). He had in his household a fair number of servants, both men and women.[30]

According to tradition there was great luxury in the houses of the high-priestly families (for polygamy see p. 94). It was reported that Martha[31] of the high-priestly family of Boethus was so pampered that she carpeted the whole distance from her house to the Temple gate because she wanted to see her husband Joshua b. Gamaliel officiate on the Day of Atonement, on which day everyone had to go barefoot (Lam. R. 1.50 on 1.16, Son. 1.47, 128). Men who had committed manslaughter, and had fled into a city of refuge, could not return until the death of the officiating high priest; accordingly the high priests' mothers maintained these exiles in food and clothing so that they would not pray for the death of their sons (M. Makk. ii.6). Further information on the expenditure of the high priests' mothers is given in connection with the Day of Atonement. On this day the high priest wore white garments during the 'corporate act of worship', to which the ceremonies in the Holy of Holies belonged, and the high-priestly robe for his own 'special part' (*Ant.* 3.159–87).[32] For this he had the privilege of wearing a special undergarment, a sort of tight-fitting tunic reaching to the knees (described in *Ant.* 3.153, cf. 159). His mother customarily provided this, while its cost was subsidized by the community to the extent of 30 minas. The mother of the high priest Rabbi [*sic*] Ishmael b. Phiabi (to AD 61) provided him with a tunic worth 100 minas, that is, one talent; while the mother of the high priest Rabbi [*sic*] Eleazar b. Harsum[33] gave him one worth 20,000 (according to the context we should read minas, but 'denarii' is the more probable, two talents) which was woven of such transparent material that the priests pronounced it inadmissible.[34]

The holder of the high-priestly office had to possess private means. One has only to think of the Day of Atonement, when the high priest

---

[30] Matt. 26.51; Mark 14.47; Luke 22.50; John 18.10, 26; servants of the high priest took part in the arrest of Jesus; so too Matt. 26.58; Mark 14.54; Luke 22.55. Servants of the high priest are also mentioned in T. Men. xiii.21; *Ant.* 20.181, 206.

[31] Lam. R. 1.50 (Son. 1.47, 128) calls her Miriam; M. Yeb. vi.4, b. Yeb. 61a and b. Gitt. 56a all have Martha.

[32] Schürer II, 319 n. 6, ET II.1, 256 n. 124.

[33] He is mentioned in Lam. R. 2.5 on 2.2 (Son. 2.4, 157) as a wealthy scribe of the time of Hadrian. Josephus gives a different ancestry for the high priests called Eleazar who held office before AD 70. Both testimonies confirm Schlatter's identification of him (*Tage*, 54–56) with 'Eleazar the Priest', the high priest who appears on the coins of the Bar Kokhba rising (AD 132 to 135 or 136).

[34] For the tunic see b. Yom. 35b Bar.; T. Yom. i.21f., 182; Schlatter, *Tage*, 54f.

had to supply the sacrifice at his own expense (*Ant.* 3.242, cf. Lev. 16.3). Over and over again, e.g. II Macc. 4.7–10, 24, 32, we find records of the high-priestly office being bought, as in the case of Joshua b. Gamaliel (*c.* AD 63–65). It was said that his wife Martha (or Miriam) paid three *qab*[35] of denarii for this purpose to 'Jannaeus' (b. Yeb. 61a). Since Jannaeus reigned from 103–76 BC this is presumably a deliberate substitution for Agrippa II who was always favourably viewed in rabbinic literature.[36]

We have no information concerning the regular income of the high priest. Josephus reports, however, that during the unsettled years before the outbreak of the Jewish war in AD 66, 'such was the shamelessness and effrontery which possessed the high priests, that they were actually so brazen as to send their servants to the threshing floors to receive the tithes due to the priests' (*Ant.* 20.181, cf. 206), 'so it happened at that time that those of the priests who in olden days were maintained by the tithes now starved to death' (*Ant.* 20.207, cf. 181). This agrees with the Tannaitic report (b. Pes. 57a Bar.) that the priests originally stored the hides from the sacrificial victims, which were their perquisites, in the Parwah Chamber in the Temple; and each evening shared them out among the course of priests who had undertaken the Temple services that day (there were twenty-four such courses who each served for a week at a time). Later, these hides were plundered by the 'men of violence', 'the big men of the priesthood', i.e. the agents of members of the high-priestly families. These two pieces of evidence lead to the conclusion that the high-priestly aristocracy had no share in the revenue of the ordinary priests[37] at least as regards some revenues and perhaps for them all. What then were their sources of income?

We must remember the remarkable wealth of the priestly aristocracy (see pp. 96–8) in contrast with the poor circumstances of the ordinary priests; and also that this aristocracy appears to have been particularly interested in the Temple treasure, and to have filled the post of Temple treasurer from the younger members of its families (b. Pes. 57a Bar.; T. Men. xiii.21, 533). We can draw a parallel to this in present-day Palestine: the Greek Orthodox clergy who belong to the monastic community of the Holy Sepulchre, and who are

---

[35] 2.02 litres (about 3½ pints) each; see Dalman, *WB*, under '*qab*'.

[36] The Talmud does not differentiate between Agrippa I and Agrippa II, and perhaps knew only one of them.

[37] *kōhēn hedyōṭ* in contrast with *gᵉdōl kᵉhunnāh*.

mainly Greek, draw a large income, while the Arab parish priests have a poor standard of living, and indeed, they went on strike for a whole year because of this during the First World War.[38] So we may reasonably suppose that the priestly aristocracy drew their regular income from the Temple treasury.

At the same time we may mention other sources of income. Some of the families may have been landowners, as for example Eleazar b. Ḥarsum if he belongs here (see n. 33). He is said to have inherited from his father one thousand villages and one thousand ships, and had so many slaves that they did not know their own master (b. Yom. 35b Bar.; cf. Lam. R. 2.5 on 2.2, Son. 2.4, 162). We must also remember the trade in sacrificial victims which may have been kept up by the high-priestly family of Annas (see p. 49), as well as the plundering of the inferior priests mentioned above, and various acts of violence and cases of bribery.[39] Besides all this we find nepotism rife (b. Pes. 57a Bar.; T. Men. xiii.21, 533) in the filling of lucrative and influential posts in the Temple, such as those of treasurer or chief priest.[40] Ananus, son of the high priest Ananias, appears in AD 52 as Captain of the Temple,[41] a rank second only to that of the high priest (*Ant.* 20.131; *BJ* 2.243). Another son of Ananias, Eleazar, held the same office in AD 66 (*BJ* 2.409; *Ant.* 20.208).

[38] I learned this from my father.
[39] b. Pes. 57a Bar.: plundering of sycamore trees in Jericho; for bribery, e.g. *Vita* 195.
[40] *ammarkāl*, Schürer II, 326f., ET II.1, 263f.: treasury official.
[41] *sᵉgan ha-kōhanīm*, Schürer II, 320f., ET II.1, 257ff.

V

THE MIDDLE CLASS

NEXT TO THE MERCHANTS, who imported goods from a distance and stored them in large warehouses, were the retail traders who had shops in one of the bazaars.[1] Then came the small industrialists or craftsmen who owned their own premises and did not hire themselves out for wages.[2] These constituted the middle classes: there were no industrial factories. This was true of the Jerusalem of the time of Jesus as it is generally true for the old city of Jerusalem today.

We rarely come across evidence for the economic situation of this class. We can disregard such extravagant statements as that a citizen of Jerusalem had a loft ('illītā) full of denarii (b.B.B. 133b), or that a tailor of Jerusalem had two kōr (about 790 litres, see p. 127 n. 17) of denarii in his possession (Lam. R. 1.2 on 1.1, Son. 70). It does not mean much, either, to find that people often invested their savings in jewellery (the custom of piercing gold pieces and wearing them as a head-dress was already known in those days, M. Kel. xii.7; Lam. R. 2.20 on 2.12, Son. 2.16, 179). It is evident, however, that the middle classes did best for themselves when they were connected with the Temple and its pilgrims. The Temple officials and workers were very well paid, as is shown by the report, exaggerated though it is, that the shewbread bakers and makers of incense received first twelve, then twenty-four (according to R. Judah as much as forty-eight) minas, or about an eighth, a quarter, or half a talent each day (b. Yom. 38a). The Old Testament precept that wages should be paid on the same day (Deut. 24.15) was meticulously followed in the Temple (*Ant.* 20.220), whereas elsewhere it was the usual practice to pay the wage daily only if it was expressly demanded; otherwise it was paid between

---

[1] The Egyptian papyri differentiate between the ἔμποροι, or wholesale merchants, and the κάπηλοι, or retail traders; MW I.1, 268.

[2] The same distinction is found in contemporary Egypt; MW I.1, 260.

twelve and twenty-four hours after the period of work ended (M. B.M. ix.11f.; Bill. I, 832). Just as it was considered a serious crime to cheat the Temple, so also it was a matter of honour for the Temple to conduct its affairs in the grand manner and contribute to social welfare (see pp. 12f.,).

The tavern trade depended almost entirely on the pilgrims (p. 60), whose main requirement was a large space with plenty of room for their mounts and beasts of burden, after the manner of the modern khan. At certain festivals people were obliged to spend the night in Jerusalem, at the first (b. Pes. 95b),[3] and according to the prevalent view, the second Passover as well (T. Pes. viii.8, 168; on the second Passover, see p. 76), at the feast of Tabernacles (b. Sukk. 47a), and at the offering of the first-fruits (b. Sukk. 47b Bar.).

The technical problems involved led to the definition of a 'Greater Jerusalem', which included Bethphage, as an area permissible for a night's stay (pp. 61f.). This concession does not seem to apply to the eighth day of Tabernacles, and for the Passover meal too it seems that all the pilgrims went into Jerusalem itself.[4]

We find a precept, propounded at least by those who held that Jerusalem had not been shared out among the tribes but remained the common property of the whole of Israel, that it was forbidden to let houses in Jerusalem because they belonged to the whole people. Indeed, R. Eleazar b. Zadoq who grew up in Jerusalem,[5] said that it was wrong even to let resting places. However there follows the description of the actual practice: 'Therefore, the inn-keepers took

---

[3] Dalman, SW 315ff.

[4] The precept was (M. Makk. iii.3, etc.) that a man should be scourged if 'he ate the Lesser Holy Things outside the wall (of Jerusalem)'. According to M. Eduy. viii.6 there was no need for the actual existence of the wall. These 'Lesser Holy Things' included the Passover. The word ḥōmā indicates the city walls of Jerusalem, but in M. Men. vii.3 and elsewhere it is interpreted to mean the (imaginary) walls of Bethphage. It may therefore have been permitted to eat the Passover within the bounds of 'greater Jerusalem'. Indeed, we see in b. Pes. 91a that a special lamb could be slaughtered on behalf of a man who was in a Gentile prison, if his release was assured, thus supposing that the prison was inside the 'walls' of Bethphage (M. Pes. viii.6). The rule was, however, that the Passover lamb must not be eaten outside the walls of Jerusalem, and we know that the strict legalists, the ḥabērīm, went further, and never ate the 'Lesser Holy Things' in the upper part of the city, one of the two biṣʿīn. For them, only the lower part of the city was admissible (T. Sanh. iii.4, 418). For the actual practice of the times we do well to adhere to what happened at Jesus' last Passover (the Synoptists regard the Last Supper as a Passover meal). Although he passed the night within the boundaries of Greater Jerusalem, he ate the meal within the city itself.

[5] This must be the Elder (Strack, Einleitung, 124, 130).

the skins of the sacrificial animals [of their guests] by force. Abbai
says, We may learn from this that it is the custom for a man to leave
his host the wineskin and the hide' (b. Yom. 12a Bar.; b. Meg. 26a).
Abbai traces back a custom that still obtained to his day (after AD
300) to the Jerusalem hosts' customary right to the hides of the
sacrificial animals. The fact that such hides, at any rate those of
Egyptian sheep, fetched from four to five *sela*,[6] i.e. sixteen to twenty
denarii,[6] shows that the custom brought in a considerable income.
In comparison, the average daily wage of a labourer was one
denarius. Occasionally a man shared his host's Passover meal as a
paying guest. If 14 Nisan fell on a Sabbath, a man would leave his
cloak with his host as security, and reckon up with him when the
feast was over (M. Shab. xxiii.1; according to b. Shab. 148b only
this meaning is possible).

The pilgrims brought considerable traffic to those engaged in the
catering trades. In the first place there were the offerings which the
pilgrims had to bring, which varied according to the purpose of their
pilgrimage. At Passover time they brought a lamb (see pp. 82f.) and
possibly a free-will offering (M. Hag. i.3); to these we have to add the
four cups of wine (M. Pes. x.1), the bitter herbs,[7] the *harōset*, and the
unleavened bread. Still more important, however, than the expense
of these ceremonial requirements was the outlay on luxury foods
which they could afford for themselves. Philo gives a spirited description of the feast days in Jerusalem as carefree breaks in a feverish
life (*De spec. leg.* I, 69; cf. *Ant.* 15.50, etc.). It was part of this full enjoyment of life to have an abundance of good food and drink. 'They
feasted seven whole days and spared no expense', says Josephus
in his picture of the people's celebration of Passover (*Ant.* 11.110).
They considered that they were not merely entitled to that kind of
luxury, but that it was actually incumbent upon them, since the
money from the 'second tithe' had to be spent in Jerusalem, and
should go, according to precept (Deut. 14.26), on meat and strong
drink and anything else they desired. Accordingly the Mishnah says

[6] Krauss, *TA* II, 113; on the high value of skins see Philo, *De spec. leg.* I, 151.
[7] Compare the shopkeepers mentioned on p. 34, who called out to the people,
'Come and buy the prescribed spices'. According to the illuminating explanation of
Professor Kahan, the phrase *taggᵉrē harāk* means 'dealers in parched corn'. For the
meaning suggested by Rashi (Hirschensohn, 133), 'dealers at the latticed window',
the plural *harakkīn* would be expected. The sellers of roasts and other dainties, who
also form part of the street scene in present-day Jerusalem, offered spices for sale at
Passover time.

(M.M. Sh. ii.1) that the second tithe was appointed to be spent on food, drink and scented oils, as Josephus puts it, 'for banquetings' (*Ant.* 4.205, 240ff.). We hear especially of their keen enjoyment of meat, an enjoyment which is still found today among the Arabs: 'As long as the Temple stood, there was no pleasure without meat' (b. Pes. 109a Bar.). They could buy themselves game, especially gazelle; if they chose fat cattle (M.M. Sh. i.3f.; iii.11) they had the option of either using the animal for a secular meal or bringing it as a peace-offering, in which case the fat parts belonged to the altar and the rest was theirs (M.M. Sh. i.3f.; *Ant.* 4.205). Thus, for example, it was a common custom to bring a festal peace-offering on the eve of the Passover, and to eat it either before or after the Passover lamb in case the portions of the latter were insufficient. On the other hand this was not customary if the Passover offering was plentiful (M. Pes. vi.3). In this connection, people often joined together to buy a whole beast. Only so can a passage in the Mishnah be explained (M. Hag. i.2f.), where the school of Shammai rules that a festal burnt-offering must cost at least two silver *māʿāh* and a peace-offering one (the burnt-offering could not be paid for from the second tithe since it was not for the offerer's pleasure) ;[8] naturally one *māʿāh*, only a sixth of a denarius (Bill. I, 293) was not enough to buy the whole beast. Households with many mouths to feed were dependent on peace-offerings, while those with fewer, and the means to do so, could better afford whole burnt-offerings (M. Hag. i.5).

Wine, which could be sweetened with honey (M.M. Sh. ii.1), was brought for drinking (M.M. Sh. i.3f.; iii.12; b. Pes. 109a Bar.), and so was grape-skin wine (M.M. Sh. i.3). The second tithe was used also for buying fish (M.M. Sh. ii.1), oil (M. Pes. vii.3), fruits such as olives, grapes (M.M. Sh. i.4), walnuts and almonds (M.M. Sh. i.3), and vegetables such as leeks (M.M. Sh. ii.1), fenugreek (M.M. Sh. ii.3), and vetches (M.M. Sh. ii.4), and baking ingredients (M.M. Sh. ii.1). The children were given rusks and nuts as titbits (b. Pes. 108b–109a Bar.). People could bring the second tithe partly in kind, but the general rule was that it was brought into Jerusalem as ready money and spent there (M.M. Sh. i.5f.). Many would deposit money with the keeper of a shop where ready-cooked food was sold, and then consume their money's worth (M.M. Sh. ii.9f.).

The rest of the trades in Jerusalem also profited to a greater or

---

[8] The school of Hillel reversed the amounts.

lesser degree from the pilgrim traffic. If a man was to fulfil the commandment to rejoice at the festival he had to see that his women-folk enjoyed themselves too. The Babylonian Jews gave their wives bright clothes for Passover, and the Palestinians white linen (b. Pes. 109a Bar.), most of which will have been bought in the city. It may generally be assumed that people would take home souvenirs of Jerusalem (p. 9), and their liberality expressed itself in gifts to the Temple, which resulted in commissions to the craftsmen of the city.

The *priests* may be regarded as belonging to the middle classes. Most of these ordinary priests lived in various places throughout the land, and were divided into twenty-four courses. Those who lived in Jerusalem seem to have reached a higher level of wealth and education, and one of these well-to-do priestly families, which had lived in Jerusalem for generations, was that of Josephus (*Vita* 1–6, see p. 108). The number of Jerusalem priests who had an education as scribes was quite large: R. Zadoq (*c.* AD 50) and his son Eleazar (pp. 286f.); Hananiah (*c.* AD 70) who was captain of the Temple (M. Pes. i.6); Eliezer b. Hyrcanus (*c.* AD 90; j. Sot. iii.4, 19a.28); the priest and Pharisee Gozorus, who took part in a mission to Galilee in AD 66–67 (*Vita* 196f., also given as Iozaros); the pupils of R. Johanan b. Zakkai, R. Simeon b. Nathaneal and the priest Jose (M. Ab. ii.8). There were probably priestly scribes in the family called Rabban Johanan in Jerusalem: it appears that there was in Jerusalem a family whose sons died at the age of eighteen. They sought the advice of Johanan b. Zakkai, who voiced his suspicion that they were descendants of Eli who had come under the curse of I Sam. 2.33, and he recommended that they should study the Law. In this way the curse was averted, and on the basis of a belief about names still found among Palestinian Jews, the family was called after Johanan so that the curse would be averted for good (b. R. Sh. 18a). Eli the priest of Shiloh (I Sam. 1.9) was of the family of Aaron,[9] so his descendants were also priests and some of them, perhaps, scribes. On the other hand, when the high priest Joshua b. Gamaliel (p. 95) is called 'Rabbi', we cannot think that this is at all likely considering what we know of the high priests; it is rather a mistake due to confusion between this man's father and the famous R. Gamaliel (Acts

[9] His grandson, Ahitub (I Sam. 14.3), had a son Ahimelek (I Sam. 22.20), who was said to be a descendant of Ithamar (I Chron. 24.3) the youngest son of Aaron (I Chron. 24.1; Ex. 6.23). We should remember that the evidence of Scripture would be sufficient to establish genealogies where the contemporaries of Jesus were concerned, and critical doubts did not arise.

5.34ff.; 22.3). As for the Levites, we find several of them who were outstanding in wealth and education, among them the chief Levite Johanan b. Gudgeda and Joshua b. Ḥananiah. The Levite Barnabas too (Acts 4.36f.), companion of Paul and leader of the first missionary journey, may belong to this group.

With regard to the income of the priests, we must distinguish clearly between what was prescribed and what actually happened. For the prescriptions we may refer to Schürer's excellent synopsis,[10] according to which we should expect to find the priests living in remarkably advantageous circumstances. What income had they in actual fact? We know that the strict legalists were most conscientious in paying certain dues, but they were only a minority. How did the majority behave? After all, when we remember the amount of the civil taxes, and add the many, heavy dues for the cultus and the priests, it seems highly unlikely that the latter were paid according to the book. In fact, we hear of numerous complaints.[11] A whole tractate of the Mishnah (M. Dem.) deals with the *demai* produce, that is, any produce which has possibly not been subject to the priests' tithe of the heave-offering (one per cent of the harvest) and the second tithe. Again, the second tithe was certainly recognized in Galilee (*Vita* 63, 80), but not the custom of devoting things to the use of priests (M. Ned. ii.4). Philo seems to know nothing at all about the heave-offering dedicated to the priests, *terūmāh*, about two per cent of the harvest (p. 107 n. 14). Finally, the expression for uneducated people, *'am hā'āreṣ*, designates them as those from whom it was useless to expect exact observance of the Law. We can see from this that the precepts of the Law were by no means generally observed.

Of great importance in judging the value of the theoretical precepts is the fact that only from the following sources of the priests' income have we any proof that they were paid at all, and even then the extent of the payment is open to question.

1. The portion of the sacrificial victims which the priests received in Jerusalem during their week of service. 'Know ye not that they which minister about sacred things eat of the things of the Temple, and they which wait upon the altar have their portion with the altar (i.e. the offerings)?' said Paul (I Cor. 9.13, cf. 10.18; Heb. 13.10). Of the two doves which Mary offered in Jerusalem (Luke 2.24) one

---

[10] Schürer II, 301–12, ET II.1, 235–48.
[11] E.g. M. Ab. v.8f.; cf. Mek. Ex. 19.1 and parr., Schlatter, *Jochanan ben Zakkai*, 67 n. 2.

was a sin-offering, which went to the priest as usual (*Ant.* 3.230). There are a number of references, such as those concerning the lottery for the priests' share (M. Shab. xxiii.2), or the Temple doctor's action in cases of stomach trouble (p. 26), or the beneficial effect of the waters of the Gihon which the priests drank to counteract their rich meat diet[12]—all these bear unmistakably the stamp of authenticity. The priests' share of the offering also included the hides of the sin-offerings, guilt-offerings and whole burnt-offerings, and we have a number of specific references to the distribution of these (b. Pes. 57a Bar., cf. b.B.K. 109a–110b; b. Tem. 20b).

2. The first-fruits too were offered. This is shown by the vivid description of the procession which was part of the ceremony (M. Bikk. iii.1–9), and especially from the information that King Agrippa (I or II?) took part in the offering (M. Bikk. iii.4).

3. The third payment due to the priests about which we have any certain proof, the tithes on agricultural produce, is quite remarkable in that it never occurs in contemporary lists of the priests' sources of income.[13] This is because the basis for the various synopses is the Mosaic law rather than actual practice. We know for certain from Josephus that the tithes, which according to Mosaic law were due to the Levites (Num. 18.21–32), were paid to the priests even before the outbreak of the Jewish war (AD 66). He records that the high priests repeatedly sent their servants to the threshing floors to seize the tithes due to the priests (*Ant.* 20.181, 206); and that his colleagues received the tithes due to them as priests in Galilee, but that he himself, although a priest, relinquished his right to them (*Vita* 63, 80). In the Epistle to the Hebrews also, we find testimony that tithes belonged to the priests: 'And those descendants of Levi who receive the priestly office have a commandment in the law to take tithes from the people' (Heb. 7.5). Again Pseudo-Hecateus of Abdera refers to the Jewish priests as those 'who receive a tithe of the produce' (*CA* 1.188). Those passages in the Talmud which state that the tithes are paid to the Levites and not to the priests (M.M. Sh. v.9; M. Ter. iv.2, etc.) are based on the purely exegetical consideration of the OT precept, and are the less significant, as other passages in the Talmud make it clear that in practice tithes were given to the priests. There

[12] *ARN*, Rec. A. ch. 35 (Goldin, 146); Neubauer, *Géographie*, 145.
[13] *Ant.* 4.69ff., 240ff.; 3.224–36; Phil, *De spec. leg.* I, 131–61; M. Hall. iv.9–11, and the addition to M. Hall. iv.11 in the Munich MS of the Talmud (variants in L. Goldschmidt, *Der babylonische Talmud* I, Berlin 1897) = b.B.K. 110b. Other rabbinic texts in Schürer II, 301 n. 6, ET II.1, 234f. n. 60.

are discussions on why the Levites had been punished by being deprived of the tithes (b. Yeb. 86a, cf. b. Sot. 47b–48a). It is reported of
the priest R. Eleazar b. Azariah, a contemporary of R. Aqiba, that
he levied tithes (b. Yeb. 86a); and there is the proverbial figure of the
priest who patrols the threshing floors (b. Ket. 105b.). Finally, it is
recorded that the high priest Johanan (Hyrcanus, 134–104 BC) had
abolished the avowal of the tithes (M.M. Sh. v.15 = M. Sot. ix.10)
because, so the rabbinic references rightly declare, tithes were no
longer paid to the Levites (b. Sot. 47b–48a).

Philo also seems to have knowledge of a priestly tithe (*De virt.* 95),
but a closer inspection of his statements raises considerable difficulties. As well as this priestly tithe he recognizes a levitical tithe, and
furthermore, defends the view that the priestly tithe not only included
agricultural produce, but also cattle.[14] As far as I can see, it has not
so far been recognized that this priestly tithe of Philo's can only be the
second tithe, which included the tithe on cattle; but this was spent in
Jerusalem by the man who owned the property. No historical value
can be given to Philo's statement, which is based simply on the literal
meaning of the scriptural text, and shows scarcely any acquaintance
with actual practice.

The priestly tithe is thus firmly established; there now remains the
question of when it was first paid. The abolition of the tithe avowal
was attributed to Johanan b. Zakkai,[15] which takes us to the last
decades before AD 70 and to the high priest John Hyrcanus (M.M. Sh.
v.15 = M. Sot. ix.10). The fact that Pseudo-Hecateus (before 100
BC) mentions the priestly tithe is a point in favour of the second name.
We know that the tithe was paid most meticulously by the strict
observers of the Law, and that they included the very smallest herbs
(Matt. 23.23; Luke 11.42) and also everything they bought—every
growing thing, that is (Luke 18.12). This last practice is attested by

---

[14] Levitical tithe: *De spec. leg.* I, 156f. His priestly tithe includes cattle, *De virt.*
95. It is interesting to compare *De spec. leg.* I, 131–44 with *De virt.* 95. The revenues
of the priests are mentioned in both passages:

De spec. leg. I, 131–44	*De virt.* 95
Dough-offering	
Tax on property (crops)	First-fruits
First-born of animals	First-born
Tax on income from crops and cattle	Tithes on crops and cattle

This comparison shows that the tax on property corresponds to the *bikkūrīm*, and
the tithe (the 'priestly' tithe, actually the 'second tithe', is considered as income tax.
It follows from this that Philo did not know the *t^erūmāh*.

[15] T. Sot. xiii.10, 230; Schlatter, *Jochanan ben Zakkai*, 29 n. 2.

the parable of the Pharisee and the publican; it was probably taken because it was not always possible to find out if the man who had sold the fruits had tithed them in the prescribed way (i.e. whether they were not *demai* produce).

We can, therefore, be certain of only these three sources of income for the priests, and this is indeed surprising. Moreover, the evidence that a considerable number of people did not pay any dues, or paid them only in part, and that many taxes were perhaps no longer paid at all, is confirmed by what we know of the financial circumstances of the priests. It would be wrong to base any estimate of this on the circumstances of Josephus the priest and writer (*Vita* 80), for he had the advantage of a good education over a number of years (*Vita* 7ff.), for some time probably in Tiberias (*Vita* 274), and was a landowner with estates near Jerusalem, probably to the west of the city;[16] he was also a member of the foremost family in the first of the twenty-four courses of priests (*Vita* 2), and so his case is not at all typical of the circumstances of the ordinary priests, the majority of whom lived in great poverty. When their threshing floors were plundered, some of them actually died of hunger according to Josephus' statement (*Ant.* 20.181, 207), which admittedly should be treated with reservation. Even Philo, who paints a glowing picture of the rich revenues of the priests in order to prove the splendour of the Mosaic Law, had to admit that the priests would have had plenty if everyone had paid his full dues, but in fact they had been reduced to poverty, because 'some of the people' (an obvious understatement) were indifferent (*De spec. leg.* I, 153–5).

---

[16] *Vita* 422. The camp of the Tenth Legion, mentioned in *Vita* 422, was in the western part of the city and its environs after the destruction of Jerusalem (*BJ* 7.5).

VI

THE POOR

THERE ARE NO Palestinian papyri which give information about Jerusalem.[1] We are therefore entirely dependent for our knowledge of the poorer classes on literary sources, and these leave much to be desired when it comes to detailed information. To be sure, we hear of a certain poor widow of Jerusalem who had only two *lepta*, or a quarter of an *as* (about one farthing) for 'all her living',[2] and cast them into the Temple treasury (Mark 12.41–44; Luke 21. 1–4). Again, we hear of a certain woman who had only a handful of meal to bring for the meal-offering, which gave rise to a scornful remark from the officiating priest (Lev. R. 3.5 on 2.1, Son. 40); or again, of the poor man who caught four turtle-doves a day, and brought two of them to the Temple even on the day when King Agrippa chose to bring a thousand offerings, and so forbade any other offerings (*ibid.* on 1.17, Son. 39). But the historicity of these three accounts is doubtful. There is, after all, a Buddhist analogy to the story of the widow's mite, and another to the story of the poor dove-catcher.[3] Dreams explain to the priest in the second case the value of the poor woman's meal-offering, and to Agrippa in the third the value of the poor man's doves; here we find a theme which is particularly clear in the Chinese translation of the Buddhist parallel to the Widow's Mite, that the value of the offerings of the poor is recognized through supernatural knowledge. So here we have no reliable information. However, even if we should often like more in-

[1] When this was first written in 1924, there were no Palestinian papyri at all. But now the position has been changed by the discoveries at Qumran, in the wadis along the south-west coast of the Dead Sea and in the Wadi ed-Daliye. Even so, it is still true (in 1968) that we have no such sources of information about Jerusalem before AD 70 as we have about the Egypt of the papyri.

[2] The daily ration of bread distributed to the poor, the barest minimum even, cost as much as two *asses* (p. 122).

[3] H. Haas. '*Das Scherflein der Witwe' und seine Entsprechung im Tripitaka*, Leipzig 1922.

formation, the sources are sufficiently adequate to enable us to form some idea who constituted the poorer classes.

We must distinguish between those of the poor who earned their own living, and those who lived, either partly or wholly, on relief.

A. SLAVES AND DAY LABOURERS

The papyri witness to the existence of the slave trade in Palestine during the third century BC,[4] and for Jerusalem in the time of Jesus we have the auction stone upon which the slaves stood (see p. 36). The impression we get from rabbinic and New Testament evidence,[5] and from Egyptian papyri,[6] is that slave ownership played no great part in the rural economy. We find most of the slaves in the city, as domestic servants, and even here, except at court, their number is not large. A Jerusalem eunuch is mentioned in the Mishnah (M. Yeb. viii.4), who was perhaps a servant in a *harem*. We find freedmen more often: 'If your daughter has attained puberty, free your slave and marry her to him', was said to be a proverb of Jerusalem (b. Pes. 113a). There was a manumitted slave in the service of the Jerusalem physician Tobias (M.R. Sh. i.7), and a freed slave woman of Jerusalem was made to drink the water of bitterness (Num. 5.11ff.) at the time of Shemaiah and Abtalion in the reign of Herod the Great (M. Eduy. v.6).

It has been stated that already during the second commonwealth it had become impossible to enslave a man who was born a Jew.[7] The passages quoted in support of this (b. Arak. 29a and the parallels b. Kidd. 69a; b. Gitt. 65a) which claim that there had only been Jewish slaves as long as the jubilee year was observed, are pure speculation. The fact that the Old Testament takes the slavery of born Jews for granted,[8] and that rabbinic literature repeatedly deals with Jewish slaves and defines their legal position as compared with heathen slaves,[9] still does not prove that this was the situation at the

---

[4] *Papiri greci e latini* (Pubblicazioni della Società Italiana per la ricerca dei papiri greci e latini in Egitto), IV, Florence 1917, No. 406.

[5] The servants in those of Jesus' parables which are concerned with the countryside were, as Matt. 20.1ff. shows, labourers hired for some period of time (cf. M.B.M. ix.11, 12).

[6] MW I.1, 260, 274.

[7] Krauss, *TA* II, 83.

[8] Ex. 21.2; Lev. 25.39, 47 (Israelite); Ex. 21.3 (wife); 21.7 (daughter); 22.2 (thief).

[9] The Jewish slave, like the heathen, was called ʿebed. Legally he was in the same

time of Jesus. What is certain is that Josephus assumes that the Old Testament precept (Ex. 22.2), by which a Jewish thief who could not pay the necessary compensation had to be sold as a slave, is valid for Herod the Great's time; he reports how the king tightened up the regulation concerning this (*Ant.* 16.1f.). For the rest, the question of whether or not there were slaves of Jewish extraction is quite immaterial, since most Gentile slaves accepted circumcision and so became Jews.[10] It had, therefore, to be decided what religious duties were obligatory for slaves (M. Ber. iii.3), and we find slaves slaughtering two Passover offerings in the Temple Court, one for themselves and one for their master (M. Pes. viii.2). Otherwise, communal life would have been impossible for a strict Jew. Freedmen at any rate must be regarded as proselytes, except, perhaps, at court where little attention was paid to religious rules. This is made clear by the counsel to marry daughters to freed slaves, and by the drinking of the 'water of bitterness' by a manumitted slave woman. In most cases therefore it is impossible to trace a slave's ancestry, and it is of no great importance.

Day labourers were much more numerous than slaves, and one of these was hired by a rich citizen of Jerusalem to act as runner in front of his horse (b. Ket. 67b Bar.). On an average their services earned one denarius a day (Matt. 20.2, 9),[11] with keep (M.B.M. vii.1). The poor man who lived by trapping doves caught four doves a day, two of which he offered each day as a sacrifice (p. 109). Since the price of doves was an eighth of a denarius in Jerusalem (M. Ker. i.7) his earnings were a quarter of denarius a day, which was considered as exceptionally small (b. Yom. 35b Bar.). It was very serious if a day labourer found no work, as happened on one occasion to Hillel in Jerusalem (*ibid.*)

B. THE SUBSIDIZED SECTIONS OF THE POPULATION

It is typical of Jerusalem that a large section of the population lived

---

position as a grown up child, and the heathen as a minor (M.B.M. i.5; M. Arak. viii.4f.; M.M. Sh. iv.4).

[10] They were given a year in which to decide, and then if they refused, were sold to non-Jews (cf. E. Riehm, *Handwörterbuch des biblischen Altertums* II, 2nd ed., Leipzig 1894, 1524a).

[11] Cf. Tob. 5.15, where Tobias' travelling companion received one drachma and his food.

chiefly or entirely on charity or relief. First of all we must mention the
scribes. It was forbidden that they should be paid for exercising their
profession (M. Ab. i.13; M. Bek. iv.6; b. Ned. 37a, 62a). The validity
of this precept in the time of Jesus is shown in the Gospels: 'Freely ye
have received, freely give. Get you no gold, nor silver, nor brass
(to carry) in your belts;[12] take no wallet for your journey, neither two
coats, nor sandals, nor staff. For the labourer is worthy of his food'
(Matt 10.8–10; cf. Mark 6.8; Luke 9.3). In the Mishnah this precept
is attributed to the Jerusalem teacher Hillel, and confirmed by another
teacher R. Zadoq, who lived in Jerusalem before AD 70 (M. Ab. iv.5;
i.13). When Schürer[13] concludes, from the fact that Hillel paid an
entrance fee to the school of Shemaiah and Abtalion (b. Yom. 35b
Bar.), that the lectures there were not free of charge, he overlooks the
fact that the fee was paid not to the teacher, but to the caretaker of the
school building. It was only later that this precept was evaded, by
permitting a scribe compensation for loss of time if he worked at a
trade, because of his service as a teacher or judge; that is, if he could
prove it.[14]

How did the scribes live? More than a hundred of the rabbis named
in the Talmud were artisans and were called after their trades.[15] Of
course, these belonged in the main to a later time. Ecclesiasticus
(early second century BC) questions the compatibility of a worldly
calling with that of a scribe (Ecclus. 38.24–39. 11), and the same question is still being discussed in the second century AD (b. Ber. 35b).
These facts raise a doubt whether it was the custom, as early as the
time of Jesus, to combine the study of the Law with manual work.
However, the particular evidence which we have (all concerning
Jerusalem) shows that there were already by that time scribes who
followed a trade. Shammai repulsed a Gentile who wanted to be a
proselyte with his carpenter's cubit (b. Shab. 31a).[16] Hillel, who
also lived at the turn of the millennium, was a day labourer, at least

---

[12] The wide sash which was also used for carrying money.

[13] Schürer II, 380 (ET omits).

[14] b. Ket. 105a; *Pesiqta de Rab Kahana* xxviii. 4, ed. S. Buber, Lyck 1868, 178a. 17;
F. Weber, *Jüdische Theologie auf Grund des Talmud und verwandter Schriften*, Leipzig
1897, 130.

[15] Delitzsch, *Jewish Artisan Life*, 78f, gives many examples; M. Weber, *Religionssoziologie* III, 410f.

[16] Cf. Mark 6.3, where Jesus is described as a τέκτων (carpenter or builder;
according to Justin, *Dial*. 88.8, a maker of ploughs and yokes), remembering also
that it was customary for a son to learn his father's trade, and that Jesus liked to
make use of metaphors which had to do with building.

during the time he was studying (b. Yom. 35b Bar.). When the apostle Paul carried on with his trade during his missionary activities (Acts 18.3), he was obviously continuing to support himself as he would as a Rabbi in Jerusalem. In the last decades before the destruction of the city, we have a report that R. Johanan b. Zakkai took part in trade, at least at the beginning of his studies, [17] and that R. Eleazar b. Zadoq (T. Betz. iii.8, 205)[18] and Abba Saul b. Batnith (*ibid.* ; b. Betz. 29a) throughout the whole of their teaching life kept shops in Jerusalem. It could, therefore, have been quite customary in the time of Jesus for scribes to follow a calling as well as their work of teaching.

However, in the main the scribes lived on subsidies. This is suggested by the conditions of Jewish teachers of Torah in Palestine before the First World War, and the sources confirm it for ancient times. Franz Delitzsch gives his opinion: 'The learned, or teachers of the wise (*talmīdē ḥakāmīm*), as they were called, with no set salary even for instruction, were dependent on the gratitude of their pupils . . . on some consideration at the distribution of tithes for the poor, and in certain cases also on support from the Temple treasury.'[19]

It was said to be meritorious to show hospitality to a scribe, to allow him a share in one's property (b. Ber. 63b) or to run his business for him as his representative (b. Ber. 34b, cf. T. Pes. x.10, 73); and Nehuniah b. Hakanah (M. Ab. iii.5), a teacher in the time of the second Temple, said that the scribes must be relieved of the yoke of the government (payment of taxes, b. B.B.8), and the yoke of worldly care (concern about their livelihood). All this is authenticated by the Gospels. On the subject of hospitality to scholars we remember the words of Jesus, that the labourer is worthy of his food (Matt. 10.10).[20] Paul regards this precept (I Cor. 9.14) as being valid also for a teacher (cf. Gal. 6.6); and we remember Jesus's exhortation to his disciples to accept hospitality during their work of evangelism (Luke 9.4; 10.7, 8), and he himself accepted the hospitality of the home of the sisters in Bethany (Luke 10.38–42; John 11.1). With regard to scribes being subsidized by well-to-do people, we must bear in mind the women among Jesus' followers who put their financial resources at

[17] b. Sanh. 41a; Siphre Deut. 357; Gen. R. 100.10 on 50.22 (Son. 1001); Schlatter, *Jochanan ben Zakkai*, 9.

[18] Hirschensohn, 133, cf. p. 32; T. Pes. x.10, 173.

[19] Delitzsch, *Jewish Artisan Life*, 80 (altered).

[20] Luke 10.7; 'wages'. The originality of the expression in Matthew is assured by rabbinic analogies as well as by the freer Pauline rendering in I Cor. 9.14.

his disposal, and other sums of money bestowed upon him and his disciples during their journeyings (Luke 8.1–3; Mark 15.41; John 12.6). On the other hand, we cannot trace specific collections for scribes in the period before AD 70.[21]

We hear more than once that the acceptance of this kind of subsidy was not always satisfactory: in *Ant.* 13.400ff. King Alexander Jannaeus (103–76 BC) warned his wife, as he lay dying, against the hypocrites who appeared like Pharisees (and most of the scribes were Pharisees) but were actually wicked and greedy (b. Sot. 22b). Their zeal was directed towards the things of this world and not of the next, a fact that is proved by the much-quoted reference to the seven kinds of Pharisee, which to-day is only partly comprehensible (*ibid.* Bar.).[22] All this fits in with the report that the Pharisees were said to have received bribes from the wife of Herod's brother Pheroras (*BJ* 1.571), that they are described as 'covetous' in the Gospels (Luke 16.14), and that the scribes were reproached for exploiting widows (Mark 12.40; Luke 20.47; this was said in Jerusalem). This last passage, with its illuminating reference to 'devouring widows' houses', can scarcely mean that the scribes accepted payment for legal advice although it was forbidden, or that they cheated widows of their rights; nor can it refer to Hillel's *prozbūl* (by which the remission of debt directed by law in the Sabbatical year was evaded) which had finally deprived widows who were in debt of the ownership of their houses. It is much more likely to refer to the scribes' habit of sponging on the hospitality of people of limited means (cf. *Ass. Mos.* 7.6, 'gluttons').

All that has been said accords with the information about the financial position of the scribes that has been handed down to us. It is doubtful if there were many rich scribes in Jerusalem at the time of Jesus. The report that Simon b. Shetah was brother-in-law to King Alexander Jannaeus and brother of Queen Alexandra (b. Sot. 47a, etc.) is a legend attributable to the queen's friendship towards the Pharisees. Furthermore, the story is told of the shopkeeper Abba Saul who sold wine, that he saved for Temple funds the froth formed by pouring the wine into measuring vessels, because it belonged to no one, and so produced three hundred clay jars full of wine (b.

[21] j. Hor. iii.7, 48a.40; the information about Rabbis collecting contributions to support the scribes belongs to the period around AD 100.

[22] Parallels in Derenbourg, *Essai*, 3 and n.1. In b. Sot. 22b the first kind is the *pārūš šikmī*, who like Shechem performed his religious duties from impure motives (Gen. 34.2–5).

Betz. 29a Bar.). But this exaggeration is merely to characterize conscientiousness. His fellow craftsman, R. Eleazar b. Zadoq, bought the Hellenistic synagogue in Jerusalem for himself.[23] This, however, was but a small building (b. Meg. 26a). If the great landowner R. Eleazar b. Harsum ever belonged to Jerusalem it was only at the time of Hadrian, and then in his capacity as high priest (see p. 97 n. 33).

On the other hand, we can be certain that there were some scribes, those who were priests for example, who drew a regular income (p. 104). The scribes employed at the Temple also had a regular income, and were paid from the money of the annual Temple tax. A few scribes are said to have been appointed to instruct the priests in the rules of slaughtering sacrifices, and others to instruct them in the prescribed performance of the food offerings (b. Ket. 106a). Again, the three or four scribes (b. Ket 105a) who were judges in a Jerusalem court, which is often mentioned (*ibid.*; M. Ket. xiii.1ff.; b. B.K. 58b), were paid by the Temple and are said to have received 99 *minas*, i.e. about a talent; but unfortunately we do not know for what period (b. Ket. 105a).

These instances of regular income must not mislead us into thinking that most of the scribes did not belong to the poorer classes. The saying that a scholar is never in want was twisted to fit the facts in the Babylonian Talmud, by saying that he was not reduced to beggary (b. Shab. 151b). The fact that the Talmud often refers to the *wife*, but never the *wives* of a scholar, is due not so much to the scribes' high regard for monogamy, but rather to the poverty of their circumstances.[24] To give some examples of such poverty from the second century AD: Two scholars of R. Gamaliel II, whose learning was so great that they 'could count the number of drops of water in the sea', had not a bite to eat, not a garment to wear (b. Hor. 10a). The famous teacher of Law, R. Aqiba, and his wife had to sleep in straw in the winter, and he had so little that he could not cheer his wife with a single jewel (b. Ned. 50a). R. Judah b. Eli, the most frequently quoted scholar in the Mishnah (over 600 times), had only one cloak, which he and his wife had to wear in turn when they went out (b. Ned. 49b–50a), and six of his pupils had only one cloak between them (b. Sanh. 20a).

[23] T. Meg. iii.6, 224; Schlatter, *Tage*, 81. The Munich codex of the Talmud (cf. L. Goldschmidt, *Der. bab. Talmud*, Berlin 1899, 643), names Eleazar b. Azariah as the purchaser, but there is no evidence of his presence in Jerusalem.
[24] J. Bergal, *Die Eheverhältnisse der alten Juden*, Leipzig 1881, 10.

When we turn to Jerusalem, we are reminded first of Hillel. Born
of a poor family of the Dispersion, he journeyed on foot from Babylonia to Jerusalem (p. 59). There he worked as a day labourer for
one *ṭeroppāʿiq*, which is half a denarius, and out of this he had to pay
the school caretaker, leaving only a quarter of a denarius for the
maintenance of himself and his family (b. Yom. 35b. Bar.). It is
related that on one occasion he could not find work, and so could not
pay the entrance fee for the school. Despite the winter weather he
stayed outside and listened through the window, and later was found
there half frozen (*ibid.*)[25] Only when he became a celebrated teacher,
with sometimes eighty pupils (b. B.B. 134a), were things better for
him. He might be able to lend a horse and a runner for a rich man in
difficulties (b. Ket. 67b Bar.), or have an ox sacrificed on his own
behalf in the Temple court.[26]

Two further cases of the poverty of Jerusalem scribes may be
mentioned. R. Johanan b. Ḥaurannith lived miserably on dry bread
during a famine (b. Yeb. 15b); and R. Eliezer b. Hyrcanus, who devoted himself to study against his father's will, lived in extreme privation until his teacher R. Johanan b. Zakkai noticed by his bad breath
that he was starving.[27] To corroborate what has been said, we may
cite the poverty of Jesus: he came from a poor family. This we know
because Mary made use of the concession to poor people, and brought
two doves as an offering for her purification (Luke 2.24; cf. Lev. 12.8);
his life was one of such privation that 'he had not where to lay his
head' (Matt. 8.20; Luke 9.58); he himself carried no money, as the
incidents of the shekel and the tribute money show (Matt. 17.24–27;
cf. Mark 12.13–17; Matt. 22.15–22; Luke 20.20–62), and he allowed
himself to depend on charity (Luke 8.1–3).[28] All things considered,
therefore, we must reckon the Rabbis among the poorer classes.[29]

When tradition talks of 'proud poverty' in Jerusalem (b. Pes. 113a),
it gives unwarranted praise, for Jerusalem in the time of Jesus was
already a centre for mendicancy; it was encouraged because almsgiving was regarded as particularly meritorious when done in the

[25] He was covered with snow, which does fall in Jerusalem, though rarely.
[26] F. Delitzsch, *Jesus und Hillel*, 3rd ed., Frankfurt-am-Main, 1875, 35.
[27] *ARN* 30 (Goldin 43); Schlatter, *Jochanan ben Zakkai*, 23.
[28] The recognition of the numerous parallels between the way of life of Jesus and
his disciples and that of the scribes must not be obscured by his opposition to the
scribes of his day in general.
[29] Cf. Weber, *Religionssoziologie* III, 409: 'A class of plebeian intellectuals'; A.
Büchler, *The Political and Social Leaders . . . of Sepphoris*, London 1909, 5: 'The rabbis
were themselves, as a rule, men of the people'; cf. Krauss, *TA* III, 66.

Holy City. It is not surprising that even in those days there were complaints of people who pretended to be blind, dumb, dropsical, deformed and lame (M. Peah viii.9; b. Ket. 67b–68a). The situation has changed so little that even lepers, whose established begging-place only a few decades ago was on the road to the Garden of Gethsemane, were also to be found in old Jerusalem. Since they were not allowed to enter the Holy City, they sat sheltering from the weather under the gates, which did not count as part of the city (b. Pes. 85b).[30]

Begging in Jerusalem was concentrated around the holy places, i.e. at that time around the Temple, but beggars were not allowed in every part of the Temple. The LXX of II Sam. 5.8 adds to the proverb, 'The blind and the lame shall not come into the house', the words, 'of the Lord'. Now lame and mutilated priests are to be found in the Court of Israel and the Court of the Priests (M.Midd. ii.5; j. Yom i.1, 38d.32; b. Sukk. 44a; cf. Bill. II, 795f.). We shall do well, then, to gather from II Sam. 5.8 LXX no more than that there were certain limitations; for indeed cripples were allowed in the Temple, but only on certain conditions. M. Shab. vi.8 rules: 'If it (the cripple's wooden stump) has a cavity for pads (to prevent friction), it is susceptible to uncleanness. And of course the knee-pads are susceptible to *midrās* (uncleanness which is communicated through pressure), yet (in spite of this) he may go out with them on the Sabbath, or enter with them into the Temple Court. A seat and its pads are (equally) susceptible to *midrās* uncleanness, yet he may not go out with these on the Sabbath, or enter with them into the Temple Court.' Cripples who could get about with a stump were obviously allowed in that part of the Temple that was forbidden to Gentiles, but for those who were altogether lame or legless and had to be carried around on a padded seat, this was forbidden. The impotent man in Acts 3.2 is probably an example of this. He lay at the 'Gate Beautiful', the Nicanor Gate, which connected the Court of Israel with the Court of the Women, of course on the side of the Court of the Women (Acts 3.8). He lay there begging (Acts 3.2, 3, 10) and had been taken there at the hour of prayer by his friends when the coming and going

[30] b. Sanh. 98a speaks of the Messiah sitting binding up his wounds amid the poor and the sick at the gates of Rome; b. Sanh. 98b, at least when the variant reading *ḥiwwārā* is accepted, says that the Messiah's sickness was leprosy. See also Rashi on Isa. 53.4–5 in Bill. I, 481 n.2. Palestinian conditions, where lepers sat at the city gates, have obviously been transferred to Rome, and b. Sanh. 98a is then a verification of what b. Pes. 85b has to say about Jerusalem lepers.

to and from the Temple was at its height. The blind and the lame who came to Jesus and asked for healing probably did so in the Court of the Gentiles (Matt. 21.14). We should find beggars elsewhere, not only in the Court of the Gentiles, but at the outer gates of the Temple area. At one of the two southern gates was the man blind from his birth, whom John says Jesus healed (John 9.1, 8). The scene immediately before this (John 8.58f.), when Jesus' opponents took up stones to throw at him, took place in the Temple, most probably in the Court of the Gentiles, where stones for building the Temple may have been lying about. The healing cannot have taken place immediately after that incident, though it follows without pause; but there may well have been a local connection in the mind of the author of the Gospel. In any case, when Jesus sent the blind man to wash in the pool of Siloam (John 9.7) he would have found him in the area south of the Temple. Again, it is as mendicants that we see the sick, the blind, the lame and the paralysed at the Pool of Bethesda (John 5.2–3). By analogy with Acts 3.2ff. (cf. John 9.1ff.) we can safely assume that the conversation between Jesus and the sick man in John 5.6, was occassioned by a request for alms. Since this pool—it remained a place of healing after AD 70, as is proved by votive offerings found there—must have been much sought after as a place of miracles, the sick had ample opportunity for begging.[31]

However there are others besides beggars that we must mention as support for the impression that Jerusalem had already in Jesus' time become a city of idlers, and that the considerable proletariat living on the religious importance of the city was one of its most outstanding peculiarities. It was said that it was of the essence of a city that it was a place where 'ten idle men' were to be found (M. Meg. i.3; cf. b. Meg. 3b), i.e. people who had renounced ordinary employment to devote themselves to worship. There were men like this in Jerusalem too. R. Eleazar b. Zadoq tells of societies whose members visited families which were bereaved, and who also took part in wedding celebrations and circumcisions and in the gatherings of the bones of the dead.[32] Such parasitic practices were forbidden to scribes.

It is amazing how many people of this kind emerged in the last decade before the destruction of Jerusalem; they formed themselves

---

[31] Cf. J. Jeremias, *The Rediscovery of Bethesda* (New Testament Archaeology Monographs 1), Louisville, Kentucky, 1966.

[32] *Semahoth* xii; T. Meg. iv.15, 226; A. Büchler, 'L'enterrement des criminels d'apres le Talmud et le Midrash', *REJ* 46, 1903, 76.

into gangs and terrorized the whole city (*BJ* 2.275), and later carried on the civil war within its walls. These revolutionaries of course included ardent patriots and men full of religious feeling, but others were simply men whom Josephus rightly describes as a rabble of slaves and the dregs of the population (*BJ* 5.443). The social factor played a large part in the Zealot movement. We can see this very clearly in the activities of these liberators of the people, who in AD 66 burnt the Jerusalem archives in order to destroy the records of their debts which were stored there (*BJ* 2.427).

VII

DECISIVE FACTORS IN DETERMINING
THE ECONOMIC CIRCUMSTANCES OF
THE PEOPLE OF JERUSALEM

A. THE ECONOMIC AND GEOGRAPHICAL
SITUATION OF THE CITY

THE POSITION OF Jerusalem was a great hindrance to the commercial life of the city. In Part I of this book we have met Jerusalem as a highland city, always short of water and of raw materials for industry, and lying in a very unfavourable position for trade and commerce. This state of affairs was bound to result in a very high cost of living.

1. *The cost of living in normal times*

We generally find that cattle and pearls (M. Arak. vi.5), crops and wine (M.M. Sh. iv.1) fetched a higher price in the city than they did in the country. In the following passage from the Talmud particular reference is made to prices in Jerusalem: 'In three ways was the land of Israel divided (between the tribes): by lot, by Urim and Thummim (oracular enquiry), and by the value of money' (j. Yom. iv.1, 41b. 49; Levy, II, 369b). If Levy's interpretation of the word is correct, the third way in which the land was divided derives from the considera-tion of the greater value of real estate in the neighbourhood of Jeru-salem. The only evidence I know of the price of a piece of land in Jerusalem is Matt. 27.6f., but this, of course, does not tell us the size of the plot. The potter's field, bought by the Temple treasurers (cf. Ex-cursus on the historicity of Matt. 27.7f., pp. 138ff.), is said to have cost thirty pieces of silver, i.e. probably 120 Roman denarii or Attic silver drachmas,[1] apparently the average price of a plot of land (p. 140).

---

[1] The thirty pieces of silver, the price of Judas' betrayal, are nearly always reckoned as sixty denarii. Actually ἀργύριον can only mean either the Roman

Fruit in Jerusalem, as is shown by one example, cost three to six times its price in the country (M. Maas. ii. 5f.; cf. p. 33). Because of the huge demand, the price of doves for sacrifice was inflated by city profiteers to as much as a hundred times the normal price (M. Ker. i. 7; cf. pp. 33f.). Luxury articles for sale in a large city were dear when compared with the price of land that has just been mentioned; thus, the precious ointment used to anoint Jesus in Bethany cost more than 300 denarii (Mark 14.5; John 12.5).

The gift which a Jerusalem father received on the betrothal of his daughter to a provincial bridegroom was said to have been particularly high, as also the dowry which a provincial bride brought to her Jerusalem bridegroom. 'When a man from a small town married a Jerusalem woman, he gave her (as a betrothal gift) his weight in gold; and a woman from a small town who married a man from Jerusalem brought him (as dowry or marriage portion) her weight in gold' (Lam. R. 4.2, Son. 216). The main reasons for these high costs in marriage settlements were the exalted status of Jerusalem as the City of the Temple, as the capital city with authority over a very wide range of ideas; but they also reflected the high cost of living in the city.

2. *The cost of living in times of emergency*

The unfavourable commercial and geographical position of Jerusalem made itself felt to the fullest extent in times of emergency (see Excursus II, p. 140), in shortages mainly of food, but also, for example, of clothing materials (*Ant.* 15. 310), and in correspondingly soaring prices. We hear of droughts following lack of rainfall, of a hurricane, of an earthquake, and of epidemics, of which one was aggravated by drought, and also of conflicts within Jerusalem and sieges of the city.

Accounts of the famine under Claudius show that Jerusalem suffered special hardships at such times. In Antioch the Christians arranged for a collection for the brethren in Judaea (Acts 11.28–30) i.e. for the church in Jerusalem, as Acts 12.25 shows (cf. 11.1 with 11.2;

---

silver denarius = one Attic silver drachma, then the commonest silver coin in Palestine (Josephus agrees with this), or the equivalent of the OT *kesep* = silver shekel, reckoned as four denarii in the Talmud, Philo, Josephus, Origen and Dio Cassius. The second meaning is the more likely, since the number thirty (Matt. 26.15; 27.3, 5f., 9) is based on an OT verse, Zech. 11.13; and, furthermore, the oldest exegetes (*Codex* D, five Old Latin MSS, two minuscules, Eusebius and the Latin version of Origen) all render ἀργύριον in Matt. 26.15 as *stater*, which implies this meaning.

11.27f. with 21.10, etc.), although the famine was said to be world-wide (11.28). Likewise the account of aid sent by Queen Helena of Adiabene because of this famine makes us realize that Jerusalem had special needs (*Ant.* 20.51). Josephus records that although a large quantity of grain was reserved in the country for ceremonial purposes, still the priests in the city had to go hungry (*Ant.* 3.321). There is also a single example in rabbinic literature which probably refers to the same emergency (b. Yeb. 15b; T. Sukk. ii.3, 193 = T. Eduy. ii.2, 457).[2] Here we read that Eleazar b. Zadoq, who was in Jerusalem at the time studying the Torah, saw his teacher R. Johanan b. Hauranit eating his bread dry. His father sent the teacher some olives, but he refused them because of their moisture content, and only accepted them when R. Zadoq assured him that they had been preserved according to the Law.

At such times prices mounted steeply and profiteers exploited the desperate situation. There is a saying that rain clouds bring 'ill luck to the profiteers (lit. fixers of market prices)' (Gen. R. 13.12 on 2.6, Son. 106).[3]

We can confirm this rise in prices from statements about the price of grain. M. Peah viii. 7 gives us the normal price: 'A poor man who is wandering from place to place should be given [out of the daily dole, from the so-called 'pauper's dish', which consisted of produce and foodstuffs], not less than one loaf worth a *dupondion* (two *asses*), [from wheat costing] one *silʿā* for four *seʾāhs*.' Thus the ration, clearly a daily ration, which a poor vagabond received from the poor fund was a loaf of bread worth two *asses* or a twelfth of a denarius (see Bill. I, 291). It must have been made from meal or grain, of which four *seʾāhs*[4] (52.5 litres, nearly one and a half bushels) cost one *silʿā*, i.e. four denarii (M.M. Sh. ii.9 *et passim*). We may deduce, then, from our quotation, first, that the price of grain or flour was one denarius for each *seʾāh* (about thirteen litres or three gallons), and secondly that the daily minimum bread ration corresponded to a price of a twelfth of a denarius, and to a grain measure of about one litre or $1\frac{3}{4}$ pints (perhaps about $1\frac{1}{4}$ lbs.).

[2] Schlatter, *Tage* 8of.

[3] Literally 'clouds which bring to nought (*šōbēr*) the mischievous designs (*ʿēdān*) of the fixers of market prices'. Either *šōbēr* or *ʿēdān* should be struck out as a gloss, a fact to which Professor Kahan has drawn my attention. The sense is then in both cases as above. See also n.2 in Son. 106.

[4] According to *Ant.* 9.85, 1 *seʾāh* = $1\frac{1}{2}$ Italian *modii*; 1 *modius* = 8.75 litres (1.925 gallons); i.e. 1 *seʾāh* = approx. 13.125 litres (about 2.9 gallons).

This is how Jesus' disciples made their reckoning in the account of the feeding of the five thousand (Mark 6.37, 44; cf. John 6.7, 10), that to provide bread for the multitude would cost two hundred denarii. They were reckoning, therefore, on a twenty-fifth of a denarius per head, which was the normal price of a half day's ration. Contemporary evidence from outside Palestine is in exact agreement with our figures. According to Cicero (*In Verrem* III, 81), twelve χοίνικες of wheat of 1.094 litres (1.926 pints) each, i.e. 13.128 litres, cost one denarius. According to Athenaeus (III, 20), one χοῖνιξ of wheat was the daily measure per head. Both the price of grain and the daily allowance of bread tally with the rabbinic evidence.

What were the prices in times of scarcity?

In the year 64 BC a hurricane had destroyed the entire harvest, 'so that a *modius* of wheat was bought for eleven drachmas' (*Ant.* 14.28); i.e. eleven drachmas were paid for 8.752 litres (just under 1½ gallons), so that one drachma would only purchase 0.796 litres (1¾ pints) instead of the usual thirteen litres (three gallons). The price was thus multiplied sixteen times. The daily allowance per head of one litre (1¾ pints) cost one and a quarter denarii instead of a twelfth of a denarius. That is more than the wages for a day's work (p. 111). Besides this, the prices during the famine under Claudius have been handed down to us by Josephus (*Ant.* 3.320): 'An *'issārōn* of wheat was sold for four drachmas.' Since the *'issārōn*[5] is 3.94 litres (7½ pints), people paid 4 drachmas for 3.94 litres, or 1 drachma per litre, i.e. the price had multiplied thirteen times.

As a result of its unfavourable position commercially and geographically the Holy City was bound to suffer particularly severely in such times of emergency.

B. THE POLITICAL SITUATION

In AD 6 Judaea lost its political independence to the Romans with the deposition of the ethnarch Archelaus, an independence which it had possessed, generally in actual fact, sometimes in name only, ever

---

[5] For the *'issārōn* of the MT, LXX at Num. 15.4 gives a tenth of an οἰφί (*'ēpāh*). Now according to *Ant.* 8.57, one *bat* (= *'ēpāh* in Ezek. 45.11; b. Men. 77a) = 72 *sextarii* at 0.547 litres (0.96 pints) each. Therefore one *'ēpāh* = 72 *sextarii* = 39.4 litres (1.08 bushels) = 3 *se*'*āh*. Likewise, according to b. Men. 77a and Targ. Onk. Ex. 16.36, one *'ēpāh* = 3 *se*'*āh*. Therefore one *'issārōn* = a tenth of an *'ēpāh* = 3.94 litres (6.9 pints).

since the days of Judas Maccabaeus (165–161 BC). Only once more before the dissolution of the Jewish state did history see a king over the Jews, in the person of Agrippa I (AD 41–44). To what extent did the political circumstances of the capital affect the fortunes of its inhabitants?

1. *Taxation*

The state asserted its rights mainly through levying taxes. Under *Herod the Great* these were ruthlessly exacted, and he was always thinking out fresh ways of subsidizing his vast expenditure: 'As his expenses were beyond his abilities, he was compelled to be harsh to his subjects' (*Ant.* 16.154). Herod, it is true, followed a cultural and political course which enhanced the economic power of the country.[6] He increased security in the land by means of strongholds and settlements; he extended the civilized areas by colonization; he promoted the commercial life of the country by founding cities and building harbours, by encouraging trade and commerce, especially by the building of the Temple (see pp. 21f.; 55). All of this improved the country which otherwise could not have borne his vast expenditure. But even with Herod's intervention on behalf of the people during the famine which broke out about AD 25, together with certain tax concessions, we should not underestimate the complaints about his extravagance that were made by his subjects in Rome after his death.[7] The expenditure within the country was matched by an even greater expenditure abroad, which brought no benefits to his subjects. We hear of bequests, of building operations, some useful and some mere luxuries, all alike of great size which were distributed among the following cities and islands: the isles of Chios, Cos, Rhodes; the cities of Laodicea, Tripolis, Byblos, Berytos, Sidon, Tyre, Ptolemais, Ascalon, Nicopolis, Olympia, Sparta, Athens, Pergamum, Antioch and Damascus.[8]

In view of this state of affairs we must admit that Josephus is right when he says that the basic motive of Herod's character was an insatiable ambition, and this was the mainspring of his lavish display (*Ant.* 16.153). In the circumstances a relatively tolerable level of taxation could have met this expenditure only to a very small extent; the people must have found much more oppressive the burden of

[6] Otto, *Herodes*, cols. 93–95.
[7] *Ibid.*, col. 95.
[8] *Ibid.*, cols. 75–77.

presents to Herod, his relations and 'friends', as well as to the tax collectors and tax-farmers[9] and their underlings,[10] the confiscation of their goods, and the extra taxes. Bitter was the popular outcry against the abuse of the whole common wealth because of despotism (*BJ* 2.84ff.; *Ant.* 17.304–10), against the squandering of money that had been wrung from the people's very life blood (*BJ* 1.524; 2.84ff.). At his death Herod left behind him an impoverished country and a demoralized populace with weakened morality,[11] resigned to misfortune (*BJ* 2.85f.; *Ant.* 17.304f.). When we consider that Herod was so poor at his accession that he had to melt down his own ornaments and valuables for ready money (*BJ* 1.358),[12] and yet so soon afterwards commanded immense wealth, we can well believe that the complaints against him were fully justified.

The ethnarch Archelaus behaved no better towards the people, and in AD 6 Caesar Augustus deposed him because of his atrocities, and banished him, confiscating his property (*Ant.* 17.342ff.; *BJ* 2.111).

Agrippa I inherited a love of splendour from his grandfather Herod (*Ant.* 19.328; *BJ* 2.218). He was such a spendthrift that he could not manage on the income of his extensive realm (*Ant.* 19.352), yet we hear of no complaints about him. Even more, it was said that the people liked him (*Ant.* 19.349), and it seems that his excessive expenditure was defrayed not by exorbitant demands upon his people, but by running into debt. Even before he became king he had contracted vast debts in various quarters, in one case more than a million Attic silver drachmas (*Ant.* 18.157, 163). As king he continued this method of procuring money (*Ant.* 19.352).

During the time of Roman rule (AD 6–41; 44–66) the burden of taxation remained constant, and the province of Judaea had to find 600 talents (*Ant.* 17.320; *BJ* 2.97). In AD 66 the Jerusalem authorities

[9] We cannot decide whether, under Herod, this was a system of state monopoly or of tax-farming. Cf. Otto, *op. cit.*, col. 97.

[10] This is as much as can be extracted with certainty from the corrupt text of *Ant.* 17.308.

[11] Hillel, who belonged to the time of Herod the Great and Archelaus, was already obliged to deal with tax evasion by smuggling goods in a hollow stick (M. Kel. xvii.16). According to the Tosephta, R. Joḥanan b. Zakkai, who taught in Jerusalem in the years before AD 70, had also to deal with this subject, clearly appealing to traditional teaching (Schlatter, *Jochanan ben Zakkai* 30). M. Kil. ix.2 discusses tax evasion by wearing several garments one on top of another, and M. Ned. iii.4 and b. Ned. 27b by perjury. See further Bill. I, 379f.

[12] This must have occurred before the confiscations which followed (*Ant.* 15.5), unless it is a duplication of a later melting down of royal valuables (*Ant.* 15.306).

exacted 40 talents of overdue taxes (*BJ* 2.405). If this represents the annual tax for the Jerusalem toparchy, it would confirm the figures, for the share of taxes, not counting customs duties, of the most important of the eleven Judaean toparchies may well have been as much as this. We know from Tacitus how the oppressive burden of taxes was resented, for he says that in AD 17 the provinces of Syria and Judaea begged for a reduction;[13] and during the siege of Jerusalem in AD 70 the refusal to pay taxes was considered to be the only cause of the war (*BJ* 5.405). This was, of course, not strictly true, but it is significant as indicating the part which taxation played in the life of the people. The gifts and bribes which had to be paid to officials and their agents were too numerous to realize. 'Do violence to no man, neither exact anything wrongfully, and be content with your wages', so John the Baptist exhorted the soldiers in his 'open-air sermon' (Luke 3.14). Matthew records an instance of the bribery of Roman soldiers in Jerusalem (Matt 28.12). The military tribune at Jerusalem, the chiliarch Claudius Lysias, had obtained his Roman citizenship by bribery or purchase (Acts 22.28). Corruption reached even the highest circles; we have only to compare the many complaints of the venality of the procurators. Pilate was reproached because of his venality (Philo, *Leg. ad Cai.* 302), while Felix held Paul prisoner in Caesarea in the hope of receiving a bribe (Acts 24.26). Josephus especially can tell us of many instances of bribery.

2. *War and spoliation*

In the political chaos of the time Jerusalem, as the capital city of Judaea and the City of the Temple, was bound to suffer particularly severely. Although under Herod the city had been peaceful, after his death, and especially under Roman rule, military oppression was again experienced.

C. RELIGION AND THE CULT

1. *Acts of charity*

Almsgiving played an important part in Jewish piety: 'The more charity, the more peace' (M. Ab. ii.7) was Hillel's teaching. Compassion for one's fellow men was regarded as a special characteristic

[13] Tacitus, *Annals* II, 42; Schürer I, 474 n. 96, ET I.2, 66 n. 93.

of a descendant of Abraham (b. Betz. 32b). As the Jerusalem proverb said, 'Acts of kindness are the salt of wealth' (in another form, 'Thrift is the salt of wealth', b. Ket. 66b).

No one should underestimate the part played by the kind of generosity to be found in Jesus' preaching. 'Sell that you have and give alms' (Luke 12.33). 'So therefore, whosoever he be of you that renounceth not all that he hath, cannot be my disciple' (Luke 14.33). The fact that this emphasis on charity towards the poor is peculiarly Lucan, does not prove that these passages are secondary, for the pericope of the rich young man appears in all three of the Synoptic Gospels (Matt 19.16–30; Mark 10.17–31; Luke 18.18–30). The severity of this pericope is reduced if we give a lower meaning to 'perfect', and 'that thou hast' (Matt. 19.21; cf. Mark 10.21, 'whatsoever thou hast'; Luke 18.22, 'all that thou hast'):

(a) We must not think of 'perfect' as referring to a special group of perfectionists, or a group striving after perfection, of which Jesus expected special accomplishments. Such meaning could quite easily have been found in Hellenistic thought (e.g. *Poimandres* iv.4, where 'perfect' virtually means 'initiated'). In later Judaism the basic meaning of 'perfect' was 'fully righteous',[14] one who keeps the whole Torah. When, therefore, Jesus said, 'If thou wouldst be perfect', he introduced no new idea into his discourse, but simply put into other words the phrase in Matt. 19.17, 'If thou wouldst enter into life', which he used to answer the young man's question (Matt 19.16). It follows then that according to Jesus' view, to give all one's possessions for the poor is part of the complete fulfilment of the Law.

(b) On the other hand the evidence of contemporary literature does not allow the 'all' to be pressed too far. According to the Mishnah (M. Arak. viii.4) a man may devote only part of his means to the Temple, and to go further than this was not valid. This passage demonstrates that men were obliged to set a limit to their generosity. It had already been recognized as a precept in the first century AD that it was not permissible to spend more than a fifth of one's means on acts of charity (j. Peah i.1, 15b.23). Zacchaeus the publican was ready to give half his goods to charity, and so to make recompense for fraud (Luke 19.8), and this intention Jesus commended. The phrase, 'to sell all that he had' (*mākar kol mā šeyēš lō*, b. Pes. 49a Bar.) cannot always be taken literally, and the evidence shows how far the demands for charity on a man's means were taken in practice. On the other

[14] *ṣaddīq gāmūr*, cf. Bill. I, 816.

hand, it was performed to the letter by such a man as R. Johanan: for the sake of studying the Torah he sold all his material possessions without even retaining enough for the needs of his old age.[15] We must, therefore, consider the possibility that 'to sell all' is not to be taken literally, but is rather a powerful expression for the demands of charity. There is no doubt in this case that such demands played a large part in the teaching of Jesus.

After this survey of the importance attached to charity at the time, let us turn to the situation in Jerusalem, and first, to such *charity as was practised privately*.

The pious citizen of Jerusalem when on his way to the Temple, would normally give alms if there was, say, a lame beggar lying at the so-called 'Gate Beautiful' (Acts 3.2ff.). Anyone who saw a poor lunatic at the gate gave him something to eat (*BJ* 6.307). Naqdimon b. Gorion practised an individual kind of charity, for it is said that on his way to the school he had woollen blankets spread out in his path so that the poor could collect them up behind him (b. Ket. 66b–67a Bar.).

We should mention here the charities which were performed by the ruling houses. Agrippa I had the reputation of a benefactor (*Ant.* 19.328, cf. 293f.), while Herod was praised for the extensive measures he took during the great famine of 25–24 (23) BC. He did not hesitate to make personal sacrifices: 'He cut up into coinage all the ornaments of gold and silver in his palace, without sparing objects made with special care, or having artistic value' (*Ant.* 15.306). Josephus (*ibid.* 309f.) describes his measures:

'For in the first place, to those who were able to provide food for themselves by their own labour he distributed grain in very exact proportions. Then, since there were many who, because of old age or some other attendant infirmity, were unable to prepare the grain for themselves, he provided for them by putting bakers to work, and furnishing them with food already prepared.' These measures indicate so clearly the conditions of a large town that we must assume that they applied principally to Jerusalem. Thirdly, 'He also took care that they should go through the winter without danger (to health), including that of being in need of clothing, for their flocks had been destroyed and completely consumed, so that they had no wool to use or any other material for covering themselves.'

---

[15] *Pesiqta de Rab Kahana* xxviii.13, ed. S. Buber, Lyck 1868, 178b.

The quite credible number[16] of 80,000 *kōr*[17] of grain distributed throughout Herod's realm gives us some idea of the extent of these measures.

Devout pilgrims practised charity as they travelled, and it was especially meritorious when practised in Jerusalem. It was not by accident that the two blind beggars in Jericho (Matt. 20.30: *two*; cf. Mark 10.46 par. Luke 18.35: *one* blind man) were sitting right beside the pilgrims' route. It was a natural misunderstanding on the disciples' part, when Judas left their company during the Last Supper, that they should think that Jesus had sent him out to dispense alms (John 13.29; cf. Matt. 26.9; Mark 14.5; John 12.5). When Paul came to Jerusalem at Pentecost (Acts 20.16) he was plainly expected to pay the expenses of the appropriate offerings for himself and for the four Jerusalem Christians performing Nazirite vows (Acts 21.24, 26; cf. 24.17, oblations). This was a not unusual form of charity. We hear of Alexander Jannaeus (103–76 BC) being persuaded by Simon b. Shetaḥ to defray the expenses for a hundred and fifty Nazirites;[18] and how Agrippa I (AD 41–44) on his accession 'paid for a very considerable number of Nazirites to be shorn' (*Ant.* 19.294). There was particularly vigorous intervention on the part of Queen Helena of Adiabene during the famine which broke out between AD 47 and 49. 'Her arrival was very advantageous for the people of Jerusalem, for at that time the city was hard pressed by famine, and many were perishing from want of money to purchase what they needed. Queen Helena sent some of her attendants to Alexandria to buy grain for large sums, and others to Cyprus to bring back a cargo of dried figs' (*Ant.* 20.51). Izates of Adiabene also took part by sending financial help (*ibid.* 53). According to the Talmud he is said to have emptied his royal treasury entirely; there he is erroneously called Monobazus of Adiabene, but there is little doubt that the same incident is referred to (b.B.B. 11a Bar.).

Josephus also makes it clear that it was the common practice for

---

[16] At the end of the last century Belgium had to import six million hectolitres (between 16 and 17 million bushels—an amount approaching 450,000 tons) of grain for human consumption annually.

[17] One *kōr* = 30 *se'āh* = 3.94 hectolitres (10.8 bushels); so 80,000 *kōr* = about 315,000 hectolitres (about 825,000 bushels—upwards of 20,000 tons). (According to Josephus, one *kōr* = 10 Attic *medimni* at 51.84 litres each; *Ant.* 15.314; cf. F. Lübker, *Reallexikon des klassischen Altertums*, 8th ed., Leipzig 1914, 1148.) *The Oxford Companion to Classical Literature*, ed. P. Harvey, 4th ed., 1951, p. 463, gives 11 gallons 4 pints as the equivalent of the Attic *medimnus*.

[18] Schürer I, 279f., ET I.1, 298ff.; Bill. II, 755f.

pilgrims in Jerusalem to give charity, when he says that the second tithe was spent there, as well as the quadrennial produce of trees and vines (pp. 134ff.), partly for charitable purposes (*Ant.* 4.227). In view of this evidence, it is worth mentioning that the text of Tob. 1.6–8 in *Codex Sinaiticus* clearly assumes that the second tithe of the third and sixth year of each seven-year period was distributed in Jerusalem for the relief of orphans, widows and proselytes. This does not exclude the possibility that this tithe may have been used in general for the local poor (cf. Deut. 26.12; 14.28f.) so far as it was discharged at all.

The *religious communities* provided a social service somewhere between the private and public services. We have evidence that the Essenes had in each city, and therefore in Jerusalem, their own agents who provided their travellers with clothing and other necessities (*BJ* 2.125), and similarly the Christian community in Jerusalem. Within the primitive Church we find a sharing of all things[19] in common (Acts 2.44–45; 4.32–37; 5.1–11) which was voluntary (Acts 2.45; 4.32; 5.4) and which extended even to landed property (Acts 2.45; 4.34, 36f.; 5.1ff.), all of which made acts of charity possible. Even if the account in Acts is merely a reading into history of an ideal, it acknowledges the extensive charitable works of the primitive Church, which were financed from the sale of property. The distri-

---

[19] Common ownership in the primitive Church has been a matter of considerable controversy. The reasons that are cited against it do not seem to me to be convincing, provided it is remembered that the participation was voluntary. The fact that only one example, that of Joseph Barnabas (Acts. 4.36f.) is given is explained by his importance. The privately owned house in Acts 12.12f. was obviously the place of assembly for the community. The existence of poverty in the community is explicable (Acts 6.1ff.) if the common ownership extended only to landed property. Whoever doubts the accounts about this primitive 'communism' must offer an explanation how they arose. There is an echo of ideal Hellenistic communal principles (Plato; Iamblichus, *Vit. Pythag.*; see E. Preuschen, *Die Apostelgeschichte*, Tübingen 1912, 28), but this is not enough to prove that the writer of Acts had transferred such ideals to the primitive Church. On the other hand it should be emphasized that such communism is understandable if one remembers (*a*) the repeated challenge of Jesus (see pp. 127f.) to devote possessions to the good of the poor; (*b*) the example of Jesus and his disciples, who depended on a common fund and forsook all their possessions (John 13.29; 12.6; Matt. 19.29 and par.); (*c*) the example of the Essenes who, like the primitive community, had communal meals (*BJ* 2.129f.). Acts 5.1–11 provides clear evidence of primitive communism, where the sin of Ananias was not his lie, but the withholding of something that had been dedicated to God; cf. v. 2, he 'kept back'; v. 3, ψεύδεσθαι + Acc., 'to cheat' (Blass-Debrunner, *Grammatik des neutest. Griechisch*, 12th ed., Göttingen 1965, 187, 4), and in v. 4 the verb must have the same meaning in spite of the dative, which is doubtless a Semitism here, cf. *kiḥēš lᵉ*.

bution was administered by the apostles (Acts 4.37; 5.2), with voluntary helpers (Acts 6.1ff.). There are further details in the section dealing with the seven deacons who were appointed to look after the poor (*ibid.*). We find them 'serving tables' (Acts 6.2) which was the provision by the Church of food for the needy.

For clearer understanding it is instructive to make a comparison between the two corresponding Jewish systems of *tamḥūy*, or 'poor bowl', and *quppāh*, or 'poor basket'. These may be distinguished as follows: The *tamḥūy* was distributed daily among wandering paupers, and consisted of food (bread, beans and fruits, with the prescribed cup of wine at Passover). The *quppāh* was a weekly dole to the poor of the city, and consisted of food and clothing (M. Peah viii.7; b. B.B. 8b Bar.; b. B.M. 38a; T.B.M. iii.9, 376, beans and fruits; M. Pes. x.1, wine). There can be no doubt therefore that these arrangements served as a model for the primitive Church. The daily distribution of aid indicates the *tamḥūy*, and the fact that local people (especially widows) were helped, indicates the *quppāh*. It is possible that Jewish poor relief was only at a later time divided into two compartments, and that originally it was simply a daily distribution to the local poor, like the Christian relief; but it is more likely that the fellowship meal that was held daily by the Christian community, entailed of itself a daily distribution of aid for its poor members.

At all events we can learn this much about Christian poor relief: (*a*) It was paid out in kind, as the wording of Acts 6.2 suggests; (*b*) it consisted of aid for 24-hour periods, i.e. two meal-times (cf. M. Peah viii.7); (*c*) It is likely that the distribution was centralized at one place. We may picture it like this: The Jerusalem Christians assembled daily (Acts 2.46; 6.1) in their meeting house (2.46),[20] probably in the evening (12.12, where the Church is assembled even at night), for a meal held within the framework of worship (2.42, 46),[21] under the leadership of the twelve apostles (Acts 6.2; 2.42). The poor, and especially widows, were served with the gifts that were brought in, and were also given provisions for the next day. The daily celebration was described in these words, 'They continued steadfastly in the apostles' teaching and fellowship (i.e. acts of charity,

[20] κατ' οἶκον is contrasted with 'in the Temple, in the sense of 'at home', as in Philemon 2. The sense is not 'in their own houses', as it is shown by the presence of all the apostles. See also Acts 12.12; 2.1–2; 1.15, where we find the whole community foregathered.

[21] 'The breaking of bread'—an expression for the Eucharist, intentionally vague, because of the *disciplina arcani.*

κοινωνία, cf. Rom. 15.26; Phil. 1.5; 4.14—16, or: table-fellowship), in the breaking of bread, and the prayers' (Acts 2.42).

Later, the resources of the primitive Church were strengthened by collections from outside communities. Such a collection was made, perhaps for the first time, in Antioch to relieve the distress of the community in Jerusalem during the famine of AD 47–49 (Acts 11.27–30; 12.25), and this was later repeated at least once during Paul's third missionary journey.[22] With reference to these collections for Jerusalem instituted by Paul in his churches K. Holl[23] would go so far as to interpret the pledge to assist the 'poor', which Paul gave to the Jerusalem apostles (Gal. 2.10), as an undertaking that the Gentile Church would make a regular contribution to Jerusalem. He can hardly be correct in this.

We come now to *public charities*. We are not concerned with a description of the OT and rabbinic legislation on social work. It is sufficient to begin by remembering only the most important regulations:

(*a*) The sabbatical year, in which all debts must be remitted (Mishnah Tractate *Shebiith*). This obligation could be evaded by using Hillel's proviso called the *prozbūl* (M. Shebi. x.4).

(*b*) The tithe for the poor (M. Peah viii.2–9; M.M. Sh. v.6 9, 10 etc. and pp. 135f.). According to this, in the third and sixth years, a tithe of the harvest produce which remained after payment of the other prescribed contributions should be given to the poor. The Mishnah (M. Ab. v.9) complains of the constant flouting of this rule, and attributes to this the prevalence of plague in the years immediately following, that is, in the fourth and seventh years of the seven-year period.

(*c*) The poor had certain legal rights during the harvest, such as field corners (M. Peah i.1ff.), gleanings (iv.10ff.), forgotten things, e.g. sheaves (v.7ff.), grapes fallen during the vintage (vii.3), and vine thinnings (vii.5). Here, too, there were complaints of evasion (M. Ab. v.9), but a number of particular details show that these rights were in many cases claimed to the full by the poor.

(*d*) In addition we may mention a list of social regulations which appear in the Talmud (b. B.K. 80b–81a Bar.) and are alleged to go back to Joshua. According to these, among other things, a man

[22] Gal. 2.10; I Cor. 16.1–4; II. Cor. 8.9; Rom. 15.25–32; Acts 24.17.

[23] K. Holl, 'Der Kirchenbegriff des Paulus in seinem Verhältnis zu dem der Urgemeinde', in *Sitzungsberichte der Preuss. Akademie der Wissenschaften*, Berlin 1921, 920–47.

could graze his cattle in woods, gather wood in private fields, and gather grass in all places except where fenugreek was growing, and fish as he wished in the Sea of Genesareth.

What public charitable institutions were to be found in Jerusalem? We already have some idea of the existence of Jewish arrangements similar to the care of the poor in the primitive Church. In connection with a legal disputation between the Jerusalem judge Hanan b. Abishalom and the chief priests, upon which Johanan b. Zakkai issued a judgement, we hear that, for example, a wife whose husband went abroad could claim maintenance from the community (M. Ket. xiii. 1–2), which she received from the poor-basket (*quppāh*). Again, when the Mishnah says that a poor man might get the four cups of wine for the Passover from the poor-dish (*tamḥūy*) if he could not procure them any other way (M. Pes. x.1), it can only refer to the time when the Passover was still celebrated in Jerusalem. An arrangement to be found only in Jerusalem is a special payment-office for the deserving poor of good families: 'There were two chambers in the Temple, the chamber of secrets (*variant*: of sins), and the chamber of utensils. Into the chamber of secrets the devout used to put their gifts in secret, and the poor of good family received support therefrom in secret' (M. Shek. v.6). Jesus may have had something like this in mind when he commended almsgiving in secret as opposed to trumpeting abroad one's generosity (Matt 6.4). Since this office was situated in the Temple, we may assume that the other arrangements for assistance were also to be found there, an assumption that is even more likely since the afore-mentioned judge Hanan, who gave judgement in the matter of maintenance, was one of the scribes paid by the Temple, and since the chief priests were involved in the matter.

Social measures were also carried out in connection with the cultus (see pp. 12f. on Temple workers). A standard of physical fitness was a prerequisite of priestly service in the Temple, and this was assessed by the Sanhedrin (M. Midd. v.4). Priests who were physically unfit were allowed to enter the Temple and were called up to perform certain functions. They used to sort out worm-eaten wood for burning, in a chamber in the north-east of the Court of Women (M. Midd. ii.5). R. Tarphon saw his uncle, a priest who was lame in one leg, blow the trumpet in the forecourt (j. Yom. i.1, 38d.32) even at the feast of Tabernacles (T. Sot. vii.16, 308). For their services these priests had a claim to that part of the revenue to which their ancestry entitled them, by virtue of their belonging to a priestly family devoted to ceremonial duties (*BJ* 5.228). In certain cases the cultus allowed considerable mitigations for poor people, as for example at the presentation of sin-offerings, when instead of a sheep two doves could be brought, and even, in cases of special poverty, a food-offering (Lev. 5.7–13; *Ant.* 3.230). People were also given the opportunity of putting their money in safe deposit in the Temple (II Macc. 3.4–6, 10–15; IV Macc. 4.1–3, 7; *BJ* 6.282)[24] and it is recorded that widows and orphans made use of this facility (II Macc. 3.10).

Finally we should mention another social measure, to be found originally only in Jerusalem. It concerned the position of widows. In Jerusalem a man took care to stipulate in his will that his widow should live in his house for the duration of her widowhood, and be supported by his estate. This became the right of all Israelite widows, and still held good even if no such provision had been made (M. Ket. iv.12.)

2. *Pilgrim traffic as a source of income*

We should be able to reach an approximate estimate of the expenditure of pilgrims in Jerusalem if it could be proved that the precepts according to which every Israelite must spend part of his annual income in Jerusalem were actually observed. These precepts were part of the rabbinic interpretation of the Mosaic Law, and involved the 'second tithe', the tithe of the herd, and the produce of trees and vines in their fourth year.[25]

The differences in the legal requirements concerning the tithe payable to the officials of the cultus on the produce of field and tree (Num. 18.20–32; Lev. 27.30.31; Deut. 14.22–26), resulted in their being interpreted as directing two tithes, the first to be delivered in kind, the second to be used in Jerusalem by the owner of the property. If a man did not wish to bring the second tithe to Jerusalem in kind, he was allowed to change it into money; but in that case he was obliged to increase it by one quarter unless he took advantage of one of the evasions listed in the Mishnah (M.M. Sh. iv.4–5). In any case, it was forbidden to use the second tithe in any place other than Jerusalem. All problems arising in this connection are dealt with in the Mishnah tractate *Ma'aser Sheni*, 'second tithe'.

The regulations concerning the second tithe show considerable alterations. The earliest evidence for a second tithe, in addition to

[24] Even in recent times in Palestine holy places were used as safe deposits. In 1914 I saw great bundles of brushwood piled up at a sacred tomb (*weli*).
[25] Schürer II, 306 n. 22.1–3, ET II.1, 240 n. 75. 1–3.

that paid over to the officials of the cultus, is provided in the LXX of Deut 26.12, in the book of Jubilees (32.8–14), and in Tobit (1.6–8)[26] according to the older of the two recensions available to us, *Codex Sinaiticus*.[27] According to this older conception, the second tithe

[26] The book of Jubilees dates from *c.* 100 BC (cf. O. Eissfeldt, *Einleitung in das Alte Testament*, 3rd ed., Tübingen 1964, 824; ET, *The Old Testament: an Introduction*, Oxford 1966, 608); Tobit is probably pre-Maccabean (*op. cit.*, 793, ET, 585).

[27] Schürer III, 243 (ET omits) rightly suggests the priority of *Codex Sinaiticus* against that of *Alexandrinus* and *Vaticanus* on Tobit, since the former in 1.6 indicates that a tithe of the herd was still due to the priests, while *Alexandrinus*, in accordance with later ruling, sets it aside. *Alexandrinus* also presents a more polished style than *Sinaiticus*. Further consideration of Tob. 1.6–8 confirms the earlier date of *Sinaiticus*.

Sinaiticus

6 'I went to Jerusalem taking the first-fruits and the first-born and the tithes of my cattle and the first shearings, and gave them to the priests, the sons of Aaron, who served at the altar.
7 And the tithe of my grain, wine, oil, pomegranates, figs and other fruit trees I gave to the sons of Levi who ministered in Jerusalem.

8 And the second tithe I converted into money in the six years, and I went and spent it in Jerusalem that year, and gave it to the orphan and the widow, and brought it to the proselytes who had joined themselves to Israel, and gave it to them in the third year, and we ate it according to the precepts.'

Alexandrinus and *Vaticanus*

6 I went to Jerusalem, taking the first-fruits and the tithes of my produce and the first shearings, and gave them to the priests, the sons of Aaron, who served at the altar.

7 Of all my produce I gave a tithe to the sons of Levi who ministered in Jerusalem. And the second tithe I sold, and went there and spent it annually in Jerusalem.

8 And the third I gave to those to whom it was due.'

Sinaiticus gives a clear meaning: v. 6 mentions dues for the priests, v. 7 those for Levites, v. 8 the remaining contributions. *Alexandrinus* and *Vaticanus* on the other hand do not give a clear meaning:

(*a*) Verse 6, in spite of the statement 'and gave them to the priests', does not really refer to the dues to the priests. For, between the first-fruits and the first shearings due to the priests, comes 'the tithes of my produce'; and since in the following passage *Alexandrinus* and *Vaticanus* mention the Levites' tithe and the second and third tithe, the passage cannot also deal with another tithe on produce due to the priests.

(*b*) Verse 6a is much more likely to refer to the entire dues which Tobias brought with him to Jerusalem, in which case the end of the verse is nonsense.

(*c*) The explanation of the matter is that *Alexandrinus* and *Vaticanus* wanted to

from the third and sixth years of each seven-year period had to be used as a poor man's tithe (Deut. 14.28–29; 26.12), and so ordinary dues would be paid only in the first, second, fourth and fifth years of the seven; in the seventh year the land had to lie entirely fallow. The book of Jubilees also takes this view that there were only two tithes, which reflects the time of its composition.

A different conception is to be found in the later text (*Alexandrinus* and *Vaticanus*) of this passage from Tobit, and this deals with three tithes. We see from Josephus (*Ant.* 4.240) that this means that the poor man's tithe of the third and sixth years was considered as a separate contribution. At the same time the second tithe was due for payment in the first six years of the seven-year period. Against this, rabbinic literature appears to have represented the older view, which was the conversion of the second tithe in the third and six years to a poor man's tithe (M.M. Sh. v.9). Finally, Philo (p. 107, n. 14) held the second tithe to be a contribution to the priests, while he allotted the first tithe to the Levites. From all these wide variations, it seems very doubtful if the second tithe was ever an entirely religious custom, and these doubts are strengthened by the fact that an entire tractate of the Mishnah (*Demai*) deals with arrangements for such produce, where it was questionable whether the producer paid both the priestly dues and the second tithe.

Similarly, the tithe of the herd (inferred from Lev. 27.32f.) belonged originally to the dues payable to the officials of the cultus. Rabbinic literature includes it in the duty which property owners must use in Jerusalem. According to this source one may not redeem the beasts if they were unblemished (M.M. Sh. i.2), but had to bring the offering in kind to Jerusalem where it had to be slaughtered as a food-offering, but without the laying on of hands (M. Hag. i.4; M. Zeb. v.8), and it could be consumed by the owner after the priests' portions had been abstracted. Even the regulations concerning tithes of cattle were very variable, as the following table shows:[28]

---

remit the tithes on the herd mentioned in *Sinaiticus* as due to the priests. This they do by carelessly substituting for 'the tithes of the herd' (where the plural is grammatically admissible) the phrase 'the tithes of my produce' (although neither the singular nor the plural of produce-tithe is suitable in the context). Therefore, *Sinaiticus* on Tobit is the earlier text.

[28] Tob. 1.6–8; Jubilees 32.15; cf. 32.2, 8; 13.26; M. Bekh. ix. 1–8, *et passim*. Philo, see p. 107 n. 14. Not much should be based on Philo's representation. He does not describe the actual position, but appears to reproduce his own view on the precepts of the Law.

	Tithe of Cattle	First Tithe (produce)	Second Tithe (produce)
Tobit (*Cod. Sin.*)	Priests	Levites	Owner
Tobit (*Cod. Alex.*)	—	Levites	Owner
Jubilees	Priests	Priests	Owner
Josephus	—	Priests	Owner
Talmud	Owner	Priests (Levites)	Owner
(Philo	Priests	Levites	Priests)

The variations are to be seen principally in the relation between the tithe of cattle, and the first and second tithes. They lead to the conclusion that, particularly in view of the silence of Josephus, this tithe of the cattle could hardly have been paid.[29]

According to the Law (Lev. 19.23–25) the produce from trees and vines could not be harvested for the first three years, and in the fourth year must be devoted to God. This is also Philo's version of the precept (*De virt.* 159). According to Jubilees the produce of the fourth year was given partly as sacrifice, and partly to the officials of the cultus (Jub. 7.36). Against this Josephus (*Ant.* 4.227) and the Mishnah (M. Peah vii.7, M.M. Sh. v.1–5) agree that it was disposed of in Jerusalem by the owner.

We are doubtful about the general carrying out of these rules. It appears from the following two examples however that the regulations concerning the second tithe and the produce of the fourth year were actually observed in many circles, for the examples bear the stamp of historicity. 'If money was found before cattle-dealers, it must be deemed to be (second) tithe; if (it was found) in the Temple Mount it may be deemed to be common money. (If it was found) in Jerusalem: at the time of a festival it was deemed to be tithe; at other times common money' (M. Shek. vii.2). Now the first tithe was for the local priests (*Vita* 63, 80), and indeed was paid in kind (*Ant.* 20. 181, 206); but here we have a kind of tithe which was brought to Jerusalem chiefly at festival times, and was changed into money. This can be only the second tithe, and the fact that the money in question was mainly used for the purchase of cattle[30] accords with this conclusion.

---

[29] This must apply to earlier times too. Benzinger, *Hebräische Archäologie*, 2nd ed., Tübingen 1907, 385, comes to the conclusion that payment of the tithe of cattle to officials of the cultus was 'simply materially impossible'.

[30] To hold money found among the cattle-dealers throughout the year to be 'second tithe' money expresses the 'more severe contingency'.

The other example is a detail contained in the statement of R. Simeon b. Gamaliel (II) to the effect that the produce of the fourth year was shared out in Jerusalem among neighbours, relations and friends, in order to decorate the bazaars of Jerusalem' (T. M. Sh. v.14, 96.10; b. Betz. 5a; b. R. Sh. 31b), so that because of the make-believe offer of crops the prices should be reduced.[31]

It can therefore be said that the various regulations quoted testify to the importance of the pilgrim traffic as a source of income for Jerusalem.

3. Income secured for the city by the cultus

The cultus provided the main source of income for the city. It maintained the priestly aristocracy, the priesthood and the Temple employees. The vast expenditure from the Temple treasury (one need think only of the rebuilding of the Temple) to say nothing of the many ceremonial activities of the devout such as sacrifices and vows —provided numerous opportunities of money-making for the trade and commerce of the city.

To sum up, the following points indicate the effect upon its inhabitants of the special character of Jerusalem:

(1) There was a large section of the population dependent on charity;

(2) There was tension caused by the social contrast that resulted from the presence of this section of the population on the one hand and, on the other, the presence of the Court and the priestly aristocracy;

(3) The city owed its well-being to its religious importance.

EXCURSUS I

The Historicity of Matthew 27.7

The account of the purchase by the high priest of the potter's field with the proceeds of Judas' treachery seems to be spurious on two counts:

(1) It could be derived from the prophetic interpretation of the passage in Zech. 11.13: 'And I took the thirty pieces of silver, and cast them to the potter in the house of the Lord' (Masoretic text);

---

[31] The divergent view of R. Simon b. Yohai is concerned only with the question whether the transport of produce in kind was required or whether its value in money could be brought to Jerusalem.

(2) It appears only in Matt. (in Acts 1.18f. Judas bought the field himself).

Nevertheless, we would make four points:

(a) The statement that Judas brought the money to the Temple cannot be said to derive from prophecy. The whole thing has been explained as follows: Matthew tried to take into account not only the *yōṣēr* (potter) of the MT of Zech. 11.13, but also the Syriac version which implies a reading *oṣar* (treasury), therefore, 'and cast it to the *treasury* in the house of the Lord'. To do this, he describes the field as the potter's field, and makes Judas bring the money to the Temple, thus giving the impression in the passage that it was paid into the Temple treasury (Matt. 27.6). From this we may conclude that neither the description of the field as the potter's field (Matt. 27.7), nor the idea that Judas brought the money to the Temple, can be historical.

This explanation, which assumes what amounts to a knowledge of textual criticism on the part of Matthew, who immediately confuses Zechariah with Jeremiah (Matt. 27.9), seems to me indefensible. Rather say that Matthew read *yōṣēr* with the MT, as in 27.10. The fact that Judas brought the money to the Temple was in accordance with custom, and must be historical.

The Mishnah indeed gives us evidence of a custom already established before the time of Jesus. In certain cases, the man who originally owned the money (i.e. the buyer of goods, e.g. of a house) might attempt to avoid accepting it back (should the seller wish to revoke the sale); then the seller would take the money to the Temple and by this means the sale could be revoked. M. Arak. ix.4 says, 'If a man sold a house . . . he may redeem it at once at any time during twelve months. . . . If the last day of the twelfth month was come and it was not redeemed, it became the buyer's for ever. . . . The buyer used to hide himself on the last day of the twelve months so that the house might be his for ever; but Hillel the elder ordained that he that sold it could deposit his money in the Temple chamber, and break down the door and enter, and that the other, when he would, might come and take his money.' Matt. 27.5 may provide an analogous instance. Judas brought the money to the Temple, not simply to make a repayment to the treasury, but so that a completed sale might be revoked; true, it was not a house that was sold, as in the Mishnah, but the person of Jesus. The procedure is this: The buyers, the chief priests and the elders, i.e. the Sanhedrin (Matt. 27.3), refused the repayment of the money. Thereupon Judas brought it to the Temple as a means of revoking the sale. In the Temple the money was deemed ownerless, and the chief priests (Matt. 27.6) became responsible for its expenditure. We may notice that in v. 3 the chief priests are spoken of as members of the Sanhedrin, but in v. 6 in their capacity as an executive body of the Temple. Hence it follows that the idea that Judas brought the money to the Temple was not dependent on prophecy; accordingly, the Temple is not the point at issue in Matt. 27.9–10.

(b) Furthermore, the chief priests' scruple about keeping the money in the Temple treasury, and their decision to buy the field 'to bury strangers in' (i.e. pilgrims), are quite credible. It is attested in the Talmud that any ill-gotten gains, or property which had become ownerless (e.g. stolen goods whose owner could not now be traced), were devoted to the treasury, but were used for some public requirement, e.g. the water supply to Jerusalem.[32]

(c) The price of a field at 120 denarii (see p. 120 n. 1) can be shown to be an average price. The price of a field mentioned in M. Arak. viii.1 as one as, 1/24 denarius,[33] is a casuistical illustration. M. Arak. ix.2 mentions 1 and 2 minas, that is 100 and 200 denarii; viii.2 tells of bidding for a field at 10, 20, 30, 40, 50 shekels,[34] that is 40, 80, 120, 160, 200 denarii. Therefore, the average price of a field is 120 denarii.

(d) The name of the field, Akeldama (Acts 1.19, cf. Matt. 27.8), as well as its use for burying strangers, does not come from prophecy. It is more likely that the name Akeldama (Acts 1.19), then in common use, originally meant 'a cemetery', and in fact the Temple authorities used it as a place of burial.

Consequently, I think it quite possible that Judas brought the money to the Temple to revoke the sale, and it was used by the Temple authorities to buy a burial ground. Particular points, such as the designation of the field, usually called Akeldama, as the potter's field, and its traditional localization in the valley of Hinnom (probably to be traced to a combination of the Zechariah passage with Jer. 19.1f.; 18.2f.) are due to the later interpretation of Zech. 11.13 as a prophecy. As regards the sum of money, the price of betrayal, a definite decision is hardly possible.

EXCURSUS II

Disasters in Jerusalem

The following survey is concerned with the period from 169 BC (the first capture of Jerusalem by Antiochus IV, Epiphanes) until AD 70 (the destruction of Jerusalem). It excludes the cases where the disaster was a direct result of war alone.

(1) When Jerusalem was besieged at the time of Antiochus V (Eupator) in 163 BC, the famine was made more severe because the ground had lain

---

[32] b. Betz. 29a Bar.; b.B.K. 94b; cf. Bill. I, 37 on Deut. 23.19.

[33] Bill. I, 291. This would buy two sparrows, Matt. 10.29, or two and a half, Luke 12.6.

[34] M. Arak. iii.3 equates an OT shekel with a *sil'ā'* = 4 denarii.

fallow in the sabbatical year of 164/3. The famine affected the besieged most of all, since they soon used up the stocks they had in the city, but it affected the besiegers also (*Ant.* 12.378; cf. I Macc. 6.49, 53f.).

(2) Some time before 65 BC (i.e. before the siege of Aristobulus II in the Temple by Hyrcanus II and the Arab king Aretas) there had been a drought. The longed-for rain followed the prayers of a pious man called Onias (*Ant.* 14.22). The rabbinic account no doubt refers to the same incident when describing how no rain had fallen by the latter part of the month of Adar (the beginning of March when the rainy season is usually coming to an end), and the prayer of Honi the 'circle-maker' produced rain. So effective was this prayer, that people had to take shelter in the Temple, because of the cloudburst which now followed, and the resultant heavy flooding. Incidentally, this shows that the event occurred in Jerusalem (M. Taan. iii.8; b. Taan. 23a Bar.).

(3) After the Passover of 64 BC a hurricane devastated the crops of the entire country (*Ant.* 14.28).

(4) The siege of Jerusalem by Herod in 37 BC fell in the sabbatical year of 38/7 BC, so that famine broke out in the city. The besiegers also suffered want, since their enemies had plundered the whole neighbourhood (*Ant.* 14.471; 15.7; *BJ* 1.347).

(5) In Herod's seventh year (reckoned from the sack of Jerusalem in 37 BC, and not from his recognition as king in 40 BC), 31 BC, an earthquake occurred which destroyed part of the livestock of the country (*BJ.* 1.370; *Ant.* 15.121).

(6) After the execution of Queen Mariamne in 29 BC the country suffered from an epidemic (*Ant.* 15.243).

(7) The famine which broke out in Herod's thirteenth year, 25/24 BC, had particularly catastrophic results, and ran its course in different stages:

(*a*) First there was a prolonged drought so that the land remained unproductive and without the smallest yield.

(*b*) Then sickness spread, an epidemic of plague that was due to a changed way of life following shortage of food. All these miseries aggravated each other, for the lack of food and care increased the epidemic sickness which had been violent from the beginning; and the death of those who succumbed robbed the survivers of the will to live, for they could see no prospect of an end to their misery.

(*c*) The second harvest also failed (*Ant.* 15.299f.).

(*d*) The people were 'in need of clothing, for their flocks had been destroyed and completely consumed, so that they had no wool to use, or any other material for covering themselves' (*Ant.* 15.310).

(8) Under Claudius Caesar (AD 41–54) there was a great famine in Palestine, the extent of which is evident from the number of different reports about it.

(a) When Helena of Adiabene made her pilgrimage to Jerusalem, a famine was raging there (*Ant.* 20.51). There are more precise details concerning the date of this in *Ant.* 20.101 where the account is introduced by ἐπὶ τούτοις.[35] If this can be taken as masculine, as in the Latin translation and consistent with the context, it implies that the famine took place under two procurators, Cuspius Fadus and Tiberius Alexander. If, on the contrary, ἐπὶ τούτοις is taken as neuter, then the famine may be placed only in the time of Tiberius Alexander. This is how the *Epitome* takes it, and this alone must be correct on the basis of Josephus' style, for he never uses ἐπί with the dative but always the genitive for indicating dates. In any case, the famine took place under Tiberius Alexander.

The following facts are known about the time the two men were in office: Cuspius Fadus took office after the death of Agrippa I, i.e. after the Passover of AD 44 (*Ant.* 20.1f.). From a decree of the year 45, we may assume that he was still then in office (*Ant.* 20.14). For Tiberius Alexander, we know only the approximate date of the end of his period of office. His dismissal is reported as coming immediately before the decease of Herod of Chalcis, which took place in the eighth year of the reign of Claudius, 24 January 48/49 (*Ant.* 20.103f.), so that it may probably be placed in the year 48. The change of office, therefore took place in 46 or 47, and the famine occurred in one of the years between 46–48.

(b) *Ant.* 3.320 mentions a famine which broke out when Claudius was emperor and Ishmael was Jewish high priest, which was particularly hard on Jerusalem. The answer to the problem of which famine in the reign of Claudius is meant here (Claudius reigned from 24 January 41–13 October 54), depends upon the dating of Ishmael's term of office. From this, one might arrive at a date later than AD 54, since Josephus first mentions the appointment of Ishmael (*Ant.* 20.179) after Nero's accession to the throne after Claudius (*Ant.* 20.148–57); but we cannot set much store by this, for in *Ant.* 20.137–59 he describes first the events in Rome connected with the family history of Nero's descendants, before turning to the situation in Palestine. On the contrary, it is quite certain that Ishmael was appointed before the nomination of Porcius Festus as governor of Judaea (*Ant.* 20.182), and therefore during the governorship of Antonius Felix. It was after the recall of Cumanus at the end of AD 52 (Tacitus, *Ann.* XII, 54), that Antonius Felix became governor of the province of Judaea (*Ant.* 20.137; *BJ* 2.247). Before this, he had simply controlled the district of Samaria (Tacitus, *ibid.*), while that of Judaea, as well as Galilee, had been under Cumanus (*Ant.* 20.100–17). The date at the end of 52 for the nomination of Antonius Felix as governor of Judaea is confirmed by

---

[35] So read all MSS, and also Eusebius, *HE* II, 12.1, where the passage is quoted, and the Latin '*horum temporibus*'. Only the *Epitome* (ed. B. Niese, Berlin 1896, 352) has the singular.

Josephus, who states that the enlargement of Agrippa II's dominions at the beginning of 53 took place after the nomination of Felix (*Ant.* 20.138; *BJ* 2.247). However, we see from Acts 23.2; 24.1 that Ananias the predecessor of Ishmael was in office under Felix, in fact for a feast of Pentecost (Acts 20.16), and therefore the Pentecost of 53 at the earliest. Since according to *Ant.* 3.320 the famine in the time of Ishmael took place at a Passover, we must consider this at the earliest to be the Passover of 54. Even this possibility is ruled out if we are to accept the chronology of Acts, according to which Paul came to Jerusalem at the earliest at the Pentecost of 55, therefore, when Ananias was still in office (Acts 23.2; 24.1). In this case, a mistake must have crept into Josephus' account since Ishmael was not high priest under Claudius. Since Josephus, in connection with his description of the reign of Claudius, knows only of the famine mentioned under (*a*), which took place in a year between 46 and 48, we must substitute for Ishmael one of his two predecessors Joseph or Ananias, and refer *Ant.* 3.320 to the same famine.

(*c*) Further, by knowing the cycle of sabbatical years, it is possible to find other references to the course of this famine under Claudius, which was prophesied by Agabus in Acts 11.28. We know that the year of autumn 47–48 was a sabbatical year, for M. Sot. vii.8 testifies to the sabbatical year of 40–41.[36] The famine must, therefore, have run the following course: Summer 47, the harvest failed; the sabbatical year 47–48 aggravated the famine, and prolonged it until the next harvest of spring 49.

(*d*) It is possible that this famine under Claudius is described in rabbinic literature. The elder Eleazar, son of R. Zadoq, records that as in his youth he was learning the Torah from R. Johanan b. Hauranit he saw him eat his bread dry, 'because it was the year of the drought' (b. Yeb. 15b; T. Sukk. ii.3.193; T. Eduy. ii.2,457). Schlatter[37] rightly deduces from this that it is more likely to refer to the famine under Claudius, than to the shortage during the siege of Jerusalem in AD 70. This period is also indicated by other information about Eleazar, especially that in T. Sanh. ix.11 (429), which tells how, when riding on his father's shoulder as a boy, he had been witness to the burning of a priest's daughter. This occurrence indicates a time when criminal justice could be executed without hindrance, and the most likely time for this was the reign of Agrippa I. Eleazar must have received instruction at a very early age, for Agrippa I, in whose time he was still a child, reigned only three years.

(*g*) Not long before AD 66 there was a shortage of water in Jerusalem during one of the three pilgrim festivals. The mention of a Roman commander-in-chief points to a time before 66, as also does the fact that Naqdemon b. Gorion is mentioned as an outstanding man. He was one of

36 Cf. my article, 'Sabbathjahr', *ZNW* 27, 1928, 100 n. 9, *Abba*, 235 n. 15.
37 Schlatter, *Tage* 8of.

the richest men in Jerusalem at the time of the Jewish war (b. Taan. 19b–20a Bar.). A similar occasion of the failure of rainfall during the decade before the destruction of the Temple is recalled by the report that Joḥanan b. Zakkai produced rain after a prolonged drought (j. Taan. iii.13, 67a.40).

(10) It must have been during the late summer of the year 69 that a drought occurred which was described by Josephus: 'For before his (Titus') coming, as you know, Siloam and all the springs outside the town were failing insomuch that water was sold by the *amphora*' (*BJ* 5.410). Moreover, the year from autumn 68 to autumn 69 was a sabbatical year.[38]

By way of appendix we must mention that the name 'Jerusalem locust' would seem to indicate occasional plagues of locusts (b. Hull. 65a).[39]

[38] Schürer I, 35, ET I.1, 41.
[39] I had experience of this in the summer of 1915, when Jerusalem was infested by a great swarm of locusts.

PART THREE

SOCIAL STATUS

VIII

THE CLERGY

A. THE HOLDER OF THE PRIMACY

The reigning high priest

B. THE CHIEF PRIESTS

The captain of the Temple

1. Cultus	*2. Custody of the Temple*	*3. Temple finances*
The leaders of the twenty-four weekly courses and of their daily courses	Temple overseers	Three treasurers

C. THE PRIESTS

Twenty-four weekly courses, each of
four to nine daily courses,
with about 7,200 priests

D. THE LEVITES (CLERUS MINOR)

Twenty-four weekly courses, each divided into:
1. Singers and musicians
2. Temple servants and guards
with about 9,600 Levites

A. THE HIGH PRIEST[1]

'While different races base their claims to nobility on various grounds,
with us a connection with the priesthood is the hallmark of **an**

---

[1] There is valuable material on the priesthood in Schürer II, 267–363, ET II.1,

illustrious line,' so Josephus confidently decides in his autobiography (*Vita* 1). In fact, Israel at the time of Jesus was a pure theocracy, and the priesthood was the primary representative of the nobility. Thus the reigning head of the priests, in times when there was no king, was the most eminent member of the nation. We must therefore concern ourselves first with him, the high priest (*kōhēn gādōl*), as the most important member of the priesthood and consequently of the whole people.

The leading position of the high priest is based upon the cultic character of his office, the 'lifelong sanctity' (*qᵉduššat 'ōlām*, M. Naz. vii.1; *character indelebilis*) of one authorized by God (b. Kidd. 23b: the priest is God's agent in the offering of sacrifices) to make atonement for the sins of the whole community (Ex. 30.10; Lev. 16). This character of office was transmitted to him by the investiture with the eight parts of the splendid high-priestly vesture.[2] This vesture possessed atoning power and each of its eight parts atoned for specific sins.[3] Consequently, for Jewry it was the very symbol of their religion. Only thus can it be understood that neither Herod the Great, Archelaus, nor the Romans later could find a more effective safeguard against rebellion than to keep the high-priestly robes in custody in the temple fortress of Antonia, handing them over to the high priest only

---

195–305; but unfortunately he does not sufficiently consider Talmudic material other than the Mishnah. See also A. Büchler, *Die Priester und der Cultus im letzten Jahrzehnt des jerusalemischen Tempels*, Vienna 1895, though his basic theory of a great revolution in the Temple in AD 62 and the following years, with the Sadducees overthrown by the Pharisees, falls to the ground because of a complete lack of concrete evidence. The Herodian Temple is described in Dalman's excellent piece of research, 'Der zweite Tempel zu Jerusalem', *PJB* 5, 1909, 29–57. W. Bousset and H. Gressmann, *Die Religion des Judentums im späthellenistischen Zeitalter*, 3rd ed., Tübingen 1926, seriously underrate the importance of the cultus and the priesthood, and ignore almost all the questions to be dealt with here.

[2] This consisted of the four priestly vestments: the white linen robe, the white linen trousers, the turban and the girdle. There were also four special items: the breastplate, the ephod (a kind of apron with shoulder-straps), the tunic, drawn on over the head, and the golden diadem, which fits on to the turban (Ex. 28–29; Ecclus. 45.6–13; Pseudo-Aristeas 96–99; *BJ* 5. 231ff.; *Ant.* 3. 159ff.; Philo, *De vit. Mos.* II, 109–35; *De spec. leg.* I, 84–91; M. Yom. vii. 5, etc.).

[3] The account of the atoning power of the eight parts of the vesture is in Cant. R. 4.7 on 4.2 (Son. 4.5, 189), and b. Zeb. 88b. In addition, there are occasional single references. In T. Pes. vi.5, 165, the golden diadem atones for uncleanness in the blood of the sacrifice and in the person offering the sacrifice, but in Nazirite and Passover offerings it atoned only for uncleanness in the blood of the sacrifice and for pollution of the offerer by a 'grave of the deep' (unnoticed pollution from a corpse buried in the ground), cf. j. Yom. i.2, 39a. 26.

on feast days. It also explains why the Jews struggled so tenaciously to have the vestments released, a struggle which ended only when the Emperor Claudius ordered their release by a decree in his own hand, on 28 June AD 45; for the campaign over the high priest's vesture was for Jewry a religious campaign (*Ant.* 18.90ff.; 20.6ff. cf. also 15.403).[4] It is especially significant, however, for the cultic character which the high priest possessed *ex officio*, that his death had power to atone.[5] As soon as the high priest died, all homicides who had fled from their avengers to the 'cities of refuge' (Num. 35.9ff.; Deut. 19.1ff.; cf. Ex. 21.23) were free and might return home (Num. 35.25; M. Makk. ii.6), and according to the prevailing opinion of the scribes they might even take up their former positions (M. Makk. ii.8). The death of the high priest had, by virtue of his office, expiated the guilt incurred by accidental homicide.

This special character of the high priest's office involved a number of unique privileges and responsibilities. The most important *privilege* was that of being the only human being with the right to enter the Holy of Holies, on one particular day of the year. The threefold entrance[6] into the Holy of Holies on the Day of Atonement signified the approach to the gracious presence of God, which was manifested in the fact that several high priests were granted divine manifestations in the Holy of Holies. Simeon the Righteous (after 200 BC)[7] and John Hyrcanus, 134–104 BC (b. Sot. 33a Bar. and par.; *Ant.* 13.282; cf. 300; 322) heard heavenly voices from the Holy of Holies. The same Simeon the Righteous (b. Yom. 39ab Bar.)[8] and Ishmael (either I, c. AD 15–16, or II, AD 55–61)[9] had visions there,

---

[4] The vesture was in Roman hands from AD 6–37, when it was released by Vitellius. When the procurator Cuspius Fadus (AD 44) tried to take it back into custody, a Jewish delegation to Rome succeeded in obtaining an edict from Claudius which confirmed the action of Vitellius.

[5] For the atoning powers of the priest's daily sacrifice, see Bill. III, 697e.

[6] M. Yom. v.1–4; quite remarkably, T. Kel. B.K. i.7, 569; Num. R. 7.8 on 5.2 (Son. 195) gives four times, and R. Jose (Num. R. ibid.) even has five times.

[7] b. Sot. 33a Bar. and par. G. F. Moore, 'Simeon the Righteous', *Jewish Studies in Memory of Israel Abrahams*, New York 1927, 348–464. In this brilliant essay Moore has proved that Simeon the Righteous lived after 200 BC, and that the alleged Simeon I, who is said to have lived in the time of Ptolemy I (323 or 306 to 285 BC) (*Ant.* 12.43; 4.157) owes his existence to a duplication by Josephus of the same person. Guthe recognized this duplication (*Geschichte des Volkes Israel* 1914, 318) but took the earlier Simeon as the historical one.

[8] This Baraita passage develops from T. Sot. xiii.8, 319, where however the name of Simeon is not mentioned.

[9] b. Ber. 7a Bar. This passage confuses a high priest Ishmael with R. Ishmael b. Elisha, who was executed c. AD 135. See Bill. II, 79 n.

and John 11.51 ascribed to the high priest, whoever he was, the gift
of prophecy. In fear and trembling (for the slightest breach of the
ceremonial rules would be visited by divine judgment), the high
priest carried out his duties in the most holy place which lay dark,
empty and silent behind the double curtain.[10]

Next, there were privileges for the high priest in the cultus,
especially that of taking part in the sacrifice at any time he liked.[11]
In addition he had the right to offer sacrifice as a mourner, which
was forbidden to the rest of the priests.[12] Furthermore, the high priest
had the right of first choice in the distribution of the 'holy things of
the temple' to the officiating priests.[13] In this distribution he could
choose: (1) a sin offering—either beast (T. Yom. i.5, 180; b. Yom.
17b) or bird (Siphra Lev. 2.3, 6d,); (2) a guilt-offering (T. Yom.
i.5, 180; b. Yom. 17b); (3) a portion of the food-offering, taken from
what remained after the offering had been made on the altar (j. Yom.
i.2, 29a. 11; Siphra Lev. 2.3, 6d); (4) four or five, or even six according to others, of the twelve loaves of unleavened shew-bread distributed each week (four to five loaves: T. Yom. i.5, 180; b. Yom.
17b. six loaves: j. Yom. i.2, 39d.64; right of first choice without
specific number: Siphra Lev. 24.9, 53a); (5) one of the two leavened
loaves of the first-fruits at the feast of Pentecost (Lev. 23.17; T. Yom.
i.5, 180; j. Yom. i.2, 38d.63; b. Yom. 17b); and (6) a hide of the
burnt-offering (j. Yom. i.2, 38d.63; i.2, 39a.2).[14] Among his

---

[10] b. Yom. 19b Bar. describes the divine punishment of a Sadducean high priest.
M. Yom. v.1; j. Yom. v.2, 42c. 17ff., rule that the high priest must say only a short
prayer in the Holy of Holies, so that the people do not take fright and become
anxious that some calamity has befallen him. When the rites of the Day of Atonement were happily ended, the high priest, accompanied by all the people, went
home rejoicing (b. Yom. 71b), and he prepared a feast for his friends 'for that he
was come forth safely from the sanctuary' (M. Yom. vii.4).

[11] M. Yom. i.2; M. Tam. vii.3. According to b. Yom. 17b this precedence
applied to all sacrifices. Cf. j. Yom. 39a.23 where it is stated that the high priest
sacrificed the votive and free-will offerings in the week before the Day of Atonement.

[12] M. Hor. iii.5. This exceptional position for the high priest was derived from
Lev. 10, where Aaron offered a sin offering despite the deaths of his two sons, and
only abstained from eating the flesh of the sacrifice (10.19).

[13] M. Yom. i.2; T. Yom. i.5, 180; j. Yom. 1.2, 38d. 63–39a.4; b. Yom. 17b;
Siphra Lev. 2.3 6d; Siphra Lev. 24.9, 53a. The conclusion drawn by R. Judah I
(d.217) from the words, 'Aaron and his sons' in Lev. 2.3, that the high priest had a
claim to half of the whole lot (T. Yom. i.5, 180, etc.), is later interpretation which
has nothing to do with the practice at the time of the Temple, when only the priority
of choice of the high priest was known.

[14] The theft of hides by the 'ruling families of the priesthood', spoken of in b.
Pes. 57a Bar; T. Zeb. xi. 16, 497, is an example of the misuse of the high-priestly
right of first choice.

additional privileges, the most prominent were the presidency of the council, the Sanhedrin, which was the highest administrative and judicial authority of Jewry; and the judiciary principle that if the high priest committed a capital offence he could be sentenced only by the Sanhedrin (M. Sanh. i.5).

The *responsibilities* of the high priest too were naturally mainly of a ceremonial nature. While the Law specifically demanded no more than that the high priest should officiate on the Day of Atonement (Lev. 16), prevailing custom involved him more deeply in cultic commitments. The Mishnah records that he had to participate in the burning of the Red Heifer (M. Par. iii.5, *et passim*; the Law concerning the 'Red Heifer' is in Num. 19), and that he had services to perform in the week before the Day of Atonement, as practice in carrying out the ritual of this Day according to the rules of the scribes of the Pharisaic party (M. Yom. i.2).[15] Then we learn from Josephus and the Talmud that it was the custom for the high priest to officiate also on Sabbaths, at the feast of the new moon, at the three pilgrim festivals (Passover or Unleavened Bread, Pentecost and Tabernacles) and at gatherings of the people (*Ant.* 15.408).[16] On the other hand, he did not have to perform personally the daily meal offering which the law said the son of Aaron must offer morning and evening[17] but simply to pay for it.[18] Other financial obligations of the

[15] 'Throughout the seven days he must, (*a*) sprinkle the blood [of the daily morning and evening sacrifice on the altar of burnt-offering] and (*b*) burn the incense [on the altar of incense in the Holy Place], and (*c*) trim the lamps [of the seven-branched candlestick], and (*d*) offer the head and the [right] hind leg [of the morning and evening sacrifices, on the altar of burnt-offering]'.

[16] Before a feast (*Ant.* 18.94: before the three pilgrim festivals and the Day of Atonement) the high priestly vestments were brought from the fortress of Antonia. There is further confirmation that the high priest officiated on days other than the Day of Atonement in I Macc. 10.21; *Ant.* 13.372; 15.51 (Jonathan, Alexander Jannaeus and Aristobulus officiated at Tabernacles). Josephus gives the most detailed account in *BJ* 5.230, where the high priest officiates 'on sabbaths, at the new moon, at family [or traditional] festivals, and any other assemblies of the people in the course of the year.' This evidence is in complete accord with the saying of R. Joshua b. Levi (*c.* AD 250), handed down by R. Uqbah, that the high priest officiated on sabbaths and festivals (j. Yom. i.2, 39a.25).

[17] Lev. 6.12–16; *Ant.* 3.257; LXX I Chron. 9.31; Ecclus. 45.14; Philo, *De victimis* 15; M. Yom. ii.3; iii.4, *et passim* in the Mishnah. Generally this offering consisted of a tenth of an ephah (3.94 litres = nearly 7 pints, probably between 4 and 5lbs.) of fine meal, kneaded with oil and baked in a pan. Afterwards the prepared cakes were broken in pieces, oil was poured over them, and half were offered in the morning and half in the evening (Schürer II, 348, ET II.1, 287f.)

[18] *Ant.* 3.257, cf. M. Shek. vii.6: at the high priest's expense. M. Yom. ii.3–5; M. Tam. iii.1; iv.3: the daily offering by the officiating priestly course.

high priest were the cost of the bullock slain as a sin-offering on the
Day of Atonement (Lev. 16.3; *Ant.* 3.242; M. Hor. iii.4), and payment of the cost of building the bridge over the Kidron Valley, which
a credible—even if slightly exaggerated—report says, had to be made
ready when the Red Heifer (Num. 19) was to be burned on the
Mount of Olives (j. Shek. iv.3, 48a.35; M. Shek iv.2).[19] The ceremony
is said to have taken place only five, or possibly seven, times during
the last three hundred years of the Temple's existence. (M. Par.
iii.5: R. Me'ir says five times, the Teachers, seven times).

Other official duties of the high priest were the carrying out of
regulations to assure his ceremonial purity. He might not touch a
corpse, or enter a house of mourning, and at a funeral he might not
follow immediately behind a bier (M. Sanh. ii.i; R. Me'ir's testimony). He was also forbidden to show the usual signs of mourning
by allowing his hair to become dishevelled and tearing his clothes
(Lev. 21.10; 10.6).[20] The fact that there was no relaxation of this
rule even for a near relative shows how strict were the regulations.
Whereas for all other priests exceptions were made, to the effect that
a priest need not avoid contact with the bodies of close relations, such
as parents, children, brothers, unmarried sisters living in a brother's
house, and wives (Lev. 21.1–4; Ezek. 44.25–27),[21] only a single
exception was made for the high priest. This was the case of the *mēt
miṣwāh* (b. Naz. 47b), that is, of a dead man who had no next-of-kin,
when the last offices were the duty of whoever found him. Even this
exception was contested. The Pharisees upheld it, placing compassion
above the strict maintenance of ceremonial purity for the high priest.
The Sadducees, however, those staunch upholders of the letter of the
law, rejected even this one exception (M. Naz. vii.1).

Especially on the Day of Atonement had the high priest to be in a
state of absolute levitical purity. For this reason, in the week before
the Day he had to undergo the seven-day period of purification prescribed in Num. 19, so as to eliminate any possibility of defilement
through contact with the dead (M. Par. iii.1; Philo, *De somniis* I,

---

[19] It is stated here that the bridge was paid for from the Temple treasury, but
Abba Saul disputed this and affirmed that the high priests had it built at their
own expense.

[20] The other priests were forbidden only to shave the head, cut off the fringe
of the beard and tattoo the skin (Lev. 21.5–6). According to Ezek. 44.20, dishevelled hair as a sign of mourning was also forbidden.

[21] The wife is not mentioned in the text, but the Rabbis interpreted the word
šeʾērō, 'his blood relation', as wife (Siphra Lev. 21.2, 46d).

214). Besides this, during the week beginning 3 Tishri, to be precise, from the conclusion of the evening sacrifice (j. Yom. i.2, 39a.22; statement of R. Joshua b. Levi, *c.* AD 250) he had to take up his lodging in his official room in the Temple on the south side of the priests' forecourt,[22] and to spend his nights there (M. Yom. i.1), so as to exclude all possibility of contracting levitical uncleanliness, particularly through his wife (T. Yom. i.1, 180: avoidance of *niddā* uncleanness, which would have kept him unclean for seven days). The nightly seclusion of the high priest in the week before the Day of Atonement may have been instituted about AD 20, as a consequence of the defilement of the high priest Simeon, son of Kamithos (AD 17–18), who on the evening before the Day, at the gathering darkness was touched by an Arab's spittle and was thereby prevented from officiating[23] on the Day.[24] So steps were taken to guard against a repetition of any such levitical defilement of the high priest before the Day of Atonement. A third precaution against his defilement at this time consisted in keeping him awake on the preceding night (M.

[22] M. Yom. i.1 calls the official room, *liškat palhedrīn* (T. Yom. i.1, 180 etc. *liškat parhedrīn*), i.e. room of the προεδροι, or, room of the court presidents. The meaning in Levy, *WB* IV, 103b, room of the πάρεδροι, room of assessors of the court, is mistaken. So is the term given by R. Jehuda, *liškat palwātīn*, room of the βουλευται (T. Yom. i.1, 180). Actually the room was clearly, in contrast to the council room, *liškat ha-gāzīt*, not for the use of all the members of the Temple court, but only for the presiding high priest. A Baraitha in b. Yom 8b. understands some contempt in calling the high priest 'the president of the council': from the time when the high priest's office was no longer lifelong, but, as in the case of a president of a civil court, for twelve months only, his official chamber had been called 'the room of the president of the council.' There is, however, no contemptuous reference in this designation. From M. Midd. v.4 we learn that the official chamber of the high priest lay in the south of the Court of the Priests, and was under the same roof as the adjoining 'Chamber of Hewn Stone' where the Sanhedrin sat, half of which was on sacred ground, and half was not (b. Yom. 25a). It was only appropriate that the official chamber of the high priests, lying as it did next to the council chamber, should be called the President's Room.

[23] Cf. A. Büchler, 'The Levitical impurity of the Gentiles in Palestine before the year 70' *JQR* 17, 1926, 1–81, esp. 8.

[24] b. Yom. 47a for an Arab's spittle. T. Yom. iv.20, 189; j. Yom. i.1, 38d.6; j. Meg. i.12, 72a. 49; j. Hor. iii.5, 47d. 11; Lev. R. 20.7 on 16.1–2 (Son. 20.11, 263); Num. R. 2.22 on 3.4 (Son. 2.26, 63); *Tanhuma, aḥare mot* 7, 433.24: spittle of an Arab sheikh. b. Yom. 47a: spittle from a certain [Gentile] lord. The variant, spittle of a Sadducee, b. Nid. 33b Bar.; T. Nid. v.3, 645, is obviously an anti-Sadducaic alteration: it is highly unlikely that a high priest would have felt himself so defiled by the spittle of a Sadducee that he could not officiate on the Day of Atonement, especially as the Sadducees were very strict about the Law (though, of course, only in accordance with Sadducaic exegesis), and the high priests themselves were Sadducees. Simeon's brother functioned as his substitute.

Yom. i.6–7) to avoid the kind of defilement mentioned at the end of
Lev. 22.4.

Next to the maintenance of his capacity to officiate which was the
object of these strict rules of purity, it was important for the high
priest to be certain of the immaculate *purity of his descent*, since according to Law his office was hereditary. This concern involved strict
rules about *marriage*, to which he was subject. The Old Testament
precept that the high priest must marry a virgin, while widows,
divorced women, violated women and prostitutes were forbidden to
him (Lev. 21. 13–15), was interpreted thus in rabbinic exegesis: On
the one hand, the concept of 'virgin' was restricted to girls from twelve
to twelve and a half years of age (M. Yeb. vi.4),[25] while, by contrast,
the range of prohibited women was enlarged. 'Widows' included a
woman whose betrothed had died before marriage (M. Yeb. vi.4);[26]
'divorced' included a girl whose engagement had been broken off
(Philo, *De spec. leg.* I, 107); a 'defiled woman' was interpreted to
mean the daughter of a priest's illegal marriage (Siphra Lev. 21.14,
47d); and 'prostitute' could mean a proselyte, a manumitted slave
and any deflorated woman, such as for example a woman taken
prisoner in wartime (M. Yeb. vi.5). This means that rabbinic exegesis
limited the right of marriage for the high priest to such an extent that
he could marry only a virgin of twelve to twelve and a half years who
was the daughter of a priest, a Levite or an Israelite of legitimate
descent. When Philo, misled by the LXX version of Lev. 21. 13, 14,[27]
restricts the precept to daughters of priests, thereby excluding the
daughters of Levites and Israelites from marriage with the high priest
(*De spec. leg.* I, 110), he must in fact have been describing not the
precepts valid in Palestine but rather the prevailing custom there; at
all events, we know of several high priests whose wives were the
daughters of priests.

(*a*) The high priest Mattaiah, son of Theophilus (5–4 BC) was,
according to *Ant.* 17.164, brother-in-law of the high priest Joazar (4

---

[25] But in the same passage another interpretation by R. Eleazar and R. Simon
refuses to restrict the concept to girls of twelve to twelve and a half years. In addition
those girls who by an unlucky chance had lost the evidence of their maidenhood
were also barred.

[26] The ban on levirate marriage (i.e. with the widow of a brother who had
died childless) in M. Sanh. ii.1 was already included in the literal meaning of
Lev. 21.14.

[27] 'And he shall take a wife in her virginity . . . a virgin of his own people
. . .'. The words, 'of his own people.', are added in the LXX.

BC). His wife and Joazar were the children of the high priest Simeon (called Boethus), *c.* 22–5 BC.

(*b*) The high priest Caiaphas (*c.* AD 18–37) married the daughter of the high priest Annas (AD 6–15, see John 18.13).

(*c*) The high priest Joshua son of Gamaliel (*c.* AD 63–65) was married to Martha (Lam. R. 1.50 on 1.16, Son. 1.47, 128: Miriam) of the high-priestly family of Boethus (M. Yeb. vi.4; b. Yom. 18a, cf. above p. 95).

Since all the wives mentioned came from high-priestly families, it may be concluded that the high priests preferred to marry women from the priestly nobility, or at least those of priestly descent. On the other hand, we hear of wives of non-priestly families only in the case of the wife of Alexander Jannaeus,[28] the Hasmonean high priest, and the wife of the high priest Pinhas of Habta, who was put into office by the Zealots in AD 67, and whom R. Hananiah b. Gamaliel (*c.* AD 120) called 'our son-in-law', i.e. a relation by marriage (T. Yom. i.6, 180; Siphra Lev. 21.10, 47c).[29] However, this last instance, which is credible, is of very little significance since Pinhas, up to the time when he took office as high priest, was a simple country priest and stonemason.

The rules affecting the marriage of the high priest were in no way mere lifeless rules; if they were broken, the whole Pharisaic party, indeed all the people, protested loudly. The Hasmonean John Hyrcanus (134–104 BC) had to listen to the Pharisee Eleazar reproving him, saying that he was an illegitimate high priest and must resign his office for himself and for his descendants, because his mother, wife of the high priest Simon (142 or 141–134 BC) had been taken captive in war under Antiochus Epiphanes IV, and so could no longer have been the legitimate wife of a high priest (*Ant.* 13. 288ff.).[30] We have already seen that a war captive was placed on the

---

[28] It is said in b. Ber. 48a *et passim* that Alexander Jannaeus was married to the sister of a non-priestly scribe R. Simon b. Shetah. Unfortunately there is no other evidence of this statement, which in any case is extremely dubious.

[29] The statement in Gen. R. 98.22 on 49.20 (Son 98.16, 966), cf. 79.13 on 30.13 (Son 79.10, 661), that the high priests preferred a daughter of the tribe of Asser is a worthless pun on Gen. 49.20.

[30] That John Hyrcanus should resign in the name of his descendants as well as for himself is shown by the fact that the reproof was repeated against his son. Josephus affirms that the reproach was unfounded. The Talmud describes the occurrence in b. Kidd. 66a: An old Pharisee demands that Alexander Jannaeus should renounce his claim to the high priesthood because his mother had been a prisoner of war. This account agrees fully with Josephus, except that the

same level as a deflorated woman (p. 154), and her son regarded as the illegitimate son of a priest and unqualified for the office of a priest (*CA* 1.35). Alexander Jannaeus (103–76 BC), son of John Hyrcanus, had to tolerate the same kind of reproach, that as the son (presumably meaning grandson) of a war captive he had no right to practise the calling of a high priest. Indeed, once at the Feast of Tabernacles, the people went so far as to pelt him with citrons ('*etrōgīm*) which each Israelite held in his hand, together with the festive wreath (*lūlāb*) at the morning liturgy of the Feast in the Temple (*Ant.* 13.371f; T. Sukk. iii.16, 197, cf. M. Sukk. iv.9).[31] The repetition of this rebuke, which had already been raised against Jannaeus' father, as well as the recording of the two instances by both Josephus and the Talmud, demonstrates the great importance attached to any breach of the high-priestly marriage laws. The Pharisees were not afraid to make their rebuke openly before the people, and even to hurl it in the face of the ruler at the apparent risk of their lives. Furthermore, it was on the basis of this rebuke that they established their rejection of the Hasmonean high priesthood as illegitimate.[32]

In yet another case an infringement of the high-priestly marriage laws is on record. Joshua b. Gamaliel (AD 63–65) was at the time of his nomination to the high priesthood betrothed to a widow, Martha, of the house of Boethus, M. Yeb. vi.4 (Lam. R. 1.50 on 1.16, Son. 1.47, 128, calls her Miriam). He consummated the marriage after his nomination, as he was entitled to do as a priest, but not as high priest.[33] The report that Martha bribed King Agrippa II with a large sum of money to allow the nomination of her fiancé as high priest to go through (b. Yom. 18a; b. Yeb. 61a. cf. p. 98) leads to the conclusion that the projected marriage with a widow was unlawful for a high priest and threatened to hinder the nomination of Joshua. It is a fair assumption that in this instance too the resentment of the

personalities are changed, John Hyrcanus being confused with Alexander Jannaeus, and the Pharisee Eleazar becomes an enemy of the Pharisees.

[31] The rabbinic passage tells how a Boethusian (Sadducean) high priest was pelted by the people with *etrōgīm*, allegedly because at Tabernacles he poured the libation of water over his feet, as the Sadducees regarded the ceremony as unbiblical. This may well be the incident involving Alexander Jannaeus.

[32] For the illegitimacy of the Hasmonian high priesthood, see pp. 188f.

[33] Alexander Jannaeus also, despite the legal ban, appears to have consummated the marriage with his sister-in-law, Alexandra (Schürer I, 277 n. 2, ET I.1, 295 n. 2).

people and of the Pharisaic party had been vociferous against this disregard of the Law. Subsequently an attempt was made to legalize the case (M. Yeb. vi.4).

Finally, among the commitments laid upon the high priest by reason of his office there was some *ceremonial* appropriate to his position, not confined to the occasions when he actually performed cultic functions. When receiving or offering condolences he appeared with an impressive retinue, with the Captain of the Temple always on his right. When he himself was a mourner, there stood on his left the director of the priestly course for the day. By contrast, when he offered condolences, the position on the left belonged to his predecessor in office (T. Sanh. iv.i, 420; cf. M. Sanh. ii.1). Another aspect of this ceremonial was that 'no one may see him naked, nor when he is shaving nor having a bath' (T. Sanh. iv.1, 420). He was also expected to take special care of his outward appearance, and we hear that he used to wear his hair in the so-called 'Julian style', cut very short (b. Sanh. 21b; b. Ned. 51a; Bill. III, 440.1).

Even after his removal from office the high priest kept his title and retained his authority. Indeed any priest who deputized for the high priest,[34] if, as sometimes happened, he was unable to fulfil his office because of defilement (T. Yom. i.4, 180), was numbered in the list of officiating high priests even though he had discharged the duty by proxy for a few hours only.

Again and again the influence of the retired high priest is discernible. Think of the part played by Annas (in office from AD 6–15) in the trial of Jesus (John 18.13, 24; cf. Acts 4.6; Luke 3.2), and of the former high priests Jonathan son of Ananus (in office from Easter to Pentecost, AD 37), who in AD 52 led an important deputation of Jews to Ummidius Quadratus, governor of Syria, and together with the reigning high priest Ananias was sent as ambassador to Caesar, and had his way over transferring control of Palestine to Felix (*BJ* 2.240ff; *Ant.* 20.162). The deposed high priests Ananus, son of Ananus (in office in AD 62; *BJ* 2.563, 648–654; 4.151ff.; *Vita* 193f; 195ff; 216ff.), and Joshua, son of Gamaliel (in office AD 63–65; *BJ* 4.160, 238ff; *Vita* 193; 204), played a leading part at the start of the uprising against Rome. The high priest retained not only a great part of his authority, but also his cultic character, after his deposal, for the

---

[34] Joseph b. Elam took the place of Mattaiah b. Theophilus in 5 BC (*Ant.* 17.166; T. Yom. i.4, 180; b. Yom. 12b; j. Yom. i.1, 38d. 1). Simon b. Kamithos (AD 17–18) had to allow himself to be represented too, see p. 153.

restrictions on marriage, as well as the ban on defilement by the dead and on undertaking mourning rites (p. 152), still had all their original force (M. Hor. iii.4). His death, too, after deposal, still had its atoning power for the homicide in a city of refuge (M. Makk. ii.6; M. Hor. iii.4). 'A high priest in office differs from the priest that is passed [from his high-priesthood] only in the bullock that is offered on the Day of Atonement and the Tenth of Ephah' (M. Hor. iii.4; M. Meg. i.9), i.e. in having to pay for the bullock and the daily burnt offering of fine meal, and to offer the bullock. We see then that the high priest retained for ever, after his deposal, the character of his office, which made him a principal member of the theocracy. He possessed a 'life-long sanctity' (M. Naz. vii.1).

This cultic character assured the high priest of a unique position in the community; but the picture is incomplete unless we enquire how far *historical circumstances* affected his position. First we must bear in mind a whole series of facts which effectively reduced the high priest's importance. The most decisive of these was encroachment by the political authority. Ancient tradition was that the high priest held office for life and bequeathed it to his descendants. The anointing prescribed by the Law (Ex. 29.7ff.; 30.22ff.) had already ceased to be practised in the Herodian-Roman period, we do not know when or why,[35] and now the consecration of the high priest by investiture took its place.[36] This was a blow to prestige. Again, the authority of the office was not increased by the fact that the political authorities ignored various precepts, as for example in Herod's appointment of Aristobulus, the last Hasmonean high priest (35 BC), at the age of seventeen (*Ant.* 15.51) when twenty was the customary canonical age for priests.[37]

It was bound to have a wholly subversive effect, when Herod dared to rob the high-priestly office of its significance by arbitrarily dis-

[35] According to rabbinic tradition (b. Yom. 52b) the holy oil was said to have been hidden away since the time of king Josiah.

[36] Namely, by putting on the four parts of the high priestly vesture, see n. 2 above.

[37] b. Hull. 24ab (par. T. Zeb. xi.6, 496, with different wording), presents three views on the matter:
1. A priest qualifies as soon as the first signs of manhood appear.
2. He qualifies at the age of twenty (on the analogy of Ezra 3.8, where this is given as the canonical age for Levites).
3. 'As soon as the first signs of manhood appear, a priest is qualified for service; but his brother priests did not allow him to take part in the service until he was twenty years old.'
The third viewpoint gives the actual practice, since in the Tannaitic Midrash Siphra Lev. 21.17, 47d) it is taught as the only tradition.

missing and appointing the high priest, and, in defiance of the privileges of the ancient Zadokite high-priestly aristocracy appointing to the office any kind of priest from some ordinary priestly family. From then on, and also under Roman rule, the office ceased to be life-long and hereditary. Herod achieved his aim, in part at least, to make the high priest wholly dependent on political authority. Cases of simony (see above p. 98; also b. Yom. 8b–9a, Bar.; j. Yom. i.1, 38c, 38 etc.), and rivalry among the chief priests were the natural outcome of the new order.[38]

In other ways the growing influence of the Pharisees made itself felt, particularly in the Sanhedrin but also in the cultus. The high priests with Sadducean sympathies had to accustom themselves to withholding their views in council, and to carrying out the Temple rites according to Pharisaic traditions. It cannot be said that the high priests themselves were blameless in the decline of their influence. Cases of nepotism (see p. 99), occasional infringements (p. 98), deviations from the high-priestly marriage laws (pp. 49f.), trading in the Temple area (pp. 155f.), perhaps occasionally insufficient training of the chief priests in scribal lore (M. Yom. i.6)[39]—all these could not fail to injure the reputation of the high-priestly office, at any rate among those people who were under the influence of the Pharisees.

However, we must take care not to exaggerate these conditions, for on the other hand the importance of the high priest greatly increased during the first century AD because, as president of the Sanhedrin and principal agent of the people at a time when there was no king, he represented the Jewish people in all dealings with Rome. Particularly at this time, there were among the high priests outstanding men who won power and prestige by their personality, men like Annas, Caiaphas and those high priests who stood out against the Romans at the beginning of the rebellion. Above all, it is

[38] Cf. j. Yom. i.1, 38c. 43, telling how the candidates for the chief priestly office bid against each other. 38d.1 tells also how Joseph b. Elam, having deputized on the Day of Atonement in 5 BC for the high priest Matthias b. Theophilus, who was unable to officiate because of uncleanness, now sought to supplant the legitimate high priest. He asked the king an apparently harmless question, 'Should the bullock [for the sin offering] and the ram [for the burnt offering] be paid for by me, or by the officiating high priest?' He hoped the king would answer, 'by you', and so confirm him as high priest, but Herod saw through him (parallels in T. Yom. i.4, 180; j. Hor. iii.5, 47d.7).

[39] A high priest who was practised in reading had to read the Old Testament during the night before the Day of Atonement to keep himself awake. If he were not practised in reading, someone read to him. 'Zechariah b. Kabutal says, "Many times I read before him from Daniel"' (M. Yom. i.6; cf. M. Hor. iii.8).

important to note that the cultic character of the high priest's office, which made him the only mortal allowed to enter the Holy of Holies, lifted him so high above his fellows that his position was not seriously affected by historical circumstances. For 'no man taketh the honour unto himself, but when he is called of God, even as was Aaron' (Heb. 5.4).

B. THE CHIEF PRIESTS AND CHIEF LEVITES

(a) The anointed high priest[40] takes precedence (in rank) over the high priest who is (only) distinguished by investiture (from the rest of the priests).[41]

The invested high priest takes precedence over the priest anointed for war (Deut. 20.2ff.).

The order of precedence continues as follows:

(b) The Captain of the Temple (sāgān).[42]

(c) The director of the weekly course (rōš ha-mišmār).

(d) The director of the daily course (rōš bēt āb).

(e) The Temple overseer ('ammarkāl).

(f) The treasurer (gizbār).

(g) The ordinary priest (kōhēn hedyōṭ).

(h) The Levite (T. Hor. ii.10, 476; j. Hor. iii.9, 48b.33).
For the continuation of the list see below p.272.[43]

It becomes clear from this survey that apart from the office of high priest there were five recognized ranks (b–f) to which we must now give attention. We should note that the offices of captain of the Temple, Temple overseer and treasurer (b, e, f) were linked to the cultus in such a way that their holders had to be permanently present in Jerusalem. In contrast, those priests who took a leading position in the twenty-four weekly courses, who were scattered about the land (c, d), had to be at the Temple only one week out of every twenty-four apart from the three pilgrim festivals.

The highest ranking priest after the high priest was the captain of

[40] The legally prescribed form for the ordination of a high priest was not used in Herodian-Roman times.

[41] The usual form for the ordination of a high priest in Herodian-Roman times (j. Hor. iii.9, 48b.33), puts 'the prophet' in the place of the invested high priest).

[42] b. Taan. 31a Bar. puts the captain of the Temple over the priest anointed for war. j. Hor. iii.9, 48b.34, omits the captain of the Temple.

[43] A corresponding list of ranks is to be found in 1 QM ii.1ff.: the high priest, his deputy, twelve chief priests, and the directors of the priests' weekly courses; twelve chief Levites, and the directors of the weekly levitical courses.

the Temple,[44] *s^egan ha-kōhanim*.[45] Josephus and the New Testament call him στρατηγὸς (τοῦ ἱεροῦ) (*Ant.* 20.131 *et passim*; Acts 4.1; 5.24, 26). His office belonged to the permanent complement of the Temple and had only one incumbent at a time. His privileged position is illustrated by the fact that he assisted the high priest in the solemn performance of his ceremonial duties, and therefore had a special place at his right hand (M. Yom. iii.9; iv.1; M. Tam. vii.3; j. Yom. iii.8, 41a.4; cf. M. Yom. vii.1; M. Sot. vii.7–8). When the high priest gave or received condolences the captain of the Temple stood on his right (T. Sanh. iv.1, 420; b. Sanh. 19a). He may at the same time have had to watch the high priest to ensure that he carried out the rite completely and correctly (M. Yom. iv.1).[46] It was also customary to appoint him as substitute for the high priest one week before the Day of Atonement, in case the latter was prevented from carrying out his duties on that day.[47]

[44] Schürer II, 320f., ET II.1, 257; Bill. II, 628–30.

[45] M. Ab. iii.2 *et passim* = director of the priests. j. Shek. v.3, 49a.30/36, substitutes the word *q^etīlīqōs*, or *k^etālīqōs* = καθολικός, and deduces wrongly from II Chron. 31.12 that there were two men of this rank, whereas the ten mentioned in II Chron. 31.13 must be the three treasury officials and seven chief men of the Temple. According to j. Shek. v.3, 49a.33, the order is, high priest, καθολικός, Temple overseer, treasurer.

[46] When the lots were cast for the two goats by the high priest on the Day of Atonement, the captain of the Temple on his right, or the director of the daily course on his left, would call on him to raise either his right or his left hand, whichever contained the lot cast for the goat 'to the Lord', and show the lot to all the people. Aqiba tells us that we have here an anti-Sadducean safeguard (b. Yom. 40b; cf. T. Yom. iii.2, 185; Büchler, *Priester*, pp. 110f.). That is, it was disputed whether the high priest had to keep the lot 'for the Lord' in his left hand, in case it came there in casting the lot (the Pharisees' view) or had to put it into the right hand from the left (the view of the Sadducees). That this raising of the hand was an anti-Sadducean provision is confirmed by the similar rule about the pouring of the libation at Tabernacles (M. Sukk. iv.9). Since the Sadducees disagreed with this libation as unbiblical, and one Sadducean high priest had once poured it over his feet (p. 156 n. 31), raising the hand while it was poured would make it as clear as possible that the rite had been fully carried out according to Pharisaic requirements. It must follow then for M. Yom. iv.1, that the captain of the Temple was there to see that the high priest carried out the ceremonies fully.

[47] T. Yom. i.4, 180: R. Ḥananiah b. Gamaliel II (*c.* AD 120) says, 'For this reason was the captain of the Temple appointed, to be the deputy of the high priest (on the Day of Atonement), lest something should happen which rendered him unfit' (Lev. 22.4). The evidence of this man is the more important in that he was a relative of the last high priest Pinḥas (p. 155). The same tradition appears in b. Yom. 39a Bar.; b. Sot. 42a Bar.: R. Ḥananiah, Captain of the Temple says, 'Why does the captain of the Temple stand at the [high priest's] right? [i.e. when casting lots for the two goats', M. Yom. iv.1 (see n. 46)]? 'In order that, if the high priest be rendered unfit, he may officiate for him.' Here is the same tradition

The importance of the office is shown conclusively in a statement in the Palestinian Talmud: 'The high priest would not be elected high priest if he had not first been captain of the Temple' (j. Yom. iii.8, 41a.5). This statement is evidently a generalization, because from the accession of Herod the Great the appointment of the high priest was frequently made arbitrarily and simply from political considerations. Nevertheless, the information must be correct in many instances. It was natural that the most senior of the chief priests should be made high priest in succession to the one who had been deposed; and in any case the captain of the Temple would certainly be selected from the families of the priestly aristocracy, as for example were the two sons of the high priest Ananias, one of whom, Ananus, held the office in AD 52 (*Ant.* 20.131; *BJ* 2.243) and the other Eleazar in AD 66 (*Ant.* 20.208; *BJ* 2.409). As further proof that the captain of the Temple was chosen from the families of the priestly aristocracy, there is the designation of the two sons of Aaron, Nadab and Abihu, as *segānē kehunnāh* (Lev. R. 20.7 on 16.1, Son. 20.10, 260; *Tanhuma*, *ahare mot*, I, 427.12). It is a reading back of a later title and relationship into the past, when two sons of the high priest Aaron were called 'Captains of the Temple'.

Finally we should mention instances of certain men being deputies for the high priest. The high priest Simon, son of Kamithos (*c.* AD 17–18) was, on the Day of Atonement, represented by his brother (see p. 153 n. 24); the high priest Matthias, son of Theophilus (mid-5 BC to 12 March 4 BC), had as his deputy on the Day of Atonement in 5 BC a relation named Joseph, son of Elam.[48] In the same way, when Aristobulus I (104–103 BC) was ill at the Feast of Tabernacles,

---

ascribed to the scribe and captain of the Temple, Hananiah himself. The Tosephta probably mentions the correct tradition: a tradition concerning Temple service seems to be traceable back to a Hananiah bearing the title of captain of the Temple. I can find (against Schürer II, 321, ET II.1, 257f.) nothing conflicting with this statement in M. Yom. i.1, which speaks of a solemn choosing of the high priest's deputy one week before the Day of Atonement; this solemn choosing at that time by no means rules out the privilege of the captain of the Temple to be deputy.

[48] Mutually consistent accounts in Josephus *Ant.* 17.166, and in rabbinic literature, T. Yom. i.4, 180; b. Yom. 12b; j. Yom. i.1, 38d.1. For the dating of Matthias' appointment in the middle of 5 BC see *Ant.* 17.78, 'after the death of Pheroras'. His deposition, according to *Ant.* 17.167, was on the day before the partial eclipse of the moon on the 13 March 4 BC. Since the Day of Atonement falls on 10 Tishri, in September–October, it follows that the deputizing on the Day of Atonement was in 5 BC.

he was represented by his brother Antigonus (*Ant.* 13.304).[49]

Since, as we have seen, it was customary for the captain of the Temple to be chosen as the high priest's deputy on the Day of Atonement, we may take it that, at least for the first two cases mentioned, the high priest's deputy held the office of Captain of the Temple, even if this is not expressly stated. If this is so, it confirms that the captain of the Temple used to be selected from the nearest relations of the high priest. The captain of the Temple had the permanent oversight of the cultus and, as the name *s^egan hakōhanīm* indicates, over the whole body of officiating priests. This agrees with the account, a little further on, about the captain of the Temple Eleazar, and the statement made by Ḥananiah, known as the captain of the Temple, about the usages in the performance of the cultus rites: 'Never have I seen a hide [of an animal found to be unfit for sacrifice] taken out to the place of burning' (M. Eduy. ii.2), a statement implying complete familiarity with Temple ritual obtained by many years' of service. In addition to the oversight of the cultus the captain of the Temple was the chief of police in the Temple area and as such had power to arrest. It was the captain of the Temple, for example, who arrested the apostles in the outer court of the Temple (Acts 5.24, 26; cf. 4.1).[50] The extent of this official's power can be gauged from this example: Eleazar, the *sāgān* of AD 66, made the decision to discontinue the sacrifice for Caesar, which was equivalent to a declaration of war against Rome, and was the immediate occasion of it (*BJ* 2.409f.). Towards the end of the same year this same man was appointed by the leaders of the uprising as commander of Idumea (*BJ* 2.566). Nothing could more clearly illustrate the power of the captain of the Temple which he exercised there, and the reputation he enjoyed.

Next in rank to the captain of the Temple were the directors of the weekly courses of priests, of which there were twenty-four, then the directors of the daily courses, of which there were about 156 since each weekly course consisted of four to nine daily courses.[51] These men lived in widely scattered parts of Judaea and Galilee, and apart from the three pilgrim festivals were in Jerusalem for only one week out of twenty-four, when it was the turn of their weekly course

---

[49] Büchler, *Priester*, 109 n. 1, rightly recognizes the fact that Antigonus was the deputy.

[50] Cf. also the Greek translation of *sāgān* as στρατηγός.

[51] T. Taan. ii.2, 216; j. Taan. iv.2, 68a.14: five to nine daily courses; b. Men. 107b: six daily courses.

to officiate in Jerusalem. During this week they had to fulfil certain specific functions in the daily ceremonial. The director of the weekly course, during his week of duty, performed the rites of purification for lepers and women after childbirth, who were pronounced clean at the Nicanor Gate when the rites were complete. It must have been the director of the weekly course who stood at the Nicanor Gate, which according to rabbinic tradition was the link between the Court of Israel and the Court of Women,[52] to receive the offering of the mother of Jesus (Luke 2.24), 'when the days of their purification according to the law of Moses were fulfilled' (Luke 2.22). It was at the Nicanor Gate too that he would make a woman suspected of adultery drink the 'water of bitterness', to determine the sentence of God.[53]

[52] By the 'east gate' M. Midd. i.4, can only mean the connection between the Court of Israel and the Court of Women, as the comparison with Josephus, *BJ* 5.198ff. proves, so M. Midd. ii.6 must be taken correspondingly. Notice, too, that according to Num. R. 7.8 on 5.2 (Son. 195); T. Kel. B.K. i.12, 570, the 'camp of the Levites' extended to the Nicanor Gate, but according to the Siphre on Num. 5.3, 2c, it reached to the gate of the innermost court. It follows that the Nicanor Gate was thus the entrance to the innermost court. Notice finally, and most particularly, that the Court of Women stood open to all who had carried out the last stages of purification, except the offering (M. Kel. i.8; T. Kel. B.K. i.10, 570); for example, a leper had to bathe in the chamber of lepers, which was in the Court of Women, before being declared clean (M. Neg. xiv.8). Therefore, the Nicanor Gate should be looked for as the point where complete cleanness was declared, before going from the Court of Women to the innermost court. So Dalman, *SW*, 301 n. 8; but Bill. II, 622–4 disagrees, placing the Nicanor Gate to the east of the Court of Women.

[53] M. Tam. v.6: 'The chief of the *ma'amād* (the name given to the group of priests, Levites and lay representatives of a weekly course) which came into Jerusalem, made the unclean stand near the eastern gates' (the Nicanor Gate, which, besides the main gate had two porches, according to M. Midd. ii.6, hence the plural). Num. R. 9.11 on 5.16 (Son. 9.13, 265f.): 'Before the Lord (Num. 5.16) at the Nicanor gate [shall the priest place the woman suspected of adultery]; this means (M. Tam. v.6), 'The head of the *ma'amād* stationed the unclean people at the Nicanor Gate.' Who was 'the head of the *ma'amād*?' 'The unclean' means people who were there because they wished to be declared clean, that is lepers, women after childbirth and women suspected of adultery (M. Sot. i.5; Num. R. 9.11 on 5.16 [Son. 9.13, 265f.]; Siphra Lev. 14.11, 35b). But for such people a priest was necessary to carry out the purification rites according to Lev. 14.11 (lepers), 12.6 (women after childbirth), Num. 5.16 (women suspected of adultery). That a priest did, in fact, carry out these rites is expressly stated in another passage, Siphra Lev. 14.11, 35b: 'The priest carrying out the rites of purification causes the man to be declared clean [the leper] to stand . . . before the Lord (Lev. 14.11) that is, before the Tabernacle [i.e.] he causes him to stand at the Nicanor gate with his back to the east and facing west.' The chief of the *ma'amād* (the entire weekly course) was therefore definitely a priest (O. Holtzmann, *Tamid* [coll. Die Mischna], Giessen 1928, 63, says quite wrongly that the title could mean, 'the special office

The director of the daily course, on the day his course was on duty, had to be present at the offering of sacrifice, and we hear that when the high priest was sacrificing he stood on his left (M. Yom. iii.9; iv. 1; cf. T. Sanh. iv.1, 420).[54] The actual conduct of the daily ceremonial, however, was in the hands of the captain of the Temple and his subordinate, the 'officer in charge of the lots' (M. Tam. i.2–3; iii.1–3; v.1–2; vi.3),[55] for only in this way could continuity be maintained in the performance of the cultus by the regularly changing weekly courses.

The last two offices of the chief priests were closely connected, and were both permanent appointments of the Temple. Their holders are often mentioned together, as for example when they took part in the tumultuous election of the priest and stone mason, Pinḥas, to the office of high priest (T. Yom. i.61, 180). They are referred to as (1) the 'ammarkᵉlin and (2) the gizbārim, the treasurers. The meaning of the word 'ammarkᵉlin is in dispute. Schürer[56] is of the opinion that it means the same as gizbārim, because in Persian the word means something like 'auditor'. But this conjecture is not decisive, since the Persian loanword which appears in the Targum had taken on in Aramaic the general meaning of 'chief of the people', then, more particularly, 'chief of the priests'. The duties of the 'ammarkᵉlin appear quite clearly in the sources, of which the most important is quoted here: 'The [seven] 'ammarkᵉlin,[57] what did they do? The seven keys of the Court [of Israel and of the priests] were in their hands, and if one of them wished to open [in the morning] he could not do so until all were assembled' (T. Shek. ii.15, 177). Now this statement is formalized, in so far as the number of seven 'ammarkᵉlin is linked with the number of seven gates to the Inner Court, so that each 'ammarkāl had in his hand one key to the Court.[58] Even so,

---

of a Levite or priest in the Temple service'!). He must therefore be identified with the director of the priests of the weekly course.

[54] If the high priest was mourning the death of a member of his family, the director of the daily course again stood on his left.

[55] The casting of lots to decide who should officiate at the daily burnt-offering (tāmīd) which was offered morning and evening, will be dealt with in full later, see pp. 201ff.

[56] Schürer II, 327, ET II.1, 263. Likewise Grätz, Topographische und historische Streifzüge, I. 'Die letzten Tempelbeamten vor der Tempelzerstörung und die Tempelämter', MGWJ 34, 1885, 193.

[57] The number is missing in the Vienna MS of the Tosephta, but occurs in the Erfurter MS (Berliner Staatsbibl. MS or. 2⁰ 1220) and in the old editions.

[58] Consistently with this, some branches of tradition calculate by the number

the whole passage is not necessarily based on pure invention; what the statement really says is that the *'ammark^{e}lîn* held the keys and the power of supervision over the Temple. This appears from M. Bikk. iii.3. As a rule the *'ammark^{e}lîn* are mentioned together with the treasurers (M. Shek. v.2; T. Yom. i.6, 180; b. Pes. 57a Bar.; Siphra Lev. 21.10, 47c and in the list already quoted on p. 160 to T. Hor. ii.10, 476). However, M. Bikk. iii.3 mentions instead the *s^{e}gānîm*, captains of the Temple, next to the treasurers. The *'ammark^{e}lîn* were therefore the Temple overseers (Luke 22.4, 52, and Josephus: στρατηγοί) and we can verify this conclusion by consulting the two lists of Temple officials. There could not be less than seven of these, according to M. Shek. v.2; T. Shek. ii.15, 177 (see also n. 57 above); and j. Shek. v.3, 49a.

Next in line after the captains of the Temple came the *gizbārîm*, the treasurers, of whom there might not be less than three (M. Shek. v.2; T. Shek. ii.15, 177). The financial affairs of the Temple—landed property, wealth and treasure, administration of the flood of tribute money and votive offerings as well as private capital deposited at the Temple; responsibility for the produce and materials needed for the cultus; supervision of the Temple monopoly in the sale of birds and other produce for sacrifice; concern for the maintenance and repair of the full complement of gold and silver vessels, of which no less than ninety-three were needed for each daily ritual—all this provided the treasurers[59] with ample scope for activity and demanded a staff of officials whom they employed.

'The three treasurers, what did they do? Into their hands were paid:

(1) the equivalent [of objects vowed to the Temple but redeemable by a money payment],
(2) and devoted property [vowed to the Temple and not redeemable],
(3) and [other] votive offerings to the Temple,
(4) and the second[60] tithe [they redeem],

---

of gates to the Court of Women, and so speak of the thirteen gates (of the inner Temple) (M. Midd. ii.6; M. Shek. vi.3, a saying of Abba Jose b. Ḥanan) and of thirteen *gizbārîm* [sic!] (b. Tam. 27a, a saying of R. Nathan).

[59] See e.g. *Ant.* 14.106ff.; *BJ* 6.390ff.; Bill. II, 37–45 for the treasure chambers in the Temple and deposits of money there. For the ninety-three vessels see M. Tam. iii.4, and for the treasurer's responsibility for these, M. Shek. v.6.
[60] So the Vienna MS and the editions.

(5) [in short] all the [financial] transactions of the Temple were carried out by them' (T. Shek. ii.15, 177).

It was therefore first and foremost the Temple income which the treasurers had to administer. We are told that they received the grain dedicated to the Temple (M. Peah ii.8), that they took payment of the equivalent of dedicated grain (M. Peah i.6), produce (M. Peah iv.8; M. Hall. iii.4) and dough (M. Hall. iii.3), that they were responsible for the use of equipment donated to the Temple (M. Shek. vi.6) and that they were entrusted with administration of the Temple tax (M. Shek. ii.1),[61] in the amount of a didrachma (Matt. 17.24), which every Israelite had to pay annually. As well as Temple income they administered Temple expenditure. They bought in wood (M. Meil. iii.8) and received the wine for the drink-offering for testing (M. Men. viii.7), as well as flour for the two loaves baked from the first-fruits at Pentecost (M. Men. viii.2).[62] Finally it was their duty to administer the stores and treasure of the Temple (see p. 166 n. 59), of which the most sacred part was the high-priestly vestment (*Ant.* 15. 408; 18. 93; cf. pp.148f.).

Further details about the Temple overseers and treasurers which we have been discussing can be found in two extremely valuable lists of 'chief men', the older of which is given below.[63]

These were the 'chief men' in the Temple:[64]

*[1] 'Joḥanan b. Gudgeda[65] was chief doorkeeper.'

*[2] 'Ben Totaphath had charge of the keys.'

*[3] 'Ben Diphai was supervisor for the festal branches for the feast of Tabernacles.'

[61] If money was lost or stolen, the messenger had to swear an oath before the Temple treasurer in case the *terūmāh* had already been taken from the treasure chamber (with the first collection of the fifteen days before Passover, the entire Temple tax for the current year passed legally into the possession of the Temple), as to the reason for the loss. If it could be proved that the messengers were guiltless, the Temple treasury bore the cost. Further see j. Shek. iii.2, 47c.31 Bar., where the temple treasurers examine the man who removes the *terūmāh* (this took place a half month before the three pilgrim festivals).

[62] From the dating (grain for the meal had to be sown seventy days before Passover), it seems to me, in connection with viii.1, that this deals not with the meal of the food offering in general, but only with that for the bread of the first-fruits.

[63] T. Shek. ii.14, 177: I follow the Erfurt MS, now in Berlin State Library, MS or. 2⁰ 1220.

[64] The numbers in square brackets indicate Levites, those in round brackets indicate priests, * = overseer, and ⁰ = treasurer.

[65] A Levite, b. Arak. 11a.

*[4] 'Arza[66] was director of music' (literally—'he was set over the *dūkān*', i.e. the platform on which the Levite singers and musicians stood).

05. 'Samuel[67] was set over the bakery.'

0(6) 'Benjamin was responsible for the baked loaves for the high priest's offering.' Obviously a priest, according to M. Tam. i.3, for the bakers of the baked loaves were called to work before sunrise (cf. iii.2), a time when their chamber near the Nicanor Gate (see p. 164 n. 52) was accessible only to priests.

0(7) 'Ben Maqlit was over the salt.' Again, a priest, for the Parwah-chamber (next to the salt-chamber in the north of the Court of Priests) where the hides of sacrificial animals were salted (M. Midd. v.3) lay in the sacred precincts (M. Yom. iii.3).

0(8) 'Ben Pelak was over the wood store.' Again, a priest, for the wood-chamber (M. Midd. v.4) lay in the sacred precincts, accessible only to priests, next to the gate through which fuel was brought in the south-west of the Court of Priests. There was also a woodshed in the north-east of the Court of Women, where the wood was inspected for worms (M. Midd. ii.4).

We have reliable criteria for determining the age of this list. To be sure, Hoffmann's attractive argument[68] that our list belongs to the period immediately before the destruction of the Temple, since it mentions as chief doorkeeper (see (1)) Joḥanan b. Gudgeda who survived the destruction, is not fully convincing, for this conclusion that Joḥanan survived the destruction of the Temple is based on a statement in the Babylonian Talmud (b. Hor. 10a–b), which, as the parallel passage in the Siphre Deut. 1.16 shows, was originally concerned not with Joḥanan b. Gudgeda but with Joḥanan b. Nuri.[69] On the other hand, we know that Joḥanan b. Gudgeda had been in office at some time before the destruction of the Temple.[70] Now there

[66] So the Erfurt MS in contrast to the Vienna MS (Vienna Nat. Library, Heb. 20), and the *ed. princ.* Venice 1521, which read 'ben Arza'.

[67] In the Vienna MS (Vienna Nat. Library, Heb. 20) and in the *ed. princ.* the names in 5 and 6 are exchanged.

[68] *Magazin für die Wissenschaft des Judenthums* 9, 1882, 96ff.

[69] Siphre Deut. 1.16, 30d. The Eleazar *ḥismā* mentioned at the same time was a contemporary of Joḥanan b. Nuri, so only his name fits the context. For the original reading of the Siphre see Bacher, *Ag. Tann.* I, 368 n. 4; G. Kittel, *Sifre zu Deuteronomium*, Stuttgart 1922, 24 n. 4.

[70] b. Arak. 11b, where he instructs the Levite Joshua b. Ḥananiah in the execution of his duties. This shows that the latter was still inexperienced, i.e. he

was an age limit of fifty years for Levites (Num. 8.25, cf. 4.3, 23, 30, 35, 39, 43, 47; j. Ber. iv.1, 7b, 63), so that Johanan, if he really did survive the destruction, was then no longer in office. The mention of this man's name in our list is therefore no certain proof that the list dates from the last years before the destruction, but rather that it points backwards to an even earlier time (see n. 70). A more reliable criterion for the dating of the list is provided by Item (3). As long as the Temple stood the festal branches were brought there on the six weekdays of the seven-day feast of Tabernacles,[71] but not on the sabbath. Now in the first ten years of the century, if the first day of the festival fell on a sabbath, the festal branch was shaken in the Temple on all seven days (M. Sukk. iv.1–2), and therefore also on the sabbath. Since it was forbidden, however, to bring anything from a private place into a public place on the sabbath, the branches were brought to the Temple beforehand on the Friday, and handed over to one of the Temple servants, a Levite (ḥazzānīm), who arranged them in the porch of the Outer Court (M. Sukk. iv.4). The next morning the Temple servants threw the branches to the people and each person caught a branch for himself. The resultant brawling was a danger to lives, so the law court ordered that the branches should no longer be shaken in the Temple on the sabbath (even when the first day of the festival fell on a sabbath), but only in the home (M. Sukk. iv.4). Since under Item (3) of our list a certain Ben Diphai is mentioned as supervising the festal branches in the Temple, the list belongs to a time before the court had altered the rules. This fits in with the fact that in the second list (below) this office no longer appears.

The fact that it mentions a smaller number of officials is further evidence of the greater age of the Tosephta list. Finally it should be noted that the director of music in the Erfurt MS bears the name Arza (see p. 168 n. 66), while in the second list the son of Arza appears as director of music. If the reading of the Erfurt MS is the original (the Vienna MS as well as the editio princeps of Venice, 1521, read Ben-Arza in the Tosephta list as well) then in the meantime the

had just reached the canonical age of twenty (Ezra. 3.8; see p. 158 n. 37) when Levites were allowed to serve. However, Joshua b. Hananiah was already a famous teacher before the destruction of the Temple (j. Hag. ii.1, 77b.32), so it is clear that the episode in b. Arak. is concerned with a period before AD 70. At that time Johanan b. Gudgeda was chief doorkeeper and consequently a man of mature age. He must therefore have already taken office in the first half of the first century.

[71] The eighth day of the festival, the closing feast, was kept as a special feast on its own. On this day the branches were not carried.

office had passed from father to son. The fact that this Arza is an otherwise entirely unknown person speaks for the originality of the Erfurt reading, although of course there is always the possibility of an inadvertent omission in the Erfurt MS. All this suggests that our list originated a few decades before the destruction of the Temple.

The second list is found in M. Shek. v.1f. [72]

v.1: 'These were the "officers" in the Temple:

[0]1. Johanan b. Phineas was over the seals.' Drink offerings and other offerings came under one rule in the Temple (see no. 4 below). If anyone wished to bring a drink offering, he made a payment to Johanan and was given a seal as receipt (M. Shek. v.4). Johanan's office was the Chamber of Seals (M. Tam. iii.3), the north-eastern room of the Chamber of the Hearth, which lay to the north-west of the Court of Priests, and was actually upon secular ground.

[0]2. 'Ahijah was over the drink offering.' In return for the receipt (see last paragraph) he handed over the corresponding drink offering.

*(3) 'Mattiah b. Samuel was over the lots.' For the casting of lots to choose priestly duties, see pp. 201ff. We can deduce from M. Tam. i.3 and vi.3 that this official was a priest: He had access to the Court of Priests. Not only had he the duty of casting the lots to determine duties, but he was also responsible for the direction and supervision of the whole ceremony of daily sacrifices (*tāmīd*) in the morning and evening (M. Tam. i.2–3; iii.1–3; v.1–2; vi.3).

[0](4) 'Petahiah was over the bird offerings.' He watched over the payments of money equivalents in the third of the thirteen trumpet-shaped[73] containers, placed on one of the colonnades surrounding the Court of Women. He also took care that the doves were presented properly. He was a priest (T. Shek. iii.2, 177).[74]

[0]5. 'Ben Ahijah was Temple physician' (literally 'he was set over the bowel-sickness'). Because of the unusually rich meat diet of the priests, who were also forbidden wine during their days of

[72] Signs as in List 1 (see above, p. 167 n. 64).

[73] Cf. 'sound a trumpet' in Matt. 6.2. This form of words is based on the shape of the receptacles for alms in the Temple, i.e. like a trumpet, wide below, and with a narrow opening to prevent thieves putting in their hands.

[74] The text here gives a later marginal note: 'This same Petahiah was Mordecai. Why was he given the name Petahiah? Because he was to "open", or interpret, sayings since he knew seventy languages.'

duty,[75] such sickness was by no means unusual, as j. Shek. v.2, 48d.26 rightly says.

*6. 'Nehemiah was over the water' (lit. 'trench-digger'), in charge of the aqueduct and the Temple cisterns, and to look after the baths.[76]

*7. 'Gabini was the herald.'

*[8] 'Ben Geber [a Levite] was over the shutting of gates.'

*[9] 'Ben Bebai was the jailer.' 'He was set over the scourge', for he had to chastise priests who sought to gain an advantage at the casting of the lots (b. Yom. 23a).[77]

*[10] 'Ben Arza was director of music' (literally 'held the cymbals') i.e. during the service he gave the Levites the signal with cymbals when to begin singing. He was most probably a Levite.

*[11] 'Hygdas (= ὄγδοος) ben Levi was director of the Levite singers.' He was probably a Levite, as the patronymic as much as the function indicates. Singing was practised by Levites exclusively, and Ogdoos had a special gift for it (M. Yom. iii.11; b. Yom. 38b etc.).[78]

⁰(12) 'The (priestly) house of Garmu was over the preparation of shewbread.' This could obviously concern only priests, since the 'Chamber of Shewbread-makers', which was the south-eastern room of the Chamber of the Hearth lying in the north-western corner of the Court of Priests, lay in holy ground accessible only to priests (M. Midd. i.6).

⁰(13) 'The (priestly) house of Abtinas (Εὐθύνοος or Εὔθυνος) was over the manufacture of incense'. A priestly family, since in the 'Chamber of Abtinas' the priests kept watch at night (M. Midd. i.1; M. Tam. i.1), which shows that it lay within the Court of Priests, therefore on holy ground (cf. M. Yom. i.5).

---

[75] Lev. 10.9; Ezek. 44.21. According to M. Taan. ii.7, this ban applied to the priests of the weekly course for the daytime only, but to those of the daily course for both day and night time.

[76] Graetz, art. cit., MGWJ 34, 1885, 204, has realized this last point.

[77] A variant translation is, 'He was over the (preparation and fixing of) wicks' (j. Shek. v.2, 48d.46), which were made from the outworn breeches and girdles of the priests (M. Sukk. v.3). However, this second meaning was disclaimed even by Abbaiah who had defended it (b. Yom. 23a).

[78] However, we come across the expression, 'his brethren the Levites' (Cant. R. 3.6, Son. 159), and also, 'his brethren the priests' (b. Yom. 38b; j. Shek. v.2, 48d. 53).

⁰(14) 'Eleazar was superintendent of curtains.' The superintendent of curtains was a priest (*Ant.* 14.106f.). For the curtains themselves see above p. 25.

⁰15. 'Pinḥas was superintendent of priestly vestments' (M. Midd. i.4; *BJ* 6.390).

v.2: 'There must never be less than seven *'amarkᵉlin*, and three treasurers. Nor were less than two persons suffered to hold office over the public in aught concerning the community,[79] save only Ben Ahijah the physician (5) and Eleazar the superintendent of curtains (14) whom the community agreed to accept.' Obviously these other officials had at least one assistant, if not more, to work with them (as e.g. nos. 1 and 2).

It is possible to place this list in a later period than the first, partly because of the omission of office no. 3 in the first list, which had been abolished, but more conclusively because of the greater number of officials. To this, we can add Josephus' report that 'the treasurer of the Temple, Phineas,' was captured in AD 70, a few days after the destruction of the Temple, and he had disclosed to the Romans 'the tunics and girdles of the priests, and an abundance of purple and scarlet cloth kept for necessary repairs to the Temple hangings, along with a mass of cinnamon, cassia and other spices, which they mixed and burnt daily to God. Many other treasures also were delivered up by him with numerous sacred ornaments' (*BJ* 6.390f). There can be no doubt that this 'treasurer of the Temple, Phineas' is the same official mentioned in the second list (15) as 'Pinḥas, superintendent of priestly vestments'.[80] This means that he was in office at the time of

---

[79] 'In money (property) matters'. This is lacking in the text of the Mishnah *ed. princ.* of the Jerusalem Talmud, Venice 1523, but it is found in ed. *Riva di Trento*, 1559, and in the Cambridge MS, ed. Lowe 1883, and in j. Shek. v.3, 49a.37 (*ed. princ.*).

[80] There is no proof of the suggestion that there were fixed names for each office, independent of the actual names of the officials e.g. that each keeper of vestments was called Pinḥas. True there was a 'chamber of Pinḥas, keeper of the vestments' (M. Midd. i.4) near the Nicanor Gate, but this designation does not mean that the keeper of the wardrobe was always called Pinḥas. The more likely explanation is that the last holder was in office for a considerable time and was an outstanding personality. It was not surprising that the name of the priest in charge of curtains was Eleazar in 54 BC, when M. Licinius Crassus plundered the Temple treasury (*Ant.* 14.106f.), and also in our list a hundred and twenty years later, since it was a common name. The fact that a certain Jesus, son of Thebuthi, in AD 70 handed over two lamps, tables, Temple furniture, curtains, priestly vestments and other treasures (*BJ* 6.387–9) does not mean that he was a treasurer; he would, in that case, have been the holder of the office 14 in the second list, and

the destruction of the Temple, and so this second list gives us the names of the last group of officials at the Temple before its destruction.

The evidence of Josephus justifies another important conclusion. He calls the Temple official, no. 15 in our list, the 'Temple Treasurer', and gives the same title on another occasion to the man in charge of curtains, no. 14 (*Ant.* 14.106f.). Now if we consider this together with the note in the second list, to the effect that there could not be less than seven Temple overseers and three Temple treasurers, it follows that our second list gives us the names and official duties of the Temple overseers and treasurers. This also applies to the first list, since both lists agree on the important officials, by somewhat different titles.

We must accordingly study the lists more closely. First, it is noteworthy that both lists give us quite a number of Levites. In the first list the doorkeeper (1) is certainly a Levite, and so most probably was the director of music (4) in charge of the Levite singers, as well as the official in charge of the Levite Temple servants at the Feast of Tabernacles (3) who would no doubt have other duties on other occasions; presumably also the keeper of the keys (2) who is named amongst these other three Levites. In the second list were two chief officials over the Levite musicians (10 and 11), two over the Levite Temple servants (8 and 9). It seems a likely conjecture that in the first list too there were two chief officials over the musicians in addition to the two overseers of the Levite Temple servants (1 and 2). This is in keeping with 4. In this case we may conjecture that the keeper of the keys (2) had the key to the room beneath the Court of Israel which opened into the court of women, where the harps, flutes, cymbals and other musical instruments of the Levites were kept (M. Midd. ii.6). In the second list the following were Levites: the man 'over the shutting of gates' (8), the director of music (10) and the director of the singers (11). Again, amongst these three chief Levites we find another office, that of jailer, (9). We may with reasonable certainty recognize in this official the head superviser, no. 3 in the first list, whose office must have a different title since the supervision of festal branches had fallen into disuse as a result of the decision of the court (p. 169). These four chief Levites (8–11) will be discussed in a separate section (pp. 207ff.). The remaining officials in both lists must have been mostly priests, since the Temple finances were in the hands of the priests.

---

the discrepancy in names would be extraordinary. He is, however, called 'one of the priests'.

In general, it is possible to establish that they were priests from the position of the places where they worked.

From the lists themselves it is possible to see which of the officials mentioned were treasurers and which 'amarkᵉlîm (overseers). In the first list numbers 5 to 8 have to do with Temple finances, while 1 to 4 have to do with the oversight of the Levite musicians and Temple servants. In the second list, as far as the physician (5) and the super-viser of curtains (14) are concerned we have the evidence of the text itself (M. Shek. v.2) that they held office as 'concerning property'. The former would in fact have to do with Temple finance, in so far as medicaments, particularly wine (j. Shek. v.2, 48d.28), were obviously provided by the Temple. For 14 and 15, we have the evidence of Josephus that they were treasurers (pp. 172f.). Besides this the keeper of the seals (1), the officials 'over drink offerings' (2) and 'over bird offerings' (4) and those who prepared the shewbread and the in-cense (12 and 13) dealt with Temple money and Temple stores, and so belong among those who held office as 'concerning property'. The fact that the number of remaining officials in the second list (3, 6, 7, 8, 9, 10, 11), for whom there is no record of connection with Temple finance, comes to seven, shows that we have here the seven 'ammarkᵉlîm with whom the paragraph at the end of the second list is concerned. This agrees both with our earlier consideration of the meaning of the word 'ammarkāl (p. 166) and also with the fact that these seven men, are officials concerned with the oversight of the Temple. We see again, then, that the accepted interpretation of the word 'ammarkᵉlîm as treasury officials (p. 165) is not tenable.

Now we can go into more detail about the Temple overseers and treasurers. Under the first heading comes the priest (List 2.3) who dealt with the daily casting of lots to choose the officiating priests of the daily course, and, as the tractate Tamid shows (p. 170), with the arrangements for the entire morning and evening services each day. Here also are the 'trench digger' (List 2.6) responsible for the main-tenance of the baths for ablutions, the cisterns and the conduits, and the herald (List 2.7) who called priests, Levites and people to wor-ship; and finally the four chief Levites (List 1.1–4; 2.8–11), in charge of the Levite musicians and Temple guards.

As for the treasurers, we get a complete confirmation of their duties as derived earlier from the sources on pp. 166f. They adminis-tered the Temple stores and issued them for use in the cultus (List 1.5–8; 2.12–13), also the Temple treasure (List 2.14–15); and after the management of the Temple revenues, their other chief concern was the control of the Temple monopoly of the trade in drink-offerings and other offerings (List 2. 1, 2 and 4).

The three spheres of duty devolving on the chief priests and chief Levites were fulfilment of the cultus, administration of Temple finances and supervision of the Temple.

In this section on the chief priests we must include an inquiry into the remarkable usage of the term 'high priest' in the New Testament, in Josephus and in the Talmud. In the Gospels and Acts alone there are no less than sixty-four references to the high priests, in the plural, although there was only one high priest at a time in office. In fact, a common expression in the New Testament is 'the high priests and elders'. We may be able to explain the use of the plural by supposing that the term 'high priests' refers not only to the high priest then in office (kōhēn-ha-mᵉšammēš), but often also the high priest no longer in office (kōhēn šeʿābar).[81] This solution, however, breaks down since all the sources repeatedly name as high priests men who do not appear in Josephus' complete list of high priests. There was for instance Skeva 'a high priest of the Jews' whose seven sons practised exorcism in Ephesus (Acts 19.14); Jesus, son of Sapphia, 'one of the high priests' (BJ 2.566); Simon, 'from the number of the high priests' (Vita 197); Matthias, son of Boethus, (BJ 4.574; 5.527–531; 6.114); the 'high priest' Levi, who rebuked Jesus for entering the Holy Place without observing the Pharisaic rules of cleanliness (Oxyrhynchus Fragment, 1908, v. 840); in the Talmud, Zadoq[82] (Lam. R. 1.49 on 1.16, Son 1.46, 127f.) and Issachar from Kephar Barqai [83] (b. Pes. 57a. Bar), are called 'high priests'.

E. Schürer, that distinguished and learned pioneer in the field of New Testament history, has attempted to solve the riddle, and the moderns all follow him[84] with the explanation that these 'high priests' were 'members of the privileged families from which the high priests were taken'.[85] He appeals to BJ 6.114, Acts 4.6 and two passages in the Mishnah (M. Ket. xiii.1–2; M. Ohol. xvii.5). To begin with, the

[81] M. Hor. iii.4. The precise description of the retiring priest, in T. Sanh. iv.1, 420 is ha-kōhēn seʿābar miggᵉdūlātō.

[82] The name Ishmael b. Elisha appears in the slightly different parallel passage in b. Gitt. 58a.

[83] There is also a report of a 'high priest' upon whom the lot fell to administer the 'waters of bitterness' (Pesiqta Rabbati 26, 129b.5), but the high priest in office was not subject to the lot (M. Yom. i.2).

[84] With the one exception of Schlatter, as I observe below, p. 177 n. 90.

[85] Schürer II, 275–77, ET II.1, 203–6.

Mishnah passages can be disregarded since, as will be shown, Schürer has mistranslated them. The passage from Josephus reads as follows: 'Among these (apostates) were the high priests Joseph and Jesus, and certain sons of high priests, namely three sons of Ishmael who was beheaded in Cyrene, four of Matthias and one of another Matthias; the last had escaped after the death of his father, who had been slain with three of his sons by Simon, son of Gioras, as related above. Many others also of the aristocracy went over with the high priests' (*BJ* 6.144).

Here it is in fact possible, as Schürer thought, to include in the term 'high priests' in the last sentence the two previously mentioned retired high priests and the eight sons of high priests, so that the term 'high priests' here might include the nearest blood-relations of the high priest. But the term 'high priests' in the last sentence could equally well indicate only the two retired high priests mentioned at the outset, and in this case the title would imply nothing else than 'the high priests no longer in office.' This passage then, is not without difficulties from Schürer's viewpoint. He does better to appeal to Acts 4.6 where 'all who were of the high-priestly family' appears as a group in the Sanhedrin, while elsewhere in the New Testament this is abbreviated to 'the high priests'. Even this passage, however, does not appear a convincing argument for calling members of the high-priestly family 'high priests'; for the question arises whether the men 'of the high-priestly' family referred to in Acts 4.6 had their seats and votes in the Sanhedrin by virtue of their family background, as Schürer has to assume, or rather by virtue of their office.[86]

So the proof texts for Schürer's hypothesis are all defective, and apart from that it is open to serious doubt. Johanan b. Zakkai met a *kōhēn gādōl*[87] in Beth Rama (Rec. B: *Rāmat beʿnē ʿanāt*), presumably in Galilee.[88] Did members of the reigning high-priestly families live in Galilee before AD 70? Highly unlikely! Furthermore, according to Schürer these men 'of the high priestly family' had seats and votes in the Sanhedrin.[89] Had this body of seventy-one members room

[86] Cf. the conference mentioned in Acts 4.6, and the nepotism practised by the illegal hierarchy in connection with the chief priestly offices, both discussed in the next section, the priestly aristocracy on pp. 181ff.

[87] *ARN*, Rec. A, ch. 12, Rec. B, ch. 27 (Goldin 71).

[88] *Bēt ʾanāt* is confirmed as being in Galilee in T. Mikw. vi.3, 658. See Schlatter, *Jochanan ben Zakkai*, 27 n. 1. The Zeno Papyrus, *Papiri greci e latini* [Pubblicazioni della Società Italiana.] vol. VI, Florence 1920, 3, no. 594 line 18, describes a Bait(i)anata in Galilee.

[89] Schürer II, 276 (ET. II.1, 205) based on Acts 4.6.

for all? If not, by what criterion, which is nowhere mentioned, were they chosen? However, the most serious objections (see also n. 83) to Schürer's argument are philological. *Kōhēn gādōl* (ἀρχιερεύς) means archpriest and nothing more. How, without further explanation, would ἀρχιερεύς to a Greek reader, and *kōhēn gādōl* to a Jewish reader, have conveyed 'a member of the high-priestly family'?

There are two passages in the Mishnah which can help us to clarify the position. In one of these, the 'sons of the high priests' made decisions in civil law (M. Ket. xiii, 1–2), and in the other they received letters from abroad (M. Ohol. xvii.5). It is a philological error when the otherwise dependable Schürer takes 'sons of the high priests' to mean 'men of importance and authority' (n. 89). For other passages, and in fact variant readings, show that the term *bᵉnē kōhᵃnîm gᵉdōlîm* does not mean 'sons of the high priests' as Schürer thought, but 'the high priests' themselves. In the same way, in the Old Testament (I Kings 20.35 etc.) the prophets were called 'sons of the prophets', and in the New Testament (Matt. 12.27) the scribes were called 'sons of the scribes'. In other words, the term 'sons of' denotes not descent but membership of a class.[90] If we apply this to the sources, we find that *bᵉnē kōhᵃnîm gᵉdōlîm*, i.e. the high priests, held a court which arrived at decisions of civil law for the priesthood. We find elsewhere a decision of this same court, that on the Day of Atonement only a priest or a Levite had the right to take the goat for Azazel into the wilderness (M. Yom. vi.3).[91] The same court is in question, as the subjects of proceedings show, when statements are made about a 'court of priests', and before this forum were heard questions concerning, on the one hand, laws affecting priests

[90] In j. Shek. iv.48a. 35 the high priests officiating at the ceremony of the Red Heifer (five times since 200 BC according to M. Par. iii.5) are grouped together as 'sons of the high priests'. For 'the high priests' in ARN, *Rec.* A, ch. 4 (Goldin 37), Rec. B, ch. 7 has 'sons of the high priests', so the two expressions are identical. Siphra Lev. 2.3, 6d, says, 'As the high priest Aaron eats [his part of the meal offering] without strife [because he had the choice], likewise the *bᵉnē kōhᵃnîm gᵉdōlîm* eat without strife.' Here the successors, the officiating high priests since Aaron, are contrasted with the first high priest, and once again it is clear that the subject is not sons of the high priests, but the high priests themselves. Schlatter, *Jochanan ben Zakkai*, 25, rightly translates *bᵉnē kōhᵃnîm gᵉdōlîm* (M. Ket. xiii. 1–2) as 'high priests'.

[91] The variant reading, 'the *priests* had established a custom', for 'the *high priests* had established' (ed. princ. Naples 1492; ed. Venice 1609; Cambridge MS, ed. Lowe 1883; *Cod. Orient.* Berlin 567. 4; *ed. princ.* of Jerus. Venice 1523) is either a correction or an inadvertent omission.

(marriage laws, M. Ket. i.5)[92] and on the other hand matters of the cultus (enquiries about signs of the new moon, i.e. the fixing of the calendar, M.R. Sh. i.7).[93] (On the other hand, when it came to condemning a priest's daughter to death for unchastity [b. Sanh. 52b] in the reign of Agrippa I, it was the Sanhedrin that acted as the court.)[94] Who were the 'archpriests' who constituted this court? They were distinguished priests, as their Sadducaic theology shows (see n. 93). They formed a well-defined body; they gave authoritative decisions on the priesthood and on questions of cultus. In other words, this court was composed of the chief priests of the Temple at Jerusalem.

This in fact is the answer to the riddle. The term *kōhēn gādōl* means the archpriest, the priest made prominent by his position over the main body of priests, and absolutely nothing else; indeed in the narrower sense the term means *the* archpriest, or high priest, and in the wider sense the archpriests or chief priests of higher rank than the majority. After the *kōhēn gādōl*, who was 'in office' (in the Holy of Holies, M. Hor. iii.4; M. Meg. i.9), who 'is dedicated by many garments' (M. Hor. iii.4; M. Mak. ii.6; M. Meg. i.9; Siphra Lev. 21.12, 47c; j. Yom. i.1, 38d.39, etc), came the other (*bᵉnē kōhᵃnīm gᵉdōlīm* the chief priests (1 QM 2.1;[95] cf. above n. 42). This linguistic interpretation is incontestable, and nowhere does it break down. It now becomes clear how the term 'high priests' could be used in the plural; how the names of 'high priests' are used which do not appear

[92] The priestly court fixed the price of the *kᵉtubbāh* (marriage contract) of a virgin who was either of a priestly family or wished to marry a priest, at 40c denarii, that is, double the usual price.

[93] When the passage speaks of two courts fixing the calendar, the college of priests and the Sanhedrin, the explanation is that originally the priests were responsible, but as they were mainly Sadducees, the Sanhedrin intervened to insist on the acceptance of Pharisaic rulings. The same two courts appear in M. Yom. i.5, where the 'elders of the court' appear with the 'elders of the priesthood'.

[94] With regard to this the following facts are certain: (*a*) Criminal law was administered without interference by the Jewish authority, which points to the time of Agrippa I (Schlatter, *Tage*, 8off.). This dating is confirmed by the evidence that R. Eleazar b. Zadoq as a small boy, had seen the execution of the sentence (T. Sanh. ix.11, 429), p. 143. (*b*) The sentence was passed, not according to Pharisaic law (M. Sanh. vii.2: 'The court at that time had not right knowledge', i.e. of the law) but according to Sadducaic (b. Sanh. 52b); for whereas the Pharisees taught that the sentence of death by burning in Lev. 21.9 required that molten lead be poured down the throat, thus burning from inside, the Sadducees taught that it should be done by heaping faggots round the accused, thus burning from outside, and this was done to the priest's daughter.

[95] Here a high priest (*kōhēn hārōš*) and chief priests (*rāšē ha-kōhᵃnīm*) are mentioned together.

in the list of officiating high priests; how a 'high priest' could live in Galilee; how he could be subject to the lot;[96] how the high priest Pinḥas was indeed descended from a high-priestly family though he did not belong to 'the high priests' (*BJ* 4.155); and how the Sanhedrin had room for the 'high priests', this being in every case a reference to the chief priests of the Temple.

In particular this explains those passages in the Gospels and Acts, of which there are no less than sixty-four, which speak of 'high priests'. For the most part this applies to the passages where they appear as members of the council in association with scribes and elders. In the trial and judgement of Jesus, and later of the apostles, and in the examination of Paul, the 'high priests' took part in their capacity as members of the Sanhedrin. They were the permanent chief priests of the Temple, who by virtue of their office had seats and votes in the Sanhedrin where they formed a well-defined group. In fact we find in one place a captain of the Temple (Acts 4.5–6; see pp. 196f., esp. n. 165) and in another a Temple treasurer (*Ant.* 20.189ff.) who belonged to the Sanhedrin. The minimum number of this chief priestly group (this is the only one we know) amounted to one high priest, one captain of the Temple, one Temple overseer (a priest), and three treasurers—six in all, to which were added the retired high priests, and those priests who were employed as overseers and treasurers. This gives a credible number in relation to the seventy-one members of the court.

At the same time there are passages in the New Testament mentioning chief priests in other combinations, either chief priests and overseers of the Temple (Luke 22.4) or chief priests and their attendants (Acts 5.17, 21). Here we are dealing with the chief priests as the independent legal and administrative authority in the Temple.[97] We have already seen from Talmudic sources that the chief priests formed an independent body competent to deal with affairs of the Temple and the priesthood (pp. 177f.). It was as the executive body of the Temple that the chief priests came to a decision over the expenditure of the money paid to Judas for his treachery, which he had returned, namely that it was the 'price of blood' and could not go into the Temple treasury (Matt. 27.6; cf. above p. 139).

[96] *Pesiqta rabbati* 26, 129b.5; p. 175, n. 83.

[97] The only exception to these passages, as context or parallels show, are those which refer to 'chief priests' in the Sanhedrin *a parte potiori:* Mark 15.3 (cf. Matt. 27.12); 15.10 (cf. 15.1); 15.11 (cf. Matt. 27.20, 'chief priests and elders'); John 12.10.

As principal authority over the Temple police they made the arrangement with Judas for Jesus' arrest (Matt 26.14–15; Mark 14.10–11;
Luke 22.4–5), which had previously been approved by the Sanhedrin
(Matt. 26.3f. and par.); they gave the orders for the apostles' arrest
in the Temple court (Acts 5.17, 21); they received from the guard at
the sepulchre the report of Jesus' resurrection (Matt. 28.11)[98] and
from the prison watch news of the apostles' escape from the custody of
the Temple police (Acts 5.24). In a similar capacity they provided
the Pharisaic zealot Saul with a contingent of Temple police for the
purpose of persecuting Christians (Acts 26.12; cf. 9.14, 21; 26.10).

So we receive the following picture. The captain of the Temple,
who was responsible for the conduct of worship and external arrangements in the Temple, was the most important priest immediately
below the high priest, and was the head of the chief priests. After
him came the leader of the weekly course of priests, whichever course
was on duty, and the leaders of the four to nine daily courses of this
week. The organization of external arrangements in the Temple was
in the hands of the seven permanent Temple overseers, to which
belonged four chief Levites; financial arrangements were entrusted
to the three permanent Temple treasurers and their colleagues. The
chief priests permanently employed at the Temple formed a definite
body who had jurisdiction over the priesthood and whose members
had seats and votes on the council.

Now this conclusion, that the Jerusalem chief priests formed a
definite body, is greatly strengthened by the statement in Acts 4.6
that the chief priests belonged to the priestly aristocracy. Thus not
every priest had access to this position. The social gulf within the
priesthood, which has been made perceptible here, is confirmed
by other evidence. Between the chief priests of Jerusalem (οἱ ἀρχιερεῖς
of the New Testament) and the rest of the priesthood an intense
antagonism had grown up in the period just before the destruction
of the Temple, as both the Talmud and Josephus agree. The Talmud
is full of complaints about the violence of the high priests who
forcibly appropriated the hides of the sacrifices, which were distributed each evening among the priests of the daily course on duty
in a Temple chamber (p. 106 above), and the measures taken against

[98] It is scarcely possible to imagine Roman soldiers keeping watch at the
sepulchre, since they would hardly have been ready to admit that they had been
asleep at their posts (Matt. 28.13). The report being made to the chief priests
points rather to Temple police (28.11). The ἔχετε in Matt. 27.65 is, therefore, taken
as indicative and not imperative.

this kind of violence, namely the procedure of having the hides distributed only once a week in the presence of the whole weekly course, did not succeed in preventing it. Complaints were also made of tyranny and nepotism (b. Pes. 57a, Bar.; T. Zeb. xi.16, 497). Quite independently Josephus reports the violent plunder of tithes due to the priests by the servants of the high priest, who raided the farmers' threshing-floors (*Ant.* 20.181, 206f.). The social gulf between the chief priests and the main body of the priesthood, revealed by these reports, only becomes intelligible if we attempt to obtain a clear conception of the priestly aristocracy.

C. THE PRIESTLY ARISTOCRACY

The high priest, and in most cases the Jerusalem chief priests, belonged to 'those who were of the high-priestly family' (Acts 4.6; *Ant.* 15.39–40), i.e. to the priestly aristocracy, about which there exist a number of inaccurate and even false conceptions, which can be corrected only by an historical review.

According to the historical conception of the Judaism of the time of Jesus, the Zadokite high-priestly family, so called after the Zadoq who was the chief priest in office under Solomon and David (II Sam. 8.17, 15.24 etc; I Kings 1.8 etc., particularly 2.35), had held the high priesthood in unbroken succession since the time of Aaron. (In actual fact the legality of the Zadokite priesthood, at least as far as we know, went back only to Solomon's time.)[99] I Chron. 6.3–15 traces their un-interrupted line from Aaron to the exile.[100] Neh. 12.10–11 gives it, likewise without a break, until the fourth century BC, and Josephus in his *Antiquities*[101] from then on to the high priest Menelaus (172–162 BC) who was in his view, certainly a mistaken one (see below), the last legitimate Zadokite high priest (*Ant.* 20.235).[102] Fourteen generations of high priests of the house of Zadoq were reckoned from the setting up of the Tabernacle of the congregation until the building of the first Temple.[103] Nine Zadokite high priests[104] must have held office in

[99] Wellhausen, *Pharisäer*, 47ff.

[100] I Chron. 6.50–53 gives a parallel list agreeing in all particulars up to Solomon's time.

[101] 11.347 to 12.239. For a critical appraisal see n. 112 below and n. 7 above.

[102] In *Ant.* 20.224–51 Josephus gives a summarized account of all the high priests from Aaron to the destruction of the Temple.

[103] I Chron. 6.3–10; Josephus, *Ant.* 20.228, reckons thirteen.

[104] So says I Chron. 6.3–15: eighteen according to the Talmud, j. Yom. i.1, 38c.37, and Josephus, *Ant.* 20.231.

rightful succession in the first Temple (of Solomon), fifteen from the exile to Menelaus (inclusive) in the second (post-exilic) Temple (*Ant.* 20.234). We do not intend to examine here the historical authenticity of these lists,[105] apart from the last of the line. We will content ourselves with establishing the historic conception of the first century AD, according to which there was an uninterrupted succession of Zadokite high priests from Aaron to the time of the Seleucid Antiochus Epiphanes IV (175–164 BC),[106] whose interference in appointments to the high-priestly office, and religious persecution, brought to an end the Zadokite line of high priests. The last high priests of the Zadokite era were:

	Term of Office	Descent	Appointed by
Onias II	to 175 BC	Son of high priest Simon	Succession
Jesus (Jason)	175–172	Son of high priest Simon	Antiochus IV Epiphanes
Menelaus	172–162	Non-Zadokite priest	Antiochus IV Epiphanes
Jacim (Alcimus)	162–159	Illegitimate Zadokite	Antiochus V Eupator (?)

EXCURSUS

THE CHRONOLOGY OF THE BOOKS OF MACCABEES

Before explaining this list, to justify the dates in it we must say something on the calculation of the Seleucid era in the two books of Maccabees. As is well known, there is great controversy as to whether the Seleucid era, which both books use for dating, should be reckoned from the spring

---

[105] The conclusion arrived at by Josephus, historian of late Judaism, that the Zadokite family held office as high priest in direct succession is correct for the post-exilic period to the time of Onias II. To trace the genealogy back to Aaron is erroneous (p. 181 n. 99), as it also is to assume that the chief priest of the Temple at Jerusalem held the primacy in the same way before the exile as after, (for detailed criticism see p. 184 n. 112).

[106] According to the list of Seleucids, B.M. 35603, published by A. J. Sachs and D. J. Wiseman, 'A Babylonian King List of the Hellenistic Period', *Iraq* 16, 1954, 202–12, Antiochus IV died between 19 November and 19 December 164 BC. This agrees with I Macc. 6.16: the year of his death was the Seleucid year 149=autumn 164 to autumn 163.

of 311 BC[107] or 312 BC,[108] or from the autumn (1 Tishri) of 312 BC;[109] or even whether there are not two systems of numbering in I Maccabees, corresponding to the different scales in Babylonia and Syria-Macedonia, giving (a) a time-scale for political events, beginning with the autumn of 312; (b) a time-scale for use within Judaism, for ecclesiastical events, beginning in the spring of 311. On the basis of the list of Seleucids referred to in n. 106, J. Schaumberger[110] has put forward this last solution. In fact this acceptance of a double time-scale in I Maccabees may well prove right, since it is the best explanation of the variations in dating political events in I and II Maccabees. Two examples may serve to illustrate this double enumeration in I Maccabees. (In II Maccabees the whole thing is much simpler, since there the dating follows the Jewish numbering apart from the two letters in ch. 11.) The first example refers to a political event, the second to an 'ecclesiastical' one within Judaism.

1. In both I Macc. 6.20–63 and II Macc. 13.1 there are reports of the campaign of Antiochus V Eupator against Judaea. According to I Maccabees it took place in the 150th year of the Seleucid era; according to II Maccabees it was the year 149. If we follow Schaumberger[111] it means not so much that one of the books of Maccabees gives false evidence, but rather that each one is based on a different reckoning of the Seleucid era. Actually they agree more readily if the campaign took place in the autumn of 163 BC, since this autumn, besides belonging, according to the Jewish reckoning used in II Maccabees, to the year 149 in the Seleucid era (i.e. spring 163 to spring 162), also belongs to the Seleucid year 150, according to the Syrian-Macedonian reckoning for political events (i.e. autumn 163 to autumn 162).

2. An examination of the report of events in the 160th Seleucid year, in I Macc. 10.1–21, shows that Jewish 'ecclesiastical' events in this book too are reckoned from the spring (of 311). After Alexander Balas set himself up as king (v. 1) Demetrius I Soter tried to win the friendship of the Jews (vv. 2–7), and as a result Jerusalem was fortified (vv. 8–14). Thereupon Alexander Balas made similar offers to the Jews (vv. 15–20). In this favourable political situation Jonathan assumed the high-priestly vestments

[107] W. Kolbe, *Beiträge zur syrischen und jüdischen Geschichte*, Stuttgart 1926, 47–57.
[108] Schürer I, 32–38 (ET I.1, 36–45), retracting his earlier opinion, and many others.
[109] Meyer, *Ursprung* II, 248 n. 1, *et alia*. According to S. Zeitlin, 'Megillot Taanit as a Source for Jewish Chronology and History in the Hellenistic and Roman Periods', *JQR*, NS 9, 1918–19, 81, the reckoning should be from the autumn of 313 BC, but this is impossible.
[110] 'Die neue Seleukidenliste B.M. 35603 und die makkabäische Chronologie', *Biblica* 36, 1955, 423–35; cf. R. Hanhart, 'Zur Zeitrechnung des I und II Makkabäerbuches', in A. Jepsen and R. Hanhart, *Untersuchungen zur israelitisch-jüdischen Chronologie* (BZAW 88), 1964, 49–96.
[111] Schaumberger, *art. cit.*, 429f.

at the feast of Tabernacles (v. 21), which was celebrated from the 15 to 21 Tishri. If the Seleucid year began in the autumn, all the principal events of the Seleucid year 160 must have taken place between 1 and 14 Tishri! But this is out of the question. On the other hand, all difficulties are removed if the Seleucid year 160 is here reckoned as 'ecclesiastical' from spring (311), in which case the Seleucid year 160 fell in the period between spring 152 and spring 151. The conclusion is that I Maccabees uses a double reckoning of the Seleucid era; political events were dated from autumn 312, and Jewish 'ecclesiastical' ones from spring 311.

To return to our list of the last high priests, on p. 182: Onias II was the last legitimate high priest in the rightful Zadokite succession, according to the reliable interpretation of the book of Daniel (9.25f.; 11.22).[112] He was replaced, at the command of Antiochus IV, in 175 BC by his brother Jesus[113] (he had adopted the name Jason) who had promised the king in return a considerable sum of money and the introduction of Greek customs into Jerusalem; and this in spite of the fact that according to the Law Onias II had a life-long right to his office, and that his son, also called Onias (III), was next in succession (II Macc. 4.7–22).[114] The disruption of the high-priestly succession began with the illegitimate appointment of Jason as high priest in 175, for the fact that Jason too had high-priestly blood in his veins did not, in the people's sense of right, alter the illegality of his assumed rank (cf. the judgment of Daniel, 9.26f.; 11.22).

However, Jason did not enjoy for long his wrongfully acquired

[112] According to Josephus' numbering he is the third of his name. Actually this Onias is the son of the high priest Simon ('the Righteous', after 200 BC), and Josephus mistakenly duplicates him, as he did Simon, cf. p. 149 n. 7 and further H. Guthe, *Geschichte des Volkes Israel*, 3rd ed., Tübingen 1914, 318. For what follows cf. I and II Macc., *Ant.* 12.237–434; *BJ* 1.31–47; also O. Holtzmann, *Neutestamentliche Zeitgeschichte*, 2nd ed., Tübingen 1906, 27–29; Schürer I, 194–226; ET I.1, 202–37; B. Stade and A. Bertholet, *Biblische Theologie des Alten Testaments* II, Tübingen 1911, 203–7, 276–9; Guthe, *op. cit.*, 318, 322–7; S. Zeitlin, 'Megillot Taanit as a Source for Jewish Chronology and History in the Hellenistic and Roman Periods', *JQR*, NS 9, 1918–19, 71–102; *ibid.* 10, 1919–20, 49–80 and 237–90; above all Meyer, *Ursprung* II, 131–66, 205–52; Schlatter, *Geschichte Israels*, 102–29.

[113] With regard to dating: Jason was appointed by Antiochus IV Epiphanes, who was king in 175, and was three years in office (II Macc. 4.23). According to Dan. 9.26f. (see p. 185 n. 117) Menelaus was already high priest by the end of 172 (murder of Onias II). Thus Jason was high priest from 175–172.

[114] Josephus' account in *Ant.* 12.237 seeks to conceal the irregularity in the succession of Jason, in that he lets Onias die a natural death in 175 and adds that his son Onias III was still a minor when his father died. This version is obviously wrong. The violent death of Onias II is certified in Dan. 9.26 and 11.22 and thus the version in II Macc. is confirmed.

title. After three years of office (II Macc. 4.23) Antiochus IV deposed him in 172 and replaced him with a non-Zadokite—an unheard-of outrage to the religious feelings of the people—one Menelaus from the priestly clan of Bilga, who had promised the king an ever higher fee (II Macc. 4.23ff.).[115] Since the people rightly saw in Onias II, still living, the rightful high priest,[116] Menelaus had him treacherously murdered at the end of 172 or early in 171 (II Macc. 4.34).[117] Onias,[118] enraged at the murder of his father, and now the rightful successor to the high-priestly title, resorted to force and succeeded in taking Jerusalem by a surprise attack, apart from the fortress[119] where Menelaus had taken refuge (II Macc. 5.5). But Onias could not hold out against Antiochus IV, who recaptured Jerusalem in 169,[120] and Onias III had to flee, while Menelaus was reinstated in office. In this desperate situation Onias

[115] He was not of Zadokite descent—v. 23, cf. 3.4 Armenian and Latin versions. Josephus tries to gloss over the fact that the legitimate succession had been broken, and speaks of Menelaus as brother of Onias II and Jason, and says that he was also called Onias (*Ant.* 12.238f; 15.41; 19.298; 20.235). It is highly unlikely, however, that the high priest Simon had two sons called Onias, i.e. Onias II and 'Onias Menelaus'. Josephus' purpose, as we have seen in n. 114 is quite obvious. His evidence on Menelaus' descent is, according to Meyer, a clumsy falsification to make the usurper Menelaus appear legitimate (Meyer, *Ursprung* II, 133).

[116] The verdict of the people, e.g. in *Ass. Mos.* 5.4: 'Those . . . who are not priests, but slaves, sons of slaves.'

[117] The account in II Macc. is preferable to Josephus's presentation in *Ant.* 12. 237, where he says Onias II died a natural death in 175 BC, since both Dan. 9.26; 11.22 and possibly also Zech. 12.10ff., confirm Onias' death by violence; Dan. 9. 26f. gives the date of Onias' murder as the beginning of the seven-year period Dec. 171 to Dec. 164.

[118] III: *BJ* 1.31; 7.423 wrongly speak of Onias II, who was then already dead, see n. 117.

[119] Josephus' account in *BJ* 1.31f., which probably goes back to Nicholas of Damascus, Herod the Great's court historian, though unquestionably preferable to the distorted account in *Ant.*, should be treated critically and with caution (see n. 118 and 120). According to *Ant.* 12.239f. and II Macc. 5.5–10 the previous high priest Jason had attempted an attack on Jerusalem. But the statement in II Macc. 5.8, that Jason had had to flee to Egypt, makes it seem likely that this originally referred to Onias III, who fled to Egypt and founded a temple at Leontopolis. The account in *Ant.* is completely distorted and prejudiced, since the account in *Ant.* 12.237ff. is dominated by the determination to conceal any irregularity in the succession of high priests (see nn. 114, 115 and 117) for which reason Josephus represented there the previous high priest, Jason, and not Onias III, as making the attack on Jerusalem in 170 BC.

[120] On his return from the first Egyptian campaign, according to I Macc. 1.20; *Ant.* 12.246 says in the Seleucid year 143, i.e. autumn 170—autumn 169 BC. According to *BJ* 1.31ff. and II Macc. 5.1–10, on his return from the second Egyptian campaign in 168 BC, but see dating in next note.

III turned to Egypt, where the Jewish community venerated him as the legitimate high priest, and obtained permission from Ptolemy VI Philometor (181–145) and his consort Cleopatra to build the temple at Leontopolis (*BJ* 1.33)[121] The fact that Onias III resolved to build a temple in a heathen land, and moreover found priests, Levites, a community and the very considerable resources necessary to pursue his plan, and finally that this rival temple in a heathen land existed for 243 years, until its destruction by the Romans in AD 73, all would be completely incomprehensible if we did not know how ingrained in the Jewish race was the awareness that Onias III, as the son of the last rightful Zadokite high priest, Onias II, was the legitimate heir to the high priesthood.[122] The legitimacy of the high priest, and the fact that the Temple of Jerusalem was desecrated by the Syrians, allayed all misgivings which must have arisen over the unhallowed place where the new temple was built. In the meantime the storm of religious persecution broke over Israel (169, or 167, to 164), with the Maccabean revolt, and in December 164 the desecrated Temple at Jerusalem was reconsecrated.

Josephus gives the impression that the Maccabees did not impugn the position of Menelaus as high priest.[123] This tolerance is not easy to explain, but may be due to an infinite respect for the authority of the high priest as such. It may also be due to the feeling that Onias III, the legitimate heir, had forfeited his claims by setting up a rival temple in Egypt, as also to the fact that the Maccabees were by no means as yet the undisputed masters of the situation: in 162, for example, they had to endure the appointment of a high priest by the Syrian king. Some such factor may underlie Josephus' account of the peaceful relations that ensued between the Maccabees and Menelaus.

[121] Further *BJ* 7.436, (where only at 7.423 is Onias III confused with his father Onias II): the temple at Leontopolis was destroyed after 343 (read 243) years of existence, in AD 73. It was therefore founded in 170 or 169 BC. According to *Ant.* 12.387; 20.236, Onias III fled to Egypt only after the high priest Menelaus was murdered and Alcimus appointed (162). This later dating is not reliable, since we have found elsewhere in *Ant.* statements which are suspect (see nn. 114, 115, 117 and 119). There is the further objection that the year 169, at the beginning of the religious persecution, is much more reasonable than 162, two years after it was over. Finally the length of time already quoted for the existence of the Temple at Leontopolis does not support the chronology in *Ant.*

[122] Cf. *BJ* 7.423–432 on Onias III's hope to bring the whole Jewish nation to his side by building this temple.

[123] *Ant.* 12.382 ff., esp. 385, says that Menelaus held the office for ten years to the beginning of 162 (when peace was concluded between Antiochus V and the Jews, for the dating of which see p. 184 n. 113.)

However, it is not certain that the Maccabees did tolerate the collaborator Menelaus as high priest, especially as I Macc. 4.42 reads: 'So he [Judas] chose priests of blameless conversation, such as had pleasure in the law.' The most we could say is that Menelaus was nominally high priest until 162.[124] It is certain that in the year 162 the ten-year-old Antiochus V Eupator, at the instigation of his guardian, the general Lysias, had Menelaus put to death in order to gain favour with the Jews.[125] The priest Jacim (Alcimus), who had by this time (162) been made high priest by the Syrians,[126] was certainly not in the direct line of succession to the last lawful high priest Onias II, but he was at least a Zadokite.[127] The fact that now, after Menelaus, there was again a man with Zadokite ancestry as high priest was enough to revive the hopes of the people, and the Hasidim (Pharisees) deserted the Maccabees and joined him (I Macc. 7.12ff.). However, they were bitterly disappointed in the man on whom they had set their hopes (I Macc. 7.16ff.; 9.54–57; II Macc. 14.3f.; *Ant.* 12.395ff.), and moreover his term of office soon ended with his death in May 159.[128]

[124] Schürer I, 215 (ET I.1, 225f.) n. 16, assumes that Menelaus 'was naturally unable, in the presence of Judas who was in possession of the actual power, to exercise the functions of the high priest's office', similarly Schlatter, *Geschichte Israels*, 116. On the other hand Meyer (*Ursprung* II, 211, 214, 224, 233) presumes that Menelaus remained in office. Unfortunately we have no source which gives clear information on the attitude of the Maccabees to Menelaus.

[125] *Ant.* 12.385; 20.235; II Macc. 13.3–8. On the dating, the execution took place in connection with the peace treaty between Antiochus V Eupator and the Jews, at the beginning of 162 according to Josephus' account, but II Macc. puts it before Antiochus V's campaign against Judaea in the late summer of 163, which sounds less likely.

[126] According to *Ant.* 12.385; 20.235 Alcimus was appointed by Antiochus V Eupator (163–autumn 162); according to I Macc. 7.5ff. and II Macc. 14.3ff., however, he was appointed by Demetrius I Soter (autumn 162–150). But II Macc. as well as Josephus (see last note) has Menelaus, Alcimus' predecessor, executed earlier under Antiochus V in 162 (II Macc. 13) and has Alcimus (14.3, 7) already appointed high priest before the time of Demetrius. Since the change of high priest was connected with the peace treaty between Antiochus V and the Jews at the beginning of 162 (*Ant.* 12.383ff.) Josephus' dating is certainly right (as against Schürer I, 216 (ET I.1, 227) n. 23, but giving no reason), and Alcimus' appointment took place as early as the beginning of 162 and not in the autumn of that year.

[127] *Ant.* 20.235: 'of Aaron's line', though not of the reigning high-priestly family. *Ant.* 12.387: 'he was not of the family of high priests'. I. Macc. 7.14: 'a priest of the line of Aaron'. In II Macc. 14.7 Alcimus describes his high priestly authority to Demetrius I as προγονικὴ δόξα.

[128] According to I Macc. 9.54, it was in the Seleucid year 153, i.e. spring 159–spring 158, in the second month.

The situation in Jerusalem had now become very confused as a result of the arbitrary interference by the Syrian kings in the high priestly succession, and of the fact that the legitimate successor, Onias III had gone to Egypt. This confusion is shown most clearly from Josephus' report that from 159–152 the highest priestly office in Judaism remained vacant (*Ant.* 20.237).[129]

Let us review again the high-priestly succession in the sixteen years in question (175–159 BC). After the deposition of the last lawful high-priest of Zadok's line, Onias II (175) there followed: (1) A Zadokite usurper, Jesus-Jason, (175–172). (2) A priest from the clan of Bilga, Menelaus, (172–162). (3) A Zadokite who was not of the lawful succession, Jacim-Alcimus (162–159). The lawful Zadokite successor to the high priesthood, Onias III, had fled to Egypt and founded a rival temple in Leontopolis, so in 159 Jerusalem was without a high priest.

For seven years this state of affairs continued, with Jewry lacking a religious leader, until autumn 152, when at the feast of Tabernacles[130] Jonathan the Hasmonean (161–143/2), then ruler of the Jews,[131] assumed the high priestly vestment. Until then the *bēt ḥašmōnay*[132] had been merely a family of priests within the

---

[129] However, according to *Ant.* 12.414 and 434 the people had already handed over the high priesthood to Judas the Maccabee after the death of Alcimus, presumably in 161, and he held the office for three years (161–158), and accordingly *Ant.* 13.46 reckons the interregnum as four years, not seven. That is obviously tendentious and cannot possibly be right, since I Macc. knows nothing of Judas being high priest and according to the dating in I Macc. 9.3, which is assuredly correct, Judas had already been killed in the first month (i.e. Nisan) of the Seleucid year 152=April 160 BC. (This calculation assumes that the 'ecclesiastical' Seleucid years were from spring to spring, see p. 183, thus 152 was from spring 160 to spring 159. But even if the Seleucid year is reckoned from the autumn, so that the Seleucid year 152 runs from autumn 160 to autumn 159, in which case Judas' death (Nisan of the Seleucid year 152) took place in April 159, he would still have been killed before the death of Alcimus which, according to I Macc. 9.54 occurred in the following Seleucid year, 153 (see previous note).

[130] I Macc. 10.21: 'In the seventh month [Tishri] of the one hundred and sixtieth year at the feast of Tabernacles'. The Seleucid year 160 is from spring 152 to spring 151. The seventh month is Tishri (September-October), and the feast of Tabernacles was held from 15–22 Tishri. Therefore, it was the beginning of October 152.

[131] The Hasmoneans later took the title of king, according to *BJ* 1.70; *Ant.* 13. 301, with Aristobulus I (104–103); but according to the evidence of coins and of Strabo (XVI, 2.40) only with Alexander Jannaeus (103–76). This is not a contradiction, for an internal use of the royal title may have preceded the official proclamation.

[132] Targum Pseudo-Jonathan I Sam. 2.4 says *ḥašmannay*. *Ant.* 12.265 calls Mattathias, the valiant priest and father of five Maccabees, 'Son of John the son

priestly clan of Joiarib, one of the daily courses of which there were four to nine in each priestly clan (weekly course).[133] The Hasmoneans earned their right to the high-priestly title, which the Syrians offered them, by their services to the people in preserving them from danger of religious extinction by the Syrian persecution. Also of influence was the fact that the Oniads, lawful successors to the high-priesthood, were serving in the temple of Onias at Leontopolis, which was not recognized in Jerusalem.

However, the origin of the Hasmonean family had not been forgotten. There were the Pharisees who regarded with suspicion the Hasmonean high priests and princes, as descendants of an ordinary priestly family, and disputed their right to the office. When they sought to bring about the resignation of the Hasmoneans from the high priesthood, by opposing John Hyrcanus (134–104) and Alexander Jannaeus (103–76) on the grounds that John's mother had been a prisoner of war (see above pp. 155f.), we must not forget that this objection was only part of their protest. Their opposition was not simply against sons of a prisoner of war, but against any descendant of an ordinary priestly family taking upon himself an office to which he was not entitled. The deep conviction of the unlawfulness of the Hasmonean high priesthood, which stemmed from an ordinary priestly family and one which had only returned to the homeland a considerable time after the end of the Exile, is shown in the following Tosephta passage:[134] 'And so they [the Jerusalem prophets] agreed with them [the twenty-four weekly courses of priests]: "Moreover if Joiarib [the priestly stock to which the Hasmoneans belonged] should have come back from the Exile, not one [weekly course] may be set aside for their sake, but they shall be simply an appendix to it [one of the weekly courses]".' This means that the Hasmoneans had not even a claim to full membership of a priestly course, not to mention the title of high priest. But the Hasmoneans made good their position, and from the first incumbent of the new position, Jonathan, it passed to his brother Simon (142/1–134) and from then on remained hereditary in the Hasmonean family.

---

of Simeon, the son of Asamonaios'; *BJ* 1.36. however calls Mattathias 'the son of Asamonaios'. A comparison of the three statements shows that the name Asamonaios (*ḥašmōnay*) was possibly not the name of his great-grandfather but a family name.

133 T. Taan. ii.2, 216; j. Taan. iv.2, 68a.14, says five to nine daily courses.
134 T. Taan. ii.1, 216; j. Taan. iv.2, 68a.8–12; b. Taan. 27b; b. Arak. 13a.

For 115 years, until the conquest of Jerusalem by Herod the Great and C. Sosius the Roman governor of Syria in July 37 BC, the Hasmoneans were high priests in unbroken succession, and provided eight high priests during this time. Then they were exterminated by Herod, for the Idumean upstart rightly saw in them the principal threat to his rule. In 35 BC there was just one more Hasmonean high priest, the seventeen-year-old Aristobulus, appointed by his brother-in-law Herod. As he walked to the altar, at the feast of Tabernacles in 35 BC, the people acclaimed him tumultuously, even with tears (*Ant.* 15.50–52; *BJ* 1.437). That was reason enough for Herod to have the young man drowned immediately after the festival, in a pool near Jericho (*Ant.* 15.53–56; *BJ* 1.437). Aristobulus was the last high priest of his family. Herod wallowed in blood. He put to death even the distant relatives of the Hasmonean line,[135] so that no single male Hasmonean was left alive to be considered as ruler and consequently as high priest.[136]

A third epoch began with the sack of Jerusalem in 37 BC, with the abolition of the life-long nature of the high priestly office together with the principle of succession. With two exceptions, Herod nominated 'insignificant persons who were merely of priestly descent' to the high priesthood (*Ant.* 20.247; T. Yom. i.7, 180), the exceptions being Ananel the Babylonian (see p. 193) and Aristobulus the Hasmonean mentioned above. He deposed the high priests and appointed others at will. This anomalous state of affairs continued until the destruction of the Temple in AD 70, and in this way no less than twenty-eight high priests filled the highest priestly office during the 106 years from 37 BC to AD 70, of whom twenty-five were of ordinary priestly families. This number should be compared with the eight Hasmonean high priests who held office in the longer period of 115 years.

We will summarize the findings in numbers once again, and for this we follow Josephus' evidence (*Ant.* 20.224ff.), whereby we observe that he reckons Menelaus as the fifteenth Zadokite to serve in the Temple, though actually his nine years of office should be re-

[135] The 'sons of Baba', murdered by Herod, were hidden at first by a leading Idumean called Costobar, but fell victim to Herod's vengeance in 28 or 27 BC. They must have been very distant relatives of the Hasmonean line, since the name does not occur anywhere else. Even so, they did not escape. They were the last surviving male members of the Hasmonean line (*Ant.* 15.260–266.)

[136] *Ant.* 15.266: 'so that none was left alive of the family of Hyrcanus'. The complete extermination of the Hasmoneans is also reported in b. B.B. 3b.

garded as an interregnum since he was not a Zadokite. Josephus calculates 83 high priests[137] from Aaron to the destruction of the Temple.

Complete List of High Priests According to Josephus

		High priests	Years
First period: Zadokite	(a) From the Exodus[138] to the building of the First Temple (Solomon's)	13	612
	(b) In the First Temple	18	466½
	The Exile	—	70
	(c) In the Second Temple (Menelaus included)	15	412
		46	1560½
Interregnum	(a) The priest Alcimus	1	3
	(b) Period without high priest	—	7
Second period:[139] Hasmonaean		8	113½
Third period:[140] Herodian and Roman (37 BC to AD 70)		28	107
	TOTAL	83	1791

This historical survey makes it possible to achieve a clear concept of the priestly aristocracy. There were in the first century AD two groups of high priestly families, one legitimate, one illegitimate. The

137 *Ant.* 20.227. For this figure, see the Talmud, where in the second Temple (Exile to AD 70) some passages give 80, some 81, 82, 83, 84 and 85 officiating high priests (j. Yom. i.1, 38c.39).

138 *Ant.* 20.230; Josephus counts from the Exodus, not from the building of the Tabernacle.

139 Feast of Tabernacles 152 to July 37, so really 114¾ years.

140 July 38 BC to 10 Ab (roughly August) AD 70, so really 106 years 1 month.

legitimate group comprised simply and solely the Zadokites serving in the Temple of Onias at Leontopolis and the families descended from this ruling line. The illegitimate were the priestly families from the midst of whom one or more members had been raised to the highest spiritual dignity by variable winds of chance and politics since 37 BC, since the Hasmoneans, who formed a group between these two and had held the high priesthood for more than a century, though descended from an ordinary priestly family, were finally exterminated. This is indeed the picture which the sources give us.

In the fourth book of his *Jewish War* Josephus describes how the Zealot leader John of Giscala took possession of Jerusalem in early November AD 67, and how the Zealots soon altered the arrangements for electing the high priest. These public benefactors, to whom nothing came amiss which would increase their own power, gambled in their dealings on the sentiments of the law-loving sector of the populace; but they may also have been partly in earnest. First, 'abrogating the claims of those families from which in turn the high priest had always been drawn, they appointed . . . low-born individuals' (*BJ* 4.148, cf. 153). This refers to the priestly families just mentioned, from whom the high priests had been nominated since 37 BC. The Zealots were right: these families were ordinary priestly families and as such illegitimate. In their stead the new masters appealed to ancient custom, whereby the high priest was chosen by lot. 'They accordingly summoned one of the high-priestly clans, called Eniachin, and cast lots for a high priest' (*BJ* 4.155).

A 'high-priestly clan'—Josephus deliberately uses the word clan as the one most suitable in this connection—can only be a family which was descended from the legitimate Zadokite high-priestly family, which had provided the high priests in Jerusalem until 172 BC, and after that in Leontopolis. This high-priestly clan lived in the country and was no different from other priestly families, particularly with regard to the training of its members. Phanni, the high priest chosen by lot who came from the village of Aphthia (Pinḥas from Ḥabtā' in the Rabbinic tradition), was a stonemason[141] and a wholly

---

[141] According to T. Yom. i.6, 180; Lev. R. 26.9 on 21.10 (Son. 338); Siphra Lev. 21.10, 47c, priestly emissaries took him away from his stone-cutting to Jerusalem. His relation Ḥananiah b. Gamaliel II (*c.* AD 120) maintained, by appealing to I Kings 19.19, 'that he had been brought from the plough to his new authority' (T. Yom. i.6, 180; Siphra Lev. 21.10, 47c) but this is a picture coloured by I Kings 19.19.

uneducated man (*BJ* 4.155). But this clan had the advantage of Zadokite descent, and this was why it came to the Zealots' minds.[142] If we disregard the high priest Eleazar of the bar Kochba rebellion, the last high priest of Jewish history was thus a Zadokite.

The Eniachin were not the only Zadokite clan. Another priestly family, descended from the lawful high priestly line, lived in Babylonia. It produced Ananel, whom Herod appointed first high priest after the sack of Jerusalem in 37 BC.[143] Thus Herod, too, as would the Zealots later, played the role of guardian of tradition, when he appointed a descendant of the legitimate Zadokite family as high priest in place of the Hasmonean 'usurper', even though he prudently chose a man of no importance.[144] Hence it follows from what has been said that in the first centuries before and after Christ there were priestly families descended from the lawful Zadokite line,[145] and that the first and the last high priest to hold office between 37 BC and AD 70 were of Zadokite descent. It is very enlightening to see that the Zadokite family, though politically obscure, stood in the popular view high above the influential but illegitimate high-priestly families. In the east, ancestry has always counted more than power, in fact it is regarded as divinely ordained, and this is something we shall have to establish again and again.

Influence and power were certainly on the side of the illegitimate high-priestly families, and thus of those from which, with three exceptions, the high priest had been nominated since 37 BC. Of the last twenty-eight Jewish high priests who were in office from 37 BC to AD 70, only the first and the last belonged, as we have seen, to a legitimate family: the Babylonian Ananel (37–36/5 BC; from 34 the second time), and the stonemason Pinḥas of Ḥabtā (AD 67/8–70). There had been, moreover, one more Hasmonean high priest in 35 BC in the person of Aristobulus. All the other twenty-five high priests

---

[142] Schürer I, 618 (ET I.2, 228): 'He was a man from the people; and this was the main thing'—but this opinion ignores the main thing, which was the ancestry of the high priest chosen by lot.

[143] *Ant.* 15.40, cf. 22; M. Par. iii.5 calls him an Egyptian.

[144] It is entirely wrong to explain the passage in *Ant.* 15.22, which says that Herod nominated none of the influential native priests, but an undistinguished foreigner, by saying, against Josephus, that Ananel came from 'an inferior priestly stock' (Schürer II, 269, ET II.1, 197, similarly Otto, *Herodes*, col. 38). That is certainly not true.

[145] To such a family belonged the celebrated priest R. Zadoq, who taught in Jerusalem before AD 70. *ARN* Rec. A, ch. 16 (Goldin 84,) reports that he was of high-priestly descent. It is no accident that he was called Zadoq!

belonged to ordinary priestly families. These families, so suddenly raised to the nobility, who came partly from abroad, partly from the provinces,[146] quickly formed a new and powerful, if illegitimate, hierarchy. There were essentially four families in this hierarchy, each of which strove to keep the highest priestly office to itself for as long as possible. Of the twenty-five illegitimate high priests of the Herodian-Roman epoch no fewer than twenty-two belonged to these four families: eight from the family of Boethus,[147] eight of Hannas, three of Phiabi and three of Kamith. It can be assumed that the three remaining high priests had some connection with these families.[148]

Originally the most powerful of the four families was that of Boethus.[149] This family came from Alexandria. Its first representative was the high priest Simon,[150] the father-in-law of Herod.[151] This family managed in time to come, to produce seven further members for the high priesthood, and its powerful influence can be seen, too, in the name 'Boethuseans' by which a section of the Sadducees, and probably even the whole party, was known (T. Sukk. iii.1, 195; b. Sukk. 43b; T. Yom. i.8, 181 etc.).

In the following period, the family of Boethus was overtaken by the house of the high priest Annas[152] whose five sons, along with his

[146] The house of Boethus came from Alexandria. The high priest Joseph b. Elam, who deputized on the Day of Atonement in 5 BC and so was included in the list of twenty-eight high priests, came from Sepphoris (T. Yom. i.4, 180; b. Yom. 12b; j. Yom. i.1, 38d.1). The high-priestly family of *bet*ᶜ*alōbay* (j. reads 'ᵃ*nōbay*) came from *ṣᵉbiyîm* (j. reads *bet ṣᵉbōʿîm*); the high-priestly family of *bet qayyāphā* (j. reads *nᵉqîphî*) came from *beth mᵉqošeš* (j. reads *bet qōšeš*): T. Yeb. i.10, 241; j. Yeb i.6, 3a.46. (b. Yeb. 15b takes the place names as proper names.) The last-named family could be that of the high priest Caiaphas, cf. p. 194 n. 21.

[147] Apart from the six members of the house of Boethus mentioned in Schürer II, 275 (ET II.1, 204); Matthias, son of Theophilus (5–4 BC), who according to *Ant.* 17.164 was the son-in-law of Simon called Boethus (22–5 BC), must be reckoned with the house of Boethus, together with Joseph, son of Elam (5 BC), who was related to Matthias, and indeed closely related since he deputized for him (*Ant.* 17.164).

[148] The three were: Jesus son of See (to AD 6), Ananias son of Nebedaeus (from c. AD 47 onwards) and Jesus son of Damnaios (c. AD 62–63).

[149] In b. Pes. 57a Bar. it is named as the first, and after it the kindred family of Qathros (Kantheras).

[150] He was occasionally called after his family, Boethus, e.g. in *Ant.* 19.297.

[151] 22–5 BC,—note the long term of office, seventeen years. On the dating: Simon was appointed after the end of the famine (*Ant.* 15.319ff.) which can be placed in 24–22 BC on the basis of the chronology of the sabbatical years (cf. my article 'Sabbathjahr', *ZNW* 27, 1928, 98f.=*Abba*, 233f.).

[152] AD 6–15, so nine years in office, Luke 3.2; Acts 4.6; John 18.13, 24.

son-in-law Caiaphas[153] and his grandson Matthias (AD 65), held the premier rank. The house of Kamithos, like that of Phiabi, provided three high priests according to Josephus, but the legendary account of the Talmud says seven, who were said to have been brothers, of whom at least one, and possibly two, must have held office as deputy for his brother who was prevented from officiating by ceremonial defilement.[154] The foundation of the power of these few families can be found in the famous lament (b. Pes. 57a Bar.; T. Men. xiii.21, 533) raised against the new hierarchy of Abba Saul b. Batnith (living in Jerusalem before AD 70—according to b. Betz. 29a Bar., before the destruction of the Temple—and teaching until about 100), in the name of (Tos: 'and') Abba Joseph b. Hanin[155] (before 70, in Jerusalem):

'Woe unto me because of the house of Baithos [Boethus]; woe unto
    me for their lances [or 'evil-speaking']!
Woe unto me because of the house of Hanin,[156] woe unto me
    for their whisperings [or 'calumnies']!
Woe unto me because of the house of Qathros [Tos: Qadhros, meaning
                       Kantheras],
    woe unto me because of their reed pens!'[157]

[153] c. AD 18–37, so nineteen years in office. Frequently referred to in the New Testament. Cf. also p. 194 n. 146. The usual dating of Caiaphas' retirement in AD 36 is unthinkable. According to *Ant.* 18.89 Vitellius, governor of Syria, sent Pilate to Rome to give account of himself, and afterwards (18.90ff.) went to Jerusalem for the Passover and on this occasion deprived Caiaphas of office (95). Now Pilate did not get to Rome until after 16 March, AD 37, after the death of Tiberius, and was therefore not dismissed from office before the end of 36, probably early in 37. This being so, Vitellius was in Jerusalem at the Passover of AD 37, and Caiaphas was then deposed. Cf. Otto, *Herodes*, col. 193ff., and notes; his mistake is simply that he confuses the first visit of Vitellius with his second, *Ant.* 18.122ff. This is quite wrong, because at this second visit Caiaphas' successor Jonathan was deprived of office. Since Vitellius received news of Tiberius' death at the second visit, when the voyage from Rome to Palestine took one to three months because of changeable winds, the second visit was definitely at Pentecost 37. Jonathan, Caiaphas' successor, was only fifty days in office, from Passover to Pentecost 37.

[154] b. Yom. 47a gives the brothers who deputized as Jeshebab and Joseph. The parallel in T. Yom. iv.20, 189, mentions only one brother as deputy; and those in Lev. R. 20.7 on 16.1–2 (Son. 20.11, 263), in j. Yom. i.1, 38d.6, in j. Meg. i.12, 72a. 49, and *Tanḥuma aḥare mot* 7, 117a. 24 etc., call him Judah.

[155] Tos.: 'Abba Jose b. Johanan, citizen of Jerusalem.' The name is the same, only the style is different. Possibly Tos. is thinking wrongly of the scribe of this name, mentioned in M. Ab. i.4, who lived about 150 BC.

[156] Tos: Alhanan, also meaning Annas. Variant reading in b., Hanin, is better.

[157] Tos. adds, 'Woe unto me because of the house of Elisha, woe unto me because of their fist!'

Woe unto me because of the house of Ishmael b. Phiabi,
    woe unto me because of their fist![158]
For they are high priests and their sons are treasurers
    and their sons-in-law are Temple overseers ['amark^{e}lin, pp. 165ff.],
And their servants smite the people [Tos: 'us'] with sticks.'[159]

This lament reveals the characteristic complaint of the people and
the *clerus minor* against the illegitimate new hierarchy, and also contains excellent historical material. Both author and writer belong to
the Jerusalem before the destruction of the Temple, and the passage
mentions the same three high-priestly families (Boethus, Annas and
Phiabi) which as we see from Josephus were the actual power in the
land.[160]

From this cry of woe we learn that the influence of the new
aristocracy depended on their power politics, exercised sometimes
ruthlessly ('lances', 'fist') sometimes by intrigue ('whisperings', 'reed
pens'), and that by this means they were able to control the most
important offices in the Temple as well as the taxes and money:
this meant all the permanent chief-priestly offices at Jerusalem, such
as that of captain of the Temple—we see on p. 162 that this was
usually filled by a near relative of the high-priest—and the Temple
overseer immediately below him, as well as the office of Temple
treasurer. Thus the text shows that they took care to choose all the
chief priests from among the sons and sons-in-law of the high priests
and former high priests.

The New Testament attests this nepotism of the new hierarchy in
a passage which is often misinterpreted. Acts 4.5–6 describes a con-

[158] These last words are missing in Tos. but they have already appeared in the
sentence before (cf. n. 157).

[159] The Tosephta text is less good, see nn. 155, 156; note especially the sudden,
extraordinary appearance of a house of Elisha. No high priest Elisha, or the son of
Elisha, is to be found in the complete list of high priests for the last 100 years before
the destruction of the Temple, which Josephus gives us. Now we have the following rabbinic references: (1) in our passage, a high-priestly house of Elisha; (2) b.
Ber. 7a Bar. and b. Gitt. 58a, we find a certain Rabbi (sic!) Ishmael b. Elisha,
ministering as high priest in the Holy of Holies; this can only mean one of the two
similarly named high priests Ishmael b. Phiabi (I, about AD 15–16; II, to AD 62),
who has been confused with R. Ishmael b. Elisha (d. AD 135); (3) The R. Ishmael
b. Elisha who was executed in AD 135 swore (T. Hall. i.10, 98) by the high-priestly
robe of his *abbā*, but he could not have meant his father since there was no high
priest Elisha, but his forefather, presumably the high priest Ishmael b. Phiabi II.
We must therefore conclude that, by the house of Elisha the Tos. text means the
house of Phiabi, and has duplicated it.

[160] The high priest Simon Kantheras was a son of Boethus, so his house belonged
to the house of Boethus.

vening of the Sanhedrin in the following way: v.5: 'On the morrow
. . . their rulers and elders and scribes were gathered together in
Jerusalem'. v.6: 'and Annas the (former) high priest was there, and
Caiaphas, and Jonathan,[161] and Alexander, and as many as were the
kindred of the high priest.' Verse 5 lists the three groups known to
form the Sanhedrin, chief priests, elders and scribes, but the word
'rulers' is used here, as in v.8 of the same chapter (cf. v.8 with v.23)[162]
and again and again in Josephus,[163] in place of the otherwise more
favoured ἀρχιερεῖς.

Now v.6 does not introduce a different group of members, other
than Sanhedrin, but as the appositional nominative shows simply
mentions individually the members of the first, most important group,
the 'high priests', i.e. the Jerusalem chief priests (see pp. 178ff.). In
this group were (a) the former high priest Annas (in office AD 6–15),
mentioned first because of his age and influence; (b) the reigning
high priest, his son-in-law Caiaphas (c. AD 18–37); (c) Jonathan, son
of Annas (AD 37), who succeeded his brother-in-law Caiaphas as high
priest a few years after the events narrated in Acts 4,[164] and so was in
all probability captain of the Temple at the time;[165] (d) an otherwise
unknown Alexander; and (e) those members of the high-priestly
family who held chief-priestly offices at the Jerusalem Temple.

Here again Acts 4.5–6 confirms the Talmudic statement, that the
new hierarchy filled all the chief influential positions in the Temple
with their own relations as a matter of course. Not only was the
son-in-law of the former high priest Annas the reigning high priest,
and his son captain of the Temple, but the ruling house of Annas had
others, and perhaps all, of the chief-priestly positions in its control.

The strength of this power which the new hierarchy had taken

---

[161] Most MSS read Ἰωάννης, but D, d, g, p, prov., tepl., Ἰωνάθας. Since John
occurs about 135 times in the NT, and Jonathan otherwise not at all, and since the
names are interchanged elsewhere (Zahn, *Die Apostelgeschichte* 1, 3rd ed., Leipzig
1922, 167 n. 88; Kirsopp Lake, *Beginnings* IV, 42; C.S.C. Williams, *Acts*, London
1957, 83), there is evidence for accepting the Western variant Jonathan.

[162] Perhaps this same usage occurred earlier in I Macc.; cf. 1.26 'rulers and
elders' with 7.33; 11.23, 'priests and elders'. 14.28 is somewhat different, where
'priests, rulers of the people and elders of the land' appear side by side.

[163] See the examples in Schürer II, 252 nn. 41f.; ET II 1, 178 nn. 483f.

[164] *Ant.* 18.95, See p. 195 n. 153 on his brief office of only 50 days.

[165] j. Yom. iii.8, 41a.5: 'The high priest was not nominated to the office unless
he had first been captain of the Temple', see p. 162. This must have been all the
more so when the family of Annas was in office, for they at that time in particular
had great power at their command: no other high priest of the first century AD had
so long a period of office as Caiaphas.

to itself—whereby they controlled not only the Temple, the cultus, the priestly court (pp. 177f.), a considerable number of seats in the highest governing body, the Sanhedrin (see p. 179), but also the political leadership of the whole nation[166]—can best be gauged from the distribution of command at the outbreak of the rebellion against Rome in AD 66. In fact, one of the two commanders in Jerusalem was the former high priest Ananus. Of the two commanders of Idumaea one was a chief priest, the other the son of the high priest Ananus. While there were three priests in command over Galilee we do not know the background of the four remaining commanding officers in Jericho, Perea, Thamna and Gophna with Acrabatta (*BJ* 2.562ff.; Galilee—*Vita* 29). Along with the political power, the priestly aristocracy through family influence obtained possession of the administration of Temple finances, a circumstance of no small importance. 'Their sons are treasurers, . . . and their servants smite the people with sticks,' says the lament of Abba Saul, which calls to mind the complaint of violence on the part of the servants, described on p. 181, in forcibly and unlawfully taking from the priests of the twenty-four weekly courses their rightful share of tributes and offerings. In fact, we have proof that most of the families in the new hierarchy had control of great wealth, as did the houses of Boethus, Annas and Phiabi.[167]

Riches and power the new hierarchy had in plenty, but these could in no way make up for their lack of legitimacy.

D. THE 'ORDINARY' PRIESTS (*kōhēn hedyōṭ*)

Over against this priestly aristocracy there stood the majority of the priesthood. At the heart of Jewry, they formed a closed circle, an hereditary community tracing its genealogy back to Aaron and inheriting thus the dignity of office. They were divided into priestly clans by ancient tradition. Already in the year 445 BC, when the Law was solemnly ratified, there were twenty-one priestly classes, or courses (Neh. 10.3–9). In the fourth century, near the end of the Persian period, there appears a second list, mentioning twenty-two; five of the older classes have disappeared, and six new ones have

---

[166] Leading priests nearly always took part in delegations, e.g. *Ant.* 20. 194, etc.

[167] I have collected the evidence on pp. 96ff. above. Cf. the precept in T. Yom. i.6, 180, that the wealth of the high priest had to exceed that of the rest of the priesthood.

been added (Neh. 12.1–7, 12–21). I Chronicles mentions for the first time twenty-four classes; again, twelve older classes have disappeared and fourteen new ones have appeared (I Chron. 24.1–19). In I Chron. 24.7 the priestly family of Jehoiarib, to which the Maccabees belonged (I Macc. 2.1; 14.29), is named in the first place, while it is completely absent in Neh. 10.3–9 and appears in Neh. 12.1–7 and 12–21 in a subordinate position. Consequently this third list must have been compiled during the Maccabean period.[168]

The division of the priesthood into twenty-four courses, each of which did service for one week in Jerusalem from sabbath to sabbath (*CA* 2.108; *Ant.* 7.365; Luke 1.8)—for which reason they were called weekly courses—was the system prevailing at the time of Jesus.[169] These twenty-four priestly clans included all the priests living in Judaea and Galilee.[170] Each priestly clan (weekly course)[171] was divided into four to nine priestly families (daily courses),[172] carrying out in turn their section of the weekly course during the seven days of their turn of duty. We have already come across an example of this division (pp. 188f.) in the form of *bēt ḥašmōnay*, a daily course forming part of the weekly course of Jehoiarib. At the head of the weekly course stood the *rōš hamišmār*, and of the daily course the *rōš bēt 'āb* (see pp. 163ff.). Thus we see the priesthood divided into twenty-four weekly courses, which in their turn were divided into about 156 daily courses.

This enquiry is not concerned at this point with a description of the liturgical activities of the priests, but in connection with the social structure of the priesthood we must discuss the question of the number of Jewish priests.

The Talmud exaggerates wildly when it says that the smallest of the weekly courses, belonging to Shihin in Galilee, alone produced

---

[168] The text of Tosephta cited above, p. 189, also shows that the classification in I Chron. 24. 7–8, which puts the priestly clan of Jehoiarib in the first place, must be of a later date.

[169] *Ant.* 7.365f.; *Vita* 2; T. Taan. ii.1, 216 and par. (p. 189 n. 134); Luke 1.5–8; Cant. R. 3.12 on 3.7 (Son. 161), *et passim*.

[170] Priests in Galilee: Shihin in Galilee: j. Taan. iv.8, 69a.53; Sepphoris: p. 194 n. 146; T. Sot. xiii.8, 319; j. Yom. iv.3, 43c.58; b. Yom. 39a; Schlatter, *Geschichte Israels*, 136; Büchler, *Priester*, 196–202.

[171] *Mišmār* (watch); *Vita* 2: ἐφημερίς, πατριά; Luke 1.5, 8: ἐφημερία.

[172] *Bēt 'āb*; *Vita* 2: φυλή. Oddly, Josephus' Greek wrongly transposes the appellations, calling the weekly course the 'daily course' (ἐφημερίς) and, on the other hand, describing the daily course under the general term 'clan' (φυλή). We find the number of daily courses to one weekly course in T. Taan. ii.1–2, 216: four to nine daily courses; and in j. Taan. iv.2, 68a.14: five to nine courses.

some 85,000 young priests (j. Taan. iv.8, 69a.53). In contrast, according to Pseudo-Hecateus[173] the number of priests was only 1,500 (CA 1.188). But this number too cannot be accepted, for, as Büchler has rightly seen,[174] this may well be only the number of priests living in Jerusalem.[175] This concurs with the evidence in Neh. 11.10–19, where there were 1,192 priests living in Jerusalem in 445 BC.[176] On the other hand, we have useful evidence in the letter of Pseudo-Aristeas, written in the last decades of the second century BC, that during his visit to the Temple, 700 priests were on duty besides the vast number of those who offered the sacrifices (Arist. 95). He intends the number 700 to represent the number of priests and Levites in the *weekly* course; to them he adds those offering the victims, i.e. the priests of the *daily* course. Thus, from Pseudo-Aristeas, we arrive at a total of about $750 \times 24 = 18,000$ priests and Levites.

It is encouraging that this number fits in with Old Testament evidence. According to Ezra 2.36–39 = Neh. 7.39–42, there returned from exile with Zerubbabel and Joshua four families of priests, comprising 4,289 men, together with 74 Levites (Ezra 2.40–42; Neh. 7.43–45), 128 singers (Neh. has 148) and 139 doorkeepers (Neh. has 138). This gives 4,630 priests and Levites (Neh.: 4,649). The historical situation explains the smallness of the number of Levites, for the priests of the high places reduced by the Deuteronomic code to the rank of Levites naturally had no desire to return from exile, and only gradually came back to Palestine. It is of a later time that I Chron. 12.26ff. speaks, when mentioning more than 3,700 priests and 4,600 Levites. (On the other hand, the number of 38,000 Levites in I Chron. 23.3–5 is an unnecessary exaggeration.) This increase in the number of Levites is explained by the fact that in the meantime the singers and doorkeepers, still distinct from the Levites in Ezra. 2.41–

[173] For the ascription of the memorandum quoted in n. 175 to Pseudo-Hecateus, who must have written late in the second century BC, see the article by B. Schaller, 'Hekataios von Abdera über die Juden', ZNW 54, 1963, 15–31.

[174] *Priester*, 48ff.

[175] Pseudo-Hecateus says: 'The total number of Jewish priests who received tithes and administered public affairs was at least 1,500.' Apart from the smallness of the number, the reference to administrative activity points to Jerusalem.

[176] The number agrees very well. The increase in the number of priests in Jerusalem was relatively small, in view of the time-lapse of about three hundred years. This is explicable if we bear in mind that with the growth of the Jewish community many families had to move out into the country (cf. Neh. 11.2). Thus, according to Neh. 11.10, the priests of the family of Jehoiarib lived in Jerusalem; while I Macc. 2.1, 18–20, 70; 13.25 says they lived partly in Modein.

58, had now become Levites, and at the same time there had been a large-scale return of priests of the high places from Babylon. The decrease in the number of priests, on the other hand, can be explained by the assumption that a large number of the families counted as priests in Ezra 2.36–39 and par. have been reckoned as Levites in our list. If we take into account the interval of time between the writing of the book of Chronicles (before 300 BC) and the writing of the letter of Pseudo-Aristeas (before 100 BC)[177] we can accept as quite reasonable the increase in the number of the priesthood from 8,300 to 18,000.

There is a second method of reckoning the numbers of the priesthood. According to M. Yom. ii.1–5 lots were cast on the morning of days of ordinary service, in four stages: $1 + 13 + 1 + 9 = 24$ services. Thus were chosen the priests who were to take part in preparing and offering the daily morning sacrifice, which consisted of the incense offering, the burnt offering of a lamb, the food offering, the baked meal offering of the high priest, and the drink offering. To these twenty-four officials three others were added[178] who were not chosen by lot, so that there were twenty-seven altogether. The same sacrifices were repeated in the evening. The purification of the Altar of Burnt Offering, which a priest must see to in the morning, appears to have been omitted in the evening, but this was compensated for by the provision of a second assistant in the evening at the Altar of Incense. Furthermore, in the evening two more priests were needed to carry the wood to the Altar of Burnt Offering (M. Yom. ii.5).

[177] For the dating of this letter see p. 200.

[178] For the incense offering two priests had to help the officiating priest who was chosen by lot for the office (cf. Luke 1.9). One brought glowing coals on a silver firepan from the Altar of Burnt Offering to the Altar of Incense in the Holy Place (M. Tam. v.5; vi.1; vii.2). The second took from the officiating priest the bowl in which the dish of incense had lain until the censing was finished (M. Tam. vi.3; vii.2). The priest who was to offer the incense chose this second assistant himself (M. Tam. vi.3). There are two traditions regarding the first assistant. According to R. Judah (b. Eli, c. AD 150) the officiating priest chose him as well (T. Yom. i.11, 181). But the tractate Tamid says of him: 'he whose lot it was to bear the firepan' (v.5; vi.2). The first assistant is thus identified with the priest who was chosen first in the four lots to purify the Altar of Burnt Offering (cf. M. Tam. i.4). The difference between these two accounts is explained by the fact that the Altar of Burnt Offering was cleaned only once each day, in the morning. Indeed M. Tam. describes the morning service, and R. Judah obviously the evening service, for only in the evening was it necessary to ask a priest to act as assistant for the incense offering, since in the evening there was no service of purification of the Altar of Burnt Offering. Again, two priests blew silver trumpets during pauses in the Levites' singing at the drink offering which ended the *tāmīd* sacrifice (M. Tam. vii.3). Thus in the morning there were three, and in the evening four, priests coopted to those chosen by lot.

For the evening sacrifice, then, there were twenty-nine priests serving. True, the same priest might find himself with more than one office per day, through the casting of lots and apportioning of services; even if we are scarcely justified in assuming that the lots cast in the morning were valid for the evening service, too, we cannot conclude from these numbers that each day there were $27 + 29 = 56$ different priests officiating. We know, however, that the priests of the daily course who were not chosen by lot that morning, were free from duty and took off their sacred vestments (M. Tam. v.3). This information implies that generally there were more than thirty priests on each daily course.

We must remember, however, that sabbaths and festivals needed a much greater number of priests than ordinary days, for on these special days, apart from the morning and evening sacrifices just dealt with (M. Tam. calls them 'perpetual'), there were other public sacrifices which reached their highest number on the first day of the feast of Tabernacles. We need not deal here with the three pilgrim festivals for, as we know, the twenty-four weekly courses of priests were all in Jerusalem at those times, and the courses not on duty were then called to help the weekly course who was (M. Sukk. v.7). We can also leave the other festivals, New Moon, New Year and Day of Atonement, since it seems likely that the daily course on duty was helped on these days by the other daily courses of the weekly course.

We will confine ourselves to the sabbath. On this day, apart from the morning and evening *tāmīd*, two more lambs would be sacrificed in public, and for each would be needed one priest to kill, one to sprinkle the blood and eight to offer the sacrifice (these numbers are found in M. Yom. ii.3–5). Furthermore, on the morning of the sabbath two more priests would be chosen by the fourth lot (M. Yom. ii.5), and together with six assistant priests they would renew the two bowls of incense on the shewbread table, and the twelve loaves of shewbread (M. Men. xi.7). So we see that on the sabbath twenty-eight other officials were added to those needed daily.

Over and above the public sacrifices we have now mentioned there was a large number of private sacrifices to offer daily. These were divided into burnt offerings, sin offerings, guilt offerings and meal offerings. Each Israelite had to pay for these offerings himself, while the public sacrifices, according to the prevailing Pharisaic opinion, were generally paid for from Temple funds. There was no apportioning of duty by lot for these private sacrifices; on the contrary, the laity themselves, on the basis of Lev. 1.5, had to do the slaughtering,[179] then the flaying and cutting up of the animal (M. Yom. ii.7). It was left entirely to the priests which one of them would undertake the actual offering (M. Yom. ii.7). We can obtain some idea of the vast number of private sacrifices offered in the Temple when we realize that whole hecatombs were repeatedly offered in the Sanctuary at Jerusalem.[180] We may presume that the daily course on duty in such circumstances was assisted at these private sacrifices by the other daily courses of the same weekly course.

Looking back on the evidence, especially that concerning the numbers on duty for the daily public sacrifices, we shall not be excessive in estimating the number of priests for one daily course at at least fifty. One weekly course comprised about six daily courses (see p. 163), and thus we have about three hundred priests for each weekly course. This number is corroborated by such evidence as this: when the veil of the Temple needed to be purified, it had to be immersed in a tank of water, and three hundred priests were needed for this (M. Shek. viii.5); and again, once three hundred priests were engaged in work on the golden vine which was above the entrance to the Holy Place (M. Midd. iii.8). Both of these illustrations come from reliable and well-informed sources: the first from Simeon, son of the captain of the Temple,[181] the second from R. Eleazar b. Zadoq, priest, scribe and merchant living in Jerusalem while the Temple was still standing (see p. 143). Thus the number 300 cannot possibly be an invention. We must regard it as the approximate number on each weekly course, and this confirms our calculations. Since there were twenty-four weekly courses, the total number of priests amounts to 24 × 300 = 7,200 priests. Then there is the number of the Levites. They also, as we have seen, were divided into twenty-four courses, and their number was considerable. According to Josephus, two hundred were needed each evening to close the Temple doors (CA 2.119). This number may include those Levites in service for the weekly course who were needed as doorkeepers and guards of the

---

[179] M. Zeb. iii.1; b. Zeb. 32a; Siphra Lev. 1.5 (Bill. II, 193). On p. 79 above I have quoted references where the laity slaughtered their own paschal victims.

[180] *Ant.* 16.14 (Marcus Agrippa, autumn 15 BC); 15.422 (Herod, 10 BC); Philo, *Leg. ad Cai.* 356 (three hecatombs during Caligula's reign); Lev. R. 3.5 on 1.16 (Son. 39); *Orac. Sib.* III, 576 and 626.

[181] M. Shek. viii.5 (ed. princ. of Jerusalem Talmud, Venice 1523) and M. Men. xi.9: (var. + Rabbi) Simeon *ben ha-sāgān*. b. Hull. 90b: R. Simeon *ha-sāgān*. This last reading must be rejected as being least attested, and improbable.

temple. To these Temple guards were added Levite singers and musicians, and their number too was large. We can reckon it too as about two hundred since, in the tradition of I Chron. 23.5, the number of Levite doorkeepers and of Levite singers was the same. Thus we arrive at a figure of around 400 × 24 = 9,600 Levites.

In I Chron. 12.26–28 we have striking proof that these figures, of 7,200 priests and 9,600 Levites, are right and in proportion with each other. As we have seen (p. 200) this text mentions 3,700 priests and 4,600 Levites, so the number of Levites surpassed that of priests, while after the exile they were very much in the minority. Thus in I Chron. the proportion of priests to Levites is 37 to 46 and for 9,600 Levites this gives us 7,722 priests, a number very close to the 7,200 we have obtained by a totally different method. Remember finally that we arrived at a total of 18,000 priests and Levites (p. 200) on the evidence of the letter of Pseudo-Aristeas, while our second calculation gives us 7,200 + 9,600 = 16,800. We may thus claim to have obtained, in this result, such historical certainty in this difficult field as can be reached with the help of the sources at our disposal today. In the time of Jesus the Jewish clergy numbered round about 18,000 priests and Levites.[182]

I have deliberately left until now the discussion of a passage in Josephus. It is much disputed because of its obscurity, but we cannot now reasonably doubt its authenticity. In a passage of his *Contra Apionem* (2.108), extant only in the Latin version, Josephus states: 'For although there are four priestly tribes, each comprising upwards of five thousand members, these officiate for one day only, and after that others succeed them.' It is clear that the last few words refer to the weekly courses. We may easily suppose that there is a textual corruption, that 'four' originally read 'twenty-four', and that Josephus in another of his exaggerations wishes his readers to believe that there were 24 × 5,000 = 120,000 priests.[183] But our preceding conclusion justifies caution and warns against a hasty rejection of the number 4 × 5,000 = 20,000. In any case, it is not impossible that

[182] This result was reached by a different method by L. Herzfeld, *Geschichte des Volkes Israel* III, Nordhausen 1857, 193. He reckons a total of 24,000 on the basis of three documents: (*a*) a text of j. Taan. iv.2, 67d.46 Bar., where the (lay) *ma'amād* (n. 53) of Jerusalem is 24,000, of Jericho 12,000; (*b*) an apocryphal letter from a consul Marcus describing the celebrations on the Day of Atonement, which speaks of 24,000 priests; (*c*) the text of *CA* 2.108, which will now be discussed. Büchler, *Priester*, 49f., on the basis of *CA* 2.108 and Pseudo-Aristeas 95, reckons 20,000 priests.

[183] Schürer II, 288f., ET II.1, 219f.: we should read *tribus quattuor* (*sc. viginti*).

Josephus has in mind in this passage a quadripartite division of the clergy, and the fact that he does not use the term 'tribe' (*tribus*) elsewhere for the weekly course, confirms this hypothesis. Indeed, T. Taan. ii.1, 216, relates how the four courses of priests who returned from exile under Ezra-Nehemiah[184] are said to have been divided into twenty-four weekly courses by the prophets of Jerusalem, and were then divided by lot into four groups of six weekly sections each. This information permits the conjecture that the ancient quadripartite division of the clergy was preserved to the first century AD in the priestly tradition, as a scheme of classification for the whole priesthood. If that is correct, the number of 20,000, which results from this text, provides us with yet another confirmation of our conclusion.

Knowledge of the number of clergy is not without importance in estimating the size of the Palestinian population at the time of Jesus. Let us consider this in a brief appendix. The priests and Levites, with women and children, would number about 50,000 to 60,000. The priests and Levites returning from exile with Joshua and Zerubbabel made up about one-tenth of the entire community (Ezra 2.36–42, cf. 2.64 = Neh. 7.39–45, 66), a generally credible proportion. Thus, Palestine in the time of Jesus had a Jewish population of $10 \times 50,000$ (or 60,000), about 500,000 or 600,000. In my opinion this is a more likely number than the million often assumed.[185] Thus for example, the official number of inhabitants in Palestine given by the British mandate[186] in 1926 was 865,000, but this included Transjordan, Samaria and other regions which at the time of Jesus were inhabited mainly or exclusively by Gentiles, and also included 103,000 Bedouin nomads. The hypothesis of a million Jews in Palestine at the time of Jesus supposes that at that time Palestine was twice as thickly populated as in 1926. This is quite improbable. On the other hand a Jewish population of 500,000 to 600,000 corresponds to the density of population in Palestine after the First World War.[187] This is a new and final confirmation of the

[184] According to Ezra 2.36–39 = Neh. 7.39–42 our priestly families returned from exile with Zerubbabel and Joshua. Still, in the time of Ezra 10.18–22, these four families formed the priesthood.

[185] E.g. R. Knopf and H. Weinel, *Einführung in das NT*, 2nd ed., Giessen 1923, 182: 'In the most generous estimation including Transjordan, less than a million Jews.'

[186] *ZDPV* 51, 1928, 238.

[187] A. v. Harnack, *Die Mission und Ausbreitung des Christentums* I, 4th ed., Leipzig 1924, 12, rightly reckons about 500,000 Jews in Palestine in the time of Jesus.

number 18,000, excluding women and children, which we have
obtained for the whole priesthood.

In each of the twenty-four weeks, and in addition at the three
annual pilgrim festivals, one of the weekly courses of priests went up
to Jerusalem to officiate from one sabbath to the next. Each course
consisted of an average of 300 priests and 400 Levites, and was
accompanied by a group of lay representatives from its district.[188] The
keys of the Temple and the 93 vessels were ceremonially handed over
by the course going off duty (*CA* 2.108). In this way the weekly course
of Abia, eighth in order, travelled from the hill-country of Judaea[189]
to the Temple, in the last years of the reign of Herod. On the day
when his daily course was on duty, the priest Zechariah had been
chosen for the privilege of offering the incense, probably at the
evening *tāmīd*,[190] and it was then he had his vision in the Holy
Place.

The cultic functions of the priests were, then, confined to two weeks
in the year, and the three pilgrim festivals. The priests lived at their
homes for ten or eleven months (according to whether the distance
from Jerusalem, and the journey to and fro five times a year, took up
more or less time). Only very occasionally did they exercise any
priestly function at home, such as declaring a leper clean after his
healing[191] before he went up to Jerusalem to obtain a final declaration of cleanness after offering the prescribed sacrifice. The tithes
and other special taxes were the priests' income, but these were by
no means sufficient to keep them in idleness throughout the year (see
p. 108). On the contrary, they were obliged to follow some profession in their own district, mostly manual work. Herod had a
thousand priests trained in carpentry and masonry, and during the
renovations to the Temple he employed them in the Temple court
and in building the Sanctuary, since no one but a priest might enter
there (*Ant.* 15.390). We have already come across Phanni, a priest
who was a stone-mason (p. 192 n. 141); R. Eleazar b. Zadoq carried

---

[188] Cf. M. Bikk. iii.2, account of the journey to Jerusalem with the first-fruits;
it says that the whole population from the district of a weekly course went to
Jerusalem with the course.

[189] Luke 1.39, εἰς πόλιν Ἰούδα, as C. C. Torrey rightly says (*HTR* 17, 1924,
83ff.), is an error in translation; *mᵉdīnāh* is inadvertently translated as 'city' instead of 'province'.

[190] Luke 1.10, cf. Acts 3.1, infers that he was on duty in the afternoon.

[191] Matt. 8.4; Luke 17.14. T. Neg. viii.2, 628, states that the leper must first
show himself to the local priests; j. Sot. ii.2, 18a.11; also Siphra Lev. 14.3, 34c,
et passim.

on a business in Jerusalem, obviously in oil.[192] A priest of Jerusalem, whose son Zechariah we meet later on, was a butcher in the Holy City (M. Ket. ii.9; see below p. 220); the priest Eleazar b. Azariah went in for wholesale cattle-breeding; and finally we shall come across a large number of priests who were scribes.

In many places, priests assisted in the local courts of justice, probably in an honorary capacity (b. Yom. 26a). Sometimes they were called there out of respect for their priestly status (*CA* 2.187), sometimes if they were trained as scribes, because of their learning (b. Yom. 26a),[193] and sometimes to satisfy biblical precepts: e.g. in cases of assessment of votive offerings which biblical precept said must be done by a priest, it was usually the duty of a priest to sit at the court (M. Sanh. i.3: because of the precept in Lev. 27.12) to defend the interests of the Temple, which claimed the equivalent of anything vowed to God (i.e. to the Temple).[194] There were, as Philo states, priests living in the country well versed in scriptural learning, who were entrusted during the synagogue worship (Bill. IV, 153ff.) with the reading and expounding of the Law,[195] but it is understandable that there were others who were not educated men.[196]

As we have already mentioned (pp. 180f.), there were profound contrasts between the great majority of priests and the senior priests who belonged generally to the priestly aristocracy. It is not surprising, then, that the mass of priests, together with the young hotheads of the aristocracy, but in opposition to the leading members of the priesthood (*BJ* 2.408ff.), threw in their lot with the people at the outbreak of the anti-Roman rebellion in AD 66.

E. THE LEVITES (CLERUS MINOR)

The Levites, descendants of the priests of the high places deposed by

---

[192] T. Betz. iii.8, 205. Comparison of this text with b. Betz. 29a Bar. implies that he traded in oil.

[193] Because of such OT texts as Deut. 17.9ff.; 21.5; Ezek. 44.24; I Chron. 23.4; cf. 26.29; Ecclus. 45.17, where the priesthood provided the judges, it is quite probable that later, too, priests tended to be nominated as judges. But in the last centuries before the destruction of the Temple, training as a scribe was the decisive factor in qualifying to be a judge.

[194] As distinct from 'the devoted thing', *ḥērem*, in which the vow must be paid in kind.

[195] Eusebius, *Praep. ev.* VIII, 7.12–13 (GCS 43.1 = Eus. VIII.1, 431f.), cites this passage of Philo.

[196] *BJ* 4.155 states that Phanni, whom the Zealots chose by lot as high priest, was so bucolic that he did not even know exactly the function of a high priest.

the Deuteronomic code, formed an inferior clergy. In theory they passed for descendants of Levi, one of the twelve patriarchs of Israel. Their relationship with the priesthood was conceived of in the following manner: the priests were the descendants of one prominent Levite, Aaron, so that they formed a privileged class within the descendants of Levi; while the legitimate high priests, as the descendants of one prominent Aaronite, Zadoq, formed a privileged class within the priesthood. Thus the Levites stood lower in rank to the priests, as a *clerus minor*, and as such took no part in the offering of sacrifice; they were entrusted solely with performing the Temple music and carrying out inferior duties. One fact particularly is characteristic of their standing: like the laity, they were forbidden, on pain of death, access to the Temple building and to the Altar (Num. 18.3; Num. R. 7.8 on 5.2, Son. 195).

The Levites, numbering about 10,000 (p. 204), were like the priests divided into twenty-four weekly courses (*Ant*. 7.367; M. Taan. iv.2: T. Taan. iv.2, 219); they took turns for service each week and each had a leader (I Chron. 15.4–12). As we have already seen (p. 173) there were in the Temple four permanent Levite officials: two overseers of the Levite musicians, namely the director of music and the director of singers, and two overseers of the Levite servants of the Temple, the chief doorkeeper and a Levite 'over the knouts'.[197] These two pairs of officers corresponded to the division of the Levites into musicians and servants, both groups roughly the same in number (see p. 204).

The singers and musicians formed the upper stratum among the Levites, and only for them was proof of pure descent necessary when they wished to be admitted to office.[198] They had to provide the singing and instrumental music for the daily morning and evening services, and on other festal occasions. At the daily services the leader of the singers and the Levite musicians and singers[199] (together with two to twelve players on reed-pipes at the feasts of Passover and Tabernacles M. Arak. ii.3–4; M. Sukk. v.1: T. Arak. i.15, 544), stood on a platform which marked the division between the Court of Priests and the Court of Israel. This was one cubit above the latter and one and a half cubits below the former (M. Midd. ii.6; *BJ* 5.226).

---

[197] Earlier called 'overseer in charge of the *lūlāb* at the feast of Tabernacles'.

[198] See in the next section, under The Hereditary Character of the Priesthood, pp. 215f.

[199] M. Arak. ii.6. There must be no less than twelve singers.

During the joyful nocturnal ceremonies which formed part of the feast of Tabernacles an imposing choir of Levites performed, standing on the fifteen steps leading from the court of women to the court of Israel (M. Sukk. v.4). But these levitical musicians never stood in the Court of Priests which enclosed the Temple building, for this was reserved for the priests alone. A Levite was permitted to enter that court only when he had a sacrifice to offer, like any layman (M. Kel. i.8).

The Temple servants had to discharge all the humbler duties which resulted from the function and maintenance of the Temple, especially those connected with the cultus. For example, these servants had to help the priest on and off with his vestments: 'The other priests [i.e. who were allotted no part in the service of the day and were thus free] they delivered to the ministers of the Temple (*ḥazzānīm*). These stripped them of their raiment' (M. Tam. v.3). They had other auxiliary duties, such as preparing the Book of the Law for reading of lessons on feast days (M. Yom. vii.1; M. Sot. vii.7–8), and arranging the *lūlāb* at the feast of Tabernacles when its first day fell on a sabbath (M. Sukk. iv.4; cf. p. 169 on the alteration in this rite). Furthermore these servants of the Temple were responsible for cleaning it (Philo, *De spec. leg.* I, 156. 'Others swept the porches and those parts of the Temple area open to the sky'), but again with the exception of the Court of Priests, which the priests themselves had to clean (M. Pes. v.8), since the Levites were not allowed there except when sacrificing (M. Kel. i.8).

Finally, the Levites formed the police force of the Temple. Philo describes their functions in great detail: 'Some of these [Levites] are stationed at the doors as gatekeepers at the very entrances, some within [the Temple area] in front of the sanctuary [πρόναο—i.e. the *ḥēl* or rampart which enclosed that part into which Gentiles were not allowed to pass] to prevent any unlawful person from setting foot thereon, either intentionally or unintentionally. Some patrol around it turn by turn in relays by appointment day and night, keeping guard at both seasons' (Philo, *De spec. leg.* I, 156). From this graphic description, completed by M. Midd. i.1, it appears that by night as well as by day the Levite Temple guard was arranged in three groups: (*a*) doorkeepers at the outer doors of the Temple: (*b*) guards at the 'rampart'; (*c*) patrols in the Court of Gentiles, and no doubt by day in the Court of Women also. In the evening the Levite Temple servants closed the doors under the supervision of the chief doorkeeper (*CA* 2.119; *BJ* 6.294; b. Arak. 11b), and then the night watchmen went to their posts, 21 in number, all lying in the secular area at the outer gates and in the Court of Gentiles (M. Midd. i.1).[200] In addition, the Temple police force was called upon for other duties. They were at the disposal of the Sanhedrin, which met in the Chamber of Hewn Stone, one of the south-western chambers of the Court of Priests.[201] They made arrests under the orders of the Temple overseers, and executed punishments under the direction of their leader (see pp. 171, 173).

If we remember that the Sanhedrin usually held their sessions in the Temple area, we can have little doubt that the band sent by this authority to arrest Jesus (Mark 14.43; Matt. 26.47; Luke 22.47; John 18.3, 12), consisted of these levitical police from the Temple, reinforced by servants of the high priest (Matt. 26.51 par.), and according to John by Roman soldiers (John 18.3, 12). John very properly distinguishes between the servants (of the high priest) and the officers (Levite Temple police). Furthermore, Jesus' words of reproach uttered at his arrest, that day after day he was in the Temple teaching and was not taken (Matt. 26.55), become most clearly understood if it was the Temple police who came to arrest him. We must also take it that the servants sent earlier by the Sanhedrin to arrest Jesus (John 7.32, 45, 46) were the Levite police from the Temple, as were the men who, at the order of 'the priests and the Captain of the Temple and the Sadducees' (Acts 4.1), arrested the apostles and brought them before the Sanhedrin (Acts 4.5–12; 5.17–18), who guarded them in prison (5.23, and esp. 24) and who scourged them (5.40). Finally, the men who dragged Paul out of 'sanctuary' (i.e. the Court of Women) and closed the gates leading to the Court of the Gentiles (Acts 21.30), during the riot leading to his arrest, were obviously members of the Temple police, more precisely the posts mounted at the 'rampart' during day-time.

---

[200] It appears from M. Tam. i.3 that the Court of Women, where the bakery was which prepared the baked cakes for the high priest's offering, was closed at nights and was part of the sector guarded by the priests: the priests themselves guarded the holy area (M. Midd. i.1; M. Tam. i.1).

[201] So says the Mishnah very definitely (M. Midd. v.5; cf. M. San. xi.2; M. Tam. ii.5; iv.3 to end). According to b. A. Zar. 8b. par. b. Shab. 15a; b. San. 41a, the Sanhedrin was exiled 'forty years' (a round number) before the destruction of Jerusalem from the Chamber of Hewn Stone to a bazaar. If Josephus means the Sanhedrin by the βουλή (or βουλευτήριον), which adjoined the sanctuary on the west side (BJ 5.144; 6.354) he makes the same assumption, as does Acts 23.10. But we have no basis for assuming that the transfer had already taken place at the time of Jesus.

Apart from the chief doorkeeper and the Levite 'over the knouts', there is mentioned a leader of Temple servants called '*iš har ha-bayit*, 'man of the Temple mount'. The Mishnah states that in the outer court there were twenty-one guard posts manned by the weekly course of Levites on duty, and 'the man of the Temple mount' had to inspect them every night, when each guard had to give the greeting of peace to show that he was awake. If the official found a sentry asleep he beat him with his stick, and indeed had the right to wake him brutally by setting fire to his clothes (M. Midd. i.1–2). It was this same official of whom Josephus tells us, that one night during the Passover feast in AD 66 the guards told the Temple overseer (τῷ στρατηγῷ) that the Nicanor Gate was standing open (*BJ* 6.294). We may assume that this leader of the levitical night-watch is the same as the chief doorkeeper.[202] Finally, it is probable that such leaders of the levitical Temple servants were the στρατηγοί with whom, according to Luke 22.4, the arrest of Jesus was arranged, and under whom it was carried out (Luke 22.52), for as we have just seen, Josephus used the same word στρατηγός to designate the leader in charge of the night watch.

By contrast the '*iš ha-bīrā*, commander of the Temple fortress (M. Orl. ii.12), had nothing to do with the officials who had oversight of the Temple, contrary to what is often suggested.[203] The *bīrā* is the fortress to the north of the Temple, otherwise called the Antonia, and Schlatter[204] has recognized that this man commanded the fortress of Antonia during the period of independence under Agrippa I (AD 41–44). This accords with the fact that he was a contemporary of Rabban Gamaliel I, who as we know from Acts. 5.34–39 was active in the fourth decade, and possible also the fifth, of the first century AD.[205] Thus the '*iš ha-bīrā* was a military commander and not a chief priest or chief Levite. Again it is a mistake, repeated time and again,[206] to identify the chief priests or Temple overseers with the

[202] Or as the man 'over the knouts', the opinion of I. M. Jost, *Geschichte des Judenthums* I, Leipzig 1857, 151f., and 152 n. 4.

[203] Schürer II, 331, ET II.1, 267, gives him the surveillance of the whole Temple.

[204] *Geschichte Israels*, 271 and n. 243.

[205] According to M. Mielziner, *Introduction to the Talmud*, 3rd ed., New York 1925, 24. Gamaliel died 18 years before the destruction of the Temple, in AD 52; Bill. II, 636, dates his activities at AD 25–50.

[206] Maimonides explains: 'the *paḥōt* are priestly *s^eḡānīm*'; J. J. Rabe, *Mischnah* I, Onolzbach 1760, 265: 'the most distinguished priests'; A. Sammter, *Mischnaioth* I, Berlin 1887, 192: 'the deputies of the priests'; K. Albrecht, *Bikkurim* (coll. *Die Mischna*), Giessen 1922, 43: 'the priestly representatives'; Schürer II, 322, ET II.1, 259, and Bill. II, 631: 'the chief priests'; Bill. IV, 644: 'the chief priests (?commanders)'. This last parenthesis contains the true solution.

paḥōt, by appealing to M. Bikk. iii.3 which says that the *paḥōt*, with the Temple overseers and chief treasurers, used to meet the processions of first-fruits at their entry into Jerusalem. Everywhere, in the Old Testament as elsewhere, the word *peḥāh* means nothing other than the Pasha, the governor with military power. The context of M. Bikk. iii.3 shows (M. Bikk. iii.4) that it describes an event during the reign of Agrippa I, that is to say during a period when there were Jewish military commanders and state officials. In the east it would be a matter of course for these men to meet the procession along with the chief priests. In 1913 I myself saw the Turkish Pasha, together with the heads of the Mohammedan clergy, go to meet the pilgrims of the Nebi-Musa festival as they entered Jerusalem.

Between the Temple musicians and the Temple servants there was a social gulf which was grounded in history. For as late as the time of Ezra neither 'singers' nor 'doorkeepers' were associated with the Levites (Ezra 2.40ff.; 7.7, 24; 10.23f.; Neh. 10.29 *et passim*) since they were not of Levite extraction.[207] The singers were first to obtain membership in the company of Levites (Neh. 11.17, 22f.; 12.8f., 24f.), and in contrast to the doorkeepers kept their higher position among the Levites. The gulf which separated the two groups at the time of Jesus is illustrated in the following sentence: 'We have it on tradition that a singing Levite who does his colleague's work at the gate incurs the penalty of death' (b. Arak. 11b). True, the actual practice was not so stringent; as we see in a Baraita passage in the same context: 'It happened that R. Joshua b. Ḥananiah [Levite and scribe] went to assist R. Joḥanan b. Gudgeda [Levite and chief doorkeeper] in fastening the Temple doors. Whereupon Joḥanan said to him: My son, turn back, for you are of the [class of] choristers, not of the Temple servants [literally, doorkeepers]' (*ibid.*).

In this context the class struggle which the Levites successfully carried out in AD 64 is instructive, and throws light not only on the division among the Levites but also on the resentment they felt against the priests, and on the revolutionary spirit stirred up in the confused years before the outbreak of rebellion against Rome. Oversight of the Temple had been transferred by the Romans to Agrippa II, and the Levite musicians, the 'psalm singers', says Josephus, demanded from him the right to wear henceforth the white linen vest-

[207] E.g. the Korahites were originally of Edomite descent, according to Gen. 36.5, 14, 18; I Chron. 1.35. I Chron. 2.42–43 said they descended from Caleb. Thus they were non-Israelites. But I Chron. 12.6 said they were Benjaminites. They were employed first as doorkeepers, I Chron. 26.1, 19; 9.19; II Chron. 31.14; then as singers, II Chron. 20.19; Pss. 42–49; 84f.; 87f.

ment of priests. Formerly the Levites had no official dress.[208] Similarly the Levite Temple servants claimed the right 'to be taught to sing hymns', thus to be on the same footing as the levitical musicians (*Ant.* 20.216ff.). Agrippa II was at that time on bad terms with the priests, who in AD 62 had gone so far as to send an envoy to Caesar who had decided their case against the king in their favour (*Ant.* 20.189ff.); so, with the agreement of the Sanhedrin, Agrippa allowed the demands of the Levites. But the people regarded these innovations in the social position of the Levites as contrary to the Law of their fathers. We see once again from this account that the musicians formed an upper stratum among the Levites; they wished to secure a position similar to the priests', whereas the doorkeepers aspired to equality with the musicians. The revolutionary spirit of the sixties allowed a partial fulfilment of their wishes, for a short period of six years.

We have very little evidence on the training of Levites. The Levite Joseph Barnabas, a leading member of the primitive Christian church, a prophet, teacher and missionary, was an outstanding man in the intellectual sphere and well versed in scripture (Acts 9.27; 11.22ff.; 12.25; 13.1ff.; 14.12ff.; 15.2ff.; I Cor. 9.6; Gal. 2.1ff.; Col. 4.10). Since he came from Cyprus (Acts 4.36) his father seems to have been one of those Levites who never served in Jerusalem, such service being in no way compulsory. We know of several Levites who were scribes (cf. CD x.5) for example the singer Joshua b. Ḥananiah who in private life was a nailsmith, and the chief doorkeeper Joḥanan b. Gudgeda.

On the whole the evidence about Levites is extraordinarily meagre,[209] but it is sufficient to enable us to form a general picture of the social position of this lower part of the clergy.

F. THE HEREDITARY CHARACTER OF THE PRIESTHOOD

The foregoing picture of the social structure of the priesthood in the Temple at Jerusalem would be incomplete if we did not conclude with a few words on its hereditary character.

---

[208] Cf. Targum Pseudo-Jonathan Ex. 29.30.

[209] The name Levi was generally borne by Levites, e.g. R. Joshua b. Levi who according to j. M. Sh. v.5, 56b.37, was friendly to the Levites. Exceptions, perhaps in appearance only: *BJ* 4.141 cites a Levi of the royal (Herodian) family; and the name Levi occurs twice in the genealogy of the Davidic Joseph, Luke 3.24, 29.

Since the offices of priest and Levite were hereditary and could be obtained in no other way than by inheritance, it was of the greatest importance that the purity of line remain unblemished. To this end, in the first place, great care was taken in tracing genealogy, and in the second there were rigid rules of marriage; if a priest could not prove his legitimate descent, he lost his rights to priestly office, both for himself and for his descendants, and to priestly revenues. If he contracted an illegitimate marriage, the son of such a marriage could not hold office.

There was in the Temple at Jerusalem a kind of archive in which the genealogies of the priesthood were kept.[210] In many cases tradition has given us genealogical tables on the forebears of the priests.[211] Thus the priest Josephus gives his genealogy on his father's side for a period of about 250 years, from two generations before the time of the high priest John Hyrcanus (134–104 BC) to the time of writing his *Vita* (after AD 100): 'with such a pedigree, which I cite as I find it recorded in the public registers. . . .' (*Vita* 6), with the record of dates of birth of his forbears.[212] This same Josephus asserts positively that, after such great wars as occurred under Antiochus Ephiphanes, Pompey, Quintilius Varus, Vespasian and Titus, the surviving priests established new genealogies from the ancient records (*CA* i.34f.). These measures were taken partly because genealogies were lost in the confusion of war, and also because they must ensure that none of the priests' wives had been made prisoners of war. In this last case they could no longer be considered legitimate wives of priests and any offspring born to them since their capture did not qualify for priestly office.

When a priest's son reached the canonical age of twenty years (p. 158 n. 37), the Sanhedrin, in session at the Temple in the Chamber of Hewn Stone, at the south side of the court of priests, examined him (M. Midd. v.4) on his bodily fitness,[213] and on the legitimacy of

---

[210] Siphre Num. Korah 116 on 18.7; further see p. 215.

[211] In OT cf. the lists in I and II Chron., Ezra, Neh. On the genealogy of the high priests, see pp. 181ff.

[212] This list contains several inaccuracies which are easily explained by the omission of two names. The long space of time between 'Matthias the hunchback' (born 135–134 BC) and Joseph (born 67 BC) and also between the latter and Matthias (born AD 6), shows that there must in each case have been a name omitted. Schürer I, 77 n. 4 (ET I.1,81 n. 3) gives a different explanation, suggesting a textual corruption (or negligence) and an author's error.

[213] Lev. 21.16–23. These provisions were extended by rabbinic law to distinguish 142 bodily blemishes that rendered a priest unfit for service (Schürer II,

his descent before admitting him for ordination. Only after he was found fit was he ordained. After a ceremonial bath of purification, he was invested with the priestly robes: 1. the long garment of byssus, 2. breeches of byssus, 3. girdle, 4. turban, and there was a series of sacrifices involving special rituals. (Ex. 29; Lev. 8). These solemn ceremonies lasted for seven days.

It is certain that a similar examination of legitimate descent was required for the Levite musicians, before being admitted to office (M. Kidd. iv.5), and there was also a canonical age for them. The Old Testament speaks of thirty years (Num 4.3, 23, 30, 35, 39, 43, 47; 1 Chron. 23.3), of twenty-five years (Num. 8.23–26) and of twenty years (Ezra 3.8; I Chron. 23.24, 27; II Chron 31.17); the first of these seems to have been the current practice at the time of Jesus (T. Shek. iii.26, 179). The examination of the young Levites also took place in the Chamber of Hewn Stone, where 'sat those who certified the genealogy of priests and Levites' (T. Sanh. vii.1, 425; T. Hag. ii.9, 235; b. Kidd. 76b.). In fact the examination seems to have been confined to the Levite musicians. Only so can the following facts be understood: it was said of the daughter of a Levite whose father had stood on the 'platform'[214] that her descent was considered pure without further examination (M. Kidd. iv.5); and the daughters of the flute-players who stood there for the feasts of Passover and Tabernacles were considered fit to marry priests, which presupposes that their fathers' descent was pure.[215] Both examples show that for the lower ranks of Levite proof of purity of descent was not required.

283f., ET II. 1, 214). The priest disqualified in this way had access to the Court of Priests, with the exception of the space between the porch and the altar (M. Kel. i.9) where he could not walk except during the procession of willow branches round the altar of burnt offering at Tabernacles (j. Sukk. iv.5, 54c.3; b. Sukk. 44a). They had a share in the revenues, but could not wear the priest's tunic (BJ 5.228). For their duties while the other priests were officiating see pp. 133f. The case of the high priest Hyrcanus II (76–67, 63–40 BC) is famous; Antigonus (40–37 BC) mutilated him by cutting off his ears (Ant. 14. 366), or biting them off (BJ 1.270) to disqualify him for service.

214 For Levite singers and musicians, see p. 208.

215 In M. Arak. ii.4 we find several points of view, on the origin of these flute-players: (a) 'they were the slaves of priests', says R. Meir. But (b) R. Jose says, 'they were from the (two) families of bēt ha-pegārīm and bēt Ṣippārayyā from Emmaus, whose daughters could marry priests. (c) As for R. Hananiah b. Hananiah, he says, 'They were Levites.' We can ignore (a), since these Temple slaves owe their existence to a purely theoretical conclusion from certain OT passages. (b) and (c) are not mutually exclusive. R. Jose (b) refutes R. Meir's opinion by unassailable historic evidence that they were not slaves but free Israelites of pure descent. R

If a priest or a Levite singer married, it was therefore necessary to examine the genealogy of his wife, in order to ensure thereby that the descendants of the marriage could qualify for priestly or levitical office. This examination of the wife's descent before the marriage took place not only in Palestine but also in Egypt, Mesopotamia and elsewhere, as Josephus affirms: 'A statement is drawn up . . . and sent to Jerusalem, showing the names of the bride[216] and her paternal ancestors, together with the names of witnesses (*CA* 1.33).

This is evidence of the great care which was taken. According to Philo, there must be examination of the purity of blood in parents, grandparents and great-grandparents (Philo, *De spec. leg.* I, 101); the Mishnah says this was necessary for four generations back of both paternal and maternal ancestry if the bride was of a priestly family, and for five if she was the daughter of a Levite or an Israelite.[217] For the daughters of serving priests and Levite musicians, as for a bride whose father was a member of a governing body (the Sanhedrin, the judiciary, or social services), examination of origin was omitted, since in such cases the father would have had to prove his legitimacy before taking office (M. Kidd. iv.5).

Lev. 21.7 gives the rules for the choice of a wife by priests: 'They shall not marry a harlot or a woman who has been defiled; neither shall they marry a woman divorced from her husband.' This proof passage has been interpreted in this manner:[218] By 'defiled' (*ḥảlālāh*) they meant the daughter of a priest's illegitimage marriage (with a woman not of equally pure descent, forbidden in Lev. 21.7); while 'harlot' included proselytes, manumitted slaves and women who had been seduced.[219] As a result there was a considerable part of the

---

Hananiah (*c*), himself a priest and according to T. Arak.i.15, 544 personally acquainted with Levites who played flutes at the altar, amplifies R. Jose's statement. (*b*) and (*c*), therefore, taken together, contain the true solution: they were Levites of pure descent, members of two well-known families from Emmaus, who played the flutes at the feasts of Passover and Tabernacles on the 'platform' reserved for the Levites.

[216] Laurentianus: τῆς γεγραμμένης, Latin: *nuptae*. This last is better; read τῆς γαμετῆς.
[217] M. Kidd. iv.4. For priests' daughters, they examined eight female ancestors for purity of line: (*a*) the mother, (*b*) the two grandmothers, (*c*) the two paternal and one maternal great-grandmothers, and (*d*) one of the great-great-grandmothers on each side. In the other cases a further generation was added. How can one explain this scheme, which seems entirely arbitrary?
[218] For what follows see Bill. I, 2f.
[219] Siphra Lev. 21.7, 47b; M. Yeb. vi.5. In detail this means: (*a*) the *ḥảlālāh*: she indeed may not herself marry a priest, but if she marries an Israelite, the

population ineligible for marriage with priests, that is, all Israelites whose descent was not pure, of whom more details are given later.[220] Only the daughter of a priest or Levite qualified to officiate, and the daughter of a pure-bred Israelite, were fit for legal marriage with a priest (M. Kidd. iii.12).

But even within this circle of legitimate families there were women excluded from marriage with a priest: a divorced woman,[221] the $ḥ^a lūṣāh$ (i.e. the woman who, after the death of her husband, is set free from levirate marriage by the ceremony of 'drawing off the shoe', Deut. 25.9) who was reckoned as divorced,[222] and the barren woman whom a priest could marry only if he already had a wife and child.[223] Ezek. 44.22 forbids also marriage of a priest with a widow unless she was the widow of a priest, while Lev. 21.14 makes this restriction only in the case of the high priest, and knows nothing of a general ban on marriage with widows for the rest of the priesthood. Later ages did not follow Ezekiel. Josephus (*Ant.* 3.277) says definitely that all priests, with the exception of the high priest, may marry

daughter of this marriage may marry a priest (M. Kidd. iv.6). (*b*) The proselyte: because of her pagan ancestry she may not marry a priest; but if she marries an Israelite, the daughter born of this marriage may marry a priest (so R. Judah b. Eli, *c.* AD 150; R. Eleazar b. Jacob, *c.* AD 150, will allow only the daughter of a male proselyte married to an Israelite; R. Jose b. Halafta, also *c.* AD 150, will allow even the daughter of a marriage of two proselytes). See M. Kidd. iv.6f. and similarly M. Bikk. i.5. One isolated voice (R. Simeon, *c.* AD 150) invokes Num. 31.18 to allow the marriage of a priest with a proselyte converted to Judaism before the age of three years and one day (j. Kidd. iv.6, 66a.10). (*c*) Manumitted slaves, as (*b*). (*d*) Women seduced by an act of prostitution: here among others belong the prostitutes (Targum Pseudo-Jonathan Lev. 21.7; *Ant.* 3.276), the women who were publicans or innkeepers (*Ant. ibid.*), and those who had been prisoners of war (*Ant. ibid*; *CA* 1.35; cf. pp. 155f., attacks on the high priests John Hyrcanus and Alexander Jannaeus). It was disputed whether or not a Jewish girl seduced by an Israelite of pure descent came in category (*d*): M. Ket. i.10 permits this girl to marry a priest; but R. Eliezer (*c.* AD 90) explains that she must be regarded as a 'harlot' and so could not marry a priest (Siphra Lev. 21.7, 47b; b. Yeb. 61b Bar.). Now this particular teacher always representes the old tradition; thus, while the Temple was still standing, the stricter opinion was in force.

[220] See ch. XV, 'Illegitimate Israelites', pp. 317ff. below.
[221] Lev. 21.7; Ezek. 44.22; M. Kidd. iii.12; M. Makk. i.1; iii.1; M. Ter. viii.1, *et passim*. The woman whose husband is declared dead and who marries again must, if her first husband returns, go back to him; she is not considered divorced from the second man since this marriage has become invalid (M. Yeb. x.3; Siphra Lev. 21.7, 47b).
[222] M. Yeb. ii.4; M. Kidd. iii.12; M. Makk. iii.1; M. Sot. iv.1; viii.3; Targum Pseudo-Jonathan Lev. 21.7; Siphra Lev. 21.7, 47b, *et passim*.
[223] M. Yeb. vi.5; R. Judah b. Elai, *c.* AD 150, forbids it in all cases; Siphra Lev. 21.7, 47b.

widows. These restrictions did not apply to the Levites; they were
forbidden marriage only with women of grave impurity (pp. 317ff.)
such as a bastard, a Temple slave, one whose father was unknown,
or a foundling (M. Kidd. iv.1.).

So much for the laws; now the actual practice: it was customary
for a priest to marry the daughter of a priest, particularly in the
circles of priestly aristocracy and among the priests of Jerusalem whose
prestige and education gave them a superior standing. The high-
priestly families especially preferred their daughters to marry priests:
the complaint quoted on pp. 195f., that the high priests pushed their
sons-in-law into the lucrative posts in the Temple, implies that they
were priests. We know of several high priests who themselves were
sons-in-law of officiating high priests; here chiefly we must mention
the high priest Matthias, son of Theophilus, and Caiaphas (evidence
on pp. 154f.). Again in two families of the priestly aristocracy
who produced high priests, among whom perhaps was the high priest
Caiaphas (p. 194 n. 146; cf. p. 94 n. 21), we hear of a girl marrying
her paternal uncle. This led to serious controversy since both women
were left widowed and childless. A levirate marriage with a woman's
own father was obviously impossible; but the question which in-
flamed the minds of Hillelites and Shammaites was whether or not
the father could contract a levirate marriage with the concubine of
his daughter's husband.[224] The point of interest here is the evidence
that, in two important families of the high priestly aristocracy in
Jerusalem, a daughter was married to her father's brother, thus that
both parties in the marriage came from leading priestly families.
There is another instance, in the marriage of Martha, of the high
priestly family of Boethus, to the high priest Joshua b. Gamaliel II,
which has already been mentioned (p. 155). In this case too both
parties came from leading priestly families.

The rest of the priesthood also preferred marriage with the daughters of priests. Thus the priest Zachariah, of the priestly class of Abia,
was married to Elizabeth, the daughter of a priest (Luke 1.5). R.
Tarphon himself a priest, had in Jerusalem a maternal uncle called
Simeon or Simšon[225], who again was a priest,[226] so that parents of
the Rabbi were both of priestly families.

[224] b. Yeb. 15b. See pp. 93f., where the case is considered in a discussion of
polygamy in Jerusalem in the time of Jesus.
[225] Simeon according to j. Hor. iii.5, 47d.37; Simšon according to Eccles. R.
3.15 on 3.11 (Son. 93).
[226] j. Yom. i.1, 38d.32; j. Hor. iii.5, 47d.37. Although lame, this uncle, as a

However, this intermarriage among priestly families was by no means exclusive; there were unions between the descendants of priests and those of Levites, as well as Israelites. Thus we see that in Jerusalem the Levite singer R. Joshua, the nailsmith, who survived the capture of Jerusalem, married a priest's daughter. As for marriages with the laity, we find (p. 155 n. 28) that the high priest Alexander Jannaeus is said to have married a sister of R. Simeon b. Shetah. Simeon b. Nathaniel, the priest and scribe, had for his wife the grand-daughter[227] of R. Gamaliel I the famous Jerusalem scholar and member of the Sanhedrin (T. A.Zar. iii.10, 464); the well-known teacher and priest Eliezer b. Hyrcanus (j. Sot. iii.4, 19a.3ff.) was married to a sister of Gamaliel II (b. Shab. 116a, *et passim*), and the priest Pinhas of Habta, later high priest (AD 67), was claimed as a relation by marriage by R. Hanina b. Gamaliel II (Siphra Lev. 21.10; 47c). Here are three priests who married daughters of the house of Gamaliel; thus it appears that among the laity the priests preferred the families of scribes. A final example: the priest and famous scribe R. Zadoq most probably had a Benjaminite wife, whose father's house was one of the distinguished families responsible for the supply of wood for the altar (pp. 286f.). Marriages, therefore, between priests and daughters of the laity were not rare, even though the Talmud occasionally frowns on such marriages (b. Pes. 49a Bar; b. Pes. 49a). We have little information on the ancestry of Levite wives; the marriage of the Levite Joshua with a priest's daughter has already been mentioned, and on p. 215 n. 215 we spoke of the legitimacy of the two Levite families from Emmaus who played the flute.

If a priest or a Levite musician contracted a marriage forbidden by law[228] ruthless action was taken: the marriage was declared illegitimate, i.e. as concubinage (b. Ket. 3a, and on this point Bill. III, 343 b), and the children barred from priestly office. Such a priest's son was called *ḥālāl* (profane) and was relegated to the group of illegitimate Israelites; his sons could no more than he take priestly office. The daughters of a priest's illegitimate marriage could not marry a priest (M. Kidd iv. 6, cf. p. 216 n. 219 (*a*)).

---

priest, blew the trumpet in the court at the feast of Tabernacles (Eccles. R. 3.15 on 3.11, Son. 93). He stood with his nephew on the platform in the court.

[227] The MS Erfurt, now in Berlin, Staatsbibl. MS *or.* 2⁰. 1220, says 'daughter'; but this is chronologically unlikely; see Bacher, *Ag. Tann.* I, 75 n. 3.

[228] As e.g. the scribe and priest Josephus, who, as a prisoner of war between AD 67 and 69, married, allegedly at Vespasian's command, a Jewish woman, also a prisoner of war, which was against the law, see p. 216 n. 219 (*d*): *Vita* 414.

These rules were by no means a dead letter. Even under Ezra (Ezra 2.61–63; Neh. 7.63–65) three priestly families who could not provide their genealogy were excluded from the priesthood. The Hasmonean high priests were forced to undergo criticism from the Pharisees of the legitimacy of their priesthood, because the mother of John Hyrcanus was said to have been a prisoner of war under Antiochus IV Epiphanes (pp. 155f.; 189f.); and later we hear of several legal proceedings against priests to deprive them of their right to office.[229] Examples will show the serious view taken on the purity of the clergy.[230] 'R. Zachariah, son of the butcher, said: "By this Temple [I swear]! Her hand [his wife's] stirred not out of mine from the time the Gentiles entered Jerusalem [doubtless when the city was taken in the Bar Kokhba war of AD 133–4] until they left."[231] They answered him: "None may testify for himself" (M. Ket. ii.9).

Thus, not only was a priest forbidden to marry a woman who had been prisoner of war, because she could not give him legitimate sons fit for the priesthood (see p. 216 n. 219), but he could not continue to live with his wife if she had merely lived in a town occupied by the enemy, and could not prove her integrity by unprejudiced evidence.[232] If he persisted in the marriage, it was regarded as concubinage and the children of the marriage were illegitimate. This rule was inexorably applied, even if her own husband could swear to her chastity on oath. Indeed the members of one family—clearly a priestly family—went so far as to refuse marriage with a priest to a young girl who had been 'left as a pledge' in Askalon (or had been taken there as hostage), even though there were witnesses to her chastity (' that she had not gone aside in secret with a man and been defiled'), and though the scribes decided this ban was not justified (M. Eduy. viii.2). Here we have a case where not only was a hostage treated as a prisoner of war, which is by no means a matter of course,[233] but her

[229] General provision for these is made in M. Makk. i.1; M. Midd. v.4. Later pages deal with special cases.

[230] For what follows cf. A. Büchler, 'Familienreinheit und Familienmakel in Jerusalem vor dem Jahre 70', Festschrift Schwarz, 133–62; ET, 'Family Purity and Family Impurity in Jerusalem before the Year 70 C.E.', Studies in Jewish History. The Büchler Memorial Volume, London 1956, 64–98.

[231] For this Rabbi's date, see Schlatter, Tage, 41. The Bar Kokhba war is to be dated 132 to 135 or 136; see C.-H. Hunzinger, RGG. V, 3rd ed. 754f.

[232] In this case a slave was allowed to testify, M. Ket. ii.9, but not her own husband.

[233] M. Ket. ii.9; 'If a woman was imprisoned by Gentiles for an offence concerning property (as hostage) she is still permitted her husband.'

own family actually increase the sentence on one of its members to remove from itself any suspicion of defilement. It was therefore the priests themselves who, despite protests from the scribes, were so concerned with family purity as to take the precept to such rigorous extremes.

It was the rule rather than an exception, that the priests themselves, contrary to the scribes' judgment, were so inexorably severe. Thus we hear that the scribes allowed the daughters of *'issāh* families (probably priestly families where the legitimacy of one member was in doubt) to marry priests,[234] but that the priests would have none of it (M. Eduy. viii.3); the mere suspicion was enough for them to hold aloof from the daughters of *'issāh* families. It was quite justifiably, therefore, that the complaint was raised by R. Johanan b. Zakkai—a man active in Jerusalem before the destruction of the Temple—that the priests followed the scribes' decisions only when they dealt with people unfit for priestly office or for marriage with priests, and ignored them when they decided in favour of leniency (*ibid.*).[235] It was this same inexorable concern for purity of priestly families which caused these priests, under Agrippa I (AD 41–44), when the Jews could exercise criminal justice, to burn publicly in Jerusalem a priest's daughter guilty of adultery (M. Sanh. vii.2; b. Sanh. 52b cf. details on p. 178 n. 94 above). For the priests offered the sacrifice as the representatives not of the people but of God (b. Kidd. 23b), and on this basis formed the sacred leadership of the people, chosen by God. All the more in the age to come would this purity be complete: 'When the Holy One, blessed be he, purifies the tribes, he will first purify the sons of Levi' (b. Kidd. 70b–71a).

[234] The word *'issāh* means 'dough' or 'mixture'. It is not easy to arrive at an exact translation. R. Meir (*c.* 150) defines it thus (b. Ket. 14b Bar.) : 'Which is the widow of an *'issāh* family? She whom possibly an illegitimate son of a priest [*ḥālāl*] is mixed.' This passage makes no sense. The word 'widow' is probably introduced inadvertently from M. Eduy. viii.3, which speaks of the *'issāh*-widow, hence the error. If we may strike out the word 'widow' in b. Ket. Bar., the sense becomes clear; a 'mixed' family is one where there is doubt over the legitimacy of one member. Büchler's explanation mentioned above, overlooks this simple solution and is therefore unconvincing; he understands by *'issāh* the illegitimate families with only a very slight blemish (see below), i.e. profane (*ḥªlālīm*), proselyte or freed slaves.

[235] M. Eduy. viii.7 recounts the case of a certain Ben Ṣion (doubtless before AD 70 since the tradition goes back to Johanan b. Zakkai) who had unjustly and by force 'removed a family and restored another'—obviously priestly families from the context—i.e. declared them illegitimate and legitimate.

IX

THE LAY NOBILITY

IN ADDITION TO THE priestly nobility there was a lay aristocracy; true, its importance was not very great, as the meagreness
of evidence shows.

It is advisable to begin by examining the composition of the Sanhedrin. According to New Testament sources this supreme court of
Judaism, consisting of seventy-one members, fell into three groups:
the chief priests who, in the person of the high priest, held the presidency, the scribes and the elders.

Who made up this group of 'elders'?[1] The history of Jewish government gives us the answer. After the exile those who reorganized the
people, by this time without a king, made the ancient ruling families
the basis of order. Originally, these had held the leadership of the
tribes and even after the settlement in Canaan their influence had
never entirely disappeared. It is probable that already in exile, that
is, with the disappearance of the monarchy, the heads of the predominant families assumed the leadership of the people, directing
the settlement of the exiled in Babylon and governing them as leaders
and judges (Ezek. 8.1; 20.1).[2] After the return from exile these heads
of families, the 'elders of the Jews' (*sābē yᵉhūdāyē*), functioned as
representatives of the people, negotiated with the Persian provincial
governor (Ezra 5.9ff.) and in association with the 'governor of the

[1] In a wider sense the word meant a non-priestly member of the Sanhedrin, both
in the New Testament (Matt. 21.23; 26.3, 47; 27. 1.3, 12, 20; 28.11f.; Luke 22.52;
Acts 4.23; 25.15 cf. 24.1) and in rabbinic literature (M. Yom. i.5; M. Par. iii.7
cf. T. Par. iii.8, 632, where the elders as representatives of the Sanhedrin and
guardians of the Pharisaic tradition appear as observers of the rites on the Day of
Atonement and the burning of the Red Heifer). This wider sense of the word, which
links the two groups of scribes and elders (in the narrower sense) in the Sanhedrin,
must be distinguished from the narrower sense which we shall examine later, which
sets the elders as a group within the Sanhedrin as distinct from the chief priests
and scribes.

[2] Cf. I. Benzinger, *Hebraische Archäologie*, 3d ed., Leipzig 1927, 269, and the
dissertation of O. Seesemann, *Die Ältesten im AT*, Leipzig 1895.

Jews' directed the reconstruction of the Temple (Ezra 5.5, 9; 6.7, 8, 14).

The Sanhedrin, supreme assembly of post-exilic Judaism, grew out of the union of these non-priestly heads of families, representatives of the 'secular nobility',[3] with the priestly aristocracy. On this point the description of Jehoshaphat's judiciary reform (II Chron. 19.5–11), which reflects the post-exilic situation, is informative; here the supreme judicial authority in Jerusalem is composed of Levites, priests and heads of families.[4] Thus it is an aristocratic senate composed of representatives of the priestly and lay aristocracy who, in the Persian and Greek periods, came to the forefront of the Jewish people. Only later, probably in the time of Queen Alexandra (76–67 BC), who held Pharisaic opinions,[5] were Pharisaic scribes admitted to this supreme assembly which until then had been wholly aristocratic. There can therefore be no doubt about the composition of the group of 'elders' in the Sanhedrin: they were the heads of the most influential lay families.[6]

The New Testament, as well as Josephus and Talmudic literature, knows this lay nobility. In the New Testament the 'principal men of the people' (Luke 19.47) appear once in place of the 'elders', as a third group in the Sanhedrin; this synonym is very informative. As a representative of this group we meet Joseph of Arimathea (Mark 15.43; Matt. 27.57; Luke 23.50f.; John 19.38–42)[7] who was a rich landowner.[8]

[3] I use the word to express the hereditary principle.

[4] Cf. further I Macc., where priests and elders of the people (7.33; 11.23) appear as representatives of the people; and especially 14.28 where the assembly of the people making a decision is composed as follows: ἐπὶ συναγωγῆς μεγάλης ἱερέων καὶ λαοῦ καὶ ἀρχόντων ἔθνους καὶ τῶν πρεσβυτέρων τῆς χώρας: Clerical and lay nobility (ἄρχοντες ἔθνους) lead the people; the elders of the community (πρεσβύτεροι τῆς χώρας) and the body of people unite with these leaders to form the assembly of the people.

[5] We meet Pharisaic members of the Sanhedrin for the first time in Ant. 13.428. As the context shows, those who in this passage are called 'elders of the Jews' (members of the Sanhedrin) are assuredly Pharisees.

[6] This what E. Meyer rightly saw in Die Entstehung des Judenthums, Halle 1896 (reprinted Hildesheim 1965), and Ursprung II, 12 and 29. See further J. Wellhausen, Das Evangelium Marci, Berlin 1909, 65: 'the lay nobility of Jerusalem'; Bill. II, 631: 'the lay members of the supreme court'. Schürer II, 252, ET II.1, 178, says: 'Such other members as did not belong to one or other of these two special classes just referred to [ἀρχιερεῖς and γραμματεῖς] were known simply as πρεσβύτεροι.' It was a way out of a dilemma.

[7] As he is called neither priest nor scribe, we must count him among the group of 'elders' in the Sanhedrin.

[8] He possessed property with a garden (John 19.41; 20.15; Matt 27.60) immediately north of the second northern wall, on the site of the present Church

In Josephus there appear, besides the chief priests, as the most influential men in Jerusalem: 'the first of the city' (*Vita* 9); 'leaders of the people' (*Vita* 194); 'the notables' (*BJ* 2.410 *et passim*), 'the leading men' (*BJ* 2.316 *et passim*); 'the nobles and the most eminent citizens' (*BJ* 2.301). These people are the 'elders' of the New Testament, and we have assurance of this from a passage in Josephus showing this tripartite division of the Sanhedrin which is common in the New Testament. The three groups are there called 'the principal citizens . . . the chief priests and the most notable Pharisees' (*BJ* 2.411).[9] This establishes beyond question the identity of Josephus' 'nobles' as the New Testament 'elders'. In other passages the 'leading citizens' are distinguished from the members of the supreme council (*BJ* 2.336),[10] and this shows that part only of the heads of leading families, certainly as representing their class, had a voice in the Sanhedrin. A comparison of two passages in Josephus confirms that the 'elders' are indeed heads of notable lay families. After his rise to power in 37 BC Herod put to death, according to *Ant.* 14.175, 'all[11] the members of this Sanhedrin'. According to *Ant.* 15.6, he put to death 'forty-five of the principal men of the party of Antigonus' (he was both king and high priest). Comparing these two passages, we gather that the principal members of the lay nobility, Hasmonean sympathisers, had a voice in the Sanhedrin. A second synonym is even more explicit. Those men called, in *BJ* 2.237, representatives of 'the magistrates of Jerusalem' are called, in the parallel passage in *Ant.* 20.123, 'those who were by rank and birth the leaders of the inhabitants of Jerusalem'. Again comparison of these two passages shows that the heads of patrician families had a voice on the Sanhedrin.

Examination of rabbinic literature leads us to the same conclusion, since it too speaks of representatives of lay nobility as a group in the Sanhedrin. Thus we have sure and certain historic evidence on the

of the Holy Sepulchre (see my *Golgotha*, Leipzig 1926, 1–33). Furthermore, the term εὐσχήμων (15.43) used in the papyri suggests perhaps a rich landowner (cf. J. Leipoldt in *Theologisches Literaturblatt* 39, 1918, col. 180f.).

[9] συνελθόντες γοῦν οἱ δυνατοὶ τοῖς ἀρχιερεῦσιν εἰς ταὐτὸ καὶ τοῖς τῶν Φαρισαίων γνωρίμοις. Cf. 2.301: οἵ τε ἀρχιερεῖς καὶ δυνατοὶ τό τε γνωριμώτατον τῆς πόλεως.

[10] 'The chief priests of the Jews, the leading citizens and the council'; 2.627: 'their leaders, with some of the magistrates'.

[11] Not to be taken literally: the Sanhedrin had seventy-one members. S. Funk, 'Die Manner der grossen Versammlung und die Gerichtshöfe im nachexilischen Judentum', *MGWJ* 55, 1911, 37–39, supposed this passage to refer to the little Sanhedrin composed, he thought, of forty-five members, but he could scarcely be right.

nature of the 'elders'. Many times in rabbinic literature there appear 'the eminent men of the generation', 'the eminent men of Jerusalem', 'the leading men of Jerusalem.' Detailed references show that they formed a limited group: the legendary tale in the Midrash in which Vespasian filled three boats with 'eminent men of Jerusalem' to deport them (Lam. R. 1.48 on 1.16, Son. 1.45, 124), is to the purpose here. There are other instances in the light of history. 'R. Zadoq, the leader of his generation' (*ARN* Rec. A, ch. 16, Goldin, 84) '*The noble women* of Jerusalem used to donate and bring it [the narcotic drink for those condemned to death]' (b. Sanh. 43a Bar.; see p. 95). 'Abba Saul (*c.* AD 150) said: "The *notable woman* of Jerusalem fed them and maintained them" (i.e. the women who brought up their children for the rite of the Red Heifer, Num. 19)' (b. Ket. 106a). Although children under age were not allowed into the Court of the Israelites (M. Arak. ii.6; T. Arak. ii.1, 544), the sons under age of the 'leading men of Jerusalem' (T. Arak. ii.2, 544.14) had a right to join in the singing of the Levites during the daily sacrifice, and so stood in the Court of the Israelites, at the feet of the Levites who were on the platform between the Court of the Israelites and the Court of Priests.[12]

One statement by the apostate Elisha b. Abuyah, born in Jerusalem before AD 70, is particularly important. 'My father Abuyah was one of the notable men of Jerusalem.[13] At my circumcision he invited all the notables of Jerusalem.'[14] This invitation shows that the father, a patrician of Jerusalem, was a very well-to-do man; and the word 'all' indicating that all the notables of Jerusalem could gather in one room, shows that the heads of leading Jerusalem families formed a small close circle.

It was members of this group who are depicted in the well-known story of three Jerusalem merchants. At the outbreak of the rebellion against the Romans they are said to have pledged themselves to provide food and wood for Jerusalem for twenty-one years (see pp.

[12] According to T. Arak. ii.2, 544, they were in the Court of Women. But, as ii.1, 544 shows, the true picture is in M. Arak. ii.6: 'nor did they stand on the Platform; but they used to stand on the ground so that their heads were between the feet of the Levites [who stood on the platform raised 1½ cubits (75 cm., about 30 ins.) above the Court of the Israelites].' G. Dalman, 'Der zweite Tempel zu Jerusalem', *PJB* 5, 1909, 43 n. 6, also rejects the placing in T. Arak. ii.2, 544.

[13] Variant in Eccles. R. and Ruth R.: 'One of the notable men of his generation'.

[14] Eccles. R.: 'And all the eminent men of the generation'. j. Hag. ii.1, 77b.33, says: 'and placed them in one room'. The par. in Ruth R. 6.6. on 3.13 (Son.6.4, 77) and Eccles. R. 7.18 on 7.8 (Son. 184) omit these words.

38f., 95f.). They are sometimes called 'three men of great wealth' (b. Gitt. 65a), sometimes 'the great ones of Israel' (*ARN* Rec. A, ch. 6, Goldin 44) or 'greatest of the town' (Gen. R. 42.1 on 14.1, Son. 340; *ARN* Rec. B, ch. 13; *Pirqe R. Eliezer* 2), and sometimes 'councillors' (Eccles. R. 7.25 on 7.12, Son. 193; Lam. R. 1.32 on 1.5, Son. 1.31, 101).[15] Some details of this story may be legendary; but there is a kernel of historical fact (see p. 96 n. 28) which contains the indication that the 'great ones of the city' sat in the Sanhedrin. This is all the more likely as 'the principal men of Jerusalem', on the Day of Atonement, had an official function to perform in connection with the rites. They accompanied, obviously as members of the Sanhedrin (cf. M. Yom. i.5), the man who led the 'Goat for Azazel' into the wilderness, as far as the first of the ten booths placed along the route (M. Yom. vi.4). A final comparison of two Midrashic passages shows that the titles 'great ones of the city' (or 'of their generation') and 'elders' appear to be synonymous.[16] This closes the circle of evidence, that in the Sanhedrin the group of 'elders' was composed of the *heads of the leading families of Jerusalem*.

During our enquiry into the composition of the Sanhedrin we have discovered convincing evidence of the existence of a lay nobility in Jerusalem, and it now remains for us to ask if we can arrive at a more precise knowledge of this section of the population. We can indeed do so. M. Taan. iv.5 hands down to us a very valuable list of the privileged families[17] who were entitled to supply wood for the altar: 'The wood offering of the priests and the people was brought nine times (in the year):

(1) on the 1st of Nisan by the family of Arah of the tribe of Judah [cf. Ezra 2.5; Neh. 7.10];

(2) on the 20th of Tammuz, by the family of David of the tribe of Judah [cf. Ezra 8.2];

(3) on the 5th of Ab, by the family of Parosh of the tribe of Judah [cf. Ezra 2.3; 8.3; 10.25; Neh. 3.25; 7.8; 10.15];

[15] In the last passage *four* councillors are mentioned through wrongly treating Naqdimon b. Gorion as two names.

[16] Lev. R. 30.7 on 23.40 (Son. 389) lists: (*a*) great ones of the city [of their generation], (*b*) private persons, (*c*) men, women and children. Cant. R. 6.11 on 6.5 (Son. 263), lists: (*a*) private persons, (*b*) children, (*c*) the $z^eq\bar{e}n\bar{\imath}m$. Comparison of these two shows that $z^eq\bar{e}n\bar{\imath}m$ probably does not indicate age but honour; cf. A. Büchler, *The Political and Social Leaders of the Jewish Community of Sepphoris*, London 1909, 10.

[17] In Neh. 10.35 we find the choice is made by lot, cf. b. Taan. 28a.

(4)   on the 7th of the self-same month, by the family of Jonadab
      the son of Rechab [cf. II Kings 10.15, 23; Jer. 35.8; I Chron.
      2.55];

(5)   on the 10th by the family of Senaa of the tribe of Benjamin
      [cf. Ezra 2.35; Neh. 3.3; 7.38; 11.9];

(6)   on the 15th by the family of Zattuel of the tribe of Judah [cf.
      Zattu: Ezra. 2.8; 10.27; Neh. 7.13; 10.15] together with the
      priests and Levites and all whose tribal descent was in doubt[18]
      and[19] the family of the Pestle-smugglers [or Mortar-smug-
      glers: b. Taan. 28a] and the family of Fig-pressers;

(7)   on the 20th of the same month [it was brought] by the family
      of Pahath Moab of the tribe of Judah [cf. Ezra 2.6; 8.4;
      10.30; Neh. 3.11; 7.11; 10.15];

(8)   on the 20th of Elul, by the family of Adin of the tribe of
      Judah [cf. Ezra 2.15; 8.6; Neh. 7.20; 10.17];

(9)   on the 1st of Tebet . . . an additional offering, and a wood
      offering [by the family of Parosh].'

First, it is surprising to find in this list mention of a Rechabite
family; indeed the latest historical record of the Rechabites is found
in Neh. 3.14 and I Chron. 2.55, for there is very grave suspicion about
Hegesippus' statement, quoted by Eusebius, *HE* II, 23.4–18, that
James the brother of Jesus was put to death by a Rechabite priest
[*sic!*]. It is surprising, too, that together with the Rechabite family
only families mentioned in Ezra and Nehemiah are named. These
two points together suggest that this list dates from a period not long
after the return from exile; probably it derives directly from the
description, in Neh. 10.35–37 and 13.31, of the casting of lots to
provide wood for the altar fire. We see therefore that the Talmudic
account[20] is quite right in saying that the privilege of bringing wood
was an ancient prerogative dating back to the time of the reorganiza-
tion of the Jewish community after the Babylonian exile. This prerogative was jealously guarded by the privileged families through the
centuries. Thus we have every reason to assume that this list preserves
the names of eminent patrician families whose precedence was based
on centuries-old privilege.

[18] Perhaps a euphemism for 'whose ancestry is not quite free from impurity'.
[19] Or 'namely'; there is no indication of tribe for the next two pseudonyms, so
they are an explanation of the preceding phrase.
[20] b. Taan. 28a; T. Taan. iv.5, 219; j. Taan. iv.2, 68a.38.

It follows that these privileged families were originally *landowning families*, as is shown by their supplies of natural products to the Temple. This accords with the fact that in Jesus' time the lay nobility consisted mostly of rich families. In the Midrash we find the sentence, 'So-and-so is rich, we will make him a city magistrate',[21] attributed to Roman officials. We shall understand this sentence if we bear in mind that the procurator was careful to choose his officials from among the 'elders' of the Sanhedrin and other heads of families—his tax officials,[22] the *dekaprotoi* (*Ant.* 20.194). These were charged with assessing the citizens liable to taxation, the tribute which Rome imposed on Judaea, and guaranteed the correct payment from their own resources.[23] This 'liturgical'[24] office of the *dekaprotos* required men of considerable means, principally men who were landowners, as we know in Egypt; this shows that the heads of patrician families, at any rate those with seats in the Sanhedrin, were men of great wealth. This appears to be true of Joseph of Arimathea and of the three great merchants of Jerusalem mentioned on pp. 225f.

In this context too is a difficult passage of the Midrash: it says that the councillors of Jerusalem with great cunning sought to persuade rich inhabitants of Bitter to accept posts as councillors, and by this means stole their property (Lam. R. 2.5 on 2.2, Son. 2.4, 160; 4.22 on 4.18, Son. 4.21, 231; j. Taan. iv.8, 69a.22). This meagre and exaggerated statement does at least tell us that the lay members of the Sanhedrin were generally men of means and—this seems to be the kernel of truth—that their office could involve financial sacrifice.

There are statements in Josephus to give us information on the intellectual and religious position of the lay nobility. 'This doctrine is received but by a few, yet by those still of the greatest dignity', he says of the Sadducees (*Ant.* 18.17); and again, 'The Sadducees have the confidence of the wealthy alone, but no following among the

[21] Gen. R. 76.5 on 32.12 (Son. 76.6, 706); see further b. Gitt. 37a: 'R. Hisda (d. 309) says, '*Būlē*, those are the rich.' For it is written (Lev. 26.19), 'I will break the pride of your power', and as R. Joseph (d. 333) explained, this means the city councillors or judges, (*būlā'ōth*; on this point see Bacher, *Ag. Tann.* I, 52 n. 6). In this reference too the councillors are rich men.

[22] *BJ* 2.405: archontes and councillors collect taxes; 407: archontes and patricians are presented to the procurator for nomination as tax officials.

[23] On the office of *dekaprotos* see C. G. Brandis, Δεκάπρωτος, in Pauly-Wissowa, *Real-Encyclopädie* IV, 1901, 2417ff.; O. Seeck, *Decemprimat und Dekaprotie*, in *Beiträge zur alten Geschichte*, ed. C. F. Lehmann, 1, Leipzig 1902; Mitteis-Wilcken, I.1, 218.

[24] This term denotes an official charge enforced by lawful authority.

populace' (*Ant.* 13.298).[25] Josephus' historical perspective confirms very convincingly these statements that the lay nobility consisted for the most part of Sadducees.[26] He depicts, for example, the Sadducees as the most distinguished and important people in the entourage of King Alexander Jannaeus (103–76 BC), who held Sadducean ideas (*Ant.* 13.411; *BJ* 1.114).

The still prevalent view that the Sadducees were a clerical party recruited, partly if not exclusively, from higher circles in the priesthood, thus stands in need of correction. It is certainly true that the later Hasmoneans and the families of the illegitimate high-priestly aristocracy, in contrast with the majority of priests, were for the most part of Sadducean opinions.[27] Thus the high priest and prince of the Jews John Hyrcanus (134–104 BC) who at the beginning of his reign favoured the Pharisees, went over in the end to the Sadduceans (*Ant.* 13.288ff.; b. Ber. 29a), thus Alexander Jannaeus (103–76 BC), high priest and king (*Ant.* 13.371f.),[28] also the high priest Simon, son of Boethus (*c.* 22–5 BC, see n. 33), the high priest Joseph, surnamed Caiaphas (AD 18–37)[29] and Ananus the younger, son of Ananus (AD 62, *Ant.* 20.199), and finally the two Sadducean high priests of rabbinic tradition whose names are not mentioned, but one of whom we must identify as Ishmael b. Phiabi II (up to AD 62).[30]

[25] Cf. in this connection *ARN*, Rec. A, ch. 5 (Goldin 39): 'And they [the Sadducees and Boethusians] used silver vessels and gold vessels all their lives' [because they denied the resurrection of the dead and thus wished to make the most of earthly life]. It is true that followers of the Sadducees belonged to wealthy circles. Let us remember too that the Hellenistic influence was evident in the theology and philosophy of life of the Sadducees, and this also indicates the wealthy classes since it was they who were most influenced by Hellenistic culture.

[26] For literature on the Sadducees see ch. XI below. Here we may mention Wellhausen, *Pharisäer*; Schlatter, *Geschichte Israels*, 165–70; R. Leszynsky, *Die Sadduzäer*, Berlin 1912.

[27] The precautionary measures in M. Yom. i.5; iv.1 and M. Sukk. iv.9 are correctly explained in b. Yom. 19b—the high priest was suspected of Sadducean tendencies.

[28] Cf. b. Sukk. 48b, where the high priest called 'a certain Sadducee' means Alexander Jannaeus.

[29] Acts 5.17 calls the Sadducees 'all they that were with him' i.e. with the high priest, who was then Caiaphas: Acts 4.6.

[30] This tradition refers to (1) a Sadducean high priest who offers the incense on the Day of Atonement, according to the Sadducean rite, b. Yom. 19b Bar.; j. Yom. i.5, 39a.45; T. Yom. i.8, 181; and (2) a Sadducean high priest who burnt the Red Heifer, T. Par. iii.8, 632, in the presence of R. Johanan b. Zakkai. This second event, therefore, could not have happened long before AD 70. Now according to M. Par. iii.5, in the first century AD there were only two high priests who prepared the Red Heifer: Elionaios, son of Kantheras (*c.* AD 44) and Ishmael, son of Phiabi (up to AD 62); thus it could only be Ishmael.

The chief priests, too, were generally Sadducees;[31] even in the time of Agrippa I their court seems to have given judgment according to the severe Sadducean law.[32] It is true moreover that these high-ranking priests took the leadership among the Sadducees; Acts shows the Sadducees as supporters of the high priest (Acts 5.17, cf. 21), and a group of Sadducees—perhaps even the whole group[33]—were called 'Boethusians' after the high priest Simon, son of Boethus.[34] But all this does not in any way prove that the Sadducees consisted exclusively, or even predominantly, of priests. Indeed, this possibility is precluded by the absence of any such affirmation in Josephus' presentation of the Sadducees; and also by the distinction drawn in Acts between priests of Sadducean opinions and Sadducees themselves (Acts 4.1).[35] It is Acts 23 which reveals the true situation. When Paul was brought before the Sanhedrin he saw that it was divided into two groups, Sadducees and Pharisees. He declared, 'I am a Pharisee, a son of Pharisees: touching the final hope and the prophecy of resurrection of the dead I am called in question' (Acts 23.6), and these words rallied the Pharisees to his side. Next day a Zealot plot was formed against Paul's life and received support from 'the chief priests and elders' (Acts 23.12–14). Since the Pharisees were on Paul's side, the plotters could only have been the Sadducean group in the Sanhedrin.

We see then that the Sadducean party was made up of chief priests and elders, the priestly and the lay nobility. Thus the patrician families stood in the same relationship to the priestly nobility as the Pharisees to the scribes. In both cases the laity formed the mass of supporters; the 'men of religion'—Sadducean clergy, Pharisaic theologians—were the leaders.

The Sadducees formed a tightly closed circle,[36] and this observa-

---

[31] It is probable that there were Pharisees among the higher ranks of priests (see pp. 256f. in the chapter on the Pharisees); but this was by no means the rule.

[32] See p. 178 n. 94.

[33] Parallel passages often use the terms Sadducees and Boethusians synonymously. In *ARN, loc. cit.* (n. 25), the distinction between them is false.

[34] T. Sukk. iii.1, 195; b. Sukk. 43b; T. Yom. i.8, 181; T.R. Sh. i.15, 210; b. Shab. 108a; b. Men. 65a; *ARN, loc cit.* (n. 25); Bill. II, 849f., 599a.

[35] A corresponding distinction between a high priest and a Sadducee is found in T. Nidd. v.3, 645; b. Nidd. 33b. For the original text of the passage (Arab sheikh instead of Sadducee) see p. 153 n. 24.

[36] Although some details of his treatment are open to question, B. D. Eerdmans, 'Farizëen en Sadducëen', *Theologisch Tijdschrift* 48, 1914, 1–26 and 223–30, saw this correctly, in contrast to Wellhausen, *Pharisäer*. It is therefore wrong to refer to Pharisees and Sadducees as 'sects', since neither group separated itself from the

tion is particularly helpful in understanding the awareness of tradition among patrician families. These facts emerge from the information that the number of Sadducean supporters was small, as Josephus says (*Ant.* 18.17), and that they possessed a *halākāh* (tradition), based on an exegesis of Scripture, which the members must follow in their conduct of life. The exclusive character of the Sadducean group is shown even more clearly by the fact that Josephus classes them with Pharisees and Essenes. In his autobiography he tells how he made a comparative survey of Pharisees, Sadducees and Essenes, in order to obtain practical knowledge of all three, and finally decided for the Pharisees (*Vita* 10ff.). We know definitely that the Pharisees and the Essenes were clearly defined communities, with conditions of admission and definite principles; it follows then that the same must be true of the Sadducees. Not everyone could gain admission to this tight circle of Sadducees.

The Sadducean 'theology' is equally instructive in understanding the lay nobility's position as guardian of tradition. They held strictly to the literal interpretation of the Torah,[37] in particular to the precepts on the cultus and the priesthood, and thus found themselves in direct opposition to the Pharisees and their oral *halākāh* which declared that the rules of purity for priests were binding on the pious laity too.[38] The Sadducees had formulated this theology in a fully developed *halākāh* based on exegesis (cf. Matt. 16.12 'the teaching of . . . Sadducees'). In addition they had their own penal code,[39] and we have much evidence of its extreme severity.[40] We have already met (p. 178) a Sadducean tribunal of chief priests, and we are reminded in several places of sentences passed according to Sadducean laws (*Ant.* 20. 199; b. Sanh. 52b). This makes the existence of Sadducean scribes quite definite; indeed we cannot really contest it, since the sources make particular mention of Sadducean scribes.[41] It shows again that

community; moreover it is wrong to dispute the aristocratic character of the Sadducees.

[37] R. Leszynsky, *Die Sadduzäer*, Berlin 1912, has given proof of this.
[38] See pp. 265f. in the chapter on the Pharisees.
[39] Meg. Taan. 10, on 14 Tammuz. cf. the Scholia on Meg. Taan. 10.
[40] Ps. Sol. 4.2; *Ant.* 20.199; Bill. IV, 349–52.
[41] *Ant.* 18.16; cf. further Acts 23.9: 'scribes of the Pharisees' party'; Mark 2.16 par. Luke 5.30: 'the scribes of the Pharisees'. Such expressions suppose that, in contrast, there were Sadducean scribes, on whom see Bill. I, 250; IV, 343–52; Meyer, *Ursprung* II, 286ff.; Schürer II, 380f., 457, ET II.1, 319f., II.2, 11; G. F. Moore in *HTR* 17, 1924, 350f.; L. Baeck, 'Die Pharisäer', in 44. *Bericht der Hochschule für die*

the patrician families of Sadducees formed a tightly closed group, with an elaborate tradition of theology and doctrine; they kept strictly to the exact text of Scripture, which shows the conservative character of these circles.

Thanks to their ties with the powerful priestly nobility, the rich patrician families were a very influential factor in the life of the nation. Especially under the Hasmoneans, up to the beginning of Queen Alexandra's reign (76 BC), was political power in their hands. Together with the leading priests they made up the Sanhedrin, and consequently they, together with the sovereign, possessed judiciary power and authority to govern. The decline of their power dates from the time of Alexandra; under her the Pharisees gained a foothold in the Sanhedrin, and the mass of people rallied more and more to them. The Sadducees were involved in hostilities with Herod the Great, in particular during the long pontificate of the high priest Simon (22–5 BC), son of Boethus after whom they were called Boethusians; this seems to have given them an opportunity of strengthening themselves internally but this could not deflect the tide of change. The decline in the political importance of the high priests during the first half of the first century AD was the cause of the decline of the lay nobility, and the Pharisees, relying on their large number of supporters among the people, saw their power in the Sanhedrin becoming stronger and stronger (*Ant.* 18.17).

Once more chance seemed to have decreed that the nobility should lead the people, in AD 66, when the uprising against Rome began, and the young nobles took into their hands the people's destiny. But it was for a matter of months only, for by AD 67 the Zealots had taken command. The decline of the state marked the decline of the lay nobility and of the Sadducean influence, which had grown from the union of the priestly and the lay nobility. The new and powerful ruling class of the scribes had everywhere overtaken the ancient class of priestly and lay nobility, founded on the privileges of birth.

Wissenschaft des Judentums in Berlin, Berlin 1927, 70 n. 87, ET, *The Pharisees and Other Essays*, New York 1947, 23.

X

THE SCRIBES

TOGETHER WITH THE old ruling class composed of the hereditary nobility of priests and laity, there grew up in the last centuries BC a new upper class, that of the scribes. At the time with which we are dealing, the first century AD until the destruction of the Temple, the struggle for supremacy between the ancient ruling class and the new reached its peak, and the balance began to be tipped by degrees in favour of the new class. How was this possible? From which circles did this new ruling class recruit its members? Upon what did their power and prestige rest that they could dare to compete with hereditary nobility of such long standing? Such are the questions which now arise.

To find answers for them we must first examine the company of the scribes of Jerusalem.[1] When we look for the origin of these scribes a varied picture emerges. In Jerusalem before AD 70 we can prove the existence of a large number of priests who were scribes (pp. 207, 243 n. 32). Among these were such leading priests as the captain of the Temple, R. Hananiah (M. Ab. iii.2 *et passim*), the chief priest Simon (Josephus, *Vita* 197), another Simon, son of a Temple captain (p. 203 n. 181),[2] Ishmael b. Elisha, grandson of a reigning high priest,[3] R. Zadoq (p. 193 n. 145) a distinguished priest of an old high-priestly family, and his son R. Eleazar (p. 203), and the writer Josephus who belonged to the first weekly course of Jehoiarib (*Vita* 1ff.).

---

[1] For the scribes and Pharisees as a factor in the community, see M. Weber, *Religionssoziologie* III, 401–42; E. Lohmeyer, *Soziale Fragen im Urchristentum*, Leipzig 1921, largely follows him.

[2] The word Rabbi as a title does not occur in every testimony.

[3] In T. Hall. i.10, 98 he swears by the vestments of his forefather (*'abbā*); this could not have been his father because in the first century AD there was no high priest called Elisha. It could be only his grandfather, probably Ishmael b. Phiabi II (until AD 62), see p. 196 n. 159. It was in Jerusalem before AD 70 that Ishmael b. Elisha began his study of the Bible, before the Romans took him captive while still a boy (b. Gitt. 58a Bar.; Lam. R. 4.4 on 4.2, Son. 218).

Besides these members of the priestly aristocracy, ordinary priests wore the robe of a scribe: the priest R. Jose b. Joezer, an expert in matters of purity (M. Hag. ii.7), priests in whose family the post of leader of the Hellenist synagogue in Jerusalem was hereditary (p. 66), the priest R. Jose, pupil of Johanan b. Zakkai (M. Ab. ii.8 *et passim*), R. Eliezer b. Hyrcanos, a very cultured priest who lived in Jerusalem before the destruction of the Temple (j. Sot. iii.4, 19a.3ff. shows that he was a priest), the priest Joezer (*Vita* 197)[4] and his father (*BJ* 2. 628), the priest R. Tarphon who in his youth had witnessed the Temple cultus (T. Neg. viii.2, 628 shows he was a priest). We do not know whether the priests Zachariah b. Qebutal (M. Yom. i.6) and Simeon the Discreet (T. Kel. B.K. i.6, 569) were ordained scribes, since the texts do not give them the title of Rabbi.

Among the scribes who lived in Jerusalem before the destruction of the Temple, we find also, members of the lower orders of clergy (p. 213): Johanan b. Gudgeda, the chief doorkeeper,[5] R. Joshua b. Hananiah, a Levite singer plying the trade of a nailmaker (b. Arak. 11b; j. Ber. iv.1, 7d.19; b. Ber. 28a), the Levite Barnabas, prophet and teacher of the early Christian community (Acts 13.1), R. Eleazer b. Jacob, nephew of a Levite (M. Midd. i.2). There were besides, as we have seen (p. 231) scribes, who came from the circle of patrician families who developed the Sadducean tradition.

Next came men from every other class of people, and these far outnumbered the rest. These other Jerusalem scribes presented in their professions a varied and multicoloured picture. We must mention Joezer, commander of the Temple fortress under Agrippa I, who was a Shammaite (M. Orl. ii.12). There were several merchants (p. 113, Johanan b. Zakkai), among them a wine merchant (*ibid.*, Abba Saul b. Batnit). There were artisans of different trades, a carpenter (p. 112, Shammai), a flax comber (Simeon b. Shetah, j. B.M. ii.4, 8c. 18), a tent maker (Paul, Acts 18.3; cf. p. 3), even a day labourer, Hillel, afterwards a very famous teacher (pp. 112f.). These petty towns-folk belonged for the most part to the unprivileged part of the population (pp. 111ff.). Among the scribes of Jerusalem, alongside men of ancient families such as Paul (Phil. 3.5; Rom. 11.1), we find even

---

[4] Γόζορος (var. Γόζαρος); the correct form of his name occurs in the parallel passage, *BJ* 2.628: Ἰώεσδρος = Joezer.

[5] On his office, see pp. 173f. According to M. Yeb. xiv.3; M. Gitt. v.5; b. Arak. 11b; b. Gitt. 55a, he was a Rabbi. b. Hor. 10a, b tells us he possessed amazing knowledge of mathematics. But the parallel, Siphre Deut. 1.16, speaks instead of R. Johanan b. Nuri, which is assuredly right, see p. 168 n. 69.

men who were not of pure Israelite descent—and the course of our investigation will show what that means—such as Shemaiah and Abtalion, the famous teachers of the middle of the first century BC, who were said to have descended from proselytes (b. Yom. 71b; b. Gitt. 57b).[6] Two other Jerusalem teachers appear to have had pagan blood in their veins, at least on their maternal side: R. Johanan, 'son of the Hauranite', c. AD 40 (M. Sukk. ii.7 et passim), and Abba Saul, 'son of the Batanean', c. AD 60 (b. Betz. 29a Bar. et passim).[7] These surprising surnames are scarcely to be explained otherwise than that their mothers were respectively Hauranite and Batanean proselytes (p. 322). Thus it is clear that if all these scribes played a prominent role, it was not as a result of their origin, but in spite of their obscure birth, in spite of their poverty, in spite of their standing as petty townsfolk.

It was knowledge alone which gave their power to the scribes. Anyone who wished to join the company of scribes by ordination had to pursue a regular course of study for several years. The young Israelite desirous of dedicating his life to such scholarship began his education as a pupil (talmīd). Many examples show that instruction usually began at an early age. Josephus makes this clear, even if we set aside a good part of his immeasurable self-praise. From the age of fourteen he had already mastered the interpretation of the Law (Vita 9). It is also clear from the story in b. Gitt. 58a Bar. and parallels about R. Ishmael b. Elisha, that he had already a thorough knowledge of Scripture when the Romans took him captive as a young man.[8]

The student was in personal contact with his teacher and listened to his instruction. When he had learned to master all the traditional material and the halakic method, to the point of being competent to take personal decisions on questions of religious legislation and penal justice, he was a 'non-ordained scholar' (talmīd hākām). It was only when he had attained the canonical age of ordination fixed—surely too late—at 40 by a post-Tannaitic reference (b. Sot. 22b), that he could by ordination (semīkāh)[9] be received into the company of

[6] Later, R. Aqiba was also considered to be a descendant of a proselyte, but this is not true.

[7] Perhaps Nahum the Mede (c. AD 50), in M. Shab. ii.1, et passim, came into this category too.

[8] Cf. Bacher, Ag. Tann. I, 166 n. 1.

[9] The corresponding custom in primitive Christianity (Acts 6.6, et passim) is a guarantee of the antiquity of this rite.

scribes[10] as a member with full rights, an 'ordained scholar' (*ḥākām*). Henceforth he was authorized to make his own decisions on matters of religious legislation and of ritual (b. Sanh. 5a), to act as judge in criminal proceedings (*ibid.* 3a), and to pass judgement in civil cases either as a member of the court or as an individual (*ibid.* 4b Bar.).

He had the right to be called Rabbi, for it is certain that this title was already used for scribes at the time of Jesus (Matt. 23.7–8).[11] However, other men who had not gone through the regular course of education for ordination were also called Rabbi, and Jesus of Nazareth is an example. This is because the title, at the beginning of the first century AD, was undergoing a transition from its former status as a general title of honour to one reserved exclusively for scribes. At all events, a man who had not completed a rabbinic education was known as μὴ μεμαθηκώς (John 7.15), and he had no right to the privileges of an ordained teacher.

Only ordained teachers transmitted and created the tradition derived from the Torah which, according to Pharisaic teaching which the mass of the people respected, was regarded as equal to (Bill. I, 81f.), and indeed above the Torah (*ibid.* 691ff.). Their decision had the power to 'bind' or to 'loose' (cf. Matt. 16.19; 18.18) for all time the Jews of the entire world. To such a student, such an 'academic', as the bearer of this knowledge and authority, there were opened key positions in the administration of justice, in government and in education. 'Academic professions' thus made their appearance, and the scribes practised them along with their teaching and their civil profession.

Apart from the chief priests and members of patrician families the scribe was the only person who could enter the supreme court, the Sanhedrin. The Pharisaic party in the Sanhedrin was composed entirely of scribes.[12] This Sanhedrin, we reflect, was not merely a court of government, but primarily one of justice.[13] Now the know-

[10] Cf. the 'families of the scribes' (I Chron. 2.55, *mišpᵉḥōt*), a 'company of scribes' (I Macc. 7.12, συναγωγή), *et passim*.

[11] See G. Dalman, *WJ*, 274, ET 333f.; *Jesus-Jeschua*, Leipzig 1922 (reprinted Darmstadt 1967), 12; ET, *Jesus-Jeshua*, London 1929, 13.

[12] In the NT the Pharisaic group in the Sanhedrin is always called 'the Pharisees', or 'the scribes' (cf. e.g. Matt. 21.45, 'the chief priests and the Pharisees', with the parallel in Luke 20.19, 'the scribes and the chief priests'); whereas nowhere do the Pharisees and scribes appear together as groups within the Sanhedrin.

[13] Matt. 26.57–66; Acts 5.34–40; *Ant.* 14.172, and the abundance of rabbinic documents.

ledge of scriptural exegesis was the determining factor in judicial decisions. Add to this the great influence that the Pharisaic group in the Sanhedrin had managed to gain in its administrative activity, and we can appreciate the importance of the scribes' privilege in forming part of the court of seventy-one. Thus, we meet in the Sanhedrin the principal scribes: Shemaiah (*Ant.* 14.172), Nicodemus (John 3.1; 7.50), R. Gamaliel I (Acts 5.34) and his son Simeon (*Vita* 190; *BJ* 2.627). Other scribes were members of tribunals: Johanan b. Zakkai (M. Sanh. v.2) and Paul (Acts 26.10–11), who had served as judges in criminal proceedings. Three other scribes made up a civil tribunal in Jerusalem (M. Ket. xiii.1ff.; b. B.K. 58b).

When a community was faced with a choice between a layman and a scribe for nomination to the office of elder to a community, of 'ruler of the synagogue', or of judge, it invariably preferred the scribe. This means that a large number of important posts hitherto held by priests and laymen of high rank,[14] had, in the first century AD passed entirely, or predominantly, into the hands of scribes.

However, the decisive reason for their dominant influence over the people has yet to be stated. The deciding factor was not that the scribes were the guardians of tradition in the domain of religious legislation, and because of this, could occupy key positions in society, but rather the fact, far too little recognized, that they were the guardians of a secret knowledge, of an esoteric tradition.[15] 'The forbidden degrees may not be expounded before three persons, nor the story of Creation before two, nor (the chapter of) the Chariot (Ezek. 1.4ff.) before one alone, unless he is a sage that understands his own knowledge. Whosoever gives his mind to four things, it were better[16] for him if he had not come into the world—what is above? what is beneath? what was beforetime? and what will be hereafter?' (M. Hag. ii.1; T. Hag. ii.1.233; ii.7.234). Esoteric teaching in the strict sense thus had as its object, as a great deal of other evidence confirms, the deepest secrets of the divine being (the vision of the

---

[14] Priests as judges before and after the exile: Deut. 17.9–13; 21.5; Ezek. 44.24. Priests as teachers: Deut. 33.10; Jer. 18.18; Mal. 2.7; Ecclus. 45.17. Levites as judges: I Chron. 23.4; 26.29. Priests, Levites, and heads of family as judges: II Chron. 19.5–11. See pp. 222f.

[15] On the esoteric tradition in late Judaism and Christianity, see my *Eucharistic Words of Jesus*, 2nd ed., ET, London 1966, 125ff. In what follows, only the most important points can be dealt with.

[16] Jerus. Talmud, Venice 1523, and Cambridge MS: *rātūy*. The reading *rā'ūy* is a correction, Bill. I, 989 n. 1.

Chariot).[17] Probably the holy name, endued with magical virtues[18] was part of this, and the secrets of the marvels of Creation.[19] Only in private, between the teacher and his most intimate pupil, were there discussions on theosophy and cosmogony as they had been transmitted in the first chapters of Ezekiel and Genesis; they spoke very softly, and during the discussion of the most sacred vision of the Chariot, they went so far as to cover their heads (b. Yeb. 6b) as a sign of deep reverence before the secret of the divine being.

It would be possible to explain as anti-gnostic polemic the later part of the text just quoted, which, in the four questions, forbids all speculation either on cosmic topography with its predictions on the celestial and the lower world, or on eternity before the creation of the world, and upon the last things.[20] But in fact apocalyptic, preserved in the pseudepigraphical writings of late Judaism, with their descriptions of eschatological events and the cosmic topography of the celestial and the lower world, formed part of the esoteric tradition of the scribes. This much is clear, if only from the repeated descriptions in the writings of the most holy vision of the Chariot (I Enoch 14.9ff.; 71.5ff.; II Enoch 20–22),[21] and of the story of Creation (Jub. 2.1–22; I Enoch 69.16–25; II [4] Esd. 6.38–56)—but there is no lack of direct evidence.

The fourth book of Esdras ends with the order given to Pseudo-Esdras to publish the twenty-four books that had been written down by him, the twenty-four canonical writings of the Old Testament, 'that the worthy and unworthy may read it' (II [4] Esd. 14.45), but the text continues,[22] 'But keep the last seventy (books), that thou mayest deliver them only to such as be wise among the people: For in them is the spring of understanding, the fountain of wisdom and the stream of knowledge.' This refers to the esoteric apocalyptic

---

[17] ma'aseh merkābāh, Ezek. 1 and 10.

[18] I Enoch 69.14–25: wonderful works of the holy name whereby God created the world, and revelation of the secret to men. Much material in Bill II, 302–333. See also my Golgotha, Leipzig 1926, 51.

[19] ma'aseh berēšīt, Gen. 1.

[20] On the hesitancy of Talmudic literature to describe the celestial paradise and the joy of its inhabitants, see Bill. IV, 1146.

[21] The Hebrew text of the book of Enoch, edited by H. Odeberg, 3 Enoch or the Hebrew Book of Enoch, Cambridge 1928, begins with the 'taking' of Enoch (Gen. 5.24), and continues, 'R. Ishmael says, As I climbed up to the heights to look upon the vision of the Chariot' (Odeberg, 3).

[22] II (4) Esd. 14.45–46. Cf. further, the keeping secret of apocalyptic writings in Ass. Mos. 1.17; Testament of Solomon Rec. C 13. 13f. (ed. McCown, Leipzig 1922, 87*), and my Golgotha, Leipzig 1926, 51 n. 4.

writings to which the majority of men were denied access. They were inspired, like the books of the canon, but surpassed these in value and sanctity.

The apocalyptic writings of late Judaism thus contained the esoteric teaching of the scribes, and knowing this fact, we can immediately perceive the extent of such teaching and the value that was set upon it. Esoteric teachings were not isolated theological writings, but great theological systems, great doctrinal constructions, whose content was attributed to divine inspiration.

We are now in a position to define the boundaries in rabbinic tradition between matters esoteric and exoteric. All the teaching of the apocalyptic literature of the pseudepigraphal writings, foreign to Talmudic tradition, or occurring there only in isolation, belongs to the esoteric tradition. Such, for example, is the teaching on the saviour *bar nāšā* ('son of man'), a fact of considerable importance in understanding the message of Jesus. It is the knowledge of the esoteric character of apocalyptic that, above all, enables us to understand rightly the organic connection between apocalyptic and Talmudic literature. Statements such as Bousset's, that apocalyptic literature contained the religion of the people and Talmudic the theology of the scribes, turns truth upside down.[23]

Certain esoteric teaching of an exegetical and juridical order was added to the theosophical, cosmological and apocalyptic esoteric teaching. Some was kept secret because of its holiness. This is particularly true of the 'Reasons of the Torah', i.e. the reasons which led God to establish particular legal prescriptions (b. Pes. 119a; b. Sanh. 21b, *et passim*). God has made known by the silence in Scripture concerning these 'Reasons of the Torah', that it is his will to leave the mass of the people in ignorance of the reasons why he had established these particular legal requirements.

Certain other teachings of this exegetical-juridical order were not divulged to the mass of people for pedagogical reasons, to avoid wrong use. This is the explanation of the prescription mentioned

[23] W. Bousset, *Die Religion des Judentums im neutestamentlichen [späthellenistischen] Zeitalter*, Tübingen 1902, 3rd ed., by H. Gressmann, Tübingen 1926. Against this conception of Bousset and Gressmann see, among others, G. Kittel, *Die Probleme des palästinischen Spätjudentums und das Urchristentum*, Stuttgart 1926, 11ff. Apocalyptic literature was none other than midrash and haggadah arising from scripture. A. Schlatter has rightly emphasized this, but only the addition of 'esoteric' midrash and 'esoteric' haggadah makes fully clear the distinction between apocalyptic and Talmudic literature.

above (p. 237) that the laws of forbidden degrees should not be explained except before two listeners. The same explanation accounts for the prescriptions on reading certain offensive stories or expressions from the Old Testament during a synagogue service. Some of these might not be read even in Hebrew; others might be read only in Hebrew without translation into the common tongue, Aramaic; and finally, others might be read only if certain coarse expressions were replaced by more acceptable circumlocutions (M. Meg. iv.10; T. Meg. iv.31ff., 228).

Pedagogic reasons also explain why there was secrecy about the miraculous magical formulae used by the Rabbis (b. Hag. 13a; cf. n. 18), and about the prescriptions that were intended to ameliorate the laws of purity (b. Ber. 22a Bar.), and those concerning work on the 'middle days' of feasts (j. Bez. i.11, 60d.64), keeping holy the sabbath (b. Hull. 15a), etc. Finally, pedagogic reasons led to the concealment of genealogical traditions of a kind likely to bring public discredit upon well-known families (b. Kidd. 70b–71a; cf. b. Pes. 62b).

As a supplementary proof of the correctness of the preceding pages we must remember the role that is played by esoteric in the New Testament writings. First, as concerns the pronouncements of Jesus, the synoptists have without doubt preserved a very exact recollection when they distinguish Jesus' words to the crowd from those to the disciples, and his pronouncement before Peter's confession at Caesarea Philippi from that which followed this event. The Fourth Gospel confirms this, and K. Bornhäuser[24] has recognized that Nicodemus comes to find Jesus by night (John 3.1ff.) to receive from him, in the course of secret converse, teaching on the innermost mysteries of the kingdom of God (3.3), of regeneration (3.3–10), and redemption (3.13ff.). In the closing discourse of John's Gospel Jesus reveals the mystery of his mission and sufferings in the course of intimate converse with his disciples (John 13–17).

The importance of esoteric is still greater in primitive Christianity. It comprises: (a) The ultimate secrets of Christology (the silence of Mark on the Resurrection appearances; the fact that all the Gospels avoid describing the Resurrection; Heb. 6.1ff., where the whole section, 6.3–10.18 reads like a lesson which must be revealed only to those capable of understanding Heb. 5.14 cf. Col. 2.2). (b) Esoteric extended to the mystery of the divine being (II Cor. 12.1–7, esp. 4), and of his plan of redemption (Rom. 11.25 et passim) particularly in its eschatological aspect (I Cor. 2.6–3.2;

[24] Das Johannesevangelium, Gütersloh 1928, 26.

15.51; all of Revelation, according to 10.7; 17.5, 7). (c) Even in the first century, men began to preserve the words of institution from profanation.

We have just spoken of the esoteric teachings of the scribes in the narrowest sense, which might not be divulged to unauthorized people. We must not forget, however, a still more important fact, that at the period we are studying, the whole of the oral tradition, particularly the *halākāh*, was an esoteric doctrine to the extent that, although taught in places of instruction and in synagogues, it could not be propagated by the written word since it was the 'secret of God',[25] and could only be transmitted orally from teacher to pupil, because it was forbidden to mingle Scripture with tradition (Ex. R. 47.1 on 34. 27, Son. 536).[26] It was not until the second century AD that, in order to counter the New Testament canon, the Jews produced a parallel complement to the Old Testament by writing down the oral Torah, which would make it accessible to all. In this way, most of the doctrine was stripped of its character of esoteric tradition.

Finally, the sacred writings of the Old Testament themselves were not immediately accessible to the masses, for they were written in the 'sacred language', Hebrew, while the common language was Aramaic. In the first century AD the leading scribes were still fighting against the spread of Aramaic translations of the Old Testament. This story about R. Gamaliel I (c. AD 30) shows the attitude in Jerusalem: Whilst in the Temple, a man brought him a copy of a targum on the book of Job (and Aramaic translation): he had it buried in a wall, as if it were a forbidden book (b. Shab. 115a).

It is only when we have realized the esoteric character of the teaching of the scribes, not only in the narrowest sense, but as concerning the whole of the oral tradition, even with respect to the text of the Old Testament, that we shall be able to understand the social position of the scribes. From a social point of view they were, as possessors of divine esoteric knowledge, the immediate heirs and successors of the prophets. 'The prophet and the scribe, to whom

---

[25] *Pesiqta rabbati* 5, 14b, 3; *Tanḥuma, wayyar*, 5, 65.30; *Tanḥuma ki thissa*, 34, 329.4.
[26] For the prophibition on writing', see Strack, *Einleitung*, 9–16. On this point we must carry Strack's excellent account (p. 14) still further, for in it the esoteric character of the scribes' knowledge is not sufficiently recognized as the decisive reason for the prohibition on transmitting by written words the oral tradition. This may be compared with Jesus' reproach to the scribes, that they took for themselves 'the key of knowledge' (Luke 11.52, par. Matt. 23.13), and so hindered other men from entering the kingdom of God.

shall we liken them? To two messengers of one and the same king',
says the Palestinian Talmud (j. Ber. i.7, 3b.56).[27] Like the prophets,
the scribes are servants of God along with the clergy; like the
prophets they gather round themselves pupils to whom they pass on
their doctrine; like the prophets, they are authorized in their office,
not by proving their origin as the priests were, but solely by their
knowledge of the divine will which they announce by their teaching,
their judgements and their preaching. It may be that a scribe is of
very doubtful origin, even of non-Israelite, but that does not affect
his prestige in the slightest. It may be that he is a beggar, like Hillel
the day-labourer from Babylonia, but his learning makes him world-
famous.

From all corners of the world young Jews streamed to Jerusalem
to sit at the feet of the masters whose teaching resounded throughout
Jewry. At the time of Herod, Hillel came from Babylonia to hear
Shemaiah and Abtalion (b. Yom. 35b), not flinching from a journey
on foot of several weeks.[28] Ḥanan b. Abishalom came from Egypt to
Jerusalem where later he was a judge (M. Ket. xiii.1–9; b. Ket. 105a),
and from Media came Naḥum, his colleague on the same tribunal
(M. Shab. ii.1; M. Naz. v.4; M.B.B. v.2; b. A. Zar. 7b). Paul came
from Tarsus in Cilicia and studied in Jerusalem under Gamaliel I
(Acts 22.3).

In the time of Jesus, then, Jerusalem was the citadel of theological
and juridical knowledge of Judaism. To be sure, at this time the
Babylonian schools were important, and from them came the *beⁿē
beⁿtīrā*[29] who, until the time of Hillel, were the leading scribes in
Jerusalem, and to whom Hillel himself owed his grounding in scribal
lore.[30] But, important as the Babylonian schools were, they could not
vie with those of Jerusalem. It is said that Hillel alone gathered eighty
pupils around him (b. Sukk. 28a Bar.). They learned from their
master in daily life as well as in the lecture room; their master's

[27] The context develops the idea that the authority of the scribe is greater than
that of the prophet, as he has no need of proof of authenticity.

[28] *ARN*, Rec. A, ch. 12; Rec. B, ch. 27 (Goldin 70). See p. 59.

[29] Their name probably comes from the colony of Bathyra in Batanea, an
establishment of Babylonian Jews set up by Zamaris of Babylon with Herod the
Great's permission (*Ant.* 17.23ff.; Strack, *Einleitung*, 118). In support of this
explanation, R. Judah b. Bathyra, living while the Temple was still standing, had
his lecture room in Nisibis in Babylonia (b. Pes. 3b); in this town, a teacher of the
same name was active at the time of the persecution by Hadrian (b. Yeb. 108b;
Siphre Deut. 12.29, 80).

[30] Bacher, *Ag. Tann.* I, 2f.

actions, even his gestures (M. Sukk. iii.9) were closely watched, and they drew from them guidance on ritual questions. The decisions and teachings of the master were propagated beyond the borders of the land (M. Yeb. xvi.7); the pupils cherished them as a precious treasure, and transmitted them by the chain of tradition.

We understand therefore that the scribes were venerated, like the prophets of old, with unbounded respect and reverential awe, as bearers and teachers of sacred esoteric knowledge; their words had sovereign authority. The Pharisaic communities especially gave their scribes unconditional obedience, and Pharisaic scribes were by far the most numerous. If the teachings of most of the Sadducean scribes disappear from tradition, the main reason is that the Sadducean role ended with the fall of Jerusalem, and the tradition handed down to us, and fixed by the written word from the second century, came exclusively from their enemies the Pharisees. It was a fact, moreover, that even before the destruction of the Temple the Sadducean scribes exercised in public life a very much less important role than the Pharisaic scribes (*Ant.* 18.17). The allegiance of the Pharisaic groups encouraged the influence of Pharisaic scribes over the people.

We have a mass of evidence attesting to the high esteem in which the majority of people held the scribes.[31] Here are some examples: According to a story in the Talmud (b. Yom. 71b), one year on the eve of the Day of Atonement, when the crowd was escorting the high priest to his home, Shemaiah and Abtalion approached; whereupon the crowd left the high priest, to his great annoyance, to go with the beloved scribes. In the days immediately before the eclipse of the moon (the night of 12 or 13 March) in 4 BC, Herod was mortally ill with the sickness of which he died some three weeks later. There were two scribes 'with a reputation as profound experts in the laws of their country, who consequently enjoyed the highest esteem of the whole nation. . .'; 'their lectures on the laws were attended by a large youthful audience, and day after day they drew together an army of men in their prime.' Herod had caused a golden eagle to be placed over the door of the sanctuary.[32] In spite of the evident mortal

---

[31] Josephus says of the masses (*Ant.* 20.264), 'They give credit for wisdom only to those who have an exact knowledge of the Law, and are capable of interpreting the meaning of the Scriptures.'

[32] *Ant.* 17.151: ὑπὲρ τοῦ μεγάλου πυλῶνος τοῦ ναοῦ; *BJ* 1.651: καθιμήσαντες σφᾶς αὐτοὺς ἀπὸ τοῦ τέγους. If this referred to the entry into the Sanctuary, the authors of the deed, pupils of the teachers, must have been priests, since only priests could go on to the Temple roof.

danger, their pupils were inspired by these two scribes to destroy it
(*Ant.* 17.149ff.; *BJ* 1.648ff.). Several decades later, Josephus recounts
(*Ant.* 19.332ff.), a scribe called Simon dared to incite the people
publicly against King Agrippa I. Again, it is said that once when a
murder had taken place, R. Zadoq, a highly respected scribe,
addressed a strong appeal to penitence directed at the priests from
the steps of the Temple porch.³³ During the first years of the rebellion
in AD 66–70 we find at the forefront of the movement such scribes as
Simeon, son of Gamaliel I (*Vita* 191, *et passim*), and the writer Josephus.

A number of smaller indications appear in the sources typifying
the esteem which the man in the street felt for the scribes. We see
people rising respectfully when a scribe passed; only tradesmen at
their work were excused this (b. Kidd. 33a). We hear them greet the
scribe very respectfully as 'Rabbi',³⁴ 'Father' (cf. Matt 23.9),³⁵
'Master' (b. Makk. 24a, *mārī*),³⁶ when he passed before them in his
scribe's robe,³⁷ which was a long mantle reaching to the feet and provided with a long fringe (Matt. 23.5). When the important men of
Jerusalem gave a feast, it was an ornament to the feast to see, for
example, two such pupils and future teachers as Eliezer b. Hyrcanos
and Joshua b. Ḥananiah (j. Hag. ii.1, 77b.34). The highest places are
kept for the scribes (Matt. 23.6 and par.), and the Rabbi has precedence in honour over the aged, even over parents. In the synagogue too,
he had the seat of honour; he sat with his back to the cupboard con-
taining the Torah, in full view of the people (*ibid.*). Finally, when it
came to marriage, the daughter of a man unversed in the Law was
considered by him only in exceptional circumstances (Bill. II, 378).

But for an exact impression of the veneration which the people
accorded to the scribes, and of the boldness of Jesus' attack upon
them, we must study Talmudic traditions relating to the sacred tombs
in Palestine,³⁸ we must follow the literature to see how, alongside the

³³ T. Yom. i.12, 181; j. Yom. ii.2, 39d.13; b. Yom. 23a; T. Shebu. i.4, 446;
Siphre Num. 35.34 (Levertoff 149).

³⁴ Mark 12.38; Matt. 23.7; Luke 20.46; j. Ber. ii.1, 4b.24, see also p. 236.

³⁵ Bill. I, 918f. gives, for olden times, examples of '*abbā* as a title of honour taken
by some teachers as a permanent title. According to A. Büchler, *Der galiläische
'Am-ha-'Ares des zweiten Jahrhunderts*, Viena 1906, 332ff., '*abbā* would be a title of
teachers ordained in Galilean schools. This may be true, but it does not exclude
the use, as in b. Makk. 24a, of the title '*abī* for other teachers.

³⁶ καθηγητής (Matt. 23.10) has no equivalent as a title in rabbinic literature, but
the corresponding ὁδηγός surely appears in Matt. 23.16 as a title.

³⁷ Mark 12.38; Luke 20.46; Bill. II, 31–33; IV, 228b.

³⁸ See my *Heiligengräber in Jesu Umwelt*, Göttingen 1958.

tombs of patriarchs and prophets, it was mainly the tombs of the Rabbis, surrounded by legend and saga, which were everywhere venerated and guarded with superstitious awe.[39] This gives us an inkling of how it was possible that the hereditary Jewish aristocracy had to endure competition from an intellectual aristocracy and, after the destruction of Jerusalem, finally to be overtaken. Tomb of Rabbi and tomb of prophet side by side; here is the solution of the enigma we encountered at the beginning of this chapter.

[39] *Heiligengräber*, 141.

XI

APPENDIX: THE PHARISEES[1]

SOCIOLOGICALLY SPEAKING, there is no question of including the Pharisees among the upper classes: their name means 'the separate ones', i.e. the holy ones, the true community of Israel,[2] and as we shall see they were for the most part men of the people, with no scribal education. But they were so closely linked with the scribes that it is difficult to separate them, the more so since the scribes' rise to power marked the rise of the Pharisees also. For this

---

[1] There is an excellent section on rabbinic documentation on the Pharisees in Bill. II, 494–519, and IV, 334–52. Schlatter, *Geschichte Israels*, 137–53, is well informed on the origin of Pharisaism. J. Wellhausen's brilliant study (*Die Pharisäer und die Sadducäer*, Greifswald 1874) is still instructive; see further Meyer, *Ursprung* II, 282–319. The growth of the movement is presented clearly by G. F. Moore, 'The Rise of Normative Judaism', *HTR* 17, 1924, 307–73, and 18, 1925, 1–38. B. D. Eerdmans, 'Farizeën en Sadduceën', *Theologisch Tijdschrift* 48, 1914, 1–26, 223–30, saw clearly the corporate character of Pharisaism. A. Büchler, *Der galiläische ʿAm-ha-ʾAreṣ des zweiten Jahrhunderts*, Vienna 1906, gives abundant material, although his basic theory, that Pharisaic communities did not appear until after the destruction of the Temple, will not hold water, since he ignores NT evidence. The work of L. Baeck, 'Die Pharisäer', in 44. *Bericht der Hochschule für die Wissenschaft des Judentums in Berlin*, Berlin 1927, 33–71, ET, *The Pharisees and Other Essays*, New York 1947, 3–50, contains some interesting observations, but entirely misconceives the corporate character of Pharisaism, and fails to distinguish Pharisees from scribes. The study by R. T. Herford, *The Pharisees*, London 1924, is even less satisfactory; the author sees no distinction between scribes and Pharisees—for him the Pharisees are 'teachers of Torah' (p. 43)—and has totally misunderstood the origin of Pharisaism as well as its corporate character. The sociological background of the movement is presented by L. Finkelstein, *The Pharisees*, 3rd ed., Philadelphia, Pa., 1962. For the problem as a whole see now R. Meyer, 'Tradition und Neuschöpfung im antiken Judentum. Dargestellt an der Geschichte des Pharisäismus', in *Sitzungsberichte der sächsischen Akademie der Wissenschaften zu Leipzig*, philolog.-hist. Kl. 110.2, Berlin 1965, 7–88.

[2] L. Baeck, 'Die Pharisäer', 34–41, ET 3–12, gives convincing proof of this. He shows that in the Tannaitic midrashim *pārūš* and *qādōš* are synonymous: see p. 249 n. 13 below. In the same way the Essene regarded themselves as the community of the 'new covenant' (CD vi.19; viii.21; xix.33f.; xx.12), as the 'remnant' (CD i.4; 1 QM xiii.8; xiv.8–9; 1 QH vi.8), as the 'escaped' (CD ii.11); their members must 'separate' themselves (1 QS v.10; viii.13; ix.20; CD vi.14).

reason we are discussing them here as an appendix to the last chapter.

If, in the following pages, we are to study the composition of the Jerusalem *ḥabūrōt* (Pharisaic communities)[3] and to describe their position within the framework of society, we must never lose sight of the fact that they formed *closed communities*. Thus the Pharisees were by no means simply men living according to the religious precepts laid down by Pharisaic scribes, especially the precepts on tithes and purity; they were *members of religious associations*, pursuing these ends.

The first appearance of the Pharisees, in the second century BC, shows them already as an organized group. The first mention of them is in the two books of Maccabees, and I Macc. 2.42 calls them 'a company of Assideans (συναγωγὴ ᾿Ασιδαίων) who were mighty men of Israel, even all such as were voluntarily devoted unto the Law' (cf. I Macc. 7.13; II Macc. 14.6). The Essenes also originated in the second century BC.[4] and whatever the foreign influences which must have affected their beginnings, they were in origin very close to the Pharisees, as witness their strict rules of purity and their efforts towards separateness.[5] It is possible, therefore, to draw from the strict life of the Essene community inferences about the communal character of the Pharisees. Among the Essene writings the *Damascus Document* especially, shows important parallels with the Pharisaic organization; we shall enlarge on that later (pp. 259ff.). In the first century AD there seem to have been several Pharisaic communities in Jerusalem alone.

In this context it is primarily the 'holy community of Jerusalem' which is meant. The Palestinian Talmud mentions once 'the holy community' (j.M. Sh. ii.10, 53d.2). In the Midrash, R. Judah I, the redactor of the Mishnah about AD 200, gives a tradition on the subject (Eccles. R. 9.7 on 9.9, Son. 237).

According to the later interpretation which the Midrash puts on the term 'holy community', it was claimed that this meant the two teachers R. Jose b. Mešullam and R. Simeon b. Menasiah, who lived about AD 180, probably in Sepphoris. Both were said to have dedicated a third of each day to study, a third to prayer and a third to manual work, and so were given the epithet 'holy community' (*ibid.*). Later, R. Isaac b. Eleazar

---

[3] The term 'community' is better than 'society' or 'association'.

[4] First mentioned about 150 BC, *Ant.* 13.172; then about 104 BC, *Ant.* 13.311; *BJ* 1.78.

[5] The remarkable appearance of the term *ḥbwr ysr'l*, used to describe the Essene community in CD xii.8, could also point to this common origin.

(about AD 280) applied the name 'holy community' to R. Joshua son of R. Timai and to R. Borgai (*ibid.*).

In both cases the fact that the expression 'holy community' is limited to two people (because of an evident misunderstanding of the Palestinian Talmud just quoted), shows that this explanation cannot possibly be right;[6] the references in the Babylonian Talmud make that quite clear. This Talmud indeed calls this same[7] association the 'holy community of Jerusalem',[8] and frequently attributes traditions to it. We hear, among other things, that the members of this association had specific customs for prayer[9] and that they had an exceptionally strict interpretation of the laws on mixed fabrics (b. Betz. 14b and par. [see n. 8]; cf. Lev. 19.19; Deut. 22.9–11).

What does this expression 'holy community of Jerusalem' mean? Bacher would like to drop 'of Jerusalem'[10] and keep the shorter 'holy community' of the Jerusalem Talmud and the Midrash; but this is merely an abbreviation. Büchler, in connection with the midrashic interpretation, sees in this association a group of Jerusalemites who had fled to Galilee, and especially to Sepphoris, after the sack of Jerusalem.[11] Certainly there is much evidence of the presence of Jerusalemites in Sepphoris after the sack of the Holy City (b. Ket. 77b *et passim*); but as we saw earlier, we must not rely too much on the interpretation of 'holy community' in the Midrash, where the expression is used to mean two Galilean teachers. Baeck and Marmorstein are right in going back to Jerusalem for the explanation.[12] The former saw in it a name for the whole community in Jerusalem, and the latter the name of an organized group already in existence there at the time of the great Tannaites.

In Paul's epistles (I Cor. 16.1; II Cor. 8.4; 9.1, 12; Rom. 15.25, 31) the primitive Christian community in Jerusalem is called 'the saints'; and Baeck appeals to that for his interpretation; but this Christian designation is entirely at variance with his views, but agrees with Marmorstein's. Indeed the members of the early Church were called themselves 'the saints' in sharp contrast with the whole community, as the true Messianic community of salvation, the remnant whom God has chosen from among the people of salvation, and thus in exactly the same way that the Pharisees called themselves 'the separated', that is 'the saints' (p. 246).

---

[6] L. Baeck, 'Die Pharisäer', 39, ET, 9.

[7] Bacher, *Ag. Tann.* II, 490 n. 2.

[8] b. Betz. 14b (= b. Yom. 69ab; b. Tam. 27b, 61b); b. Betz. 27a; b. R. Sh. 19b; b. Ber. 9b (cf. Bill. II, 692). These pass on traditions of the second century AD, mostly of the second half of the century.

[9] b. Ber. 9b. One custom they had was to recite the Eighteen Benedictions each morning immediately after the *š^ema*ʿ.

[10] *Ag. Tann.* II, 490 n. 6.

[11] Büchler, *Priester*, 39–41.

[12] L. Baeck, 'Die Pharisäer', 39, ET, 9f.; A. Marmorstein, 'Eine angebliche Verordnung Hadrians', *Jeschurun* 11, Berlin 1924, 152ff.

We have now reached the point where Marmorstein's views too need supplementing. *Qādōš* (saint) and *pārūš* (separated, a Pharisaic epithet) are used synonymously in the Tannaitic Midrashim.[13] We must take into account too the customs of life and the traditions of the 'holy community', in particular their faithful observance of fixed times for prayer, which is universally praised (Eccles. R. 9.7 on 9.9, Son. 237; b. Ber. 9b; see p. 248 n. 9); we must compare this with the fact that in the first century AD the observance of fixed hours of prayer was recognized as a distinctive sign of a Pharisee.[14] All this leads inevitably to the conclusion that in all probability the 'holy community of Jerusalem' was a Pharisaic community in the Holy City in the first century AD.

It is the period before the destruction of the Temple, too, which is suggested by the following Tosephta: 'R. Eleazar b. Zadoq[15] said: This is the custom of the *ḥabūrōt* [communities] in Jerusalem: some [of the members of a *ḥabūrāh*] go to a betrothal feast, others to a wedding feast, others to a feast of circumcision, others to a gathering of bones [for the purpose of final burial];[16] the first go to a joyful feast, the others to a house of mourning' (T. Meg. iv.15; *Semaḥot* xii).

What was the nature of these associations in the Holy City? Several times in rabbinic literature we come across references in the second century AD to private charitable associations (*ḥeber ʿīr*) in certain parts of the country; they made it their duty to devote themselves to charitable works of all kinds, among them those indicated in the Tosephta passage just quoted, and to observe liturgical obligations.[17]

13 L. Baeck, 'Die Pharisäer', 36f., ET, 5–8. Siphra Lev. 19.2, 44b: 'Be *qᵉdōšīm*, that is to say, *pᵉrūšīm*'; Siphra Lev. 11.44, 39a: 'Be *qᵉdōšīm* for I am *qādōš*', that is: 'As I am *qādōš*, so should you be *qᵉdōšīm*; as I am *pārūš*, so should you be *pᵉrūšīm*.' Similarly in Siphra Lev. 11.45, 25a; Siphra Lev. 20.26, 46d; Lev. R. 34.4 on 19.2 (Son. 307).

14 b. Ber. 47b Bar.: 'Who is an *ʿam hā-āreṣ* (a non-Pharisee)? He who does not recite the *Shᵉmaʿ* morning and evening.' This is the view of R. Eliezer (about AD 90, the representative of the ancient tradition among the teachers of his time).

15 As the context shows, this was R. Eleazar I, born soon after AD 35 in Jerusalem and living there until the destruction of the Temple; see p. 143.

16 If the body was put in a tomb hewn out of the rock, the bones were gathered into an ossuary about a year after the burial.

17 On these associations, see A. Büchler *Der galiläische ʿAm-ha-ʾAreṣ des zweiten Jahrhunderts*, Vienna 1906, 207–21; J. Horovitz, *ḥbr ʿīr*, Frankfurt 1917; Bill. IV, 607–10. The question is, should it be pronounced *ḥeber ʿīr* (a city charitable association) or *ḥābēr ʿīr* (city teacher, or a member of a charitable association)? In spite of Horovitz' objection, the balance is tipped in favour of the first reading (A. Geiger, *Urschrift und Übersetzung der Bibel*, Breslau 1857, 122f.; Levy II, 9b; Eliezer b. Jehuda, *Thesaurus totius hebraitatis* III, Berlin 1911, *sub verbo*, 1433; H. Grätz, *Geschichte der Juden* III.1, 4th ed., Leipzig 1888, 78; A. Büchler, *op. cit.*, 210–12; Schürer II, 503 n. 10, ET II.2, 58 n. 47; Dalman, *WB*, 136a; Bill. IV, 607ff., who takes only T. Meg. iv.29, 228, for discussion). In what relation to the Pharisaic communities did these charitable associations stand? This question is not yet settled.

The ḥabūrōt of Jerusalem mentioned in this Tosephta passage are incontestably linked with these charitable associations; they are the oldest organization of this kind spoken of in the sources. It is true that neither in this passage, nor in others which deal with the ḥeber ʿîr, is there any question of the members being bound by the obligations which the members of Pharisaic communities had to accept, on the strict observance of laws pertaining to purity and the tithe; thus it is quite possible that this Tosephta passage too speaks of private charitable associations which must have existed in Jerusalem.[18]

Nevertheless we may ask if things are quite so simple. First, we must notice that this passage does not use the exact expression ḥeber ʿîr, but the term ḥabūrāh which, apart from associations and other bodies, is used to mean the Pharisaic communities too (e.g. T. Dem. ii.14, 48, et passim). Moreover, we must remember that the Pharisees themselves attached the greatest importance to works of supererogation and good works; what is more, the accomplishment of works of supererogation was an integral part of the very essence of Pharisaism and its ideas of meritorious behaviour.[19] Another fact is worthy of note: a document from the beginning of the first century AD, the Assumption of Moses, reproaches the Pharisees for being men who 'at every hour of the day love to banquet and gorge themselves', who 'from morning till evening love to say: we want feastings and plenty to eat and drink'.[20] These reproaches lead us to look among the Pharisees —if we are not to write them off as mere drunkards and gluttons—for customs similar to those which our Tosephta passage describes among the 'communities' of Jerusalem.

We must take a final point into consideration. In Talmudic sources we occasionally meet 'the sons of the synagogue' (benē ha-kenēset, M. Bekh. v.5; M. Zab. iii.2; b. M.K. 22b Bar.; Semaḥot xi), who bound themselves to observe liturgical rules and to take part in (liturgical) funeral ceremonies. They were, then, an organization similar to the charitable associations mentioned earlier. M. Zab. iii.2 assumes that these synagogue associations follow the Pharisaic laws of purity in food preparation.[21] Thus we have clearly outlined here the link between the Pharisees and public charitable associations ministering to the needs of synagogues.

The presence in Jerusalem of purely private charitable associations for

---

[18] See Büchler, op. cit., 208–12.

[19] To demonstrate the importance which the Pharisees attached to works of supererogation, we shall quote but a few of the many NT references: Tithes of supererogation: Matt. 23.23; Luke 18.12; laws on purity: Matt. 15.1–2; Mark 7.1–4; Matt. 23.26 and par.; fasting: Luke 18.12; Matt. 9.14 and par.; prayer: Matt. 6.5–8 (this passage is directed against the Pharisees, see p. 254); almsgiving, Matt. 6.2–4.

[20] Ass. Mos. vii.4, 7–8. The context shows clearly that the Pharisees are the subject.

[21] Büchler, Der galiläische ʿAm-ha-ʾAres, 74 n. 2.

the common good is nowhere attested; and so with all the documentation we have studied we are forced to conclude that the *ḥabūrōt* mentioned in our Tosephta passage are related to the Pharisaic communities, if not actually identical with them.

The Pharisaic communities of Jerusalem, several of which are known as we have seen, had strict rules of admission, which again shows their character as a closed society. Before admission there was a period of probation, one month or one year,[22] during the course of which the postulant had to prove his ability to follow the ritual laws. Josephus for example tells us how he submitted himself successively the Pharisaic, to Sadducean and to Essene laws, and finally at the age of nineteen chose the Pharisees (*Vita* 10ff.). This specific example confirms that there was a probationary period before admission to a Pharisaic community.

Once this period was over, the candidate committed himself to observe the rules of the community. In the earlier period, which is the only time to concern us here, this pledge was taken before a member who was a scribe.[23] The new member of the community bound himself to observe the Pharisaic laws on purity and tithes.[24] Henceforward the Pharisee was a member of an association. These associations had their leaders (*Ant.* 15.370; *BJ* 2.411; Luke 14.1ff.: 'a chief Pharisee', *et passim*) and their assemblies (Matt. 22.15 and par.; cf. 12.14; 22.41); these last it seems, were linked with a common

[22] In the first century AD there was a divergence of opinion between the Shammaites and the Hillelites on the length of the probation time in T. Dem. ii.12, 48: 'After how long [probation] is he [the candidate] accepted? The followers of Shammai require thirty days for liquids [this means the seven "liquids causing impurity": dew, water, wine, oil, blood, milk, honey; when solid or dried foods come into contact with something impure, they do not become impure unless moistened beforehand by one of these seven liquids. The candidate had to prove that he had paid attention to these rules and observed them, and had kept these seven liquids away from his fruit, vegetables and other dry foods], and twelve months for raiment [clothing became impure by pressure or by contact with someone levitically impure, which the Pharisees strove to avoid]. But the followers of Hillel content themselves for both (proofs) with thirty days.' See on this Bill. II, 505f.

[23] In b. Bekh. 30b Bar. (ar. T. Dem. ii.13, 48 according to the Vienna MS and *ed. princ.*), the oath, according to Abba Saul (about AD 150) was taken before a member who was a scribe. Later, admission was before three Pharisees (b. Bekh. 30b Bar.). Bill. II, 506, was quite right in seeing the ancient custom in Abba Saul's words; this is confirmed by the analogous practice among the Essenes, see p. 260, cf. CD xiii.11–13; xv.7ff.: reception by the supervisor, who was a scribe, xiii.6.

[24] For the laws of purity see Matt. 15.1–2; Mark 7.1–4; Matt. 23.25–26; Luke 11.39–41. Those on the tithe: Luke 18.12; Matt. 23.23; Luke 11.42.

meal,[25] particularly on Friday evening at the beginning of the sabbath (b. Erub. 85b, see n. 25). It seems that Pharisaic associations sometimes made a public appearance, e.g. to express condolences or to take part in festal occasions (p. 249). They had their own internal code of rules, and could agree among other things on the expulsion of a member (b. Bekh. 31a Bar.).

We shall do well not to overestimate the number of members of these Pharisaic *ḥabūrōt*. From a reliable source, transmitted to us by Josephus who probably had it from Nicholas of Damascus, the intimate counsellor and historian of the court of Herod the Great—thus from a semi-official source—we learn of 'more than six thousand' Pharisees during Herod's time throughout his kingdom.[26] By way of comparison, let us quote other figures. The population of Jerusalem was about twenty-five to thirty thousand (p. 84); the priests and Levites together raised that number by about eighteen thousand (p. 204); the Essenes were four thousand strong (*Ant.* 18.20). Incidentally, these numbers confirm that as far as the Pharisees are concerned, we are dealing with a marked group; and the size of their number confirms that in Jerusalem during the first century AD, there must have been several Pharisaic communities.

The composition of these Pharisaic communities is clouded in obscurity, and they are often confused with the scribes (p. 246 n. 1; p. 254 n. 31). There are several reasons for this. First, the fact that the term *ḥābēr*, meaning a member of a Pharisaic community, was after the New Testament period used for a non-ordained teacher ('colleague of the teachers'), but especially the fact that Matthew and

---

[25] b. Pes. 101b–102a, if the *bᵉnē ḥabūrāh* named here and in b. Erub. 85b are members of a Pharisaic community. See too Luke 7.36–50; 11.37f., 14.1. Perhaps we should also consider as communal meals the Pharisees' meals in Jerusalem mentioned by Abba Saul. (T. Sanh. iii.4, 418; j. Sanh. i.2, 19b.57; b. Sheb. 16a Bar.). Especially should we remember the communal meals among the Essenes.

[26] *Ant.* 17.42. I. Elbogen 'Einige neuere Theorien über den Ursprung der Pharisäer und Sadduzäer', in *Jewish Studies in Memory of Israel Abrahams*, New York 1927, 135–48, expressed on p. 136 doubts on this number 6,000: (*a*) it concerns only the Pharisees who refused the oath to Herod; (*b*) the number 6,000 appears also in *Ant.* 13.373 and 379. I cannot share these doubts. Indeed, (*a*) in *Ant.* 17.42. Josephus seems to assume that all the Pharisees refused the oath; (*b*) the two other passages which quote the number 6,000 deal with events of about eighty years earlier.—The evangelists show that there were many Pharisees in Galilee, Matt. 9.11, 14 *et passim*. According to Luke 5.17 they came 'from all the cities of Galilee and Judaea and from Jerusalem'. It is doubtful if there were Pharisees in foreign parts. In Acts 23.6, Paul of Tarsus calls himself Φαρισαῖος . . . υἱὸς Φαρισαίων, but these last two words could equally mean (p. 177) that he was a pupil of Pharisaic teachers or a member of a Pharisaic association.

Luke very often lump together 'the scribes and the Pharisees';
Matthew in the discourses of Jesus, and Luke in the narrative parts
of his Gospel, frequently use this expression;[27] on the other hand
Mark and John do not know it.[28] It is disastrous that Matthew in
particular (with the exception of 23.26), unites the two groups, even
in the words of Jesus against the scribes and Pharisees in Matt. 23.
Indeed Matthew introduces in exactly the same way, by 'Woe unto
you, scribes and Pharisees', the words against the vanity and lust for
honours among the teachers, and those against the hypocrisy of the
Pharisees in their observance of religious laws on purity and tithes;
and thereby he obliterates the difference between the two groups.
More happily, the parallel tradition in Luke guards against wrong
conclusions; indeed Luke makes a clear distinction between Jesus'
discourse against the theologians, the scribes (Luke 11.46–52; 20.46;
cf. 11.43) and his discourse to 'the men of practice', the Pharisees
(Luke 11.39–44).[29]

We shall perceive very clearly the difference between the two if we
bear in mind the reproaches which Jesus, according to Luke,
addresses to each separately. The scribes (Luke 11.46–52; 20.46; cf.
11.43—see n. 29) are reproached for (a) imposing very strict religious
laws on other people, while avoiding them themselves; (b) building
'tombs of the prophets' while ready to condemn to death men sent
by God; (c) keeping their learning secret and so cutting off the
people's access to the kingdom of God, while making no use themselves of their own knowledge; (d) inordinate pride in dress, in
salutations and in order of seating, particularly with regard to the
synagogues. As we see, these reproaches have a general bearing on
their scribal education and its resulting privileges in social life.

Jesus' reproaches to the Pharisees, listed in Luke 11.39–42, 44, are

[27] Matt. 5.20; 12.38 (Luke 11.29: the crowds); 15.1 (Mark 7.1: the Pharisees
and those scribes come from Jerusalem); 23.2, 13, 15, 23, 25, 27, 29; Luke 5.17, 21
(Matt. 9.3; Mark 2.6: several scribes); 5.30 (Matt. 9.11: the Pharisees; Mark 2.16:
the scribes of the Pharisees); 6.7 (Matt. 12.10; Mark 3.2: they); 7.30; 11.53; 14.3;
15.2.
[28] In Mark 7.5, the article refers to what precedes it; it is not used in a general
way. In John 8.3 the expression is used in the pericope of the 'adulterous woman'
which was interpolated into the Fourth Gospel.
[29] In 11.43 an error has slipped into the Lucan tradition; but a parallel
tradition elsewhere in the same gospel and in Mark corrects it entirely. Indeed,
in Luke 20.46, with which Mark 12.38–39 is in accord, the reproach on their
ambitious lust for the highest places in the synagogues and the first salutations in
the bazaars is rightly described as being addressed to the scribes; on the other
hand, Luke 11.43 has it erroneously addressed to the Pharisees.

of an entirely different kind. They are accusations of (a) hypocrisy in carrying out the laws on purity, while remaining impure inwardly; (b) hypocrisy in paying tithes on green and dry vegetables not required by the Law, while neglecting the religious and moral obligation of the Law. We can see that these reproaches have absolutely nothing to do with a theological education; they are levelled at men who lead their lives according to the demands of the religious laws of Pharisaic scribes.

Luke shows plainly, and in full accord with references in contemporary sources, that the parallel discourse in Matt. 23 falls into two parts: the first (vv. 1–22, 29–36) is levelled at the scribes, and the second (vv. 23–28) at the Pharisees. Matthew himself makes this clear on several occasions, for example when he introduces the fifth 'woe' (Matt. 23.25–26) by the words: 'Woe unto you, scribes and Pharisees', and then continues (v. 26) by the single phrase: 'thou blind Pharisee.'

In the same way the first two chapters of the Sermon on the Mount contain a discourse against the scribes and one against the Pharisees. In Matt. 5.20 the two groups are named at the beginning, under the heading of scribes; but then there comes first, in 5.21–48, a discourse against the scribes who transmit and explain the 'tradition of the ancients'; then, in 6.1–18, the discourse turns on the 'hypocrites' (in Matthew's Gospel this word means the Pharisees, except in a few cases).[30] These verses are no longer directed against doctrinal tradition, but against men who in everyday life made a great show of works of supererogation (almsgiving, prayer, fasting, cf. Luke 18.12).

We must therefore make a distinction between scribes and Pharisees, and reject the completely false idea that the Pharisees were the same as the scribes.[31]

One point only is true: that the *leaders* and influential members of Pharisaic communities were *scribes*. Tradition tells us that the following scribes belonged to a Pharisaic community or ruled their lives according to Pharisaic laws: before 162 BC, Jose b. Joezer (M. Hag. ii.7); about 50 BC Abtalion and Shemaiah (*Ant.* 15.3 and 370);

---

[30] In Matt. 23.13, 29 (probably also 23.15) the hypocrites are the scribes; in 24.51 the godless; in 7.5, deceitful men.

[31] E.g. W. Bousset, ed. H. Gressmann, *Die Religion des Judentums im späthellenistischen Zeitalter* 3rd ed., Tübingen 1926, 187: 'The Pharisees are educated men.' It is a totally false judgment but very prevalent.

about 20 BC perhaps Hillel;[32] about AD 30, in the time of Jesus and
the early Christian Church, Nicodemus (John 3.1ff.), and further the
anonymous Rabbi who questioned Jesus on the great commandment (Mark 12.28), and several other scribes who came into contact
with Jesus (Mark 2.16; Luke 5.30; Matt 15.1–9; Mark 7.1–13),[33] R.
Gamaliel I (Acts 5.34; T. A. Zar. iii.10, 464) and Saul of Tarsus
(Acts 23.6);[34] about AD 50, Johanan son of the Hauranite, who ate
food according to the rules of levitical purity (b. Yeb. 15b and par.),
and R. Zadoq, the celebrated priest who also observed those rules for
his food (M. Sukk. ii.5); about AD 60 Josephus (*Vita* 12) priest and
writer, and Simeon b. Gamaliel I (*Vita* 191);[35] at the time of the
destruction of the Temple, the son of this R. Simeon, R. Gamaliel II,
who is said to have eaten his food according to the Pharisaic laws on
levitical purity and always kept his garments in a state of the utmost
levitical purity (T. Hag. iii.2, 236),[36] and Joezer, priest and scribe
(*Vita* 197; on the form of this name, see p. 234 n. 4).

The sum total of these names is, as we see, not very great. Truth to
tell, we know only a small number of names of scribes who belonged
to a Pharisaic community; actually their number was much greater.
Further, it must be noted that we know of a large number of scribes
who opposed Sadducean teachers, and championed Pharisaic ideas,
but we have been given no specific evidence that they belonged to a
habūrāh. Johanan b. Zakkai, for example, upholds Pharisaic opinions
against Sadducean in M. Yad. iv.6, holding that the holy books

[32] We must conclude this from the story told by Gamaliel of his father (M.
Erub. vi.2), if the father of Gamaliel I was Hillel. (The Simeon mentioned only
in b. Shab. 15a Bar., said to have been president of the Sanhedrin after Hillel and
before Gamaliel I, is named nowhere else, and was never said to be Gamaliel's
father.) However, we do not know if the account in M. Erub. vi.2 comes from R.
Gamaliel I or R. Gamaliel II; only in the first case could we make any deduction
about Hillel.

[33] The Pharisees who discussed with Jesus the exegesis of Deut. 24.1 (Matt.
19.3; Mark 10.2) are also theologians.

[34] Paul was an ordained scribe. Acts 26.10, where he speaks of his functions as
a judge, makes this quite certain.

[35] If we take it that the account in M. Erub. vi.2 comes from Gamaliel II (see
n. 32), it concerns his father R. Simeon b. Gamaliel I.

[36] Gamaliel was already active before AD 70, as the following references confirm: T. Sanh. ii.6, 416: he wrote, on the steps of the Temple area, a decree of
Galilee (we must attribute this to Gamaliel II, with Bill. I, 154 and Dalman, *WJ*,
3, ET, 3); M. Pes. vii.2: he had his paschal lamb roasted in Jerusalem by his slave
Tabi (this must refer to Gamaliel II, as we know the name of his slave); M. Sukk.
iii.9 (this event may well belong to the liturgy of the Temple, as Bill. II, 788e,
agrees; thus it was before AD 70, which presumes that R. Gamaliel II was already
by that time a recognized authority).

soiled the hands; but he speaks here of the Pharisees in the third person to such effect that on the basis of this text he has been held to be a Sadducee (*sic!*).[37] In Luke 11.45, after Jesus' reprimand to the Pharisees, a scribe says to him: 'Master, in saying this thou reproachest us also.' This scribe champions the Pharisees, too, without explicitly including himself among them. In cases like that we may without hesitation presume that the scribe who is defending Pharisaic opinions himself belongs to a Pharisaic community; but we still must not underestimate the number of teachers who did not belong to a Pharisaic *ḥabūrāh*. In all cases this number is considerably higher than the Talmudic tradition would have it, the tradition derived from a purely Pharisaic point of view.

To my mind the example of Simeon b. Nathaniel is particularly instructive. He lived about AD 70, and was a priest and a pupil of R. Johanan b. Zakkai (M. Ab. ii.8) whose Pharisaic ideas we have just studied. Simeon married a grand-daughter (p. 219 n. 227) of the Pharisee R. Gamaliel I (T.A. Zar. iii.10, 464). However, he refused to eat his 'common' food according to the Pharisaic laws of purity, and because of his marriage he was forced to pledge himself not to demand that his wife should prepare 'pure' food in his house, since he himself would not have observed levitical purity (*ibid.*). Among the very little information we have about him, we find a criticism of prayer becoming 'somewhat too fixed'; for thus the intimacy of prayer suffered (M. Ab. ii.13). Evidently Simeon criticized the establishment of fixed hours of prayer, to which the Pharisees attached such importance (p. 249 n. 14 *et passim*).

This particular case shows us that it is important not to underestimate or overestimate the number of non-Pharisaic scribes, and that a part only—to be sure, more important than the other part—of the scribes belonged to Pharisaic communities.

For the most part, the members of the *ḥabūrōt* were not scribes. First, we know that a large number of priests were Pharisees. Among the Pharisaic scribes which we have listed we find the following are priests: Jose b. Joezer, R. Zadoq, Josephus and Joezer. To these we may add the clergy who were Pharisees but had not had a scribal education. Thus Josephus tells us that John Hyrcanus (134–104 BC), high priest and prince, was at the beginning of his reign 'a disciple of

---

[37] B. D. Eerdmans, 'Farizeën en Sadduceën' in *Theologisch Tijdschrift* 48, 1914, 9ff. A grave mistake! Other passages also (b. Men. 65a *et passim*) show unmistakably that Johanan b. Zakkai's position was categorically anti-Sadducean.

theirs (the Pharisees) and greatly beloved by them' (*Ant.* 13.289; b. Ber. 29a); furthermore, a fragment of an apocryphal gospel names Levi as a Pharisaic chief priest;[38] and finally we must mention the Levite Joḥanan b. Gudgeda, whom we have met already as chief doorkeeper in the Temple (pp. 167, 212, 234).

The conscientiousness of the members of the priesthood in matters of Pharisaic demands on purity is shown very informatively in the following quotation from M. Ḥag. ii.7:[39] 'Jose b. Joezer [before 162 BC] was the most pious in the priesthood, yet for them that ate of Hallowed Things his apron counted as suffering *midrās* uncleanness. Joḥanan b. Gudgeda [about AD 40] always ate [his common food] in accordance with [the rules governing] the cleanness of Hallowed Things, yet for them that occupied themselves with the sin offering water his apron counted as suffering *midrās* uncleanness.'

According to this passage, Jose b. Joezer, even in daily life outside the Temple, conscientiously observed the rules of purity which held good for priests, and in particular kept his garments so pure that he could always eat the heave-offering without having to change his clothes; he had only to do this to eat the meat of sacrifices. As for Joḥanan b. Gudgeda, he voluntarily imposed upon himself a degree of purity even more severe, going well beyond the letter of the Pharisaic laws on purity. While he was a Levite, in all his food he observed the degree of purity demanded for the meat of sacrifices; so much so that, if he had been a priest, he would have had the right to eat the meat of sacrifices in his everyday clothes, and would have had to change them only for the aspersion by the water of purification (Num. 19). Earlier we made the acquaintance of a priest called Simeon b. Nathaniel, who refused to submit to the Pharisaic law on purity, so we can see that priestly obedience to this law was by no means a foregone conclusion.

The priests took part to a great extent in the Pharisaic movement, and this is explained by the fact that this movement had its origin in the Temple. It sought to raise to the level of a general norm the practice of purity laws even among non-priestly folk, those laws which need only be enforced for priests when they ate the heave-offering.

But the scribes we have just named, priests and Levites, were only the leading faction among the Pharisees. The *laity* who joined the Pharisaic communities and undertook to observe the Pharisaic laws on tithes and purity were far more numerous, as we can see from the frequent occurrence of the 'scribes and Pharisees' in the New Testament. This expression shows that besides the leaders who were scribes, the great majority of members had not had a scribal education. The Talmud expressly says of a Pharisee who turned against Alexander Jannaeus, that he was a 'simple Israelite' (b. Kidd. 66a); Josephus says that two high-ranking people who took part in a deputation to Galilee in AD 67 were Pharisees, and lay people at that (*Vita* 197). The 'men of Jerusalem' who concealed their fig-cakes in water—evidently during the years of the rebellion in AD 66–70—'because of usurping owners', and were concerned about their ritual purity until the scribes reassured them (M. Maksh. i.6), were Pharisees of Jerusalem, simple men of the people without learning. In another place we find 'men of Jerusalem' zealously performing their religious obligations for the feast of Tabernacles, such as participation in synagogue worship, visits of condolence, sick-visiting, attendance at schools and prayer (b. Sukk. 41b; T. Sukk. ii.10, 195; j. Sukk. iii.14, 54a.38); these too perhaps were Pharisees (cf. the exposition on pp. 249–51), and if so most likely pious laymen.

Again, there were in Jerusalem wine and oil merchants whose conscientiousness led them to fill 300 jars with froth from wine which was sold, and 300 jars with oil which remained in their measuring cups; they delivered it to the Temple treasurers, because they could not consider that these leavings were their property (b. Betz. 29a Bar.); thus in all probability they were Pharisees. The incense makers[40] mentioned in connection with the question of keeping the sabbath (M. Erub. x.9) were perhaps Pharisees too. The Pharisee in Luke 18.9–14 was priding himself on fasting twice a week and paying tithes on all he acquired (such as fruits of harvest);[41] he must also be considered as a layman, since nothing is said to the contrary.

The innumerable rules on commercial dealings between Pharisee

[40] The word can equally mean a fatstock dealer. According to R. Jose it meant wool dealers (M. Erub. x.9.)

[41] This can be translated as: (*a*) 'I pay tithes on all my produce', or (*b*) 'on all I earn, I give a tenth for works of charity', see Bill. II, 244f. We have chosen for our translation the sense (*c*), that he was boasting of paying tithes on all he bought, not merely on all he himself produced (since he did not know for certain if the seller had already paid the tithe, even if he insisted he had). This last meaning is much the most probable, since it comprises most unmistakably one of the characteristics of a Pharisee (M. Dem. ii.2; T. Dem. ii.2, 47).

and non-Pharisee give us more insight into the circles of the Pharisaic community (M. Dem. ii.2–3; vi.6; T. Maas. iii.13, 85, *et passim*). These passages leave no doubt that above all it was merchants, artisans and peasants who made up the *ḥabūrāh*. In short, the Pharisaic communities were mostly composed of petty commoners, men of the people with no scribal education,[42] earnest and self-sacrificing; but all too often they were not free from uncharitableness and pride with regard to the masses, the *'ammē hā-'āreṣ*[43] who did not observe the demands of religious laws as they did, and in contrast to whom the Pharisees considered themselves to be the true Israel.[44]

Analogies to the specific character and the organization of Pharisaic communities as we have just described them, appear in the *Damascus Document* (CD),[45] and more recently but in less proportion, in the *Manual of Discipline* (1 QS).[46] Before the Qumran discoveries the Damacus Document was almost universally thought to be a Pharisaic writing (the first edition of this section in 1929 was of the same opinion). Since the publication of the Qumran writings, it is quite certain that they are Essene in origin. Proof of this is in the resemblance of subject matter and the fact that fragments of the Damascus Document have been found at Qumran.[47]

But the Essene origin of the Damascus Document does not alter the fact that it is of help in understanding the organization of Pharisaic communities, indeed Pharisees and Essenes both obviously owe their origin to the *ḥasīdīm* of Maccabean times (p. 247). This goes far in explaining resemblances between the two movements, and these appear with greater force in the Damascus Document than in the Manual. Indeed, the former, which was probably intended for Essene groups dispersed throughout the land, assumes patterns of

[42] We must note that when Jesus discusses exegetical questions with the Pharisees (Matt. 22.41–6 and par.) and other theoretical questions, he deals with their leaders, the scribes.

[43] In the singular this word means literally 'people of the land (of Israel)'. Originally it described the vast multitude of the people of Israel; then it was applied to the mixed Jewish-pagan population which resulted from the pagan influx into Palestine during the Babylonian exile; finally in the second century BC it was used for anyone who did not know the Law, especially the non-Pharisee.

[44] For the meaning of the word 'Pharisee', see p. 246 n. 2.

[45] S. Schechter, *Documents of Jewish Sectaries* I, Cambridge 1910.

[46] M. Burrows, J. C. Trever, W. H. Brownlee, *The Dead Sea Scrolls of St. Mark's Monastery*, II, 2, New Haven 1951. D. Barthelemy, in *Qumran Cave 1* (*Discoveries in the Judaean Desert*, 1) Oxford 1955, 109–111.

[47] In Cave 4 (J. T. Milik, *RB* 63, 1956, 61) and in Cave 6 (M. Baillet, *ibid.*, 513–523).

community life like those of Pharisaic rule, whereas the Manual organizes the stricter life of an isolated monastery at Qumran.

If we examine the organization of Essene communities, we see first of all that we are dealing with tightly closed groups. A list of members[48] was made (CD xiii.12, cf. x.2), in which was kept the sequence of priests, Levites, Israelites and proselytes (xiv.3ff.), which was also valid for assemblies. Precise rules governed admission to the community. Only 'those whose days are completed' could be included among 'them that are mastered' (x.i–2, cf. xv.5–6); as it appears from Num. 1.3, this fixed the minimum age of entry at twenty years (1 QSa i.8 expressly states twenty years as the limit).

First of all there was a preliminary examination by the supervising scribe (CD xiii.11–12; xv.11)—of which more later—who had sole right of accepting candidates (xiii.12–13),[49] and to whom the postulant must present himself (xv.7–8). The supervisor then made known to him the secret legal maxims[50] of the community (xv.10–11); the candidate took the oath of entry (xv.6), then was put on the list of members (xiii.12). Next, according to the Manual of Discipline (1 QS vi.13ff.; cf. vii.19ff.; viii.24f.) there was a period of two years' probation. Serious transgressions were punished by temporary or permanent expulsion (CD xx.1–13; see also the rules of punishment in the Manual, 1 QS vi.24—vii.25).

These details are mainly in agreement with the result of our earlier examination of Pharisaic communities (pp. 251ff.); this becomes particularly clear if we remember that the synagogue, in contrast to these two movements, knew nothing of expulsion and of the admission of adults except in the case of a converted pagan.

As for the administration, there was at the head of each 'camp' a supervisor ($m^e baqq\bar{e}r$) who had to be between thirty and fifty years old (CD xiv.8f.). He was a scribe, who could inform on the exact meaning of the Law (xiii.7f.). Transgressions had to be reported to him (ix.18f., 22). He alone had the right to admit a candidate to the community (xii.12f.); he examined and classified the new recruits (xiii.11f.; cf. xv.8.11). Moreover he was the spiritual father of the community; he had 'pity on them like a father upon his sons' (xiii.9). His dealings with the community were pictured as those of a shepherd

---

[48] 1 QS v.23; vi.(10) 22, (26); vii.2, 21; viii.19; ix.2; cf. 1 QSa i.21.

[49] 1 QS v.8, 20ff.; vi.19, has it otherwise, that priests and members together carried out admissions.

[50] Their legal decisions followed their own judicial rules.

with his sheep (*ibid.*); and that is why he took care that no one in the community was oppressed or beaten, in that he loosed 'all the fetters that tie them' (xiii.10; with 'bind' and 'loose' cf. Matt. 16.19). He, with the judges, received gifts for charity from the community and saw to their distribution (xiv.13).

Taking into account the similarities of organization between Essene and Pharisaic communities which we have studied above, we can represent the functions of the Pharisaic ἄρχοντες (Luke 14.1), on which the sources tell us very little, as analogous to the functions of the Essene *mᵉbaqqēr*. The fact that this *mᵉbaqqēr* also shows some affinity with the Christian bishop is also in favour of the analogy. All that has been said up to the present on the derivation of this last office (bearing in mind that the term ἐπίσκοπος in Syrian cities meant members of a public building commission,[51] and among the Jews the ruler of the synagogue),[52] is not conclusive. We must make two observations here:[53] first, the title *mᵉbaqqēr* corresponds literally with the Greek ἐπίσκοπος; and next, the position and the functions of the *mᵉbaqqēr* are identical with those of a bishop in the Syrian *Didaskalia*. These two facts pose the question of whether the function of the leader of an Essene community, as we know it from the information in the Damascus Document on the *mᵉbaqqēr*, was not the model for the Christian ἐπίσκοπος (and this poses a second question: whether this influence was not felt rather through the Pharisees than through the Essenes).

There have been objections to the hypothesis of such connections for allegedly, we find in the Damascus Document beside the supervisor of each separate camp, xiv.8f., the 'supervisor of all the camps', a monarchical head. It would be highly improbable that the Christian communities of the New Testament period should have taken over only the function of the ἐπίσκοποι of particular communities (note the plural in Phil. 1.1), and not the monarchical episcopacy—a concept which appears for the first time in the work of Ignatius of Antioch.

Our reply must be that it is extremely doubtful whether the Damascus Document knew of the monarchical function of a 'supervisor in chief'. The critical expression *mᵉbaqqēr lekol ha-maḥanōt* (xiv.

---

[51] A. Schlatter, *Geschichte der ersten Christenheit*, Gütersloh 1926, 95; M. Dibelius, *An die Philipper*, 3rd ed., Tübingen 1937, on Phil. 1.1.

[52] K. G. Goetz, *Petrus*, Leipzig 1927, 49ff.

[53] G. Hölscher, *ZNW* 28, 1929, 39.

8–9) can have several interpretations. The translation 'supervisor for each camp' agrees with the sense of the passage and indeed the rules which follow (xiv.9ff.) cannot be applied to a single chief supervisor. As we see from ix.17ff., these rules are intended much more for a supervisor of each camp.

To sum up: we may make use of our information on the organization of Essene 'camps', though with the greatest caution, to give clearer outline to the picture of the organization of Pharisaic communities which emerges from the rare references we have.

The influence which these Pharisaic communities and their scribal leaders are known to have gained is astonishing and at first puzzling. Their first great success that we know of historically was achieved during the six years of bloody insurrection and civil war under Alexander Jannaeus (103–76 BC); the great multitude of the people rallied to the Pharisees who were contesting the legitimacy of the Hasmonean high priesthood (pp. 155f., 189). Several times on the brink of ruin, Alexander Jannaeus finally forced a peace (*Ant.* 13. 372–382; *BJ* 1.88–98) but only at the price of a frightful blood-bath. The Pharisees however had triumphed. The king on his death-bed counselled his wife Alexandra (76–67 BC) to align herself with the Pharisees (*Ant.* 13.401–404). Then they gained entry to the Sanhedrin which, up to that time, had consisted exclusively of representatives of the religious and lay aristocracy, and withdrew their opposition to the ruling family. Alexandra ruled, but since she was a woman she could not also be high priest, and this fact must have facilitated the Pharisees' change of mind. During that time, supported by the power of the queen, they were the real leaders of the state (*BJ* 1.110f.).

After the death of Alexandra, the Pharisees' power diminished under Aristobulus II (67–63 BC), and accordingly they took up their old opposition to the royal family and, in 63 BC, persuaded the people to send a legation to Pompey to demand the suppression of the national monarchy (*Ant.* 14.41),[54] and they did not hide their joy when this plan succeeded (*BJ* 1.170). It was particularly in the reign of Herod the Great (37–4 BC) that the extent of their power was apparent. At his accession Herod put to death the leaders of the lay nobility, his most powerful enemies in the Sanhedrin; in contrast, he spared the Pharisaic leaders and gave them honours (*Ant.* 15.3ff.).[55]

[54] It has generally been presumed, quite rightly, that the legation was instigated by the Pharisees.

[55] The Pharisees had advised the surrender of Jerusalem to Herod.

When subsequently the Pharisees refused to take the oath of fidelity to Herod and to Caesar, the king contented himself by imposing a money fine on them, while for the same crime he had other people put to death.[56] The Pharisees had complete access to the court in Jerusalem and exercised great influenced on the harem and on domestic arrangements (*Ant.* 17.41ff.; cf. 15.3f.).

The reason for the king's toleration of the Pharisees is to be found chiefly in their power: Herod had to keep continually before him the fact that the Pharisees had the support of the people (*ibid.*).[57] Although Wellhausen has scant reason to say that 'the Pharisees had their period of prosperity under Herod',[58] for this period came in fact after the destruction of Jerusalem in AD 70, one thing is certain: while the priestly families of the new illegitimate hierarchy depended completely and abjectly on the good graces of Herod, the Pharisees were entirely undisturbed. They had again asserted their influence in the Sanhedrin. Only in 6 BC, two years before his death, did Herod, as a result of court intrigues, break with the Pharisees (*Ant.* 17.36–46; *BJ* 1.569–71).

In the following era, until the beginning of the revolt against Rome (AD 66) the influence of the Pharisees on the political life of the Jewish people was limited. To be sure, they were still represented on the supreme council, but it was the priestly and lay aristocracy, the Sadduceans, who had the determining role. The Pharisees could always make their voice heard on the Sanhedrin during sessions and had close relations with Herod Antipas, Tetrarch of Galilee (Mark 3.6; Luke 13.31; Mark 12.13, par. Matt. 22.15–16); this at least is the opinion of the evangelists and the writer of Acts (Acts 5.34–39; 23.6). According to the Fourth Gospel, the condemnation of Jesus was the work of the Pharisees, but this can scarcely be true (John 7.32, 45–52; 11.46; 12.42; cf. 'the Jews' in 7.13; 9.22; 19.38; 20.19). Yet we do know that the Pharisee Paul was commissioned with the active persecution of Christians (Acts 9.1–4; 22.3–8; 26, 9–14).[59] Generally speaking, however the Pharisees' influence on politics and

---

[56] It is probable, as shown by Otto, *Herodes*, col. 64 n. (in conjunction with Wellhausen), that the two accounts in Josephus, *Ant.* 15.368–370 and 17.42, are of the same event, but from two different sources, one anti-Herod and favouring the Pharisees (15.368ff.), the other well-disposed to Herod and rejecting the Pharisees (17.42: doubtless Nicholas of Damascus).

[57] They were ready even to declare war on the king and to do him injury.

[58] *Pharisäer*, 109.

[59] On the dating of this: according to Gal. 1.18; 2.1, the conversion of Paul took

the administration of justice in Palestine before AD 66 must not be exaggerated.[60] Their only real importance during this time was in the realm of religion, and here they, not the Sadducees, were supreme. The religious life, and especially the liturgy, was ordered by Pharisaic laws (*Ant.* 18.15). The last Jewish king, Agrippa I (AD 41–44) himself lived according to Pharisaic rules (*Ant.* 19.331).[61]

The Sadducean high priests, however unwillingly, had to fulfil the liturgical ceremonies according to the Pharisaic interpretation of the Torah; for example, the drawing of lots for the two goats (p. 161 n. 46) and the burning of incense on the Day of Atonement (T. Yom. i.8, 181; b. Yom. 19b Bar.; j. Yom. (i.5, 39a.46), the libation of water at Tabernacles (p. 161 n. 46) and the rite of the Red Heifer (T. Par. iii.8, 632);[62] this was true even with rites which had no biblical foundation, such as the libation of water at Tabernacles.[63] The complete calendar, especially the feast of Pentecost, was fixed according to Pharisaic reckoning.[64] About 20 BC Hillel had already established that the Paschal lamb could be slain even on the sabbath day, and so on this point too he had abolished the Sadducean practice hitherto in use (T. Pes. iv.1–2, 162). The following fact shows how powerless the Sadducees were: they once tried by a trick to fix the calendar according to their calculation for the feast of Pentecost, and to do this they sought through false witness to mislead the commission appointed by the Sanhedrin to deal with the calendar (T.R. Sh. i.15, 210).

---

place 17 years—or 15 in the modern reckoning—before the Apostolic Council held at the end of AD 48, and so about AD 33 (see my article 'Sabbathjahr').

[60] With the outbreak of the revolt against Rome they succeeded in breaking into the administration of justice. The Sadducean penal code was now abolished and that day celebrated as a national day (cf. *Meg. Taan.* 10, on 14 Tammuz). This abolition took place neither under Alexandra (76–67 BC) nor Agrippa I (AD 41–44), but at the time of the revolt against Rome (AD 66). Indeed, when a daughter was condemned to death under Agrippa I (see p. 178 n. 94) this was done according to Sadducean law.

[61] Schürer I, 554ff., ET I, z, 156ff. Cf. the favourable opinion of him in the Talmud (Bill. II, 709f.).

[62] On this point see A. Büchler, *Das Synedrion in Jerusalem*, Vienna 1902, 67f. and 95.

[63] b. Taan. 3a traces the rite to the *halākāh* of Moses on Sinai; according to j. Shebu. i.9, 33b.50, it was a command of the earlier prophets. R. Judah b. Bethyra (*c.* AD 110) and R. Aqiba (d. 135), b. Taan. 2b, as well as R. Nathan (*c.* 160), b. Taan. 3a Bar., all try to find scriptural proof.

[64] The Pharisees' calculation of the date of Pentecost is first found in LXX Lev. 23.11. In the first century AD Philo, *De spec. leg.* II, 176; *De decal.* 160, and Josephus, *Ant.* 3.250ff., testify to the importance of the Pharisaic observance to fix the date of Pentecost.

The older generation of Sadducees was quite resigned, because they well understood that it was impossible to succeed against the all-powerful Pharisees. In the Talmud[65] we hear of a Sadducean high priest who performed the burning of incense on the Day of Atonement according to the Sadducean rite; he poured the incense on the burning coals while he was still in the Sanctuary, and not when he had entered the Holy of Holies, as the Pharisees required. Then his father said to him, 'My son, though we are Sadducees, we fear the Pharisees [and conduct ourselves according to their interpretation].' In another passage, a Tannaitic tradition tells of some Sadducees' wives who were said to observe Pharisaic laws on purity, for otherwise the Pharisees would have considered they were impure because of their 'custom of women' and thus made their husbands continually impure (T. Nidd. v.3, 645; b. Nidd. 33b Bar.). Josephus agrees entirely with these statements, and says of the Sadducees (*Ant.* 18.17), 'they are able to do almost nothing of themselves; for when they become magistrates, unwillingly and sometimes by force they addict themselves to the notions of the Pharisees, because the multitude would not otherwise bear them.' So we see that the people wholeheartedly supported the Pharisees, and Josephus in particular never tires in pointing this out.[66]

In order to understand this development, we must realize that the Pharisaic movement developed as an opposition to the Sadducean. Among the priesthood this opposition grew up in the second century BC, that is under the Seleucid domination before the beginning of the Maccabean wars,[67] when a group of priests, the Pharisaic section, instituted great changes. Whereas the Torah laid down rules of purity and rules on food for the officiating priests alone, the Pharisaic group made these rules a general practice in the everyday life of the priests and in the life of the whole people.[68] In this way they meant to build

[65] b. Yom. 19b Bar.; T. Yom. i.8, 181; j. Yom. i.5, 39a.46; Bill. II, 78f. and 848f.

[66] *Ant.* 13.288: the people believe the Pharisees even if they speak against a king or a high priest; 13.298: the multitude was on their side; 17.41 (see p. 263 n. 57); 18.15: the whole of the cultus was performed according to Pharisaic directions; 18.17.

[67] Cf. p. 247: the Pharisees were already in existence at the time of the Maccabean wars, *c.* 162 BC (I Macc. 2.42). Likewise p. 257: Jose b. Joezer, mentioned in M. Hag. ii.7, lived until 162 BC.

[68] In T. A. Zar. iii.10, 464, R. Meir (*c.* AD 150) defined the non-Pharisee thus: someone who 'did not take his common food according to levitical purity (prescribed for priests in the Torah)'. Schlatter, *Geschichte Israels*, 138, says very clearly and precisely: 'The Temple and the priesthood constituted the centre of the

up the holy community of Israel, the 'true Israel' (for this is the meaning of the word 'Pharisee', see p. 246 n. 2). The Sadducean group, on the other hand, was conservative and held that the priestly laws were limited to the priests and the cultus, in conformity with the text of Scripture.

The conflict between Pharisees and Sadducees sprang from this opposition. It dominated the profound religious revolution of Judaism between the Maccabean wars and the destruction of Jerusalem, and we may judge for ourselves the bitterness of the conflict by reading the Psalms of Solomon.[69] The champions of the ancient orthodox theology and tradition, inflexible defenders of the letter of the written biblical text, wrestled with the champions of the new tradition, the unwritten Law.[70] The struggle became particularly severe because social opposition was added to religious: the old conservative nobility, i.e. the priestly as well as lay nobility, opposed the new ruling class of scriptural interpreters and community members, who were drawn from all walks of life, but especially from the petty bourgeoisie. They voluntarily submitted themselves to priestly rules and thus prepared the way for a universal priesthood.

We see, therefore, that doubtless the Pharisees were the people's party; they represented the common people as opposed to the aristocracy on both religious and social matters. Their much-respected piety and their social leanings towards suppressing differences of class, gained them the people's support and assured them, step by step, of the victory.

There is something very impressive about the way in which the people unreservedly followed the Pharisees. For the Pharisees fought on two fronts; not only did they oppose the Sadducees, but as the true Israel they drew a hard line between themselves and the masses, the 'ammē hā'āreṣ who did not observe as they did the rules laid down by Pharisaic scribes on tithes and purity.[71] This opposition

---

movement, and it was the priestly law which the movement caused to be adopted.' Cf. I Abrahams, *Studies in Pharisaism and the Gospels* II, Cambridge 1924; I. Elbogen, 'Einige neuere Theorien über den Ursprung der Pharisäer und Sadduzäer', in *Jewish studies in memory of Israel Abrahams*, New York 1927, 137; L. Baeck, 'Die Pharisäer', 58, ET, 41f.

[69] Josephus, *Ant.* 18.12, emphasizes the intractable and fanatical character of the Pharisees.

[70] Josephus, *Ant.* 13.297f., shows vividly the opposition of written versus oral Law.

[71] John 7.49; Luke 18.9–14; Bill. II, 505ff.; Schürer II, 468f., ET II.2, 22f.

between the members of Pharisaic communities and the ʿammē hā-
āreṣ was largely based on the latter's neglect of tithing (pp. 105ff.),
and became acute probably during the years when John Hyrcanus
(134–104 BC) published his famous decrees on the tithe, intended to
prevent the neglect of payment of the tithe on agricultural produce
(b. Sot. 48a Bar.; cf. T. Sot. xiii.10, 320; Bill. II, 500). This opposition grew to the dimensions of a caste distinction on the part of the
Pharisees. Commerce,[72] marriage,[73] and hospitality[74] to the non-
Pharisee, who could be suspected of impurity unless proved otherwise, were, if not entirely forbidden, at least protected by very
scrupulous limitations.

The people as a whole were not disconcerted by this situation, in
spite of some angry outbursts against this new ruling class, and
evidence of an intense desire to throw off the yoke of a contempt
based on religious superiority. To this desire we may trace, partly
at least, the motive to follow Jesus among those who 'travailed'
and were 'heavy laden', were the 'publicans' and 'sinners'. But as a
whole the people looked to the Pharisees, in their voluntary commitment to works of supererogation, as models of piety, and as embodi-
ments of the ideal life which the scribes, these men of divine and
secret knowledge, had set before them. It was an act of unparalleled
risk which Jesus performed when, from the full power of his consciousness of sovereignty, he openly and fearlessly called these men
to repentance, and this act brought him to the cross.

[72] T. Maas. iii.13, 85: 'They must not sell [cereals, except wheat, grapes and
olives] except to a ḥābēr [Pharisee] who kept himself in the laws of purity.' M.
Dem. ii.3 forbids the sale to non-Pharisees of moist or dry vegetables and fruits,
and the purchase of moist ones.

[73] An exception in T. A. Zar. iii.10, 464, see p. 256.

[74] Mark 2.16; Matt. 9.11; Luke 5.30; cf. Luke 15.2. M. Dem. ii.3 forbids going
as a guest to an ʿam-hāʾāreṣ or receiving him as a guest while he is wearing his own
clothes.

PART FOUR

THE MAINTENANCE OF RACIAL PURITY

Up to the present, it has not been sufficiently recognized that from a social point of view the whole community of Judaism at the time of Jesus was dominated by the fundamental idea of the maintenance of racial purity. Not only did the priests, as the consecrated leaders of the people, watch anxiously over the legitimacy of priestly families, and weed out all priestly descendants born of an illegitimate union (pp. 213–221); but the entire population itself, in the theory and practice of religious legislation at the time of Jesus, was classified according to purity of descent. Only Israelites of legitimate ancestry formed the pure Israel. All families in which some racial impurity could be established were excluded from the pure seed of the community. As in the case of the priesthood, the reason for this was a religious one: the nation was considered God-given and its purity was God's will; the promises of the age to come were valid for the pure seed.

Because this division of the people into social classes was entirely ruled by the principle of maintaining racial purity, the single breach of this principle took on heightened importance: in the case of pagans converted to Judaism, they could not of course become part of the pure seed of the Israelite people, but they were indeed received into the larger community of the people and had the right to marry non-priestly Israelites of pure ancestry. Here again, the reason was a religious one: the fact that they belonged to the religious community weighed more heavily than their ancestry.

XII

THE STRUCTURE OF THE NATIONAL COMMUNITY

FOR THE STUDY which is to follow we have a list, of basic importance, to help us understand the criteria of classification into groups of the Jewish community at the time of Jesus. This list comes to us in different redactions and thus our first task is to find which form of the tradition must be considered as the earliest.

These three forms of the list which the reader is asked to compare carefully are in agreement only at the beginning (1–3), for Israelites of legitimate descent; for the rest they seem to disagree entirely. Actually their agreement goes quite deep, for their main concern is the *tripartite division of society* according to ancestry, a division which is the basis of each of the three forms of the list.

M. Kiddushin, immediately after the first list, continues, 'the priestly, levitic and (full-)Israelitish stocks may intermarry. The levitic, Israelitish, impaired priestly stocks, proselyte, and freedman stocks may intermarry.

'The proselyte, freedman, bastard, *nātīn* [Temple slaves], *šetūqī* [fatherless] and *'ᵃsūpī* [foundlings][1] may all intermarry.'

This document divides society into three groups:

(a) families of legitimate descent: priests, Levites and full Israelites. Only these families had the right to marry into priestly families.

(b) Next, families of illegitimate descent with only a very slight blemish. These families were not entitled of course to marry into priestly families, but could marry Levites or legitimate Israelites.

(c) Last, families with grave blemishes of ancestry. They were on no account to marry into legitimate families, or if they did the

---

[1] On the subject of fatherless children and foundlings, R. Eliezer (*c.* AD 90) defends a different point of view: because of uncertainty over their origin, he forbids them to marry bastards or each other (M. Kidd. iv.3).

marriage was illegitimate, merely concubinage (b. Ket. 3a; Bill. III, 343b).

I	II	III
M. Kidd. iv.1	T. Meg. ii.7, 223[2]	M. Hor. iii.8 (par. T. Hor. ii.10, 476 etc.)
(a) 1. Priests 2. Levites 3. Israelites (full)	1. Priests 2. Levites 3. Israelites (full)	1. Priests 2. Levites 3. Israelites (full)
(b) 4. Illegitimate children of priests (impaired stock) 5. Proselytes 6. Freedmen	4. Proselytes 5. Freedmen	4. Bastards 5. Temple slaves
(c) 7. Bastards 8. Temple slaves (*n*e*tīnīm*) 9. Fatherless (*š*e*tūqīn*) 10. Foundlings (*'*a*sūpīn*)	6. Illegitimate children of priests[3] 7. Temple slaves 8. Bastards	6. Proselytes 7. Freedmen
	9. Eunuchs[4] 10. *Ṭumṭūm*[5] 11. Hermaphrodites	

[2] Text of the Erfurt MS, now in Berlin, *Staatsbibl.* MS or. 2⁰ 1220; par. T. Ber. v.14, 12 and T.R. Sh. iv.1, 212. These three texts, particularly T. Meg. and T.R. Sh., divide the list into 4 parts (1–3, 4–5, 6–8, 9–11). In T.R. Sh., ed. Zuckermandel, 212 line 6 does not appear very clearly for, against all the evidence (MSS of Erfurt and Vienna, Alfasi) Zuckermandel has dropped the 'and' before 'Israelites' which separates the first group. Two other parallels are in T. Men. x.13, 528 and x.17, 528, lacking only the *ṭumṭūm* and the hermaphrodites. In these passages too the list is clearly divided into four groups.
[3] The word *ḥalālīm* is lacking in T.R. Sh. iv.1, Erfurt MS, but is included in the MS of Vienna, and by Alfasi.
[4] There are four kinds of eunuch listed.
[5] A man of deformed sex.

This tripartite division is the basis of each of the three forms of the list; only in list III are groups (*b*) and (*c*) in reverse order. This list therefore deals unfavourably with proselytes and freedmen, by placing them socially lower than bastard Israelites because of their Gentile origin. This may reflect an ancient tradition.

The list of exiles in Ezra 2.2–63, par. Neh. 7.7–65, gives the following order:

(*a*) Families of pure descent:
      Lay people: Ezra 2.2–35, par. Neh. 7.7–38.
      Priests: Ezra 2.36–39, par. Neh. 7.39–42.
      Levites: Ezra 2.40–42, par. Neh. 7.43–45.
(*b*) Temple Servants: Ezra 2.43–54, par. Neh. 7.46–56.
      Royal slaves: Ezra 2.55–58, par. Neh. 7.57–60.

Appendix—Israelites and priests
with no genealogy.   Ezra 2.59–63, par. Neh. 7.61–65.

It is possible that list III was drawn up on this scheme, or on some analogous scheme of some antiquity, when adding proselytes and freedmen. However, a different explanation appears more likely to me. With the growth of Christian communities, the attitude of Judaism towards the mission and proselytes altered unfavourably. After the destruction of Jerusalem proselytes were judged more severely, especially from the time of the Bar Kokhba revolt (AD 132–5) when the intense missionary activity of Judaism which is reflected in the New Testament[6] came to an end. There was a similar change in judgement on Gentiles, which began in the pre-Christian era and then established itself securely as the religious laws on levitical purity of the Gentiles continued to be tightened. It may be that list III reflects this later situation, when it modifies the order of the scheme given in lists I and II, and places the bastard above the proselyte.

The differences between lists I and II are by comparison much less important. If we take out the details of no importance,[7] the differences are limited to differences of opinion on the position of illegitimate children of priests: list I puts these (4) *before* the proselyte (5) and

---

[6] Matt. 23.15, and especially the references in Acts to proselytes and demi-proselytes in the diaspora. Cf. G. Rosen, F. Rosen and G. Bertram, *Juden und Phönizier*, Tübingen 1929.

[7] List I puts the bastard before the *nātîn* (Temple slave), while list II reverses this; but this is unimportant since, at the time of Jesus, the Temple slave was a purely theoretical factor (see pp. 342f.). List I ends with fatherless children and foundlings, while list II has a fourth group (eunuchs etc.). This is of no importance.

the freed Gentile slave (6), while list II puts them *after* the Gentiles converted to Judaism and side by side with the despised bastards.

We need not hestitate over an explanation for this last point. As we saw earlier (pp. 219ff.), there was a profound divergence of opinion between priests and scribes on the position of illegitimate children of priests, because the priests took up an inexorably rigorous stand in order to preserve racial purity in their class. This suggests the hypothesis that list I, with its more favourable attitude to the illegitimate children of priests, was edited by the scribes, while list II, with its more severe attitude, was edited by the priests. Apart from this difference of opinion on the illegitimate children of priests, lists I and II are in full accord on the classification of the national community according to ancestry, and here we must see a good, ancient tradition. One account even claims that the division into ten groups, in list I, goes back to Hillel (b. Yeb. 37a; b. Kidd. 75a).

So here we have the course of our study: First of all we must describe the 'pure seed' of the people (ch. XIII); and on this subject we must not omit other factors beside ancestry which determined social position (ch. XIV). Then we must deal with groups of people with slight or grave blemish in their ancestry (ch. XV). Next we must put, between Jews and Gentiles, Gentile slaves (ch. XVI) and the Samaritans (ch. XVII). A final chapter deals, as an appendix, with the social position of women (ch. XVIII).

XIII

THE ISRAELITES OF PURE ANCESTRY

A. LEGITIMACY OF ANCESTRY[1]

Together with the clergy (priests and Levites), the Israelites of pure ancestry made up the pure Israel.

Pure ancestry had to be proved for a man to exercise any civic rights, and this fact confirms our conclusion that it was not only the priests who, without exception, had to produce their genealogy before being allowed to take office (pp. 214f.); even the simple Israelite knew his immediate ancestors and could point to which of the twelve tribes he belonged. After the return from exile, the pure families separated themselves from those who had mixed with Gentiles (Ezra 9.1–10, 44); consequently, from this time onwards, proof of legitimate ancestry had become the very foundation of the community of returned people. The families of pure race, and they alone, made up the 'true Israel'. The genealogical tables in the books of Ezra and Nehemiah, and especially the detailed genealogies of the twelve tribes, I Chron. 1–9, reflect the interest of the post-exilic period in family trees; in the following eras, these passages formed the basis for establishing a genealogy. This interest showed itself too by the fact that during the post-exilic times men began to use as surnames the names of the patriarchs of the twelve tribes (evidence on p. 296), and so already proclaimed their membership of the tribe by their name.

[1] Bill. I, 1–6; IV, 792ff.; A. Büchler, 'Familienreinheit und Familienmakel in Jerusalem vor dem Jahre 70', *Festschrift Schwarz*, 133–62; ET, 'Family Purity and Family Impurity in Jerualem before the Year 70 C.E.', *Studies in Jewish History. The Büchler Memorial Volume*, London 1956, 64–98; L. Freund, 'Über Genealogien und Familienreinheit in biblischer und talmudischer Zeit', *Festschrift Schwarz*, 163–92; G. Kittel, 'Die γενεαλογίαι der Pastoralbriefe', *ZNW* 20, 1921, 46–69; A. Büchler, 'Familienreinheit und Sittlichkeit im Sepphoris im zweiten Jahrhundert', *MGWJ* 78, 1934, 126–64; S. Klein, 'Kleine Beiträge zur Erklärung der Chronik Dibre hajamim', *MGWJ* 80, 1936, 195–206.

As regards the time of Jesus, we have already seen (pp. 226f.; M. Taan. iv.5) that certain families of the lay nobility had the privilege of carrying the wood to the Temple on certain days;[2] this fact shows that the genealogical tradition was well preserved among the *lay nobility*. But at the time of Jesus the rest of the families of pure origin knew their ancestry too. Thus—and this too we have seen already— every Israelite, even if living in a foreign country, if she wished to marry into a priest's family had to produce her genealogy for five generations (p. 216; M. Kidd. iv.4); and each candidate for a public position also had to supply proof of his legitimacy (p. 216; M. Kidd. iv.5). These statements assume that each Israelite knew at least the last few generations of his ancestors.[3]

Detailed references confirm these general statements. The greater part of the references concerns membership of the *tribe of Judah*,[4] and especially among them those concerning membership of the *line of David*. This is understandable: E. Sellin has shown that it is probable that even after the downfall of Zerubbabel, the *gens davidica* remained the foremost lay family in post-exilic Judaism; and from their midst, probably up to the time of the Maccabeans, came the supreme civil head of the γερουσία.[5] Furthermore the messianic hope rested in this royal family, and this is the reason why tradition often has occasion to mention Davidic origin.

Here we must recall, first of all, that according to the unanimous witness of the New Testament (pp. 290ff.) Jesus Christ was of David's line, since according to the Jewish family laws he had legally (e.g. for purposes of inheritance) to be considered the son of the Davidic Joseph of Nazareth. Again, Eusebius—following Hegesippus (*c.* AD 180)—says that the Emperors Vespasian (Eusebius, *HE* III, 12), Domitian (*ibid.* III, 19–20) and Trajan (*ibid.* III, 32.3–4) had persecuted the family of David so that no descendant of the kingly line

---

[2] Cf. further the genealogical notes of a member of one of these families (p. 286).

[3] Even today a Palestinian feels it important to know his pedigree. P. Kahle, 'Die Samaritaner im Jahr 1909 (AH 1327)', *PJB* 26, 1930, 89–103, has shown this in his findings on genealogies of Samaritans still living in 1909: he counted 173.

[4] Cf. the list in M. Taan. iv.5, given earlier, pp. 226f., which gives evidence of the existence of six families of Judah for the period before AD 70.

[5] E. Sellin, *Geschichte des israelitisch-jüdischen Volkes* II, Leipzig 1932, 82ff., 121 and especially 168f. There is support for Sellin's evidence: as we shall soon see, the exiliarchs were most likely Davidic. See further G. Dalman, *WJ*, 266, ET, 323, who refers to the *Breviarium temporum* of Pseudo-Philo giving a series of Davidic princes (*duces*) extending to the Hasmonaeans.

should remain; thus we see that the number of those claiming Davidic origin was by no means small. The Talmud tells that R. Ḥiyya the elder (*c.* AD 200) was a descendant of David (b. Ket. 62b; cf. j. Taan. iv.2, 68a.48 *et par.*). The learned exiliarch Rab Huna, chief of the Jewish community of Babylonia, who lived also *c.* AD 200, was of the family of Judah[6] and perhaps Davidic; at this, no doubt points the report (j. Kil. ix.4, 32b.51) that he belonged to the family of R. Ḥiyya the Elder whom we have just mentioned.

Finally, it seems that among the messianic pretenders of the first century AD there was at least one family claiming to be of Davidic descent; at all events, this is the most illuminating explanation of the well-known legendary tale which transfers to Bethlehem, the town of David, the birth of the messianic child Menaḥem b. Hezekiah (j. Ber. ii.4, 5a.18)—this is the leader of the revolt which began in AD 66, Menaḥem (*BJ* 2.433ff.)[7] son of Judah of Gamala, son of Hezekiah.[8] For more than a hundred years members of the family of Hezekiah distinguished themselves time and time again by their mutinies and pretensions to the throne;[9] this too makes it seem probable that this family was of royal descent.

Next to the descendants of *Judah* came those of *Benjamin*. The first book of Chronicles enumerates the Benjaminite families of that time (I Chron. 7.6–11; 8; 9.7–9). Certainly Menelaus, illegally created high priest in 172 BC (p. 185) and executed ten years later (p. 187),

---

[6] j. Kil. ix.4, 32b.30 and par. This testimony is guaranteed by the fact that it comes from R. Judah I, the Palestinian patriarch and rival of the exiliarch, who in the same context admits that as a Benjaminite he is of less illustrious family than the exiliarch. See further b. Sanh. 5a; b. Hor. 11b Bar., where the promise in Gen. 49.10, 'The sceptre shall not depart from Judah', is applied to the exiliarchs, which shows that they were members of the house of Judah. Origen, *De princ.* IV, 1.3 (GCS 22 = Origen V, 297) knows the tradition that the exiliarchs were Judahites and that Gen. 49.10 referred to them.

[7] Schürer I, 487, ET I.2, 81.

[8] Cf. my article 'Erlöser und Erlösung im Spätjudentum und im Urchristentum', *Deutsche Theologie* 2, Göttingen 1929, 116f.

[9] In 47 BC Herod put to death the brigand Hezekiah, and this considerably heightened the hostility of the Sanhedrin against Herod (*Ant.* 14.159; *BJ* 1.204). In 4 BC Hezekiah's son Judah, who aspired to the throne, led a revolt (*Ant.* 17.271f.; *BJ* 2.56). In AD 6 came another revolt by Judah (*Ant.* 18.1ff.; *BJ* 2.117ff.; Acts 5. 37). We must suppose this is the same Judah, as Schlatter says, *Theologie*, 82 n. 2. About AD 47 James and Simon, the two sons of Judah, were executed by the procurator Tiberius Alexander (*Ant.* 20.102). In 66 Menaḥem, son of Judah, seized power in Jerusalem and claimed the title of king (*BJ* 2.433ff.; cf. j. Ber. ii.4, 5a. 14ff.). In 73 Eleazar, a kinsman of Menaḥem and descendant of Judah, led the defence of Masada (*BJ* 7.253ff.; cf. 2.447).

was not a Benjaminite;[10] on the other hand Mordecai, hero of the book of Esther,[11] as also the apostle Paul[12] and his teacher R. Gamaliel I,[13] were so beyond doubt. There was a Benjaminite family of high rank, that of Senaa, which is well attested for the time before the destruction of the Temple in AD 70 (M. Taan. iv.5, see p. 227; b. Taan. 12a, see p. 286).[14]

Naturally there are only very isolated claims to belong to one of the ten[15] or nine-and-a-half[16] 'lost' tribes of Israel. Tobit was designated a descendant of the tribe of Naphthali (Tob. 1.1–2); Judith was said to be of the tribe of Simeon (Judith 8.1; 9.2), and the prophetess Anna, daughter of Phanuel, of the tribe of Asser (Luke 2.36). We have already mentioned (p. 227) a Rechabite family (cf. too Neh. 3.14)[17] during the period before the destruction of the Temple. But it is open to question[18] whether R. Jose b. Ḥalaphta, celebrated teacher and leather-worker who lived c. AD 150, was in truth a Rechabite (j. Taan. iv.2, 68a.48 and par.). Hegesippus mentions a Rechabite priest (Eusebius, HE II, 23.4–18) but this is certainly wrong if we must take this as implying Rechabite descent; for nowhere else[19] do we find the slightest allusion to the fact that the Rechabites (II Kings 10.15, 23; Jer. 35.2–19; I Chron. 2.55) would have been considered a priestly family at any later time.[20]

---

[10] He is erroneously said to be so in LXX II Macc. 3.4; the Latin and Armenian translations are correct, see p. 185 n. 115.

[11] Esth. 2.5; LXX addition to Esth. 1.1; Ant. 11.198.

[12] Rom. 11.1; Phil. 3.5. The completely unjustified doubt cast by K. Kohler, JE XI, 1904, 79, on the subject of this reference to the apostle is very properly rejected by W. G. Kümmel, Römer 7 und die Bekehrung des Paulus, Leipzig 1929, 112 n. 1: 'Paul surely did not invent that!'

[13] See p. 287. Gamaliel was an ancestor of R. Judah whose Benjaminite ancestry is well authenticated.

[14] On the other hand the attribution of Benjaminite origin to B. Ṣiṣīt hakassāt, an important wholesale dealer in Jerusalem who lived at the time of the destruction of the Temple, is entirely worthless (j. Taan. iv.2, 68a.46 and par.; see p. 284).

[15] The number current in II (4) Ezra 13.39ff., et passim. Bill. IV, 903–6.

[16] Syriac Baruch 77.17ff.; 78.1ff.

[17] On Neh. 3.14 see E. Sellin, Geschichte des israelitisch-jüdischen Volkes II, Leipzig 1932, 7.

[18] This reference forms part of the genealogies transmitted by R. Levi (c. AD 300). For a criticism of these genealogies see Israel Levi, in REJ 31, 1895, 209ff. ('a popular fancy') and pp. 284f.

[19] Not even on the basis of Jer. 35.19 (where the Lord promises the Rechabites that they 'shall not want a man to stand before me for ever') has anyone dared to conclude that they were priests. Siphre Num. 78 on 10.29 applies this verse in Jer. to the descendants of Rechabite daughters who married priests.

[20] S. Klein in MGWJ 70, 1926, 413, and 80, 1936, 200 shows more confidence in the historicity of references to the Rechabite.

On the whole the verdict must be that the laity also had their traditions on their own ancestry. These traditions derived almost all their families from the tribes of Judah and Benjamin, and this is in accord with the picture we get from I Chron. 1–9, particularly 9, and with the contents of the list given earlier (pp. 226f.); but especially does it correspond to the historical situation: these two tribes, with the priests and Levites, constituted the core of post-exilic Judaism. The following passage shows us the extent of these genealogical traditions: 'Mar Zutra [d. 417] said: Between Azel [I Chron. 8.37f.] and Azel [I Chron 9.43f.] he [Rab, d. 247] loaded him [Rammi bar Judah] with four hundred camel-loads of exegetical interpretations' (b. Pes. 62b). I Chronicles provides genealogical lists between Azel and Azel, and besides priests and Levites, these deal exclusively with references to families of the lines of Judah and Benjamin. This confirms, then, that the bulk of the genealogical tradition consists of information on the families of these two tribes.

After this, we need not be surprised to find that not only do we hear in general of genealogical traditions of lay families, but side by side with the written genealogies of priests which we have studied earlier (pp. 213ff.) we find similar written ones for lay people. For the earlier times, the Chronicler's account of the registration of the whole[21] nation on its return from exile and its reinstatement in its own country (Neh. 7.6–7; Ezra 2.1–2; Neh. 11.3; Ezra 8.1) gives some important proof. On the basis of older documents (Neh. 7.64 par. Ezra 2.62)[22] the names of the heads of each family were recorded, with information on his ancestors,[23] and thus the *lay genealogies* were made up. As for the other members of each family, only their number was indicated (Ezra 8.3–14; Neh. 7.6–69 par. Ezra 2.1–67). There was always particular note made of families whose Israelite ancestry was uncertain (Neh. 7.61–65 par. Ezra 2.59–63) and Israelites married to Gentiles (Ezra 10.18–44) who thus had blemished their descendants (10.44). We have a basis for saying that these genealogies, begun on the analogy of the carefully kept family trees of the priests, were at

21 W. Rothstein and J. Hänel, *Kommentar zum ersten Buch der Chronik*, Leipzig 1927, xxviii and 188 (on I Chron. 9.1a).
22 The genealogies in I Chron. 1–7 are connected with the genealogical references in Gen., Ex., Num., Josh., Ruth, I and II Sam. and I Kings.
23 Ezra 8.1–14; cf. Neh. 7.6–69; Ezra 2.1–67. Neh. 11.3–24 gives information on heads of families who settled in Jerusalem after the exile. The parallel list in I Chron. 9.1–17 which, according to 9.1–3, pretends to go back to the period of the monarchy, must be dated accordingly to Neh. 11.1–3.

least partially kept up. In I Chron. 3.1–24 the genealogy of the house of David is carried in a continuous line to the time of the Chronicler; and likewise I Chron. 2.34–41 carries the genealogy of the Sheshanites, a branch of the clan of Caleb,[24] perhaps to the time of the Chronicler.

For the later period, too, there are several instances of a written form of lay genealogies. We must first mention here the two genealogies of Jesus given to us in Matt. 1.1–17 and Luke 3.23–28;[25] Matthew adheres to I Chronicles.[26] Again, Simeon b. Azzai (c. AD 110) found in Jerusalem a roll of genealogies;[27] according to later tradition (j. Taan. iv.2, 68a.54ff., pp. 284f.) it deals with genealogical details which almost exclusively concern lay families. We must also quote the Christian physician Julius Africanus (c. 160–240), who, in his *Letter to Aristides* preserved by Eusebius, says, in connection with the alleged burning of genealogies ordered by Herod (see below): 'A few careful people had records of their own, having either remembered the names or recovered them from copies, and took pride in preserving the memory of their aristocratic origin.'[28]

The following account provides further evidence: 'Rabbi [Judah I, c. AD 200] was engaged [in marriage arrangements] for his son into the family of R. Ḥiyya [the Elder]; but when the contract was about to be signed, the maiden died. "Is there, God forbid" said the Rabbi, "any taint [that God should prevent the union]?" They sat down and made enquiry into the [genealogy of the] families; [they discovered that] Rabbi descended from Sheptaiah son of Abital [II Sam. 3.4: son of David], and R. Ḥiyya from Shimei [*sic*—in II Sam. 13.3, Shimea] the brother of David' (b. Ket. 62b; pp. 288f.).

---

[24] W. Rothstein and J. Hänel, *op. cit.* (see n. 21), liif., 27f.

[25] It is with Luke's genealogy that the malicious reference in b. Sanh. 106b is connected: 'I have seen a chronicle of Balaam [on 'Balaam' used to denote Jesus see H. L. Strack, *Jesus, die Häretiker und die Christen*, Leipzig 1910, 26, n. 2] where it is said, Balaam the lame was thirty-three years old when Pinḥas Listā'ā [Pontius Pilate] killed him.' This reference doubtless goes back to Luke 3.23.

[26] Matt. 1.2–6a; I Chron. 2.1–15; Matt. 1.6b–12; I Chron. 3.5–19. In Matt. 1.12 Shealtiel (in the Hebrew of I Chron. 3.19, Pedaiah) is the father of Zerubbabel; this is explained by LXX use which the MSS A and B in I Chron. 3.19 give as Σαλαθιηλ (rec. of Lucian: Φαδαιας). This does not exclude the existence of a Semitic origin for the Matthean genealogy (see p. 294 n. 84), for the translator may have used LXX I Chron.

[27] M. Yeb. iv.13: 'R. Simeon b. Azzai said: I found a family register in Jerusalem m^egillat y^eḥusin and in it was written, "Such-a-one is a bastard through [a transgression of the law of] thy neighbour's wife".'

[28] *Die Briefe des Sextus Julius Africanus an Aristides und Origenes*, ed. W. Reichardt (Texte und Untersuchungen XXXIV.3), Leipzig 1909, 61, lines 17ff., cited by Eusebius, *HE* I, 7.14.

Thus the existence of written lay genealogies is certain; but we must now test the statement that lay genealogies were publicly kept. Julius Africanus in his *Letter to Aristides*[29] asserts: 'But in the archives were still [to the time of Herod] inscribed [first] Hebrew families and [second] those descended from proselytes, such as Achior the Ammonite[30] and Ruth the Moabitess, and people of mixed blood[31] who came out of Egypt at the same time [as the Jews]. Herod, who had no drop of Israelite blood in his veins, was stung by the consciousness of his base origin, and burnt the registers of these families, thinking to appear nobly born if no one else was able by reference to public documents to trace his line back to the patriarchs or [to proselytes and][32] to those called γιῶραι [mixed blood].'[33]

Is this account worthy of belief? There is certainly mentioned a burning of genealogical documents under Herod, in the Syriac *Treasure-cave*, whose original elements date back to *c.* 350;[34] but this *Treasure-cave* is dependent on Julius Africanus.[35] In b. Pes. 62b we read: 'Rami, the son of Rab Judah, said in the name of Rab (d. AD 247): Since the day that the book of genealogies was hidden, the strength of the sages has been impaired and the light of their eyes has dimmed.'[36] But this passage is useless as proof; since both the preceding as well as the following context shows, that Rashi is right in his

[29] Reichardt, p. 61; Eusebius, *HE* I, 7.13.

[30] Instead of ὡς Ἀχιώρ, TERMD say ἕως Ἀχιώρ—'up to Achior'.

[31] For the ἐπίμικτοι, cf. LXX Ex. 12.38 and Num. 11.4.

[32] With E. Schwartz and W. Reichardt we must consider προσηλύτους τε and τοὺς ἐπίμικτους as pre-Eusebian glosses. They came about because of the loanword γειῶραι which the first copyist interpreted correctly as 'proselytes' and the second wrongly as 'mixed blood, mongrels'.

[33] This is the Aramaic *giyyōrā*, 'proselyte', i.e. full proselyte; cf. LXX Ex. 12.19 and Isa. 14.1: γιώρας.

[34] *The Book of the Cave of Treasures*, (translated by E. A. Wallis Budge, London 1927, 195) distinguished three burnings: (*a*) In the time of Antiochus IV (Epiphanes); (*b*) a gap in the text: according to A. Dillmann's translation of the Ethiopic *Book of Adam* (Göttingen 1853, 133) it should read 'at the destruction of Jerusalem' (?); [the English *Book of Adam and Eve*, translated by S. C. Malan, London 1882, 200, gives 'in the days of Qablar the great king of Mosul'!] (*c*) '. . . in the days of Herod when Jerusalem was destroyed'.

[35] A. Götze, 'Die Schatzhöhle. Überlieferung und Quellen' (*Sitzungsberichte der Heidelberger Akademie der Wissenschaften*, philos.-hist. Klasse 13, essay 4), Heidelberg 1922, 80–85 and 91, has shown that the chronology of *The Treasure-cave* is based on Julius Africanus' chronology.

[36] There is a connection between b. Pes. 62b and the note by Julius Africanus, according to M. Sachs, *Beiträge zur Sprach- und Alterthums-forschung aus jüdischen Quellen* II, Berlin 1854, 155ff.; F. Rosenthal, '*Über 'issah*', in *MGWJ* 30 (1881), 118ff.; Krauss, II, 434 n. 91; G. Kittel, 'Die γενεαλογίαι der Pastoralbriefe', in *ZNW* 20, 1921, 52.

commentary on b. Pes. 62b, when he sees in this 'book of genealogies' the biblical books of Chronicles.[37],[38] This Talmudic passage, then, speaks of the time when the traditional interpretation (see n. 37) of I Chronicles was reckoned among the esoteric material (p. 240)[39]— *nignaz*, 'to be hidden', is the technical term for the removal of certain material from public teaching—and deplores the trouble caused to genealogical traditions by this measure.

Julius Africanus' note on the burning of these genealogies is therefore an isolated one. True, we should not attach too much importance to Josephus' silence on this point; he might not report a burning of genealogies by Herod, since in his history of the reign he largely follows Nicholas of Damascus, the court historian and panegyrist of the king. Herod would have been entirely capable of such an act of destruction. We know that he wished to conceal his base origin (*Ant.* 14.9), and moreover, in destroying the genealogical documents he may have hoped to check the messianic claims attached to the line of David, claims which were a continual menace to his power.

Still keeping within the bounds of possibility, another observation will take us even further. According to Julius Africanus, the Hebrew families were registered in the archives first and the proselytes second. This fits very well with what is said in the Damascus Document on the registering of all members of the new covenant: 'They shall be written down by name, each man after his brother, the priests first, the Levites second, the children of Israel third and the proselytes fourth' (*CD* xiv.4–6). Here too we have the Israelites before the proselytes. We may assume that this registration practised at Damascus uses older models; so we cannot relegate entirely to the realm of fable Africanus' statement that there were in the archives genealogical lists such as he describes (according to Rufinus he meant the secret archives of the Temple),[40] as long as we do not take it that he is

---

[37] He thinks this passage has in view the oral interpretation of Chronicles.

[38] The connection between b. Pes. 62b and the note by Julius Africanus is contested by Freund, 'Über Genealogien und Familienreinheit', in *Festschrift Schwarz*, 173 n. 3 and 187ff. Freund relates the references in b. Pes. 62b to secular genealogies in agreement with L. Ginzberg, in *MGWJ* 56, 1912, 665 n. 4, and L. Goldschmidt, *Der babylonische Talmud* II, Berlin 1930, 496 n. 72. Strack, *Einleitung*, 12, and Bill. I, 6, rightly relate them to Chronicles.

[39] b. Pes. 62b expressly says that the interpretation of the 'book of genealogies' formed part of the esoteric material of the scribes; R. Johanan (d. AD 279) refused to teach R. Simla (c. AD 260) about the 'book of genealogies'.

[40] In his Latin translation of Eusebius, *HE* I, 7.13 (GCS 9.1 = Eus. II. 1, 61 lines 3–4) Rufinus says of Africanus' statement: Quod per idem tempus omnes Hebraeorum generationes descriptae in archivis templi secretioribus habebantur.

referring to a complete census of the population.[41] He is much more likely to mean writings concerned with the genealogical tradition. The mention of the 'mixed multitude' coming out of Egypt with the Jews, of Ruth the Moabitess and Achior the Ammonite of the book of Judith, shows that its contents must have had a strong legendary flavour.

Finally, another statement of Josephus ought to be noted; but unfortunately its value is reduced by uncertainty of the reading of a key word. He speaks (CA 1.29) of the care with which his nation has always kept public documents; he continues (ibid. 30f.): 'Not only did our ancestors in the first instance set over this business men of the highest character, devoted to the service of God, but they took precautions to ensure that the priests' lineage should be kept unadulterated and pure. (31) A member of the priestly order must, to beget a family, marry a woman of his own race, without regard to her wealth or other distinctions; but he must investigate her pedigree, obtaining the genealogy from the archives,[42] and producing a number of witnesses' (see p. 216). If, then, the right reading is ἐκ τῶν ἀρχείων, the lay families of the period, according to Josephus, found in the archives a basis which allowed them to furnish authentic proof of their ancestry. There, too, we may give credit to this reference, if we are careful not to imagine that Josephus was speaking of a complete census of the whole population. Much more is he thinking of the priestly genealogies (pp. 213ff.) found in the Temple archives (which also contained particulars of the wives of the priest descended partly from lay families: II Chron. 31.18; Vita 4), as well as records of debts and other documents put in the archives for safe keeping (BJ 2.427), the genealogical data of which could serve as a basis for lay families wishing to establish their ancestry.

All this, then, establishes the existence of both oral and written genealogical traditions among lay families, of both private and public character. Now another question arises: what is their historical value?

[41] The Protevangelium of James 1.3 (M. R. James, Apocryphal New Testament, 2nd ed., Oxford 1953, 39), mentions a 'record of the twelve tribes'. This does not mean a total census, but most likely has I Chron. 1–9 in mind.

[42] (So the reading in Loeb). Instead of ἐκ τῶν ἀρχαίων ('from the ancient families'?) A. Gutschmid, Kleine Schriften iv, Leipzig 1893, 398, suggests ἐκ τῶν ἀρχείων, ('from the archives'). This conjecture which makes very good sense, becomes all the more certain when we remember that the text itself rests on a single MS, Cod. Laurentianus, eleventh cent. Thus Th. Reinach, Flavius Josèphe, Contre Apion, Paris 1930, is right in introducing it into the text.

B. THE HISTORICAL VALUE OF LAY GENEALOGIES PARTICULARLY THOSE IN MATT. 1.1–17 AND LUKE 3.23–38

The genealogies of priestly families were, in general, authentic,[43] at least for one or two centuries back. There is no doubt of this fact, taking account of the hereditary character of the priesthood which was strictly maintained, and of the careful examination of genealogies before admission to the priesthood, together with the fact that the priests were divided into clans and families (pp. 198f.). It is certain too that the priests made enquiries into the family purity of their brides before contracting marriage, especially when the bride was not of a priestly family.[44] Taken altogether, this completely excludes the possibility that the genealogical traditions of the lay families, whose existence we have proved on pp. 275ff., may be pure invention.

I

Now it is true that occasionally in an allegedly genealogical tradition we find a quite worthless play on words, because genealogical conclusions are drawn from a verbal pun on the name. The following passage is an example:[45]

R. Levi (c. AD 300):

'A genealogical scroll was found in Jerusalem in which it was written that:

1. Hillel (c. 20 BC) was descended from David.
2. Ben [the family of] Yasaph, [Yasa] from Asaph.
3. Ben [the family of] Sisit ha-kassat (c. AD 70) from Abner.
4. Ben [the family of] Qobesin [Kobshin], from Ahab.
5. Ben [the family of] Kalba Shabua (c. AD 70), from Caleb.
6. R. [the family of] Yannai (c. AD 225), from Eli.
7. Ben (read thus, instead of *min*) [the family of] Yehud [Yehu], from Sepphoris.
8. R. Ḥiyya Rabba (c. AD 200) from Sheptaiah, son of Abital (II Sam. 3.4).

---

[43] We must reckon with several discrepances of the kind indicated on p. 214 n. 212.

[44] See the sections on the legitimate and illegitimate priestly aristocracy, pp. 181ff., and on the hereditary character of the priesthood, pp. 213ff.

[45] j. Taan. iv.2, 68a.45ff.; Gen. R. 98.13 on 49.10 (Son. 98.8, 956). j. Taan. gives the older tradition, for this text alone gives the pun Yasaph—Asaph. Important variations in the parallel tradition of Gen. R. are indicated in square brackets and the order is different in Gen. R.

9. R. Jose bar Ḥalaphta (*c*. AD 150), from Jonadab b. Rekab (II Kings. 10.15).
10. R. Neḥemiah (*c*. AD 150), from Neḥemiah the *Tiršātā* (Neh. 8.9).'

Two remarks will serve to show the quality of this list: (*a*) it is claimed to have been found in Jerusalem, where it must have come into existence in the third century AD—R. Yannai (6) was active about AD 225. Now after the bar Kokhba rebellion (AD 132–5) Jerusalem became a Roman colony, Aelia Capitolina, and entry into the Holy City was forbidden to Jews on pain of death.[46] The only time they could enter was on 9 Ab, the anniversary of the destruction of Jerusalem, to make their lamentations in the holy place.[47] (*b*) The genealogical statements in nos. 2 and 5 are the result of a pun; that in no. 10 results from a similarity of names; and that in no.1 we shall shortly show to be historically false (pp. 287ff.).

Consequently, this genealogy allegedly found in Jerusalem is a product of the imagination[48] which first came into existence in Sepphoris about AD 250.[49] It is impossible[50], too, that the first five items should be in a list found at Jerusalem before AD 70 and completed later.[51] Naturally the genealogical passages in the Old Testament opened up a wide field for similar genealogical deductions, using puns and interpretations.[52]

However, this does not prove that all genealogical traditions are historically worthless; it merely means that we must be cautious and critical in our approach to the traditions. For example, the genealogical statements in Tob. 1.1; Judith 8.1; Esth. 2.5 must be viewed with caution, as they appear to be in the same vein as the rest of these historical novels.

II

In two cases we have material which enables us to make a critical

---

[46] See my *Golgotha*, Leipzig 1926, 19f.
[47] Origen, *In librum Jesu Nave* xvii.1 (GCS 30 = Origen VII, 401f.); *Itin. Burdigalense* (ed. P. Geyer, *Itinera Hierosolymitana saeculi IIII–VIII*, CSEL 38, 1898, 22); Jerome, *In Soph.* 1.15ff. (PL 25. 1354); Schürer I, 703, ET 1.2, 320; *mÿ Golgotha*, 20 n. 13.
[48] I. Lévi, 'L'origine davidique de Hillel', *REJ* 31, 1895, 209ff.
[49] As shown by A. Büchler, *Priester*, 43.
[50] Not until the third century AD was the Davidic ancestry of the Hillelites asserted.
[51] Against Büchler, *op. cit.*, 42.
[52] G. Kittel gives evidence in *ZNW* 20, 1921, 59–67; see also b. Pes. 4a.

examination of lay genealogies in the Talmud. The first concerns R. Eleazar b. Zadoq, the scribe of Jerusalem, active there before its destruction.[53] Eleazar maintains that he is descended from the son of Senaab (*sic!* Ezra 2.35; Neh. 3.3; 7.38; M. Taan. iv.5: Senaa), of the tribe of Benjamin, one of the families whose privilege it was to carry wood to the Temple (p. 227). He tells how 10 Ab, a feast day when this high-ranking family had to carry the wood (M. Taan iv.5), coincided one year with the anniversary of the destruction of Jerusalem on 9 Ab, which had been transferred this year to 10 Ab, because in that year 9 Ab fell on a sabbath, and they would wish to avoid that day as a day of mourning for Jerusalem.[54]

We can see that there is such concrete evidence in this passage that we can undoubtedly accept the fact that R. Eleazar b. Zadoq belonged to a Benjaminite family of high rank. On the other hand there is the statement that his father, R. Zadoq, was of high-priestly[55] descent, i.e. of legitimate Zadokite stock (p. 193 n. 145). We might be inclined to regard this evidence as worthless, a derivation from the name Zadoq; but this is impossible. Indeed, there is a well-attested and credible account[56] of how one day, when there had been a murder in the Temple, R. Zadoq spoke to the priests of the Temple from the steps of the Temple porch, and made a strong appeal for penitence. No lay person could have entered so far, so R. Zadoq must have been a priest. Both these statements on Eleazar's origin contain absolutely authentic material, so the Tosaphists[57] may be right in assuming that Eleazar b. Zadoq was of Benjaminite descent on his mother's side. This conclusion is all the more likely since Eleazar does not speak of his Benjaminite descent in connection with a genealogical statement, but quite casually in the course of discussion of

---

[53] For the chronology see the analysis above, p. 143. He was still a boy at the time of Agrippa I (AD 41–44). At the time of the famine in Claudius' reign (AD 47–49, see my article 'Sabbathjahr'), he was already a pupil of R. Joḥanan the Hauranite. He was therefore born at the end of the decade 30–40.

[54] b. Taan. 12a; b. Erub. 41a; j. Taan. iv.6, 68b.44; j. Meg. i.6, 70c.13. On this point see J. N. Epstein, 'Die Zeiten des Holzopfers', *MGWJ* 78, 1934, 97–103; he concludes that this passage (in opposition to M. Taan. iv.5) considers that 9 Ab was the day when the family of Senaa delivered the wood.

[55] *ARN*, Rec. A, ch. 16 (Goldin, 84).

[56] T. Yom. i.12, 181; T. Shebu. i.4, 446; Siphre Num. 35.34, 28c; j. Yom. ii.2, 39d.13 Bar.; b. Yom. 23a Bar.

[57] Tosaphoth on b. Erub. 41a. Bill. I.5, is of the same opinion, also V. Aptowitzer, *HUCA* 4, 1927, 238; S. Klein, 'Zur jüdischen Altertumskunde', *MGWJ* 77, 1933, 192.

the celebration of 10 Ab. There is therefore no need to reject these statements on his descent.

The second case concerns the ancestry of R. Judah I (AD 135 to after 200), the Palestinian patriarch and descendant of Hillel.[58] There is contradictory evidence on his ancestry.[59]

(a) He came, on his father's side, from the tribe of Benjamin, and only on his mother's side from the tribe of Judah;[60]

(b) He came from the tribe of Judah (b. Sanh. 5a; b. Hor. 11b Bar.) and more precisely, he was descended from David.[61]

(c) Another tradition adds that he was a descendant of Shepatiah, son of David and Abital (II Sam. 3.4; b. Ket. 62b; p. 287). So we have a mass of contradictions, but in fact the case is quite clear.

1. Judah I himself said that the Babylonian exiliarch Rab Huna was of a more illustrious ancestry than he (Rab Huna was probably of Davidic line, p. 277 n. 6), for he (Judah) was a Benjaminite and could only have come from the tribe of Judah on his mother's side (n. 60). This autobiographical evidence is authentic;[62] for on the one hand the patriarch here places himself below the exiliarch, and on the other hand there is no doubt of the truth of the report that the family of R. Judah I kept genealogical records.[63]

2. The passage itself, however, makes it clear that it was very painful for R. Judah I to be reminded that the Babylonian exiliarch was of a more noble family than he (cf. b. Hor. 11b). Immediately after this autobiographical note of R. Judah, we find this: 'One day, R. Ḥiyya the elder (himself of Davidic line (p. 277)) and who wanted to make R. Judah I aware of his inferior ancestry) went into the house of the Rabbi and said to him, Rab Huna [the then exiliarch and relation of R. Ḥiyya, p. 277] is outside. Then Rabbi (Judah I) went pale with anger, and to appease him R. Ḥiyya replied, His coffin is

58 It is not absolutely proved that the family of Gamaliel were descended from Hillel, but it is very probable.

59 The text of the three following quotations is translated in Bill. I, 4–5.

60 j. Kil. ix.4, 32b.30; j. Ket. xii.3, 35a.37; Gen. R. 33.3 on 8.1 (Son. 261f.). A critical edition of the text is given in G. Dalman, *Aramäische Dialektproben*, 2nd ed., Leipzig 1927 (reprinted Darmstadt 1960), 27f.

61 R. Judah I from David: b. Shab. 56a. Hillel from David: j. Taan. iv.2, 68a. 46, and par.; see p. 284.

62 I. Lévi, 'L'origine davidique de Hillel,' *REJ* 31, 1895, 209ff., has given decisive proof. He emphasizes particularly that the claim of the family of Hillel to be of Davidic descent is not met before AD 200.

63 b. Ket. 62b. Again, Josephus, *Vita* 191: R. Simeon b. Gamaliel I (great-grandfather of R. Judah I) came from a 'very illustrious family', that is a family with an authentic family tradition.

going by' (j. Kil. ix.4, 32b.31 and par: see n. 60). The result of this incident was a thirty-day ban on R. Ḥiyya and a temporary breach between the two men.

This incident holds the key to contradictory evidence on the ancestry of R. Judah I. So that the line of Palestinian patriarchs should not appear inferior to the Babylonian exiliarchs, tradition gives R. Judah I a Davidic origin; this appears for the first time in b. Sanh. 56a where it is given by Rab (d. 247), a pupil of R. Judah and nephew of R. Ḥiyya. This revaluation was facilitated by the fact that the patriarch was indeed descended from the tribe of Judah, even if only on his mother's side.

The motive for this falsification of history is shown particularly clearly in b. Sanh. 5a Bar., (cf. b. Hor. 11b; b. Sanh 38a), the Baraita known to Origen (cf. p. 277 n. 6) where Gen. 49.10a—'the sceptre shall not depart from Judah'—is applied to the exiliarchs, and 49.10b —'nor the ruler's staff from between his feet'—to the Palestinian patriarchs. As this Talmudic passage shows, it was not only 'socially' that the patriarchs were to be put on a level with the exiliarchs; they were to have, in the same way as the exiliarchs, a part in the promises of Gen. 49.10 and so probably a legitimate claim on messianic power. It is instructive to notice that the Baraita does not bring about a complete equality between the two, but clearly shows the superiority of the exiliarchs, who 'rule over Israel with a staff', over the patriarchs who 'have the right to teach publicly in Israel.' In order to lend the falsification of history its full weight, the Palestine tradition, in the third century AD,[64] projected it back to Hillel, the ancestor of R. Judah I, by marking him as the descendant of David.

3. Together with the idea of the relationship between patriarchs and exiliarchs, the comparison of R. Judah with R. Ḥiyya the Elder was decisive in the formation of the tradition. It seemed intolerable that R. Ḥiyya should be of more illustrious ancestry than the patriarch who belonged to the tribe of Benjamin. Here the situation was saved by a further step: not only was R. Judah I made a descendant of David, but the whole of R. Ḥiyya's genealogy[65] was simply transferred to him, thereby making him a descendant of Sheptaiah, son of David and Abital. As for R. Ḥiyya, he became a descendant, not of David but of a collateral of the royal family, and

---

[64] The oldest witness is R. Levi (c. AD 300); j. Taan iv.2, 68a.45ff. See the passage on p. 284.

[65] Supposing this to be correctly given in j. Taan. iv.2, 68a.48. See p. 284.

David's brother Shimea was said to be his ancestor (b. Ket. 62 b).

The remarkable lesson to be learnt from this is not that we have here a case when history was falsified in the third century AD for the greater glory of the Palestinian patriarchal line, but that the genuine tradition was not to be supplanted. All efforts to obtain recognition of the Davidic ancestry of Hillel's line could not prevent the Benjaminite origin from remaining common knowledge. The material contents of the genealogical tradition were too substantial for falsification to displace them so unceremoniously.

The work among scribal circles in handing on traditions on the legitimacy and illegitimacy of certain families was the main contribution to this solidity of genealogical tradition. The incentive towards this tradition was the rigour we have already described (pp. 220f.) with which the priests kept their class free from taint of illegitimacy, either directly or from descendants of priests whose legitimate ancestry was in doubt. For their part, this rigour led the priests to hold firmly to tradition, in order to know which priestly families were legitimate and which doubtful (the *'issāh* families, p. 221 especially n. 234). The scribes, for their part, approved neither the rigour nor the point of view of the priesthood on this, and so were led to preserve the traditions of families which they considered had been wrongly declared legitimate or illegitimate by the priests.

A tradition of R. Joḥanan b. Zakkai (d. *c.* AD 80), evidently from a period when the Temple was still standing, asserts: 'the family of Beth Zerepha was in the land beyond Jordan and Ben Zion removed it afar by force (i.e. declared it illegitimate). And yet another (family) was there, and Ben Zion brought it night by force (declared it legitimate)' (M. Eduy. viii.7. Also T. Eduy. iii.4, 459.30; j. Yeb. viii.3, 9d.8; j. Kidd. iv.1, 65c.51; b. Kidd. 71a Bar.). We may presume that this passage is speaking of priestly families, and the decision of b. Zion, of which the scribes did not approve,[66] was the decision of the tribunal of priests we met on pp. 177f. How the scribes dealt with such cases is shown in the Tosephta (T. Eduy. iii.4, 459; j. Kidd. iv.1, 65c.53), which goes on: 'And the scribes did not wish to make the state of affairs public, but handed them [the names of the families wrongly declared legitimate] down to their sons and pupils once in every seven years [secretly].'[67]

[66] This R. Joḥanan b. Zakkai, the originator of our tradition, complains about the priests' inflexibility, cp. p. 221.
[67] Cf. b. Kidd. 71a Bar.: 'There was yet another [family forcibly declared

With the passage of time this kind of tradition, which was put forward mainly through exposition of the genealogical details in I Chron., took on such importance (see the extent of such tradition's in b. Pes. 62b, quoted above p. 279), that there were inevitably fears that some distinguished families might be disgraced if blemishes in their ancestry were made public.[68] And so it was decided (b. Pes. 62b.; pp. 240 and 282)—when, we do not know, but assuredly before the time of R. Johanan (c. AD 199–279)—to forbid public exposition of I Chron. and to relegate it to the traditional esoteric material (on this see pp. 237ff.).

The conclusion of this second section is this: there are certainly falsifications of history in the genealogies, but these cannot be constructed at random as there are possibilities for verification. We have now arrived at a criterion for assessing the New Testament genealogies of Jesus, the only one, apart from the New Testament material itself, which is at our disposal.

III

What is the historical value of these genealogies of Jesus? Matthew (1.1–17) and Luke (3.23–38) each give us one. Both give the ancestry of the carpenter Joseph, and both try to show his Davidic origin.[69]

We must give credence to this assertion that Joseph descended from David. Of course we could conjecture that later, on the basis of Jesus' messianic character, Davidic ancestry would have been attri-

---

legitimate, Rashi, *in loco*] which the sages declined to reveal, but the sages confided it [the name] to their children and disciples once a septannate'. For examples of a secret tradition on illegitimate families, see b. Kidd. 70b.

[68] b. Kidd. 71a; par. j. Kidd. iv. 1,65c.54; j. Yeb viii.2, 9d.11: 'R. Johanan (d. 279) said: By the Temple! It is in our power [to reveal the families of impure birth in Palestine], but what shall we do, seeing that the greatest men of our time are mixed therein.' *Ibid*: 'In the days of R. Pinhas [b. Hama, c. AD 360] it was desired to declare Babylon as 'dough' ['*issāh*, expression meaning 'of doubtful lineage', p. 221] in comparison with Palestine. He [Pinhas, who wanted to prevent this] said to his slaves: When I have made two statements in the house of study, take up my litter and flee. When he entered he said to them: (1) A fowl does not require ritual slaughter by the Torah. While they were sitting and meditating thereon he said to them: (2) All countries are dough in comparison with Palestine, and Palestine is dough in comparison with Babylon. [Thereupon] they [his slaves] took him up in his litter and fled. They [his audience] ran after him but could not overtake him. Then they sat and examined [their genealogies] until they came to the danger [of discovering impure descent], and so they separated.' Cf. Bill. I, 1.

[69] The ancient and modern attempts to see one as Mary's genealogy have all failed.

buted to Joseph; but against this hypothesis is the united witness of the New Testament[70] that Jesus was of David's line. There is also the record of Hegesippus, writing about AD 180, on the Palestinian tradition: the grandsons of Judas, brother of Jesus, were denounced by Domitian as descendants of David, and confessed at their trial that they were indeed so (Eusebius, *HE* III, 19; 20.1–6). In the same way Simeon, a cousin of Jesus, and James' successor as head of the Jerusalem community, was denounced as being of David's line and crucified (*ibid.* III, 32.3–6). Julius Africanus confirms that relations of Jesus boasted of their Davidic descent.[71] Added to all this is the fact that nowhere, during the lifetime of Jesus and his apostles, can we find the Jews ever questioning the Davidic origin of Jesus.[72] Jewish polemic would scarcely have ignored such a powerful argument against Jesus' messianic claims.

However, the two genealogies differ entirely. From Abraham to David they agree, for both follow the Old Testament (Ruth 4.12, 18–22; I Chron. 2.1–14). Then the differences appear: (1) Matthew follows the succession through Solomon, Luke through David's son Nathan. (2) Surprisingly, at the time of the Babylonian exile the lists agree on the name of Shealtiel, but give him different fathers (Matt. 1.12: Jeconias, cf. I Chron. 3.17;[73] Luke 3.27: Neri). (3) From Zerubbabel onwards, whom both lists indicate as Shealtiel's son (Matt. 1.12; Luke 3.27) the lists again diverge completely. They

---

[70] Rom. 1.3; II Tim. 2.8; Heb. 7.14; Matt. 1.1–17, 20; Luke 1.27, 32; 2.4; 3.23–38; Acts 2.25–31; 13.23, 34–37; 15.16; Rev. 5.5; 22.16; cf. 3.7. The title 'Son of David' as applied to Jesus: Mark 10.47–48 and par.; Matt. 9.27; 15.22; 21.9, 15; cf. Mark 11.10; Matt. 12.23; it is of course primarily a messianic title, but at the same time it emphasizes Davidic origin (G. Dalman, *WJ*, 262, *ET* 319). In Mark 12.35–37 and par. Jesus resists the political idea of Messiah, appealing to Ps. 110; at no point do we find Jesus denying his Davidic origin.

[71] *Letter to Aristides*, ed. W. Reichardt, *Die Briefe . . . an Aristides und Origenes*, Leipzig 1909, 61, lines 20ff. = Eusebius, *HE* I, 7.14.

[72] The polemic led by unbelieving Jews, John 7.42, is directed against Jesus as a Galilean. David is mentioned simply to support the statement that the Messiah will come from Bethlehem. Ulla (*c.* AD 280) says that Jesus was 'near the government' (*qārōb lemalkūt*), b. Sanh. 43a, and one is inclined to see in that a Talmudic recognition of Jesus' Davidic descent (Derenbourg, *Essai*, 349; F. Delitzsch, *Jesus und Hillel*, Frankfurt 1875, 13; S. Krauss, *Das Leben Jesu nach jüdischen Quellen*, Berlin 1902, 205 *et passim*). But H. L. Strack, *Jesus, die Häretiker und die Christen*, Leipzig 1910, 18*n. 8, rightly draws this conclusion, with reference to b. B. K. 83a: 'near the government' means in both cases 'connected with the heathen government'.

[73] Matthew rightly reads, or places, the article before *'assīr* (I Chron. 3.17), and so has seen this term as describing Jeconiah 'the prisoner' and not as a proper name, a mistake made in MT and LXX.

continue through two different sons of Zerubbabel (Matt. 1.13: Abiud; Luke 3.27: Rhesa). (4) The lists meet again only at Joseph[74] and so before him they differ on the name of Jesus' grandfather: according to Matt. 1.16 he was called Jacob, but in Luke 3.23, Eli.

Since the many attempts to harmonize such completely different genealogies, from Julius Africanus onwards, have failed, we may be inclined to regard both as completely worthless. The progress of our enquiry does not justify such complete scepticism, but challenges us to examine them to see if one is preferable to the other.

A comparison of the two lists with regard to their authenticity gives the following results:

1. Matt. 1.17 states explicitly that his list falls into three sections of fourteen names each. These numbers have a symbolic meaning; there is a *gematria* (play on numbers) based on the fact that in Hebrew the letters of the name David have a value of $4 + 6 + 4 = 14$. In Jesus the number of David is completed for the third and last time.[75]

Luke gives, according to the text of ℵ L T sa. bo., a list of seventy-seven names including Jesus. This may be on the basis of a number of symbolism similar to that we studied in n. 75, dividing the history of the world into twelve periods.[76] Jesus appears at the end of the eleventh week of the world, which precedes the messianic week.[77] However this hypothesis is very difficult to justify. First we must notice that textual

[74] It is possible that they agree on Joseph's grandfather (Matt. 1.15–16: Matthan—Jacob—Joseph; Luke 3.23–24: Matthat—Eli—Joseph), cf. K.H. Rengstorf, *Das Evangelium nach Lukas*, 10th ed. (NT Deutsch 3), Göttingen 1965, 60. But it is not certain if the name Matthat in Luke is original; p. 293.

[75] There may be another symbolic idea behind Matt. 1.17. I Enoch 93.1–10 and 91.12–17 shows that as early as the second century BC world history, from the creation to the end of the world, was divided into ten 'weeks' of seven generations each. On the basis of the tribal lists in Genesis, according to which Abraham belonged to the twentieth generation since the creation, the first three weeks were counted as the pre-Israelite period of man (I Enoch 93.3–5). Thus there were seven weeks left for Israelite history; the last week contained the messianic period (91.15–17). If Matt. 1–17 has this scheme in mind, the division of human history from Abraham to Jesus into 3×14 generations would mean that the sixth of the seven cosmic weeks of Israelite history would end with Jesus; so the last cosmic week, the messianic one, would follow as the seventh and last. Bill I, 44f., and more confidently K. Bornhäuser, *Die Geburts- und Kindheitsgeschichte Jesu*, Gütersloh 1930, 16ff., consider this very possible. We may concede the possibility of an allusion to this scheme, but ask ourselves why Matthew did not make the allusion clearer.

[76] Bill. iv.986f.; Syr. Bar. 53–72; Latin and Arabic translations of II (4) Esd. 14.11; cf. Apocalypse of Abraham 29.

[77] K. Bornhäuser, *op. cit.*, 22; C. Kaplan, 'Some New Testament Problems in the Light of the Rabbinics and the Pseudepigrapha', *Bibliotheca sacra* 87, Dallas 1930, 465–71; K.H. Rengstorf. *op. cit.*, 61.

tradition is not unanimous: B N U *et al.* give only seventy-six names; Syr. sin. has only seventy-three (or actually seventy-two with a gap large enough for only one name); Irenaeus, *Adv. Haer.* III, 22.3, has only seventy-two. But it is in the highest degree likely that, in the current text with seventy-seven names, the following names are not original: Luke 3.27: Rhesa (originally not a proper name but an attribute of Zerubbabel = 'prince', see p. 296); v.31: Melea, or Menna (a dittography);[78] v.33: Aminadab (rightly omitted in B and Syr. sin; some annotator added the name on the basis of LXX I Chron. 2.10 and Ruth 4.19–20; he did not understand that the following name, Admin, was only an abbreviation of Aminadab).[79]

Further, in v.24, the names Matthat and Levi are doubtful, for Julius Africanus (Eusebius, *HE* I, 7.5) and probably Ireneus also (since he has only seventy-two names) read neither of them[80]; moreover, they are repeated in v.29! Consequently the Lucan genealogy can originally have comprised only seventy-two names. Altogether it is doubtful if Luke counted the names; and in any case, if he was also giving a symbolic meaning to the number of Jesus' ancestors, we would have expected a similar remark from him corresponding to Matt. 1.17.

2. In his genealogy Matthew adds the names of four women (1.3, Tamar; 1.5, Rahab and Ruth; 1.6, Bathsheba), all women to whom God's power was revealed, therefore types of Mary.[81] Luke has nothing to correspond to this.

3. Matthew follows I Chronicles (see n. 26) for his first part, Abraham to Zerubbabel. The Lucan source, on the other hand, does not yet regard the books of Chronicles[82] as Holy Scripture (see pp. 295f. on the total divergence of the lists in Luke 3 and I Chron. 3).

4. A threefold error finds its way into Matthew or his source.

(*a*) In the list of kings after David, Matt. 1.8–9 omits three names, obviously in error, as the following comparison shows. Matt. 1.8–9: Ιωραμ-Οζιας-Ιωαθαμ. I Chron. 3.11–12: Ιωραμ-Οζιας (A V; Οζεια B;

---

[78] See A. Schlatter, *Das Evangelium des Lukas*, Stuttgart 1931, 218.

[79] Cf. G. Kuhn, 'Die Geschlechtsregister Jesu bei Lukas und Matthäus nach ihrer Herkunft untersucht', *ZNW* 22, 1923, 217 n. 2.

[80] Schlatter, *loc. cit.*

[81] Cf. E. Klostermann, *Das Matthäusevangelium*, 2nd ed., Tübingen 1927, 2; A. Schlatter, *Der Evangelist Matthäus*, Stuttgart 1929, 2f. There is a different opinion in G. Kittel, *TWNT* III, 1938, 1f.

[82] The inclusion of Chronicles in the canon took place in Palestine between 20 BC (*terminus post quem*) and AD 60 (*terminus ante quem*), cf. Schlatter, *Theologie*, 131 n. 2.

$O\chi o\zeta\iota a(s)$ plurimi)—$I\omega as$-$A\mu a\sigma\iota as$-$O\zeta\iota as$ (Lucian; $A\zeta a\rho\iota as$ A; $A\zeta a\rho\iota a$ B)
—$I\omega a\theta a\nu$.[83]

(b) As a result of the similarity between the names Jehoiaqim
and Jehoiakin, the first of these two kings has been omitted[84] in
Matt. 1.11.

(c) Contrary to the claim in Matt. 1.17, the third group (Matt. 1.
12–16) does not contain fourteen names but only thirteen; Jehoiakin
is named twice, rightly as the last member of the second group, and
again in error as the first member of the third group. Matthew, or his
source, has therefore not been very exact, or maybe has been led
into inaccuracies because of the scheme based on the number
fourteen.

5. Matthew gives twelve names for the period from Zerubbabel
to Jesus (inclusive of both). It is far too small a number for a round
six hundred years,[85] since it would mean each generation represents
fifty years. Perhaps the list was shortened in the interests of the number fourteen. Luke gives for the same period eighteen names, which
gives a much more credible number of thirty-three years for each
generation.[86]

6. Finally—and this is particularly important—Matthew traces
the genealogy of Jesus back to David through the reigning line (i.e.
Solomon), but Luke traces it through a non-reigning branch (Nathan).

All these points lead to the same conclusion: in comparison with
Matthew, Luke presents a more reliable tradition.[87] It is hardly likely

---

[83] The error may also go back to the original Semitic form (assumed in the
following note) of the genealogy: in the Hebrew text of II Chron. 22.6 (as in Matt.)
Ahaziah and Azariah are also confused (C. C. Torrey, The Four Gospels, London
1933, 289). But it is more likely that the omission of the three names first happened when it was translated into Greek.

[84] The error goes back to the Semitic original.

[85] Zerubbabel was born c. 570 BC, see E. Sellin, Geschichte des israelitisch-
jüdischen Volkes II, Leipzig 1932, 89.

[86] Let us compare this with the numbers on p. 191 on the subject of high priests.
According to Josephus' calculations, this gives for each generation an average
time of 26 years in the time of the first Temple, and 27½ years in the time of the
second Temple until 162 BC.

[87] This is generally recognized today: K. Bornhäuser, Die Geburts- und
Kindheitsgeschichte Jesu, 28 (while the genealogy in Matthew is concerned with the
succession in the royal family, that in Luke rests on 'consanguinity of its members');
A. Schlatter, Lukas, 216 (Luke's genealogy seemed to him better attested than
Matthew's; C. C. Torrey, The Four Gospels, 305 (Luke has inserted a genealogy
'which he believes authentic, in contrast with the evident artificiality of the one
in Matthew'); K. H. Rengstorf, Das Evangelium nach Lukas (NT Deutsch 3),
Göttingen 1965, 62 agrees with Bornhäuser.

that the list in Matthew is a pure invention; in default of exact information, he has used the material of another Davidic list.

But this does not decide the question of the actual value of the genealogy in Luke. We have two criteria for criticism: first, the difference between Luke and I Chronicles, and second an enquiry into the names of the Lucan list.

The *difference between Luke and I Chronicles* is threefold:

(i) According to Luke Zerubbabel was the son of Shealtiel (Luke 3.27); but according to the Hebrew text of I Chronicles he was the son of Padaiah (I Chron. 3.19).

(ii) According to Luke, Zerubbabel descended from David through Nathan (Luke 3.27–31); but according to I Chronicles, through Solomon (I Chron. 3.10–19).

(iii) Luke gives as Zerubbabel's son one Rhesa (Luke 3.27), who in I Chron. 3.19–20 does not appear among the sons of Zerubbabel.

The reasons for Luke's divergence from I Chronicles is not that he had rejected the statements in I Chronicles—perhaps because he had better material—but much rather because the author of the genealogy in Luke (in contrast to Matthew who assuredly knew I Chronicles, see p. 280 n. 26) did not know the books of Chronicles[88] which even in Palestine were included in the canon only in the course of the first century AD.[89] As for the differences, we can check them thus:

(i) Thanks to the concurring evidence in Hag. 1.1, 12, 14; 2.2, 23; Ezra 3.2, 8; 5.2; Neh. 12.1, also LXX A* B I Chron. 3.19; *Ant.* 11.73; and Matt. 1.12 it is absolutely certain that Luke is right, as against I Chronicles, and that Zerubbabel was the son of Shealtiel.[90] But this by itself does not prove that the genealogy in Luke is authentic, but is simply evidence that he followed the canonical books he knew.

(ii) On the second difference, one fact speaks in favour of Luke— I Chronicles makes Zerubbabel a descendant of the reigning Davidic line (as does Matt. 1.1–17, following I Chron.); but Luke makes him a descendant of the non-reigning branch. Now, nowhere else in the Old Testament is it said, as I Chron. 3.17–19 says, that Zerubbabel was a grandson of the king Jehoiakin who was taken into exile. Could I Chronicles wrongly have considered as the grandson of the last reigning king, the restorer of the Temple upon whom for a long

---

88 Th. Zahn, *Das Evangelium des Lukas*, 3rd and 4th eds., Leipzig 1920, 218.

89 Schlatter, *Theologie*, 131 n. 2: between 20 BC and AD 60.

90 E. Sellin, *op. cit.*, 83f. has shown that I Chron. 3.19 is wrong in saying Zerubbabel was the son of Pedaiah.

time political hopes were concentrated, and upon whose descendants still in later years the messianic hope was fixed ?[91]

(iii) The third difference is only apparent. Luke gives ‘Ρησά as the son of Zerubbabel, and ’Ιωανάν as the son of ‘Ρησά (3.27). As A. Hervey[92] has already recognized, Rhesa is merely the Aramaic *rēšā* = chief, prince; this word was originally an attribute of Zerubbabel.[93] So originally ’Ιωανάν was given as the son of ‘Zerubbabel the prince’ = Hananiah son of Zerubbabel, I Chron. 3.19. It is only after this that Luke and I Chronicles diverge: ’Ιωδά (Luke 3.26) does not appear among the sons of Hananiah in I Chron. 3.21.

On the whole, the differences between Luke and I Chronicles suggest a favourable judgement on the value of the Lucan genealogy, at least for the post-exilic part.

On the other hand, an enquiry *into the names* leads to an adverse judgement for the pre-exilic part. R. Fruin[94] has reminded us that the custom of using the names of the twelve patriarchs as personal names did not arise until after the exile. In fact, the name of Joseph first appears in Ezra 10.42; Neh. 12.14; I Chron. 25.2, 9; the name of Judah, Ezra 3.9; 10.23; Neh. 11.9 etc. and the name of Simeon, Ezra 10.31. The name Levi as a personal name appears only during the Maccabean era[95] and in New Testament times.[96] Luke gives for the period of the ancient monarchy the names of Joseph, Judah, Simon and Levi as the sixth[97] to the ninth descendants of David, but this is an anachronism, and shows that the pre-exilic part of the Lucan genealogy has no historical value.

It is hardly necessary to extend this adverse judgement to the whole

[91] See *Tanḥuma, toledoth*, 14, 48b.9f.: ‘and from whom (what descent) will he be born [the Messiah]? From Zerubbabel.’

[92] *Genealogies of Jesus Christ*, Cambridge 1853.

[93] Among the followers of Hervey, we can quote *inter alia* A. Plummer, *The Gospel According to St Luke*, 5th ed., Edinburgh 1922, *in loc.*; C. C. Torrey, *The Four Gospels*, London 1933, 306; F. Hauck, *Das Evangelium des Lukas*, Leipzig 1934, 57.

[94] ‘Oudchristelijke Studiën’, *Nieuw Theologisch Tijdschrift* 20, 1931, 222. Cf. the remark by F. Delitzsch, in *Riehms Handwörterbuch des biblischen Altertums* I, 2nd ed., Bielefeld—Leipzig 1893, 919b; R. de Vaux, ‘Binjamin—Minjamin’, in *RB* 45, 1936, 402.

[95] Pseudo-Aristeas (written between 145 and 100 BC), 48 gives Λευις . The same form of the name comes in III Esd. 9.14.

[96] Mark 2.14 (par. Luke 5.27, 29). Levi is also the name of the father of two contemporaries of Josephus, John of Giscala (*BJ* 2.575 *et passim*) and John of Tiberias (*Vita* 131). Similarly the name appears in the first century AD on a Jerusalem ossuary (*CIJ* II, no. 1340).

[97] τοῦ Μελεὰ τοῦ Μεννά (Luke 3.31) is evidently a dittography, and so counts as a single name.

of the post-exilic part of the Lucan genealogy. If we consider first, that it has emerged as superior to the Matthean, and, secondly, all that we have to establish immediately on the value in civil and religious life of keeping up the tradition of legitimate ancestry, and if we take into account, thirdly, that the carpenter Joseph belonged not only to one of the families privileged to supply wood for the altar (p. 226) but also to the royal family whose tradition was carefully kept, of which we have positive proof, and, finally, our results on p. 290 on the value of contemporary lay genealogies, we shall not hesitate to assume that Luke, or his source, may have preserved authentic material, at least for the last few generations before Joseph.[98]

C. THE CIVIL RIGHTS OF FULL ISRAELITES

The value of establishing pure ancestry for a family by means of genealogical traditions and records was not merely theoretical; it assured the family in question of civil rights which full Israelites possessed. The most important privilege was to be known as a family 'who [could] marry [their daughters] to priests' (M. Kidd. iv.5; M. Sanh. iv.2; M. Arak. ii.4 *et passim*). Only women of pure Israelite descent were qualified to bear sons worthy of serving before the altar in Jerusalem (pp. 154, 219ff.).[99] Again we see the intimate connection between social stratification and religion. Only those families who had preserved the divinely ordained purity of the race, which Ezra restored through his reforms, belonged to the true Israel.

But this right of legitimate families to contract marriages with priests was not their only privilege. On the contrary, all the most important honours, positions of trust and public posts were reserved for full Israelites.[100] Proof of pure ancestry was required to become a

[98] The same result is reached by a completely different method by G. Kuhn, 'Die Geschlechtsregister Jesu', *ZNW* 22, 1923, 206–28, especially 209 and 222. He traces the list in Luke 3.23–26 (Jesus to Matthat) back to ancient documents 'which passed from one generation to another in Jesus' family' (p. 222); and these list, he thinks, originally agreed with the one in Luke 3.29–31 (Jesus to Matthat). I cannot agree with his analysis and his somewhat bold surmises (for one thing, the fact that Julius Africanus according to Eusebius *HE* I, 7.9–10, did not read the names Matthat and Levi in Luke 3.24; this removes immediately the mainstay of his conjectural reconstruction of a double list). But I am entirely with him in his positive assessment of the beginning of the Lucan genealogy.

[99] For the examination of the genealogies of priests' brides, pp. 216ff.

[100] The most important passage, M. Kidd. iv.5 says: 'They need not trace descent [of the bride of a priest or Levite musician] beyond the Altar [if her father is an officiating priest, her legitimacy is assured] or beyond the Platform [of

member of the supreme councils,[101] that is the Sanhedrin[102] and any of the criminal courts of 23 members (M. Sanh. iv.2; cf. b. Sanh. 36b; b. Kidd. 76b) which, according to the Mishnah[103] had the right of passing capital sentence. A later source (j. Kidd. iv.5, 65d.49) maintains that this right extended to the clerks and bailiffs of the court too.

Proof of pure ancestry was demanded also for public officers (M. Kidd. iv.5; j. Kidd. iv.5, 65d.48)[104]—and here we should think especially of the seven-member local councils of the Jewish communities[105]—and trustworthy men whom the community appointed as almoners (M. Kidd. iv.5; j. Kidd. iv.5, 65b.48f.; b. Pes. 49b Bar.). In every case, genealogies were examined before appointment. We know only of one exception to this, and that is questionable: the two famous scribes Shemaiah and Abtalion (c. 50 BC) of whom the first was definitely a member of the Sanhedrin,[106] were said to have descended from proselytes (p. 235).

Further, R. Simeon b. Gamaliel II (c. AD 140) states that in

Levite singers] or beyond the Sanhedrin, and all whose fathers are known to have held office as public officers or almoners may marry into the priestly stock and none need trace their descent.'

[101] This also explains why b. Shab. 139a speaks of 'families of judges'.

[102] M. Kidd. iv.5; b. Kidd. 76b. Similarly in M. Hor. i.4: Proselytes, bastards and Temple slaves could not sit on the tribunal (the Sanhedrin here: M. Hor. i.5). T. Sanh. iv.7, 421 gives further evidence, saying that the private copy of the Torah which the king had to possess, according to Deut. 17.18–19, and from which he had to read the lesson in the Temple for a feast of Tabernacles following a sabbatical year, was corrected by 'the court of priests, Levites and Israelites who could marry (their daughters) with priests'. In j. Sanh. ii.7, 20c.48 this is replaced by 'court of seventy-one'. Thus only Israelites of pure ancestry could be members of the Sanhedrin.

[103] G. Allon, 'Zur Erforschung der Halacha bei Philon', in *Tarbiz* 5, 5694 = 1933/4, 28–36 and 241–6, upholds the view that according to Philo, only the Great Sanhedrin at Jerusalem could pass capital sentences.

[104] It is true that, according to b. Kidd. 76b, this applied only to Jerusalem. When R. Simeon b. Jehozadek (c. AD 225) recommends, in b. Yom. 22b that no one should be appointed to a leading post in the community unless he had 'a basket of reptiles' on his back (i.e. blemishes in his ancestry), this was meant as a protection from arrogance; at the same time, it gave the community a chance to be rid of unpopular leaders (by pointing out the blemishes); this is good evidence for the fact that purity of ancestry was the normal requirement for holding office.

[105] On these councils cf. Schürer II, 224–6, ET II. 1, 150–3; Bill. II, 641f. and IV, 145. Siphre Deut. 17.15: 'We do not appoint an official who is not' one from among your brethren' (Deut. 17.15). According to b.B.B. 3b, this excluded proselytes.

[106] *Ant.* 14.172–6; 15.4; Σαμαίας mentioned in *Ant.* 15.4 is certainly Shemaiah and not Shammai (Schürer II, 422–4, ET II.1, 358f.; Schlatter, *Theologie*, 199 n. 1).

earlier times the marriage contracts of women ('of pure descent' adds
j. Sanh. i.2, 19c.9 Bar.) were signed only by priests, Levites or
Israelites of pure ancestry (T. Sanh. vii.1, 425). In contrast to the
Hillelites, the Shammaites are said to have admitted to their schools
only sons of good families (*ARN*, Rec. B, ch. 4, Goldin 26). Finally
we should mention the Essenes, who enrolled new members according to their ancestry (CD xiv.3ff.), and attached great importance to
this order of descent (*ibid.* xiv.6).

There were some parts of Palestine whose inhabitants were
particularly exclusive, where the privileges of legitimate Israelites
were extended much further than we have shown up to now. There
is an account in M. Kidd. iv.5 concerning Sepphoris, which may
have been the capital of Galilee[107] when Herod Antipas came to the
throne: 'R. Jose [*c.* AD 150] says: Also any whose name was signed
[as a witness][108] in the old archives [i.e. as a member of the govern-
ment] at Sepphoris [no further proof of ancestry was required].[109] R.
Ḥananiah b. Antigonus says: Also any whose name was recorded in
the king's army.' The 'king's army' or 'camp' may be identical with
the 'old castle of Sepphoris' which is mentioned in another passage
(M. Arak. ix.6; T. Shab. xiii.9, 129), so we look for that too at
Sepphoris.[110] In this case, R. Ḥananiah's reference belongs to the
time when there was a Jewish garrison in the castle[111] in the service
of one of the Herodian princes.

Unfortunately, we have far too little information about the extent
of Jewish army service under the Herodian princes. Certainly the law
of the sabbath, forbidding an attack on that day, would severely
limit the usefulness of Jews in the armed forces. However, we know
that Herod the Great installed Jewish military colonies in Batanea
(*Ant.* 17.23–28); and again the commander-in-chief of the army of
Agrippa I, whose domain included Sepphoris, may well have been a
Jew, judging by his name Silas = *Šeʾilā*[112] (*Ant.* 19.299; 317ff.). So
it is not impossible that at some time, under Herod the Great, Herod
Antipas,[113] or Herod Agrippa I, there may have been quartered at

[107] Schürer II, 211 n. 496, ET II.1, 138 n. 362.

[108] In the best MSS the word *ʿēd* is suppressed.

[109] Schürer II, 211 n. 495, ET II.1, 138 n. 361, has given the correct explanation of this passage.

[110] Büchler, *Priester*, 198 n. 2.

[111] For a Gentile garrison at the castle of Sepphoris, see T. Shab. xiii.9, 129.

[112] Josephus mentions four people of this name, and all were Jews.

[113] J. Wellhausen, *Das Evangelium Matthaei*, Berlin 1904, 35: 'Indeed the soldiers of Antipas may also have been Jews.'

Sepphoris a Jewish corps, whose officers or higher ranks (for R. Ḥananiah's reference was probably limited to these) had to furnish proof of their legitimate ancestry. So it appears that in Sepphoris proof of pure Israelite descent was required not only to become a magistrate, as was the rule in any Jewish town, but even to hold a position in the garrison there.

Along with Sepphoris in Galilee (M. Kidd. iv.5) and Emmaus–Nikopolis (M. Arak. ii.4),[114] it was chiefly Jerusalem which was renowned for the care taken to protect the rights of pure Israelites, and this is quite correct.[115] It was claimed that in the Holy City every public official was of pure ancestry (b. Kidd. 76b). Another report claims that noble-minded men of Jerusalem would not sign any document, nor sit as judge in any court, nor accept any invitation without first assuring themselves of the kind of men their co-signatories, colleagues in court or fellow-guests were; that is, they desired to know, among other things, if they were pure Israelites.[116] Thus we see to what extent the families of Jerusalem kept themselves exclusive even in minor details of everyday life.[117]

So we see that very important civil privileges were reserved for full Israelites;[118] but we have not yet indicated the most important advantage which these families had. This was in the religious sphere. Thanks to their pure origin, they could share in the merits of their forefathers, which were hereditary and theirs by proxy in two senses. First, the common teaching said that the whole of Israel participated in the merits of the patriarchs, of Abraham in particular. These merits made prayers acceptable, protected from danger, helped in war, were a substitute for each man's lack of merit, expiated sins, appeased the wrath of God and warded off his punishment, saved from *Gehinnom* and assured a share in God's eternal kingdom.[119] But,

[114] See p. 215 n. 215 on this passage; today Amwas, south-east of Lydda.

[115] The passage in M. Kidd. iv.5 which we studied on pp. 297ff., no doubt refers principally to circumstances in Jerusalem.

[116] b. Sanh. 23a Bar. and par. Cf. too M. Gitt. ix.8 on the care taken by 'the more scrupulous in Jerusalem' on signing bills of divorce.

[117] Cf. b. Sanh. 19a Bar., where the jealousy of two families of Jerusalem is recorded, and that each claimed the right to go first to offer ceremonial condolences.

[118] An exception was made for men who had no sons; even if they were of pure ancestry, they were refused membership of the Sanhedrin (M. Hor. i.4; b. Sanh. 36b Bar.; according to T. Sanh. vii.5, 426 they were also refused membership of the criminal court of twenty-three), for the fact of having no son was regarded as a blemish and divine punishment; cf. *Protevangelium of James* i.2 (M. R. James 39).

[119] Evidence in Bill. I, 116–20; F. Weber, *Jüdische Theologie auf Grund des Talmud und Verwandter Schriften*, 2nd ed., Leipzig 1897, 292–4, 296f.

in addition, each Israelite had a share in the merits and intercession of his own particular ancestors if there were righteous men among them;[120] and conversely if he chose a wife who was not of equal purity of birth, vengeance would come on his children (b. Kidd. 70a). 'A father endows his son with [the blessings of] beauty, strength, riches, wisdom and length of years' (j. Kidd. i.7, 61a.27f., par. M. Eduy. ii.9). 'The prayer of a righteous man [who is] the son of a righteous man is not like the prayer of a righteous man [who is] the son of a wicked man' (b. Yeb. 64a).

But even now we have not said the last word. The prophet Elijah was to be the forerunner of the Messiah, to set the community in order, to restore the original purity of Israel, so that the people were ready both inwardly and outwardly for final salvation.[121] The main task in this re-establishment of Israel was 'to restore the tribes of Jacob' (Ecclus. 48.10), i.e. according to rabbinic exegesis, to 'declare impure', or 'pure' to 'remove' or 'bring nigh' the families who had wrongly been declared legitimate or illegitimate.[122] Only families of pure Israelite descent could be assured of a share in the messianic salvation,[123] for only they were assisted by the 'merit of their legitimate ancestry'.[124] Here we have the most profound reason

[120] F. Weber, *op. cit.*, 294–7. Two examples may be given: R. Eleazar b. Azariah, a descendant of Ezra of the tenth generation, was entrusted with the direction of the school at Jabne because of 'the merits of his ancestors' (b. Ber. 27b). R. Joshua at first refused to grant R. Gamaliel II's request for pardon; but later when the request was renewed with the words 'For the honour of my ancestors', R. Joshua relented (b. Ber. 28a).

[121] Cf. J. Jeremias, art. *'Ηλίας, TWNT* II, 1935, 930–43.

[122] M. Eduy. viii.7. In this text Elijah's task is limited to cases where families had been declared legitimate or illegitimate by force; this limitation is clearly a later exegesis of an old tradition where it was not known.—In the middle of the second century, there were two opposing tendencies: one very rigorous in which Elijah simply had to 'remove' illegitimate families, and a milder one, which eventually triumphed, in which he had simply to restore those families wrongly declared illegitimate, cp. Bill. IV, 792–4.

[123] b. Kidd. 70b: 'R. Hama b. R. Hanina [*c.* AD 260] said: When the Holy One, blessed be He, causes His divine Presence to rest [on Israel in the Messianic age] it is only upon families of pure birth in Israel, for it is said [Jer. 31.1]: "At that time, saith the Lord, will I be the God of all the families of Israel." It is not said "of all Israelites" but "of all families".' According to b. Kidd. 70a, Elijah writes down, at the time of marriage, any who marry wives not their equal in purity of descent.

[124] Midrash Ps. 20.2, ed. S. Buber, Vilna 1891, 88a4: 'At that time your people shall all be delivered (from *Gehinnom*), everyone who shall be found written in the book [Dan. 12.1]. By whose merit [will they be saved?] . . . R. Samuel b. Nahman (*c.* AD 260) said: Through the merit of the legitimacy of their ancestry—as it says [in Dan. 12.1, quoted above], everyone whose name shall be found written in the book [kept by Elijah on the legitimacy of marriages, see n. 123].'

for the behaviour of these pure Israelite families—why they watched so carefully over the maintenance of racial purity and examined the genealogies of their future sons- and daughters-in-law before marriage (b. Kidd. 71b). For on this question of racial purity hung not only the social position of their descendants, but indeed their final assurance of salvation, their share in the future redemption of Israel.[125] However, this was not the view of John the Baptist, who exhorted even the legitimate descendants of Abraham to repentance, as an indispensable condition of participation in the Kingdom of God (Matt. 3.9, par. Luke 3.8); nor was it the view of Jesus, who pointed out to his fellow Israelites claiming descent from Abraham (John 8.33, 39) that the one and only way to salvation was redemption by the Son (John 8.36).

[125] Along different lines Philo, in his discussion of nobility ('De nobilitate') in *De Virt.* 187–227, strenuously defends the idea that true nobility lies not in ancestry but in a virtuous life; he is influenced by Hellenistic ideas, and especially by the Stoic ideal of the wise man as the only noble one (cf. F. H. Colson, *Philo* [Loeb Classical Library] VIII, London 1939, 449).

XIV

DESPISED TRADES AND JEWISH SLAVES

A. DESPISED TRADES

ALTHOUGH THE QUESTION of racial purity determined to a large extent the social position of the Jew of New Testament times within his own community, we must not conclude from chs. XII and XIII that this question was the only determining factor. As we have already seen in ch. X, an inferior position because of blood or social rank was by no means prejudicial to the social position of the scribes. Conversely, we must show in the following pages that there were circumstances—quite independent of ancestry —which carried a social stigma in public opinion. First of all, there was a whole series of trades which were despised, and those who practised them were, to a greater or less degree, exposed to social degradation.[1] A number of lists of such occupations was drawn up, and here we give the four most important (trades for which there is evidence in Jerusalem are in italics.)

The first impression given by a cursory glance over these four lists is that there can be few reputable trades left, since they give such a large number of suspect trades and each list is composed in a whimsical manner, from an entirely subjective point of view. But actually this is not the case at all.

In list 1, nos. 1–6, Abba Saul (c. AD 150; p. 305 n. 6) quotes the trades which a father should not teach his son for they are the 'craft of robbers' (M. Kidd. iv.14), i.e. they were particularly notorious for leading to dishonesty. This is clear for trades 1–4, which are trades concerned with transport. There the temptation was great for men to embezzle some of the goods entrusted to them. In fact the list has all forms of transport which existed at that time with the exception

---

[1] For what follows see my article 'Zöllner und Sünder', *ZNW* 30, 1931, 293–300.

I M. Kidd. iv.14[2]	II M. Ket. vii.10[8]	III b. Kidd. 82a Bar.[9]	IV b. Sanh. 25b[12]
1. *Ass-driver*	1. Dung-collector	1. Goldsmith (Tos: sieve- maker)	1. Gambler with Dice
2. Camel- driver	2. Copper- smelter	2. *Flaxcomber*[10]	2. Usurer
3. Sailor[3]	3. *Tanner* (p. 6)	3. (Handmill) cleaner	3. Pigeon- trainer[13]
4. *Carter* (pp. 31f.)[4]		4. *Pedlar*	4. Dealer in pro- duce of the sabbatical year
5. *Herdsman*[5]		5. *Weaver* (pp. 4f.25) (Tos: adds *Tailor:* pp. 5.20, 34)	5. *Herdsman* (n. 5)
6. *Shopkeeper*[6] (pp. 3ff., 113, 234)		6. *Barber* (p. 18.26)	6. *Tax collector* (p. 125)
7. *Physician* (pp. 17f.)		7. *Launderer*	7. *Publican* (p. 32)[14]
8. *Butcher* (pp. 8, 220)[7]		8. Blood-letter	
		9. Bath- attendant	
		10. *Tanner* (p. 6)[11]	

[2] I quote the beginning of the list (1–6) from the best tradition, which is in j. Kidd. iv.11, 66b. 25ff., which quotes our Mishnah as an anonymous Baraita.

[3] The text of the Mishnah in the Palestinian Talmud (*ed. princ.*), j. Kidd. iv.11, 65a.40, reads *sappār, sappān* (sailor, barber); in M. Kidd. iv.14, Stettin 1865, this is reversed. It is obviously a dittography, since 'barber' does not fit in with trades connected with transport, and it is therefore rightly omitted from our text (see n. 2) and from the text of the Mishnah in the Bab. Talmud, Lemberg (=Lvov, 1861.

[4] The text of the Mishnah in the Palestinian Talmud (j. Kidd. iv.11, 65a.40 and that of the Babylonian Talmud, Lemberg 1861, have here *qaddār* (pottery merchant), which is surprising among transport workers. Our text (see n. 2) gives the answer by reading *qarār* (carter), *qaddār*. The context shows that the original read *qārār*, and that *qaddār* is another example of dittography.

[5] Herdsmen in the service of Jerusalemites: according to b. Ket. 62b, R. Aqiba

of carriers, doubtless because they were employed for short distances only and so could be better supervised. A similar suspicion weighed on herdsmen (5) who did not enjoy a very good reputation.[15] As proved by experience, most of the time they were dishonest and thieving; they led their herds on to other people's land (b. Sanh. 25b; Bill. II, 114), and pilfered the produce of the herd. For this reason it was forbidden to buy wool, milk or kids from them (M.B. K. x. 9; T.B.K. xi.9, 370). As for the shopkeeper (6), he was tempted to cheat his customers. R. Judah (c. AD 150) passes stern judgment on physicians (7) and butchers (8): 'The best among physicians is destined for Gehenna, and the most seemly among butchers is a partner of Amalek' (M. Kidd. iv.14). Physicians, who elsewhere also are assessed unfavourably,[16] are included among

---

was in his youth herdsman in the service of b. Kalba Shabua, a rich merchant of Jerusalem.

[6] With regard to the author of the first part of list 1 (1–6), the text of the Mishnah of the Babylonian Talmud and the Stettin ed. 1865 says: 'Abba Gorion [c. AD 180? Bill. I, 187] said in the name of Abba Goria . . .' Another dittography. The right version is in the Mishnah of the Palestinian Talmud (ed. princ.), j. Kidd. iv.11, 65a.39, which reads: 'Abba Gorion of Sidon said in the name of Abba Saul. . . .'

[7] Trades 7 and 8 were added by R. Judah (c. AD 150), M. Kidd. iv.14.

[8] Cf. T. Ket. vii.11, 269; j. Ket. vii.11, 31d. 22; b. Ket. 77a.

[9] Trades 1–7 are found also in T. Kidd. v.14, 343 with the following differences, the sieve-maker comes first, the tailor is added to no. 6; the order is different:
1. Sieve-maker
2. Flaxcomber (read with b. Kidd. 82a Bar.: hassᵉrīqīm)
3. Weaver
4. Pedlar
5. (Handmill) cleaner
6. Tailor
7. Barber
8. Launderer

[10] A flax merchant in Jerusalem appears in j. B.M. ii.5, 8c.18. cp. n. 36.

[11] Read habbursī instead of habbursᵉqē (tannery). Bill II, 695. Trades 8 to 10 were added in b. Kidd. 82a Bar.

[12] The first four trades, M. Sanh. iii.3 = M.R. Sh. i.8.

[13] Pigeon racing was a game of chance, involving gambling.

[14] Luke 18. 10–14. Nos. 5–7 were added in b. Sanh. 25b Bar. Similarly T. Sanh. v.5, 423 adds, as nos. 5–8.
5. Brigands
6. Herdsmen
7. Authors of acts of violence
8. Those suspected of cheating in money matters.

[15] We notice that herdsmen appear again in list IV; see below, pp. 310f., for remarks on this list.

[16] LXX Isa. 26.14: ἰατροὶ οὐ μὴ ἀναστήσωσιν, and LXX Ps. 87 (88). 11: ἢ ἰατροὶ ἀναστήσουσιν (from the dead) καὶ ἐξομολογήσονταί σοι. In b. Pes. 113a we find a warning against staying in a town where the leading citizen is a physician.

'crafts of robbers' because they were suspected of dancing attendance on the rich and neglecting the poor who could pay only a little.[17] Butchers were suspected of being dishonest because they were tempted to sell for human consumption meat from *t^erēpāh* (b. Sanh. 25a), which according to the rabbinic interpretation of the word *t^erēpāh*[18] is flesh of animals with some fatal physical blemishes.[19]

However extensive were the adverse judgments in list I, we must not forget that more favourable opinions on these 'crafts of robbers' were not lacking. So we hear of an ass-driver (1) well versed in the Scriptures, whom R. Jonathan (*c.* AD 220) honoured in word and deed (Gen. R. 32 on 7.19, Son. 32.10, 255). R. Judah (*c.* AD 150) opposes Abba Saul (*c.* AD 150) by saying that camel-drivers (2) are on the whole reliable men, and that sailors (3), because of the constant danger they face, are generally good men (M. Kidd. iv.4). As far as herdsmen (5) are concerned, the favourable picture of the shepherd which we are given in Jesus' teaching is quite isolated; in rabbinic literature in general there are unfavourable references to herdsmen, if we abstract those passages which have developed from Old Testament texts, and present Yahweh, the Messiah, Moses and David as shepherds. Turning to shopkeepers (6) we find very respected scribes in Jerusalem who kept shops (pp. 113 and 234). As for doctors (7), we should remember how highly they are praised in Ecclus. 38.1–15; Theudas (T. Ohol. iv.2, 600 = Theodore), a physician of Lydda, appears in the Mishnah as the authority for a tradition (M. Bekh. iv.4; b. Sanh. 93a Bar.). With regard to butchers (8), Rabbi (d. 217) for example vigorously protests against condemning a whole profession because of an individual (b. Hull. 94b).[20] There is moreover no evidence that these trades in list I would have been despised because of their social standing, with the exception of the herdsman who reappears in list IV. On the contrary, we know that a number of rabbis were shopkeepers (6); and we learn that Tobias, a physician (7) of Jerusalem, was on one occasion allowed to witness that he had seen the new moon (M.R. Sh. i.7), and

[17] Rashi on b. Kidd. 82a Bar., (Babylonian Talmud, Lemberg 1861, Rashi's commentary line 53), gives three reasons for an unfavourable view of physicians: (*a*) they soothed their patients and so kept them from seeking God; (*b*) they had many human lives on their conscience; (*c*) they neglected the poor. The third reason fits best in the context.

[18] In the biblical sense it is 'torn flesh', i.e. an animal killed by a beast of prey.

[19] Whether the animal died from this blemish (caused either naturally or by man or beast of prey), or perhaps had been slaughtered before its time.

[20] We have already met, p. 220, a Jerusalem Rabbi whose father was a butcher.

that once the advice of all the physicians of Lydda was asked on a question of ritual purity (T. Ohol. iv.2, 600). We must therefore take it that list I, in its enumeration of 'crafts of robbers', is a personal judgment of Abba Saul, representing widely held but certainly not universal opinions.

The same holds good for several shorter lists giving professions which never bring in their wake 'a sign of blessing' i.e. even the smallest blessing.[21] We add the lists here, with the trades established for Jerusalem again in italics:

1a b. Pes. 50b Bar. (par. T. Bikk. ii.16, 102)	1b b. Pes. 50b Bar.	1c b. Pes. 50b Bar. (par. T. Bikk. ii.15, 102).
1. Dealer in produce of the sabbatical year[22]	1. *Writer*[23]	1. *Those who write*[23] *scrolls*
2. Small cattle breeder	2. Interpreter	2. Those who write *tephillin*
3. Those who cut down beautiful trees	3. Those who do business with orphans' money	3. Those who write *mezūzōt*
	4. *Those engaged in maritime commerce* (p. 34)	4. Sellers of scrolls,[23] *tephillin* and *mezūzōt*
		5. Sellers of purple wool[24]

The people mentioned in list 1a were suspected of transgressing certain demands of religious laws, such as the law of the sabbatical year (Ex. 23.10–11; Lev. 25.1–7), the rabbinic ban on pasturing

[21] In b. Pes. 50b Bar. traders in cane and jars appear as the first group. They have no blessing because the shape of their wares draws upon them the evil eye. This superstition does not belong in our study, which must concern itself with despised trades.

[22] Read *tagge͑rē še͑mittāh*, with Tos., ed. A. Schwarz, Vilna, 1890, instead of *tagge͑rē sēm͑tā* (street merchants) which does not make sense in the context.

[23] Jerusalem: b. B.B. 14a; Sopherim iv.9 = j. Meg. i.9, 71d. 57 Bar. In our passage it referred to writers of the Torah scrolls.

[24] Purple (or blue) wool was used in making fringes (*ṣīṣīt*): the par. T. Bikk. ii. 15 quotes in the fourth place those who 'concern themselves with recovering money'.

small cattle in the land of Israel, except on the steppes (M.B.K. vii. 7), or the biblical law on the protection of trees (Deut. 20.19–20). The men in lists 1b and 1c trade in sacred things: the writer, who makes money from copying holy books; the interpreter, who makes money from work done during service and that on the sabbath (so b. Pes. 50b); the men who do business with orphans' money, who are tempted to harm those protected by God; ('maritime commerce' does not fit in here at all well); finally, in list 1c, the makers and dealers in ritual objects. These lists 1a–1c are not, any more than the others, juristic documents; no one pursuing any of the trades in lists b. and c. was necessarily a social outcast.[25] We should rather regard these lists as a warning to act with a good conscience, a warning, truth to tell, based on some concrete, unpleasant experiences.

List II has three trades which were certainly not considered dishonourable, but were repugnant[26] especially because of the foul smell connected with them.[27] Dung-collectors and tanners went together,[28] since the former collected the dung needed for fulling and tanning. If anyone engaged in one of the three trades in this list, his wife had the right to claim divorce before the court, and to be paid the sum of money which had been assured her in the marriage contract in case the marriage was dissolved or her husband died (T. Ket. vii.11, 270). She could even claim a divorce if she knew when she married her husband that he was engaged in one of the three trades in question, and had married him on condition that he could continue in his trade. In this case, at least in the opinion of R. Meir (c. AD 150), she could explain: 'I thought that I could endure it, but now I cannot endure it' (M. Ket. vii.10). Otherwise the wife, from the age of thirteen years[29] could only claim divorce if her husband

---

[25] List 1c concludes with the words: 'But if they engage (therein) for its own sake (i.e. and not for money) they see (signs of blessing)'. R. Meir (c. AD 150) practised the trade of writer, b. Erub. 13a; This shows how little it dishonoured the person. Cf. further b. Sukk. 26a Bar., where it is said that the men named in list 1c were freed from the commandments ordered in the Torah, for their profession meant that they accomplished them.

[26] As a repugnant trade, b. Pes. 113a adds flaying: 'Flay carcases in the market place and earn wages' (i.e. it is better to earn a living with the lowliest trade than to beg).

[27] Cf. the opposition of a spice merchant and a tanner in b. Kidd. 82b Bar.

[28] In T. Ket. vii.11, 269 they were the same man, and in fact the tanner must often have been a dung-collector.

[29] If a man is betrothed or married to a girl who is a minor (she was a qᵉṭannāh until the age of twelve years and a day, b. Yeb. 100b), she could eventually, by

demanded vows unworthy of her (Bill. I, 318f.), or if the husband was afflicted (M. Ket. vii.10; T. Ket. vii.11, 270) with leprosy[30] or polypus;[31] in all other cases[32] the right of divorce was exclusively on the husband's side. Bearing all this in mind, we can see the extent to which the men who engaged in the trades cited in list II were deprived of civil rights. But we must always observe that there is no *moral* stigma attached.

Those who were engaged in the trades in list III had to suffer for it even more severely, for the trades had to do with women and so the men were suspected of immorality; this was why they must not be left alone with women (M. Kidd. iv.14; T. Kidd. v.14, 343; b. Kidd. 82a Bar.).[33] Of these it was said, 'From their midst shall no man be king or high priest,[34] not because they are unworthy but because their work is despised' (b. Kidd. 82b Bar.). Here, king and high priest are mentioned simply as examples of public officers, as this saying of R. Jose (c. AD 150) shows: 'Leech, tanner and bath-attendant [cf. list III, 8–10], from these no overseer is set over the congregation.'[35] According to this sentence, even the post of leader of the congregation was forbidden to these engaged in these trades; this is shown by another passage which says that it was unusual to accept the witness of weavers. So we see that those engaged in trades suspected of immorality carried a stigma in their public and legal life; not, it is true, *de jure*—*de jure* these men were 'worthy' to be public officers and witnesses—but indeed *de facto*.

---

right of refusal, annul the betrothal or marriage: (a) during the lifetime of her father, only if she had already been divorced once (M. Yeb. xiii, 6; the former marriage had removed her from her father's power); (b) after her father's death, if she had been given in betrothal or marriage by her mother or brothers (M. Yeb. xiii.2; a marriage concluded without her father, if she was a minor, is only valid in certain circumstances).

30 Conclusion of J. Preuss, *Biblisch-talmudische Medizin*, Berlin 1911, 399f, from b. Ket. 20b; M. Ker. iii.7; b. Taan. 21a, *mukkēḥ seḥin* is a man mutilated with leprosy.

31 On this malady see Preuss, *op. cit.*, 340.

32 According to a later ruling the inability of the husband to support his wife was also a reason for annulment, b. Ket. 77a.

33 For special reference to the suspicion attached to pedlars (itinerant spice merchants), see A. Büchler, 'Familienreinheit und Sittlichkeit in Sepphoris im zweiten Jahrhundert' in *MGWJ* 78, 1934, 138 n. 2.

34 Notice that it is taken entirely for granted that a priest might follow a trade, (pp. 206f.).

35 *Derek ereṣ zuta* 6 (Bill II, 642). This passage does not occur in the A. Tawrogi ed., Königsberg 1885.

It is no accident that among the large number of scribes whom we know to have been engaged in manual work or trade, there is only one of whom we can certainly say followed any of the trades in list III.[36] The stigma was attached particularly to weavers (5) and to tanners (10), the former because in addition to suspicioned immorality in Palestine the weaver's trade was considered woman's work.[37] There is one particularly significant incident showing the social position of weavers in Jerusalem: a case in which the scribes accepted the witness of two weavers of Jerusalem (who moreover lived near the Dung Gate which led to the Valley of Hinnom (pp. 5 and 17; cf. Bill. IV, 1030 n. 1) is recorded by tradition as an extraordinary one, marking special generosity on the part of the scribes (M. Eduy. i.3). To the suspicion of immorality attached to tanners was added the fact that their trade was repugnant, because of the smell (see list II, no. 3). 'Woe to him who is a tanner!' cried Rabbi (d. AD 217; b. Kidd. 82b Bar. par. b. Pes. 65a Bar.). While on this subject we must not overlook Acts 9.43, which says very simply, not even stressing the last word: 'And he (Peter) stayed in Joppa many days and lodged with one Simon, a tanner.'

But it was to the trades in list IV that the greatest stigma was attached, and it meant nothing less than the loss of civil and political rights. In this list are gathered the trades which were based entirely on trickery and were therefore banned *de jure*. The first four of the seven trades in this list are quoted in the Mishnah (M. Sanh. iii.3 = M.R. Sh. i.8); the last three are added in a Baraita (b. Sanh. 25b Bar.). Gamblers with dice, usurers,[38] organizers of games of chance and dealers in produce of the sabbatical year (1–4) were in fact notorious tricksters. We have already looked into the question of shepherds (5) misappropriating other people's property (p. 305, and p. 311 n. 42f.). In the same way experience had shown that tax-collectors (6) and publicans (7), whose post went to the highest bidder, together with their subordinates, almost always abused their position to enrich themselves by dishonesty. 'For herdsmen, tax

[36] In j. B.M. ii.5, 8c.18, we hear that R. Simeon b. Shatach 'worked with flax', which may mean a comber (List III, no. 2) or a flax merchant. The context tells how his pupils offered him a donkey so that his work would not tire him so much, and this rather suggests a merchant. He could however have done both, as often happened in those days.

[37] *Ant.* 18.314, cf. *BJ* 1.479: Alexander and Aristobulus threatened their women folk with forced labour at the looms when they came to power.

[38] Who transgressed the OT rules on interest, Ex. 22.24; Lev. 25.36f.; Deut. 23.20f.

collectors and publicans is repentance hard', it was once said (b. B.K. 94b Bar.). The reason was that they could never know every person they had injured or cheated, and to whom they must make amends.

Characteristically, linguistic custom associates tax-collectors and thieves (M. Toh. vii.6), publicans and robbers (M.B.K. x.2; b. Shebu. 39a Bar.; cf. Luke 18.11; M. Ned. iii.4; *Derek ereṣ* 2); tax-collectors, robbers, money-changers and publicans (*Derek ereṣ* 2); publicans and sinners (Mark 2.15f.; Matt. 9.10f.; Luke 5.30; Matt. 11.19 par. Luke 7.34; Luke 15.1f.);[39] publicans and Gentiles (Matt. 18.17); publicans and harlots (Matt. 21.31f.); extortioners, impostors,[40] adulterers and publicans (Luke 18.11); murderers, robbers and taxgatherers (M. Ned. iii.4); indeed 'publican' was generally almost a synonym for 'sinner' (Luke 19.7). It was forbidden to accept alms for the poor or to use money for exchange, from 'the counter of excisemen or from the wallet of tax-gatherers',[41] for such money was tainted. If tax-collectors and publicans had belonged to a Pharisaic community before taking on the office, they were expelled and could not be reinstated until they had given up the posts (T. Dem. iii.4, 49; j. Dem. ii.3, 23a.10).

But men who followed the trades in list IV were not only despised,[42] nay hated,[43] by the people; they were *de jure* and officially deprived of rights and ostracized. Anyone engaging in such trades could never be a judge, and his inadmissibility as a witness[44] put him on the same footing as a gentile slave (M.R. Sh. i.8). In other words he was deprived of civil and political rights to which every Israelite had

[39] Cf. Matt. 5.46: 'For if ye love them that love you, what reward have ye? do not even the publicans the same', with par. Luke 6.32: 'And if ye do good to them that do good to you, what thanks have ye? for even sinners do the same'.

[40] In the context of Luke 18.11, ἄδικοι has this exact meaning; cf. E. Klostermann, *Das Lukasevangelium* 2nd ed., Tübingen 1929, *in loc.*

[41] M.B.K. x.1—'but it may be taken from them at their own house or in the market.'

[42] See also Midrash Ps. 23.2, ed. Buber, Vilna 1891, 99b.12: 'There is no more disreputable occupation than that of a shepherd.' Philo, *de agric.* 61:' Such pursuits (looking after sheep and goats) are held mean and inglorious.' See also b. Yeb. 16a.

[43] T.B.M. ii.33, 375: 'One does not rescue from pits *gōyīm* and those who breed and pasture small cattle' (because they often also bred swine—Bill. IV, 359. They are not mentioned in the par. b. A.Z. 26a–b Bar.).

[44] In M. Sanh. iii.3, par. M.R. Sh. i.8, this extends to the first four trades in list IV; in b. Sanh. 24b to the other three. It is quite extraordinary that the Jewish community of Caesarea Maris should choose the Jewish customs officer as their representative (*BJ* 2.287). Schlatter, *Theologie*, 186, explains this by the fact that this community was not under Pharisaic direction.

claim, even those such as bastards who were of seriously blemished descent. This makes us realize the enormity of Jesus' act in calling a publican to be one of his intimate disciples (Matt. 9.9 par.; 10.3), and announcing the Good News to publicans and 'sinners' by sitting down to eat with them.

B. JEWISH 'SLAVES'[45]

The Jewish slave too must be reckoned among the socially oppressed. We have already seen, in the section on slaves and day-labourers (pp. 110f.), that in New Testament times there were in Palestine Jewish slaves (which are the only ones to concern us here). Billerbeck has emphasized this too (IV, 689).[46] Here let it be noted that the Talmudic evidence on the price of a Jewish slave was based on actual circumstances. This price was from one to two minas (b. Arak. 30a Bar.; Abadim ii.10); according to another statement, from five to ten minas (b. Kidd. 18a Bar.), while a Gentile slave fetched up to one hundred minas (M.B.K. iv.5; see pp. 346f., for further details). The reason for this great discrepancy was that the period of service for a Jewish slave was only six years, while for a Gentile it was for life. The number of Jewish slaves in Palestine was actually not very large, and their position was regulated in accordance with the humane Old Testament prescriptions.

There were three ways in which a Jew might become a slave:

1. *Ex furto*, which seems to have been the most usual way; e.g. the case of a thief who was not in a position to make equivalent restitution[47] for the stolen goods. On the basis of Ex. 22.2 the court would forcibly sell him (Mek. Ex. 21.7, 28b.17, 20 [L III, 20]; Siphre Deut. 15.12, 43a; b. Kidd. 14b, 17b *et passim*). The sale, which applied only to adult male Israelites (Mek. Ex. 21.20, 30c.42 [L III,

---

[45] The term 'slave' does not correspond exactly to the legal position, in that it does not mean 'bondage'. The small Talmudic tractate on slavery has been edited by R. Kirchheim, *Septem libri talmudici parvi hierosolymitani*, Frankfurt 1851, 25–30, and translated by L. Gulkowitsch in *Angelos* I, Leipzig 1925, 89–95. The value of Gulkowitsch's introduction is lessened by the fact that he often mixes the rules on the treatment of Jewish and Gentile slaves. Bill. IV, 698–716, gives an excellent anthology, in his Excursus 26, of rabbinic pronouncements about Jewish slaves.

[46] This point of view has come under renewed attack by S. Zucrow, *Women, Slaves and the Ignorant in Rabbinic Literature and also the Dignity of Man*, Boston 1932.

[47] According to *Ant.* 16.3, the thief must restore the value fourfold, but this is probably a mistaken generalization of Ex. 21.37b. In Luke 19.8, the fourfold restitution is voluntary.

57]), could be only to a Jewish owner (*Ant.* 16.3; Siphre Deut. 15.12, 43a). However, Herod decided to rid the country of a rabble of convicts and, vigorously opposing their rights, to sell thieves to foreigners and non-Israelites (*Ant.* 16.1f.). Here there may arise the question of a greater tightening up of penal rights being introduced at this time. Indeed, the *halākāh* knows nothing of the sale of married women (Bill. I, 798)[48] or adult daughters (Mek. Ex. 21.20, 30c.43 [L III, ever, only adult Lsraelites (p. 312 last l.), and only in the case of Jesus, it is taken for granted that a man's wife and children are sold because of his debt, but this is more likely to reflect circumstances outside Palestine.

2. *Ex concessu*, by voluntarily selling himself (Lev. 25.39–43). However, only adult Israelites (p. 312 last l.), and only in the case of extreme poverty (Siphra Lev. 25.39, 55c), had the right to sell themselves (Mek. Ex. 21.7, 29a.27 [L III, 20]). It was forbidden to Israelite women (Mek. Ex. 21.7, 29a.24, 28 [L III, 20]). Sale to a non-Jew was valid, but responsibility for redemption lay with the relatives (Lev. 25.47–52; b. B.B. 8b; b. B.M. 71a Bar.; b. Arak. 30b; Abadim ii.9. M. Gitt. iv.9 differs). Usually, it was an act of despair by a man hopelessly in debt.

3. So far (except for Matt. 18.25) we have dealt only with the sale of adult male Israelites. Israelite girls, however, could also be sold, but only minors (Mek. Ex. 21.7, 29a.7 [L III, 18]; 21.20, 30c.43 [L III, 57]), and then only under the age of 12 years.[49] On the basis of Ex. 21.7 *patria potestas* gave a Jewish father the right to sell his underage daughters to another Jew.[50] In practice this usually meant that the girl was destined later to marry her owner or his son (Abadim i.10f.).

Josephus (*Ant.* 16.1ff.) and the New Testament (Matt. 18.25) are in agreement on this point, that the compulsory sale because of theft mentioned under 1. above was not unusual. The case of a young

[48] In M. Sot. iii.8 a woman could not be sold even for a theft which she herself had committed.
[49] The girl had then to be freed if neither her master nor his son wished to marry her; p. 314.
[50] Mek. Ex. 21.7, 29a.19ff. [L III, 18]; cf. M. Sot. iii.8. A father could not sell his son (Mek. *ibid.*). M. Gitt. iv.9 differs: 'If a man sold himself and his children (*bānāw*) to a Gentile, they may not redeem him;' but this is concerned with an illegal method, which is why there was no redemption. The children could be redeemed only after their father's death (M. Gitt. iv.9). After the return from exile, there were times of distress when fathers sold their sons and daughters into slavery, Neh. 5.2, 5.

under-age girl left as a pledge—and to Gentiles at that—may be attested in the passage we studied earlier (M. Eduy. viii.2; see p. 220); however this may mean that it was done under duress, i.e. she was left as a hostage.

The *state of slavery* to a Jewish master could last six full years[51] and no longer,[52] unless the male slave (the females had no such right, Mek. Ex. 21.7, 29a.32 [L III, 20f.] *et passim*) voluntarily renounced his freedom and changed his six years to lifelong service (Ex. 21.5–6; Deut. 15.16–17), which ended only with the death of his owner.[53] This generally happened when a Jewish slave was the father of children of a female Gentile slave who belonged to the same master (see next para.) and did not wish to leave her and his children (Ex. 21.5; *Ant.* 4.273). This however seems to have happened only rarely.[54] The slave's term of service could be ended before the six years were up, if he was given his freedom or redeemed, or if he redeemed himself.[55] Further, the Jewish woman slave was freed if her master died (Mek. Ex. 21.6, 29a.6 [L III, 18]; M. Kidd. i.2 *et passim*), whereas the male slave (Mek. Ex. 21.6, 29a.5 [L III, 18], *et passim*) passed into the power of the son (though no one else had the right of inheritance of a slave). The slave girl who attained her twelfth year was also freed, but in this case the custom was for her master or his son to marry her (Mek. Ex. 21.8, 29b.4 [L III, 24]; Abadim i.7–10 *et passim*). Whether these regulations were always observed is another matter: We must not forget, in Ecclus. 7.21, the admonition not to defraud a servant of his liberty.

As to the *legal position* of the Jewish slave, we must state that slavery was not considered disreputable, and his master must spare the Jewish slave the more humiliating tasks of slavery.[56] In law he was equal to the elder son of the family, and had a right to the same

[51] Ex. 21.2; Deut. 15.12; cf. John 8.35; 'And the bondservant abideth not in the house for ever.' See further *Ant.* 4.273; 16.3 and the *halākāh* in Bill IV, 701f.

[52] A unique statement in b. Kidd. 14b Bar.: 'He who sells himself may be sold for six years and for more than six years.' R. Eliezer (*c.* AD 90), that immovable defender of the old tradition, rejects this possibility (*ibid*). If a slave ran away he must afterwards serve for the length of time that he was away, Bill IV, 702ff.

[53] In this case, the owner's son did not inherit the slave, Mek. Ex. 21.6, 29a.1, 6 [L III, 17f.]; M. Kidd. i.2; b. Kidd. 17b Bar., *et passim*.

[54] Rabbinic precepts sought to tighten up the law here; Bill IV, 707.

[55] We need not consider the regulations for the year of Jubilee, since they were not in force.

[56] Mek. Ex. 21.2, 28b. 42ff. [L III, 5f.], e.g. washing his master's feet, putting on his shoes etc. See further Siphra Lev. 25.39, 55c; Abadim ii.1. He must not be asked to do things which would publicly brand him as a slave.

treatment as his master: good food, good clothing, a good seat at table and a good bed (Mek. Ex. 21.5, 28d.22 [L III, 14]; Siphra Lev. 25.39, 55c, Abadim ii.2 *et passim*; cf. Matt. 10.24f.). Unlike the Gentile slave, he could acquire possessions by finding (M.B.M. i.5) or as gifts,[57] and he could shorten his term of service by payment. Again unlike the Gentile slave, his master could not declare him devoted (M. Arak. viii.5). If he were married, his master was obliged to maintain his wife and children (Mek. Ex. 21.3, 28c.36 [L III, 10], *et passim*). In short, the legal status of the Jewish slave was regulated according to the Old Testament prescription: 'He shall be with you as a hired servant' (Lev. 25.40). He was 'a worker whose labour was leased by a certain master for six years; the purchase price was, as it were, a payment of wages in advance for the whole of that period' (Bill. IV, 709).[58]

In one respect only was he deprived of a right, and then only in the case of a male slave. This was on the basis of the rabbinic exegesis of Ex. 21.4, where the Law prescribes: 'If his master give him [the Jewish slave] a wife, and she bear him sons or daughters, the wife and her children shall be her master's, and he shall go out by himself.' Since an adult Jewess could not be slave to a Jew, this passage is interpreted thus: the master had the right to give a Gentile woman slave to a Jewish slave as wife,[59] even against his will (b. Kidd. 14b: R. Eliezer's opinion; cf. M. Tem. vi.2). When the slave was freed, the wife and children remained in the master's possession.

Harsh reality was often grimmer than rabbinic legislation, as we know from Herod's order to sell thieves to foreigners (*Ant.* 16.1ff.). How unscrupulously the Law was occasionally flouted is shown by the behaviour of Antigonus the Maccabean: in 40 BC he promised the Parthians, besides 1,000 talents, 500 women on condition that they would help him to win the throne (*Ant.* 14.331, 343, 365; *BJ* 1.248, 257, 273). To make up this number he had included 'most of their own' (i.e. the women folk of his enemies, Hyrcanus, Phasael and Herod: *BJ* 1.257), which means that they were Jewesses. In general

---

[57] On the other hand, the gain from his work as a slave belonged entirely to his master (cf. Matt. 25.14–30; Luke 19.13–27).

[58] L. Gulkowitsch, 'Der kleine Talmudtraktat über die Sklaven', *Angelos* I, 1925, 88, says that the Jewish slave had no right of witness. But this is not so: the text he quotes, b. B.K. 88b, is speaking of Gentile slaves.

[59] According to R. Eliezer (*c.* AD 90) who probably represented old tradition, this held good for the slave sold *ex concessu* as well as the slave sold *ex furto* (b. Kidd. 14b). The limitation to a slave already married (to a Jewess) appeared first in the fourth century (b. Kidd. 20a).

however, it must be said that in normal times the Old Testament legislation which so powerfully protected Jewish slaves, closed the door on too arbitrary a behaviour on the masters' part. There is a characteristic saying, 'Whoever buys himself a Jewish slave buys himself a master' (b. Kidd. 20a.22a *et passim*); and Jesus' words, 'A disciple is not above his teacher, nor a slave above his master; it is enough for the disciple to be as his teacher and the servant like his master' (Matt. 10.24f.; John 13.16; 15.20), can also give us a glimpse of the humane treatment of Jewish slaves.

XV

THE ILLEGITIMATE ISRAELITES

A. ISRAELITES WITH SLIGHT BLEMISH

IN THIS SECTION WE shall examine three groups of people, illegitimate children of priests, proselytes, and freed slaves. Of these the proselytes were by far the most numerous. The members of the three groups had one thing in common, the fact that a marriage between them and Levites or Israelites of pure descent, was recognized as legitimate. But they could not marry into priests' families; that was the exclusive right of Levites and full Israelites. Their social position was thus appreciably lowered; the exclusion of alliance with priestly families was not only a social deprivation but in the end a religious one. Furthermore, these groups were deprived of important civil rights: they were disqualified from seats on certain courts and tribunals, and from the most sought after positions of honour (listed on pp. 297–300).

1. *Illegitimate descendants of priests*

Among those Israelites with slight racial blemish were first of all 'the profane' (*ḥālāl*, a technical term based on Lev. 21.15; *ḥalālāh*, Lev. 21.7, 14). These were the illegitimate children of priests, and were the children born of a marriage between a priest and a woman who was not of pure descent, or ineligible for other reasons (b. Kidd. 77a–b). We have already examined (pp. 216ff.) the circumstances under which the marriage of a priest was forbidden, and his descendants were illegitimate. In accordance with Ezra 2.61–63 and Neh. 7. 63–65, such an illegitimate son could not hold priestly office, nor could his descendants (p. 220).[1] Furthermore, he could not marry the

---

[1] Nor could he pronounce the priestly benediction in the synagogue worship, b. Sot. 38b. 40a.

daughter of a priest (M. Kidd. iv.1).[2] If the illegitimate son of a priest had a half-brother who was of legitimate descent (i.e. the same father, but a mother who was the priest's equal in purity of descent), and the latter died childless the former could not contract a levirate marriage with his widow (M. Yeb. ix.1), since because of his illegal descent he was not in a position to pass on to his sons the 'name' (Deut. 25.6) of a legitimate priest. The illegitimate daughter of a priest could not marry a legitimate priest (M. Kidd. iv.6; T. Kidd. v.3, 341) even by levirate marriage (M. Yeb. ix.2). What is more, the widow of a *ḥālāl*, even if she herself were of legitimate descent, could not marry a priest, according to the priestly code;[3] by marrying an illegitimate son of a priest, she herself had become illegitimate[4] and her own legitimate descent counted for nothing. These strict rulings show again (pp. 219ff.) the inflexibility of the priests' determination to keep themselves pure and to exclude any taint of illegitimacy.

Even the more leniently disposed Pharisees (pp. 220f.) supported in principle the exclusion of illegitimate descendants of priests from the priestly status, and they did not hesitate to demand that the high priests John Hyrcanus and Alexander Jannaeus should resign their office, since in their eyes they were illegitimate children of priests (pp. 155f.). On the other hand the scribes could not approve the priests' rigorous attitude on questions of marriage with the illegitimate descendants of priests, especially in cases where the illegitimacy was not proved but merely presumed. This concerned the *'issāh* families[5] already mentioned on p. 221, with whom priests would not intermarry. On the basis of textual criticism, I have earlier (p. 221 n. 234) given a

---

[2] The lenient opinion of R. Judah (*c.* AD 150): 'Proselyte, freedman and *ḥālāl* may marry a priest's daughter' (T. Kidd. v.2, 341) was not in line with ancient law.

[3] b. Kidd. 75a: 'R. Ḥisda (d. AD 309) said: Do not all agree that an *'issāh* widow ['*issāh*, see next paragraph] is unfit for [marriage with] a priest?' What applied to the *'issāh* widow applied even more for the widow of a *ḥālāl*, whose standing with regard to purity was lower.

[4] Cf. the similar decision for proselytes, b. Kidd. 78a: 'A proselyte renders [a legitimate Israelite daughter] unfit [for marriage with a priest] by having cohabited [with her]'.

[5] Bibliography: F. Rosenthal, 'Über *'issā*. Ein Beitrag zur Sittengeschichte der Juden vor und nach der Zerstörung des zweiten Tempels', *MGWJ* 30, 1881, 38–48, 113–23, 162–71, 207–17; A. Büchler, 'Familienreinheit und Familienmakel in Jerusalem vor dem Jahre 70', *Festschrift Schwarz*, 133–62, ET, 'Family Purity and Family Impurity in Jerusalem before the Year 70 C.E.', *Studies in Jewish History. The Büchler Memorial Volume*, London 1956, 64–98; see the criticism of Büchler's view, p. 221 n. 234.

solution to the ʿ*issāh* problem: they were the priestly families where there was some doubt on the legitimacy of one or more members. I have discovered confirmation of this solution by proving that the Tosaphists uphold the same conception of ʿ*issāh*,[6] as well as Maimonides and Obadiah di Bertinoro.[7] In these doubtful cases of legitimacy of priests' children, scribes of the school of Hillel wished to make them cases of conscience; that is, they were ready to accept the declaration of the ʿ*issāh* family if made in good faith, and thus decided in favour of the legitimacy of the children of this family.[8] But the priests inexorably rejected the ʿ*issāh* families, always and on sight, and if there was the slightest suspicion would not marry the daughters of such families (M. Eduy. viii.3; see n. 8). In all cases concerning purity of priestly descent, they decided on principle on the strictest line (p. 217, end of n. 217 pp. 220f.).

Altogether it must be said that the number of illegitimate priestly families does not seem to have been very large.[9]

---

[6] On b. Ket. 14a: 'A family in which it is possible one or more *ḥᵃlālīm* have been included [i.e. mixed].'

[7] On M. Eduy. viii.3: 'A family in which it is possible a *ḥālāl* has been included, so that each son is suspected of being illegitimate.'

[8] M. Eduy. viii.3: 'R. Joshua (*c.* AD 90) and R. Judah b. Bathyra (after AD 100) testified that (the widow *'almānat*: this word should be omitted as in the Tos. passage soon to be quoted) (which belonged to) an ʿ*issāh* family was eligible for marriage with a priest; (and) that the members of an ʿ*issāh* family are qualified to bear testimony as to which (of themselves) is unclean or clean, and which must be put away and which may be brought near. Rabban Simeon b. Gamaliel (II, AD 140) said: We accept your testimony, but what shall we do? For Rabban Johanan b. Zakkai decreed that courts may not be set up concerning this. The priests would hearken to you (only) in what concerns putting away but not in what concerns bringing near.' T. Eduy. iii.2, 459 said, obviously commenting on the first two phrases of this Mishnah passage: 'A later court taught: [the testimony of] the ʿ*issāh* is acceptable (*neʾemānat*) to declare for purity or impurity, to forbid or allow [marriage], to put away or bring near [to the priesthood]. But they have settled nothing concerning the ʿ*issāh* widow.' This last sentence proves that the word 'widow' in M. Eduy. viii.3 does not belong to the original tradition (we have already verified this on other grounds, p. 221 n. 234). According to the *halākāh*, then, the ʿ*issāh* family itself has to give testimony to the legitimacy or illegitimacy of that one of its members whose descent is doubtful. Rosenthal (see n. 5) on p. 43 of his article has a useful suggestion: In his opinion, the Tosephta passage shows that originally the first sentence of this Mishnah passage read not *'lmnt* ʿ*sh* but *n'mnt* ʿ*sh*. The faulty reading in M. Eduy. viii.3 is the source of much confusion over the meaning of ʿ*issāh*.

[9] T. Kidd. v.2, 341; par. b. Ket. 14b Bar.: 'The Israelites know *nᵉtīnīm* (Temple slaves, see pp. 342f.) and bastards in their midst, but not *ḥᵃlālīm*.' A. Büchler, in *MG WJ* 78, 1934, 159ff., gives some instances of *ḥᵃlalim* in the second century AD. See also j. Gitt. i.2, 43c.39; Bill. II, 377.

2. The proselytes

The proselytes[10] formed another group of Israelites with a slight blemish, and they were much more numerous than the *ḥalālim*. We are concerned here with full proselytes, the 'proselytes of righteousness' (*gērim = gērē ṣedeq*), i.e. Gentiles converted to Judaism who had been circumcised, baptized[11] and had offered sacrifice. They must be clearly distinguished from the 'God-fearers' (*yir'ē šāmayim*. LXX, NT and Josephus: φοβούμενοι [σεβόμενοι] τὸν Θεόν), who simply confessed faith in one God and observed part of the ceremonial laws, without total commitment to Judaism. Legally they were still regarded as Gentiles.

In the first century AD, which is our main study, it is true that the era of forcible conversion[12] to Judaism was over, such as had taken place in the time of the Maccabees, particularly under John Hyrcanus in Idumaea (*Ant.* 13.257) and Aristobulus I in the Kingdom of Iturea (*Ant.* 13.318).[13] In this first century, even in the Diaspora it seems to have been no easy task to win proselytes, to judge by Matt. 23.15; this is hardly surprising when we consider the spread of anti-Semitism in the Greco-Roman world.[14] Schürer rightly decides that 'formal conversions to Judaism do not seem to have been as frequent as a loose attachment in the form of σεβόμενοι'.[15] However the baptism of proselytes in the pool of Siloam in Jerusalem was not a rare occurrence. It is easy indeed to imagine that Gentiles came to Jerusalem for their conversion to Judaism (*Pirqe R. Eliezer* 10), if only to offer the sacrifice demanded by the occasion.[16]

---

[10] Bibliography: Tractate Gerim, ed. G. Polster (text, trans., and notes) in *Angelos* 2, 1926, 1–38. Bill. II, 715–23; I. Levi, 'Le prosélytisme juif', *REJ* 50, 1905, 1–9; 51, 1906, 1–31. Earlier bibliography in Schürer III, 150 n. 1, ET II.2, 292 n. 232. Schürer himself (150–88, ET, 292–327) deals with the success of Jewish proselytizing and the different categories of proselyte; 168f., ET, 308f., he touches on the questions we are about to examine, but only very briefly and not very usefully since the only source he uses is the Mishnah.

[11] On the antiquity of proselyte baptism as an initiation ceremony see Bill. I, 102–8; also my book *Die Kindertaufe in den ersten vier Jahrhunderten*, Göttingen 1958, 29–34, ET, *Infant Baptism in the First Four Centuries*, London 1960, 24–29.

[12] Cf. M. Nidd. vii.3: there are places almost entirely peopled with proselytes.

[13] In *Ant.* 13.319 Josephus appeals to a passage, which he quotes, from Strabo, now lost.

[14] Cf. Schürer III, 126f., and 150ff., ET II.2, 273ff., 291ff.; J. Leipoldt, *Antisemitismus in der alten Welt*, Leipzig 1933.

[15] Schürer III, 177 (ET omits).

[16] b. Ker. 81a = 9a; Gerim ii.5. The sacrifice usually consisted of a pair of doves.

It was in Jerusalem during the last decades BC that there were three Gentiles converted to Judaism, who were rejected by Shammai but welcomed by Hillel.[17] Another event, recorded in connection with a dispute between the schools of Shammai and Hillel, belongs to the period before AD 30. The Shammaites declared admissible the baptism of a convert on the day of his circumcision, but the Hillelites required an interval of seven days between circumcision and baptism (M. Pes. viii.8; M. Eduy. v.2; T. Pes. vii.13, 167), because they attributed to the Gentile the same impurity as a corpse. The text adds an illustration of the older practice, that of the Shammaites (T. Pes. vii.13, 167; j. Pes. viii.8, 36b.47): 'There were in Jerusalem soldiers as ['as' in j. Pes., 'and' in T. Pes.] doorkeepers; [on 14 Nisan] they received baptism and ate the Passover in the evening' ['although they had been circumcised that day' must be added to complete this, as M. Pes. viii.8 and b. Pes. 92a Bar. show]. Unfortunately we know no more of this story, so we do not know of which soldiers it speaks. One thing only is certain—these were Gentiles converted to Judaism (according to the context of the passage), and this took place before AD 30 because, as the New Testament shows the Shammaite point of view was no longer in force at the time of Jesus.[18] Between AD 30 and 33 we meet in Jerusalem Nicholas, a proselyte from Antioch who became a member of the early Christian Church (Acts 6.5). Finally, in connection with proselytes in Jerusalem, we should remember meeting some distinguished teachers in the Holy City who were of proselyte descent (p. 235).[19] One 'Judah, son of Laganion the proselyte',[20] and a proselyte called Mary[21] are mentioned in Jerusalem ossuaries.

Let us look at the *origin* of Palestinian proselytes, particularly those of Jerusalem. Most of them came from regions near the boundaries of Jewish territory. Idumea was the home of the Herodian royal family.

[17] b. Shab. 31a Bar.; *ARN*, Rec. A, ch. 15, Goldin 79ff. In this context too are the traditions concerning Hillel and the proselyte Ben He-He (b. Hag. 9b, cf. Bacher, *Ag. Tann.* I, 8f.).

[18] See my article 'Der Ursprung der Johannestaufe', *ZNW* 28, 1929, 312–20; again John 18.28, cf. Matt. 8.8: Gentile houses in Jesus' time were considered unclean by a corpse. Likewise in *Ant.* 18.94.

[19] Cf. also T. Sukk. i.1, 192.11; j. Sukk. i.1, 51d.24: it was said that the seven sons of Queen Helena of Adiabene, who was converted to Judaism, were all scribes (*talmīdē ḥakāmīm*). See further p. 331 n. 71, the explanation by R. Joshua of Deut. 10.18.

[20] *CIJ* II, 1385, Greek. But this inscription may be a falsification.

[21] *CIJ* II, 1390, Hebrew.

The mothers of the two scribes mentioned earlier (p. 235), R. Joḥanan (*c.* AD 40)[22] and Abba Saul (*c.* AD 60) came from Auranitis and Batanea respectively. Since 23 BC both these regions formed part of the dominion of Herod the Great; from 4 BC to AD 34 they belonged to the tetrarchy of Philip, and after AD 53 to the dominion of King Agrippa II.

Again, because of Deut. 23.4–9 there were discussions on admitting Ammonites and Moabites for conversion,[23] and the question arose as to whether Edomite and Egyptian proselytes of both sexes could marry Jews immediately on conversion.[24] These were no mere theoretical debates, as is shown by the following reports: In the time of Rabban Gamaliel II (after AD 90) an Ammonite proselyte called Judah was admitted to conversion in the house of study at Jabneh (M. Yad. iv.4; T. Yad. ii.17f., 683; b. Ber. 28a Bar.);[25] and among the pupils of R. Aqiba there was an Egyptian proselyte called Minjamin[26] who was married to an Egyptian proselyte woman (T.

---

[22] I read 'R. Joḥanan *ben ha-ḥōrōnīt*' with T. Sukk. ii.3, 193, Erfurt MS; T. Eduy. ii.2, 457, Erfurt MS; M. Sukk. ii.7 in *ed. princ.* of Babli, Venice 1522, and the Munich MS of Babli. However there is strong evidence for the reading 'Joḥanan *ben ha-ḥōrōnī*', cf. H. Bornhäuser, *Sukka (Die Mischna)* Berlin 1935, 69f., who leaves the question open.

[23] Deut. 23.4 forbids the acceptance of Ammonites and Moabites into the community of Israel. As it makes no mention of women of either nation, it was concluded that women were not forbidden (M. Yeb. viii.3). The reproach made to Ammonites and Moabites in Deut. 23.5 applied only to men, not to women (j. Yeb. viii.3, 9c.9; b. Yeb. 77a; Siphre Deut. 23.4, 249, 50c); from the story of Ruth the Moabitess and Naomi the Ammonitess (I Kings 14.21) it was concluded that God had 'loosed the bonds' (Ps. 116.16) binding the women of Moab and Ammon (b. Yeb. 77a). Some went even further: M. Yad. iv.4 shows that about AD 90 the whole of Deut. 23.4 was no longer carried out, but was applied only to ancient times. Cf. K. H. Rengstorf, *Jebamot* (coll. *Die Mischna*), Giessen 1929, 104–6; Bill. IV, 378ff.

[24] According to Deut. 23.8–9, only third-generation proselytes from Edom and Egypt could belong to the community of Israel. This was applied to both men and women (here too R. Simeon, *c.* AD 150, excluded women: M. Yeb. viii.3; Siphre Deut. 23.9, 253, 50c), and this was taken to mean that two generations of Edomite and Egyptian proselytes, counting from the time of conversion (T. Kidd. v.4, 342), could not marry a Jew (M. Yeb. viii.3). As shown in T. Yad. ii.17, 683 and T. Kidd. v.4, 342, from AD 90 this rule was taken as applying to ancient times, and now no longer in force.

[25] The decision of the majority was against Gamaliel's vote.

[26] The Vienna MS and older editions (against Zuckermandel) say 'Benjamin'. R. de Vaux, 'Binjamin—Minjamin', *RB* 45, 1936, 400–2 takes the view (without knowing our passage) that Minjamin is another form of Binjamin, and that the name Minjamin-Binjamin expresses membership of the tribe of Benjamin. Our passage, about an Egyptian proselyte with the name Minjamin, must considerably modify this opinion.

Kidd. v.4, 342). Nicholas the proselyte, a member of the early Christian Church in Jerusalem (Acts 6.5), is mentioned in connection with the capital of the Roman province of Syria. The discussion on the acceptability of the Qarduans, i.e. the Armenians (Qardu is the biblical Ararat) and the Palmyrenes as proselytes (b. Yeb. 16a–b, Bar.; j. Yeb. i.6, 3a.59ff., *et passim*) was occasioned by concrete instances (the Hillelites supported them, the Shammaites opposed), as we know from ossuaries found at Sha'fat, three kilometres north of Jerusalem, which doubtless formed part of a cemetery for the Jewish Diaspora; there are Palmyrene names there, some written in Palmyrene writing.[27] We find too a mention of a certain Miriam of Palmyra offering a Nazirite sacrifice in Jerusalem (M. Naz. vi.11; T. Naz. iv.10, 299); she was perhaps a proselyte.[28] From an even more distant country, the kingdom of Parthia, came the proselytes of Adiabene, at their head the royal family of Adiabene whom we meet in Jerusalem during the last decades before AD 70 and during the revolt (66–70).[29] Even further to the east was the country of Nahum the Mede (*c.* AD 50; M. Shab. ii.1 *et passim*); we do not know whether his ancestors were Jews from Media or native-born Medes, the former seems even more likely.[30]

What was the *legal status* of proselytes? The ruling that the converted Gentile must be considered 'in all things as an Israelite' (b. Yeb. 47b) does not mean that the proselyte enjoyed the same rights as a full Israelite, but merely that he was bound, like all Jews, to observe the whole Law (Gal. 5.3; Mek. Ex. 12.49, 7c). The legal status of the 'stranger' (*gēr* = proselyte) was contained in the following principle: '*ēn 'āb lᵉgoy*: 'the heathen has no father.'[31] In this legal principle, fundamental to the ancient laws on proselytes, we find reflected the extraordinarily pessimistic judgement of rabbinic Judaism (Bill. III, 62–74) on the heathen and particularly on their moral life:

---

[27] F.-M. Abel, *RB* 10, 1913, 262–77, and *CIJ* II, 1214–39.

[28] S. Klein, *Jüdisch-palästinisches Corpus inscriptionum*, Vienna and Berlin 1920, 25 n. 5.

[29] See pp. 13f., 24, 67f., 92, 129. We find in Jerusalem, on a sarcophagus of the tombs of the royal family of Adiabene, the bilingual inscription 'Queen Sadda' in Hebrew and Syriac, which has aroused must interest; see e.g. S. Klein, *op. cit.*, 26; *CIJ* II, 1388.

[30] Since proselyte descendants seem to have been known by their mother's name (p. 235) on the Jewish principle that Gentiles, have no legitimate father (cp. following note).

[31] Ruth R. 1.8 (Son. 35) a saying of R. Meir (*c.* AD 150); b. Yeb. 98a; *Pesiqta rabbati* 23–24, 122a.11.

all heathen women, even married women, were suspected of having practised prostitution,[32] and so on principle it was taken that no Gentile knew his own father (Bill. I, 710 n. 1). So we see why scribes of Gentile origin, such as R. Johanan 'son of the Hauranite woman' (c. AD 40) and Abba Saul 'son of the Batanean woman' (c. AD 60) were called after their mothers (p. 322)—'they had no fathers.'

It was probably not until much later—but certainly in Tannaitic times—that even relationship to his mother was denied the proselyte if she were still a heathen when he was born. This was by invocation of the principle that 'at his conversion (to Judaism), the proselyte is like an infant new-born'.[33] Actually this sentence meant originally—as its wording and usage in the older passage (b. Yeb. 48b Bar.; Gerim ii.6) and the existence of similar expressions in rabbinic literature (Pesiqta rabbati 16, 84a.8; Cant. R. 8.1 on 8.2, Son. 303) and the New Testament (see 7 lines down) shows—that 'God forgives the proselyte all his sins (at the moment of his conversion)' (j. Bikk. iii.3, 65c.61).[34] Thus the comparison of a proselyte with a new-born child is originally a religious one, and expresses in a vivid way the blessings of salvation which conversion to Judaism brings, the *tertium comparationis* being the innocence of the new-born child. When Paul says that by baptism men become 'a new creation' (Gal. 6.15; II Cor. 5.17), when I Peter 2.2 compares baptized persons with 'children new-born', we see here the image[35] in the same religious sense.

It was only later that this comparison of the proselyte to a new-born child became a legal principle; then it meant that the converted heathen must be regarded as newly created, i.e. 'without father,

---

[32] Cf. M. Yeb. vi.5: 'The harlot [Lev. 21.7] refers only to a female proselyte or to a freed bondwoman, or to one [Israelite by birth] that suffered connexion of the nature of fornication.'

[33] b. Yeb. 48b Bar., 22a, 62a, 97b; Gerim ii.6 ed. Polster, *Angelos* 2, 1926, 6f.

[34] See particularly b. Yeb. 48b Bar., where R. Jose (c. AD 150) explicitly rejects the theory that the proselytes' sufferings and vexations were a punishment for their failure to keep the Noachic precepts incumbent upon Gentiles before their conversion. R. Jose (Gerim ii.6: R. Judah, c. AD 150) bases his rejection on this principle: 'The proselyte on his conversion is like a new-born child.' Thus according to him this sentence means that sins committed before conversion are forgiven him (Gerim ii.6: 'They are remitted unto him [by God]').

[35] We find in Paul's teaching (Rom. 6.2ff. *et passim*) Hellenistic influence in his explanation of Christian baptism, but these are only secondary. Cf. my article 'Der Ursprung der Johannestaufe', *ZNW* 28, 1929, 312–20, which shows the dependence of I Cor. 10.1ff., on the teaching about baptism in later Judaism and early Christianity.

without mother nor any (other) relation'.[36] Consequently this era refused the proselytes any relationship with their mother as well. This hardening attitude, resulting partly from the isolationism of Judaism in face of the spread of Christianity, expressed itself too in many ways elsewhere.[37] We see it in the significant pronouncement by R. Helbo (c. 300), that proselytes were as bad for Israel as leprosy (b. Nidd. 13b and par.). But, as we have just seen, the legal interpretation of the comparison of a proselyte with a new-born child is later;[38] it was still being discussed in the fourth century (b. Yeb. 22a, 97b) and R. Naḥman for example did not recognize it (b. Yeb. 22a). It was on the old legal principle that 'the heathen has no father'[39] that the ancient laws about proselytes were built, such laws as those on incest relating to proselytes (see Bill. III, 353–8).

The ancient laws developed from this legal principle, were chiefly concerned with *matrimonial right*, on which we must note:

(*a*) Female proselytes were not fit for marriage with a priest (T. Kidd. v.3, 341; j. Yeb. viii.3, 9b.29; *CA* 1.31). Before their conversion they might have been guilty of prostitution, and according to Lev. 21.7 the 'harlot' has no right of marriage with a priest (M. Yeb. vi.5; Siphra Lev. 21.7, 47b; see p. 216).[40] In the second century an attempt was made to soften this severe ruling, so R. Simeon b. Yoḥai (c. 150) gave an exception: 'A proselyte woman who was converted before the age of three years and one day may marry a priest' (j. Kidd. iv.6, 66a.10).[41] In the second century also there were

---

[36] Rashi on b. Sanh. 57b Bar.; Bill. III, 354 n. 1.

[37] But there were also contrary tendencies more favourable to proselytes, see p. 326.

[38] The idea that the proselyte is 'without mother' is found for the first time in Bar. b. Sanh. 57b–58a, which says that the proselyte has no relationship after the flesh with his mother unless she was converted during her pregnancy: 'A proselyte born but not conceived in sanctity [both parents were heathen, but they, or at least the mother, became converts before his birth] possesses kin on his mother's side but not on his father's.' Thus, only if the mother of a proselyte is converted before his birth is his blood relationship to her recognized; and this means that if she were not converted when he was born, the proselyte is 'without father or mother'. T. Yeb. xii.2, 254 confirms this explanation.

[39] This is how we must correct the explanation given by K. H. Rengstorf in his article γεννάω κ.τ.λ., in *TWNT* I, 1933, 666 lines 14ff.

[40] It may be that this suspicion of immorality which was laid on proselytes was behind the teaching of R. Aqabya b. Mehalalel (c AD 70) who wished to exclude the female proselytes and freed slaves from the prescriptions in Num. 5.11–29 for the woman suspected of adultery. He was alone in this, and in fact was put under a ban for refusing to abandon his rigorous attitude (Siphre Num. 5.12, 7, 3b and par.).

[41] As scriptural proof, Num. 31.18 was quoted: 'But all the (Midianite) women children, that have not known man by lying with him, keep alive for yourselves',

discussions to decide to what extent the ban on priestly marriages for proselytes applied also to their descendants (M. Kidd. iv.6–7; cf. M. Bikk. ii.5; for details see p. 216 n. 219), and the more lenient view prevailed (that of R. Jose b. Ḥalaphta, c. 150; he allowed the daughter of two proselyte parents to marry a priest, b. Kidd. 78b; the halākāh was of the same opinion). However, the priests opposed this relaxation with a passive resistance (pp. 220f.; cf. M. Eduy. viii.3); they and their daughters[42] kept themselves as far as possible from proselytes and their descendants (b. Kidd. 78b; j. Bikk. i.5, 64a.27).

(b) Beyond this, proselytes of both sexes could marry without restriction among other groups of the population (M. Kidd. iv.1; see p. 272), i.e. among Levites, Israelites of pure descent,[43] and Israelites with a slight or grave blemish[44] in their ancestry.[45] The biblical precepts concerning incest applied to proselytes only as they related to consanguinity on the mother's side (Bill. III, 353–358); the rabbinic laws, which applied to the second degree of relationship,[46] were not applicable to them (b. Yeb. 22a). The right which the proselyte had of contracting a valid marriage with, for example, a bastard or with his own half-sister,[47] is explained by the 'lesser sanctity' (cf. b. Yeb. 22a) of proselytes, as opposed to the 'greater sanctity' of Israelites of pure descent, kept strictly apart.[48]

---

and added to it was: 'And Pinhas [the priest] was among them [i.e. the men addressed in Num. 31.18, thus 'yourselves' in the scriptural text, included priests]'; par. b. Yeb. 60b; b. Kidd. 78a. Cf. also j. Bikk. i.5, 64a.31 et passim.

[42] R. Judah (c. AD 150) said: 'Proselyte, freedman and ḥālāl may marry with the daughter of a priest' (T. Kidd. v.2, 341; b. Kidd. 72b Bar.), but this did not represent ancient teaching nor general custom.

[43] There were, however, those who said 'Proselytes . . . may not enter into the community (i.e. may not marry legitimate Israelites)', T. Kidd. v.1, 341.

[44] Later marriage between a proselyte and a bastard was forbidden, as R. Judah said (c. AD 150), b. Kidd. 67a Bar., 72b Bar.

[45] According to M. Yeb. viii.2, the marriage of a proselyte woman even to a man with mutilated or crushed organs was valid; such a union was forbidden to Jews by birth, because of Deut. 23.2.

[46] To safeguard the laws on incest in Lev. 18, the rabbis had added to the forbidden degrees of relationship another degree on each side, above and below. These eight rabbinic (not biblical) degrees of forbidden relationship (šᵉniyyōt) are given in T. Yeb. iii.1, 243; b. Yeb. 21a Bar.

[47] This marriage was allowed when brother and sister were both proselytes with the same father and different mothers. In this case, brother and sister were not related, since the proselyte 'has no father'.

[48] From this there came further details on matrimonial laws: two brothers, one of whom was conceived before his mother's conversion, were not held by obligation of levirate marriage (M. Yeb. xi.2) for legally they had not the same father; this

The *right of succession* is very closely bound up with the matrimonial right. Two questions arise in this connection: (1) What right has the proselyte to inherit from his heathen father? (2) What right of inheritance from their father have the children of a proselyte whom he begot before his conversion?

As to the first question: the proselyte was allowed to take by inheritance from his heathen father only things, such as money and crops, which were not connected with the worship of idols. 'If a proselyte and a Gentile (who were brothers) inherited jointly from their father who was a Gentile, the proselyte may say to the other, 'Do thou take what pertains to idolatry and I will take the money' or 'Do thou take the wine (which might be used for libations) and I will take the produce' (M. Dem. vi.10; T. Dem. vi.12, 57).[49] True, the proselyte had no right to profit directly or indirectly, as in the example given, from that part of his inheritance from his heathen father which had been or could have been used for worship if idols, but he was permitted to profit indirectly, so that he had no occasion to lapse into paganism.[50]

As to the second question: here again the principle of 'no father' came into play. The children begotten before the proselyte was converted could therefore claim no part of the estate, even if they were converted with their father. For example: 'If a man borrows from a proselyte whose sons have become proselytes with him (to Judaism) he need not (if the proselyte dies) repay the debt to the sons' (M. Shebi. x.9). Rabbinic law says that the wife usually has no right of inheritance (M.B.B. viii.1); so the inheritance of a proselyte who 'died without heirs'—i.e. without children conceived after his con-

---

was even more so when the two brothers were born before their mother's conversion (M. Yeb. xi.2). In the case of a proselyte woman conceived or born before her mother's conversion, whose husband accuses her of not being a virgin when he married her, it was not permitted to use the ruling about paying an indemnity to her father (Deut. 22.19) if the accusation were false, nor the ruling that she should be taken to her father's door, and there stoned (Deut. 22.21) if the accusation were true, M. Ket. iv.3; for indeed in law she had no father. Cf. also M. Ket. i.2, 4; iii.1–2: for the marriage contract etc., only those proselytes who were less than three years and one day when converted were put on an equal footing with Jews by birth; for only in that one case was it believed to be certain that they were virgins.

[49] But certain particularly scrupulous proselytes acted like Aquila, the translator of the Bible (c. AD 120), who 'made more rigorous decisions for himself and threw his share [of the inheritance from his heathen father] into the Dead Sea', T. Dem. vi.13, 57.

[50] W. Bauer, *Dammai* (coll. *Die Mischna*), Giessen 1931, 50f.

version—was regarded as without owner. This applied to all his goods (b. Gitt. 39a; Gerim iii.8),[51] and so included his fields (b. Gitt. 39a; Gerim iii.9–10), cattle (M.B.K. iv.7; Gerim iii.13), slaves (Gerim iii.8, 13) and the money due to him (M. Shebi. x.9; M.B.K. ix.11); the only exception was that part of his possessions which were owing to a creditor (Gerim iii.11–12), or to the widow on the basis of a marriage settlement.[52] Anyone at all could appropriate these ownerless goods (Gerim iii.8),[53] and the one who first carried out the 'seizure' of possession' (Gerim iii.9–10. 13) could keep them. Thus slaves who were of age could declare themselves free (Gerim iii.13; iii.8; cf. b. Gitt. 39a; b. Kidd. 23a) and take for example the very flocks they were tending (Gerim iii.13); the widow too could carry out this 'seizure' of ownerless goods (Gerim iii.11).

Now let us turn to the right of the proselyte to *hold office*. He was forbidden a seat on the great Sanhedrin (M. Hor. i.4–5; pp. 297f.) and on the twenty-three member tribunals which tried capital crimes (M. Sanh. iv.2; b. Sanh. 36b); if he participated in a decision taken by one of these courts, the decision was invalid (M. Hor. i.4). Nor could he sit on the three-member court[54] before whom the *ḥaliṣāh*, the removal of the shoe to refuse levirate marriage (Deut. 25.9–10) took place. On the other hand he was not prohibited from making a decision in lawsuits over goods, as a member of a three-member court.[55]

Finally it must be emphasized that the lack of an authentic Israelite genealogy had consequences for the proselytes which were not merely legal but religious as well. The proselyte had no part in the vicarious virtues of Abraham (Num. R. 8.9 on 5.10, Son.

---

[51] Gerim iii.8–13 deals with the full proselyte, in contrast to iii.1ff., which is concerned with the half-proselyte (*gēr tōšāb*).

[52] *Ketubbāh* (Gerim iii.11). However, the creditor and the widow had to prove their claims in time.

[53] Here we must read *qetānīm*, with b. Gitt. 39a: 'If the servants are still minors, a man could acquire by taking them for himself (instead of lawful acquisition, e.g. buying from the market)' Gerim iii.9–13.

[54] Siphre Deut. 25.10, 291.53a; *Midrash ha-gadol* on Deut. 25.10, ed. D. Hoffmann, *Midrasch Tannaïm*, Berlin 1908–9, 167. This prohibition was based on the words 'in Israel' in Deut. 25.10, because the same word in v.7 was said to exclude proselytes. L. Ginzberg, *Eine unbekannte jüdische Sekte* I, New York 1922, 126, doubts if the disqualification of proselytes from public office should be taken as an ancient *halākāh*, and there is some truth in that, see p. 298.

[55] M. Sanh. iv.2, and Obadiah di Bertinoro on this passage; b. Sanh. 36b. In some places, it is true, the proselyte seems to have been excluded completely from public office, b. Kidd. 76b.

232), for these were reserved for the blood-descendants of the patriarch (Bill. I, 117ff.).[56] The proselyte, then, had to rely absolutely on his own merits for justification.[57]

By contrast, with regard to *charity for the poor*, proselytes were on an equal footing with impoverished Israelites.[58] The humane social legislation of the Old Testament always demanded that the stranger (*gēr*) in need should have a share in the poor relief; but rabbinic exegesis restricted the original meaning of *gēr* by seeing it as a designation of the proselyte. The needy proselyte, then, had the following rights:

(*a*) At harvest time he was entitled to the poor man's share, i.e. to harvest round the edge of the field (from Lev. 19.10; 23.22), to glean the field (Lev. 23.22) and the vine (Lev. 19.10; Deut. 24.21), and to take the forgotten sheaf (Deut. 24.19); all these biblical texts refer explicitly to the *gēr*.[59]

(*b*) Further, from Deut. 14.29; 26.12 the poor proselyte was taken into consideration when the poor man's tithe was distributed.[60] Tob. 1.6–8 (reading in *Sinaiticus*, see p. 135) shows that this ruling was actually observed.

(*c*) Finally he had a right to public assistance (b. A.Zar 20a): there is a story often told[61]—much exaggerated after the manner of legends —giving an example of this for a well-known family in Jerusalem: 'A family called Nebellata[62] (Antebila,[63] Nabtela)[64] was living in

---

[56] The proselyte did not belong, M. Bikk. i.4. The opposing view that the proselyte could, on the basis of Gen. 17.5, be counted among Abraham's descendants, did not appear before the second century: T. Bikk. i.2, 100, first limited to the Qenites, then generalized, j. Bikk. i.4, 64a.15.

[57] b. Kidd. 70b: 'Rabba bar Rab Huna (*c.* AD 300) said: This is the superiority of the Israelites (legitimate, from the context) over the proselytes: While to the Israelites it is said (unconditionally), I will be their God and they shall be my people (Jer. 31.33), to the proselytes it is said (a condition implied), He that hath boldness to approach me, saith the Lord . . . Ye shall be my people and I will be your God (Jer. 30.21, 22)'.

[58] So it happened that some Gentiles sought conversion solely in order to benefit from public charity, i.e. 'to be cared for like the (Israelite) poor', *Yalqut Shimeoni* i.645 on Lev. 23.22, Zolkiew 1858; 471.46.

[59] Siphra Lev. 19.10, 44d affirms that *gēr* here means full proselyte.

[60] On this too, Siphre Deut. 14.29, 110, 42c affirms as in n. 59.

[61] T. Peah iv.11, 23, and with some differences j. Peah viii.8, 21a. With no genealogy of the family: Siphre Deut. 14.29, 110.42c; Siphre Deut. 26.12, 303, 53d; *Midrash ha-gadol* on Deut. 26.12, ed. Hoffmann, 179.

[62] Reading in Tosephta, Erfurt MS. On the basis of Neh. 11.34, where Nebellat is mentioned as a place name, S. Klein, in *MGWJ* 77, 1933, 189f., is in favour of this reading. H. S. Horovitz and L. Finkelstein, *Siphre zu Deuteronomium* in *Corpus*

Jerusalem, and traced its genealogy back to Arauna the Jebusite (thus they were proselytes).[65] The teachers granted them (when they became needy) 600 shekels of gold (as aid); they (the teachers) did not wish them (the family) to leave Jerusalem' (T. Peah iv.11, 23). We can take it that this was an actual happening, and that thanks to public assistance a family in Jerusalem which had fallen on hard times was saved from having to leave the city. As the amount of assistance they received was extraordinarily high, from the story.[66] this family must have been very rich and influential before.[67] Later tradition[68] considered this to be a family of proselytes, which shows that proselytes had a share in poor relief as a matter of course.

In practical, everyday life the legal restrictions placed on proselytes did not play a large part; heathen origin was a 'slight blemish'.[69] If, according to the Damascus Document (pp. 259ff.), the Essenes observed the rule that in every settlement of their sect members must be registered according to origin: priests, Levites, Israelites, proselytes (CD xiv.3–6), this was probably not to underline the inferior position of proselytes in the sect, but much more likely to make a

---

Tannaiticum 3.3), Breslau 1936, 171, 9 (110 on Deut. 14.29) agree with this.

[63] Reading of Yerushalmi; H. Grätz, 'Eine angesehene Proselytenfamilie Agathobulos in Jerusalem', in *MGWJ* 30, 1881, 289–294, takes Antebila as corresponding to Agathobolus, but it is difficult to support this.

[64] Tosephta, Vienna MS, and Siphre Deut. 26.12, 303.

[65] The genealogical reference is lacking in Siphre Deut. 110 and 303, and also in the *Midrash ha-gadol*, see p. 329 n. 61.

[66] Supposing the weight of a shekel to be 16.36 gr., these 600 shekels would represent 20 pounds of gold, in round numbers.

[67] On a principle of acts of charity the assistance given must be in conformity with the condition of the person assisted, i.e. according to the former way of life of the impoverished person, cf. Bill. I, 346f., and IV, 538, 544f.

[68] In one part of the tradition (p. 329 n. 61) the words which connect the story with descendants of Arauna (and therefore proselytes) are missing. The fact is very rightly questioned by S. Klein, 'Zur jüdischen Altertumskunde', *MGWJ* 77, 1933, 189–193. He takes it as referring originally to descendants of the *bᵉnē 'Arnān*, mentioned in I Chron. 3.21, who were descendants of Zerubbabel. Even if this is correct, the fact still remains that later in the second century this was applied to a family of proselytes.

[69] So Josephus sometimes calls proselytes Ἰουδαῖοι (*Ant.* 18.258), cf. W. Gutbrod, art. Ἰσραήλ κ.τ.λ., in *TWNT* III, 1938, 372f. Philo according to the views on p. 302 n. 125, has a very good opinion of proselytes in *De virt.* 187–227 *et passim*; Abraham, who passed from polytheism to monotheism, is 'the standard of nobility for all proselytes', 219. Truth to tell, a certain disdain for proselytes appears in rabbinic literature, e.g. in the ruling forbidding them to keep a Jewish slave (b. B.M. 71a Bar.), or the principle whereby their past must be forgotten (M.B.M. iv.10).

definite line between proselytes and Israelites tainted with a grave blemish, 'the excrement of the community',[70] for which see pp. 337ff. We have two significant facts which demonstrate the social position of proselytes before the destruction of the Temple: we have already met scribes whose mothers were proselytes,[71] and also the royal family of Adiabene, converts to Judaism, were always spoken of with great pride.[72] The early Christian Church totally rejected any discrimination against proselytes among its members; Acts 6.5 tells how a proselyte belonged to the committee of seven who had charge of poor relief.

The *Herodian royal family* too belonged to the proselyte sector of the population. Herod the Great had no Jewish blood in his veins. His father Antipater was from an Idumean family (*Ant.* 14.8; *BJ* 1.123; see also *Ant.* 14.403); his mother Kypros came from the family of an Arab sheik.[73] In vain did Herod try to hide his proselyte origin, that he was what Josephus calls a 'half-Jew' (*Ant.* 14.403), by having his court historian, Nicholas of Damascus, spread it around that he was descended from the first Jews who returned from exile in Babylon (*Ant.* 14.9);[74] he even tried to claim a priestly descent, according to Strabo,[75] and descent from the Hasmonean royal family, according to the Babylonian Talmud (b. B.B. 3b, 4a; cf. b. Kidd. 7ob). Was Herod as some claim, a (freed) slave,[76] more precisely the grandson of a temple slave in the shrine of Apollo at Ascalon?[77] We cannot truthfully answer yes to that question. It may be a malevolent in-

---

[70] L. Ginzberg, *Eine unbekannte jüdische Sekte* I, New York 1922, 124f.

[71] See p. 235, cf. also Gen. R. 28.20 (Son. 638); R. Joshua (*c.* AD 90) sees in the vestments that God, on the basis of Deut. 10.18, promises to give to the proselyte (the word *gēr* always means this in the Midrash) the mantle of honour (of teachers), Bill. II, 843.

[72] See p. 323 n. 29; Schürer III, 169–72, 173, ET II.2, 308–11, 313f.

[73] *BJ* 1.181: τούτῳ γήμαντι γυναῖκα τῶν ἐπισήμων ἐξ ᾿Αραβίας Κύπρον τοὔνομα. *Ant.* 14.121 is disputed; most MSS read πλείστου τότε ἄξιος ἦν (Antipater) καὶ παρ᾽ Ἰδουμαίοις (reading in eight cases; only the Palatinus Vaticanus gr. 14 reads: ᾿Ιουδαίων οἷς), παρ᾽ ὧν ἄγεται γυναῖκα τῶν ἐπισήμων ἐξ ᾿Αραβίας Κύπρον ὄνομα. H. Willrich, *Das Haus des Herodes*, Heidelberg 1929, 172, speaks for a Jewish origin for Kypros; but the variant is too poorly authenticated to be considered as the original text. On the basis of *BJ* 1.181, referred to at the beginning of this note, Schlatter, *Theologie*, 185 n. 1 suggests that the original text read: παρὰ τοῖς Ναβαταίοις.

[74] Josephus rightly rejects this false claim. See further pp. 28lf., on the burning of Jewish genealogical records, ordered by Herod.

[75] ᾿Ιστορικὰ ὑπομνήματα XVI, 765. *Ass. Mos.* vi.2, emphasizes that Herod was not of priestly stock.

[76] b. B.B. 3b; 'Slave of the Hasmonean family', cf. b. Kidd. 7ob. *et passim.*

[77] Julius Africanus, in his *Letter to Aristides*, ed. W. Reichardt (Texte und Untersuchurngen xxxiv. 3), Leipzig 1909, 60 lines 15ff.

vention of Jewish (see n. 76), Samaritan[78] or Christian[79] tradition, especially as it contradicts Josephus' claim of an exalted origin for Antipater (*BJ* 1.123)[80] However if, as seems likely, this quotation goes back to Ptolemy of Ascalon (beginning of the first century AD)[81] the date is a strong argument in favour of its authenticity.

As the descendant of proselytes, perhaps even of freed slaves, Herod had no claim whatsoever to the Jewish royal throne; Deut. 17.15 expressly forbids it: 'One from among your brethren you shall set as king over you; you may not put a foreigner over you, who is not your brother.' Rabbinic exegesis of this passage too excluded proselytes from the monarchy, as we see in b. B.B. 3b: 'He [Herod] said: Who are they who teach, 'one from among. . . .' [etc., Deut. 17.15]? [They said] The Rabbis. He therefore arose and killed all the Rabbis [for their teaching did not please him].'[82] The Pharisees refused to take the oath of fidelity to Herod (*Ant.* 15.370; 17.42). According to the Law, Herod was an illegitimate usurper, and this may have been reason enough for their refusal.

Agrippa I, Herod's grandson, had to suffer indignity from a Rabbi called Simon, who called together the people of Jerusalem and aroused them against the king by demanding 'that he might justly be excluded out of the Temple (more precisely, from the Court of Women and the Court of Israel) since it belonged only to native Jews' (*Ant.* 19.332). Thus Agrippa I, descendant of proselytes, was called a non-Jew, and this exaggeration shows the fierce disdain which characterized the people's contempt for the origin of the Herodian princes. The Mishnah has preserved for us an account of how Agrippa I sought to appease the people's anger by a calculated show of humility.

---

[78] See the chronicle, ed. E. N. Adler and M. Seligsohn, 'Une nouvelle chronique samaritaine', in *REJ* 45, 1092, 76 lines 14–15: 'And Herod was a bastard.' About this chronicle, see my study *Die Passahfeier der Samaritaner* (*BZAW* 59), 1932, 57.

[79] Schürer I, 292 n. 3, ET I.1, 314 n. 3.

[80] True, it is different in *Ant.* 14.491: [ἡ ἀρχὴ]μετέβη δ'εἰς Ἡρώδην τὸν Ἀντιπάτρου οἰκίας ὄντα δημοτικῆς καὶ γένους ἰδιωτικοῦ καὶ ὑπακούοντος τοῖς βασιλεῦσιν. Cf. also p. 282.

[81] Eusebius, *HE* I, 7.12, tells that Julius Africanus said of his evidence on Herod's ancestry (see p. 331 n. 77): καὶ ταῦτα μὲν κοινὰ καὶ ταῖς Ἑλλήνων ἱστορίαις. Now we know that Ptolemy of Ascalon, at the beginning of his work on Herod, had spoken of the origin of Jews and Idumeans (Schürer I, 48f. ET I.1, 57). We may therefore easily surmise that Julius Africanus when referring to 'Greek history' is thinking of the work of Ptolemy of Ascalon and this was his source.

[82] Because, of course, their exegesis excluded proselytes like him from the monarchy. There are other references, too, on this exclusion of proselytes, e.g. b. B.K. 88a.

Deut. 31.10–13 prescribes that there should be a reading of the Law on the evening of the first day (15 Tishri) of the feast of Tabernacles that followed a sabbatical year;[83] the custom had grown up—probably under the Hasmoneans, when king and high priest were the same person—that the king, seated for the occasion on a wooden platform erected in the Court of Women (M. Sot. vii.8), should do this reading of the law.[84] The sabbatical year 40–41 ended on 1 Tishri of the year 41; therefore Agrippa had to read the Law on 15 Tishri 41. He remained standing throughout the reading, to show to the people his humility. But there was a further opportunity to demonstrate it, for 'when he reached, Thou mayest not put a foreigner over thee which is not they brother (Deut. 17.15), his eyes flowed with tears; but they called to him, "Our brother art thou! Our brother art thou! Our brother art thou!"'[85] Historians have disputed whether this story refers to Agrippa I[86] or to Agrippa II.[87] In the second case it would have happened on 15 Tishri, AD 55 or 62 (54–5 and 61–2 were sabbatical years,) but it is far more likely to refer to Agrippa I.[88]

[83] On this subject see my article 'Sabbathjahr'.

[84] Deut. 1.1–6.3; 6.4–9; 11.13–21; 14.22–29; 26.12–15; the section on the king: 17.14–20; 27.1–26; 28.1–69 (M. Sot. vii.8, with variant reading in the MSS, and parallel traditions).

[85] M. Sot. vii.8 and par.; Siphre Deut. 17.15, 157; Midrasch Tannaim, ed. D. Hoffmann, Berlin 1908–9, p. 104, on Deut. 17.15.

[86] D. Hoffmann, Die erste Mischna, Berlin 1882, 15ff., and Magazin für die Wissenschaft des Judenthums 9, 1882, 96ff.; Schürer I, 555, ET I.2, 157; Schlatter, Geschichte Israels, 435 n. 244; Theologie, 83 n. 1, 135 n. 1; Bill. II, 709f.; Jeremias, 'Sabbathjahr', ZNW 27, 1928, 100 n. 9 = Abba, 235 n. 15; V. Aptowitzer, 'Spuren des Matriarchats im jüdischen Schriftttum', HUCA 5, 1928, 277–80.

[87] Derenbourg, Essai, 217; M. Brann,' Biographie Agrippa's II', in MGWJ 19, 1870, 541–548; Büchler, Priester, 12ff. Büchler appeals to (a) j. Sot. vii.7, 22a.31 Bar.: 'R. Hananiah b. Gamaliel (c. AD 120) said: Many were slain in that day because they flattered him.' As there is no evidence of an uprising in AD 41, this must refer to Agrippa II. Büchler however overlooks that the context speaks of the Passover feast; This passage obviously refers to the count of animals which Agrippa II ordered at a Passover (T. Pes. iv.3, 163; cf. BJ 6.424) where many were crushed to death in the press. This event has been confused, as is the way of legendary tales, with M. Sot. vii.8, which is indeed referred to Agrippa II, but this has no historical value. (b) Büchler also appeals to T. Sot. vii.16, 308: 'They say in the name of R. Nathan (c. AD 160): The Israelites made themselves guilty of destruction because they flattered Agrippa.' Mention is made previously of a feast of Tabernacles, in which R. Tarphon took part, and he was still a young man at the time of the destruction of the Temple in AD 70; thus it can only refer to the year 62.—But it is not stated that R. Nathan's words refer to that same feast in which R. Tarphon took part.

[88] For the following reasons: (a) the narrative in M. Sot. vii.8 agrees with the constant efforts made by Agrippa I to win the favour of the Law-fearing circles (Acts 12.3 et passim). (b) In AD 62 there was sharp conflict between Agrippa II and

Whenever it took place, the incident is utterly characteristic of the people's attitude to the Herodian royal family. The Herodians themselves knew very well that as descendants of proselytes they had no right to the throne and must pay due regard to public opinion. It was only the tears of a king publicly admitting his inferiority which won the people's sympathy and called forth the pitying cry, 'āḥīnū 'attāh, which seems to hark back to Deut. 23.8: 'Thou shalt not abhor an Edomite; for he is thy brother.'

3. Freed Gentile slaves

The institution of manumitting slaves was borrowed from Roman law. These manumitted slaves formed the third section of the community of Israelites tainted with a slight racial blemish. They were men and women of Gentile birth (there was a different law governing Jewish slaves, see pp. 312ff.) who had passed as bondslaves into the service of a Jew, and had then accepted circumcision and baptism,[89] and later on were freed.[90]

The manumission[91] could come about in several ways:

(a) by the free decision of the owner (b. Gitt. 38b *et passim*)[92] which he could express by tacit recognition,[93] a solemn, sacramental liberation in the synagogue,[94] a clause in his will (M. Peah iii.8 etc.) or a deathbed wish (b. Gitt. 40 a etc.),

---

the leaders of the people with the priesthood (*Ant.* 20, 189ff.). This broke out before Albinus took office (*Ant.* 20.197) and he was certainly in office at the feast of Tabernacles in 62. In such a tense situation a demonstration of sympathy by the people for the king is highly improbable. (c) According to Josephus, *Ant.* 4.209, the high priest had to read the Law at the feast of Tabernacles; so this must have been the practice in the period before the destruction of the Temple, as Josephus saw in case he himself attended the feast of 62 while a young priest of twenty-four years of age. The alteration in the rite, whereby the reading was no longer done by the king but by the high priest, doubtless took place in the year 48 (feast of Tabernacles after the sabbatical year 47–8) when there was no king. In M. Sot. vii.8, it is the king who reads, therefore the event took place before 62.

[89] On this baptism see b. Yeb. 46a–47b Bar., and Bill. I, 1054f.; IV, 724, 744.
[90] Only Gentile slaves who had been circumcised (see pp. 348ff. on circumcision of Gentile slaves) could be freed according to Jewish laws.
[91] Bill. IV, 739–744; Krauss, *TA* II, 98–101.
[92] It was however in dispute whether the master had the right to free his slaves at will, cf. b. B.K. 74b.
[93] This tacit recognition was deemed to have taken place when the master treated the slave as a free man, Bill. IV, 740, 742f.
[94] See the evidence on inscriptions, Schürer III, 23f. 93f. (ET omits); A. Deissmann, *Licht vom Osten* 4th ed., Tübingen 1923, 271 ET, *Light from the Ancient East*, 2nd ed., London 1927, 321.

(b) by the slave buying his freedom, with someone else's help (M. Kidd. i.3; Abadim iii.4),[95]

(c) by means of a forced liberation, decided by a court, if in the presence of witnesses (b. B.K. 74b) an owner knocked out the eye or the tooth of a slave (Ex. 21.26–27), or mutilated him[96] at one of the 'twenty-four tips of members' (M. Neg. vi.7: tips of fingers, toes and ears, tip of nose, of male organ, and nipples in a woman; b. Kidd. 25a Bar.; Abadim iii.4). Slaves could also qualify for half-freedom,[97] but in this case the slave had to sign a bill promising to pay half[98] of his value (M. Gitt. iv.5.) to the remaining owner or owners.

(d) As we have already seen (p. 328) a slave gained his liberty by his master's death, if the master were a proselyte without children, as heirs, conceived after his conversion.[99]

(e) Finally, a slave not yet passed into the full possession of his owner through 'ritual ablution with the object of becoming a slave' (p. 334 n. 89), could gain his own freedom by declaring it a 'ritual ablution with the object of becoming a free man' (Mek Ex. 12.48, 7; b. Yeb. 45b, 46a).

On the whole it must be said that the chances of a Gentile slave obtaining his freedom were very small. If a freedman had accepted the ablution 'with the object of becoming a free man', which was pre-scribed in every case, then all the *potestas* of his former master was at an end, and from then on the freedman was legally the equal of other full proselytes. However the Sadducean courts of priests (pp. 177f.) made distinctions in spite of all. For example, such a court would not allow a freed slave of Tobias, a Jerusalem physician, to testify to see-ing the new moon (M.R. Sh. i.7), thus placing him on a level with a bondslave (M.R. Sh. i.8) who was ineligible for such witness. Freed slaves of both sexes were thus seperated into a special group, apart from full proselytes, and a distinction was also made between their sons and other descendants of proselytes (T. Kidd. iv.15, 341), al-

[95] The Gentile slave himself could neither possess goods nor acquire them. If a Jew sold his Gentile slave to a Gentile or into a foreign land, the Gentile slave must be ransomed, then freed, M. Gitt. iv.6.

[96] b. Kidd. 24a Bar.: a deduction from Ex. 21.26–27, by means of the her-meneutical rule *binyān 'āb*.

[97] This could happen e.g. when two or more people inherited one slave, and one owner gave him his freedom.

[98] Two-sixths or two-thirds etc., depending on the number of owners who had a share in him and the number who renounced their share by freeing him.

[99] In this case the slaves, if adult, could declare themselves free (as goods with-out an owner), Gerim iii.13. b. Kidd. 23a includes slaves under age too.

though prevailing opinion had it that there should be no difference in legal status. The reason for the distinction was that, in the freed slaves, to the stigma of Gentile birth was added a second stigma of their former slavery. This, particularly for a female freed slave, was a heavy moral burden, for it was quite unthinkable that a Gentile slave should never have been violated. That is why the word 'harlot' in Lev. 21.7 is legally explained, in a forthright manner: 'The harlot refers only to a female proselyte, or to a freed bondwoman, or to one that suffered connexion of the nature of fornication' (M. Yeb. vi.5; Siphra Lev. 21.7, 47b; see p. 216 n. 219); thus every freed woman slave was regarded *ipso facto* as a harlot! In view of this she was lower than a proselyte: 'Why does every man require marriage with a proselyte and not with a freed bondwoman? Because it is presumed that the proselyte has remained chaste [if she were still a small child when her parents were converted], while the freed bondwoman is in general a harlot' (T. Hor. ii.11, 477; par. j. Hor. iii.9, 48b.56).

The number of freed slaves was not great, and towards the end of the first century AD the Rabbis were even disputing as to whether after all manumission was permissible.[100] However, it is certain that the prevailing rule and actual practice ruled that it was. Josephus mentions in the Herodian court freed slaves who took part in the funeral rites of Herod the Great (*BJ* 1.673).[101] With regard to Jerusalem, rabbinic literature mentions, in the middle of the first century BC, a freed bondwoman called Karkemith,[102] who was married to a Jew; and elsewhere a freed slave is mentioned (M.R. Sh. i.7). The ossuaries of a primitive cemetery which was discovered at Sha'fat, about two miles north of Jerusalem, carry inscriptions in Hebrew, Palmyrine and Greek.[103] Among other names we find here the names of slaves, and the names Αφρεικανος Φουλειος, Φουλεια Αφρεικανα.[104] It is

[100] They disputed over the sentence in Lev. 25.46: 'Ye shall take your bondmen for ever', whether or not it meant a complete prohibition on manumission, b. Gitt. 38b.

[101] 500 slaves and freedmen. Freed bondmen at the court of Pheroras (*Ant.* 17. 61); Eutychus, freed by Agrippa I (*Ant.* 18.168); Philip son of Jacim, a high-ranking officer in the service of Agrippa II, has freedmen in his household (*Vita* 48 and 51).

[102] M. Eduy. v.6; Siphre Num. 5.12, 7; b. Ber. 19a Bar.; Num. R. 5.31, 56b (Son. 328ff.). On this text see Bill. IV, 309f.; S. Mendelsohn in *REJ* 41, 1900, 32; K. G. Kuhn, *Sifre zu Numeri*, (*Rabbinische Texte* II.3) Stuttgart 1959, 33, who gives a more extensive bibliography.

[103] F.-M. Abel, in *RB* 10, 1913, 262–277; *CIJ* II, 1214–1239.

[104] = Furius Africanus, Furia Africana, Abel, *art. cit.*, 3 and 4, 272f.; *CIJ* II, 1227a and b.

possible but not certain that some of the dead were freed slaves.[105]

The following saying, from Jerusalem, characterizes the social position of freedslaves: 'If your daughter has attained puberty [older than twelve and a half years] free your slave and give [him] to her [as a husband]' (b. Pes. 113a); that is to say, if your daughter is beyond the age of betrothal (Bill. II, 374; twelve or twelve and a half years), have no scruples in giving her in marriage to your freedman. Here we find the freed slave mentioned as a member of the lowest group in the community who could marry an Israelite of pure descent; for immediately after this group in the social hierarchy came the Israelites tainted with grave racial blemish, with whom legitimate Israelites could not marry. We see that freed slaves were treated with much disdain,[106] and it showed a very deep popular contempt that the members of the Herodian royal family were reckoned among them (p. 331 n. 76). The whole of Christian humility is to be seen in Paul's description of a Christian as 'the Lord's freedman' (I Cor. 7. 22), while in matters of conscience and questions of faith the Christian is slave to no man, even if his status is that of a slave (I Cor. 7. 23).

B. ISRAELITES WITH GRAVE RACIAL BLEMISH

We have just been studying those classes, with only slight racial blemish, who were forbidden only marriage into priestly families. Now we turn to groups who were forbidden marriage with Levites also, with legitimate Israelites and with illegitimate descendants of priests.[107] This prohibition, which was based on Deut. 23.2–3, excluded from 'the assembly of the Lord' (Deut. 23.2–3) all Israelites tainted with grave racial blemish, they were the 'excrement of the community' (*pesūlē qāhāl*).

1. *Bastards*

First came the bastards, *mamzērīm*.[108] 'Who is accounted a bastard?

[105] F. Bleckmann, *ZDPV* 38, 1915, 239.

[106] j. Hor. iii.9, 48b.58; 'R. Johanan (d. 279) said: Do not trust a slave until the sixteenth generation [after he has been freed].'

[107] M. Kidd. iv.1 (see p. 272); iii.12; M. Yeb. ii.4; viii.3; ix.2–3; M. Makk. iii.1 (following the text of *ed. princ.*, Naples 1492, and of the Mishnah in *ed. princ.*, of the Babylonian Talmud, Venice 1520ff.).

[108] Originally the word *mamzēr* probably meant the mixed population of the Philistine plain in the Persian era (S.I. Feigin in *The American Journal of Semitic Languages and Literature* 43, 1926, 53–60; M. Noth, *ZAW* 45, 1927, 217). On the meaning of this term in ancient rabbinic literature see A. Büchler, 'Familienreinheit

(*a*) [The offspring from] any [union of] near of kin which is forbidden [in the Law] by "Thou shalt not enter". So R. Aquiba (d. after AD 135). (*b*) Simeon of Teman (*c*. AD 110) says: [The offspring of any union] for which the partakers are liable to extirpation at the hands of heaven. And the *halākāh* [the rule in force] agrees with his words. (*c*) R. Joshua (b. Hananiah, *c*. AD 90) says: [The offspring of any union] for which the partakers are liable to death at the hands of the court [of the land]' (M. Yeb. iv.13).[109] As we can see, the learned men of the second century AD were not in agreement on the legal concept of a bastard. Three opinions were extant:

(*a*) R. Aqiba represented the strictest views. He declares as bastards all offspring of unions forbidden in the Torah (incest, adultery etc);[110] and he excludes only the offspring of a union, forbidden in Lev. 21.14, between the high priest and a widow,[111] an exception based on the same text, Lev. 21.15 ('he shall not profane', *lō yᵉhallēl*, so the children are not *mamzērîm* but *ḥᵃlalîm*). It is characteristic of Aqiba's severity that he goes even further than the text of the biblical Law: he also declares bastard the offspring of a marriage forbidden only by the rabbis. A few examples: he considers bastard the child of a union with a *ḥᵃlūṣāh*,[112] with relations of a *ḥᵃlūṣāh*,[113] with a divor-

---

und Familienmakel in Jerusalem vor dem Jahre 70'. *Festschrift Schwarz*, 140ff., ET, 'Family Purity and Family Impurity in Jerusalem before the Year 70 C.E.', *Studies in Jewish History. The Büchler Memorial Volume*, London 1956, 72ff.; V. Aptowitzer, 'Spuren des Matriarchats im jüdischen Schrifttum', Excursus ii: 'Das Kind einer Jüdin von einem Nichtjuden', *HUCA* 6, 1928, 267–77; A. Büchler, 'Familienreinheit und Sittlichkeit in Sepphoris im zweiten Jahrhundert', *MGWJ* 78, 1934, 126–64.

[109] More detailed in Siphre Deut. 23.2, 248; j. Kidd. iii.14, 64c.44. Cf. too T. Yeb. i.10, 241 (R. Simeon's opinion); j. Yeb. vii.6, 8c.1ff. (R. Joshua's opinion). The opinion of R. Aqiba is often quoted.

[110] b. Kidd. 64a, 68a, 76a. According to Aqiba the child is a bastard even if Scripture mentions no punishment (condemnation to death or extirpation). Thus e.g. the child is a bastard when a husband takes his divorced wife again, if during the interval she has contracted another marriage (cf. p. 339 n. 116); Deut. 24.1–4 forbids this without mentioning a punishment in case of transgression.

[111] b. Kidd. 64a, 68a; b. Ket. 29b: he declares the children *ḥᵃlālîm* and not *mamzērîm*. According to T. Yeb. vi.8, 248, Aqiba would also have excluded the children of a marriage between a priest and a divorcee or a *ḥᵃlūṣāh* (on this see next two notes) although this marriage too was prohibited (p. 217).

[112] = wife of a brother who died childless, whose brother-in-law refuses levirate marriage with her. M. Yeb. iv.12; T. Yeb. vi.5, 247; b. Yeb. 44b. Aqiba appeals to Deut. 25.9: *lō yibneh*; K. H. Rengstorf, *Jebamot* (Coll. *Die Mischna*) Giessen 1929, 64.

[113] M. Yeb. iv.12; T. Yeb. vi.5, 247; b. Yeb. 44b. Aqiba puts the *ḥᵃlūṣāh* on the same level as a divorced woman, and applies Lev. 18.18 to her.

ced woman, whose 'folded and closed'[114] bill of divorce carried the signature of a slave instead of a missing witness (b. Giṭ. 81a Bar.),[115] etc.[116]

(b) The second opinion on the meaning of this term *mamzēr* arises from the observation that unions forbidden in the Torah are sometimes threatened with extirpation, sometimes with death (e.g. Lev. 20.10–16: death; 20.17–21: extirpation). Simeon of Teman, whose opinion was during the second century raised to be the rule in force (M. Yeb. iv.13) declared bastard only those offspring of unions threatened in Scripture with extirpation, i.e. by rabbinic exegesis, with an untimely death through divine judgment. As we see from the grouping in M. Ker. i.1 of the thirty-six faults threatened with extirpation (Bill. I, 272), they were concerned with children born of particular cases of incest.[117]

(c) The third opinion on the meaning of *mamzēr*, defended by R. Joshua, considered as bastards only those children born of a union which, in the Torah, is punishable by death. In M. Sanh. vii.4–xi.6

[114] A bill of divorce was complicated. It was drawn up with one line written and one line left blank; in the blank lines the bill was folded and closed. In this way there was a series of folds; on the outside of each fold there had to be at least one signature of a witness. This complex process was intended to provide an opportunity of reconciliation for impetuous husbands.

[115] The bill of divorce was invalid, so the children were conceived in adultery.

[116] Other cases: (i) M. Yeb. iv.12; T. Yeb. vi.5, 247; j. Yeb. x.1, 10c.62ff.; b. Yeb. 44b: if in defiance of the ban in Deut. 24.1–4 anyone took back his divorced wife after she had remarried in the interval, the child was a bastard, according to Aqiba. (ii) M. Yeb. x.1: if, after a mistaken announcement that her husband had died, a woman remarried, her child was a bastard whether it be her first husband's or her second. Here Aqiba is not actually quoted, but as K. H. Rengstorf has rightly remarked (*Jebamot*, [coll. *Die Mischna*,] *in loco*) this corresponds exactly with his outlook. (iii) M. Yeb. x.3: T. Yeb. xi.6, 253: other instances of false information on the immediate circumstances of the husband's death: the children are bastards. (iv) j. Yeb. x.1, 10c.61: Aqiba says that the child born from the union of a husband with a wife suspected of adultery is a bastard. Other instances: M. Yeb. x.4; T. Yeb. xi.6, 253; T. Giṭt. viii.6, 332; b. Kidd. 64a and par.; b. Yeb. 49a.

[117] Examples of Simeon's opinion: a child born of intercourse with a sister-in-law was a bastard (M. Yeb. x.3, 4; cf. Lev. 18.16); or of intercourse with the sister of the divorced wife (M. Yeb. iv.12; cf. Lev. 18.18). In both these cases the punishment of extirpation is given in Lev. 18.29. Simeon does not count as bastards those children who were conceived during a menstrual period (T. Yeb. vi.9. 248) although the case, according to M. Ker. i.1 (punishment of extirpation) might belong to this group; furthermore, according to M. Yeb. iv.13, Simeon seems not to have counted as bastard the child conceived in adultery, either, though the adultery might belong to the faults mentioned in M. Ker. i.1. Both these things may be explained by the fact that Simeon's opinion is limited to the prohibitions on incest which are punishable by extirpation (T. Yeb. i.10, 241; T. Kidd. iv.16, 341; b. Kidd. 75b).

the four legal forms of the death penalty (stoning, burning, beheading, strangling) are grouped together, and this shows us that according to this third opinion specified cases of incest, and adultery too,[118] resulted in the children being bastards.

The interesting problem is to find which is the oldest view. Who were regarded as bastard in Jerusalem before the destruction of the Temple? Traditional teaching allows only the following conclusion to be drawn. M. Yeb. iv.13 relates: 'R. Simeon b. Azzai (c. AD 120)' said: I found a family register in Jerusalem and in it was written: Such-a-one is a bastard through [a transgression of the law of] thy neighbour's wife.' We see then that in Jerusalem children conceived in adultery were declared bastards, and another fact reinforces this statement: R. Eliezer (c. AD 90), the staunch upholder of the old tradition, puts forward the same idea on many occasions;[119] moreover it was the teaching of Hillel (c. 20 BC) and the teachers of his time,[120] and it is also assumed in Heb. 12.8.

If we look back over the three divergent opinions on the meaning of 'bastard' at the beginning of this section, we see that this last one corresponds to the opinion of R. Aqiba and R. Joshua; on the other hand it is not the opinion of R. Simeon of Teman which was accepted during the second century as the rule in force. It follows that the an-

---

[118] According to R. Joshua children conceived in adultery were bastards; M. Yeb. iv.13 says so explicitly. According to M. Sanh. vii.4–xi.6 the union of a betrothed woman with another man was also threatened by the death penalty. M. Sanh. vii.5 *et al.* A. Büchler, 'Familienreinheit und Sittlichkeit', *MGWJ* 78, 1934, 140, quotes other cases.

[119] b. Nidd. 10a Bar.: children of the wife of an impotent man were bastards. See further b. Ned. 20 a–b.

[120] T. Ket. iv.9, 264 (par. j. Ket. iv.8, 28d.69; b. B.M. 104a Bar.): after their betrothal (and before marriage) Jewish women in Alexandria were taken and violated. Hillel argues, from the fact that they were not married, the rejection of the opinion of doctors of his time who said the children were bastards: 'He [Hillel] said to them [the children]: Bring me your mothers' marriage contracts, They brought them to him and [it appeared that] there was written: So soon as thou enter my house [thus from the time of marriage and not of betrothal, Bill. II, 392] thou shalt be my wife according to the law of Moses and of Israel.' Hillel well knew that at the betrothal the Jews of Alexandria followed an Egyptian custom (I. Heinemann, *Philons griechische und jüdische Bildung*, Breslau 1932 [reprinted Darmstadt 1962], 298 and 301f.) and gave written promises of marriage (Heinemann gives on p. 301 an example of the text), whose wording was different from the marriage contracts (*ketubbāh*) of Palestine (cf. Philo, *De. spec. leg.* III, 72). As, in the present case, there were only written promises of marriage and not marriage contracts, the marriage had not begun with the betrothal; thus the children were not conceived in adultery. This incident implies that Hillel and his contemporary teachers declared the child conceived in adultery to be a bastard.

cient conception of a bastard was more rigorous than in the second century, and we find confirmation of this elsewhere too.[121] Consequently we must assume that the class of population who, with its descendants, was called by that name was quite large. The remark about the 'family register in Jerusalem', in the preceding paragraph, shows that it was well known that there were families with this grave blemish of *mamzēr*,[122] although they did their best, of course, to keep it secret (cf. the incident in Lev. R. 32 on 24.10, Son. 32.7, 416).

What was the legal position of bastards in society? The Bible had ruled: 'A bastard shall not enter into the assembly of the Lord, even to the tenth generation . . .' (Deut. 23.3). Rabbinic exegesis formulated this: 'The *mamzērim* and the *n^etinim* (Temple slaves, see pp. 342f.) are forbidden [to enter the community of Israel, i.e. for sexual union], and forbidden for all time, whether they are males or females' (M. Yeb. viii.3, cf. Siphre Deut. 23.3; 248.50b). This forbids marriage for bastards, and levirate marriage too,[123] into families of priests, Levites, Israelites and illegitimate children of priests (M. Kidd. iv.1; see p. 272). Bastards could marry only into families of proselytes, freed slaves and Israelites with grave racial blemish. If the daughter of a priest, a Levite or a legitimate Israelite forms a union (legitimate marriage being impossible) with a bastard, whatever the circumstances (M. Yeb. vi.2), she is henceforth unfit for marriage with a priest (M. Yeb. vi.2). If she is a priest's daughter, she may no longer eat the heave-offering for priests in her father's house (M. Yeb. vii.5). The

[121] The LXX shows a more extensive (therefore more rigorous) conception of the term when in Deut. 23.3 the translation ἐκ πόρνης is given for *mamzēr*, which figures only twice in the Old Testament (Zech. 9.6: ἀλλογενής, see on this A. Geiger, *Urschrift und Übersetzungen der Bibel*, Breslau 1857, 52–55).—It seems that in the first century AD a unique opinion assumed that even a child born of a Jew and a Gentile woman was a bastard. R. Zadoq, who was a prisoner in Rome after the capture of Jerusalem in 70, repulsed a bondwoman by emphasizing that he was of high-priestly origin and did not wish to swell the number of bastards (*ARN*, Rec. A, ch. 16, 63a, Goldin 84). A. Büchler, 'Familienreinheit und Familienmakel', *Festschrift Schwarz*, 146, ET (see n. 108), 79f., rightly regards this as an extension of the term bastard to include the child born of a Jew and a Gentile woman. V. Aptowitzer's opposing view ('Spuren des Matriarchats im jüdischen Schriftum', *HUCA* 5, 1928, 266f.) is not convincing and his explanation is very artificial. Against him see A. Büchler, *MGWJ* 78, 1934, 134 n. 4.

[122] T. Kidd. v.2, 341: 'The Israelites know the Temple slaves and the bastards among them.'

[123] M. Yeb. ix.1: 'An Israelite who married the daughter of an Israelite and has a bastard brother; a bastard who married a woman that is a bastard and has a brother who is an Israelite; these are cases in which the women are permitted in marriage to their husbands and forbidden to their brothers-in-law [in levirate marriage].' Other instances in ix.2.

child of any such union is a bastard (M. Kidd. iii.12);[124] and this goes for any descendant of a male bastard;[125] the older era seems to have been more indulgent in its judgement on descendants of a female bastard.[126]

With regard to the right of inheritance, we must establish that at the end of the first century the rights of a bastard to inherit were in dispute.[127] They had no right to public office, and if they took part in a decision of the Sanhedrin or the court of twenty-three, the decision was invalidated (M. Hor. i.4; b. Sanh. 36b). The only right permitted them was to be judge in decisions of civil law in a court of three members (b. Sanh. 36b).

When we consider that the stigma of bastardy marked every male descendant (see n. 126 for female descendants) for ever and indelibly, and that a bastard family's share in Israel's final redemption was most vigorously disputed (Bill. IV, 792ff.), we shall understand that the word 'bastard' constituted one of the worst insults to a man; and anyone using it was sentenced to thirty-nine lashes with the whip (b. Kidd. 28a Bar.).

2. Temple slaves, fatherless, foundlings, eunuchs

Among this class of Israelites with grave racial blemish were the Temple slaves, neṯînîm. Josh. 9.27 narrates that Joshua made (lit.

[124] 'If the betrothal was valid (i.e. not forbidden by the law of incest) but transgression befell (by reason of the marriage) the standing of the offspring follows that of the blemished party.'

[125] Only later was the following rule established: 'A female [Gentile] slave is a purification for all the unworthy [i.e. for those with grave blemish in their ancestry]', T. Kidd. v.3, 342. This means that in the union of a bastard with a female (Gentile) slave, the child follows the standing of its mother, and so becomes a slave; but a slave may be freed and so enter the class (see pp. 334ff.) of Israelites with only slight racial blemish who could marry legitimate Israelites. So R. Tarphon (c. AD 100) taught: 'The mamzērîm may become pure. How? If a bastard marries a [Gentile] slave, the son is a slave. If he is freed, the son [of a bastard] becomes a free man.' But the older view was different. The text continues: R. Eliezer (c. AD 90, representative of the ancient tradition) said: 'See, he is a bastard slave [the taint of the bastard continues in all circumstances]' (M. Kidd. iii.13).

[126] According to b. Yeb. 78b, R. Eliezer (c. AD 90) gave the following explanation: 'Were anyone to present me with a female bastard of the third generation . . . I would declare her pure.' It seems that R. Eliezer limited the prohibition on bastards being admitted to the community (Deut. 23.3) to male bastards. In contrast the prevailing teaching in the second century extended Deut. 23.3 to include female bastards and their descendants.

[127] T. Yeb. iii.3, 243.26 and on this subject K. H. Rengstorf, in Rabbinische Texte, Erste Reihe: Die Tosefta, Band III, Stuttgart 1933, 34 n. 21.

'gave'—*wayyittᵉnēm*) the Gibeonites hewers of wood and drawers of water for the people and the Temple. Now because there are, in the post-exilic books of the Old Testament, several references to slaves of Levites (Ezra 8.20) as *nᵉtīnīm* ('given') it is assumed that these Temple slaves were descendants of the Gibeonites. What the rabbinic literature tells us about these Temple slaves can be reduced to the explanation of the ban, from II Sam. 21.2 ('now the Gibeonites were not of the children of Israel'), on sexual relationship with them; in no case do we ever find the slightest indication[128] that in Jesus' time, either in Jerusalem or other Jewish territory, there were still slaves of the Temple. To be sure, there are several references to 'servants of the Temple' (see pp. 209f.) who carried out the inferior tasks in the Temple; but as we may see particularly from a passage in Philo (*De spec. leg.* I, 156; cf. p. 209), these were the νεωκόροι, i.e. Levites.

We have no information worthy of note on the *fatherless* (men whose father was unknown) and the *foundlings*. They were forbidden marriage with both Israelites of pure descent and with illegitimate children of priests (M. Kidd. iv.1; see p. 272), for their father, or their parents, were unknown. In fact, they were suspected of bastardy (cf. M. Ket. i.8–9); and on the other hand the possibility could not be excluded that they might without being aware of it, contract a forbidden marriage with a relation (b. Kidd. 73a).

Nor could *eunuchs*, according to Deut. 23.2, enter the community of Israel, i.e. they were forbidden marriage, and of course levirate marriage too (M. Yeb. viii.4; T. Yeb. ii.6, 243), with legitimate Israelites.[129] However, rabbinic exegesis limited this ban to those who had been castrated by men.[130] They could not be members of the Sanhedrin (b. Sanh. 36b Bar.) nor of the criminal court (T. Sanh. vii.5, 426). The discussions on the subject of the eunuch's legal position were not merely academic controversies, as is shown by the fact that there were many of them, particularly in the royal court and

---

[128] M. Arak. ii.4, par. T. Arak. i.15, 544.8, does not belong here, as we have shown, p. 215 n. 215. See also the passages quoted by A. Büchler, 'Familienreinheit . . .', *Festschrift Schwarz*, 153, 154f., ET (see n. 108), 88, 89f.

[129] They could marry proselytes and freed slaves (M. Yeb. viii.2) as well as female bastards, for the first two had originally no part in the community of Israel, and female bastards could not get a part of the community (Deut. 23.3).

[130] This comes from M. Yeb. viii.6: 'If a priest that was a eunuch by nature married the daughter of an Israelite, he gives her the right to eat of Heave-offering.' This means that the marriage is valid, for the illegitimate wife of a priest was ineligible to eat the heave-offering in her husband's house (M. Yeb. vi.2–3).

harem, as we have seen (pp. 87ff.). This is confirmed by an event described in the Mishnah (M. Yeb. viii.4).[131]

To sum up, it must be said that bastards and eunuchs were included among those Israelites with grave racial blemish. Rabbinic legislation, appealing to Deut. 23.2–3, was ever watchful to keep the community, and the clergy in particular, apart from these elements by marking them as a caste outside the law.

[131] 'R. Joshua b. Bathyra testified of ben Megusath who lived in Jerusalem [and was] a man-made eunuch, that [after his death] they [his brothers] contracted levirate marriage with his wife.'

XVI

GENTILE SLAVES[1]

THE CLASS OF PEOPLE we are to study now, descending the social scale, is that of the Gentile slaves. They were in a curious, intermediate position, being in very close contact with the Jewish community but not counted as belonging to it.

The claim that slavery, in Judaism, 'was very rare . . . at the time of the second state'[2] is certainly not true.[3] To be sure there is no evidence that in Palestine at the time of Jesus there were any industries requiring a large number of slaves; nor were there many *latifundia* with slave labour on a large scale,[4] but we most assuredly meet domestic slaves of Gentile origin in great numbers, in the important households in Jerusalem; we must remember first the Herodian court,[5] and then the houses of the priestly nobility, where there were also large numbers of slaves.[6] Moreover, detailed evidence is

[1] R. Kirchheim, *Septem libri talmudici parvi hierosolymitani*, Frankfurt 1851, 25–30: 'Abadim'; Bill. IV, 716–44. J. Winter, *Die Stellung der Sklaven bei den Juden in rechtlicher und gesellschaftlicher Beziehung nach talmudischen Quellen*, Halle 1886; R. Grünfeld, *Die Stellung der Sklaven bei den Juden nach biblischen und talmudischen Quellen* I (Jena Dissertation), Jena 1886 (limited to biblical statements); Krauss, *TA* II, 83–111; G. F. Moore, *Judaism in the First Centuries of the Christian Era* II, Cambridge 1927, 135ff.; I. Heinemann, *Philons griechische und jüdische Bildung*, Breslau 1932 [reprinted Darmstadt 1962], 329–45. R. Salomon, *L'esclavage en droit comparé juif et romain*, Paris 1931, is worthless, since it depends entirely for rabbinic documentation on Z. Kahn, *L'esclavage selon la Bible et le Talmud*, Paris 1867.

[2] L. Gulkowitsch, 'Der kleine Talmudtraktat über die Sklaven', *Angelos I*, 1925, 89.

[3] The rejection of slavery by the Essenes (Philo, *Quod omnis probus*, 79; *Ant.* 18.21, but see pp. 348f.) and by the Therapeutae (Philo, *De vita contemplativa*, 70) had no effect on the situation.

[4] Jesus' sayings and parables, using agricultural images, do indeed often mention slaves (Matt. 13.27–30; Luke 17.7–10; 15.22) but more often day labourers (Matt. 9.37–38; 20.1–16; Luke 10.2; 15, 17, 19; John 4.36).

[5] See pp. 87f. Slaves in the royal court, in the New Testament: Matt. 22.3–10; Luke 19.12–27.

[6] *Ant.* 20.181, 206f.; b. Pes. 57a, par. T. Men. xiii.21, 533, and the mention of the high priest's servants in the Passion narrative, particularly Mark 14.47 and

not lacking. R. Eleazar b. Zadoq who was brought up in Jerusalem reports that at the feast of Tabernacles, the Jerusalemite visiting the 'house of study' customarily had his slave carry the *lūlāb* to the house (T. Sukk. ii.10, 195; par. b. Sukk. 41b). We hear of a girl (this was certainly in Jerusalem) who was taken prisoner with six female slaves (*ARN*, Rec. A, ch. 17, Goldin 89).[7] On an ossuary discovered at Shaʿfat, about two miles north of Jerusalem, is the name of a slave Epictetus;[8] and Rhoda, the servant of the house of John Mark's mother mentioned in Acts 12.13, was also a slave as her name implies.[9] In conclusion we may remember the derisive saying by Hillel, who is no doubt contemplating the situation in Jerusalem when he warns: 'The more bondwomen the more lewdness; the more bondmen the more thieving' (M. Ab. ii.7).

Slaves of both sexes were either bought or born in the house. It may well be that the slave-traders, with their 'merchandise' for the slave market in Jerusalem, came chiefly from Phoenicia (II Macc. 8. 11). Malchus the servant of the high priest (John 18.10) was probably as his name implies, an Arab from Nabatea[10] and from there too came Corinthus, Herod's bodyguard (*BJ* 1.576f.; *Ant.* 17.55–57). Altogether Arabia may well have supplied the majority of Gentile slaves in the possession of Jews in Palestine, for there is evidence that there was a very large number of Arabian prisoners of war taken by the Jews in the Herodian wars (*BJ* 1.376).

The price of slaves varied very much, according to their age, sex and mental and bodily qualities or defects. Current events too affected this: in wartime there was a glut of slaves and prices fell, while in peacetime prices rose. In the Roman empire prices rose steeply under

par.; John 18.18 (distinguishes between δοῦλοι and ὑπηρέται); 18.26. On John 18.10 see n. 10.

[7] One of the slaves told her new master that the girl's mother had 500 bond-women.

[8] F.-M. Abel, in *RB* 10, 1913, 276 no. 16, and *CIJ* II, 1238: Φειδωνος ος και Επικτητος Κωμα του Σητου.

[9] See E. Preuschen, *Die Apostelgeschichte*, Tübingen 1912, 78, on Rhoda as a slave name.

[10] This is a common name in Nabatean and Palmyrene inscriptions; H. Wuthnow, 'Eine palmyrenische Büste', *Orientalische Studien E. Littmann überreicht*, Leiden 1935, 63–69, gives us several examples, especially for Palmyra. Two Nabatean kings bore the name: Malchus I (50–28 BC) and Malchus II (AD 40–71). An inscription at Hauran: *RB* 41, 1932, 403 and 578. See also the index to Josephus.—However the name occurs also in Syria: Le Bas and Waddington, *Inscriptions grecques et latines recueillies en Grèce et en Asie mineure* III, Paris, 1870, gives 28 examples from Syria.

Augustus. Horace quotes prices ranging from 500 drachmas to 100,000 sesterces (according to the Ptolemaic and Syrian values, this was from 5 to 152.8 minas); and Martial quotes from 600 denarii to 200,000 sesterces (from 3 to 305.6 minas).[11] In the first century BC the average price was about 20 minas, and in the first century AD about 30 minas.[12] In Palestine too the prices varied considerably. During the Maccabean wars Nicanor, who was certain of victory in 166–165 BC, promised Jews for sale to Phoenician slave-traders, at ninety Jews for one talent (II Macc. 8.11);[13] this is a ridiculous price when we remember that several decades earlier[14] Hyrcanus, son of Joseph the Palestinian tax-farmer, had paid one talent in Alexandria for each male or female slave, carefully selected of course (*Ant.* 12.209). The Mishnah (M.B.K. iv.5) mentions a price for a slave of between a quarter of a mina and one hundred minas[15] (reckoning the mina at one hundred denarii); this is a relatively low price compared with current prices outside Palestine. This was doubtless to do with the fact that the better kinds of slave (men who were eunuchs or tutors, women who played musical instruments or were courtesans) who commanded the highest prices, played only a minor role in Palestine. The average price of 15–20 minas which we can deduce from M.B.K. iv.5 is confirmed by Josephus: in Gen. 37.28 Joseph's brothers sold him for twenty pieces of silver (*šeqel*); on the basis of LXX (Gen. 37.28: εἴκοσι χρυσῶν!) Josephus quotes 20 minas (*Ant.* 2.33), which naturally represents the current price of slaves in his time, i.e. the end of the first century AD.[16] We get an idea of the value of this sum by comparing it with the average wage of a day-labourer at this time, which was one denarius. Consequently the price of a slave, twenty minas (= two thousand denarii), corresponds to two thousand times the daily wage of a labourer.[17] So a slave, male or female, constituted a very valuable possession.

Any description of the *social position* of Gentile slaves must start

[11] O. Roller, *Münzen, Geld und Vermögensverhältnisse in den Evangelien*, Karlsruhe 1929, 14 n. 17.

[12] Roller, *op. cit.*, 15.

[13] Unfortunately we do not know the value of the talent in question.

[14] For the dating of this event in the period before 198 BC see Schürer I, 183 n. 4 (ET omits).

[15] The reading in the Palestinian Talmud, of 0.25 to 1 mina, favoured in Bill. IV, 716f., cannot be considered, as this is far too low a price.

[16] Josephus finished his *Antiquities c.* AD 94.

[17] Though present-day comparisons may be dangerous, we may say that the possession of a slave then corresponded to the possession of a luxury car now.

from the fact that they were the absolute property of their master. The slave could possess no goods at all; it was his master who possessed not only all the products of his work, but also anything he found (M.B.M. i.5), anything he was given (j. Kidd. i.3, 60a.28), anything he received as compensation for an injury received or a humiliation endured (b.B.B. 51a)—in short 'everything that is his (even his children) belongs to his master' (Gen. R. 67.5 on 27.37, Son. 609). Like any other possession he could be sold, given away, pledged (M. Gitt. iv.4), devoted (M. Arak. viii.4), and formed part of his master's inheritance. As is always the case where slavery exists, this situation was felt most in that male slaves had absolutely no protection against harsh treatment, brutal punishment or violent abuse,[18] and that female slaves had to submit themselves to their master's pleasure (T. Hor. ii.11, 477; M. Yeb. vi.5; M. Ab. ii.7; Num. R. 10 on 6.2, Son. 10.7, 369f.; M. Ket. i.4 etc.). However the treatment of slaves here was on the whole a great deal more humane than elsewhere in the ancient world: as we have seen (p. 335), certain mutilations which the master caused his slaves in the presence of witnesses (which was a necessary requirement, at least according to R. Joshua, c. AD 90) could bring about the release of the slave, on the basis of the exegesis of Ex. 21.26–27, which was liberal at that time;[19] moreover—at least this was the rule theoretically in force—the premeditated putting to death of a slave had to be treated as murder, and merited capital punishment if the slave died within twenty-four hours (Bill. IV, 737–9).

Gentile slaves of both sexes who became the property of a Jew were made to accept baptism 'to the end of becoming a slave', Bill. I, 1054f. If the slave were a woman this baptism signified *conversion to Judaism*;[20] male slaves had to complete this conversion by submitting to circumcision (Gen. 17.12–13; Jub. 15.13 [c. 120 BC]). How

[18] Cf. the drastic advice in Ecclus. 30.33–38: torture, torment and fetters for a bad and disobedient slave.—Abuse: Abadim iii.5; b. Kidd. 25a *et passim*.—Slaves being maimed: Bill. IV, 730ff.; Krauss, *TA* I, 246; II, 86, 95f.—Instruments of punishment and torture: Bill. IV, 734; Krauss, *TA* II, 95f.—R. Gamaliel II, whose attitude towards his slave Tabi was considered exemplary, blinded him in one eye (b.B.K. 74b); but according to the par. j. Ket. iii.10, 28a.13 he merely broke a tooth; we do not know which is the older tradition.—Cf. too Luke 12. 46–48.

[19] Bill. IV, 729–31 and 735–7. But there was certainly no question, on that basis, that 'all bodily injury resulted in immediate freedom' (L. Gulkowitsch *Angelos* I, 1925, 89).

[20] Targum Pseudo-Jonathan on Deut. 21.13, on the subject of women prisoners of war: 'And thou shalt cause her to be baptized and shalt make her a proselyte.'

obvious this was is apparent from CD xii.10–11: 'And his slave and his maidservant he [the member of the new covenant] must not sell to them [Gentiles] for as much as they came into his house [with him] into the covenant of Abraham.' In the third century AD (R. Joshua b. Levi, *c.* 250) a slave was given twelve months for reflection; if he then refused conversion, his master had to sell him back to Gentiles (b. Yeb. 48b). By contrast the earlier age seems to have insisted on immediate circumcision,[21] on the basis that the Gentile might make food ritually impure (*Pirqe R. Eliezer* 29; b. Yeb. 48b).

The equivocal position of the Gentile slave is explained by the fact that though circumcised he was still in slavery. By circumcision he had become 'a son of the covenant' (Mek. Ex. 20.10, 26b.51 [L II, 255]), but at the same time, since he was not a freedman he could not belong to the community of Israel (b.B.K. 88a).[22] He had 'lost the status of a heathen, but . . . not yet attained that of a Jew' (b. Sanh. 58b). This equivocal position determined both his religious duties and his rights, and both were limited by consideration of the rights of his owner.

Let us first consider the *religious duties* of a slave which resulted from his conversion. These were governed by the principle that he should perform only those which were not related to any particular moment,[23] since he was not the master of his own time. So the Gentile slave was not bound by the obligation to recite the *š^ema^c*, which an Israelite had to do daily at sunrise and after sunset (thus at particular moments); nor did he have to wear phylacteries (M. Ber. iii.3). He was not obliged either to join the pilgrim feasts in Jerusalem at Passover, Pentecost and Tabernacles (again at particular times, M. Hag. i.1), or to live in booths at Tabernacles (M. Sukk. ii.1 and 8) and to wave the *lūlāb* (b. Kidd. 33b Bar.; see Bill. II, 784ff.), or to sound the

---

[21] In Mek. Ex. 12.44, 7b, R. Eliezer (*c.* AD 90) who in every dispute was a staunch supporter of the ancient tradition, defends this opinion. *Ed. princ.* or Venice, 1545, 7b.20ff., attributes to him an opposite opinion from the fact that some words are dropped; but according to the correct reading in *Yalqut Shimeoni* i.211, Vilna ed. 1898, 134a. 14, this opposite opinion is that of R. Ishmael (d. AD 135). There is some doubt, however, since b. Yeb. 48b Bar. speaks of R. Aqiba as the author instead of R. Eliezer.

[22] 'The slave is not eligible to enter the community.'

[23] Bill. III, 562 and IV, 722f.; true, the principle was only a general rule and did not cover every eventuality, for there was a series of rules which slaves (like women) were not bound to observe, although they were not tied to any particular moment of time, cf. Bill. III, 559 (e.g. study of the Torah etc.).

horn at the New Year (T.R. Sh. iv.1, 212). On the other hand he was bound to say the benediction after meals and the daily recitation of the *tephillah* or 'Eighteen Benedictions' (M. Ber. iii.3), which could be said any time 'until sunset' (M. Ber. iv.1), and he must put the *mezūzāh* at the door (M. Ber. iii.3).[24] On the whole the number of religious duties laid upon a slave was very small. They were much the same as a woman had to perform and in this she was on a level with a slave, for she too had a master over her.[25]

The religious and civil rights which were due to a slave by his conversion to Judaism were, like his religious duties, limited by his slavery; it was the reverse side of the coin, extremely serious for his position. The advantages of the Jewish religious laws were only accorded to the slave in so far as they did not encroach upon his master's rights over him. First, and most important, on the basis of Ex. 20.10 and Deut. 5.14 he had the same right to sabbath rest as every other Israelite; he also had the right to take part in the feast of the Passover, including the Passover meal.[26] Finally, his master could not sell him to a Gentile (M. Gitt. iv.6).[27] As we have seen already, the Damascus Document was especially insistent on this point (CD xii. 10–11; see pp. 348f.); so we may conclude that in the earlier period this prescription had the force of law, at least in the circles of those who were strict in their observance of the Law.[28] These were practically all the rights which a slave gained by conversion.[29] In fact, he had no rights at all. First let us consider the religious side: In the Temple he could not, for example, lay his hands (on the head of the sacrificial victim) nor weigh out the portions (T. Men. x.13 and 17, 528); in the synagogue he was not allowed to make up the minimum number of ten present which was necessary for public prayer,[30] and he could not be called upon for the reading (this appears from b. Gitt. 40a);

[24] According to b. Men. 43a Bar. he must also wear tassels on his outer garments.
[25] 'Women, slaves and minors' were often mentioned together, e.g. M. Ber. iii. 3; M. Sukk. ii.8 *et passim*. Women and slaves together: M.R. Sh. i.8 *et passim*.
[26] Passover meal: Ex. 12.44; b. Pes. 88a Bar.; T. Pes. vii.4, 166. On the basis of Lev. 22.11 the Gentile slave of a priest could eat the heave-offering for priests, M. Yeb. vii.1.
[27] This passage forbids even the sale to a Jew living outside Palestine. Scriptural basis for this was Deut. 23.16, cf. Siphre Deut. 23.16, 259, 50d.
[28] It is difficult to believe that this prescription was widely observed; we hear of the pledging and the sale of slaves to Gentiles, b. Gitt. 43b–44a.
[29] To complete the list, we must mention that he had the right of making vows, but only in so far as they did not inconvenience his master—in which case the latter must give his consent, Bill. IV, 723.
[30] Once R. Eliezer freed his slave to make up the quorum, b. Gitt. 38b.

at table he was not allowed to be among the number of people invited to say benediction after a meal (M. Ber. vii.2). Moreover, he had no right to bear witness; except in a few exceptional cases,[31] he was ineligible as a witness (*Ant.* 4.219; M.R. Sh. i.8). Last, and most important, he was deprived of any rights of matrimony. A slave, man or woman, could under no circumstances contract a valid marriage with any Israelite (M. Kidd. iii.12; M. Gitt. ix.2, *et passim*), even with one tainted with very grave racial impurity; any child born of a union between an Israelite and a slave woman was a slave, like its mother,[32] and belonged to her master. So in this respect slaves of both sexes, despite their conversion to Judaism, were still regarded as Gentiles.

This abysmal social position, which made the word 'slave' one of the worst of insults and punishable by anathema (b. Kidd. 28a Bar.), explains the furious protest of Jesus' listeners when he called them 'bondservants' (John 8.32–35).

[31] E.g. he could bear witness that when a town had been taken by Gentiles, the wife of a priest had not been touched, M. Ket. ii.9; Rashi on M.R. Sh. i.8 gives two further examples (cf. Bill. III, 560).

[32] M. Kidd. iii.12; b. Kidd. 68b; M. Yeb. ii.5; b. Yeb. 17a, 22b, 23a; *Pirqe R. Eliezer* 36 *et passim*, following the legal ruling that a child born of an invalid union belongs to its mother's side. Gal. 4.21–23 assumes that this legal principle is in force. It is also confirmed by John 8.41: Jesus calls his audience 'bondservants of sin' 8.34, and says they are not the spiritual descendants of Abraham, 8.39; they protest against the accusation of being born ἐκ πορνείας. These Jews are assuming that the principle just mentioned is in force; only on the assumption that this principle applied to them could Jesus, in their opinion, have the right to make the accusation. According to ancient law the reverse holds good too, and a child born of the union of a male slave and a Jewess was a Jew; here too we have an invalid union, with the child belonging to its mother's side (see V. Aptowitzer, *HUCA* 5, 1928, 267ff.; A. Büchler, *MGWJ* 78, 1934, 143ff.). Aptowitzer, 'Spuren des Matriarchats im jüdischen Schrifttum', *HUCA* 4, 1927, 207–40, and 5, 1928, 261–97 has shown most convincingly that the two legal principles quoted in this note are the remains of an ancient matriarchal law; these remains are so much the more interesting since, by the time of the biblical era the patriarchal law had superseded it throughout the whole of the legislation.

XVII

THE SAMARITANS[1]

DESCENDING TO THE lowest degree of the scale, we come to the Samaritans. During the post-biblical period the attitude of the Jews towards their neighbours the Samaritans, who were regarded as a mixed Judaeo-Gentile race, underwent great changes and run into extremes. The older accounts tended to overlook this, with the result that they gave a false picture.

After the separation of the Samaritans from the Jewish community and the construction of their temple on Mount Gerizim (at the latest in the fourth century BC),[2] there must have been much tension between Jew and Samaritan. We have the evidence, for the beginning of the second century BC, of the spiteful remark in Ecclus. 50.25–26: 'With two nations is my soul vexed, and the third is no nation [cf.

---

[1] There is a basic collection of sources in Bill. I, 538–60. There is very little which is relevant to our discussion in the little Talmudic tractate Kutim on the Samaritans, since this applies throughout to a later date; it has been edited by R. Kirchheim, *Septem libri talmudici parvi hierosolymitani*, Frankfurt 1851, 31–37, and translated by L. Gulkowitsch in *Angelos* I, 1925, 48–56. J. A. Montgomery, *The Samaritans*, Philadelphia 1907; Schürer II, 18ff. (ET II.1, 5ff.) 195ff., (his remarks on the Samaritans' position with regard to religious laws are not correct for the first century AD but only apply to the different circumstances in the second century); Schlatter, *Theologie*, 75–79; J. Jeremias, *Die Passahfeier der Samaritaner* (*BZAW* 59) 1932; J. Macdonald, *The Theology of the Samaritans*, London 1964.

[2] Samaritan tradition places the construction of the Temple in the time of the second return from exile, thus in the fifth century BC (*Et-taulida*, ed. A. Neubauer, in *Journal asiatique*, 6th series, 14, 1869, 401, lines 16–18; *Liber Josuae*, ed. Th. G. J. Juynboll, Leiden 1848, ch. 45; *Abul-fath*, ed. E. Vilmar, *Abulfathi annales samaritani*, Gotha 1865, 61ff., in the Arabic text; *Samaritanische Chronik*, ed. E. N. Adler and M. Séligsohn, in *REJ* 44, 1902, 218ff.). Against this Samaritan tradition we have Josephus' view that the temple was built in 332 BC (*Ant.* 11.324; cf. 13. 256). E. Sellin, *Geschichte des israelitisch-jüdischen Volkes* II, Berlin 1932, 169–71, argues in favour of this last date. A. Alt, 'Zur Geschichte der Grenze zwischen Judäa und Samaria', *PJB* 31, 1935, 106–11 (reprinted in his *Kleine Schriften* II, Munich 1953, 357–62), places the construction of the temple on Gerizim in the latter part of the Persian era, a little before Alexander reached Asia, thus in the middle of the fourth century.

Deut. 32.21]: They that are the inhabitants of Seir and the Philistines, and that foolish people [cf. Deut. 32.21] that dwelleth in Sichem' (hebr. Text). Josephus tells the story, for the period immediately before 150 BC, of a religious quarrel between Egyptian Jews and Samaritans, taken before Ptolemy Philometor (181–145 BC), on the question of rivalry between the two sanctuaries at Jerusalem and Gerizim (*Ant.* 13.74ff., cf. 12.10). It was during the reign of the Hasmonean John Hyrcanus (134–104 BC) that these tensions reached their peak; not long after the death of Antiochus VII (in 129) John seized Sichem and destroyed the temple on Gerizim (*Ant.* 13.255f.). It is not surprising that after this the atmosphere was continuously charged with hatred.[3]

It is possible that towards the end of the first century BC there was a temporary relaxation. Herod married a Samaritan woman (p. 358), and Schlatter concludes from this that the king had made an attempt —the only attempt—to disperse the hatred between the two communities.[4] In favour of this hypothesis we can quote the fact that during Herod's reign the Samaritans seem to have had access to the inner court of the Temple at Jerusalem (*Ant.* 18.30). But they must already have lost this right some twelve years after Herod's death when one Passover at the time of the Procurator Coponius (AD 6–9), some Samaritans strewed human bones in the Temple porches and all over the sanctuary in the middle of the night (*Ant.* 18.29f.). This was obviously an act of revenge for something about which Josephus is characteristically silent. This appalling defilement of the Temple, which probably interrupted the Passover feast, added fresh fuel to the old fires of hatred.

From this time onwards the hostility became more and more implacable, as all the New Testament evidence shows us, as well as Josephus' contemptuous references to the Samaritans and the severity of the old rabbinic law toward them (pp. 356ff.). When the Galilean Jews of the first century AD journeyed to Jerusalem, especially at feast times, they used, it is true, to take the road leading through Samaria (*Ant.* 20.118; *BJ* 2.232; Luke 9.51–55; John 4.4–42); but there were always incidents (Luke 9.53; John 4.9) and sometimes even bloody encounters.[5] In the second century AD relationships

---

[3] Test. Levi vii.2: 'From this day forward [a reference to Gen. 34.25–29] shall Shechem be called a city of imbeciles, for as a man mocketh a fool so did we mock them.'

[4] *Theologie*, 75.

[5] One incident is characteristic: Josephus tells of it because of its far-reaching

again improved. The Samaritans were judged much more leniently than in the first century, as we see from the Mishnah regulations on relations with them; they were regarded 'as Israelites wherever their behaviour corresponded with the ideas of Pharisaic religious legislation' (Bill. I, 539) and only on other points were they treated as non-Israelites. This milder attitude was mainly due to the authority of R. Aqiba; Billerbeck (I, 538) has assumed that by this friendly bearing Aqiba perhaps aimed to win their support against the Romans in the bar Kokhba revolt (132–5[6]). Then, before AD 200, the attitude to the Samaritans hardened again, and about 300 the breach was complete; ever after that they were regarded as Gentiles (Bill. I, 552). The opposition to them was so bitter that, according to an account by Epiphanius, Samaritans converted to Judaism had to be circumcised anew; the Samaritans replied to this by taking the same measure.[6] As a result Judaism forbade altogether any conversion of Samaritans.[7]

Thus, in the first century AD with which we are now concerned, we are in one of the periods of embittered relationships between Jews and Samaritans. When Jesus crossed Samaria he could find no shelter, for he was going to the hated Temple in Jerusalem (Luke 9.52–53). He was refused even water to drink (John 4.9) and this shows the burning hatred of the Samaritans for the Jews: the ruin of their temple on Gerizim was a constant provocation. The Jews for their part began to call the Samaritans 'Cutheans' (see p. 355 n. 11f.) and the word 'Samaritan' was a gross insult in the mouth of a Jew (John 8.48; b. Sot. 22a). These and other indications[8] make us realize the contempt with which the Jews looked on this mixed race.

---

political consequences (*BJ* 2.232–46; *Ant.* 20.118–36): In AD 52 some Jewish guerrillas attacked Samaritan villages in vengeance for the murder of one (*BJ*) or more (*Ant.*) Galilean pilgrims, who were going to Jerusalem for a feast, and while crossing Samaria had been attacked on the northern boundary of Samaria, in the frontier village of Ginae (i.e. Jenin).

[6] Epiphanius, *De mens. et pond.* xvi.7–9 (ed. P. de Lagarde, *Symmicta* II, Göttingen 1880, 168f.), says: 'There was in the time of Verus a certain Samaritan teacher called Symmachus, who became a Jew. He was not honoured by his own people, and eaten up with ambition for power he was angry with his fellow citizens. He became a proselyte and was recircumcised. Do not be surprised at this, dear reader, for Jews who take refuge with the Samaritans . . . are recircumcised, as also Samaritans that go to the Jews' (it is doubtful whether Symmachus was a Samaritan; according to Eusebius, *HE* VI, 17, he was an Ebionite).

[7] *Tanḥuma, wayyešeb*, 2, 117, 38; *Pirqe R. Eliezer*, 38.

[8] In Luke 10.37 the scribe avoids saying the word 'Samaritan', but uses the

These changing relationships between Jew and Samaritan naturally brought corresponding changes in religious legislation as applied to Samaritans. Thus it is very difficult to discover from our sources, which for the most part were written much later, what ruling was in force during the first century AD. However we are not without some assistance. In addition to the evidence in the New Testament and Josephus, there are especially the words of R. Eliezer (c. AD 90) to help us clarify matters; for on the subject of Samaritans, as in other matters, he stands immovably for the old tradition, and many other Tannaitic teachers support him on this point.[9]

The Samaritans then, as still today, attached great importance to the fact that they were descended from the Jewish patriarchs.[10] This claim was contested: they were 'Cutheans',[11] descendants of the Median and Persian colonists (Luke 17.18: ἀλλογενής —stranger in the land), foreigners.[12] Such was the Jewish view current in the first century AD (see n. 10f.), in order to refute any Samaritan claim to blood affinity with Judaism (Ant. 11.341). Even their recognition of the Mosaic Law[13] and their meticulous observation of its prescriptions did nothing to alter their exclusion from the community of Israel, because they were suspected of an idolatrous cult from their veneration of Mount Gerizim as a holy mountain.[14] The fundamental

---

circumlocution 'He that showed mercy on him.'—When the sons of Zebedee (Luke 9.54) wished to call down fire on the inhospitable Samaritan village, their national hatred obviously filled them with righteous indignation at this violation of the laws of hospitality.

[9] R. Ishmael (d. AD 135), R. Judah b. Eli (c. 150), R. Simeon b. Johai (c. 150); cf. Bill. I, 538ff.

[10] John 4.12; Ant. 9.291; 11.341, 345 (in both these passages Josephus insists that, according to circumstances, the Samaritans sometimes claimed kinship with the Jews, and sometimes denied it; but this is surely a biased account); Gen. R. 46.8ff. Son. 873: 'R. Meir met a Samaritan and said to him: Whence are you descended? He replied: From Joseph'.

[11] The name Kūtīm for the Samaritans is not found in the Old Testament, Aramaic parts included. It appears for the first time in Josephus: Χουθαῖοι, once (Ant. 13.256, variant) Κουθαῖοι, besides Σαμαρεῖται, Σαμαρεῖς, more frequently. In the Mishnah kūtīm is already exclusively applied to Samaritans.

[12] The 'men of Cuth' (II Kings 17.30, cf. 17.24) were one of the tribes installed as colonists in Samaria by the Assyrians in the eighth century BC. Josephus explains that their country is the land of the Medes and Persians (Ant. 12.257); cf. Ant. 9.288: they had been removed from the country of Cutha in Persia to Samaria.

[13] The Pentateuch was the basis of the Samaritans' religion; they recognized no other sacred writing in the Jewish canon.

[14] M. Hull. ii.7 (where we must read lᵉkūtī, with the text of the Babylonian

reason for their exclusion, however, was their origin and not the cult of Gerizim; there had been no breach with the Jewish community in Egypt, in spite of the existence of the temple at Leontopolis, for there were no analogous hindrances there.[15]

This principle held against the Samaritans had as its first and most important consequence that from the beginning of the first century AD they were regarded as being on a level with the Gentiles in all things ritual and cultic. As we have seen (p. 353), they were probably forbidden access to the inner courts of the Temple from about AD 8. This is confirmed by a Mishnah passage, obviously old, probably dating from when the Temple still stood. In it, it was forbidden to accept the Temple tax from Samaritans, or sin offerings, or guilt offerings and bird offerings [for women after childbirth and with haemorrhage]; only votive offerings and freewill offerings were to be accepted, as in the case of Gentiles (M. Shek. i.5).[16] This inclusion of Samaritans among the Gentiles in ritual and cultic matters is attested too by some words of R. Judah b. Eli (c. AD 150, who represented the older tradition as regards the Samaritans): He said that a Samaritan may not circumcise a Jew, for he would direct his intention[17] towards Mount Gerizim (T.A. Zar. iii.13, 464; b. A. Zar. 27a Bar.; Kutim i.9b). We find the same thought behind the ban enunciated by R. Eliezer (c. AD 90) on eating at Passover unleavened bread belonging to a Samaritan, 'for the Samaritans are not versed in the precepts of the commandments',[18] and on eating an animal killed by a Samaritan (see p. 355 n. 14) 'since an unexpressed intention in a Gentile [while slaughtering] is directed to idolatry' (M. Hull. ii.7).

By the very fact of this inclusion of Samaritans among Gentiles we understand that there could be no question of marriage with them.[19]

Talmud, ed. Frankfurt 1721, and Lemberg 1861; cf. Bill. I, 538), a saying of R. Eliezer (c. AD 90).

[15] Schlatter, Theologie, 79.

[16] On sacrifices by heathens see Bill. II, 549–51; Schürer II, 357–63, ET II.1, 299–305.

[17] He circumcised *lešōm* (= in the name of, or with intention to) Mount Gerizim. In a similar way, we must take the words 'in the name of' in NT baptism to express the intention inherent in the baptism.

[18] b. Kidd. 76a Bar.; b. Hull 4a Bar.; T. Pes. i.15, 156. In this last passage, we must read 'R. Eliezer' as in Tos. *ed. princ.* by Alfasi, and not R. Eleazar as in the Vienna and Erfurt MSS.

[19] We often find this ban expressed: M. Kidd. iv.3; T. Kidd. v.1f., 341; b. Kidd. 74b–76b; Kutim i.6; ii.9 *et passim*. We should probably include M. Shebi. viii.10

On this point the Jews were inflexible. Their intention was to set every obstacle in the way of marriage between Jews and Samaritans; and to this end, as we see from a later[20] report, but one worthy of belief,[21] a very important rule was put into force during the last decades before the destruction of the Temple;[22] this was that the Samaritans were considered 'from the cradle' [i.e. always] as impure in a very high degree, and as causing impurity.[23] Only once in the

---

here too: 'Moreover they declared before him [R. Aqiba, d. after AD 135]: R. Eliezer [c. AD 90] used to say: He who eats the bread of a Samaritan [for this reading see Bill. III, 420 n. 1, and IV, 1183] is like one that eats the flesh of swine. He replied: Hold your peace, I will not say to you what R. Eliezer has taught concerning this.' According to this tradition, R. Eliezer would have absolutely forbidden any eating of Samaritan bread. But many different traditions say that he allowed Samaritan leavened bread and cakes to be eaten after the Passover (j. Orl. ii.7, 62b.55; j. Shebi. viii.10, 38b.60 (he treated Samaritan unleavened bread differently, see p. 356 n. 18). His words reported in M. Shebi. viii.10 must therefore have a different meaning, as is shown too in Aqiba's dissatisfied answer. Thus R. Jose (c. AD 350) is probably right when he says (j. Shebi. viii.10, 38b.59) that 'to eat bread' in R. Eliezer's sentence is a euphemistic circumlocution for marriage.

20 R. Nahman bar Isaac (d. AD 356) b. Shab. 16b–17a.
21 M. Nid. iv.1 and M. Toh. v.8 show that the ruling was in force in the second century. Now, as we know (pp. 353f.), the second century was a favourable time for Samaritans, so it is hardly possible that the rule was not made until then.
22 In b. Shab. 16b–17a, R. Nahman insists that this rule was one of the Eighteen Enactments fixed in the loft of Hananiah b. Hezekiah b. Garon, after joint consultation of the Hillelites and the Shammaites which took place before AD 48. (Paul Billerbeck, in a conversation I had with him shortly before his death, 23 December 1932, at Frankfurt/Oder agreed with my dating of these enactments before the Apostolic Council in 48. According to M. Hengel, Die Zeloten, Leiden and Cologne 1961, 207 n. 4, the famous Eighteen Enactments were not promulgated until the time of the first revolt against the Romans. Even in this case, however, we must admit the possibility that they were already being partly observed before being raised to the rank of obligatory halākōth.)
23 This refers to the rule that Samaritan women were considered to be 'as menstruants from the cradle', and their husbands as perpetually unclean for that reason (cf. Lev. 15.24), M. Nidd. iv.1; T. Nidd. v.1, 645. Because of this any place where a Samaritan lay was levitically unclean (ibid.), and likewise any food or drink which had touched the place. Thus a traveller through Samaritan territory who accepted food and drink from them could never know if it was clean or not. By the same rule, moreover, the spittle of a Samaritan woman was unclean; and if one such woman stayed in a town, all spittle there was unclean, M. Toh. v.8— For the reason stated in n. 21 a similar regulation in the Mishnah probably belongs to the first century: Samaritans were suspected of throwing abortions into 'places of uncleanness' (bēt ha-tum' ōt = 'latrine'), so that such places conveyed corpse uncleanness to anyone who went there (M. Nidd. vii.4).—We may realize more fully the deadly severity of these enactments when we remember that until AD 8 it was probable (p. 353) that the Samaritans had access to the inner courts of the Temple, so that until then there was no levitical reason to exclude them from the Temple.

post-biblical period do we hear of a Jew marrying a Samaritan woman, and that was Herod the Great;[24] but it is possible that Herod did this, as we have said (p. 353), to try to bridge the gap between Jews and Samaritans. We must also add that this marriage took place before the deterioration in relationship described on p. 353.

We see, then, that before AD 70 the Jewish attitude to the Samaritans was very much the same as their attitude to Gentiles. They 'have no law nor even the remains of a law; therefore they are contemptible and corrupt' (j. Pes. i.1, 27b.51) declares R. Simeon b. Johai (c. AD 150), who represented the older tradition on the Samaritans.[25] Contact with Samaritans was as difficult, at least for those Jews who observed Pharisaic laws on purity, as that with Gentiles. The ancient commentator in John 4.9[26] spoke the truth when he said: 'The Jews have no dealings with the Samaritans.'

Only against the background of this over-all contemporary situation, which we have just described, can we fully appreciate the New Testament attitude towards the Samaritans or measure, for example, the impact of Jesus' words on his listeners: He put before these Jews the picture of a Samaritan as a model, humiliating for them to contemplate, of gratitude (Luke 17.17–19) and of neighbourly love triumphing over deep-rooted national hatred (Luke 10.30–37).

[24] Malthake, *BJ* 1.562; Σαμαρεῖτις; *Ant.* 17.20: ἐκ τοῦ Σαμαρέων ἔθνους. H. Willrich, *Das Haus des Herodes*, Heidelberg 1929, 172, doubts if Malthake belonged to the 'religious sect of the Samaritans', but there is no basis for doubt.

[25] According to Schürer II, 23, ET II.1, 8, the Samaritans were on a level with Sadducees, in matters of religious legislation. But as this statement is based on Mishnah passages reflecting the more favourable attitude towards the Samaritans of the second century AD, it does not hold good for the first century.

[26] This sentence is missing in ℵ* Dabde.

XVIII

APPENDIX: THE SOCIAL POSITION OF WOMEN[1]

EASTERN WOMEN TAKE no part in *public life*. This was true of
Judaism in the time of Jesus, in all cases where Jewish families
faithfully observed the Law. When the Jewess ;of Jerusalem left
her house, her face was hidden by an arrangement of two head veils,
a head-band on the forehead with bands to the chin, and a hairnet
with ribbons and knots, so that her features could not be recognized.[2]
It was said that once, for example, a chief priest in Jerusalem did not
recognize his own mother when he had to carry out against her the
prescribed process for a woman suspected of adultery (*Pesiqta rabbati*
26, 129b). Any woman who went out without this headdress, i.e.
without her face being hidden, committed such an offence against

[1] The abundant literature includes the following: Krauss, *TA* II; M. S.
Zuckermandel, *Die Befreiung der Frauen von bestimmten religiösen Pflichten nach Tosefta
und Mischna* (reprinted from *Festschrift zu Israel Lewys 70. Geburtstag*), Breslau 1911;
S. Krauss, 'Die Ehe zwischen Onkel und Nichte', *Studies in Jewish Literature Issued
in Honour of Prof. K. Kohler*, Berlin 1913, 165–75; J. Neubauer, *Beiträge zur
Geschichte des biblisch-talmudischen Eheschliessungsrechts. Eine rechtsvergleichend-historische
Studie* (Mitteilungen der vorderasiatischen Gesellschaft, 24–25), I-II, Leipzig
1920; J. Leipoldt, *Jesus und die Frauen*, Leipzig 1921; V. Aptowitzer, 'Spuren
des Matriarchats im jüdischen Schrifttum', *HUCA* 4, 1927, 207–40, and 5,
1928, 261–97, especially 4, 232ff. (marriage with a niece) and 5, 281ff. (right
of purchase, right of succession, endogamy); Bill. IV, 1928, Index s.v. 'Frau';
S. Bialoblocki, *Materialen zum islamischen und jüdischen Eherecht*, Giessen 1928;
M. Friedmann. 'Mitwirkung von Frauen beim Gottesdienst', *HUCA* 8–9, 1931/2,
511–27; I. Heinemann, *Philons griechische und jüdische Bildung*, Breslau 1932, 231–
329; Schlatter, *Theologie*, 162–70; S. Zucrow, *Women, Slaves and the Ignorant in
Rabbinic Literature*, Boston, Mass., 1932; A. Gulak, *Das Urkundenwesen im Talmud
im Lichte der griechisch-ägyptischen Papyri und des griechischen und römischen Rechts*,
Jerusalem 1935; J. Leipoldt, *Die Frau in der antiken Welt und im Urchristentum*,
Leipzig 1955; Z. W. Falk, *Jewish Matrimonial Law in the Middle Ages* (Scripta
Judaica VI), Oxford 1966. For present-day Palestine, H. Granqvist, *Marriage
Conditions in a Palestinian Village* I-II, Helsinki 1931–5, which gives further
bibliography.

[2] Bill. III, 427–34; cf. Susanna 32; I Cor. 11.5; *Ant.* 3.270.

good taste that her husband had the right—and indeed the duty (T. Sot. v.9, 302)—to put her away from him, and was under no obligation to pay the sum of money to which, on divorce, the wife had a right by virtue of the marriage contract (M. Ket. vii.6). There were even women so strict that they did not once uncover their head in the house, women like Qimḥit, who, it was said (p. 195), saw seven sons admitted to the high priesthood, which was regarded as divine reward for her extreme propriety: 'May it [this and that] befall me if the beams of my house have ever seen the hair of my head' (j. Meg. i.12, 72a.53; j. Hor. iii.5, 47d.15; j. Yom. i.1, 38d.9). Only in her wedding procession was a bride seen with uncovered head, and then only if she were a virgin, not a widow (M. Ket. ii.1).

Accordingly, a woman was expected to remain unobserved in public. There is a recorded saying of one of the oldest scribes we know, Jose b. Joḥanan of Jerusalem (c. 150 BC): 'Talk not much with womankind', to which was added, 'They said this of a man's own wife: how much more of his fellow's wife!' (M. Ab. i.5).[3] Rules of propriety forbade a man to be alone with a woman (M. Kidd. iv.12; b. Kidd. 81a; John 4.27), to look at a married woman,[4] or even to give her a greeting (b. Kidd. 70a–b). It was disgraceful for a scholar to speak with a woman in the street (b. Ber. 43b Bar.). A woman who conversed with everyone in the street could, like the woman who worked at her spinning in the street, be divorced without the payment prescribed in the marriage settlement.[5]

It was considered preferable for a woman, and especially an unmarried girl, in general not to go out at all. Philo (De spec. leg. III, 169) said: 'Market places and council-halls, law-courts and gatherings, and meetings where a large number of people are assembled, in short all public life with its discussions and deeds, in times of peace and of war, are proper for men. It is suitable for women to stay indoors and to live in retirement, limited by the middle door (to the men's apartments) for young girls,[6] and the outer door for married women.' Elsewhere Philo[7] says that the Jewish women of Alexandria

---

[3] See the story in b. Erub. 53b, and Josephus' remark in BJ 1.475: Antipater was 'perpetually coaxing and working upon his aunt's [Salome's] feelings, as though she had been his wife.'

[4] Bill. I, 299–301; Schlatter, Geschichte Israels 161f., and 417 n. 145; Schlatter, Der Evangelist Matthäus, Stuttgart 1929, 175f.

[5] M. Ket. vii.6. On the marriage contract, see below, p. 367 n. 45, and p. 368.

[6] Philo had in mind a Hellenistic household.

[7] In Flaccum II, 89. On Philo see I. Heinemann, Philons griechische und jüdische Bildung, 233–5.

were kept in seclusion, 'never even approaching the outer door. As for their maidens, they remained confined to the inner chambers (the women's quarters), and for modesty's sake avoided the sight of men, even of their closest relations.' There is a great deal of evidence that this segregation of women, unknown in biblical times, was customary elsewhere than in Alexandrian Judaism. 'I was a pure maiden and I strayed not from my father's house,' said the mother of the seven martyrs to her sons (IV Macc. 18.7).[8]

The following references take us to Jerusalem for a glimpse of the strict customs observed among the leading families. When Ptolemy IV, Philopator, wished to go into the Holy of Holies in 217 BC, 'The virgins who had been shut up in their chambers rushed forth with their mothers, and covering their hair with dust and ashes, filled the streets with groanings and lamentations' (III Macc. 1.18, cf. 1.19). There were similar signs of agitation again in the year 176 BC. On learning that Heliodorus, King Seleucus IV's chancellor, tried to rob the Temple treasury, 'the virgins that were kept in ward ran together, some to the gates, others to the walls, and some leaned out of the windows', and the women dressed in mourning and thronged the streets (II Macc. 3.19). It was an absolutely un-precedented thing when in 29 BC Alexandra the queen mother, with no regard for propriety, ran through the streets of Jerusalem reviling her daughter Mariamne with loud abuse as she was condemned to death (Ant. 15.232f.).[9] Similarly the Talmud sees in the words of Ps. 45.14: 'The king's daughter is all glorious within' a description of the restricted life of women who never left their apartments (b. Yeb. 77a).[10] We see then, that the daughters of the leading houses in Jerusalem, who were strict in observance of the Law, were accustomed to stay within the house before marriage, as far as possible; married women left it only with their faces covered.[11]

However, we must not generalize about this at all. In the royal households, for the most part, no one was greatly troubled over these

---

[8] Cf. Pseudo-Phocylides 215 (ed. E. Diehl, *Anthologia lyrica graeca* [coll. Teubner], 3rd ed., fasc. 2, Leipzig 1950, 107): 'But guard the maiden in close-locked apartments.' The same advice appears in Ecclus. 26.10; 42.11–12.

[9] Cf. also *Actus Vercellenses* (= Acts of Peter) 17: The noble Eubola had never appeared in public, so her appearance caused a great sensation. This scene is set in Judaea, i.e. Jerusalem, but is of no use in deciding the situation in Palestine.

[10] The same biblical text is applied to Qimhit (see p. 360) in j. Yom. i.1, 38d.11.

[11] This strict custom helps us to understand (see I. Heinemann, *op. cit.*, 235) why the Talmud is so disapproving of the 'haughtiness' of the prophetesses Deborah and Huldah, b. Meg. 14b.

customs. Consider Queen Alexandra who for nine years (76–67 BC) kept in her hands the reins of power, ruling with discretion and energy in no way differing from the Ptolemaic and Seelucid princesses.[12] Or consider the sister of Antigonus (the last Maccabean king 40–37 BC), who defended the fortress of Hyrcania against Herod the Great's troops (*BJ* 1.364). Consider too Salome, dancing before the guests of Herod Antipas (Mark 6.22; Matt. 14.6). Furthermore, even where the custom was strictly observed there were exceptions. Twice a year, on 15 Ab and the Day of Atonement, dances took place in the vine-yards around Jerusalem, when the maidens extolled their own excellence before the young men (M. Taan. iv.8; b. Taan. 31a Bar.).[13] According to the Palestinian Talmud maidens of the best families also took part in these dances.[14]

Above all, the stern seclusion could not be generally observed. Ordinary families could not adhere strictly to the totally retired life of the woman of rank, who was surrounded by her household of servants; and the main reasons for this were economic ones. For example, a wife had to help her husband in his profession, perhaps by selling his wares (M. Ket. ix.4). We may also see this relaxation of custom among ordinary people in the description of the popular feasts which took place in the Court of Women, during the nights of the feast of Tabernacles; the crowds were so exuberant that finally it became necessary to construct galleries for the women, to separate them from the men (T. Sukk. iv.1, 198.6).[15] Moreover in the country there were further relaxations. Here, the maidens went to the well (M. Ket. i.10; Gen. R. 49 on 18.20, Son. 49.6, 425); the married woman engaged in agricultural work together with her husband and children (M.B.M. i.6),[16] sold olives at the door (b. B.K. 119a), served at table (Mark 1.31 and par.; Luke 10.38ff.; John 12.2). There is no indication that the custom of wrapping up the head was observed as strictly in the country as in the town; rather was there in this respect a difference between town and country similar to what we see in

[12] H. Willrich, *Das Haus des Herodes*, Heidelberg 1929, 49.
[13] R. Eisler, in *Archiv für Religionswissenschaft* 27, 1929, 171ff., sees in these dances a survival of ritual Dionysiac mysteries; W. Wittekindt, *ibid.*, 28, 1930, 385–92, on the other hand, has shown that the dances in the vineyards were a survival of the rites of Marduk's marriage feast, which was celebrated in Babylon at the feast of the new year.
[14] j. Taan. iv.11, 69c.17, says even the king's and the high priest's daughters.
[15] Abin (*c.* AD 325) said: 'The sorest spot of the year [in a moral sense] is the feast,' b. Kidd. 81a.
[16] A woman 'came in from the harvest', M. Yeb. xv.2; M. Eduy. i.12.

present-day Palestine. However, a woman must not be alone in the fields (b. Ber. 3b), and it was not customary even in the country for a man to converse with a strange woman.[17]

The woman's *position in the house* corresponded to this exclusion from public life. In their father's house, daughters came behind the sons. Their education was limited to learning domestic arts, especially needlework and weaving, and they looked after their smaller brothers and sisters (b. B.B. 141a; b. Nidd. 48b Bar.). Towards their father they certainly had the same duties as the sons, to give him food and drink, to clothe and cover him, to help him in and out when he grew old, and to wash his face, hands and feet (T. Kidd. i.11, 336). But they had none of their brothers' rights; the succession, for example, passed to the sons and their descendants (M.B.B. viii.2; Siphre Num. 27.4)[18] before the daughters.[19]

The *patria potestas* was extraordinarily far-reaching over the minor before her marriage; she was totally dependent upon it. There were very precise distinctions between the minor (*q^etannāh*, small girl to the age of 'twelve years and one day'), the young girl (*na^{ca}rāh*, between twelve and twelve and a half), and the maiden of full age (*bōgeret*, above twelve and a half). Up to the age of twelve and a half years, her father had full power over her.[20] She had no rights of possession; the proceeds of her work and anything she found belonged to her father (M. Ket. iv.4; b. Ket. 40b *et passim*).[21] A girl under twelve and a half had just as little right to dispose of herself, for her

[17] As we see from the disciples' amazement at seeing Jesus in conversation with a Samaritan woman, John 4.27.

[18] See also on this point K. G. Kuhn, *Sifre zu Numeri, Rabbinische Texte* II, 3, Stuttgart 1959, 539 n. 44, 542 n. 18.

[19] If there were sons, they were the sole heirs. They were obliged only to support their unmarried sisters until they were married, M.B.B. ix.1, and to pay them a dowry, M. Ket. vi.6. This right of the sisters had complete priority, so that if the family were poor the daughters must be supported even if the sons had to go begging at the gates, M.B.B. ix.1. True, the Sadducees championed the claim that the daughter of a dead man should be on an equality at least with the daughter of his son (the dead man's grand-daughter) for rights of inheritance, b.B.B. 115b; but they did not prevail against the Pharisees on this point: see V. Aptowitzer, 'Spuren des Matriarchats im jüdischen Schrifttum', *HUCA* 5, 1928, 283–9 (Excursus 5: 'Daughters' rights of succession among the Sadducees').

[20] At least unless she has not already, in her minority, been betrothed and separated; then the marriage removes her from her father's power (e.g. b. Ket. 40a etc.).

[21] To her father, too, belonged any money paid as compensation for 'indignity and blemish', and pain because of violation (Deut. 22.29; M. Ket. iv.1; iii.8; b. Ket. 29a, 40b *et passim*).

father could cancel her vows;[22] he represented her in all legal matters;[23] acceptance or refusal of a marriage offer in particular was exclusively[24] in his power or in that of his deputy (M. Ket. iv.4; M. Kidd. ii.1).[25] Up to the age of twelve and a half, a girl had no right to refuse a marriage decided by her father,[26] and he could marry her even to someone deformed (b. Ket. 40b).[27] Furthermore, a father could even sell his daughter into slavery, as we have already seen (p. 313),[28] though certainly only if she were under twelve. Only the girl come of age (over twelve and a half) was independent; she could not be betrothed against her will (b. Kidd. 2b, 79a). However, even in her case, the marriage money which her fiancé had to pay on the betrothal belonged to her father (b. Ket. 46b; b. Kidd. 3b). This very extensive paternal power naturally led to daughters, and especially minors, being considered mainly as cheap labour and a source of profit. There is a laconic saying (j. Ket. vi.6, 30d.36): 'Certain men marry off their daughters and put themselves to some expense; others marry them off and receive money for them.'[29]

The *betrothal* ceremony,[30] which in our opinion, though not by Oriental standards, took place at an extremely early age, began the

[22] Siphre Num. 30.4, cf. Kuhn, *Sifre zu Numeri*, 616ff.

[23] J. Neubauer, *Beiträge zur Geschichte des biblisch-talmudischen Eheschliessungesrechts* II, 159ff.

[24] 'If a minor (*qᵉtannāh*, under twelve years) during her father's lifetime betroths herself or is married, the betrothal is no betrothal, and the marriage is no marriage (both are invalid)', T. Yeb. xiii.2, 256. See p. 363 n. 20 for an exception.

[25] If the father died, this right passed to the nearest relation, usually the mother or brothers. E.g. this is the situation envisaged in S. of S. 8.8–10 where the brothers are discussing how best they may profit from their sister's marriage (cf. S. Krauss, 'Die Rechtslage im biblischen Hohenliede', *MGWJ* 80, 1936, 330–339); further see Josephus, *CA* 2. 200, and *Ant.* 20.140: Agrippa II, in about AD 53 gave his sister Mariamne to Archelaus 'to whom her father Agrippa (I, d. in 44) had previously betrothed her'. But the minor whose mother or brothers had betrothed or married her after the death of her father was entitled to annul the marriage by declaring that she refused it, M. Yeb. xiii.1–2.

[26] She could merely express a wish to stay in her father's house until puberty.

[27] It could even happen that a thoughtless man forgot to whom he had betrothed his daughter, M. Kidd. iii.7.

[28] He had no longer this right in the case of the *naʿᵃrāh* (between twelve and twelve and a half years old), and of the girl who had come of age, M. Ket. iii.8.

[29] Cf. also b. Kidd. 18b Bar., where giving a daughter under twelve in bethrothal is called 'selling the daughter for marriage', a saying which bears traces of an ancient right.

[30] On the legal aspect see J. Neubauer, *Beiträge zur Geschichte des biblisch-talmudischen Eheschliessungsrechts* I-II, Leipzig 1920; Bill. II, 384ff.; A. Gulak, *Das Urkundenwesen im Talmud*, Jerusalem 1935.

transfer of the girl from her father's power to her husband's. The usual age for a girl's betrothal was between twelve and twelve and a half (Bill. II, 374); but there is incontestable evidence of betrothals and marriages at an even earlier age (p. 363 n. 26).[31] It was very common to be betrothed to a relation,[32] and this not only in the leading families where it was difficult for young people to meet because the daughters were kept secluded from the world. Thus for example we hear of a father and a mother in dispute because each wanted the daughter to marry into his or her own family (b. Kidd. 45b). In cases where the daughters were heirs, in default of sons, the Torah even ordered them to marry relations (Num. 36.1–12). The book of Tobit (6.10–13; 7.11–12) tells us of a case where this ruling was applied, and it is still in use in arabic Palestine.[33] Priests in particular were accustomed, as we have seen (pp. 154f. and p. 218) to choose their wives from among priestly families. Lay marriages between relations are attested e.g. in Tob. 1.9; 4.12; Judith 8.1–2. On this last point the book of Jubilees seems to recommend marriage with a cousin; indeed we find frequent stories, outside the biblical narratives, of the patriarchs who before and after the flood married the daughters of their father's sister (Jub. 4.15, 16, 20, 27, 28, 33; 11. 14) or brother (Jub. 8.6; 11.7). The later period represented marriage with a niece,[34] i.e. the daughter of one's sister, as a desirable[35] and even pious act;[36] so we hear of many occasions when a young man

---

[31] During his lifetime Agrippa I betrothed his two daughters Mariamne (born (34–35) and Drusilla (born 38–39), *Ant.* 19.354. As he died in 44, Mariamne was at most ten years old when she was betrothed, and Drusilla six.

[32] Marriage within the tribe and the family was normal and desirable, j. Ket. i.5, 25c.34; j. Kidd. iv.4, 65d.46. Probably with an eye to Num. 36.1–12, Philo says that those having control of fatherless daughters should marry them to relations. Josephus, *CA* 2.200, says (according to majority evidence) that according to the Law's requirements, those wishing to marry should 'sue from him who is authorized to give her away one who is not ineligible on account of nearness of kin' (MS L: τὴν ἐπιτήδειον; Eusebius, *Praep. ev.* VIII, 8.33 [GCS 48.1 = Eus. VIII.1, 439], Cod. BJ: ἐπιτήδειον; Latin, *oportunam.* Reading in other codd. of Eusebius: ἐπιτήδειον 'of him who is qualified by relationship').

[33] H. Granqvist, *Marriage Conditions in a Palestine Village* I, Helsinki 1931, 76ff.

[34] S. Krauss, 'Die Ehe zwischen Onkel und Nichte', in *Studies issued in honour of Prof. K. Kohler*, Berlin 1913, 165–175; A. Büchler, *JQR* 3, 1912–1913, 437–442; S. Schechter, *JQR* 4, 1913–1914, 454f.; V. Aptowitzer, 'Spuren des Matriarchats', *HUCA* 4, 1927, 232ff.

[35] T. Kidd. i.4, 334, 'Let no man take a wife until his sister's daughter has grown up.'

[36] b. Sanh. 76b Bar.; b. Yeb. 62b: a marriage with one's sister's daughter means that one's prayers are granted.

marries his sister's daughter.[37] In the same way marriage with a brother's daughter was not infrequent;[38] we have already seen (p. 218) that such marriages took place also among the high-ranking priestly families. The violent polemic in the Damascus Document against marriage with a niece, which deals as much with the brother's as with the sister's daughter,[39] testifies to the frequency of such unions. Finally the references in Josephus to marriages in the royal Herodian family[40] also show how widespread was marriage between relations. Most of these refer to marriages between relations, e.g. marriage with a niece (daughter of a brother[41] or of a sister),[42] with a cousin[43] and a second cousin.[44]

[37] M. Ned. viii.7 discusses the case of someone who is obliged to marry his sister's daughter. *ibid.*, ix.10: after an earlier refusal a man is led by R. Ishmael (*c.* AD 135) to marry his sister's daughter. On the advice of his mother, R. Eliezer b. Hyrcanus (*c.* AD 90) married his sister's daughter (j. Yeb. xiii.2, 13c.50; *ARN*, Rec. A, ch. 16, Goldin 84f.), and the same with R. Jose the Galilean (before AD 135), Gen. R. on 2.18, Son. 134.

[38] Abba married the daughter of his brother Rabban Gamaliel II, b. Yeb. 15a. See too the discussions in b. Yeb. 15b–16a, especially at the beginning of 16a. V. Aptowitzer, *art. cit.*, 211f., also indicates b. Sanh. 58b which interprets Gen. 20.12 thus (Abraham says that Sarah is his half-sister on his father's side): 'She is the daughter of his brother.' On the question of the antiquity of marriage with a niece, especially the brother's daughter, the point made by S. Krauss, *op. cit.*, 169, is significant in Hebrew 'paternal uncle' is *dōd*, i.e. 'well-beloved'.

[39] CD v.7ff. based the ban on the laws of incest, Lev. 18. The position of S. Krauss, *op. cit.*, 172, is untenable. He says that in CD the ban on marriage with a niece came from Sadducean circles; they were led to it after a Roman law of AD 49 permitted a woman to marry her father's brother, but not her mother's. This construction by Krauss is built on the erroneous opinion of the Damascus Document as a Sadducean writing (see pp. 259f. against this), and also on a too late dating of this document: it dates from approximately 100 BC.

[40] Cf. the genealogical tree of the Herodians at the end of Otto's *Herodes*.

[41] Marriages are recorded between:

Herod the Great	and the daughter (name unknown) of a brother.
His son Herod	and Herodias (grand-daughter of Herod the Great).
Herod Antipas (son of Herod the Great)	and Herodias (grand-daughter of Herod the Great).
Herod Philip (son of Herod the Great)	and Salome (grand-daughter of Herod the Great).
Herod of Chalcis (grandson of Herod the Great)	and Berenice (great-grand-daughter of Herod the Great).

[42] Herod the Great married a daughter (name unknown) of his sister Salome. As for the marriage of Joseph, Herod the Great's uncle, with his niece Salome, we do not know if she was the daughter of Joseph's brother or sister.

[43] As in the case of:

Phasael (nephew of Herod the Great)	and Salampsio (daughter of Herod the Great).

Betrothal, which was preceded by courtship and the drawing up of the marriage contract,[45] signified the 'acquisition' (*qinyān*) of the woman by the man, and thus the valid settlement of the marriage. The betrothed woman is called 'wife', can become a widow, be put away by divorce and punished with death for adultery (Bill. II, 393ff. has the evidence). It is characteristic of the legal position of the betrothed woman[46] that the 'acquisition' of a wife is compared with that of a Gentile slave: 'She is acquired by money, or by writ, or by intercourse' (M. Kidd. i.1);[47] in the same way: 'A Canaanitish bondman is acquired by money or by writ or by usucaption' (M. Kidd. i.3).[48] There is therefore a negative answer to this question: 'Is there then any difference between the acquisition of a wife and the acquisition of a slave?' (j. Ket. v.4, 29d.52; j. Shebi. viii.8, 38b.51).

Aristobulus (son of Herod the Great)	and Berenice (niece of Herod the Great).
Antipater (nephew of Herod the Great)	and Kypros (daughter of Herod the Great).
Joseph (nephew of Herod the Great)	and Olympias (daughter of Herod the Great).
Pheroras' son (nephew of Herod the Great)	and Roxane (daughter of Herod the Great).
Pheroras' son (nephew of Herod the Great)	and Salome (daughter of Herod the Great).
Aristobulus (great-grandson of Herod the Great)	and Salome (great-grand-daughter of Herod the Great).
[44] As in the case of:	
Agrippa I (grandson of Herod the Great)	and Kypros (grand-daughter of Phasael, Herod the Great's brother).
Herod of Chalcis (grandson of Herod the Great)	and Mariamne (grand-daughter of Joseph, Herod the Great's brother).

[45] The basic importance of this marriage contract consisted of legal rulings on financial matters between the two parties. Its main dispositions were: (*a*) Establishing what the bride's father was to pay—the marriage portion (*niksē mᵉlōg* = goods of usufruct, i.e. goods which remain in the ownership of the wife while the husband has right of usufruct), and the dowry (*niksē ṣōn barsel* = goods of reserve stock, i.e. goods which became the property of the husband, but the equivalent of which must be guaranteed to the wife in case of divorce). (*b*) Establishing the written marriage bond (*kᵉtubbāh*, i.e. the sum which reverted to the wife in case of separation or the death of her husband).—Cf. Bill. II, 384–393; S. Bialoblocki, *Materialien zum islamischen und jüdischen Eherecht*, Giessen 1928; A. Gulak, *Das Urkundenwesen im Talmud im Lichte der griechisch-ägyptischen Papyri*, Jerusalem 1935 (Gulak's distinction between betrothal, 36ff., and marriage contract, 52ff., do not apply to Palestine in the time of Jesus).

[46] S. Bialoblocki, *op. cit.*, 26f.

[47] At the time of the Mishnah, betrothals were usually completed by a betrothal gift to the woman.

[48] In the third place, for the woman as for the slave there is an action which is part of the new duties of the person acquired.

But it is only with the *marriage* itself, which ordinarily took place one year after betrothal (M. Ket. v.2), that the girl definitely passed from her father's power to her husband's (M. Ned. x.5). The young couple lived with the husband's family as a rule.[49] This meant that the young wife, usually still very young, had the heavy and often difficult task of adapting herself to a family circle strange to her and often hostile too.[50] Legally, the wife differed from the slave in the first place because she kept the right of possession (but not of disposition) of the goods she had brought with her as a marriage portion;[51] in the second place by the assurance of the marriage contract (*keṭubbāh*) in fixing the sum to be paid to her in case of separation or the death of her husband.[52] 'What is the difference between a wife and a concubine? R. Meir (*c.* AD 150) said: The wife has a marriage contract, the concubine has none' (j. Ket. v.2. 29d.16, cf. b. Sanh. 21a).

In *conjugal life*, that is after the marriage itself, the husband was obliged to support his wife, and she could demand this before a court (b. Ket. 77a, 107a). He had to provide her with food, clothing and shelter, and to fulfil his connubial duty; and furthermore to redeem his wife in case of her later captivity (M. Ket. iv.4, 8–9; T. Ket. iv.2, 264), to give her medicines if she were ill (M. Ket. iv.9), and to provide a funeral for her if she died—even the poorest man had to procure at least two flute-players and one woman mourner; and moreover, where it was the custom to make a funeral oration for a woman, he had to provide that too (T. Ket. iv.2, 264; M. Ket. iv. 4).

---

[49] Krauss, *TA* II, 40. This is still the custom today, H. Granqvist, *Marriage Conditions in a Palestine Village* II, Helsinki 1935, 141ff. Mark 1.29–31 must not necessarily mean that Peter lived at his mother-in-law's house.

[50] It was a principle of the legal dispositions to suppose that the mother-in-law and her daughters, the concubine, sister-in-law (by marriage) and step-daughter (daughter of her husband by another woman) are all jealous of the wife, M. Yeb. xv.4; M. Sot. vi.2; M. Gitt. ii.7. Cf. Granqvist, *op. cit.* II, 145ff.

[51] On the marriage portion see above, p. 367 n. 45. It could be increased after the marriage had taken place by gifts or inheritance, Bill. II, 384f. The husband generally had the usufruct of the marriage portion (apart from the exceptions mentioned in b. B.B. 51b), but it remained in the ownership of the wife; cf. S. Bialoblocki, *op. cit.*, 25.

[52] Bill. II, 387–392. This sum comprised, besides a basic amount (with supplements), the wife's dowry brought by her (as distinct from the portion, see n. 45). By putting a general mortgage on all his goods the husband was liable for the sum laid down in the marriage contract, b. Ket. 82b Bar.; M. Ket. iv.7; M. Yeb. vii.1. This ruling was no doubt influenced by Hellenistic law (there are illustrations of this in Egypt for Ptolemaic and Roman times in A. Gulak's *Urkundenwesen im Talmud*, 57f.).

The wife's first *duties* were household duties. She had to grind meal, bake, wash, cook, suckle the children, prepare her husband's bed and, as repayment for her keep (b. Ket. 58b), to work the wool by spinning and weaving (M. Ket. v.5).[53] Other duties were that of preparing her husband's cup, and of washing his face, hands and feet (b. Ket. 61a, cf. 4b.96a). These duties express her servile relationship with her husband; but his rights over her went even further. He laid claim to anything his wife found (M.B.M. i.5—in this she resembled a Gentile slave, see p. 348), as well as any earnings from her manual work, and he had the right (because of Num. 30.7–9) to annul her vows (M. Yeb. x.1). The wife was obliged to obey her husband as she would a master—the husband was called *rab*—indeed this obedience was a religious duty (*CA* 2. 201). This duty of obedience went so far that the husband could force a vow upon his wife, but any vows which put the wife in a discreditable position gave her the right to demand divorce before the court (M. Ket. vii.1ff., see pp. 308f.). Relationships between children and parents were also determined by the woman's duty of obedience to her husband; the children had to put respect for their father before respect for their mother, for she was also obliged to give a similar respect to the father of her children (b. Kidd. 31a; saying of R. Eliezer, *c.* AD 90; M. Ker. vi.9). In a case of danger to life, the husband must be saved first (M. Hor. iii.7— unless the wife's chastity was threatened).

Two facts are particularly significant of the degree of the wife's dependance on her husband:

(a) Polygamy was permissible,[54] the wife had therefore to tolerate concubines living with her. Of course, we must add that for economic reasons the possession of several wives was not very frequent. Mostly we hear of a husband taking a second wife if there was dissension with the first, but because of the high price fixed in the marriage contract he could not afford to divorce her (b. Yeb. 63b; see also p.

[53] In M. Ket. v.9 a weekly stint of weaving is prescribed, which the wife of a poor man had to do; this was reduced only if she was suckling a child.

[54] See pp. 90, 93f. for evidence of polygamy in Jerusalem. Cf. Schlatter, *Theologie*, 165. The violent protest of the Essene emigrants from Jerusalem (CD iv.21 etc.) against polygamy also proves its existence in Jerusalem. In Mark 10.6–9, Jesus appears to refer to polygamy, and rejects it; in Mark 10.6 and Matt. 19.4, he quotes Gen. 1.27, i.e. the very same passage on which CD iv.21 bases its rejection of polygamy; in Mark 10.8 and Matt. 19.5 he quotes Gen. 2.24 in its anti-polygamic form, i.e. with the words οἱ δύο which are found only in LXX, Syr., Vulg. and Targum, Pseudo-Jonathan, cf. J. Leipoldt, *Jesus und die Frauen*, Leipzig 1921, 60.

372 n. 64). We have a numerical guide to the frequency of polygamy in the information given by H. Granqvist,[55] that in 1927, in the village of Artas near Bethlehem, out of 112 married men twelve (that is, nearly one in ten) had more than one wife, eleven had two wives and one had three. However, we must treat these figures only as a rough guide, and not as portraying the exact picture of things in Jesus' time.

(b) The right to divorce was exclusively the husband's.[56] The few cases in which the woman had the right to demand a legal annulment of her marriage are mentioned above, pp. 308f. In Jesus' time (Matt. 19.3) the Shammaites and the Hillelites were in dispute over the exegesis of Deut. 24.1, which gives, as a reason for a man divorcing his wife, a case where he finds in her 'some unseemly thing', *'erwat dābār*. The Shammaites' exegesis was in accord with the meaning of the phrase, but the Hillelites explained it as, first the wife's unchastity (*'erwat*), and secondly something (*dābār*) displeasing to the husband; either gave him the right to put away his wife (Siphre Deut. 24.1, 269, 51b; b. Gitt. 90a Bar.). In this way the Hillelite view made the unilateral right of divorce entirely dependant on the husband's caprice. From Philo (*De spec. leg.* III, 30) and from Josephus (*Ant.* 4.253),[57] both of whom knew only the Hillelite point of view and championed it, it appears that this must already have been the prevailing view in the first half of the first century AD. However, reunion of the separated parties could take place;[58] also, by reason of divorce, there was a public stigma on the husband as well as on the wife and daughters (M. Ned. ix.9); then, too, when he divorced his wife, the husband had to give her the sum of money prescribed in the marriage contract; so in practice these last two facts must often have been obstacles to any hasty divorce of the wife.[59] As

---

[55] *Marriage Conditions in a Palestinian Village* II, Helsinki 1935, 205.

[56] When Herod the Great's sister Salome sent her husband Costobar a bill of divorce (*Ant.* 15.259f.), this, as Josephus is quick to point out, was in contravention of Jewish laws by which only the husband had the right to send such a bill.

[57] Cf. Josephus' own behaviour in putting away his wife because he was 'not content with her nature', *Vita* 426.

[58] T. Yeb. vi.4. 247: 'The divorced wife may return to her husband'; M.M.K at i.7 *et passim*. But this was not permitted if she had meanwhile remarried (Deut. 24. 1–4; Jer. 3.1; M. Yeb. vi.5), or if the divorce had been on the grounds of her sterility (M. Gitt. iv.8), or suspicion of her adultery, or because she had often made vows against her husband's will (M. Gitt. vii.7). However, scholars disagreed on some points, e.g. on vows (Bill. I, 310f.). From what has been said on p. 217, we see that priests were not allowed to take back a divorced wife.

[59] b. Yeb. 89a, 63b; b. Pes. 113b.—Gen. R. 17.3 on 2.18 (Son. 133), is

for the wife, she could occasionally take things into her own hands and go back to her father's house, e.g. in case of injury received (T. Yeb. vi.6, 247; b. Ket. 57b).[60] But in spite of all this, the Hillelite view represented a considerable degradation of women. Altogether we must be very cautious in drawing conclusions from the legal dispositions about the practice of divorce, conclusions e.g. on the number of divorces. H. Granqvist[61] has established that, in the village of Artas near Bethlehem, out of 264 marriages which took place in the space of a century—from c. 1830 to 1927—only eleven, that is, four per cent were broken by divorce. This is an emphatic warning against over-estimation of the number of divorces. If, as we may assume,[62] in case of divorce the children remained with their father, this would be the greatest hardship for the woman who divorced him.

It is extremely unlikely, as we see on p. 313, that the woman was so much the property of her husband that she could be sold into slavery to repay a theft he had committed.

Naturally, within these limits the position of the wife varied according to particular circumstances. There were two factors of notable importance. On the one hand a woman had ties of blood with her relations, particularly with her brothers, and this had significance for her position in married life. It was meritorious for a man to marry his niece (see p. 365), and this is connected with the fact that a woman found here a greater protection by reason of her blood relationship with her husband.[63] On the other hand, to have children, particularly sons, was extremely important for a woman. The absence of children was considered a great misfortune, even a divine punishment (b. Pes.

---

significant: R. Jose the Galilean (before AD 135) had a bad wife, but he could not divorce her because the sum of money fixed by the marriage contract was too high. So his pupils brought him the necessary money.

[60] In the Hellenized circle of the princely Herodian families, it often happened that a woman left her husband. Thus Herodias left Herod (*Ant.* 18.136; Mark 6.17 —where Philip is mistakenly named in place of Herod). In the same way all three of Agrippa I's daughters left their husbands: Berenice left Polemon of Cilicia (*Ant.* 20.146); Drusilla left Azizus of Emesa (20.142); Mariamne left Julius Archelaus (20.147). It must be remembered that the last two were cases of betrothals of children (see p. 365 n. 31). Cf. also p. 370 n. 56.

[61] *Op. cit.*, II, 268.

[62] As happens among Arabs in present-day Palestine, see Granqvist, *op. cit.*, II, 287.

[63] Granqvist, *op. cit.*, I, 67ff. The woman who came from a distance had the least protection, *ibid.*, I, 94. Cf. also II, 144, 218ff.

113b; Luke 1.25; II (4) Esd. 9.45).[64] As the mother of a son the wife was respected; she had given her husband the most precious gift of all.

As a widow too a woman was still bound to her husband, that is if he died without leaving a son (Deut. 25.5–10; cf. Mark 12.18–27). In this case she had to wait, unable to make any move on her side, until the brother or brothers of her dead husband should contract a levirate marriage with her or publish a refusal to do so; without this refusal she could not remarry.[65]

The conditions we have just described were also reflected in the prescriptions of religious legislation of the period. So from a *religious* point of view too, especially with regard to the Torah,[66] a woman was inferior to a man. She was subject to all the *prohibitions* of the Torah (except for the three concerning only men, Lev. 19.27a; 19. 27b; 21.1–2—M. Kidd. i.7), and to the whole force of civil and penal legislation,[67] including the penalty of death (b. Kidd. 35a; b. Pes. 43a). However, as to the *commandments* of the Torah, here is what was said: 'The observance of all the positive ordinances that depend on the time of year is incumbent on men but not on women' (M. Kidd. i.7 cf. T. Sot. ii.8, 295). Because of this formula, which is not al-together precise,[68] there is quoted a series of commandments from which the wife is exempt: to make pilgrimage to Jerusalem at the

[64] Cf. Luke 23.29.—After ten years of childlessness, the husband had to take a second wife, M. Yeb. vi.6.

[65] The publication of the 'refusal' (*ḥalīṣāh*, 'putting off the shoe', cf. Deut. 25.9–10) is often reported (K. H. Rengstorf, *Jebamot*, Giessen 1929, 31f.*). As for the fulfilment of levirate marriage in Jerusalem in Jesus' time, we have evidence of three cases (M. Yeb. viii.4; T. Yeb. i.10, 241), cf. *Theol. Literaturzeitung* 54, 1929, col. 583. Following J. Wellhausen (*Das Evangelium Marci*, 2nd ed., Berlin 1909, 95), K. H. Rengstorf (*Die Tosefta, Seder Naschim, Rabbinische Texte* I.3, Stuttgart 1933, pp. 18ff.) claims that, on the contrary, levirate marriage was completely out of use in Jesus' time; his arguments do not convince me. According to Rengstorf, the *ben mᵉgusat* mentioned in M. Yeb. viii.4 is a proselyte, since he is called by his mother's name, and therefore the levirate law did not apply to his widow. This explanation is unreliable; there is nothing to prevent us from seeing, like Dalman, *WB* 224a, *mᵉgusat* as the name of a man. Above all, Rengstorf must take the verb *yibbēm*, in M. Yeb. viii.4 in a general sense, 'to marry one's sister-in-law'; but this is against established usage (cf. Rengstorf himself in his edition of *Jebamot* [coll. *Die Mischna*] Giessen 1929, 3*) and against the context of M. Yeb. viii.4, where *yibbēm* has the ordinary technical meaning 'to contract levirate marriage with the widow of a brother who died with no male heir'.

[66] See Bill. III, 558–62, for what follows.

[67] Only one point is doubtful: we do not know if in older times a wife was sold because of a theft, see p. 313; the Mishnah forbids her sale, M. Sot. iii.8.

[68] Bill. III, 559; see p. 349 n. 23. There were some commandments from which a wife was exempt although they were not tied to any particular time, e.g. studying the Torah, which we shall mention shortly.

feasts of Passover, Pentecost and Tabernacles (M. Hag. i.1);[69] to live in the booths (M. Sukk. ii.8; T. Kidd. i.10, 335) and to shake the *lūlāb* at the feast of Tabernacles (T. Kidd. *loc. cit.*); to sound the *šōpār* at the new year (T.R. Sh. iv.1, 212); to read the *mᵉgillāh* (book of Esther) at the feast of Purim (T. Meg. ii.7, 224); to recite daily the *šᵉma'* (M. Ber. iii.3) which consisted of Deut. 6.4–9; 11.13–21; and Num. 15.37–41; and so on. Further, she was exempt from study of the Torah; R. Eliezer (*c.* AD 90), tireless upholder of the old tradition, says impressively, 'If a man gives his daughter a knowledge of the Law it is as though he taught her lechery' (M. Sot. iii.4).[70] The idea that the Torah should be taught to daughters also (M. Ned. iv.3)[71] and only the oral Law kept from them[72] was in no way representative of the old law. In every case, schools were solely for boys, and not for girls.[73] Of the two sections of the synagogue mentioned in the law of Augustus, σαββατεῖον and ἀνδρών (*Ant.* 16.164), the first, where the liturgical service took place, was open to women too; but the other part, given over to the scribes' teaching, was open only to men and boys as its name suggests. In the better class families, however, the girls were given a secular education; for instance, they were taught Greek 'for it is an ornament to them' (j. Peah i.1, 15c.16).

As a woman's religious *duties* were limited, so were her religious *rights*. According to Josephus, women could go no further in the Temple than into the Courts of the Gentiles and of Women (*Ant.* 15.418f.; *BJ* 5.199).[74] During the time of their monthly purification, and also for a period of forty days after the birth of a son (cf. Luke 2.22) and eighty days after the birth of a daughter (Lev. 12.2–5; Bill. II, 119f.), they were not allowed even into the Court of Gentiles (*CA* 2.133; M. Kel. i.8). It was not customary for women to lay their hands on the head of the sacrificial victims,[75] or to wave the portions

---

[69] Very often, however, wives took part voluntarily in these, especially at Passover, Luke 2.41; T. Ned. v.1, 280; b. R. Sh. 6b, and b. Erub. 96a Bar. See Bill. II, 141f. on the attempt to correlate theory and practice.

[70] Here is another of this scholar's sayings: 'Better to burn the Torah than to teach it to women', j. Sot. iii.4, 19a.7.

[71] M. Sot. iii.4, a saying of Ben Assai (*c.* AD 110). Cf. also b. Kidd. 29b, 34a; b. Sanh. 94b.

[72] Krauss, *TA* II, 468 n. 373e.

[73] M. S. Zuckermandel, *Die Befreiung der Frauen von bestimmten religiösen Pflichten*, Breslau 1911, 22.

[74] T. Arak. ii.1, 544 says that they could also go into the inner court, but only to offer sacrifice; cf. G. Dalman in *PJB* 5, 1909, 34, and his *SW* 298 n. 4.

[75] T. Men. x.13, 528 says it was not customary. M. Men. ix.8 says it was not permitted.

of the sacrifice;[76] when occasionally we read of women being permitted to lay their hands on the victim, this is added: 'Not that that was customary for women, but was to appease the women' (b. Hag. 16b). By virtue of Deut. 31.12, women, like men and children, could participate in the synagogue service (b. Hag. 3a Bar., and par.; j. Hag. i.1, 74d.35, etc.).[77] but barriers of lattice separated the women's section. Later[78] they even went so far as to build a gallery for women with a special entrance. In the liturgical service, women were there simply to listen. To be sure, in older times they do not seem to have been excluded from being called upon to read the Torah, but by Tannaitic times it was not customary for them to obey the call to read.[79] Women were forbidden to teach (M. Kidd. iv.13).[80] In the house, the wife was not reckoned among the number of persons summoned to pronounce benediction after a meal (M. Ber. vii.2). Finally we must record that a woman had no right to bear witness,[81] because it was concluded from Gen. 18.15 that she was a liar.[82] Her

[76] T. Men. x.17, 528 says it was not customary. According to M. Zeb. iii.1, a woman was permitted to slaughter the sacrifice, though this was not customary either.

[77] See also Philo, De spec. leg. III, 171; De vita contempl. 69. The Jews of Sardis, e.g., met in their local shrine 'with wife and children', Ant. 14.260.

[78] The Mesopotamian synagogue of Dura-Europos, discovered in 1932, dates back to AD 245, and had no gallery. According to C. H. Kraeling (Bulletin of the American Schools of Oriental Research 54, April 1934, 19) this is a type of synagogue older than those in Galilee which were built between the third and the seventh century.—C. Watzinger, Denkmäler Palästinas II, Leipzig 1935, 108, dates back to Hellenistic times the type of synagogue with galleries. He bases this on the description in the Talmud of the great synagogue of Alexandria as 'Diplostoon', a term which Watzinger says means 'in two storeys, i.e. with galleries over the aisles'. But, as the same passage of the Talmud shows (T. Sukk. iv.6, 198) the word diplostoon means 'a double colonnade', intending to show the synagogue as a building with five aisles, two rows of columns on each side.

[79] T. Meg. iv.11, 226: 'All are qualified to be among the seven [who read the Torah in the synagogue on sabbath mornings], even a minor and a woman. But a woman should not be allowed to come forward to read [the Torah] in public.' Par. b. Meg. 23a Bar. I. Elbogen, Der jüdische Gottesdienst in seiner geschichtlichen Entwicklung 3rd ed., Frankfurt 1931 (reprinted Hildesheim 1962), 170, concludes from this that originally women were actually called to read the Torah. Bill. III, 467, assumes, however, that women were called simply to do them honour, but that they never actually did so.—Only in the Diaspora did it happen that by reason of foreign influences women received the title of ἀρχισυνάγωγος, Schürer II, 512, ET II.2, 65.

[80] II Tim. 3.14 assumes that Timothy had been instructed in Scripture from his earliest years, and so obviously by his pious mother and grandmother (1.5). But this was teaching within the home, and was moreover a special case because Timothy's father was a Gentile (Acts 16.3).

[81] M. Shebu. iv.1; Siphre Deut. 19.17, 190; b.B.K. 88a; Ant. 4.219.

[82] Yalqut Shimeoni i. 82, Vilna ed. 1898, 49a below.—Ant. 4.219: 'Let not the

witness was acceptable only in a few very exceptional cases, and that of a Gentile slave was also acceptable in the same cases (M.R. Sh. i.8): e.g. on the remarriage of a widow, the witness of a woman as to the death of the husband was accepted (M. Yeb. xvi.7).

On the whole, the position of women in religious legislation is best expressed in this constantly repeated formula: 'Women, (Gentile) slaves and children (minors)' (M. Ber. iii.3; M.R. Sh. i.8; M. Sukk. ii.8; M.B.M. i.5 *et passim*). Like a non-Jewish slave and a child under age, a woman has over her a man who is her master (b. Kidd. 30b, Bill. III, 562); and this likewise limits her participation in divine service, which is why from a religious point of view she is inferior to a man.[83]

We may add to all this that there were plenty of disdainful opinions expressed on women.[84] It is striking to see how these opinions outweigh opinions of high esteem, which were by no means lacking.[85] It is typical that joy reigned at the birth of a boy (Jer. 20.15),[86] while the birth of a daughter was often greeted with indifference, even with sorrow (b. Nidd. 31b).[87] We have therefore the impression that Judaism in Jesus' time also had a very low opinion of women, which is usual in the Orient where she is chiefly valued for her fecundity, kept as far as possible shut away from the outer world, submissive to the power of her father or her husband, and where she is inferior to men from a religious point of view.[88]

Only against the background of that time can we fully appreciate

---

testimony of women be admitted because of the levity and boldness of their sex.'

[83] A prayer recommended for daily use says: 'Blessed [be God] that hath not made me a woman', T. Ber. vii.18, 16. J. Leipoldt, *Jesus und Paulus*, Leipzig 1936, 37, repeats an observation by Prof. R. Meyer: Neither the Old Testament nor the Mishnah knows the feminine form of the Hebrew adjectives *ḥasid* (pious), *ṣaddīq* (just), *qādōš* (holy).

[84] J. Leipoldt, *Jesus und die Frauen*, Leipzig 1921, 3ff. Abundant evidence in Bill., see the Index, IV, 1226f. Philo, in his judgements of women is as severe as the Talmud.

[85] See Bill., Index.

[86] Mek. Ex. 12.6, 3c gives as a supreme example of 'good news' the announcement of the birth of a son; b. Nidd. 31b.

[87] b. Kidd. 82b (par. b. Pes. 65a Bar.): 'Woe to him whose children are daughters!' R. Hisda's words: 'Daughters are dearer to me than sons' (b.B.B. 141a) appear so incredible to later commentators that they have recourse to some astonishing explanations: Rashi: he had more delight in his daughters because his sons were dead; Tosaphot: his daughters must have married eminent teachers, etc.; cf. S. Zucrow, *Women, Slaves and the Ignorant*, Boston, 1932, 34f.

[88] *CA* 2.201: 'The woman, says the Law, is in all things inferior to a man.'

Jesus's attitude to women. Luke 8.1–3; Mark 15.41 and par. (cf. Matt. 20.20) speak of women following Jesus, and this was an unprecedented happening in the history of that time. John the Baptist had already preached to women (Matt. 21.32) and baptized them;[89] Jesus, too, knowingly overthrew custom when he allowed women to follow him. He could do this because he required from his disciples an attitude to women of complete chastity: 'Every one that looketh on a (married) woman to lust after her hath committed adultery with her already in his heart' (Matt. 5.28). Jesus was not content with bringing women up onto a higher plane than was then the custom; but as Saviour of all (Luke 7.36–50), he brings them before God on an equal footing with men (Matt. 21.31–32).

What was more, Jesus' attitude to the subject of marriage was an entirely new one. He was not content to stand up for monogamy (see p. 369 n. 54); he completely forbade[90] divorce when talking to his disciples (Matt. 19.6), and unhesitatingly and fearlessly criticized the Torah for permitting divorce because of the hardness of human hearts (Matt. 19.8).[91] Marriage to him was indissoluble to the extent of seeing the remarriage of divorced persons, whether men or women (Matt. 5.32; 19.9; Mark 10.11–12; Luke 16.18), as adultery because the first marriage still stands. By this estimation of marriage, and this unexampled sanctification of it, Jesus puts into practice the scriptural saying that marriage is an ordinance created by God (Gen. 1.27; 2.24; Mark 10.6–7).

[89] *Gospel of the Nazarenes:* Ecce mater domini et fratres eius dicebant ei: Joannes Baptista baptizat in remissionem peccatorum; eamus et baptizemur ab eo (Jerome, *Dial. adv. Pelag.* III, 2, PL 23, 570). See also on this J. Leipoldt, *Jesus und die Frauen,* Leipzig 1921, 15f.

[90] The exception παρεκτὸς λόγου πορνείας is found only in Matt. (5.32, cf. 19.9); but it appears neither in Mark 10.11 nor in Luke 16.18. As Paul knows nothing of this exception we must consider it an interpolation into that Gospel.

[91] b. San. 99a Bar. may be a response to Jesus' words: 'If anyone should say: "The whole Torah is from heaven save this [single] verse which Moses said from his own mouth and not God" to him applies [the saying]: "He hath despised the word of the Lord" (Num. 15.31).'

COMPLETE LIST OF HIGH PRIESTS FROM 200 BC TO AD 70

Simon the Righteous (after 200 BC)	149
Onias II (to 175 BC)	182, 184–189
Jesus (Jason) (175–172 BC)	182, 184f., 188
Menelaus (172–162 BC)	182, 184–188, 190
Jacim (Alcimus) (162–159 BC)	182, 186, 188, 191

The eight Maccabean high priests (152–37 BC)

Jonathan (152–143/2 BC)	151, 183, 188
Simon (142/1—134 BC)	155, 189
John Hyrcanus I (134–104 BC)	6, 107, 149, 155, 189, 214, 229, 256, 267, 318, 320, 353
Aristobulus I (104–103 BC)	151, 162, 188, 320
Alexander Jannaeus (103–76 BC)	70, 90, 94, 98, 114, 129, 151, 155f., 188f., 217, 219, 229, 262, 318
Hyrcanus II (76—67 BC 63–40 BC)	35, 64, 90, 141, 190, 215, 217
Aristobulus II (67–63 BC)	141, 262
Antigonus (40—37 BC)	90, 215, 224, 362

The twenty-eight high priests from 37 BC to AD 70

1.	Ananel (37–36 BC: again from 34 BC)	66, 69, 190, 193f.
2.	Aristobulus III, the last Maccabee (35 BC)	151, 158, 190, 193
3.	Jesus, son of Phiabi (to c. 22 BC)	(194)
4.	Simon, son of Boethus (c. 22–5 BC)	69, 155, 194, 229f., 232
5.	Mattaiah, son of Theophilus (5 BC–12 March 4 BC)	154, 157, 159, 162, 194, 218
6.	Joseph, son of Elam (5 BC)	157, 159, 162, 194
7.	Joezer, son of Boethus (4 BC)	154 (194)
8.	Eleazar, son of Boethus (from 4 BC)	(194)
9.	Jesus, son of See (until AD 6)	194
10.	Annas (AD 6–15)	96, 155, 157, 159, 194f., 197
11.	Ishmael b. Phiabi I (c. AD 15–16)	149, 196
12.	Eleazar, son of Annas (c. AD 16–17)	194

13. Simon, son of Kamithos (AD 17–18)   157, 162

14. Joseph Caiaphas (c. AD 18–37)   94, 96, 155, 159, 194f., 197, 218, 229

15. Jonathan, son of Annas (Easter to Pentecost AD 37)   157, 195, 197

16. Theophilus, son of Annas (from AD 37)   (194)

17. Simon Kantheras, son of Boethus (from AD 41)   196

18. Matthias, son of Annas   (194)

19. Elionaius, son of Kantheras (c. AD 44)   94, 229

20. Joseph, son of Kami   143

21. Ananias, son of Nebedaius (AD 47 to at least 55)   49, 96, 99, 143, 157, 162, 194

22. Ishmael b. Phiabi II (until AD 61)   97, 142f., 169, 196, 229, 233

23. Joseph Qabi (until AD 62)   94, 176

24. Ananus, son of Ananus (AD 62)   157, 198, 229

25. Jesus, son of Damnaius (c. AD 62–65)   176, 194

26. Joshua b. Gamaliel (c. AD 63–65)   95, 97f., 105, 155–7, 218

27. Matthias, son of Theophilus (AD 65–67)   195

28. Pinḥas of Ḥabtā (AD 67–70)   155, 161, 165, 179, 192f., 197f., 206f., 219

THE JERUSALEM SCRIBES

Rabbān Johanan b. Zakkai   104, 113, 116, 125, 133,
                                                  144, 176, 221, 229, 234,
                                                  237, 255f., 289, 319

Rabbān Simon I b. Gamaliel I   33, 237, 244, 255, 298
Hananiah, Captain of the Temple   6, 104, 161f., 233
'Abbā Joseph b. Hanin   195
Eleazar b. Zadoq, priest (born shortly after AD 35)   31, 104, 113, 115, 118,
                                                  122, 143, 203, 206, 233,
                                                  249, 286, 346

Abba Saul, son of the Batanean   31, 113f., 195, 198,
                                                  234f., 242, 322, 324

Rabbān Gamaliel II   60, 94, 115, 219, 255,
                                                  301, 319, 322, 348, 366

The following studied in Jerusalem c. AD 70

Eliezer b. Hyrcanus, priest   104, 116, 217, 219, 234,
                                                  244, 249, 271, 314f.,
                                                  340, 349f., 355–7, 366,
                                                  373

Joshua b. Hananiah, Levite   94, 168, 212f., 219, 234,
                                                  244, 301, 319, 331,
                                                  338f., 340, 348

Jose, priest   104, 234
Simon b. Nathaniel, priest   104, 219, 256f.

INDEX OF NAMES AND SUBJECTS

INDEX OF REFERENCES

OLD TESTAMENT

NEW TESTAMENT

APOCRYPHA AND PSEUDEPIGRAPHA

QUMRAN WRITINGS

THE MISHNAH

(Tractates are alphabetically arranged)

THE TOSEPHTA

THE BABYLONIAN TALMUD

THE JERUSALEM TALMUD

THE EXTRA-CANONICAL TRACTATES

MIDRASH RABBAH

JOSEPHUS

PHILO